The first passenger train arrives in Morgantown, February 14, 1886. (From a painting by Diane Lenhart.)

The Monongalia Story

A Bicentennial History

IV. Industrialization

By Earl L. Core

West Virginia University
and
Morgantown Public Library

McClain Printing Company
Parsons, West Virginia
1982

International Standard Book Number 0-87012-411-0
Library of Congress Catalog Card Number 74-79040
Reprinted in the United States of America
Copyright © 2000 McClain Printing Company
Parsons, West Virginia
All Rights Reserved
2000

Reprinted 2000

To
Those who
came before
us.

Preface

This is the fourth volume of a projected five-volume work designed to constitute a bicentennial history of Monongalia County, West Virginia. The first volume, published in 1974, is a prelude to the history, including a general description of the land, with an account of the exploration and early settlements, ending with the political establishment of the county in 1776.

The second volume, bearing the date 1976, deals with the history of the pioneer period, from 1776 to 1826.

The third volume, with the date 1979, deals with the fifty-year period from 1826 to 1876. It is subtitled DISCORD, and the bitterness of the Civil War period is the central theme.

The present volume deals with the next fifty-year period, from 1876 until 1926. This is appropriately subtitled INDUSTRIALIZATION and deals with the profound changes in the socio-economic life of the county wrought by the building of railroads and paved roads.

Acknowledgements of assistance in the preparation of this volume are due hundreds of persons who have provided materials of value and many of these are recognized in footnote and other citations. Special appreciation is expressed to members of the staff of the West Virginia University Library, the Morgantown Public Library, and the Monongalia County Courthouse, as well as to members of the Monongalia Historical Society.

I am especially indebted to Miss Diane Lenhart for the sketches and maps which she designed particularly for this work. The map of Monongalia County in 1876 used on the back endpaper was also drawn by Miss Lenhart from source materials of that period.

It is a pleasure to recognize also the unusually careful work of Miss Doris A. Geiler, who typed the entire manuscript.

A substantial portion of the material in this volume has been included in weekly columns in the *Sunday Dominion-Post* and appreciation is expressed to publishers of that newspaper.

It might be appropriate to comment on material here included. For the earlier volumes it was sometimes difficult to discover enough material on a given subject. But in the preparation of the later volumes there was an "embarrassment of riches" and it is obvious that a selection of materials is necessary. It is certain that many very important items have been omitted and for these omissions I am regretful. Many items that have been included may seem to be insignificant, but often they were included because they made it easier to picture a situation existing at a particular time in the county's history.

July 1, 1981   EARL L. CORE

Contents

Introduction

The half century from 1876 until 1926 witnessed the greatest changes yet made in the history of Monongalia County, an industrial revolution. A community that had been almost entirely based on agriculture, by the end of that period, had been transformed by the development of various types of industry. The key to the great change was the development of new forms of transportation: railroads, slack water on the river, finally, gasoline-propelled vehicles and paved roads.

Senator Waitman T. Willey had predicted the coming changes in an address delivered at the celebration of Morgantown's centennial anniversary, in 1885, the year before the railroad arrived:

"The long wished for railroad is at our doors. We welcome its advent. And yet, to us, there comes with it some regrets. The venerable homogeneity of our society will be broken . . . Heretofore, in consequence of our isolated situation, . . . we have been . . . compelled into closer personal relationships, begetting friendships all the more intense because thus limited and concentrated. But with the railroad the stranger will intrude upon us and the influx of new outside influences, social, moral and material, will less or more modify the existing conditions of society."

Senator Willey's forecast was not long in coming about. Within two decades the railroad had brought not only numerous factories, but with them a host of strangers speaking a multitude of unknown tongues. Morgantown quickly grew from a village to a small city, and the 1885 conditions of society were indeed modified—more rather than less.

But Senator Willey could scarcely have foreseen the revolution that would come about by the time the county celebrated its 150th anniversary, in 1926. Monongalia County citizens, by 1926, no longer led a life of isolation and more or less self-reliance. No longer did they depend almost entirely upon their gardens for vegetables, their orchards for fruit, the streams for ice. No longer did they cut their own wood for the fireplace and the kitchen range, pump their water by hand, light their houses with candles or kerosene lamps. No longer was a trip in the buggy to church or the next community center a matter of hours.

Now, in 1926, nearby chain stores provided fresh fruits and vegetables. Kitchen and bathroom are provided with eager water, waiting behind the faucet. Refrigeration is made simple by convenient ice deliveries or by wire. Electricity brings good lights, makes cleaning easy, cooks the food. As if by magic the old mud turnpikes have been transformed into a network of hard-surfaced roads, over which flows an unending stream of automobiles, trucks, motor coaches. Airplanes roar overhead with passengers and freight. Provincialism is broken down, culture is stimulated, patriotism heightened.

Through the medium of the radio the Monongalia County citizen, once so isolated, now sits quietly in his home and listens to music, lectures, sermons, plays; he sits in on the opening of Congress or a debate in the legislature.

It was almost as if fairy tales were coming true.

CHAPTER ONE HUNDRED ONE

1877

As Monongalia County began its second hundred years a remarkable and largely unforeseen change began to take place. During the county's first century it was chiefly a community of farmers, as was most of America. But in the three decades following the Civil War an unprecedented development began to take place, spurred by the steady increase in labor-saving machinery which led to better working conditions and a growing investment in education.

Monongalia County's industrial revolution was a little late in its development. Although the main line of the Baltimore and Ohio Railroad, from 1827 on, seemed likely to pass through the county, it eventually detoured around and in 1877, after fifty years, the nearest railroad was still twenty-five miles away. But there was a feeling in the air that something great was just around the corner.

The Borough of Morgantown. As Monongalia County began its second century, its county seat town was still governed under the provisions of the charter of 1860, adopted just before the Civil War. The mayor and a council of five members, elected by the people annually, met in a monthly session. The minutes were accurately kept by the recorder and may still be consulted in the city hall. The proceedings consisted largely of reports of permits or licenses granted, payment of bills to people who rendered services to the town, orders for improvements on streets, and assessments of fines for breaking town ordinances.

The population of the borough in 1870 was only 787, a gain of 38 since 1860, so growth was not very rapid. In 1877 a survey indicated that there were, within the borough limits, 82 horses, 47

1

cattle, 80 hogs, 44 carriages, 182 watches and clocks, 31 pianos and melodeons, and 159 voters.

There was no police force, no fire department, no sewer system. Occasional arrests were made by the sheriff or the town sergeant. Usually good order prevailed. Rare exceptions were animated arguments between university students and town boys, sometimes marked by physical blows, or altercations among citizens, mostly set off by intoxication.

The principal streets were macadamized but they were not very smooth and often had deep holes in them. Sidewalks were scarce and mostly made up of planks nailed to underlying supports. To protect the public health the council was taking steps to abolish privies and sources of filth along the edges of streams. Sanitation was further improved by eliminating hitching racks for horses around the courthouse and by prohibiting the courthouse janitor from cleaning the public spittoons at the town pump.

The general tenor of life was quiet and there was little evidence that an awakening was only a decade away.

The Boy President. The Board of Regents of West Virginia University, on January 11, 1877, elected the Reverend John R. Thompson to be the second regular president of the university.[1] The Reverend Mr. Thompson was described as "the brainy, brilliant and eloquent pastor of the Methodist Episcopal Church in Morgantown," otherwise known as "the Boy Preacher." He now became the "Boy President," since he was a little short of his twenty-fifth birthday at the time of his appointment.

In response to their newspaper advertisements, the regents had received thirty-nine formal applications for the position. The Reverend Mr. Thompson was not among the applicants and was generally regarded as preeminently a preacher of the evangelical type, so his selection was a surprise to many persons. The *Wheeling Daily Register,* on January 26, 1877, quoted a Morgantown correspondent as saying that "the best men in the faculty are humiliated," a statement promptly denied by the faculty.

John R. Thompson was born at Carrollton, Ohio, on March 14, 1852. He was licensed to preach at the age of seventeen and at nineteen was graduated from Mount Union College, Alliance,

1. *Weekly Post,* January 20, 1877.

Ohio. In February 1873, he was married at Alliance to Mary Virginia Cox, the daughter of Rev. William Cox. He served a two-year pastorate at the Chapline Street Methodist Episcopal Church in Wheeling and then accepted a call to the Morgantown church, where he at once attracted wide attention for his eloquence. He was small physically, but a strong personality, able, courageous, aggressive.

The Reverend Alexander Martin, first president of the university, had resigned in the face of difficulties in 1875 and Vice-President John W. Scott had been named acting president.[2]

Under the acting presidency of Professor John W. Scott the university threatened to become "a rapidly disappearing quantity." Following President Martin's removal the enrollment dropped to ninety-three and in January 1877 only forty-two students were enrolled.

The "Boy President" concluded, at the beginning of his administration, that it would require a "long time, great industry, unflagging energy, a creative and practical mind, a tender and loving heart, a tenacious and invincible will" to create that "lofty spirit of State pride" needed to establish and maintain a real university.[3]

In general, the press and the public approved of him and the future appeared more auspicious.

"He entered upon the duties as president in March . . . , and threw himself into the work with all his most remarkable energy. Passing from town to town, often from one country neighborhood to another, attending picnics, Sunday-school conventions and church dedications, as well as educational meetings and sessions of ecclesiastical bodies, he preached, lectured, and visited from house to house, becoming familiar with public men as well as with the life of the common people."[4]

New appointments to the faculty during 1877 included D. Boardman Purinton, professor of logic; and Israel C. White, professor of geology and natural history.

Students mostly lived in private homes or boarding houses. The first of the larger boarding houses was the two-story building

2. Earl L. Core, *Monongalia Story*, vol. 3, p. 686.
3. Charles H. Ambler, *History of Education in West Virginia*, p. 197.
4. Samuel T. Wiley, *History of Monongalia County*, p. 415.

constructed in 1874 by William Dann at the corner of Hough and Front streets. It was sold in June 1877 to James M. McVicker and William C. McGrew and was managed thereafter by James Davis.

Free Public Schools. The system of free public schools, with compulsory attendance, was little more than a decade old, but was working most satisfactorily. Alexander L. Wade on August 7 was reelected county superintendent, with no opposition. By an amendment of the state school law, provision was made for the appointment of three trustees for each sub-district, by the board of education; previously they had been elected, but this did not work very well. Graduates who received diplomas this year numbered 110. There were eighty-two school buildings in the county, with eighty-eight teachers employed, and 3,845 pupils enrolled. District alumni associations were formed.[5]

Commissioners of the Morgantown School District were Henry S. Hayes, A. W. Lorentz, William C. McGrew, Samuel Sears, and William Hoge.[6] Members of the boards of education of the various districts were: Clinton, James S. Watson, Henry Austin, A. J. Frum, and Ezekiel Trickett; Morgan, Coleman Vandervort, J. C. Davis, and Leonard Selby; Union, James Hare, Leonard Warman, Jesse Lewellen, and W. L. Coombs; Cass, James Sanders, John T. Fleming, and J. J. Wharton; Grant, Ulysses Camp, I. C. Rich, and Ambrose Walters; Clay, A. W. Tennant and Malin Tennant.

A Narrow-Gauge Railroad? For half a century civic leaders of Monongalia County had sought to have railway connections for the community. All the many efforts to secure the necessary capital having failed, in 1877 attention was directed towards the narrow-gauge railway. Such roads were usually of three-foot gauge, while the standard-gauge was five feet eight-and-one-half inches. The narrow-gauge made possible a close fitting of the road-bed to the contour of the ground, with a consequent great saving in the cost of construction. Additional savings resulted from the use of smaller cross-ties and lighter rails. Steeper grades

5. Wiley, pp. 369, 370, 371, 373, 378, 379, 380, 383.
6. Wiley, pp. 597, 629, 657, 692, 709, 730, 751.

than could be used on the standard-gauge are also practicable; this might save distance. "As the difference between the cost of the narrow-gauge and the standard-gauge increases in favor of the former in proportion to the roughness of the country, it would seem that the narrow-gauge is a railway peculiarly adapted to the mountain regions of West Virginia."[7]

At this time the people of Kingwood were agitating a project of building a narrow-gauge road to Morgantown, thence connecting with Pittsburgh by steamboats on the Monongahela River. A joint meeting was held in the courthouse at Morgantown on August 30. Waitman T. Willey was elected chairman of the group and Henry M. Morgan secretary. A committee of Morgantown citizens consisting of the Honorable Mr. Willey, George Hall, Joseph Moreland, John J. Brown, Ashbel Fairchild, George C. Sturgiss, and Henry M. Morgan was appointed for further discussions with the Kingwood group.

Meanwhile the attention of Monongalia County people was turned to the Pittsburgh, Castle Shannon and Washington Narrow-Gauge Railroad. The object was to secure an extension of this railway, through Waynesburg, Mount Morris, and Morgantown, to some point on the Baltimore and Ohio Railroad. A meeting was held at the courthouse on November 3, at which company representatives proposed to make the extension, providing the people along the route would subscribe, in money or labor, an amount sufficient to grade the road, build the bridges, and furnish the cross-ties.[8]

Dolls Run Christian Church. The new red brick building of the Dolls Run Christian Church was dedicated November 18, 1877, after having been under construction for the past year. Bricks were made in a nearby brickyard across the road. A year earlier it was reported: "There is a brickyard here in full blast carried on by the Brand Brothers. We are going to have a new church in this place. Jack Brand has moved in his new shop ready for biz."[9]

The arrangement of the interior of the church was modeled

7. Wiley, pp. 113, 114. Numerous articles in the *Weekly Post* during 1877 advocated the advantages of narrow-gauge lines.

8. Wiley, pp. 113-15. A narrow-gauge railroad was completed from Washington to Waynesburg in 1877.

9. *Morgantown Post*, September 2, 1876.

Fig. 1. Dolls Run Christian Church.

after the building erected by Alexander Campbell in Bethany, with the pulpit in the front of the church, between the two doors, one for the men, the other for the women. Rev. Campbell Jobes, an itinerant minister, had charge of the dedication services, which attracted large crowds. The church was one of the strongest in the area, with a membership of around two hundred, and it was the rallying point for great revivals. The brick church replaced a frame building which had been constructed thirty years earlier (see *Monongalia Story*, vol. 3, p. 124).[10]

Destructive Floods. On Tuesday, January 16, 1877, the highest waters in years caused great damage in the county. Heavy snows that had accumulated went off with a torrential rain on Monday night and the river stood at twenty-seven feet at Morgantown—the highest since 1852. "The destruction to roads and bridges on Dunkard Creek, . . . by the late flood, is estimated at

10. The dedicatory address was by W. K. Pendleton, state superintendent of schools. *Weekly Post*, November 3, 1877.

several thousand dollars. We learn that five bridges were washed away on Dunkard, and the damage to other streams was great."[11] "The flood on Dunkard last week washed out the following bridges: At South's, Brown's, Strosnider's, and the mouth of the stream."[12]

Rebuilding Bridges. The destruction of the bridges at Strosnider's Mill, Adam Brown's ford, and South's ford, so soon after their completion (see vol. 3, p. 641), was a heavy blow to the citizens, but the county court quickly called for bids for raising the abutments and building new superstructures. There was considerable discussion about the relative merits of wooden and iron bridges, it being generally believed that the new bridges should be of wood, since the material would be cheaper, and the money would be spent at home, whereas if iron bridges were built the money would leave the county. Bids were asked for both types. Emrod Tennant was the lowest bidder for wooden (covered) bridges, at the price of thirty-nine hundred dollars, and the King Iron Bridge Manufacturing Company, of Cleveland, Ohio, was the lowest for the iron bridges, at forty-five hundred dollars.

There was some dissatisfaction expressed, therefore, when the contract was let to the King Iron Bridge Company. The contract called for the raising of the abutments, wing walls, and parapets three feet higher and the work was to be completed not later than July 15, 1877. John E. Price, N. L. South, and A. Fairchild served on the commission appointed by the court to supervise the replacement of the bridges. The span at South's ford was 104 feet long, that at Adam Brown's 90 feet, and at Strosnider's 110 feet. The bridge at Adam Brown's was constructed, finally, of wood, perhaps as a sort of compromise.[13]

Adam Brown. Adam C. Brown, son of Abraham and Elizabeth Core Brown, died July 13, 1877. He was born May 16, 1820, and located in 1855 at the fording place on Dunkard Creek bearing his name. He married Elva Anne, daughter of Jacob and Catherine Pickenpaugh Shively and they had nine children, Michael S.,

---

11. *Morgantown Weekly Post,* January 27, 1877.
12. *Waynesburg Independent,* January 26, 1877.
13. Earl L. Core, *Chronicles of Core,* pp. 114, 115.

Morrison, John S., Abraham, Jacob, Catherine, Sabina, Christina, and Emanuel. "He was a strict and conscientious member of the Dolls Run Christian Church."[14]

Terrible Hailstorm. "On July 5, 1877, in the afternoon, a terrible hailstorm passed over the head-waters of Stewart's run, and broke into two water-spouts, one on the head-waters of Stewart's run and the other on Indian Creek, where the storm hurled logs against Silas Hawkins's house and damaged it greatly."[15]

"Sallytown." In the days when Morgantown was a village, the section north of North Boundary Street (later Willey Street) and east of the future North High Street was called Sallytown, in honor of an eccentric old woman by the name of Sally Thomas. She lived in a little house at the corner of Spruce and Willey streets. The only members of her household were "successive generations of cats and kittens."[16]

Miscellany. In 1877: Dr. F. G. Howell began the practice of medicine in Morgantown (Wiley, p. 584). . . . W. R. White and Samuel Steele were ministers of the Morgantown Methodist Episcopal Church (Wiley, p. 590). . . . J. C. Jordan was appointed minister of the Morgantown Baptist Church (Wiley, p. 595). . . . The Mount Calvary Methodist Church, in Clinton District, was added to the Morgantown Circuit (Wiley, p. 627). . . . Mary E. Roderick, wife of G. T. Loar, of Clinton District, died (Wiley, p. 639). . . . E. A. Haldeman established a wagon and buggy factory at Stewartstown; soon he was making fifty vehicles per year (Wiley, p. 674). . . . Isaac Hastings began operation of Ice's Ferry (Wiley, p. 680). . . . Charles M. Conway was minister of the Avery Methodist Circuit (Wiley, p. 689). . . . The Flickersville flour mill, built in 1833, was destroyed by fire in February (Wiley, p. 724). . . . A vote was held on the question of the location of the state capital, with the following results in this county: for Charleston, 626; for Clarksburg, 1,188; for Martinsburg, 4 (Wiley, p. 769). . . . Ministers of the Monongalia Methodist Circuit were J. E. Wasson and C. J. Price; the month of the annual conference meeting was changed from March to October, consequently there were

14. *Chronicles of Core*, p. 115.
15. Wiley, p. 738.
16. *Sesqui-Centennial of Monongalia County*, p. 256.

two conferences and two appointments; those appointed in October were J. E. Wasson and C. S. Harrison (Wiley, p. 773). . . . Eleanor Ray, wife of L. H. Dorsey, died; she was a sister of Thomas Patrick Ray (see *Monongalia Story*, vol. 3, p. 215). . . . In August J. W. Anderson established a line of coal wagons to deliver coal from the Koontz mine (Callahan, p. 213). . . . Rev. John P. Varner was minister of the Miracle Run Methodist Church (Dodds and Dodds, p. 134). . . . A large black bear, weighing three hundred pounds, in May, passed through Pleasant Valley, crossed the river at Big Falls, and was shot by Edgar Wilson, on Miracle Run (*Weekly Post*, June 23, 1877). . . . O. B. Johnson's store was broken into and robbed on the night of August 26 (*Weekly Post*, September 15, 1877). . . . The ninth annual county fair was held September 25-27 (*Weekly Post*, September 29, October 6, 1877). . . . Rev. William H. Satterfield, of Pleasant Valley, committed suicide on September 18; he was sixty years of age (September 29, 1877). . . . Joseph Jolliff, of Smithtown, died October 13; the son of William Jolliff, he was born May 20, 1798 (*Weekly Post*, October 27, 1877). . . . Miss Elizabeth Cade, of Morgantown, died November 7, aged forty-four years (*Weekly Post*, November 17, 1877). . . . "The oldest woman in town," Mrs. Deborah Thompson, relict of John W. Thompson, died November 19, aged eighty-eight years; her husband had died November 27, 1863 (*Weekly Post*, November 24, 1877). . . . Rev. J. B. Dickey, of the Morgantown Presbyterian Church, was being recognized for his "wonderful power in reading the scriptures and hymns, and in oratory" (*Weekly Post*, December 8, 1877). . . . Mrs. Margaret Tennant, wife of Richard D. Tennant, of Mooresville, died December 8 (*Weekly Post*, December 15, 1877). . . . Mellon's Chapel M.E. Church, near Rock Forge, was dedicated by Rev. S. Lowther, on May 27 (*Weekly Post*, June 2, 1877).

CHAPTER ONE HUNDRED TWO

1878

In 1878, Alexander L. Wade, Monongalia County superintendent of schools, was preparing to write a book which would be among the most influential ever written by a local author. Entitled "A Graduating System for Country Schools," it would be published in Boston in 1881 and sold throughout the country.[1]

The first constitution of the new state of West Virginia had included this injunction: "The Legislature shall provide, as soon as practicable, for the establishment of a thorough and efficient system of free schools." And the very first legislature, on December 20, 1863, had passed a long act establishing the free school system. But the state, and the entire country, were in the midst of a long and bitter war and the implementation of the system, so different from that of old Virginia, was mostly delayed until the coming of peace, in 1865.

A Graduating System for Country Schools. Alexander L. Wade, in 1871, became principal of the Morgantown public school, which was making use of the old building of the Monongalia Academy, constructed in 1828, given to the state when West Virginia University was located here, and sold by the state to the borough of Morgantown for $13,500.

The Wade family was among the pioneer settlers of the Monongahela Valley, but George and Anna Wade, Alexander's parents, were among those who "went West" in the early nineteenth century, in search of greener pastures. Alexander was born near Rushville, Indiana, February 1, 1832. Then the family, unlike most of those who "went West," came back to Monongalia County in 1839. Here the father died, in 1846, "leaving," says

1. See *Weekly Post,* January 15, 1881.

Wiley[2], "no fortune save the force of a Christian example. Alexander, being the eldest of five children, and at the time of his father's death but fourteen years of age, undertook to aid his mother in maintaining the family, a work which he continued till after he reached his majority."

In 1848, only sixteen years of age, he began teaching school, his first assignment being in a log schoolhouse on Pedlar Run. He married, in 1854, Hattie Sanders and they had six children, Clark, Spencer, Mary, Anna, Charles, and Hattie.

He advanced rapidly. In 1861 he was elected clerk of the county court, and in 1863, county recorder, a position he held for eight years. In 1866, when the first telegraph line was built into Morgantown, he became the first operator.

In January 1871 he was elected clerk of the county board of school supervisors and in the autumn of that year he became principal of the Morgantown public school. In the autumn of 1873, in order to broaden his experience as an educator, he engaged with Superintendent Cox to visit all the county schools. This work he continued for the next two years.

On August 13, 1875, he was elected county superintendent of schools, without opposition, and on August 7, 1877, was reelected, again without opposition.

Wiley[3] tells of the birth of the idea that led to Wade's greatest fame: "He had long entertained the belief that there is entirely too much waste in country school work; and, while County Superintendent, he saw this fact in a still clearer light. He saw that average students in academies and colleges complete more branches in a single year, than average pupils in country schools complete in the entire school period. After much careful study he became satisfied that the chief cause of difference is found in the fact, that in all higher schools there is a definite work to do, a definite time in which it ought to be done, and a test as to whether it is well done; while in country schools no such provisions exist. He, therefore, determined to introduce into the country schools of his county, a system of graduation, similar to that of academies and colleges."

He began to organize graduating classes in the autumn of 1874

2. *History*, p. 372.
3. Pp. 373, 374.

and the first classes graduated, the first common school diplomas were granted, in the spring of 1876. The first common school catalog was published that autumn.

The annual report of the chief of the National Bureau of Education for 1878 said of the system: "Of all the plans developed none has excited more attention than that known as the 'Graduating System for Country Schools,' devised by A. L. Wade, County Superintendent of Monongalia, W.Va. . . . It has been reviewed by all the educational journals and has excited the attention of the principal State Superintendents of the Country."

Within the next few years the system was adopted by three other counties in West Virginia, fifteen counties in Pennsylvania, and by the state of Maine. It was being studied in most other states and a modification of the system is still in use today.

Law and Medicine. In 1878 the regents of West Virginia University created the "Chair of Law and Equity" and elected the "Hon. D. B. Lucas of Jefferson County, to fill the same." However, after some delay, he declined the appointment and suggested the appointment of his brother-in-law and neighbor, St. George Tucker Brooke, a lawyer and ex-Confederate soldier who had participated in the battle between the *Monitor* and the *Merrimac.* The appointment was made and Professor Brooke began to offer regular courses in law and equity in the 1878-79 term, with the understanding that they would be developed into a professional school of the university.[4]

The University Catalog for 1878-79 announced the establishment of a "Medical Department," with Dr. H. W. Brock as professor.

Hugh Workman Brock was born at Blacksville on January 5, 1830, the son of Fletcher and Rachel Brock.[5] At the age of sixteen he began studying under Dr. Charles McLane and graduated from Jefferson Medical College in 1852. He then returned to Morgantown to become a partner of Dr. McLane, an arrangement which continued until the onset of the Civil War, when he became an army surgeon, serving in Sheridan's Field Hospital at Win-

4. Ambler, *History of Education in West Virginia,* pp. 195, 196.
5. See vol. 3, p. 486.

Fig. 2. I. G. Lazzelle.   Fig. 3. Hugh Workman Brock.

chester, Virginia. After the war he returned to practice with Dr. Joseph A. McLane, leaving this in 1874 to enter into practice with his younger brother, Luther Sansom Brock (born December 19, 1844), who had graduated from Jefferson Medical College that year.

In 1868-69 Dr. Hugh Brock had become a part-time professor at the university with the title of lecturer in anatomy, physiology, and hygiene. The course he gave was doubtless intended to be popular in nature, but, beginning with the school year 1878-79, "the work given by Dr. Brock became more professional in name and in content. . . . The work . . . was designed to serve as a nucleus around which it was hoped to establish a fully organized medical department.

"It is quite apparent that the course covered a wide area—perhaps too wide for the small number of hours devoted to it. However, in view of the limited knowledge of the day and the primitive state of medical education, the course may have been more useful than it seems to us at the present time."[6]

6. Edward J. Van Liere and Gideon S. Dodds, *History of Medical Education in West Virginia*, pp. 8, 9.

Dr. Brock was a man of high ideals and was a dedicated physician, going to New York or Philadelphia almost every year to attend lectures and clinics so he could keep up with advances in medicine. He was one of the founders of the West Virginia Medical Society, which held its organizational meeting at Fairmont, April 10, 1867.

Dr. McLane is Dead! Morgantown's most famous physician passed away May 22, 1878; for more than half a century his presence had dominated the field of medicine in the county (see vol. 3, pp. 213, etc.). He was born September 4, 1790, and had come here from Lancaster, Pennsylvania, in 1823.[7]

Medical education was in a primitive state at the time and young men who wished to become practicing physicians often "read" medicine by working with a well-known and successful doctor. Numerous young men, through the years, studied under Dr. McLane.

About 1850 Dr. McLane had formed a partnership with Isaac Scott, formerly of Parkersburg, for the manufacture and sale of McLane's Improved Liver Pills and Scott's White Circassian Liniment, the name of the firm being C. McLane and I. Scott. The project was remarkably successful; sales increased rapidly and by 1855 more than a dozen people were required to make and fill orders from every state and even from foreign countries.

Dr. McLane also, about the same time, formed a partnership for the practice of medicine, with his son, Joseph, and with Drs. Scott and H. W. Brock. Their practice extended to Uniontown and Waynesburg, in Pennsylvania, and to Kingwood, Grafton, and Clarksburg, in Virginia. They of course made house calls and had the reputation of never refusing a call, no matter how great the distance or how bad the weather. Charles and Joseph McLane were similar in their love of life and people and had an inexhaustible supply of anecdotes and good stories, which may have played a part in the healing process by taking the patients' minds from their troubles.

Charles McLane married Elizabeth, daughter of Jacob Kerns, and they had eight children, namely, William C. (died 1821),

7. *Weekly Post,* May 25, 1878. See biography by A. L. Wade, *Weekly Post,* March 5, 1887.

Catherine C. (died 1832), Joseph A., Eliza Emily, Ann Lavinia, Mary Louise, John Wesley, and Virginia. Eliza Emily married Dr. Isaac Scott.[8]

Slack Water Comes Closer. In 1878 the frustrating and long-drawn-out efforts to secure slack-water navigation for Monongalia County were at last on the verge of success. In pioneer times the Monongahela River had played an important role in westward migration; even though the river flowed to the north, many immigrants crossed the mountains by wagon or horseback or afoot to Morgantown or other points on the river, then took flatboats for the remainder of the journey to Ohio, to Kentucky, to Indiana, or Illinois.

But the river's promise in providing reliable transportation facilities was by no means satisfactorily realized. Much of the time the water level was too low for dependable movement of craft, or too high and swift for safety.

The first steamboat reached Morgantown in 1826,[9] the cause of great excitement, and thereafter a few steamboats usually arrived each year, causing only slightly less excitement, but their value in the transportation picture was limited because of their irregularity.

Finally the federal government began to enter the picture and at last progress began to be made. Congressman James C. McGrew secured the passage of an act by the Forty-first Congress, authorizing a survey of the Monongahela River from New Geneva to Morgantown, which was made in the summer of 1871. The Forty-second Congress, in 1872, appropriated $25,000.00 to begin the work of slacking the river between the two points, and later another $66,000.00. In 1872 a contract for building a lock and dam went to Smith, Hawkins and Davis for $54,641.75. This was to be known as Lock No. 9, even though Locks 7 and 8 were not yet built (or even started).

The work proceeded slowly, with many delays. In 1875 Congressman J. Marshall Hagans secured another appropriation of $22,000 to continue work on the lock and also the passage of an

8. James Morton Callahan, *Making of Morgantown*, pp. 96-98; *Weekly Post*, June 1, 1878.

9. Vol. 2, p. 510. See vol. 3, various entries, for progress on slack water from Pittsburgh south to the state line.

act authorizing a survey of the Monongahela River from Morgantown to Fairmont. This survey was made under the direction of
Captain T. P. Roberts, whose report gave the distance as twenty-
eight miles, with a fall of fifty-five feet in the river, which would
require six dams. It is obvious that the fall from Fairmont to
Morgantown is much more rapid than that from Morgantown to
Pittsburgh.

In March 1876 the contract was awarded to Smith and Hawkins for construction of the dam at Hoard's Rocks. The contract
price was fifty thousand dollars and the work was to have been
completed by November 15; it was suspended in October, however, because of the exhaustion of funds and the failure of Congress to make further appropriation.

The work was at last resumed in 1878. A part of the earlier
work was found defective and had to be torn out and rebuilt.
Then the work was again suspended.[10]

After a century of such frustrating delays, it might have been
felt that the people of Monongalia County would have given up in
despair their efforts to secure slack-water navigation. But at last
success was about to crown their efforts.

Working for a Railroad. Even while earnestly striving to secure
slack-water navigation for the county, many civic leaders were
working on the project of securing a railroad. At the meeting on
November 3, 1877 (p. 5), a committee had been appointed to
solicit subscriptions and three thousand dollars had been subscribed by those at the meeting.

In 1878 the name of the railroad was changed to the Pittsburgh, West Virginia, and Southern Narrow-Gauge Railroad, and
on January 31, at a meeting in Grafton, George C. Sturgiss was
appointed general manager of the enterprise in West Virginia.
The road was designed to run from some point in Cass District to
Morgantown and on to Grafton, to connect with the B&O. The
people along the route were asked to subscribe three thousand
dollars for each mile of the road.

Meetings were held at Maidsville and Cassville, and one at the
courthouse, on March 16, where $11,999 was subscribed. On
June 14, Morgan District, by a vote of 467 to 6, subscribed

10. Wiley, pp. 130, 131; *Weekly Post,* August 10, 21, 1878, etc.

$20,000 to aid in the construction of the road through her territory. But on November 9 Cass District voted on a proposition to subscribe $15,000 and, by a vote of 107 for and 123 against, refused to contribute her portion, thereby effectively defeating the project, since all later efforts to raise the money by private subscription failed.[11]

The County Fair Closes. The ninth and last annual fair sponsored by the Monongahela Valley Agricultural and Mechanical Society was held October 1-3, 1878. The fair had been well attended but receipts had not been sufficient to meet expenses. E. H. Coombs was the last president of the society.[12]

The Second Judicial Circuit. This circuit had been constituted in 1872, including Wetzel, Marion, Monongalia, Taylor, Doddridge, and Harrison counties. Charles S. Lewis was elected judge for a term of eight years.

Judge Lewis died January 22, 1878,[13] and A. Brooks Fleming, of Fairmont, was appointed on January 30 to fill his position. In October he was elected to fill the unexpired term.

Aretas Brooks Fleming was born October 15, 1839, the son of Benjamin Franklin and Rhoda (Brooks) Fleming. He studied law at the University of Virginia and with E. B. Hall, and was admitted to the bar in 1861. He was a member of the West Virginia Legislature from Marion County for two terms.[14]

Morgantown Building Association. Morgantown's first building and loan company, the Enterprise Building Association of Morgantown, formed in 1872, closed up its business in May 1878, paying off its stockholders in full. "Not a cent was lost in any manner, it is said, during its entire course of business."[15]

While its affairs were being wound up, another similar association was organized and incorporated April 2, 1878, as the Morgantown Building Association. The first officers were Manliff Hayes, president; John C. Wagner, treasurer; E. H. Coombs,

11. Wiley, p. 115.
12. Wiley, p. 248; *Weekly Post*, October 12, 1878.
13. See editorial, *Weekly Post*, February 2, 1878.
14. Wiley, pp. 309, 331, 332; *Weekly Post*, February 9, 1878.
15. Wiley, p. 555.

secretary; J. M. Hagans, solicitor; M. L. Casselberry, W. C. Mc-
Grew, E. Shisler, W. W. Dering, and William Wagner, directors.[16]

Mount Olive Methodist Church. The third church building to
serve the Pentress (New Brownsville) section was dedicated December 22, 1878, by members of the Methodist Episcopal congre-

Fig. 4. Mount Olive Methodist Episcopal Church. (Courtesy Ruth S. Conn.)

gation. Like the Dolls Run Christian Church, completed a year
earlier, it was built of red bricks made at the site. A. W. Brown
was the contractor.

The dedicatory sermon was given by Rev. J. R. Thompson, who
was assisted by Rev. J. W. Bolton and Rev. Gideon Martin. The
church became a member of the Blacksville Circuit.

Ground for the building was given by Nicholas Johnson. The
first trustees were Nicholas Chalfant, John Brown, Albert Chap-

16. Wiley, pp. 555, 556; *Weekly Post,* March 23, 1878, etc.

lin, George W. Johnson, A. W. Brown, Titus Lemley, Lindsey Blaker, Abraham Hawkins, and C. E. Hawkins.[17]

Cross Roads. A post office was established June 17, 1878, at Cross Roads, Battelle District, with Griffin S. Cross as the first postmaster. The location was on one of the corners where two roads crossed. The first school, called the Sutton, was built about 1820. The first church was built by a Baptist congregation about 1835.

Improved Mail Service. "The much needed semi-weekly mail from Morgantown to Burton by way of Granville, Randall, Cassville, Pedlars Run, Mooresville, Pentress, Miracle Run, Blacksville, Wadestown, and Cross Roads has been established. Formerly there was but one mail over this route each week, which was a matter of serious inconvenience to the large number of our citizens who resided between here and Burton. This will be hailed with satisfaction by the many who could heretofore get mail but once each week."[18]

Miscellany. In 1878: D. C. Hoffman introduced registered Jersey cattle from Maryland and fine Merino sheep from Greene County, Pennsylvania (Wiley, p. 247). . . . George M. Reay erected a firestone coke-oven at the Durbannah Foundry, about eight feet in diameter, for burning forty-eight-hour coke (Wiley, p. 264). . . . Thomas H. B. Staggers, son of Harvey Staggers, was admitted to the Monongalia County bar on March 22 (Wiley, pp. 317, 357). . . . University President J. R. Thompson, convinced of the state's great need of an educational paper, in November began the publication of the *West Virginia Journal of Education* (Wiley, p. 415). . . . The Reverend Stephen H. Hunter and his wife, Sallie H. Moreland Hunter, sailed for China as missionaries under the Presbyterian Board of Foreign Missions (Wiley, pp. 449, 450). . . . D. H. Chadwick and Company opened a store in Morgantown (Wiley, p. 583). . . . J. Keener Durr tore down the old Na-

17. Dodds and Dodds, pp. 128, 129; *Chronicles of Core*, p. 117; Hugh M. Shafer, *The Mt. Olive United Methodist Church, 1878-1978.* 39 pp., 1978; "At Olive United Methodist Church: Century of Service is Achieved." *Panorama* (*Sunday Dominion-Post*, July 23, 1978).

18. *New Dominion*, July 27, 1878.

tional Hotel building and erected a new four-story brick building
on the site, opposite the courthouse, which he named the Com-
mercial Hotel (Wiley, p. 586; *Weekly Post*, March 16, 1878). . . .
W. C. Snodgrass was appointed minister of the Morgantown
Methodist Episcopal Station (Wiley, p. 590). . . . A. T. Crolle was
Methodist Protestant minister at Morgantown (Wiley, p. 594).
. . . M. J. Jones opened a store at Smithtown (Wiley, p. 615). . . .
An iron bridge was built across Booths Creek at Uffington, at a
cost of fifteen hundred dollars (Wiley, p. 619). . . . Final services
were held in the Smithtown Presbyterian Church (Wiley, p. 625;
see vol. 3, p. 93). . . . Easton Grange, No. 390, Patrons of Husban-
dry, was organized, with twenty-five members (Wiley, p. 676).
. . . M. D. Lee was minister of the Forks of Cheat Baptist Church
(Wiley, p. 686). . . . Eli J. Wilson was appointed minister of the
Avery Methodist Circuit (Wiley, p. 689). . . . J. S. Pickenpaugh
took over the Frederick Furman store in Cassville upon Furman's
death (Wiley, p. 702). . . . S. J. Acklin took over D. T. Miller's
store at Brown's Mills (Wiley, p. 747). . . . J. E. Wasson and C. S.
Harrison were ministers of the Monongalia Methodist Circuit
(Wiley, p. 773). . . . Edward Price, who had come from England in
1842, and who made chairs with the aid of a foot lathe he brought
with him, established a furniture business under the firm name of
E. Price and Sons (Callahan, p. 136). . . . Rev. James E. Meredith
became pastor of the Miracle Run Methodist Church (Dodds and
Dodds, p. 134). . . . The old poor house property, south of Mor-
gantown, was sold by the overseers to Hosea Stansberry for
twelve hundred dollars (*Weekly Post*, April 13, 1878). . . . Mrs.
Ann Summers, wife of Alex Summers, died June 13, aged fifty-
four years (*Weekly Post*, June 22, 1878). . . . Frederick Furman,
merchant of Cassville and Jimtown, died on May 3 (*Weekly Post*,
June 1, 1878). . . . Mrs. Lurana Jarrett, widow of John Jarrett, of
Cheat Neck, died on October 18, aged eighty-seven years (*Weekly
Post*, October 26, 1878). . . . "Aunt Clarissa" Brown, former
faithful slave of Guy R. C. Allen, died October 24, aged eighty-
four years (*Weekly Post*, November 2, 1878). . . . Elizabeth, wife
of Joseph Smell, died April 1, aged fifty-six years (*Weekly Post*,
April 6, 1878).

CHAPTER ONE HUNDRED THREE

1879

One of the great days in the history of Monongalia County was September 29, 1879, when about fifteen hundred people gathered along the Monongahela River at Hoards Rocks[1] to celebrate the completion of Lock and Dam No. 9, providing slack-water navigation most of the way from Morgantown to Pittsburgh. Addresses were made by Congressman J. Marshall Hagans and by Morgantown attorney Joseph Moreland.

The struggle for aids to navigation on the Monongahela had been a very long and frustrating one, almost overwhelming because of its tremendous cost. As early as 1817 a Monongahela Navigation Company had been chartered by the Virginia General Assembly, but nothing came of all the efforts until a Pennsylvania corporation by the same name organized in 1837, began work at Pittsburgh. Locks and Dams Nos. 1, 2, 3, and 4 were completed by 1844 and the river was made navigable between Pittsburgh and the National Road at Brownsville. From 1844 to 1852 the company carried over 745,000 passengers. By 1856 Locks and Dams Nos. 5 and 6 were completed, bringing slack water to New Geneva.

Work was then suspended for a long time, partly because of the tremendous cost of the improvements and the relative sparseness of the population in the upper Monongahela, partly because of the intervention of the Civil War.

The Dam at Hoards Rocks. At last, in 1872, the United States Congress was induced to enter the project (a logical move since more than one state was involved) and the first small federal ap-

1. Near the site of the 1772 settlement of John Hoard (see vol. 1, pp. 192, 211).

propriation of twenty-five thousand dollars, was made to begin
the work of slacking the river from New Geneva to Morgantown.
    Because of strong public sentiment in Morgantown it was de-
cided to bypass temporarily Locks and Dams Nos. 7 and 8 and to
proceed at once to No. 9, the first one to be constructed south of
the state line. Work was begun in 1876.
    A Uniontown newspaper, the *Genius of Liberty*, published a de-
scription of the completed lock and dam, furnished by William
Weston, engineer in charge:
    "The dam is over 300 feet from shore to lock-wall. It is built en-
tirely of stone and cement, and is vertical on the upper side and
slants from a width of four feet on top to fourteen at the bottom.
It is built in the form of an arch, circling up the river. A line
drawn from the middle of the base of the arch to the middle of the
top of the dam is twenty feet. The foundation stones are bedded
in solid rock with a shoulder of five or six inches to rest against.
The stones are not only cut keystone fashion to prevent moving
down, but each successive layer is held down by being cut with
copings and thus dovetailed in the wall below each stone in the
top layer which reaches across the top of the dam, and is cut
smooth and round so as to prevent drift catching the walls. No
loops or hooks of iron are used to hold the stone together, as this
is unnecessary. From the standing water below, the dam is nineteen feet high, and slacks the water five feet at Morgantown, a
distance of eight miles by river.
    "The lock walls are the most complete piece of masonry along
the river. The walls within the gates are 200 feet; entire length of
walls 300, and the distance between the walls fifty feet. The
wicket gates are in the walls on the sides of the lock; the water
above the upper gates pass in arches; when these wickets are
opened to the center of the side walls then perpendicular down to
the bed of the river, then returns to the center table walls above
and under the upper gates, and thence through arches in the table
walls into the lock. These arches, though very crooked, will admit
a volume of water sufficient to fill the lock in a short time. There
are five inch grooves in each wall above the upper gates, and
below the lower gates for the purpose of slipping down five-inch
boards (like the front boards are put in a granary as it fills up), to

Fig. 5. Dam at Hoards Rocks, under construction. (Courtesy Clifford Hoard.)

Fig. 6. Lock No. 9. (Courtesy Clifford Hoard.)

keep the water off the gates if they need repair. The four gates weigh thirteen tons each."[2]

Clifford Hoard, a descendant of John Hoard (vol. 1, p. 192), supplied the following:

"Since the dam was built in the form of an arch, it caused a back wash. The back wash acted in this manner: After the water came over the dam, it would flow straight down the river for a hundred yards or so and then from the center it would turn sharply to the left and to the right and flow directly back to the dam on the shore side. Now the higher the water the faster the back wash would move. When high water was running and the water hit the built-in bench at the base of the dam, it made an awesome spectacle. The roar of the water was tremendous. It could be heard from every hill top in the vicinity, and some of these hill tops were a mile away.

"This back wash formed a serious hazard for a boat approaching from down river. The pilot had to be extremely careful or the back wash would take him on the outside wall."[3]

The big boats had their problems but small boats often got into very serious difficulties, the whirling water taking them directly into the rush of water coming from the dam. Clifford Hoard continues: "Your writer recalls one instance when a poor panic-stricken man yelled out, 'God Almighty save me!' We are happy to report that no one ever met with disaster because my father, the lock tender, or Uncle Ben, the lock master, always got a line to them and pulled them to the lock wall."

Railroad Discussions. Although disappointed by the vote in Cass District late in the previous year (p. 17), promoters of the proposed Pittsburgh, West Virginia and Southern Narrow-Gauge Railroad continued to hold discussions. A corps of engineers under N. McConaughty surveyed the route of the road from Morgantown to the Pennsylvania line. Dr. George P. Hayes, president of the company, addressed meetings in its interest at Morgantown and at Cassville.[4]

2. Quoted by Wiley, pp. 131, 132; see also *Morgantown Weekly Post*, October 4, 1879.

3. Pers. comm.

4. Wiley, p. 115.

The Monongalia Agricultural Association. The old Monongahela Valley Agricultural and Mechanical Society, which had held nine annual fairs at Morgantown, dissolved in 1879 and a new organization, the Monongalia Agricultural Association, took its place in an effort to continue the fairs. The group was organized June 23, 1879, with the following stockholders: Col. Joseph Snider, Frederick Breakiron, Major W. W. John, Edward W. Brand, Manliff Hayes, S. B. McVicker, P. F. Harner, E. J. Evans, A. Garrison, Edward W. St. Clair, and J. E. Dent. Col. Joseph Snider was elected president and Edward W. Brand vice-president.[5]

The first fair was held October 14-16 at the old fairgrounds.

"Wednesday opened bright, warm and dusty, with the mercury dancing around the eighties somewhere at noon. The advent of the Pt. Marion Brass Band, in their crimson chariot, drawn by four horses, about 9 o'clock Wednesday morning, was a signal for a general turn-out and at that hour Main street was alive with pedestrians and moving vehicles, filled with human freight, wending their way to the Fair grounds.

"The exhibition of horses, cattle and sheep on Wednesday and Thursday was *the largest and best* ever seen at a Fair in Monongalia County. . . .

"Capt. Alpheus Garrison had charge of the Agricultural and Manufacturers' Hall. The Society made a wise selection in appointing Capt. Garrison as Marshal. He made an excellent officer, and was assisted in the discharge of his duties by Mr. Elza Sheets."[6]

Public Schools. The legislature of 1879 made some radical changes in the state school law. It reduced the annual salary of the county superintendent to a maximum of $125, repealed the provision requiring him to visit the schools, and made him little more than a clerk. The act also specified that the district boards of education should consist of a president and four commissioners, who should appoint a trustee for each sub-district. The board was to appoint the teachers and fix their salaries.

Bruce L. Keenan was elected county superintendent on Au-

---

5. Wiley, p. 248.

6. *Morgantown Weekly Post*, October 25, 1879.

gust 17, receiving 663 votes to 646 for Alexander L. Wade. Mr. Wade, who had been superintendent since 1875, had left the impression that he did not want to continue in the office and did not promote his interests.[7]

A County Teachers Institute conducted by F. H. Crago was held for one week, beginning August. 4.[8]

The Morgantown School opened September 1 with a large attendance but there were complaints that the eight months term was too long. A newspaper editor said: "Six months is enough schooling to give young children in any one year, and we hope the School Commissioner will never again order an eight months school. It is entirely too confining and a child's mind will warp and shrivel instead of expanding into brightness and buoyancy."[9]

John W. Scott. The first vice-president of West Virginia University, John W. Scott, D.D., LL.D., died in North Carolina July 25, 1879. He was born in York County, Pennsylvania, in 1807, and graduated from Jefferson College in 1827. He served in the ministry, in the Presbyterian Church, then turned his attention to education and was president of Washington College for twelve years. He became principal of Woodburn Seminary and was the last principal of Monongalia Academy. He was appointed to the faculty of West Virginia University in 1867, as vice-president and professor of languages.

In the fall of 1875, upon the resignation of President Alexander Martin, he was appointed acting president and served in that capacity until March 28, 1877. He was a profound scholar and a man of great force of character.[10]

Deaths. A former resident of Clinton District, Samuel Newman, died in Ohio in 1879. When the road from Clinton Furnace to Halleck was built, about 1873, a beech tree was found with the inscription, "S. N. 1818," cut in the bark. It was afterwards learned that Samuel Newman had killed a deer there and cut his initials to mark the spot.[11]

A former instructor at Monongalia Academy, John Mills, died

7. Wiley, pp. 369-71.
8. Wiley, p. 380.
9. *Morgantown Weekly Post,* September 6, 1879.
10. Wiley, pp. 409, 417, 418.
11. Wiley, p. 634.

near Morgantown June 11, 1879. He was born in Dunbarton, New Hampshire, August 6, 1806. He came to Morgantown in 1835 and took a position in the Monongalia Academy, which he retained until 1844. He was then discharged by the trustees, it is said, because he refused to vote for Henry Clay on the grounds that he was a duelist. He thereupon started a school of his own, which he operated successfully for four years, then, his health failing, he purchased a farm near Morgantown and lived there the remainder of his life.[12] He married Mahala Berkshire and they had two surviving children, Mrs. Jane M. Wood and Rev. William J. Mills.

Albert C. Rude, of Union District, died suddenly at his home June 14, 1879, of pneumonia, aged about fifty-eight years. He "was a clever man and good citizen. He was two or three times elected Magistrate of Union District, and was regarded as a strictly upright and honorable man."[13]

The widow of Captain James Hurry, Mrs. Margaret Hurry, died October 16, aged eighty-three years. Her husband died in 1832. They had seven children, those who survived being Captain Frank Hurry, Mrs. Rebecca J. Lynch, Mrs. Cornelia Davidson, Mrs. Mary Sinsel, and Mrs. Sarah Wood. Her father, Captain William Elsey, was a Revolutionary War soldier.[14]

Fidelio Hughes Oliphant, one of the pioneers of the iron industry in Fayette and Monongalia counties, died at his home at Oliphants Furnace, Fayette County, on November 10. He was born January 4, 1800, the son of Col. John Oliphant. He married Jane C. Duncan and they had eleven children.[15]

Rawley Evans Dent, youngest of the twelve children of Capt. John and Margaret Evans Dent, died near Laurel Point on November 24. He was born February 29, 1808, and lived all his life in the same neighborhood. "He was full of life and energy and brave as a lion. Being exceedingly fond of amusement and a great promoter of fun, he was a general favorite." He married Maria Miller, then Nancy Barker, and the following children survived:

12. See lengthy sketch of his life, *Morgantown Weekly Post*, June 28, 1879.
13. *Morgantown Weekly Post*, June 21, 1879.
14. *Morgantown Weekly Post*, October 25, 1879.
15. *Morgantown Weekly Post*, November 22, 1879, a two-column biography copied from the *Uniontown Republican Standard.*

Maria Christy, J. Clark Dent, Imlah Judson Dent, Ann Amelia Thorn, Eugenie Yeager and E. Coleman Dent.[16]

"The Range." A note from West Warren stated: "Mr. John Ewing, of Washington, Pa., is here gathering and shipping his grain—the proceeds of the extensive farm known as 'the Range,' which consisted of 4,000 acres at the time he purchased it. He has since sold and narrowed it down to 1200 acres. Jacob M. Haught, the chief tenant, has lived on this farm for 46 years. Who in the State can beat this?"[17]

The Fur Trade. Many men and boys of the county were engaged in hunting or trapping fur-bearing animals, especially skunks. Johnny Bean, a celebrated skunk hunter, often dug them out of their holes, in spite of their strong odor ("one healthy cat will furnish enough perfumery to innoculate a whole neighborhood"), but they were commonly captured by "dead-falls," or traps.

Prices were about as follows: white skunk, 50 cents; black, $1; common, 25 cents; fox, 75 cents to $1; coon, 40 to 50 cents; muskrat, 10 cents. One buyer, Peter Brown, agent of a New York City firm, expected to buy nearly $4,000 worth of pelts in the county during 1879.[18]

Odd Fellows Pic-Nic. Members of the Odd Fellows Lodge had a "pic-nic" at Cassville on August 28, with music by a cornet band and an address by George C. Sturgiss. An observer commented that "he never saw as many buggies, carriages, and spring wagons at a small pic-nic in his life as there were at Cassville." "Now, what's the use of our people crying 'hard times,' " he said. "There never was a time in the history of this country, since the war, when crops were so good and prices so low, and still the people from country and town who can now afford to ride in fine carriages and wagons, are the ones that complain."[19]

Educational Meetings. To acquaint the public with the programs carried on in the relatively new free schools, numerous educational meetings were held, in all parts of the county. These were

16. *Morgantown Weekly Post,* November 29, 1879.
17. *Morgantown Weekly Post,* October 4, 1879.
18. *Weekly Post,* March 8, 1879.
19. *Morgantown Weekly Post,* September 6, 1879.

well attended, partly because the citizens certainly were genuinely interested in their schools, and partly because the meetings were outlets for social proclivities.

Typical of such meetings was this: "An educational meeting was held at the Dolls Run Christian Chapel on Monday night, January 27, in the interest of the Dolls Run, Sugar Valley, and Pedlars Run schools. J. E. Price was elected president and Squire S. P. Tennant vice-president. After a song from the choir and organ, the president introduced Prof. [Alexander] Wade, county superintendent, who gave reports of the above-named schools. . . . Mr. Wade spoke for about one and a half hours to a very attentive and quiet audience. The president then introduced S. W. Ramsey, teacher of the Dolls Run School, who . . . remarked in his speech that should he teach again he would visit every family before the opening of school. Mr. [Jonathan C.] Murphy[20] was then introduced and spoke in high terms of the character of his patrons . . . E. P. McGinnis[21] was next introduced and spoke upon the necessity of a hearty cooperation among the patrons, pupils, and teachers . . . Mr. Zimri Ammons . . . was next introduced, who said that he would go farther to attend an educational meeting than any other. He made a very good speech. Capt. [Alphaeus] Garrison was next called for and responded in his usual fervent style. . . . The whole thing passed off quietly and pleasantly."[22]

Churches. J. T. Eichelberger became minister of the Smithtown Methodist Circuit. J. C. Jordan became minister of the Forks of Cheat Baptist Church. D. H. Davis was appointed minister of the Avery Methodist Circuit. J. B. Dickey was pastor of the Sugar Grove Presbyterian Church.

Miscellany. In 1879: Clarence B. Dille was admitted to the Monongalia County bar on March 20, Frank Woods on March 19, and Ulysses Arnett on March 22 (Wiley, pp. 317, 318). . . . The *West Virginia Journal of Education,* published for the past year by University President John Rhey Thompson, was merged with the *New England Journal of Education* (Wiley, p. 415). . . . John

20. Teacher of the Sugar Valley School.
21. Teacher of the Pedlar Run School.
22. *Morgantown Weekly Post,* January 31, 1879.

J. Brown on January 2 was elected president of the Merchants'
National Bank of West Virginia at Morgantown (Wiley, p. 463).
. . . William W. Price died at the age of ninety-two (Wiley, p. 472).
. . . Lazier, Finnell and Company, L. Weaver, and S. D. Hirshman
opened stores in Morgantown (Wiley, p. 582). . . . Dr. R. E. Brock
began the practice of medicine in Morgantown (Wiley, p. 584).
. . . M. L. Hutchinson opened a store at Smithtown (Wiley, p.
615). . . . Shay and Bayles opened a store at Easton (Wiley, p.
676). . . . Steam machinery was installed in G. A. Burke's wagon-
making shop at Blacksville (Wiley, p. 745). . . . The heavy slate
roof of the courthouse was repaired in September by the insertion
of iron rods to hold the walls together (Callahan, p. 215). . . . The
old tannery of Martin Callendine, on Front Street at Maiden
Alley, had become a nuisance and the borough council notified
him that he must provide abatement, or have the old house pulled
down and the vats filled (*Morgantown Post*, May 23, 1879).
. . . Thomas Arnett and Sons' steam flouring mill at Arnettsville
was destroyed by a fire from the furnace on June 20 (*Morgantown Weekly Post*, June 28, 1879). . . . Capt. Alphaeus Garrison's
store on Pedlar Run was robbed on the night of January 30 and
Wilson and Hutchinson's store at Smithtown the following night
(*Weekly Post*, February 8, 1879). . . . Two convicts recently
liberated from the penitentiary, "the notorious Taylor and
Jones," were arrested for the thefts on February 7 (*Weekly Post*,
February 15, 1879). . . . Bishop Simpson presided over the
Thirty-third West Virginia Conference of the M.E. Church, at
Morgantown, in October (Wiley, p. 446).

CHAPTER ONE HUNDRED FOUR

1880

The census of 1880, the second since West Virginia had become a separate state, indicated that Monongalia County was beginning to recover from the rigors of civil discord and that growth was proceeding more briskly. The 1860 census showed a growth in population of only 5 percent over 1850 and the 1870 census showed even less growth, only 4 percent over 1860.

The Census of 1880. But in 1880 the population of the county was given as 14,985, a gain of 11 percent. Of the total population of the county in 1880 the report showed that 8,843 were born in West Virginia, 4,318 in Virginia, 1,462 in Pennsylvania, 69 in Ohio, 130 in Maryland, 14 in Kentucky, 3 in British America, 25 in England and Wales, 22 in Ireland, 3 in Scotland, 14 in Germany, and 2 in France. There were 317 black people, up from 231 in 1870. Females slightly outnumbered males, 7,571 to 7,414.

The population of Morgantown was 745, a reduction from 797 in 1870. The census provided estimates for the population of several unincorporated villages, as follows: Arnettsville, 54; Blacksville, 106; Cassville, 80; Durbannah, 127; Granville, 122; Hamilton, 44; Hoffman's Addition, 86; Maidsville, 44; Sallytown, 67; Stringtown, 29; and West Morgantown, 51.

The population of the seven districts, with 1870 figures for comparison, follows on page 32.

It will be noted that the most substantial increases were in the two westernmost districts, Battelle and Clay, and the conclusion to be drawn is that more farm families were moving into the rich agricultural lands in the valley of Dunkard Creek.

Agriculture was still the most important occupation, with wheat, corn, oats, and livestock important products. The production of hops fell, as the production of alcoholic beverages was no

31

	1870	1880
Battelle	1,856	2,293
Cass	1,449	1,459
Clay	1,972	2,522
Clinton	1,900	2,126
Grant	2,216	2,156
Morgan	2,536	2,722
Union	1,618	1,707

longer a Monongalia County industry. Home-made linen was giving way to factory-made cotton fabrics and the raising of flax was ending; 5,998 pounds had been raised in the county in 1860, only 225 pounds in 1880.

Maple sugar, maple molasses and sorghum molasses were important products. The making of maple sugar was an early spring activity, while sorghum molasses making was a feature of late summer.

The census reported "21 flour-and-grist mills in the county, with a capital of $86,500, 35 employees, with $6,022 paid in wages and a total value of the products amounting to $176,164. There were 13 sawmills, capital $15,500, 36 employees, with $4,700 paid in wages, and a total value of the products of $27,660."

Those named to take the Monongalia County census were: Battelle, Dr. A. B. Mason and J. H. Showalter; Cass, G. C. Cole; Clay, M. S. Garrison; Clinton, Joseph H. Powell; Grant, J. A. Thompson; Morgan, W. W. Houston; Morgantown, James H. Winger; Union, J. T. McCloskey.[1]

Churches and Religious Life. The religious character of the people of Monongalia County in the 1880s was attested by the fact that churches were located in every section of the county, all of them, of course, built by the money and hard labor of the worshipers.

The religious needs of the Morgantown community were supplied by five churches within the corporate limits of the borough.

1. Wiley, p. 765.

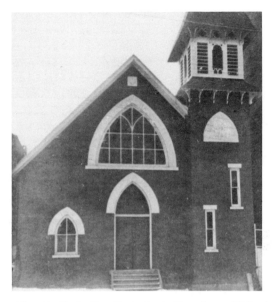

Fig. 7. Methodist Protestant Church on Walnut
Street. (H. L. Grant, *Greater Morgantown*, 1902.)

The Methodist Episcopal Church, built in 1850, after the original
building on the site had been destroyed by fire, stood at the corner of Pleasant Street and Long Alley (Chestnut Street). The
Presbyterian Church, built in 1868, stood on the corner of High
Street and Kirk Alley (Kirk Street). The Baptist Church, on the
corner of Long Alley and Bumbo Lane (Fayette Street), had been
constructed in 1846. The Methodist Protestant Church, on Walnut Street between High and Spruce streets, was built in 1880;
from 1874 until 1880 the congregation had worshiped in the old
academy building (then used as a public school building), following destruction of their original building by fire. The first church
building for black people in the borough was an old log house on
Long Alley between Maiden Alley (Wall Street) and Bumbo Lane.
In 1868 black Methodists purchased an old house on Long Alley
and converted it into a church. Later this old building was removed and (in 1870) a small frame church was erected on the site.

   There were eight churches in Clinton District, the Pisgah (organized in 1813), Fairview (1851), Halleck (1854), and Summers

(1846) M.E. churches; the Hopewell and Mount Calvary (1869) M.P. churches; and the Goshen (1837) and Smithtown Baptist churches.

Morgan District, outside of the borough of Morgantown, had several churches, including Mellon's Chapel (1876) Rock Forge (1810) and Drummond's Chapel (1835) M.E. churches and the Pleasant Hill Baptist Church. Woodland (1857) was used by all denominations.

In Union District was the Forks of Cheat Baptist Church, the oldest in the county, founded 1775, older than the county itself. There were two M.E. churches, Pierpont's (1800) and Fletcher (1859). Brown's Chapel, a Presbyterian church at Stewartstown, was organized in 1830, but in 1880 was not being regularly used. M.P. churches included Zion (1833), Avery (1842), Eden (1840), and Calvary (1852). Mount Union German Baptist Church, on the Stewartstown road, was built in 1883.

Across the river, in Cass District, there were four M.E. churches and three M.P. churches. The M.E. churches included Bethel (1824), Fort Martin (1778), the second oldest church in the county, Cassville (1880), and Wade's, while the M. P. churches included Maidsville, Cassville, and Gustin Run.

In Grant District M. E. churches included Cold Spring, Snider's Temple (1846), Laurel Point (1835), Granville (1850), Union (1856), Bend of the River (1865), and Arnettsville (1873). The Sugar Grove Presbyterian Church dates from 1835, some of the early members being from the Burnt Meeting House (see vol. 3, p. 268).

In Clay District there were four M.E. churches, namely, Point Pleasant (1863), Mount Hermon (1835), Mount Olive (1878), and Blacksville (1851). There were two Baptist churches, one at Mc-Curdysville (1805) and one at Blacksville (1849). The Church of Christ or Christian Church (often called Campbellite) had congregations at Dolls Run (1835), Pleasant Valley or Mooresville (1871), and Antioch (1879), at Ponetown.

Battelle District, the farthest from the county seat, had three M.E. churches, Park's (1846) on Miracle Run, West Warren (1845), and Highland (1866), near Flyblow. There was a Baptist Church at West Warren (Wadestown), organized in 1854. The Liming Church (1849) belonged to the Christian or Church of Christ denomination.

Besides religious services, the churches afforded abundant occasion for social enjoyment, especially at Thanksgiving, Christmas, and Easter. Christmas, then as now, was the great holiday of the year, but the religious aspects were more strongly emphasized a hundred years ago.

The Election. Two amendments to the state constitution were voted on, an amendment to Section 13 of Article III and an amendment to Article VIII. Both were ratified, the first by a vote of 1440 to 1270, the second by a vote of 1450 to 1277. The second amendment reconstituted the judicial circuits, Monongalia, with Marion and Harrison, falling into the Second Circuit. A. Brooks Fleming was reelected judge of the Circuit.

S. C. Malone. The son of J. C. Malone, of Clinton District, S. C. won distinction as an artist and penman. In 1880 he designed and executed a handsome picture entitled "From the Log Cabin to the White House," portraying Garfield and the leading events of his life. It was lithographed in New York and a large edition published. The original was presented to President Garfield and upon his death was returned to the artist.[2]

The University. Prior to 1880 the legislature had never appropriated over $16,000 a year for operation of the university. In 1880 the regents were planning to increase the endowment to $200,000, with an assured annuity of $12,000, thus placing the institution "upon an independent and permanent footing."

Although President Thompson was forced to pinch pennies, many people in the state thought too much money was being expended on the university. A Wheeling newspaper attacked an item of three thousand dollars for current and contingent expenses in the 1879 budget as extravagant and "enough to startle every economist in the State." The editor investigated the "proportions" of the university and its "accomplishments," finding that there were only forty students in the college proper and that twenty-two of these were taking "contingent courses." There were only twenty students in course of graduation and only two in the senior class. There were eighty-nine students in the preparatory department, fifty-two of these (and twenty-one in the college) being residents of Monongalia County. "In view of these findings the editor suggested that a commission be authorized to

2. Wiley, p. 632.

sell the University to the highest bidder with a view to closing it or to converting it into a private or denominational institution."[3]

President Thompson, answering this editorial, deplored the attitude of those seeking to injure or destroy their own university. "There was however no denying that the institution was a university in name only and that its patronage was largely local, for the campus meetings of the regents were then largely given over to political and bargaining caucuses to determine who would be the treasurer of the board, the secretary of the executive committee, and the superintendent of buildings and grounds." On the recommendation of President Thompson, the 1879 legislature vested the duties of these officers in members of the faculty, who were required to perform them without additional pay.[4]

President Thompson approached problems of student discipline with a foresighted attitude. He wished to rid the university of an "outgrown puritanical regime" and its "reform school and inebriate asylum methods" and to substitute "an element of personal moral influence." With this in mind he made horseback trips with students into the surrounding country and complied with a faculty rule forbidding the hitching of horses on the campus.

But he took every opportunity to denounce those who distracted students from their work. This caused some antagonism and a story is told of an angry person who accosted the president, club in hand, and accompanied by friends, to force him to change his attitude. He said, "You do not need that club and you do not need this crowd. You can crush me to earth with your fist, but you cannot terrorize me. As long as I am President of the University I shall continue to denounce you and your nefarious business and to do all I can to annihilate it."

As early as 1868 the regents were planning a university composed of colleges, but in 1880 the institution still adhered to "the college plan," functioning through seven departments, namely, the classical, scientific, agricultural, military, engineering (1869), law (1878), and medical (1878). There were neither schools nor colleges in the organization, but the law and medical departments were being developed into professional schools.[5]

3. Ambler, pp. 197, 198.
4. Ambler, *History of Education in West Virginia*, pp. 197, 198.
5. Ambler, pp. 199, 200.

The Second National Bank. A charter was issued on February 24 for the Second National Bank of Morgantown, with a capital of sixty thousand dollars and privilege to increase it to one hundred thousand dollars.

This organization was started as a banking business known as Hoffman and Company, in April 1868 by J. H. Hoffman and Charles S. Finnell. On March 23, 1874, it was chartered as a state bank under the name of the Morgantown Bank. William Price was the first president, J. H. Hoffman, cashier. G. W. John was the first president of the National bank.

At this time the only other bank in Morgantown was the Merchants' National Bank of West Virginia at Morgantown, organized October 1, 1865.[6]

Temperance Societies. The subject of temperance was a much debated issue in the final quarter of the nineteenth century. There were various temperance societies and temperance meetings were held frequently, the attendance indicating a decided anti-saloon sentiment. The Morgantown borough council, however, granted liquor licenses in June 1878 and in April 1879 to J. K. Durr and to F. H. St. Clair. A license was also granted in 1879 to J. F. Hopkins. In December 1880, following a large temperance meeting, leading "drys," including President J. R. Thompson, W. C. McGrew, L. S. Hough, G. M. Reay, J. A. Dille, E. H. Coombs, and George C. Sturgiss, took steps to petition the legislature to submit to popular vote the question of a prohibition law.[7]

Outside of Morgantown, no liquor licenses were granted at the time by the county court.

A Buggy Accident. Dr. A. B. Mason, of West Warren, "was returning home in his buggy when the horse took fright and ran over the high bank west of town, which is near 60 feet high, and a grade not far from 60 degrees. Mr. P. V. Rice, who was with him, jumped out at the brink unhurt. The doctor was thrown out about half way down the bank, and whirled end over end a distance of 40 feet before he struck the ground. Rice thought he was dead, but by the time he got to him he had rallied so he sat up, and enquired for his horse, which had run down the creek and become

6. Wiley, pp. 462-64.
7. Callahan, p. 216.

detached from the buggy, with no damage except the breaking of the shafts. The doctor met with no serious injury."[8]

Too Big A Load. "On the occasion of the recent departure of a carriage load of lawyers from Morgantown, to attend the late term of court at Kingwood, the vehicle contained Hons. Waitman T. Willey, J. Marshall Hagans, Judge R. L. Berkshire, and Philip H. Keck—bright and shining lights of the legal fraternity. The road was rough and the mud deep and sticky. Of course in such a crowd of gentlemen, after exhausting other subjects, that of politics would naturally crop up. It would be almost impossible for a party of gentlemen of the character named to ride twenty-two miles over a slow and muddy road, and not broach the approaching Presidential contest. . . . The wheels bore up well, until the name of Sam Tilden was broached, when whack! went the single tree and down came the carriage bed into the mud!"[9]

Blacksville Baptist Church. Members of the old Minorsville Baptist Church (see vol. 3, p. 318), perhaps because they were so few, joined with Baptists along Rush Run, across the state line, in Pennsylvania, meeting in various homes. The group then built a church near Johnson's School, in Greene County. Later, in 1880, they built a church in Blacksville, which thereafter became their center for worship. The building had two doors and two aisles, so that the men and women could sit on separate sides.[10]

New Poor House Superintendent. The contract for keeping the poor of the county was awarded, on January 29, to John L. Jones. The contract called for him to receive $1.31 per person per week, for which he was to furnish all necessary bedsteads, beds, bedding, clothing, boarding, medicine, fuel, tobacco, nurses and attendants necessary for the health and comforts of the paupers. There were about thirty persons living in the county poor house at Cassville.[11]

Halleck. A post office called Halleck (from Civil War hero, General Henry W. Halleck) was established March 18, 1880, with

---

8. *Weekly Post,* June 19, 1880.

9. *Weekly Post,* April 3, 1880.

10. Dodds and Dodds, *Churches of Monongalia County,* p. 122; *Weekly Post,* August 21, 1880.

11. *Weekly Post,* February 7, 1880.

Charles H. Duncan as the first postmaster. It was near the Taylor County line, along the old Kingwood to Clarksburg road, and was the highest post office in the county, at 1850 feet above sea level, on Chestnut Ridge.

The County Fair. "The Second Annual Fair of the Monongalia Agricultural Society came off at the Fair Grounds near town, Oct. 13th, 14th, and 15th.

"The first and second days there was not as much interest manifested as there should have been, and the last day of the Fair about as many people stood on the outside and watched from the hills as there were inside the enclosure.

"The pacing race Thursday was pretty good, and the sweepstakes trot Friday were only tolerable. The time made was poor.

"There was a fair exhibition of stock—some very fine horses and blooded cattle, sheep and hogs.

"The display in the Halls were meagre. Our people, we are sorry to see, are losing their interest in the County Fair to a great degree."[12]

Michael Core. A farmer of Dolls Run, Michael Core, died May 19, 1880. Born November 25, 1801, he was the son of Christopher and Hannah Snider Core. He married Christena, daughter of Abraham and Mary Shriver, and their children were Asa, Benjamin, Abraham, Christopher, Isaac, and Edgar Wilson. Their old log house, along the Dunkard Creek Turnpike, was built around 1840 and was still standing in 1980.[13]

Passing of a Pioneer. James Arnett, Jr., died February 25, 1880, at his home in Arnettsville. He was born September 10, 1796, and was numbered among the Monongalia County pioneers. He was "an upright and respectable citizen, and for many years a faithful and consistent member of the M.E. Church. . . . The writer of this remembers his old home (now on the farm of his son, D. M. Arnett) as one of the places of holding meetings, before our Churches were built."[14]

Miscellany. In 1880: W. C. Lough and Brothers opened an establishment at Cassville for the manufacture of buggies, spring-

12. *Weekly Post*, October 23, 1880.
13. *Chronicles of Core*, pp. 118, 119; *Weekly Post*, May 29, 1880.
14. *Weekly Post*, March 6, 1880.

wagons, and general woodwork (Wiley, p. 262). . . . Admitted to
the Monongalia County bar were Ledrew W. Wade, March 1;
John W. Davis, July 14; Waitman W. Houston, April 16; J. S.
Brookover, September 2; and Isaac C. Ralphsnyder, October 8
(Wiley, pp. 317, 318). . . . The West Virginia Press Association
held its annual meeting in Morgantown, on June 9 (Wiley, p. 439;
Weekly Post, June 10, 1880). . . . Elizabeth Semore died at the
age of ninety (Wiley, p. 472). . . . Mary McVicker, widow of
William John, and mother of Dr. George W. John, died (Wiley, p.
477). . . . George Kiger, Jr., succeeded T. P. Reay as operator of
the Morgantown office of Western Union Telegraph Company,
moving the office to the Commercial Hotel (Wiley, p. 555). . . . J.
Keener Durr resumed operation of the Commercial Hotel (Wiley,
p. 586). . . . L. W. Roberts was named minister of the Smithtown
M.E. Circuit (Wiley, p. 626). . . . Samuel F. Kelley in April opened
a blacksmith shop in Easton (Wiley, p. 676). . . . E. P. Brand was
minister of the Forks of Cheat Baptist Church (Wiley, p. 686).
. . . Jacob T. Eichelberger was minister of the Arnettsville M.E.
Circuit (Wiley, p. 728). . . . E. J. Rinehart opened a store at the
corner of High Street and Maiden Alley (Callahan, p. 209).
. . . Shisler's New Hardware Store was equipped in an up-to-date
manner, including in its stock fertilizers and farm equipment,
along with wallpaper and paints (Callahan, p. 210). . . . L. J.
Holland provided twenty-cent baths in the basement of the Commercial Hotel (Callahan, p. 212). . . . The Sarver School, on the
mountain five miles from Dellslow, was built, used both for a
school and a church; the first ministers were Ephraim Cohen and
Marion Burns (Dodds and Dodds, p. 81). . . . Hosea Stansberry,
in February, captured a large otter in a trap (*Weekly Post,* February 28, 1880). . . . "Mr. J. M. Neil, who runs a line of flat boats
from New Geneva to Morgantown, arrived Saturday last with a
large load of goods for our merchants, and for some of the county
merchants who receive their goods by river" (*Weekly Post,*
May 8, 1880). . . . Joseph Piles, of Days Run, was killed May 8 by
a log rolling over him; he was fifty years of age (*Weekly Post,*
May 15, 1880). . . . In April, several university students with
their girls, on a trip to near Reedsville, drove one horse to death
and nearly killed another, causing an outcry in town (*Weekly
Post,* April 17, 1880). . . . John Hoard died December 11, aged
seventy-nine years (*Weekly Post,* December 18, 1880). . . . Mrs.

Mary Evans died December 12, aged ninety-one years (*Weekly Post,* December 18, 1880). . . . Isaac Shriver, of the Dunkard Valley area, died March 30, aged seventy-three years (*Chronicles of Core,* p. 119; *Weekly Post,* April 10, 1880).

CHAPTER ONE HUNDRED FIVE

1881

By an amendment of the eighth article of the constitution of West Virginia, in 1880, the county court was abolished, and, beginning the next year, was no longer composed of two justices of the peace from each district, but was to consist of a board of three commissioners. This board held its first meeting January 3, 1881.[1]

The County Court. The original county courts date from 1623, in the early colony of Virginia. When Virginia became a commonwealth, in 1776, the governor was empowered to name its members, called justices of the peace, from a list submitted (after the first court had convened) by the court itself, so that it tended to be a self-perpetuating body. Furthermore, they recommended to the governor from their own body names for appointment to the offices of sheriff and commissioner of the revenue.

The pioneers found the county courts prime targets for their spleen. Clothed with executive, legislative, and judicial powers, they ruled the county but residents of the county had no voice in their appointments.

Nevertheless, despite bitter debate, the system was scarcely modified by the new Virginia constitution of 1830 and remained virtually unchanged until the members of the county court became elective, under the terms of the constitution of 1852. Beginning that year, the court consisted of four justices each from the seven magisterial districts, or a total of twenty-eight.

---

1. Curiously, although this body no longer handled judicial affairs, it continued to be called the county court until January 1, 1975, when an amendment changed the name to the county commission. Even yet (1981), it is popularly known as the county court, even though its members have for a century now been called commissioners.

This system continued until 1863, when, in the constitution for the new state of West Virginia, the county court was abolished, and in its place was substituted a county board of supervisors, consisting of one member from each of seven townships. Much of the supervisory work now developed upon the townships, each of which had two justices, two constables, a clerk, a treasurer, an overseer of the poor, in addition to the one supervisor (a member of the county board).

The new state constitution, to replace the one quickly adopted under the rigors of civil war, was approved in 1872. All advocates of the new constitution were emphatic in expressing their wish to abolish the township system, which they said was a new and expensive importation from the northern states. They desired to restore the old county court system. So the new constitution did away with the townships as subdivisions of the county and these were reconstituted as magisterial districts, as they had been before the war. They retained the same names, however; thus Clay Township became Clay District, etc.

By the 1880 amendment, as stated above, the county court was no longer composed of trial justices, but became largely an administrative board for county business affairs, chiefly police and fiscal. It appointed coroners, overseers of the poor, and other officers. Each district then elected its own magistrates (justices of the peace) and constables, and its own board of education, composed of the president and two other members.

Starting in 1881, the first members of the new county court were A. W. Brown, W. W. Dering, and S. P. Barker, the latter elected president. W. T. Willey was sworn in as clerk of the county court on November 7, 1882, succeeding John W. Madera. George W. McVicker had been sheriff since 1880, James M. Stewart county surveyor, and B. M. Jones assessor. Benjamin S. Morgan was elected county superintendent of schools in 1881.

President Thompson Resigns. At the time of the appointment of the Reverend John R. Thompson as president of West Virginia University, on January 11, 1877, the institution was "a rapidly disappearing quantity." From a high of 166 students for the 1870-71 term, the enrollment had fallen to 93 for the 1876-77 term, and in January 1877 only 42 students were actually enrolled.

But, as expected, the new, youthful president at once began a program designed to bring about an upward trend. At the request of the board of regents, he devoted his full time during the spring months of 1877 to travel about the state in an effort to restore confidence in the university. It was quite discouraging; at the end of three months he reported that he was "surprised and startled that such ignorance and apathy, and suspicion and distrust, and downright opposition should prevail among the citizens of West Virginia concerning their own university.

Despite this apathy, the enrollment did begin an upward trend, showing 118 for 1877-78, 135 for 1878-79, 132 for 1879-80, and reaching 177, the highest in history, for the 1880-81 term.

But there continued to be difficulty in providing for adequate financing. Prior to 1880 legislative appropriations for the university had never exceeded sixteen thousand dollars for a single year, except for capital expenditures. An annuity of twelve thousand dollars was available from endowments, but it is obvious that the president had to study his budget very carefully.

Although the enrollment continued to increase, there were many both inside and outside the faculty who felt that the presidency should be in the hands of an educator and not a minister. Political differences between "pro-Virginians" and "pro-Northerners" on the faculty and on the board of regents became more and more uncompromising and finally President Thompson submitted his resignation, effective March 12, 1881. The board accepted his resignation, with formal expressions of appreciation for his success as an administrator.

President Thompson did indeed contribute to the advancement of the university, in a very difficult period. Even his critics admitted his success.[2]

The regents were unable immediately to agree upon his successor and named Vice-President Daniel B. Purinton as acting president. He thus functioned for the remainder of the academic year and served as chief administrative officer and professor of mathematics during the 1881-82 term.

The annual Commencement Week exercises were always interesting. They consisted of the baccalaureate sermon, the

2. Wiley, pp. 414-16; Ambler, *History of Education in West Virginia*, pp. 294, 295.

literary contests, addresses to the literary societies, senior exercises, and the graduation exercises.

In 1881 an innovation in the program was a tournament. The
young men, mounted on fine horses, performed on the fairgrounds as knights of old. The fairest young lady in the crowd
was crowned by the victor. A boat race was also a feature, and on
one evening a grand ball was held, lasting far into the night.[3]

The Iron Valley and Morgantown Railroad. On March 1, 1881, articles of incorporation of the Iron Valley and Morgantown Railroad were filed with the secretary of state and the corporation
commenced its existence on March 15. Incorporators were Col.
Felix Nemegyle and Charles E. Kimball, of New York; J. N. Camden, of Parkersburg; John T. McGraw, of Grafton; and William C.
McGrew and George C. Sturgiss, of Morgantown.

The purpose of the company was to construct a railroad from
Hardman's Switch, on the B.&O. Railroad in Preston County,
"along the meanders of Three Fork Creek, to the Irondale Furnace, in the said county, and from said Irondale Furnace, along
said creek, to the watershed between the said Three Fork Creek,
and Deckers Creek, and from thence along and over the most
practical route of the said last named creek to the town of
Morgantown," and from Morgantown along the Monongahela
River to the Pennsylvania line. Or, the articles continued, from
Hardman's Switch to Morgantown by any other route "found
upon a survey to be practical and convenient."[4]

On April 2 the county court passed an order submitting to the
voters of Morgan District a proposition to subscribe $40,000 of
preferred capital stock to be expended in the construction of the
road. The election was held May 17 and the subscription was
authorized by a vote of 478 to 5. On the same day Valley and
Lyons districts, of Preston County, voted subscriptions to the
road totaling $31,000. The estimated length of the line was
thirty-four miles, the estimated cost $680,000.

The corporators organized on September 19, with Daniel R.
Davidson, president; William C. McGrew, vice-president; and
George C. Sturgiss, secretary. Directors were Daniel R. David-
son, James B. Young, and Robert Pitcairn, of Pittsburgh; Wil-

3. Callahan, p. 231.
4. Wiley, pp. 116, 117.

liam C. McGrew and George C. Sturgiss, of Morgantown; Col.
Felix Nemegyle, of New York; and John W. Guseman, of Preston
County.

The West Virginia and Pennsylvania Railroad. So many new railroads were being discussed that the editor of the *Weekly Post* occasionally apologized for mentioning another one. But he did tell
of a meeting held at Fairmont on March 21 in the interest of a
road projected to run south from Pittsburgh along the Monongahela River into West Virginia. Harrison and Marion counties
voted subscriptions to it, but Monongalia, engrossed with the
Iron Valley proposal, did not.

A certificate of incorporation was issued July 26, 1881, to the
West Virginia and Pennsylvania Railroad, to "commence at the
Pennsylvania line in the county of Monongalia, and run thence by
the most practicable route, by way of Morgantown and Fairmont
or Palatine to Clarksburg." Among the corporators, from Monon-
galia County, was W. T. Willey, J. M. Hagans, Ashbel Fairchild,
George C. Sturgiss, N. N. Hoffman, W. S. Cobun, Thomas F.
Watson, Shelby P. Barker, J. S. Hood and W. E. Watson.[5]

Slack Water Developments. Because of a weakness in Lock No. 9,
completed about two years earlier (p. 21), it was found necessary
to lower the height by four feet, and this was completed in January 1881.[6] Col. W. E. Merrill, engineer in charge of the work, said
that Lock and Dam No. 8 should have been built before No. 9, and
that the proper location of No. 9 should have been at Collins
Ferry, four miles below Morgantown, but no good foundation
could be found there. Building at Hoards Rocks, four miles further down, caused the lift to be increased beyond what it should
have been.

At last, in July 1881, the contract for construction of Lock No.
8 was awarded to Shipman and Carmody, of Fairfax County, Virginia, for $46,236. On December 24 the contract for Lock No. 7
was let by the Monongahela Navigation Company of Pennsylvania to Harold, McDonald and Company.[7]

5. Wiley, pp. 118, 119.
6. *Weekly Post*, January 29, 1881.
7. Wiley, pp. 132, 133.

William Price. The son of Michael and Elizabeth Price, who came to America from Wales, William Price, died May 14, 1881. He was born in Greene County, Pennsylvania, on November 21, 1803, and moved to Monongalia County in 1826, settling on Dunkard Creek. He married Catherine Brown and they had thirteen children, George (married Elizabeth Jane Tennant), Abraham Brown (married Elizabeth Ann Morris), Elizabeth, Mary (married Thomas D. Pugh), Michael Core, John Evans (married Elizabeth Chalfant), Jeremiah Oliver, Albert Clay (married Mary Adeline Garner, then Sarah Sarepta Bell), Mariah Louisa, Thomas Horner (married Georgia Wylie), Christina, Jane B. (married A. E. Lough), and Sarah Black (married W. A. Bane).

He was educated at Jefferson Academy, Jefferson, Pennsylvania, and came to Monongalia County to teach his first term of school. He was a justice of the peace under the 1851 constitution and was county surveyor in 1863, running the township lines that year. He represented the county in the house of delegates in 1869 and was elected to the state senate in 1864, 1867, and 1870. Newspapers over the state spoke highly of him; a county paper declared that "his many acts of charity and kindness will live in the memory of many years after his body has crumbled to dust."[8]

His wife, born January 22, 1814, died April 27, 1869.[9]

The Public Schools. At the election on May 17 Benjamin S. Morgan was chosen as county superintendent. He graduated from West Virginia University in 1878 and took the law course there in 1881-82.[10]

Superintendent Morgan prepared an Outline Course of Study for the public schools that was highly commended. Its purpose, as explained by Morgan, was:

"To secure uniform work throughout the county, a better classification of pupils, and the proper order of studies; to prevent promotions to the higher grades of study before the child is prepared profitably to pursue them, and the going over of the same parts of any branch term after term until all hope and ambition literally dies in the child; and to encourage pupils to complete all of the elementary branches."

8. *Weekly Post*, May 21, 1881.
9. Wiley, pp. 287, 288; *Chronicles of Core*, p. 121. See his portrait, vol. 3, p. 705.
10. Wiley, pp. 370, 371, 376, 379.

The plan divided the schools into five grades, the First and Second requiring one year each, the Third, Fourth, and Fifth two years each.[11]

He also suggested and urged the introduction of the county newspapers into the free schools; a copy of each paper published in the county, he said, should be subscribed for and placed in each school room.

The Last County Fair. The last of a series of twelve annual county fairs closed on September 15, 1881. Efforts had been made as early as 1854 to establish a fair, but without much success (vol. 3, p. 414). On January 7, 1869, the Monongahela Valley Agricultural and Mechanical Society was incorporated and this society held nine fairs, the last one in the fall of 1878 (p. 17). This society was succeeded by the Monongalia Agricultural Association, organized June 23, 1879, which held three fairs.

The fairgrounds were across Deckers Creek from Morgantown, on a level tract of land near the old Kerns Fort, a section just beginning to be called Greenmont. The site was reached by crossing the creek on a covered bridge behind and below the old Monongalia Academy on Walnut Street.

A great deal of effort went into the promotion of these fairs but, although some of them were financial successes, most of them were not, and, receipts not being sufficient to meet expenses, the fairs were discontinued and the association was dissolved (in 1882).

Local newspapers, which had given great publicity to the fairs, deplored the lack of success and especially lamented the fact that nearby towns (e.g., Fairmont and Waynesburg) continued to hold fairs which were well attended.[12]

New County Jail. A new stone building for the county jail, replacing the one constructed in 1850, was erected in 1881. A contemporary description states: "It is said to be as fine a jail as can be found in West Virginia. A fine two-story brick [sic] is attached for a jailer's residence. The jail is a two-story structure. Iron cells are on the first floor for dangerous criminals, and strong and secure rooms are fitted up in the second story, for the reception of other

11. Wiley, p. 379.
12. See *Weekly Post*, August 20, 27, 1881.

prisoners. . . . The cost of the jail, when completed and furnished, was estimated at eighteen thousand dollars."[13]

"As early as 1874 civic leaders of Morgantown had led an agitation for a new jail to replace the old one from which several prisoners had recently escaped, and to provide additional facilities for the detention of culprits who had recently committed robberies in the county. Some of the outlying districts objected on the ground that the county could not afford to build a new jail, others because they thought that "the county should expend its money and efforts in constructive ways to create an atmosphere which would not require jails."[14]

Churches. The Reverend Thomas B. Hughes was appointed minister of the Morgantown M.E. Station. He was born in Fayette County, Virginia, in 1836; his father was a relative of the pioneer, Jesse Hughes (vol. 1, p. 220; vol. 2, p. 191). In 1876 the Reverend Mr. Hughes had been presiding elder of the Buckhannon District.

The Reverend G. B. Foster was named minister of the Morgantown M.P. Church.

Eli Westfall was appointed as minister of the Avery Methodist Circuit.

G. J. Martin was appointed minister of the Arnettsville M.E. Circuit. J. T. Eichelberger was minister of the Monongalia Circuit.

Methodists at Wise were holding services in the schoolhouse on the James Eakin farm; James Eakin, J. R. Robinson, Josiah Cross, Isaac Cross, Levi Stiles, Sarah H. Morris, and others were organizing a new congregation.

Coasting Carnival. "During the almost unprecedented season of sleek sleighing, our citizens—young and old—men and women and children—have been enjoying the coasting, as well as riding behind spanking teams. The streets, which have been almost 'a glare of ice' have afforded fine sport for sledding and from the University to the wharf—down to the water's edge, have our young men and women, too, enjoyed the fun and frolic of coasting."[15]

13. Wiley, p. 575; specifications are set forth in the *Weekly Post*, September 4, 1880.
14. Callahan, p. 215.
15. *Weekly Post*, January 22, 1881.

James Robb. "There died in a secluded but richly appointed home, near Cincinnati, yesterday, one whom the world was fast forgetting, but in other days had delighted to honor. We refer to Mr. James Robb, whose career, beginning as a poor and friendless boy, was in point of dazzling achievements in business and princely social surroundings with hardly a parallel in American history."[16]

His career began in Morgantown in 1834 as cashier of the Merchants' and Mechanics' Bank (vol. 3, pp. 105, 447).

Wise. A post office named Wise, for a pioneer family (see vol. 3, various references), was established May 2, 1881, with John R.

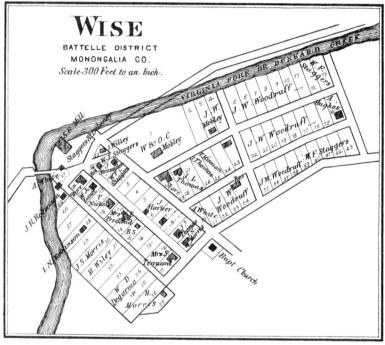

Fig. 8. Map of Wise. (From *Atlas of . . . Monongalia County,* 1886.)

Robinson as the first postmaster. It was located in a small community along Dunkard Creek, in Battelle District, on the mail

---

16. *Cincinnati Commercial,* July 31, 1881, a four-column biography reprinted in the *Weekly Post,* August 13, 1881. Another biography was in the *Wheeling Standard,* March 2, 1878.

route from Morgantown to Burton. Locally the community was sometimes referred to as Wiseville.

Miscellany. In 1881: Fish culture in ponds in Monongalia County was begun on April 29 when William S. Cobun and Lewis Runner received ninety German Carp from the State Fish Commission[17] (*Weekly Post,* April 30, 1881). . . . Machinery at the old Anna Furnace at Ice's Ferry, was taken out and sold. Any hopes that the county's iron works might revive were gone (Wiley, p. 257). . . . Thomas Anderson hauled ninety bushels of Connellsville coal from near Pierpont church to Fairchance Furnace for coking; Supt. R. L. Martin pronounced it a fair grade (Wiley, p. 264). . . . Dr. James P. Fitch opened an office in Morgantown for the practice of medicine (Wiley, p. 585). . . . On December 15 the Morgantown Bridge Company contracted with J. W. Shipman, of Buffalo, New York, for twelve thousand dollars for repairs to the suspension bridge across the river (Wiley, p. 588). . . . In May, John Kerns, of near Halleck, was found dead in the road; a coroner's jury decided that his death had been accidental, the result of a fall (Wiley, p. 633). . . . J. P. Snider sold his store at Flickersville to J. B. Price (Wiley, p. 725). . . . Thomas H. Laidley, son of pioneers Thomas and Sarah Laidley, died; he was born in 1793 (Callahan, p 83). . . . Laishley Weaver succeeded Ray Willey as a storekeeper at the southwest corner of Walnut and High streets (Callahan, p. 209). . . . The Real Estate Agency, owned by George C. Sturgiss and Company, opened for business (Callahan, p. 211). . . . A post office called Blaine, in Clinton District, was established July 7, 1881, with Ezekiel Trickett as postmaster (Wiley, p. 620). . . . Rev. Silas Billings, who had been principal of the Monongalia Academy about twenty-five or thirty years ago, died in Winchester, Virginia, in January (*Weekly Post,* January 22, 1881). . . . James S. Morris, of Dolls Run, died January 12, aged thirty-five; he was a son of Ezekiel Morris (*Weekly Post,* January 22, 1881). . . . Mrs. Elizabeth Cordray, relict of Curtis Cordray, died January 11, on Stewarts Run, aged seventy-two years (*Weekly Post,* January 22, 1881). . . . James W. Tapp, of near Rosedale, committed suicide by hanging himself, January 21; he was aged fifty-seven (*Weekly Post,* January 29, 1881). . . . Michael

17. The carp didn't last long. The *Weekly Post,* on September 16, 1882, reported that they had been stolen and the project abandoned.

White, of Cass District, died August 9, aged eighty-six years
(*Weekly Post,* August 13, 1881). . . . Stephen Gilbert, of Morgantown, died August 21, aged eighty-five years (*Weekly Post,*
August 27, 1881). . . . Mrs. Mahala Stewart, widow of Daniel W.
Stewart, died September 24, aged eighty-one years (*Weekly Post,*
October 1, 1881). . . . The driest summer month on record in the
entire history of Morgantown was August 1881 when only four-
tenths of an inch of rain fell[18] (*Dominion-Post,* September 14,
1980).

18. The wettest summer month was June 1939 with 13.36 inches.

CHAPTER ONE HUNDRED SIX

1882

In 1882 public transportation into and out of Morgantown was still dependent upon stagecoach lines, as it had been for more than half a century. More and more communities throughout the nation were being served by railroads, which had even reached the Pacific coast shortly after the close of the Civil War, but Monongalia County's efforts to secure a railroad line had been constantly subjected to defeat.

Stagecoach lines. As early as 1830 efforts had begun to establish stagecoach connections, particularly with the through lines of stages on the National Road (vol. 3, pp. 48, 89). On May 9 of that year a meeting was held at the courthouse and a committee appointed to contact the postmaster general "to cause mail to be carried in stages from Uniontown, Pa., by way of this place" to Clarksburg. The mail, it was hoped, would provide a subsidy for what might otherwise be an unprofitable enterprise.

The project was eventually approved and regularly scheduled stagecoach service through the county was started early in 1833. It was a line of four-horse stages from Uniontown to Morgantown by way of Ice's Ferry, operated by Col. Richard M. Johnson, who was already operating stages on the National Road. A year later a tri-weekly line was established from Uniontown to Morgantown, continuing on to Clarksburg by way of Smithtown.

For the next twenty years these stages operated on a more-or-less regular basis, delayed or occasionally canceled only by bad weather. For much of the time service was on an every-other-day schedule—one day north, the next day south.

A great change came about in 1852, with the completion of the Baltimore and Ohio Railroad from Cumberland to Fairmont and Wheeling. The great stage lines that had followed the National Road quickly dwindled away, as mail and passengers were carried by rail. Morgantown, however, was still served by stagecoaches, the only difference being that the principal connection with the outside was now at Fairmont rather than at Uniontown.

Stages now left Morgantown daily at 7:00 a.m. for Fairmont, "connecting with the cars on the Baltimore and Ohio Rail Road." Returning, the stages left Fairmont at 1:00 p.m. for Morgantown, here connecting with stages for Uniontown. To these lines there was added, in July 1855, a tri-weekly stage to Brownsville, there connecting with the evening steamboat to Pittsburgh. After slack water reached New Geneva, in 1856, the coaches had a shorter trip and met the boats at that point. Alexander Hayes was a prominent operator in those days. Perhaps the most famous of Morgantown's stagecoach operators was Elcaney C. Bright, familiarly known throughout the area as "Uncle Caney," traveling between Morgantown and Fairmont in the 1850s and 1860s (vol. 3, p. 432).

But in 1882 Morgantown's stagecoach days were about to come to a close. The railroad was knocking at the door.

The Iron Valley and Morgantown Railroad. Discussions continued through 1882 on the proposed Iron Valley and Morgantown Railroad. At a directors' meeting on May 11, William C. McGrew was elected president of the company; John W. Guseman, vice-president; and George C. Sturgiss, secretary and general manager. Directors were John W. Guseman, William C. McGrew, Daniel R. Davidson, Ashbel Fairchild, William Morehead, John T. McGraw, and Alexander Strausz.

A preliminary survey was made to a point on the B.&O. and a final location made from Morgantown to Masontown. Citizens of Newburg and vicinity, in March, subscribed several thousand dollars to the road, on condition that Newburg be made a terminal point.[1]

Other Proposed Railroads. The Monongalia County court, on April 29, entered an order in response to several petitions, submitting to the voters a proposal to subscribe one hundred fifty thousand dollars to the capital stock of the proposed West Virginia and Pennsylvania Railroad. Friends of the scheme held several meetings in its support, but at the election on June 10 the

1. Wiley, p. 118.

proposal lost by a vote of 1,486 to 1,045—32 less than the required three-fifths majority.

Friends of the proposal did not give up, however, and at a meeting on June 16 a new proposal was prepared which, it was hoped, would win favor in all parts of the county. This provided for a subscription of one hundred thousand dollars to the West Virginia and Pennsylvania Railroad, one of sixty thousand dollars to a narrow-gauge railway from Morgantown to Blacksville, and one of fifteen thousand dollars to the Iron Valley and Morgantown Railroad.

The Blacksville and Morgantown Narrow-Gauge Railway was incorporated by E. P. Lantz, Thompson Strosnider, E. Tennant, A. Garrison, D. South, A. W. Brown, and G. A. Burke, with a capital stock of one hundred thousand dollars to two hundred thousand dollars. It was to extend from the Pennsylvania line on Roberts Run, in Blacksville, by way of Dunkard Creek, Dolls Run, Scotts Run, and the Monongahela River to West Morgantown. Two meetings in support of the proposal were held in Blacksville in October.

The county court on November 9 ordered a special election on this proposition to be held on December 30, but, dissatisfaction having developed, the order was rescinded on December 5.[2]

More About Slack Water. A meeting was held at Morgantown on March 13 in the interest of slack-water navigation, with D. B. Purinton president and E. Shisler secretary. A committee composed of George C. Sturgiss, Joseph Moreland, A. Fairchild, J. M. Hagans, and I. C. White was appointed to ask Congress for an appropriation to complete Lock No. 8 and to repair Lock No. 9. On June 9 Congress agreed to appropriate twenty-five thousand dollars for this purpose.[3]

Bridge Bonds Issued. In March 1882, a deed of trust bearing date of January 7, 1882, with John Marshall Hagans and L. S. Hough as trustees, was executed to secure bonds that were issued thereunder to the amount of eleven thousand dollars. The payment of the bonds was personally guaranteed by George C. Sturgiss. The amount thus secured, together with about four thousand dollars already on hand, was expended in strengthening and improving the river bridge, in building two iron truss bridges as approaches,

2. Wiley, pp. 119, 120.
3. Wiley, p. 133.

in rebuilding a part of the stone masonry, and in repairing and rebuilding the wood work.[4]

A part of the so-called debt of West Virginia alleged to be due to Virginia was created by the appropriation of funds by the General Assembly of Virginia for construction of certain buildings, roads, and bridges, before the Civil War. The people of the territory now in West Virginia, of course, were paying their fair share of the taxes.

Revolutionizing Agriculture. New types of agricultural implements were bringing about a revolution in methods of farming. The threshing machine was developed in New England in the 1830s and, with the introduction of the reaper, efforts were spurred to improve it. By the 1860s threshers were turning out thirty bushels per man per hour, compared with only seven bushels flailing out the grain. Steam came to be used as a power source, and the first steam threshing machine was brought into Monongalia County in 1882 by Lucian Snider.

Cultivators, sulky plows, wheat drills, corn planters, reapers, mowers, horse rakes, etc., provided other labor-saving devices. Thomas Anderson was using a sulky corn-plow in this county by 1882.

William Sanford Cobun. The county clerk of Monongalia County, W. S. Cobun, died October 29, 1882. He was born near Masontown, Preston County, on March 12, 1838, the son of Samuel W. and Susan Guseman Cobun. The family moved to Barbour County and, upon his father's death, came to Monongalia County in 1844. Young Sanford was "industrious, truthful and energetic" soon becoming the main support of the family. He attended Monongalia Academy, clerked and taught school. In 1861 he enlisted as a private in Capt. Frank W. Thompson's Company. In 1864 he reenlisted, was promoted to first lieutenant, and was honorably discharged October 6, 1865. He then served in the West on the Great Plains against the Indians, returning home in June 1866. Mr. Cobun resumed the work of clerking and teaching, continuing until 1870, when he was elected county recorder. In 1872 he was elected county clerk and in 1878 was reelected.[5]

---

4. "History of the Morgantown Bridge," by "J.C.B.," *Daily Post,* June 14, 1907.

5. Wiley, pp. 354, 355; *Weekly Post,* November 4, 1882.

He married Delia Eckhardt on July 3, 1870, and they had six children.

Teachers' Institute, Etc. The annual county teachers' institute was held in Morgantown for one week, beginning August 7, conducted by F. H. Crago. The enrollment was 112, with 98 as the average daily attendance. Of these, four teachers had taught ten years or more, eight had taught less than ten but at least five years, 56 had taught at least one year but less than five, and 23 less than one year. Starting for the first time were 27 persons.

It was reported that there were ninety-two school buildings in the county, mostly one room.

Teachers' certificates were graded as No. 1, No. 2, and No. 3. In 1882, thirty-two No. 1 certificates were granted, sixty-five No. 2, and three No. 3.

A total of 365 pupils were enrolled in Morgantown schools, requiring seven teachers, including the teacher of the "colored" school (50 pupils).

Morgantown High School. The first "high school" in Monongalia County was established at Morgantown in 1882, with Thomas E. Hodges as the first principal.

Only very gradually had the Morgantown High School grown out of the Morgantown Graded School. West Virginia's first school law authorized township boards of education, which were to operate the public schools (mostly in one-room buildings) but also to establish certain central schools "of higher grade," where instruction could be given in bookkeeping, algebra, geometry, and surveying, and in such other branches pertaining to the natural sciences and general literature as the boards might determine.

This authority was repeatedly renewed, but by 1873 only three high schools had been established in the state: one in Fairmont, one in Parkersburg, and another at Charleston. It was lamented that only "a very small portion of the youth of the state had any opportunity to prepare for college," and for this reason a Preparatory Department was maintained at the university until 1912.

In 1885 the high school in West Virginia was still officially considered "a factor of transcendant importance in the education of the people" but its inadequacy was described as "the greatest defect in the educational system of the State." Among the reasons for this failure: "Most potent among these reasons was the traditional aversion to higher education, going back to the time when it was considered a patriotic duty to oppose it, as financed in eastern Virginia for 'nabobs.' Thus, many a young West Virginian who later found his way to an institution of higher learning, kept his record, even a good one, from the folks at home for fear of being misunderstood. In other words, the environment was not conducive to higher education. Generally, the cause was attributed to poverty, but this explanation ignored the fact that poverty, under other conditions, was a touchstone to education."[6]

This explanation, while doubtless true for most of the state, probably does not tell the full story of Morgantown's slowness in developing a high school. This community, from early pioneer times, had shown a strong interest in higher education. Monongalia Academy, as mentioned above, was founded in 1814; by the outbreak of the Civil War there were three academies here, and Morgantown was widely known as an educational center.

The most important reason for Morgantown's delay in establishing a high school was that one already existed, essentially, in the Preparatory Department of the university. Of the 124 students enrolled during the university's first year, only six were in the university proper; the remainder were in the Preparatory Department, and most of these were from Monongalia County. The total enrollment in the university in 1878-79 was still only 135 and the *Wheeling Intelligencer* recommended selling the school to the highest bidder, since 89 of these students were in the Preparatory Department and 52 of them, with 21 in the college proper, were residents of Monongalia County.

The University. At their annual meeting in June, the board of regents abolished the earlier curriculum (embracing the freshman, sophomore, junior, and senior classes), and adopted an elective system, distributing the course of study into ten independent schools, eight academic and two professional. A laboratory of practical chemistry was established by Woodville Latham, assisted by Dr. H. B. Lazier and Jesse Fitch. An appropriation of twenty-seven hundred dollars was made in 1882 for the purchase of apparatus, most of which was bought in Europe.

6. Ambler, pp. 249, 250.

William Lyne Wilson was elected the third president of the university by the regents in June and entered upon the office September 6, succeeding D. B. Purinton, who had been acting president since March 1881. He was born May 3, 1843, in Jefferson County, the son of Benjamin and Mary (Lyne) Wilson. He was educated at the Charlestown Academy, Columbian College, D.C.,

Fig. 9. J. R. Thompson. (West Virginia University Library.)

Fig. 10. W. L. Wilson. (West Virginia University Library.)

where he received the B.A. degree in 1860, and at the University of Virginia. He served in the Confederate army and, tradition says, was in Morgantown with Jones's raiders, preventing the burning of the suspension bridge (vol. 3, p. 543). In 1865 he joined the faculty of Columbian College as professor of Ancient Languages, then serving as professor of Latin from 1867 until 1871. During this time he studied law and graduated in the law department of that institution in 1867. He resigned his professorship in 1871 and began the practice of law in Charles Town. He served for three years as county superintendent of schools in Jefferson County.

He was a delegate to the National Democratic Convention at Cincinnati in 1880 and was chosen Elector-at-Large on the Hancock ticket in West Virginia.

On September 20, 1882, only a few days after his selection as president of the university, he was nominated by acclamation as the Democratic candidate for Congress in the Second District and was elected in October. He thereupon resigned the presidency, to take effect the following spring.[7]

A significant feature of university work at this time was the increased interest in the study of geology, under the instruction of Prof. I. C. White. In May 1882 he took his senior students on their first long geology excursion—by horseback through Webster and Braxton counties to the Kanawha, and by train from Charleston to the University of Virginia.

Churches. In 1882 the Morgantown Presbyterian Church had eighty-four members and contributed $1,258 for salary of the pastor and other purposes. The Sugar Grove Church had forty-two members and paid $92 for the pastor's salary, etc.

Rev. Daniel G. Helmick was named minister of the Morgantown Methodist Protestant Church.

Rev. W. B. Treevy was minister of the Blacksville M.E. Circuit.

A new Methodist church was organized at Saint Cloud, four miles north of Wadestown, known as Oak Forest. Among the founders were John White, Solomon Russell, John Hostutler, Wesley Gilmore, Alex Hennen, and Hager Six. The white frame church was built on a hill with a scenic view of a valley covered with farms and forests.

Georgetown. Along the Fairmont Pike in Grant District a post office had been established March 8, 1876, by the name of Cedar Valley, with William N. Stewart as the first postmaster. In 1881 Henry Clay Miller opened a store nearby and the post office was moved to his store, with Miller as the postmaster. On March 8, 1882, the name was changed to Georgetown, in honor of George Pratt, one of the oldest residents.[8]

James Vance Boughner. Perhaps more widely known than any other person in the county, Dr. J. V. Boughner, died February 8, 1882, of stomach cancer.

---

7. Wiley, pp. 405, 407, 408, 409, 411, 416, 417, 419.
8. *Weekly Post,* August 5, 1882.

He was born at Clarksburg April 9, 1812, the son of Daniel and Mary Vance Boughner. When only sixteen years of age he became postmaster at Greensboro, Pennsylvania, where it was said of him that "possessed of an active and ambitious mind, he made up for want of early opportunities by extensive and general reading and study, and acquired a very thorough knowledge of the standard English classics and of general history."

He attended lectures at Cincinnati Medical College and located at Mount Morris, Pennsylvania, practicing medicine in both Greene and Monongalia counties. On May 8, 1885, he married Louisa J., daughter of Andrew Brown, and soon thereafter moved to Brown's Mills. In 1859 he retired from the practice of medicine and moved to Morgantown.

He was active in politics during the Civil War and was a delegate to the Wheeling Convention of May 13, 1861. He was named a paymaster in the Union army in 1864 and was later collector of internal revenue. He was elected to the West Virginia Legislature in 1867.

His children were Rosalie, Mary L., William L., Martha, Emma, and Andrew Brown.[9]

Miscellany. In 1882: Smyth Bros. (William B. and John H. Smyth) started a furniture and undertaking establishment at Maidsville (Wiley, p. 263). . . . Admitted to the Monongalia County bar were A. G. Davis (June 16), George C. Cole (October 12), Leonidas V. Keck (October 13), Ben S. Morgan (October 18), Francis T. Haymond (October 23), Madison T. Garlow (June 20), and Arthur L. Cox (Wiley, pp. 317, 318). . . . The Goshen Baptist Association, composed of the Forks of Cheat, Morgantown, Pleasant Hill, Goshen, and Zoar Baptist churches, had a membership of 574 (Wiley, pp. 441, 450). . . . The county court appointed Drs. L. S. Brock, G. M. Fletcher, and E. H. Coombs as members of a new county board of health, authorized by the legislature March 15, 1882 (Wiley, p. 468). . . . E. J. Rinehart opened a store on Lot 81, following Lazier, Finnell and Company (Wiley, p. 582). . . . Dr. Jesse J. Hall joined Dr. Horatio N. Mackey in the practice of medicine in Morgantown; other new Morgantown physicians were Dr. W. C. Kelley, Dr. James P. Fitch, and Dr. Dorsey P. Fitch (Wiley, pp. 584, 585). . . . A large skeleton of an

9. Wiley, pp. 479, 480.

Indian, in a sitting position in a rock grave, was unearthed in Clinton District by Mr. and Mrs. F. M. Fetty (Wiley, p. 608). ... David Savage was operating a gristmill at Easton (Wiley, p. 676). ... The Mount Union Cemetery, in Union District, was incorporated (Wiley, p. 689). ... Dr. Charles H. McLane, Cassville physician, closed his office there and moved to Zanesville, Ohio (Wiley, p. 702). ... Lewis Chisler started a wagon-making shop at Flickersville (Wiley, p. 725). ... The Hennen Brothers furniture factory refurnished the Morgantown Grade School with new seats and desks, of their own design and manufacture, varying in size to fit pupils of different ages, the first equipment of this kind which had appeared in the county (Callahan, p. 208). ... Rev. Samuel Clawson,[10] a former Monongalia County M.P. minister, died in Westbon on September 4 (*Weekly Post,* September 9, 1882). ... George Weaver, of near Wharton's Mills, Cass District, died on June 2; he was fifty-six years of age (*Weekly Post* June 10, 1882). ... Mrs. Rachel Wells, wife of Moses Wells, died November 21 on Jakes Run, as the result of a fire when her chaff bed ignited from a spark from the grate (*Weekly Post,* November 25, 1882). ... Repairs on the suspension bridge across the river were completed and the bridge was ready for travel late in the year; Charles M. Chalfant was named Toll-Gatherer for 1883 (*Weekly Post,* December 21, 1882).

10. See story about him in *Weekly Post,* January 21, 1888; see also James Robison, *Recollections of Rev. Samuel Clawson* (Pittsburgh, 1883), 246 pp.

CHAPTER ONE HUNDRED SEVEN

1883

On December 1, 1883, Samuel T. Wiley published his scholarly and voluminous *History of Monongalia County*,[1] one of the best county histories ever published for any county in the state. He doubtless intended it to be a centennial history but: "Unexpected difficulties in the way of obtaining some information essential to the book, and a spell of sickness, has prevented its completion at the time contemplated by the author."

Wiley's History. Samuel Thomas Wiley was born May 25, 1850, at Smithfield, Fayette County, Pennsylvania. He was injured when only twenty years of age by the fall of a heavy beam and suffered off and on for the remainder of his life from pulmonary hemorrhage, finally losing use of his left lung entirely. But though sorely handicapped, his accomplishments were very great. He taught in various academies and small colleges, mostly in one-room schools.

But his first and best love, and the area of his greatest achievement, was the literary field. A biographer commented that, especially in the domain of history, "his knowledge was deep, comprehensive, and discriminating, and it brought him a renown most justly deserved."

His *Legends of Fayette County* and *Story of the Catawha Warpath* were published in 1879, and the *History of Preston County* in 1882.

Most of his life was spent on the eastern slope of Chestnut Hill (Laurel Ridge), in his native county, although he traveled widely

1. *History of Monongalia County, West Virginia, From its First Settlement to the Present Time; with Numerous Biographical and Family Sketches*, illustrated, 776 pp. (Kingwood: Preston Publishing Co., 1883).

trying to find a climate better suited for his health. He died in a sanitarium in Oil City November 10, 1905.

A book of 776 pages, the *History* was published by the Preston Publishing Company, at Kingwood. Fine cloth volumes sold at $4.00, library sheep at $5.00, and morocco antique at $6.00. Agents were sent out in advance to secure prepublication orders. A. J. Arnett, of Arnettsville, was one of these; in a letter with a printed letterhead, giving the name of the book, written April 6, 1883 to Abraham Wisman, he said: "I want to sell you and Frank a History of our county before we quit selling. Expect to be through canvassing by 20 or 25 of April. . . . If you want a copy I will let you have it at $3.75 allowing you 25 cents for staying all night."

In setting forth upon the task, Wiley recognized the magnitude of his project: "To write the history of Monongalia County from its creation by legislative enactment in 1776, down to the re-corded events of the present,—and to confine the work to the limits of the present territory of the county,—to gather a large portion of the events of this history from scant records and im-perfect sources,—is an undertaking of no small degree. While it unavoidably possesses considerable to make it a wearisome task, it also necessarily contains much to render it a work of pleasure."

Some aspects rendered the enterprise rather dramatic: "Mon-ongalia! the age of the Republic numbers thy years! Monongalia, mother county of Northern West Virginia! five generations sleep in thy cemeteries, and thousands of loving hearts, the Great Re-public over, cherish thee fondly as the land of their birth and the home of their fathers."

Wiley's style is free-flowing and quite readable and he carefully checked his sources to avoid errors. Printers' proofs were also carefully checked and typographical errors are almost non-existent. As compared with some county histories, his arrange-ment is orderly and logical and the student consulting his fin-ished product can have assurance that what he reads is correct.

There are thirty-four chapters, plus an appendix of additions and corrections. The first two chapters deal with the Mound Builders and Indians, then follow chapters on "Monongalia under Orange," . . . "under Augusta," and ". . . in West Augusta," leading to the formation of Monongalia County (Chapter 6).

Fig. 11. Samuel T. Wiley.

Fig. 12. I. C. White.

Fig. 13. Frank Cox.

Fig. 14. Marmaduke Dent.

The next eight chapters deal with the history of the county during the Revolution, the close of the Indian wars, the Mason and Dixon line, the Whiskey Insurrection, various losses of territory, internal improvements, finally Monongalia under the Reorganized Government of Virginia and under the new state of West Virginia.

A dozen chapters then follow, on various aspects of the county's history: its physical history, agricultural, industrial, political, judicial, educational, journalistic, religious, financial, medical, military, finally, miscellaneous, history.

The author then approaches his subject from yet another viewpoint, giving a detailed history, chapter by chapter, of each political subdivision. There is a chapter on Morgantown borough, then one on each of the seven magisterial districts, namely, Clinton, Morgan, Union, Cass, Grant, Clay, and Battelle.

Numerous biographical sketches are included, classified in general according to the segment of the county's history which the subject represented, as political, religious, etc., or the district in which the person resided. There are twenty-eight full-page portraits.

In addition, there are two illustrations of public buildings, one of the Morgantown Public School (formerly Monongalia Academy), the other of West Virginia University.

Wiley had a high opinion of the county's schools, churches, and press; the latter, he said, wielded "a potent influence for the public weal" and contributed "to the high moral character the county has abroad for peace and good order."

He writes soberly and straightforwardly, "making a faithful presentation of facts"; this, he feels, "may not render it acceptable to the extreme enthusiastical, too prone to over-exalt; or the over-critical, too liable to under-estimate."

Posterity, however, has uniformly given him a high rating. He did a magnificent job.[2]

2. We can point out only one shortcoming: there is no index to the 776 pages, with thousands of proper names. As a postscript, however, we may point out that Norman B. Shively, of Shinnston, working under the direction of the Monongalia County Bicentennial Committee, did prepare such an index (*Index to Samuel T. Wiley's History of Monongalia County, West Virginia* (1883), 109 pp. Monongalia Historical Society. 1976); it was published posthumously on July 4, 1976. This remarkable work, appearing almost a century later than the book it indexes, includes 109 pages, with approximately 9,300 entries, and was so carefully done that I have yet to find a mistake in it. The book and the index go together beautifully.

Discouraging Railroad Developments. No progress having been made on plans for the Iron Valley and Morgantown Railroad, officials of the company, with considerable fanfare, on March 22, 1883, held a groundbreaking ceremony at J. Joseph and Son's mill, on Deckers Creek, doubtless with the idea of stimulating investment. A force of twenty to thirty men continued work of grading for a few days, and then the work was stopped. Morgantown newspapers, on March 28, carried notices calling for bids "for the graduation, masonry, trestling and bridging of 14½ miles of the Iron Valley and Morgantown Railroad." Several proposals were received but no action was taken. No one made a public announcement to the effect, but the proposal was dead.[3]

A new proposition was then prepared, providing for a subscription of one hundred thousand dollars to the West Virginia and Pennsylvania Railroad, one of sixty thousand dollars to a narrow-gauge railway from West Morgantown to Blacksville, and one, of fifteen thousand dollars to the Iron Valley and Morgantown Railroad. This did not come to a vote, however, and the subscription to the Iron Valley road was deleted. The revised proposition was submitted to the voters on February 17, 1883, and was defeated by a vote of 1,383 for and 1,479 against.

A separate proposal to subscribe to the stock of the West Virginia and Pennsylvania Railroad was submitted to the voters of Cass and Grant districts, on the grounds that it would be built on their side of the river. The vote was held in May 1883 and it, too, was defeated, 51 to 143 in Cass, and 63 to 244 in Grant.[4]

All these defeats were most discouraging, considering the amount of effort and time devoted to the projects by Morgantown's civic leaders. But it was clear to everyone that outside financial assistance was necessary before a railroad could be built into the county.

The University. In June 1883 the board of regents abolished or suspended the office of the presidency of West Virginia University and replaced it with "Chairman of the Faculty."[5] Robert C. Berkeley was appointed to the position. Born in Hanover County,

3. Wiley, pp. 117, 118.
4. Wiley, pp. 120-22.
5. This was an old Virginia idea, of a university without a president.

Virginia, in 1837, Professor Berkeley graduated from the University of Virginia in 1861 and taught at Washington College, Chestertown, Maryland, from 1867 to 1873, when he was appointed professor of ancient languages and literature at West Virginia University. He served as librarian and secretary of the faculty from 1875 to 1883.

In September 1883 three or four Morgantown girls continued agitation for admission of women to the university by actually enrolling in Prof. William P. Willey's class in history. From the university's beginning no ruling had barred them—it was simply inferred that the school was for men only. A co-education bill was defeated by the legislature in 1881.

Lake Monongahela. In 1883 Prof. Israel C. White, a teacher at West Virginia University, explained his theory concerning the various terraces upon which the town of Morgantown was located, and was already on his way to becoming a world-acclaimed geologist.

According to his theory, these terraces, together with immense deposits of stratified clays and boulder beds, above the level of the upper slopes of the river gorge, are explained by the existence of a former glacial lake which he named Lake Monongahela, formed by a great ice field descending from the north and effectually stopping the drainage of the pre-glacial river into the Lake Erie basin. Eventually the waters of the lake escaped through the newly formed Ohio River Valley.

I. C. White was born November 1, 1848, in western Monongalia County, on the headwaters of Dunkard Creek. He was the son of Michael and Mary Ann White.

He graduated at West Virginia University in 1872 and taught school in Pennsylvania and New Jersey. He became connected with the Second Geological Survey of Pennsylvania in 1875 and took a postgraduate course in geology and chemistry at Columbia College. In 1876 he worked along the Ohio line and harmonized the Ohio and Pennsylvania geological surveys. In 1877 he was elected to the chair of geology and natural history in West Virginia University. His geological excursions, with university seniors, through Virginia and West Virginia, soon became well known and of great value.[6]

6. Wiley, p. 421; Callahan, pp. 19, 20.

Public Schools. The Free School System in Monongalia County, not yet twenty years old in 1883, had made remarkable progress, but significant challenges still lay ahead.

"With but one school-house a score of years ago now they stand to greet us beside every highway. This is a revolution that can not go backwards. It creates its own momentum. It moves by a power within, which increases as it moves, and which strikes out the light and heat of its own vitality. An average of the estimates made by many large operators, working many thousands of hands, gives, as a result, that a knowledge of only the elements of a primary education adds twenty-five per cent to the value of man, as a simple laborer. This fact teaches that to educate the rising generation is the most practical way to utilize our resources. The wealth of our hills and valleys, and the number of our population, will be but barren blessings, if we add not the intelligence and the virtue which make the true glory of a State."[7]

Benjamin S. Morgan, on May 15, 1883, was reelected county superintendent of schools, without opposition.

Names of Schools. Every section of Monongalia County was served by a public school in 1883 and these were listed by Wiley[8] and Hastings[9] as follows:

Clinton District. Watson (Pine Grove), Smithtown, Kincaid, Halleck (Smith), Brown, Clinton, Pleasant Valley, Frum, Woodland, Price, McBee (Stony Point), Smell, Martin (Laurel Run), Carroll (Union Grove), Gum Spring.

Morgan District. Flatts, Woodland, Dug Hill, Vandervort, Summers, Rock Forge, Sarver, Dorsey.

Morgantown Independent District. Morgantown.

Union District. Baker, Bush, Oak Grove, Jennewine, Pierpont, Pleasant Hill, Sugar Grove, Wood Grove.

Cass District. Fort Martin, Maidsville, Lazzell, Jimtown, Mountain Tea, Stumptown, Laurel Hill, Buckeye, Osageville, Cassville.

Grant District. Granville, Stony Point, Sugar Grove, Cool Spring, Peter's Temple, Arnettsville, Laurel Flat, Union, Bend of

7. Wiley, p. 393.
8. *History of Monongalia County,* pp. 628, 657, 692, 709, 730, 751.
9. *School and Local History,* vol. 1.

the River, Laurel Point, Harmony Grove, Barb, Stewart, Georgetown.

Clay District. Point Pleasant, Dolls Run, Pedlars Run, Price, Mooresville, Democrat, McCurdysville, Head of Days Run, Wilson, Sugar Valley, Emrod Tennant, New Brownsville, Blacksville, Varner, Union, Garfield, Bellaire.

Battelle District. Wise, Valley Chapel, Mount Tabor (White), Oak Forest (Saint Cloud), Camp Run, Saint Leo, West Warren, Harmony, Cross Roads, Barr, Miracle Run (Darrah), Scotts Run, Paw Paw, Efaw.

George W. John. One of Monongalia County's most distinguished citizens, Dr. G. W. John, died January 26, 1883. The son of William and Mary McVicker John, he was born February 4, 1827, at Stewartstown. He received his education at the common school in that community and at Monongalia Academy.

About 1850 he began the study of medicine with Dr. U. L. Clemmer, of Smithfield, Pennsylvania, and attended lectures at the Cincinnati Eclectic Medical Institute. He began the practice of medicine at Stewartstown in 1852; "He was an ardent advocate of reform, and his efforts were devoted principally to the elaboration and perfection of the *materia medica.* Such was his love for his profession, that he continued to practice it until a short time before his death."

In 1860 he opened a general store at Stewartstown, and also had stores at New Geneva and Rosedale, in Pennsylvania. In 1871 he moved to Durbannah and opened a store in Morgantown. In 1874 he bought a High Street property opposite the Wallace House and located his store in the store-room on that property. He also had branch stores at Uffington and Reedsville. He engaged also in the lumber business.

He married Sisson, daughter of John S. Dorsey, on August 31, 1849. Their children were Alice (married William Moorhead); Ellenora (married Joseph M. Wood); and George M. John.[10] Following Dr. John's death, the store he had operated at the corner of High Street and Maiden Alley was taken over by his son, George, and his son-in-law, William Moorhead.

Dr. Marmaduke Dent. Another of Monongalia County's substantial citizens, Dr. Marmaduke Dent, died only a few days later, on

10. Wiley, pp. 477-79.

February 10, 1883. Born February 25, 1801, he was a son of John and Margaret Dent, pioneer settlers on Dents Run.

He attended the subscription school at Laurel Point. "Being of delicate health and afflicted with the asthma, upon arriving at his majority, he determined upon the study of medicine," beginning in the office of Dr. Enos Daugherty. After three years, in 1825, he began the practice of medicine in Kingwood, the first resident physician of Preston County. Here, in 1827, he married Sarah, daughter of William Price. In 1828 they moved to Laurel Point and Marmaduke engaged, with his brother Nimrod, in the business of milling, merchandising, and distilling. In 1830 he sold out to Nimrod and moved to Granville, where he opened an office for the practice of medicine. In 1839 he opened a store there and continued in both activities until shortly before his death. He had a very wide medical practice.

Eight children survived to adult life: Marshall Mortimer; Dr. William Marmaduke; Margaret L., married Frank M. Chalfant; John Evans; Dr. George Washington; Dr. Felix Jackson; James Evans; and Sarah Virginia, married Thomas P. Reay.[11]

Addison S. Vance. A distinguished civic leader, A. S. Vance, died April 22, 1883. He was born in 1812 in Frederick County, Virginia, and came to Morgantown in 1835. He began carrying the first daily mail into Morgantown about 1854. He was a member of the last primary school board appointed under the state of Virginia, October 29, 1862.

Augustus Haymond (portrait, vol. 3, p. 552). A prominent member of a pioneer family, Augustus Haymond, died October 9, 1883. The son of William Haymond, Jr., and Cynthia Carroll Haymond, he was born at Palatine Hill, Monongalia (now Marion) County, May 17, 1812. In 1835 he came to Morgantown and engaged in merchandizing. He was elected justice of the peace in 1856 and reelected in 1860; in the latter year he was president of the county court. He served as coroner from 1842 until 1856.

He was elected clerk of the circuit court and took office on the day West Virginia became a state, June 20, 1863. He was reelected in 1866, 1872, and in 1878.

11. Wiley, pp. 482-85.

He was married twice, the first time to Rebecca Madera, who bore him three children, William C. Haymond, Mrs. Eunice M. Lemley, and Mrs. Susan M. Proctor. His second wife was Dorcas Thompson and their children were Francis T. and George.[12]

Victor Mills. During the summer of 1883 E. C. Allender built the Victor Mills, along Front Street at the corner of Walnut Street. The building was three stories high, fifty by thirty-four feet, with

Fig. 15. Victor Elevator and Mills Company.

an engine house twenty by thirty-four feet. It was equipped with the latest improved milling machinery and was run by a sixty-horsepower engine. The mills used the gradual reduction system of making flour. The estimated cost of the building and machinery was ten thousand dollars.[13]

U. S. Mail. Six mail routes to and from Morgantown transported the mail in 1885, traveling by stage, buggy, or horseback.

12. Wiley, pp. 352-54, 774.
13. Wiley, p. 579; *Weekly Post*, September 15, 1883; November 17, 1883.

The Fairmont mail, West Side, went by stage daily except Sunday, by way of Laurel Point, Georgetown, Arnettsville, and Rivesville, to Fairmont. Lowsville mail was dropped off by this route at Arnettsville.

The Fairmont mail, East Side, went every other day by way of Uffington, Whiteday, Mount Harmony, and Palatine, to Fairmont. At Uffington mail was dropped off for Clinton Furnace, Halleck, and Gladesville.

The Fairchance mail went by hack daily except Sunday by way of Easton, Laurel Iron Works, and Wymp's Gap to Fairchance.

The Smithfield mail went by hack on Mondays, Wednesdays, and Fridays by way of Stewartstown, and Morris Cross Roads to Smithfield and returned the same days.

The Burton mail, on Mondays and Fridays, went by way of Randall, Cassville, Pedlar Run, Andy, Mooresville, Pentress, Blacksville, Miracle Run, Wise, Wadestown, and Crossroads, to Burton. At Pentress mail was dropped off for Center, Jake's Run, and Basnett.

The Dunkard mail, on Mondays and Fridays, went by way of Randall, Maidsville, Rosedale, and Mount Morris to Dunkard, returning the same days.[14]

"**Cassville's Pride.**" "A few days ago we had the pleasure of walking through the extensive buggy, carriage and wagon manufactory of W. C. Lough & Bro., at Cassville, . . . and were surprised to see the rapid strides being made in the establishment. A large addition has recently been built to the manufactory to accommodate their growing trade and their finishing apartments are full of beautiful buggies and wagons. The firm is young but full of energy and progress. Their work is durable and finely finished, and their prices very moderate. We saw many handsome buggies and wagons finished up to perfection, which are for sale at very low figures, and we advise all who need anything in their line to call and see them."[15]

Churches. Rev. G. B. Foster became pastor of the Morgantown Baptist Church.

Asby Stevens was minister of the Smithtown M.E. Circuit.

14. *Weekly Post*, August 18, 1883.
15. *Weekly Post*, May 19, 1883.

The Hopewell M.P. Church, in Clinton District, was repaired, repainted, and re-dedicated.

John Conwell was minister on the Arnettsville M.E. Circuit.

Rev. S. L. Finney succeeded J. B. Dickey[16] as pastor of the Morgantown and Sugar Grove Presbyterian Churches.

T. H. Trainer was minister of the Monongalia M.E. Circuit.

A Church of the Brethren was organized by ministers who came from Big Sandy Creek in Preston County. A building was constructed three miles north of Morgantown, on the Point Marion road, and was called Mount Union.[17]

A new church building was constructed by the West Warren Baptist congregation.

J. T. Eichelberger organized the Mount Tabor M.E. Church in the White Settlement of Battelle District.[18]

O'Neal Post Office. A post office by the name of O'Neal was established May 28, 1883, with John N. Conway as the first postmaster.[19] It was located in the rather isolated area of Grant District surrounded on three sides by the Monongahela River and generally referred to as the "Bend of the River" section. Beside the post office was the Bend of the River School; out the road a short distance was a public scale for weighing cattle, and there was a sawmill about two miles away, at the mouth of Flaggy Meadow Run. At the tip of the region a ferry connected with Little Falls.

Miscellany. In 1883: C. W., J. M., and Conn Pixler brought a steam threshing machine into the county (Wiley, p. 245). . . . Kern and Kern's buggy factory, along the river just above the mouth of Deckers Creek, suspended operations (Wiley, pp. 260, 261). . . . Frank Cox was admitted to the Monongalia County bar on June 18 (Wiley, p. 357). . . . On July 4 a soldiers' reunion was held on the university grounds, with four hundred veterans present; steps were taken to effect a permanent organization (Wiley,

16. For biography of the Reverend Mr. Dickey, see Moreland, *First Presbyterian Church*, p. 54.
17. The congregation, however, did not thrive in this locality; see p. 364.
18. Dodds and Dodds (p. 134) say 1893 but this is a misprint. The church is shown in D. L. Lake's "Atlas" (1886), on the map of Battelle District. See Alvah J. W. Headlee, "Old Mount Tabor Cemetery" (MS, 1970), where the date 1883 appears.
19. *Weekly Post*, August 11, 1883.

p. 520). . . . Thomas Jackson, Sr., of Clinton District, died; he was born in Yorkshire, England, and came here in 1853 (Wiley, p. 644). . . . Elizabeth Stewart, of Union District, died; she was eighty-four (Wiley, p. 675). . . . W. I. Vandervort and Company opened a farmer's store at Easton in April; salesmen were E. S. Stewart and Elza Stewart (Wiley, p. 676). . . . John T. Bates sold his store at Laurel Iron Works to W. J. Donaldson (Wiley, p. 690). . . . Mrs. Ann Brown opened a grocery store at Hamilton (Wiley, p. 704). . . . E. J. Rinehart opened a store in the old Wallace store room on High Street (Callahan, p. 209). . . . S. Hitchens opened a store in Morgantown, adding tinware and glassware to the usual line of groceries and provisions (Callahan, p. 210). . . . Seth Hulings and others, representing the Morgantown Gas and Water Company, in October, were granted rights-of-way through borough streets for gas and water pipes, "provided they begin the work of providing the town with gas or water within one year" (Callahan, p. 217; *Weekly Post,* November 10, 1883). . . . James Domer Stimmell, aged twenty-five, was accidentally shot and killed at Hagedorn's Mill, on the way home from hunting; his breech-loading shotgun fell and discharged (*Weekly Post,* April 21, 1883). . . . Thomas Martin, of Dolls Run, died June 24, about thirty years of age (*Weekly Post,* July 14, 21, 1883). . . . George W. Laishley, a county commissioner, was seriously injured in a threshing machine accident on September 28 (*Weekly Post,* October 6, 1883). . . . The usual peace and quiet of Morgantown was unexpectedly broken on Saturday evening, October 27, by a series of fist fights (*Weekly Post,* November 3, 1883). . . . Mrs. Mahala Mills, widow of John Mills, died on December 27, at the age of seventy-two; she left two children, Mrs. A. C. Wood and Rev. William Mills (*Weekly Post,* January 5, 19, 1884). . . . Lamps were first placed on the Morgantown suspension bridge (*Daily Post,* June 14, 1907).

CHAPTER ONE HUNDRED EIGHT

1884

After more than a half century of frustrating efforts to secure a railroad line through Monongalia County, in 1884 success at last seemed about to crown the efforts of community leaders.

The defeat of the proposed bond issue in May 1883 was discouraging to friends of the West Virginia and Pennsylvania Railroad, which had been incorporated July 26, 1881. But they did not abandon the project of trying to secure rail connections between Fairmont and Pittsburgh, by way of Morgantown.

The Railroad Comes Closer. Discussions now took a somewhat different trend. Why should not the Baltimore and Ohio, with hundreds of miles of track already in operation, build a connection between Fairmont and Uniontown, towns which it already served? Rumors of this grew steadily throughout the year and in December 1883 a new company, the Fairmont, Morgantown, and Pittsburgh Railroad, was incorporated under the laws of West Virginia. Two of the directors, W. C. McGrew and Ashbel Fairchild, were Morgantown men. The Baltimore and Ohio promised financial assistance.

These efforts, however, were in competition with supporters of the West Virginia and Pennsylvania Railroad, who had not yet admitted final defeat. The two groups, both working to secure a railroad for Monongalia County, unfortunately found themselves in conflict with each other.

Across the Pennsylvania line the State Line Railroad was incorporated April 11, 1884, with the proposal of building a line from Uniontown to the state line, there to connect with the road coming from Fairmont. Construction was promptly begun, but progress was very slow; eight years later it had been extended only to Smithfield.

At last, late in 1884, construction got under way at both ends of the Fairmont-to-Morgantown extension. A temporary bridge across Deckers Creek was started at the Morgantown end, and a much larger, permanent bridge across the Monongahela River at the Fairmont end. At Fairmont the work was delayed by a contest with the West Virginia and Pennsylvania company concerning right-of-way. A similar contest at Point Marion delayed the proposed connection with the Pennsylvania road, but this was not of much immediate concern to Morgantown people.

A University Without a President. For the two years (1883-85) the university operated in a chairmanship interim between presidents, it was featured by antagonism and indirection. Professor Berkeley, the chairman, bore the brunt of criticism and the faculty was rent by controversies between "Virginians" and "Northerners." The chairman had difficulty to maintain faculty control and there were also heated debates relative to keeping "coeds" out of the university.

To increase the enrollment, the regents, in June 1884, abolished tuition charges, except for the law and medical "schools" and for nonresidents, allowing free tuition to one student for each five hundred people in each county, and, in addition, five cadets from each senatorial district were allowed free tuition, textbooks, and stationery.[1]

An amusing but mysterious incident took place in April 1884. A group of students found a steer in a pasture near the campus and then:

"Someone caused the steer to mount the steps leading into Martin Hall, up the stairway to the second floor where he (or they) left the steer overnight in the faculty assembly room. The next morning the steer had his head and horns sticking out the window looking East and the room was a shambles. No one ever discovered who the culprits were."[2]

1. Ambler, *History of Education in West Virginia*, pp. 302, 303.
2. Worth K. Rice, doing research for Dean James Morton Callahan in 1922, came across and duly noted this item. In 1934, Rice, then practicing law in Saint Paul, Minnesota, was told by James C. Michael, Judge of the Saint Paul District Court, that on a "warm and drizzly afternoon in April, 1884, some of the boys and I coaxed a steer into Martin Hall." See "It's No Bull. A Steer in Martin Hall," *West Virginia Hillbilly*, April 29, 1978.

The School Journal. The *West Virginia School Journal* began publication in November 1881 as the organ of the state department of free schools, with State Superintendent Bernard L. Butcher as editor of the official department and T. B. McCain, of the Wheeling public schools, as editor of the professional columns. The *Journal* continued under Butcher's management until October 1884 when it was sold to his successor, Benjamin S. Morgan. Under Superintendent Morgan's editorship and management, assisted by J. F. Cork, the size of the publication was changed from octavo book form to sixteen page (eleven-by-fourteen-inch) magazine form, and the place of publication from Wheeling to Morgantown, with J. E. Fleming as printer and T. E. Hodges, of the Morgantown Graded School, as business manager.[3]

The Little Red School House. Dozens of one-room schoolhouses were advantageously located throughout the county. They were not always painted red, it is true, but they were all real community centers. "During election campaign years the different political parties held local partisan rallies in the school house. The teachers sponsored spelling bees and ciphering matches frequently during the school term. . . . School exhibitions, often lasting three hours, celebrated the 'last day' of the school term. Songs, readings, recitations, dialogues, both serious and comic, composed the main features of such exhibitions."[4]

Forks-of-Cheat Baptist Church. A new brick building[5] for the historic Forks-of-Cheat Baptist congregation, oldest in the county, was dedicated August 31, 1884. It was the fourth building to serve the congregation.

The building committee was composed of Rev. E. P. Brand, E. W. St. Clair, Lancelot John, Hannah Hunter, G. W. Sisler, and William L. Jaco. The cost was about twenty-two hundred dollars.

The dedicatory sermon was delivered by Elder D. W. Rogers to a crowded house. "Dinner was served on the ground where Mother Earth served for our table and the Heavens for the canopie. A grand crowd enjoyed a social hour, after which the sound of the bell caused the crowd to witness the solemn cere-

3. Ambler, *History of Education in West Virginia*, p. 216.
4. Hastings, *School and Local History*, vol. 1, pp. 67, 68.
5. Still used in 1976.

mony of the ordination of two deacons, William Jaco and W. H. West."[6]

On the Monongahela. "The present season of bad roads and bad weather has caused a turn in the direction of travel over our miserable mud pikes, and most of our citizens now avail themselves of the pleasures of steamboat navigation on our river. The steamer *Harry* makes regular daily trips from Morgantown at 7 a.m. for Greensboro, where she connects with the line boats every morning at 10 a.m., for all points between here and Pittsburgh."[7]

Morgantown Improvement Company. On November 15, 1884, the Morgantown Improvement Company was organized "for the purpose of boring for natural gas near the town for heating, lighting, and domestic and manufacturing purposes, and ultimately to petition for the establishment of water works." Prominent citizens interested in the project included George C. Sturgiss, I. C. White, L. S. Brock, and D. B. Purinton. The borough council, approving the plan of the company, granted privileges for thirty years, but specified that the work must begin within sixty days and that the delivery of gas must begin within twelve months. Certain exemptions from taxation were allowed on real estate to be acquired.

Work was begun in December on a gas well, located between Foundry Street and Deckers Creek.[8]

Fire Watch. In the early history of Morgantown destructive fires were frequent, especially arising from defective flues and chimneys or from the fall of burning coals from the open grate to the floor. Following the Civil War the borough councils made special efforts to prevent such disasters. A tour of inspection was usually made of the town by each incoming council, to observe whether all premises were in sanitary condition, and whether chimneys and roofs were in proper condition to reduce the danger of fires. After such inspections the council issued orders to various people to abate nuisances or to repair chimneys or roofs. This close watch was evidently helpful, because very few dangerous fires were recorded between 1865 and 1885. One of these was

6. Gluck and others, *Forks-of-Cheat Baptist Church*, pp. 31, 32.
7. *Weekly Post*, March 29, 1884.
8. Callahan, pp. 217, 260.

on Christmas night, in 1884, when J. K. Durr's barn burned.[9] Arson was suspected and the council offered one hundred dollars reward for evidence that would lead to the conviction of the person who set it afire.[10]

The sale of firecrackers, squibs, etc., was prohibited within the limits of the corporation, and there was a fine of twenty dollars and costs for each offense. The penalty for buying, setting off, or shooting firecrackers, squibs, or other combustible matter within the town limits was a fine of not less than five dollars nor more than fifty dollars and costs for each offense. In 1884, when the Democrats were celebrating the election of Cleveland, they were refused permission to set off fireworks from a platform in front of the Commercial House.[11]

Post-Election Stunts. Among community events contributing substantially to social life were patriotic celebrations, great political rallies, and humorous post-election stunts to pay off pre-election wagers. For example, on November 14, 1884, to fulfill an election agreement, J. Pres Reay, preceded by a band and flag, pushed George Hall in a wheelbarrow from the courthouse down High Street to Foundry and back to the courthouse. At the same time Frank Cox wheeled Charles Allebaugh in the torchlight parade the Democrats were allowed in lieu of a display of fireworks.[12]

Shanks' Mill. The old Core Mill property, on Dunkard Creek at Core's Ford (see vol. 2, p. 419), was sold June 5, 1884, by Benjamin and E. W. Core to Leonard Shanks, who was to operate it very efficiently for more than thirty-five years. The mill property had been developed by Abraham Brown, son-in-law of pioneer settler Michael Core. John Brown, a son of Abraham, sold it to Daniel R. Tennant in 1863; Tennant transferred it to Isaac Core in 1868; and Isaac sold it to Benjamin and E. W. Core in 1871.[13]

Mills were still essential to the economic life of the county and were important community centers, where farmers gathered, ex-

9. *Weekly Post,* January 10, 1885.
10. *Proceedings of the Council,* January 10, 1885.
11. Callahan, pp. 195, 196.
12. Callahan, pp. 233, 234.
13. *Chronicles of Core,* pp. 122, 123, 251.

changing news and views while the grain was being ground into flour or meal.

Deaths. A Clay District farmer, Barton Morris, died October 30, 1884. Born April 14, 1799, he was the son of Levi and Elizabeth Morris. He married Comfort King, October 22, 1826, and they were the parents of three children, Eli, David Snyder,[14] and Sarah.

A farmer of Dolls Run, Asa Lemley, died November 2, 1884. He was a son of Isaac and Margaret Snider Lemley and was born June 25, 1806. He married Elizabeth Evans, who died March 9, 1873; he was survived by five children, namely, Lee Roy, Lewis, Alexander, David E., and Martha.[15]

A farmer of Dunkard Ridge, near the Pennsylvania line, Joseph Inghram, Sr., died November 9, 1884. He was born January 22, 1801. He and his wife, Mahala, were the parents of Eleazar, Harriet, Margaret, and Joseph, Jr.[16]

An early settler in Berry Hollow, a branch of Dolls Run, James Berry, died June 23, 1884. He was born in 1798. He married Ruth Pointer (1799-1879) and they were the parents of Robert C., Samuel W., Hyson G. P., William, Zanie (married Henry Cunningham), and J. Washington (married Margaret Barrickman).[17]

Miscellany. In 1884: Demain's Cheap Grocery, supplanting the A. L. Wright Company, put in a new stock of goods advertised to be sold "dirt-cheap" (Callahan, p. 210). . . . One of Morgantown's first full-time barbers, Adam Bowers, opened a shop in the Stine building (Callahan, p. 212). . . . S. S. Wade began the practice of medicine in Morgantown (Callahan, p. 214). . . . Liquor licenses were authorized by Morgantown's borough council for J. K. Durr, F. H. St. Clair, and James C. Wallace (Callahan, p. 216). . . . The steamer *Harry*, Capt. J. M. Neil, arrived at Morgantown on January 3 (*Weekly Post*, January 5, 1884). . . . Elizabeth E. Willey, wife of Waitman T. Willey, died on January 9 (*Weekly Post*, January 19, 1884). . . . Mrs. Elva Ann Brown, widow of Adam Brown, died January 29, aged sixty-seven (*Weekly Post*, Febru-

---

14. *Chronicles of Core*, p. 123; a grandson of David Snyder was Coleman Morris, a well-known cartoonist of Seattle, Wash.

15. Headlee, *George Lemley . . . and . . . Descendants*, p. 106.

16. *Chronicles of Core*, p. 123.

17. *Chronicles of Core*, p. 123.

ary 9, 1884). . . . The Baltimore Clothing House opened for business on Walnut Street on February 23 (*Weekly Post,* February 23, 1884). . . . The operetta *Genevieve* was presented on February 22 in Academy Hall by ladies of the Presbyterian Church (*Weekly Post,* March 1, 1884).

CHAPTER ONE HUNDRED NINE

1885

The General Assembly of Virginia, in October 1785, passed an act establishing "a town, by the name of Morgans-town," being "fifty acres of land, the property of Zackquill Morgan." The town was to be laid out in lots of half an acre each, "with convenient streets." Samuel Hanway, John Evans, David Scott, Michael Kearnes, and James Daugherty were named as trustees.

As the time for the centennial approached, Morgantown's citizens showed an increasing interest in local history, which had been stimulated by the observance of the centennial of the county and the nation, in 1876.

Morgantown's Centennial. Community leaders planned a new centennial celebration, to mark the close of a century of gropings in various areas, and the beginning, they hoped, of a period of awakening and more rapid growth and expansion under more intelligent direction.

The observance was scheduled to be held in October and it was hoped that it might occur on the day of the opening of the new railroad service to Morgantown, a most significant event in itself. But work on the new line did not proceed as rapidly as had been expected, so that this aspect of the celebration had to be postponed.

The editor of the *New Dominion*, as early as November 4, 1884, had urged the observance: "It would be disgraceful to let the occasion pass without some adequate manifestation of interest.— Our self respect demands it.—Besides, our centennial year is more full of hope for our town than any other period of our history."

The movement grew rapidly, under the leadership of Senator Waitman T. Willey, Col. James Evans, Joseph Moreland, John J. Brown, Judge John A. Dille, E. Shisler, N. N. Hoffman, Prof. W.

P. Willey, John C. Wagner, J. M. Hagans, George C. Sturgiss, William Morehead, W. C. McGrew, L. S. Hough, and others. When postponement of the celebration was threatened because of delay in completion of the railroad, young men, such as Julian E. Fleming and Joseph Moreland intervened; they were resolved to make the observance successful, and to hold it during the centennial month of October. Alfred K. Smith's persistent determination was largely responsible for securing the necessary financial aid.

The general executive committee, at its final meeting before the celebration, adopted a coat of arms designed by Lillie Hagans, showing the figure of an erect woman with a background of mountains and a river at her feet, under which was the inscription "Regina Monongahelae" (Queen of the Monongahela).

The women spent a week in placing appropriate street decorations and then on Wednesday, October 28, disregarding lowering clouds and intermittent rain, a large crowd gathered for the celebration.

"Old men with whitened hair and wrinkled face returned from afar to view old landmarks familiar to their boyhood, or perhaps to trace in the countenances of a young generation some features which recalled the memory of old friends no longer living. The middle-aged, who had migrated to other places in childhood, returned like children to receive the embrace of a fond mother. The young men and maidens, with all the flush and flame and flourish of youth, dashed in behind their foaming horses. Before evening the hotels and boarding houses were filled, and rooms offered in private homes were quickly occupied. For the accommodation of late arrivals the court rooms and jury rooms were opened and placed in charge of a special officer."[1]

The next morning (Thursday, October 29) the crowd watched a long procession through the muddy streets, and then gathered in front of the courthouse to hear the address of welcome by the distinguished and venerable Waitman T. Willey, who was introduced by Col. James Evans, a grandson of John Evans, one of the first trustees. On the platform was Zackquill Morgan, of Pittsburgh, son of Capt. Zackquill Morgan, who died at Bladensburg in the War of 1812, and grandson of Zackquill Morgan, the founder of the town.

1. Callahan, p. 235.

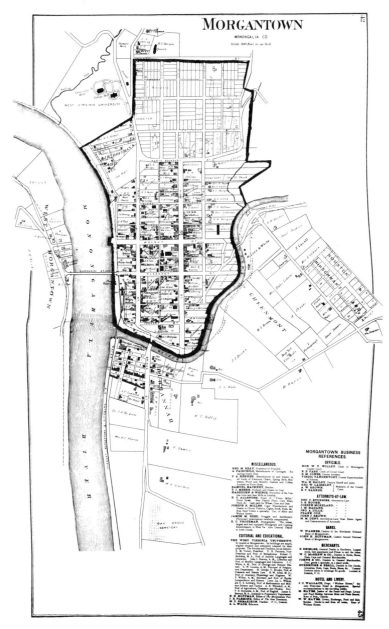

Fig. 16. Map of Morgantown at its Centennial. (From *Atlas of . . . Monongalia County*, 1886.)

The large audience reassembled at 1:30 p.m. and a promising young poet, Waitman Barbe,[2] read an appropriate poem. After reference to the pioneer work of the forefathers, and commendation of the virtues of the small town ("a city only in thy larger dream"), he closed with:

> "And now old stream, that cut thy channel long
> Before the sachem's shout and twanging thong
> Were heard the lonely mountain site along,
> Speed thee, and this our sacred message bear
> To every listening bank thy waters wear—
> Beside the New Dominion's fairest stream
> A sister town is waking from her dream;
> That, though she's just a hundred years today,
> Her heart's as young as the winsome heart of May,
> Her feet keep time to the merriest roundelay,
> And her tresses wear no streakings of the gray."

Senator Waitman T. Willey then delivered the historical address of the occasion, epitomizing the hardships of the town's earlier history and closing with a worthy tribute to its later educational advantages, developing through various academies and seminaries, culminating in the relatively new West Virginia University. Hardly anyone failed to realize that the speaker had himself played a very prominent role in the town's history.

The exercises closed at 8:00 p.m. with a display of fireworks in the public square in front of the courthouse.

"The look backward doubtless stimulated the determination to join in a greater forward movement for which events were preparing the way."[3]

Progress on the Railroad. As noted above, construction of the railroad to Morgantown was actually under way, after more than fifty years of only talking about it.

Morgantown, welcoming an enterprise which appeared likely to awaken the community from a long period of lethargy, quickly granted a right-of-way for the railroad and for the new depot, to be located at the foot of Cherry Alley. In October 1885, a contract

2. For whom the Morgantown Public Library was later named.
3. Callahan, p. 236.

for construction of the depot was awarded. Excavation began at once: bricks and timbers were assembled. Before the end of the year rails were received by the construction company to lay the track at Morgantown.

But construction of the line down the river from Fairmont, already under construction for over a year, was delayed by numerous landslides, and the opening of service was delayed week after week, much to the distress of Morgantown people, eagerly awaiting sight of the first train.

Towards the end of December many Morgantown train enthusiasts traveled seven miles through mud and slush to Little Falls to see the train. The next issue of the Fairmont newspaper, the *Index*, described the population of Morgantown as sitting around the half finished depot watching it grow towards completion.

Meanwhile, local concerns continued to operate their stagecoach from Morgantown to Fairmont daily, as they had for many years in the past. The trip in summer was not bad, taking only four or five hours, but in winter it might require twelve hours or more, because of the deep mud through which the horses could pull the hack only with the greatest difficulty. For over sixty years the stagecoach had been Morgantown's most reliable mode for public transportation. At last a change was about to be made.

Eli Marsh Turner. West Virginia University ended its two-year period without a president on June 11, 1885, when Eli Marsh Turner of Clarksburg, was elected by the regents to the position. He was a graduate of Princeton (1868), taught Greek there from 1869 to 1872 and was assistant librarian in 1872-73. He returned to Clarksburg in 1873 to enter law and politics. He was elected to the state senate in 1876. In 1884 he moved to a farm near Clarksburg.

"With tastes essentially intellectual, President Turner was eager to resume educational work and was generally considered well suited to the University presidency. A widely circulated report that he was Paris greening potatoes when word came to him of his election did not detract from his popularity. West Virginia was then 85 per cent rural."[4]

"Significant of the changing order, many persons were pleased with the fact that the new president was a Southerner, liberal

4. Ambler, p. 303.

Fig. 17-A. West Virginia University Campus, late 1880s. (Morgantown Public Library, Moreland Collection.)

Fig. 17-B. The university faculty, 1885. From *left, seated,* St. George T. Brooke, D. B. Purinton, President E. Marsh Turner, B. W. Allen, A. W. Lorentz, and J. S. Stewart; *standing,* J. I. Harvey, R. C. Berkeley, Lt. James L. Wilson, P. B. Reynolds, A. R. Whitehill, I. C. White, and William P. Willey. (West Virginia University Library.)

enough to get his education in the North. Such persons predicted that he would be an even better president than Wm. L. Wilson had been. In faculty circles the restored presidency was thought to have been strengthened by the election of Dr. Alex R. Whitehill to head the school of agriculture, chemistry and physics in succession to Professor Woodville Latham, who as a result of a long trial involving Governor Jackson and other prominent persons, had been advised 'to avoid the very appearance of offense in the future' in the use of intoxicants. The faculty was strengthened also through the election of P. B. Reynolds, President of Buckner College, Arkansas, and former president of Shelton College, West Virginia, to head the school of English in succession to Professor F. S. Lyon, former head of the pro-Northern faction."[5]

Co-Education Defeated. For the second time, the state legislature, in February 1885, defeated a bill to allow the admission of women at West Virginia University. Commenting on the vote, D. B. Lucas, of the Eastern Panhandle, wrote to Professor R. C. Berkeley:

"We today defeated the co-education bill after a severe fight. . . . When we are prepared to substitute the half civilization of the northwest for the culture of the Atlantic seaboard we shall be prepared for co-education. I hope that its advocates, having been defeated twice in the legislature, will give us a rest. If they do not, I have made up my mind what to do. I will get up a memorial to establish a college east of the Alleghenies and petition the legislature that one-half of the endowment and the annual appropriations may be accorded us. The Third District will support me in it, and I think such a proposition could have been carried this session without difficulty. The Democratic party, by an overwhelming and almost unanimous vote, have declared against co-education, and the continued local agitation of the subject will render it nigh impossible to get our appropriations."[6]

The Anticlinal Theory of Petroleum Geology. The idea of using structural geology in the exploration for oil and gas was due almost exclusively to the efforts of Professor I. C. White, at West

5. Ambler, p. 304.
6. Callahan, pp. 228, 229.

Virginia University, who published his initial article, introducing his theory to the public, in 1885.[7]

"My excuse for writing the article," he said, "was that I might be of some service in preventing the waste of capital that has been going on within a radius of fifty miles of Pittsburgh, by an indiscriminate search for natural gas."

In outlining the events that led to his conclusions on the anticlinal theory, Professor White gave the following narrative:

"The first oil producer to undertake this study in a systematic way was Mr. J. J. Vandergrift, of Pittsburgh, Pa., then President of the Forest Oil Company and the United Pipe Lines.

"In the spring of 1883, Mr. Wm. A. Earseman, a veteran oil operator, who was then in the employ of the Anchor Oil Co. and who had noted the fact that many of the great gas wells of Pennsylvania were located along the lines where anticlinal axes had been drawn on the maps of the State Geological Survey of Pennsylvania, secured Mr. Vandergrift's assent and financial support to undertake a geological investigation of the occurrence of natural gas. Mr. Earseman then began correspondence with myself upon the subject, the result of which was an engagement in which the writer agreed to devote the month of June, 1883, to an investigation of the subject for Mr. Vandergrift. In the work I was often accompanied by Mr. Earseman, who communicated freely to me his ideas on the subject of anticlinals, though he did not then possess the necessary geological attainments to enable him to verify or disprove his suspicions. After visiting and studying the geological surroundings of all the great gas wells that had been struck in the Appalachian district, the conclusion was reached that the rock disturbance caused by anticlinal waves was the main and important factor in the occurrence of both petroleum and natural gas, and this announcement was made to Mr. Vandergrift in a written report at the close of June, 1883."[8]

The Public Schools. Virgil Vandervort in 1885 followed Benjamin S. Morgan as county superintendent of schools.

Women teachers were becoming more numerous. A county

7. "The Geology of Natural Gas," *Science,* June 26, 1885.

8. *West Virginia Geological Survey,* vol. 1, pp. 159-63. 1899. See also Thoenen, *History of the Oil and Gas Industry in West Virginia,* pp. 119-27.

board of examiners, composed of the county superintendent and two experienced teachers gave teacher examinations and certified teachers. Applicants took an examination based on difficult questions from the subject fields of the elementary school curriculum, then in a rather fluid state. More and more women were among the applicants, in contrast to the pioneer days, when nearly all of the teachers were men.

A teacher with a certificate then began a search for a vacant school, meeting with the local trustees. A successful school term was not always a guarantee of reappointment, because of local politics and jealousies.[9]

Drugstores. By 1885 there were two thriving drugstores in Morgantown. J. M. Reed, druggist and apothecary, advertised that he carried a full stock of drugs, books, perfumery, wines, liquors, paints, oils, notions, etc. Henry B. Lazear, who had kept a drugstore and bookstore on the Courthouse Square since 1866, carried about the same line, emphasizing, however, mixed paints, oils, varnish, and "Yankee notions," rather than strictly drugs or medicine. At both drugstores, patent medicines which had a good sale included Hostetler's Bitters, Well's Health Renewer, St. Jacob's Oil, Ayer's Sarsaparilla, and McLane's Vermifuge.[10]

Real Estate Agencies. The sale of real estate in and around Morgantown was stimulated by sanguine expectations of railroad connections. The first real estate agency was managed by George M. Hagans, an industrial promoter who offered for sale not only town lots, but also suburban property, timberland, coal mines, and farms. During the early seventies, his agency had a rapid growth. After his death in 1874, another agency was opened, in 1875 by Fitch and Moreland, who were also successful. In 1881 a new real estate agency, owned by George C. Sturgiss and Company, opened for business and met with prompt success.[11]

Little Falls and Lewisville. A post office was established at Little Falls, along the Monongahela River in Clinton District, on November 9, 1885, with J. Marshall Jacobs as the first postmaster.

The falls in the river had been noted in the earliest pioneer

9. Hastings, *School and Local History*, vol 1, p. 68.
10. Callahan, p. 211.
11. Callahan, p. 211.

times as obstructions in canoe travel and Jacob Hall was given a land grant "nearly opposite the falls of the River to include his actual Settlement made in 1775" (vol. 1, p. 286). There was a "Little" Falls, with a drop of about six feet, near the mouth of Toms Run, and a "Big" Falls, with a drop of about eight feet, at Round Bottom. Both of these were problems in steamboat navigation, except at times of moderately high water.

Lewisville post office, in Morgan District, was established August 25, 1885, with John B. Cunningham as postmaster. The name Lewisville was in honor of Lewis Hagedorn, who operated a gristmill along Deckers Creek, near the post office.

Churches. In 1885 the religious needs of the people of Morgantown were served by five churches within the borough limits. The Methodist Episcopal Church, at the corner of Pleasant Street and Long Alley, had been completed in 1850. The Presbyterian Church, built in 1868, stood at the corner of High Street and Kirk Alley. Rev. Spencer L. Finney, pastor of the Presbyterian Church, died December 9, 1885; he had succeeded the Reverend Mr. Dickey in 1883. The Baptist Church, at the corner of Long Alley and Bumbo Lane, was built in 1846. Black people had worshiped at the Jones African Methodist Episcopal Church, on Long Alley between Maiden Alley and Bumbo Lane, since 1869.

After a long delay, the new Methodist Protestant Church on Walnut Street had been completed, replacing the structure that burned in 1874. The congregation was unable to start rebuilding at once and the members scattered. In 1877 Rev. J. F. Cowan,[12] a young man just entering the ministry, was appointed pastor of the Morgantown Circuit. He hunted up the scattered remnants and held services in the old academy. In 1878, he was succeeded by Prof. A. T. Crolle, "a scholarly gentleman and a fine preacher," under whose pastorate the new building was begun. It was completed in 1885, under the pastorate of Rev. D. G. Helmick.[13]

Miscellany. In 1885: Isabella, the Marchioness of San Roman (vol. 3, p. 447), died in lonely retirement (Callahan, p. 100). . . . Phoebe Davis Hayes, widow of Alexander Hayes (vol. 3, p.

---

12. Later an editor of the *Christian Endeavor World*, in Boston.
13. *Daily New Dominion*, August 19, 1899.

132, etc.), died June 20, aged eighty-one (courthouse records).
. . . The Morgantown Gas and Water Company, finding no gas at
its Deckers Creek well, abandoned the enterprise in March (Callahan, p. 218). . . . Morgantown, in a May 11 election, voted 119 to
36 to subscribe five thousand dollars for a water works system[14]
(Callahan, pp. 218, 261). . . . The Reverend G. A. Gibbons, rector
of the Fairmont Episcopal Church, who had helped to establish a
Morgantown Parish in 1876, resigned in June to accept a call to
Romney and Moorefield (Callahan, p. 229). . . . A roller skating
rink was opened in Morgantown and for a time roller skating was
the most popular amusement here (Callahan, p. 231).

14. However, no action was taken in the matter.

CHAPTER ONE HUNDRED TEN

1886

February 14, 1886, was one of the great days in the history of Morgantown—the first passenger train arrived in town!

On January 16, 1886, the *Fairmont Index* reported that the track had been completed from Fairmont to Uffington, only three-and-one-half miles from Morgantown, and added: "If the Athens City Council will kindly order the bars down, in ten days Major Whiting will ride the snorting, cinder-belching steed through the grass-grown streets of the good old town, and then we shall be glad to see her spread herself."[1] The *Morgantown Post* was inclined to doubt this statement (without, apparently, sending a reporter to check it), replying that the *Index* was "a little previous"—that the only part of the railroad that had been completed to Uffington was the roadbed, ballast, and crossties. But on February 6 the train did reach the carriage shop in Durbannah, just south of the unfinished bridge across Deckers Creek. A week later, on February 13, railroad officials announced that the first passenger train would leave Morgantown for Fairmont on Monday morning, February 15, at 6:45 a.m.

The First Passenger Train. The train came down from Fairmont on Sunday afternoon, to be ready for the first regularly scheduled trip from Morgantown to Fairmont the following morning. The first ticket for Morgantown was purchased by R. C. White, of Lattas, Ross County, Ohio, and was retained as a souvenir by conductor K. D. Walker. The trip of twenty-five miles from Fairmont took two hours and fifty minutes, having been delayed considerably by a large rock which had fallen on the track and had to be removed.

1. Quoted by *The Post*, January 16, 1886.

The *Morgantown Weekly Post* reported the excitement of its arrival in town: "At 5½ p.m. the train pulled around the bend and came in sight in Durbannah, and there was a suppressed 'hurrah!' in the crowd that was hard to keep down. A number of young men and boys had gone to Uffington to come down on the train, and there was great enthusiasm aboard. Handkerchiefs waved from fair hands at the depot, and there was a spontaneous and hearty response from the passengers aboard the first through train for Morgantown, and white cambric fluttered and flapped a hearty 'how-de-do' everywhere. When the train stopped there was a cordial good feeling all around, and a hand-shaking was the order of the day. A number of railroad officials and others came down."[2]

Fig. 18. Morgantown in the late 1880s, showing the new railroad depot. (Morgantown Public Library, Moreland Collection.)

The next morning the first tickets from Morgantown to outside points were sold by Major W. C. McGrew, the first railway sta-

2. *Weekly Post,* February 20, 1886.

tion agent at Morgantown. Among passengers on the first out-
bound train were N. N. Hoffman, George Keener, Mary Dille, Dr.
George Morris, E. C. Protzman, Clarence McVicker, Z. F. Yost,
Waitman Barbe, and J. E. Fleming.

The popular local enthusiasm, says Callahan, "was not un-
mixed with regret. The conservative element of the town
lamented that the homogeneity of its society would be broken—
that the quiet of a hundred years would disappear, and be succeeded by the hum of industry with its accompanying changes in
-the social order. These conservatives, nevertheless, realized that
the time had come for their community to awake from her sleep.
While regretting the retirement of their past life of social equality
and quiet they joined in the universal local rejoicing."[3]

Senator Waitman T. Willey, in his centennial address the previous October, had included remarks in the same vein:

"The long wished for railroad is at our doors. We welcome its
advent. And yet, to us, there comes with it some regrets. The
venerable homogeneity of our society will be broken. Our old time
hospitality and our earliest family-like social relations will be
marred. Heretofore, in consequence of our isolated situation, cutting us off from easy intercourse with the wide world around us,
we have been somewhat in the condition of the ships coming
crossing the seas. We have been compelled into closer personal
relations, begetting friendships all the more intense because thus
limited and concentrated. But with the railroad the stranger will
intrude upon us and the influx of the new outside influences,
social, moral, and material, will less or more modify the existing
conditions of society. Among these we may hope to see established in our midst new industries and an increase of enterprise in
all of our pursuits. But we may as well disabuse ourselves at once
of the delusion possessing some of us that a railroad is all we
want. We shall want the energy and enterprise to make available
the opportunities which it will afford. To the farming interests of
any country through which they pass, railroads must always be
beneficial; but to inland towns like ours, they are of little value
excepting the conveniences of ingress and egress, unless capital
can be attracted by them and invested in profitable industries."

The outlook was not wholly bright, however, as some were still

3. *Making of Morgantown*, p. 244.

fearful (see vol. 3, p. 291) that the locomotives would scare the horses, especially at road crossings. "Therefore, THE POST points out, in time, the great dangers that will threaten our people at these crossings, and would warn them, like the Dutchman, to always 'look a leedle oudt' when they are traveling a mud pike alongside a railroad."[4]

But the opening of the railroad was the beginning of a new chapter in the county's history. Travel was stimulated, excursions were arranged, more visitors arrived from outside, student enrollment at the university increased. The increased demands for raw materials provided new opportunities for labor and there was a pronounced growth in local hauling. There were great expectations for new business enterprises which would tap resources of the community, increase the value of real estate, and stimulate many improvements in civic life.

In these great expectations the community would not be disappointed.

The first schedule included one round trip daily, as follows:

Northward (Read up)		Southward (Read down)
P.M.		A.M.
5.20	Morgantown, Lv.	6.45
4.55	Uffington	7.10
4.22	Little Falls	7.43
3.43	Opekiska	8.22
3.18	Catawba	8.47
2.50	Houlttown	9.15
2.40	F. M. & P. Junction	9.25
2.30	Fairmont, Ar.	9.35

"It is thought that in one month the passenger train will make two trips a day instead of one, as now. The connection at Fairmont will be made such that a man can leave here in the morning, go to Wheeling and spend eight or nine hours on business and return at night. This will be a great convenience to all the people along this line, and certainly one appreciated."[5]

4. *Weekly Post*, January 16, 1886.
5. *Weekly Post*, February 27, 1886.

The new timetable went into effect on May 31, as follows:

Read down			Read up	
P.M.	A.M.		A.M.	P.M.
2.15	5.30	Morgantown	10.30	9.10
4.45	7.00	Fairmont	8.00	7.40

Atlas of Monongalia County. It is remarkable that the two best known and most noteworthy books dealing with Monongalia County were published during the 1880s, without any particular connection with each other. We have already noted[6] Samuel T. Wiley's *History of Monongalia County,* which appeared in 1883. Three years later in 1886, there was published in Philadelphia, Pennsylvania, a remarkably detailed Atlas of the county.[7]

The book measures 17 3/4 by 14 1/2 inches and includes seventy-two pages, mostly full page colored maps.

The maps were drawn from "actual surveys" made by J. M. Lathrop, H. C. Penny, and W. R. Proctor. We may picture these engineers, equipped with a measuring line and notebook, walking the full length of every single road and street in the two counties, and recording the results so accurately that they never missed a curve in the road, nor misspelled the name of a geographical feature. According to the title page, the surveyors were assisted by H. C. Mead, E. W. Dixon, S. W. Lincoln, M. D. Bartlett, and A. Y. Peck.

Preliminary pages list the table of contents, a table of distances in the two counties, and population data, by districts, in the counties. Villages listed in Monongalia County, with mileage from Morgantown are Arnettsville (11.5), Blacksville (21.0), Cassville (7.5), Easton (3.2), Granville (2.2), Jimtown (3.3), Lowsville (11.5), McCurdysville (16.0), Smithtown (11.8), Stewartstown (7.0), Wise (28.0), and West Warren (29.1).

The first map is a double-page representation of the two counties, drawn to a scale of 600 rods to an inch. Principal roads are shown, towns and villages, streams, coal banks, and railroads.

---

6. P. 63.
7. Actually, the full title of the work is *Atlas of Marion and Monongalia Counties, West Virginia,* and it was published by D. J. Lake & Co., No. 27 South Street, in Philadelphia.

The next several maps are of the magisterial districts and towns of Marion County.

Monongalia County is treated in the same manner. Battelle District is shown in a full page map, 200 rods to an inch; Cass District has a full page map, 200 rods to an inch; Clay District has a full page map, 200 rods to an inch; Clinton District has a full page map, 1 1/3 inches to the mile; Grant District has a full page map, 200 rods to an inch; Morgan District has a double page map, 2 inches to the mile; and Union District has a full page map, 1 1/2 inches to the mile.

In Monongalia County Morgantown is the only town and it is shown in a double-page map on a scale of 300 feet to an inch. Enlarged sketches, however, show the details of several villages, including Cassville, Smithtown, Jimtown, Granville, Arnettsville, West Warren, Blacksville, Wise, McCurdysville, and Lowsville.

The most remarkable feature of the district maps is that every house is shown by a dot, alongside which is given the name of the owner. I have not found a misspelled name, and the locations known to me are precise, indicating the painstaking care and scholarship used in preparation of the work. Schools, churches, mills, stores, cemeteries, coal banks, distilleries, furnaces, and other works of man are also given. Turnpikes are indicated by a symbol different from other roads, although most of them were scarcely different in character.

Following the maps there appear the names of several hundred "patrons," evidently persons who had subscribed in advance to help pay the costs of producing the work. For each of these is given the size of his farm, his post office address, his occupation, the place of his nativity, and the date he settled in the county (or date of birth, if he was born in the county).

In an appendix there appear tables showing the population of the United States by counties (there were only thirty-eight states), principal cities, with their population, the presidents and their cabinets, members of the Forty-ninth Congress, etc. A double-page map shows Virginia and West Virginia, with counties indicated, another shows the United States, with states and territories indicated, while a third double-page map shows the entire world.[8]

---

8. It does not need pointing out that this Atlas, so carefully done, was of great value at the time of its publication, and of even greater, historical, value today. The Monongalia Historical Society, as one of its bicentennial activities, republished, in black-and-white, maps of the seven districts of Monongalia County and these are available for purchase at the Morgantown Public Library.

A College of Medicine? Efforts to develop the school of anatomy, physiology and hygiene at West Virginia University into a professional school continued. Prof. B. W. Allen having vacated the chair in 1886, it was occupied by Dr. L. S. Brock during the next academic term.

President Wilson in 1883 had recommended that establishment of a medical school was one of the university's most "pressing needs," and later Chairman Berkeley had advised the board of regents to take some definite action, either to abolish the "School of Medicine" or make it what its name implied. His personal opinion was that such a school should not be established at Morgantown, because of the lack of funds and clinical facilities, but that it should be located at Wheeling, the largest city in the state, if established at all.

President Turner shared this opinion and in 1886 he and Col. D. D. Johnson, president of the board of regents, indicated that Wheeling should be the site of the proposed University College of Medicine. In "the consenting opinion of the medical profession," however, the proposal was considered impractical. The medical profession went on record, considering the absence of state funds for development, as opposed to the establishment of a state supported medical school in West Virginia at that time.[9]

W.V.U. Alumni. Up until and including the 1880 catalog, a complete list of alumni was included each year, and half or more of the alumni returned regularly for participation in the commencement exercises. At the beginning of President J. R. Thompson's administration the participation, in 1877, became the "Alumni Gathering," the chief feature of which was the Alumni Banquet, arranged from year to year by D. B. Purinton.

J. B. Stewart, '77, was the first president of the Alumni Association (1886-87) and J. H. Hawthorne, '77, the first secretary (1886-88).

The Protestant Episcopal Church. Morgantown Episcopalians had always been relatively few in number and for many years shared meeting facilities with the Presbyterians (vol. 2, pp. 448,

---

9. Board of Regents *Bien. Rpt.*, 1886-88, pp. 17, 18; *Wheeling Daily Intelligencer*, June 11, 1888; Ambler, p. 307; Van Liere and Dodds, *Medical Education in West Virginia*, pp. 10, 11.

449, 499-501; vol. 3, pp. 498-500). In 1874, chiefly through the leadership of Thomas Rogers and Prof. R. C. Berkeley, they reorganized their congregation and thereafter held monthly services in the old academy building, conducted by Rev. G. A. Gibbons, rector of the church in Fairmont. In February 1876 the Morgantown Parish was organized at a meeting presided over by the Reverend Mr. Gibbons (vol. 3, p. 680). In 1886 the congregation built a small frame church on High Street, under the supervision of Rev. Howard MacQueary, who had succeeded the Reverend Mr. Gibbons in 1875.[10]

New Post Office Building. Joseph Moreland constructed a two-story frame building next to his office on Pleasant Street, the contract going to Fairchild, Lawhead and Company, Isaac Weaver doing the foundation. The post office was then moved into this eighteen-by-thirty-foot building, from its previous location on High Street.[11]

Morgantown's outside mail now arrived daily at 5.15 p.m., via the railroad. The stagecoach was still running through Arnettsville, carrying only local mail.[12]

Dellslow and Opekiska. A post office called Dellslow was established along Deckers Creek, in Morgan District, on July 26, 1886, with James P. Burbridge as the first postmaster.

The post office in the community had originally been called Lewisville (see p. 92), in honor of Lewis Hagedorn, a miller, but the mail kept getting confused with Lowsville so Mr. Hagedorn was asked to suggest a new name. He proposed Delsloh, after Freidelsloh,[13] Germany, his birthplace, but the Post Office Department spelled it Dellslow.

Abraham Guseman was the first settler in the community, living, tradition says, under Pioneer Rocks, in 1793, while building his log house. He constructed the first flour and carding mill in 1807 and the community was thereafter known as Guseman's

---

10. On a site later occupied by the Morgantown Hardware store. Callahan, pp. 229, 257; Dodds and Dodds, p. 75; *Weekly Post*, April 10, 1886. James P. Chaplen, of New Martinsville, was the contractor.

11. *Weekly Post*, January 23, 1886.

12. *Weekly Post*, March 20, 1886.

13. I.e., a free town near a slough, or swamp.

Mills. It was bought by Lewis Hagedorn and Peter Weinig in 1869 and the area thereafter was called Hagedorn's Mills.[14]

A post office by the name of Opekiska was established April 14, 1886, with Thomas F. Watson the first postmaster. The post office was located along the Monongahela River at the mouth of White Day Creek and was served by trains of the B.&O. Railroad. Opekiska, dating from pioneer times, was said to have been the name of an Indian chief (the equivalent of White Day), who sometimes visited there (vol. 1, p. 235).

Antioch Church of Christ. A congregation affiliated with the Restoration Movement (vol. 3, p. 125) of Alexander Campbell was organized about 1850 near Daybrook, on Days Run, and a small log building was constructed on a hillside. Later (about 1879) the congregation moved about a quarter of a mile closer to the village and built a frame church. Abraham Lemley, in 1886, deeded land to the Antioch Church for church purposes.[15]

Zoar Baptist Church. Another in the long list of congregations founded by Rev. G. F. C. Conn (vol. 3, p. 280, etc.), the Zoar Church, was established in 1886 on Dents Run about a mile north of Laurel Point. The Morgantown Baptist Church gave letters of dismission, recorded in the church book July 15, 1886, to nearly all of its members on the west side of the river, who then became members of the new congregation. The small frame church was built on a knoll adjacent to the Dents Run Cemetery and overlooking the old eighteenth century "State Road" to Fishing Creek (vol. 2, p. 237).[16]

Dunn Chapel. In 1886 a Methodist congregation was organized in the Dunn Settlement ("Dunntown," vol. 1, p. 302; vol. 3, p. 243) in Union District and built a small frame church on land provided by John McCarney. The foundation was built by John N. Fields and Clark Molisee. The lumber was furnished by Zackiel Dunn

14. See MSS, "History of Dellslow," by Charles A. Hagedorn and another by Fay Hagedorn, in Morgantown Public Library.

15. Wiley, p. 751; Core, *Morgantown Disciples*, pp. 17, 18, 19; Dodds and Dodds, p. 124.

16. *New Dominion, Woman's Edition,* December 30, 1896; Dodds and Dodds, pp. 99, 100. An organization had existed earlier (cf. p. 61).

and Tommy Fields, and the building was constructed by Sammy Sanders and Billy Phillips.[17]

Methodist Conference. The West Virginia Conference of the Methodist Episcopal Church was held in Morgantown, beginning on September 22. Numerous distinguished clergymen were in attendance. The *West Virginia Conference Daily*, edited by W. T. Barbe and published by J. E. Fleming, included numerous biographies of ministers, including Rev. J. B. Feather, Dr. Gideon Martin, and Rev. Clark Crawford. W. R. White was appointed minister of the Morgantown Station, J. B. Feather for Morgantown Circuit, C. W. Cox for Arnettsville, T. H. Trainer for Blacksville.[18]

New Brownsville and Cassville. Along the Dunkard Valley Turnpike, New Brownsville (Pentress P.O.) and Cassville were developing into bustling villages. At New Brownsville it was said in 1886: "William Davis and Son are the blacksmiths; then there is T. Lemley, carpenter, cabinet maker, and farmer, who, by the way, is one of the good Republicans that has been tried and not found wanting. Then there is John Sine, our handy man, 'Jack of all trades,' and a dyed-in-the-wool Democrat. Emrod Tennant is our justice and lawyer. Everybody knows him, so I'll not try to say anything about the 'Squire.' Last but not least is Jim Downey, constable; he is also road supervisor, bridge builder and stonemason."[19]

Concerning Cassville, it was said that there are "three stores, two blacksmith shops, a shoe shop, a buggy factory, a saddler shop—all of which are doing a good business."[20] Cassville, from the presence of the county poorhouse there, usually had a resident physician. Dr. Tom M. Hood located there early in 1886.[21]

17. Dodds and Dodds, pp. 152, 153. The name was later changed to Mount Union and then to Tyrone. Some of the early ministers were Revs. K. P. Burns, Raider Nicholson, T. A. McMillon, and Zinn Fink.
18. *Weekly Post*, October 2, 1886.
19. *Weekly Post*, April 2, 1886.
20. *Weekly Post*, February 13, 1886.
21. In September 1887 he was appointed assistant physician at Weston State Hospital, and was succeeded by Dr. D. H. Courtney; Core, *Chronicles of Core*, p. 125.

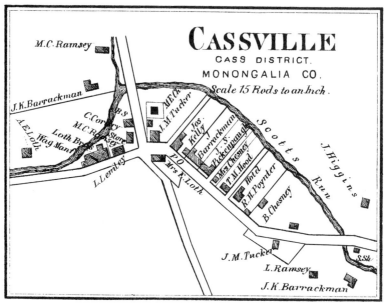

Fig. 19. Map of Cassville. (From *Atlas of... Monongalia County,* 1886.)

Oil Excitement. A flurry of oil excitement developed in the fall of 1886. At Mount Morris, just across the state line, it was reported that a well being drilled by E. M. Hukill, a promoter from Oil City, Pennsylvania, had struck a gusher in the third sand, at about twenty-six hundred feet depth. Intense excitement developed at the strike and it was reported that Hukill had refused twenty thousand dollars for the well.[22]

A month later it was said: "The oil excitement continues and the leasing is still going on. Quite a large tank is being erected at Mt. Morris. The light from the burning gas, supposed to be at the Mt. Morris and the Willow Tree, was observed several evenings last week against the northern horizon; the flickering motion of the light like that of a candle was very discernible."[23]

Willeyton. Residents of Dubannah petitioned admission to the town of Morgantown by extension of the town limits southwards across Deckers Creek but the council, on November 6, 1886, re-

22. *Weekly Post,* November 22, 1886.
23. *Weekly Post,* November 22, 1886.

fused to consider it. Thereupon they proposed incorporation of a new town, to be called Willeyton, in honor of Waitman T. Willey.

Miscellany. In 1886: Heavy snows fell in January and on the nineteenth it was reported that "enormous snow drifts are in every direction. Clark Wade got his hack snowed under between Mount Morris and Waynesburg" (*Weekly Post*, January 19, 1886). ... Plans were being made for construction of the Iron Valley Railroad to run from Morgantown to near Newburg (*Weekly Post*, May 29, 1886). ... Two hundred pupils, teachers, and friends of the Morgantown High School rode the train for an outing and picnic at Little Falls on May 27 (*Weekly Post*, May 29, 1886). ... Albert G. Madera, son of Nicholas B. Madera, died May 27, aged fifty-eight (*Weekly Post*, June 6, 1886). ... Zeri Ramsey was seriously injured on July 13 when his mare became frightened near Berry's Mill, at Cassville, and upset the buggy (*Weekly Post*, July 17, 1886). ... McLure and Comley's steam threshing machine broke down the bridge over Robinsons Run near Tapp's Mill while crossing; the machinery was badly damaged and George Davis severely injured (*Weekly Post*, July 24, 1886). ... Fully eight hundred people witnessed two games of baseball between Morgantown and Wheeling at the old Fair Grounds, on August 13 and 14; the first game ended in a 5-5 tie, in the second Wheeling won, 10-5 (*Weekly Post*, August 21, 1886). ... Thomas E. Hodges, principal of the Morgantown High School, having accepted the position of principal of Marshall College, Huntington, resigned and was succeeded by Nacy Waters (*Weekly Post*, August 21, 1886). ... John Pounds, an alleged horse thief, escaped from the county jail on October 1, causing great excitement (*Weekly Post*, October 9, 1886). ... Edgar C. Hoard, of Stewartstown, aged sixty-five, died December 3 as the result of an accident in which his wagon upset on a road as he was returning from Mount Morris, Pennsylvania (*Weekly Post*, December 11, 1886). ... Alba R. Campbell, Mooresville merchant, died on June 6; he was born July 16, 1860 (*Chronicles of Core*, p. 125). ... Enos Myers, of Pedlar Run, son of early pioneer John Myers, died December 7, aged seventy-four; his wife was Elizabeth Statler and their children were John, Elroy, Sylvester, Oliver, Michael, Charlotte, Melissa, Louisa, and Barbara Ellen (Core, *Chronicles of Core*, p. 126).

CHAPTER ONE HUNDRED ELEVEN

1887

The thriving suburb of Morgantown known for years as Durbannah, just south of Deckers Creek on the banks of the Monongahela River, in February 1887, by an order of the circuit court, was incorporated as a separate borough. The name Durbannah had been suggested by George Kramer for F. M. Durbin, who built several houses there about 1844 (vol. 3, p. 341).

The Borough of South Morgantown. Nevertheless, after considering various other names (including Willeyton, p. 104), the name South Morgantown was finally selected for the new borough.

"Our election for corporation officers will come off March 19th. Already there are fears of rioting at the polls, and a strong force of military will be promptly on hands in case of any trouble. We trust the voters will elect active members of the Council. We want good government that will give us good streets and sidewalks."[1]

The Athenaeum. On November 3, 1887, a new publication by students at West Virginia University, called for some unexplained reason *The Athenaeum*,[2] made its initial appearance. U. S. G. Pitzer, "a gentleman with considerable experience in journalism," was named editor-in-chief and Phil A. Shaffer business manager.

The first student publication at the university had been the *University Bulletin* (vol. 3, p. 676), published irregularly during 1873-76. The *University Daily* (p. 211), begun in 1877, was published during commencement week until 1896.

On March 4, 1887, a new student-sponsored publication, the

1. *Weekly Post,* March 5, 1887.

2. *Athenaeum* was the name of a school in ancient Rome for the study of the arts, from *Athenaion,* a temple in Athens where poets read their works.

Fig. 20. Durbannah Bridge over Deckers Creek, about 1885.

Echo, was published. It was edited by J. W. Smith, assisted by H. C. Ogden, J. A. Jackson, J. L. Roemer, E. P. Rucker, and J. A. Crawford. Although shortcomings were pointed out, it was nevertheless a financial success.

With the opening of the 1887-88 term, therefore, members of the Parthenon and Columbian Literary societies voted unanimously to establish a college newspaper. An editorial board was appointed, consisting of, in addition to Pitzer, Frank Snider and H. H. Ryland, Columbians, and Stuart F. Reed, D. L. Jamison, and J. E. Brown, Parthenons.[3]

County Schools. William E. Glasscock, a native of Grant District, was elected county superintendent of schools in 1887.

Reading, writing, and arithmetic were still the basic subjects in the public school curriculum. More ambitious pupils, by special arrangement with the teacher, might study history, geography,

3. Ambler, pp. 356, 357.

grammar, higher arithmetic. A few teachers were able to instruct in algebra or Latin.

The first board of teacher examiners appointed by Superintendent Glasscock was composed of Sarah R. Coyle, of Morgantown, and Zimri Ammons, of Cass District.[4]

The "Black Bottle" Railroad. The completion of the railroad from Fairmont revived the old project of a line up Deckers Creek (pp. 45, 67). In the spring of 1887 grading for this road was actually begun, under the direction of the West Virginia Railway Company, which proposed to construct it via Masontown, Reedsville, and Hardmans Furnace to Independence, on the B.&O. eleven miles east of Grafton.[5] Work was done on the first eight miles of the road,[6] known popularly as the "Black Bottle,"[7] but the company was unable to dispose of its bonds and suddenly collapsed, producing much anger among its unpaid Hungarian and Italian workmen and considerable friction in the legal settlement of its affairs.[8]

Noted Tree To Be Felled. "On the pasture lot belonging to the William Lazier heirs, near the bridge over Deckers Creek as you approach Mackey's mill from Morgantown (formerly the Rogers gristmill), stands an old locust tree that has a history. Seventy years ago the man Clemens, of near Clarksburg, was hung upon that tree. It has often been pointed out to the younger generation by old people who remember the event. It is now about to be cut

4. Hastings, *School and Local History,* vol. 1, pp. 66, 69.

5. *Weekly Post,* April 23, 1887.

6. Dirt was flying by May (*Weekly Post,* May 7, 1887) and Tennant and Johnson, the contractors, were cutting through the Hogback by June (*Weekly Post,* May 21, 1887). Newspaper publicity continued through the summer, full of optimism; a two-column account gave details, saying 750 men were working (*Weekly Post,* July 23, 1887).

7. It is said that the name Black Bottle was given to the projected railroad because the owner of the Irondale Furnace, a Hungarian named Colonel F. Nemegeyle, always set out a black bottle and a number of glasses at the meeting of his board of directors. They were promoters of the road for transportation of their product. Pittsburg *Post,* quoted by *The Post,* July 13, 1895. For biography of Nemegeyle (Nemegyei), see Wiley, *History of Preston County,* pp. 497, 498.

8. *Weekly Post,* August 27, 1887; Callahan, pp. 246, 252. George C. Sturgiss, the promoter who had told the laborers the work must cease, was forced to hide to escape their wrath.

down and destroyed under the march of modern enterprise. The Black Bottle Railroad will take its place.

"By-the-way, it has been over half a century since any one was hung in Monongalia. The negro Joshua was the last person publicly strangled on the gallows. He expiated (for another's crime, it is said) upon the scaffold near the present residence of Michael R. Chalfant, just beyond the University grounds, nearly 60 years ago."[9]

A New Courthouse? As early as 1884 the old county courthouse, completed in 1848, was pronounced a dangerous place for public meetings. In 1887 the county court employed a Pittsburgh architect to prepare plans and specifications for a new building, and to estimate the cost of its construction. These plans were delayed, however, by numerous objectors who proposed temporary repairs until sufficient funds were available for a new structure. Other persons maintained that public sentiment favored improved roads over a modern courthouse.[10]

Local Business and Professional Men. Advertisers in the *Weekly Post* during 1887 included George M. Reay ("stoves, fronts, grates, furnaces"), H. N. Mackey ("flour, meal, and feed"), J. M. Reed and Company ("drugs, books, stationery, notions, wines, etc."), Fairchild Lawhead and Company ("carriages, buggies, barouches, phaetons, spring wagons, village carts"), George C. Baker ("insurance"), A. D. Bowers ("new barber shop"), and H. B. Lazier ("drugs, books, stationery, Yankee notions").

Physicians included Brock and Wade (L. S. Brock and S. S. Wade), James P. Fitch, and W. C. Kelley. Morgantown attorneys included Sturgiss and Baker (R. L. Berkshire, Geo. C. Sturgiss and Geo. C. Baker), Keck and Son (P. H. and L. V. Keck), Frank Cox, W. W. Houston, Joseph Moreland, and Thomas H. B. Staggers.

Monongalia's Horse Market. "John Clark, a horse buyer of Uniontown, Pa., left Morgantown last Friday with another car

---

9. *Weekly Post*, May 7, 1887. For the hanging of Abel Clemans, see vol. 2, p. 345. A long recital of the "Abel Cummins" murder case appeared in installments in the *Weekly Post*, from September 27 to November 22, 1890.

10. Callahan, pp. 265, 266.

load of horses purchased in Monongalia County. They were good horses—every one of them. He paid on an average $140 for them and he told a POST representative that he had purchased, in this county, the present season, *over one hundred horses* at $140 each—or, in other words, left from $15,000 to $18,000 in cash with our farmers. He has shipped six car loads from here inside of two or three months."[11]

Fish Ponds. Many Monongalia County farmers supplemented their agricultural production through operation of fish ponds. There were problems, such as the following:

"C. Shriver's fish pond [near Ponetown] went dry a few days ago, causing the death of about eleven thousand young fish. Mr. Shriver took some twenty-five or thirty of them, weighing from two to five pounds, and put them in a small hole of water in Days Run to keep them alive, but some sneak thief stole them the same evening."[12]

What Monongalia Misses—Slack Water. "THE POST has always contended that if we had Slackwater completed to Morgantown there would be more summer visitors come to this county during the heated term than at any other point along the river. A ride from Pittsburgh, in those elegant steam packets, to the 'head of navigation' would be a trip eagerly sought by all. Thousands already avail themselves of the opportunity to come up as far as Greensboro—some come on to Pt. Marion, and many as far as Mr. [C. D.] Ley's up the Cheat river; but if we had Slackwater, nearly all the visitors would come to this immediate vicinity."[13]

The Dunkard Creek Turnpike. The road linking the Dunkard Valley, in the western end of the county, to Morgantown was the Dunkard Creek Turnpike. Originally incorporated by the Virginia General Assembly on February 1, 1839, it was revived by the West Virginia Legislature February 23, 1871. However, as with all other Monongalia County turnpikes (vol. 3, p. 641), it failed to reach the goals set by its promoters, and its operation never yielded any profit. Nevertheless, it did serve the purpose of providing a relatively good road to the county seat.

11. *Weekly Post,* June 25, 1887.
12. *Weekly Post,* July 30, 1887.
13. *Weeky Post,* October 8, 1887.

At the beginning of 1887 a New Brownsville correspondent was rejoicing that "all the toll gates are off the mud pike now, and it is free for all."[14] At Cassville, in June, it was reported: "The travel upon our road to and from town has been equal to that of a city thoroughfare."[15]

The White Settlement. In the western end of the county, on the headwaters of Dunkard Creek, a settlement had been developing from which came a man already on his way to international fame. The first American ancestor of this family was Stephen White, who came to Maryland in 1659. His son, Stephen II, had a son, John, and John's son Stephen III, was the father of Grafton (1752-1829), who came to the Monongahela Valley in pioneer times.[16]

William (1783-1850), one of the nine children of Grafton White, settled in western Monongalia County, on land where the Maple Post Office was later located. He married Mary Darling and they were the parents of eleven children; all but one of them married and located in the vicinity, forming what became known as the "White Settlement."

Michael, son of William and Mary White, married Mary Anne Russell and their children were Henry Solomon, William Thomas, Lydia Ann, Catherine, Israel Charles, and John. Michael, "a strong, virile citizen, a born leader of men," was a member of the commission selected in 1863 to divide the county into townships (vol. 3, p. 547) and suggested the name Battelle for the western-most township, in honor of the Rev. Gordon Battelle (vol. 3, p. 400).

Israel Charles White was born on his father's farm, on November 1, 1848. His older brother, Henry, wrote concerning his boyhood:

"Israel was a reserved and studious boy and efficient in all of his work. From the age of eight or nine years he was a persistent

14. *Weekly Post,* January 29, 1887.
15. *Weekly Post,* June 18, 1887.
16. Lloyd L. Brown (*West Virginia History* 8(1946): 5, says he settled in 1774 in what was to become Monongalia County, but his land grant of four hundred acres on "Robeson Run" was dated 1789. Grafton married Margaret Dinney and their tombstones are in the midst of a deep second growth forest near Maidsville, where they were discovered by Clarence Willard, who showed them to the author.

collector of fossils. In 1861 he went to school to me, three miles away, over one mountain and up another, or sometimes a little longer route down one stream and up another; but Israel was always behind, hunting specimens along the streams."[17]

When he entered West Virginia University "he demurred to the requirements to learn farming, claiming that he was already a graduate farmer, having begun farm work by planting corn with a red string on his big toe, when he was eight years old."

New Post Offices. Four new post offices were established in the county during 1887.

The Hagans Post Office, near the head of Indian Creek, in Clay District, was set up February 2, with Michael E. Fetty as the first postmaster. It was named for Morgantown attorney John Marshall Hagans, who secured the establishment of the office.

"Hagans is situated on Big Indian Creek about 3½ miles above Arnettsville. We can boast of four dwelling houses, a church, a school house, a store and postoffice, and, last but not least, a gigantic sugar-tree under which the lads and lassies of this region assemble every Sabbath—and, oh, how they do enjoy themselves."[18]

A post office by the name of Jay was opened April 23, with Milton Hall as postmaster. It apparently hardly got into operation; the U.S. Post Office Department records state succinctly "no papers, May 18, 1887," implying that the postmaster's appointment was not confirmed.

A post office called Maple, in Battelle District on the headwaters of the Pennsylvania Fork of Dunkard Creek, just south of the state line, was established January 6, 1887, with Simon L. White as the postmaster.

Another Battelle District post office, Saint Leo, was established on the headwaters of the West Virginia Fork of Dunkard Creek, southwest of Wadestown, on May 18, 1887. Joseph M. Hall was the first postmaster. Saint Leo is said to have been named for Leo XII, who became pope in 1878.

17. *West Virginia History* 8(1946): 9. The outcrops were of what was generally recognized as Permian age and there were many imprints of leaves of trees and casts of stumps and portions of stems of tree ferns (*Psaronius* sp.). See Gillespie, Clendening, Pfefferkorn, *Plant Fossils of West Virginia*, 1978.
18. *The Post*, May 19, 1894.

James Summers. James, son of Joseph and Julia (Tarleton) Summers, died in 1887. He was born in 1850 and married Elmira Knapp (1863-1947), daughter of Robert Waugh (1831-1906) and Mary Wooddell (1831-1906) Knapp. Joseph Summers was the son of Rev. Alexander (1778-1847) and Mary Ann (1776-1832) Summers, both of whom died in Monongalia County. Julia Tarleton was the daughter of Caleb (1776-1861) and Margaret (Bean) (1781-1831) Tarleton; both were born in Maryland and are buried at Pisgah, Clinton District.[19]

Miscellany. In 1887: The east end of Lot 15 in Morgantown was conveyed for $6,000 by A. W. Lorentz, commissioner, to E. M. Turner (Callahan, p. 311). . . . Thornton Pickenpaugh, in April, conveyed parts of Lots 99 and 100 to Job S. Swindler, who, in October, sold them to Elizabeth Hair for $1,550 (Callahan, p. 324). . . . Rev. John Ambler came to Morgantown as the first resident minister of the Protestant Episcopal Church (Dodds and Dodds, p. 75). . . . Parmelia, wife of James Troy, of Clay District, died February 22, aged seventy-three (Core, *Chronicles of Core,* p. 127). . . . Thomas, son of Michael Barrickman, died June 14, aged thirty, survived by his wife, Belle Rice (Core, *Chronicles of Core,* p. 127). . . . Joseph Inghram, Jr., of Dunkard Ridge, died June 17; he was born December 5, 1826, and married Sarah Cosgray (Core, *Chronicles of Core,* p. 127). . . . The old Zion Methodist Church, in Cheat Neck, was repaired, and rededicated on December 19 by Rev. Jos. B. Feather and John Conwell; "Uncle Jack" Baker, who helped to build it in 1837, delivered an appropriate address (*Weekly Post,* January 8, 1887). . . . The suspension bridge was sold on March 12 to holders of the mortgage bonds, operating under the name of West Morgantown Bridge Company; the sale price was $7,525 (*Weekly Post,* March 19, 1887). . . . A community called Parkville (from the Park family, especially William A. Park, local merchant) was developing on Miracle Run (*Weekly Post,* March 19, 1887, etc.). . . . William Main and Company's Consolidated Shows gave two performances in Morgantown on June 30 (*Weekly Post,* June 25, 1887).

19. *One Hundred Seventy-Fifth Anniversary Celebration*, p. 445.

CHAPTER ONE HUNDRED TWELVE

1888

In 1888 an important and far-reaching new industry was opening in Monongalia County, an industry that was relatively new in the nation, but which was destined to have a fantastic future.

The Discovery of Oil. Oil was first discovered in western Virginia in 1807 along the Kanawha River in connection with drilling for salt wells. At first it was used for medicine and for lubricating wagon wheels. By 1826 it was beginning to be used in lamps.

By 1836 oil had also been found at the mouth of the Hughes River. Not far away, on the Little Kanawha River, was Burning Springs, where natural gas escaped from springs. Thomas Jefferson, as early as 1781, had reported that this gas burned with unusual brilliance when a lighted candle was held in it.

In 1859, at Burning Springs, Gen. Samuel D. Karnes, of Pittsburgh, Pennsylvania, drilled a well on land leased from William P. Rathbone. At a depth of 303 feet he struck oil, in July 1860, and about one hundred barrels a day flowed from the well for several weeks.

Within a few weeks, however, the harsh realities of the Civil War stopped the drilling and the rumors; men now talked of war who only a short time before had talked only of oil. On the now abandoned derricks the flag of the United States was hoisted.

Application of Structural Geology. After the war a new trend became evident and the scientific method was utilized in exploratory geology. Geologists sought, from surface indications, to solve the fundamental problems of the origin of petroleum and its conversion, its reservoirs and accumulation points, structure and migration, the permeability and porosity of sands, pressures and sedimentary capping. Many geologists, over the next twenty years, developed a sizable literature.

The idea of using structural geology in the exploration for oil and gas was due almost wholly to the efforts of a native of Monongalia County, Dr. I. C. White.

I. C. White. Israel Charles White was born November 1, 1848, on the headwaters of Dunkard Creek, in western Monongalia County, the son of Michael and Mary Anne (Russell) White.[1] He was one of the early students at West Virginia University, graduating in 1872. He taught school in Pennsylvania and New Jersey, worked on the Pennsylvania Geological Survey, and took a postgraduate course in geology and chemistry at Columbia College. In 1877 he was elected a professor at West Virginia University. By 1883 he held the chair of Geology and Natural History and was already "acknowledged throughout the United States as a leading geologist."[2]

It was while he was serving with the Pennsylvania Geological Survey that Dr. White received the training and experience that led him to develop the anticlinal or structural theory for use in the location of oil and gas. As is well known, a well referred to as the first oil well in the United States was drilled by Edwin Laurentine Drake near Titusville, Pennsylvania. His crew struck oil on August 27, 1859, at a depth of seventy feet, and other wells were quickly drilled, including the ones at Burning Springs.

Dr. White's initial article, introducing his theory to the public, was published in 1885.[3] Promoters were quick to give his theory a trial, hoping to make money, and while it was not always successful, it did break the "impasse between geology as a science and its practical application."

A great increase in the demand for natural gas drove exploration south from Pittsburgh to the borders of West Virginia. Monongalia County has a long border with Pennsylvania, and, passing from west to east a series of anticlines (the Amity, Mooresville, Indiana, Fayette, and Chestnut Ridge) enters West Virginia from the north, with the intervening synclines (the Robinson, Whiteley, Lambert, and Connellsville-Uniontown). At

1. See Lloyd L. Brown, "The Life of Dr. Israel Charles White." Master's thesis, West Virginia University, 1936; *West Virginia History* 8(1946):5-104; Ruth I. Hayhurst, "The Life of Israel Charles White. . . ." *Newsletter W.Va. Geol. Surv.* 16th issue (1972), pp. 12-16.
    2. Wiley, p. 421.
    3. "The Geology of Natural Gas," *Science,* June 26, 1885.

Mount Morris by the fall of 1888, the pool was producing five hundred barrels of oil a day from nine wells, and Dr. White and others were ready to test out the anticlinal theory south of the line.

Bank of the Monongahela Valley. In 1888 Morgantown was beginning to get started on its transition from a village to a city. A railroad provided connection with main line trains at Fairmont and the completion of slack-water facilities was about to open an age of packet boats.

The expansion of the community was reflected in the growth of its banking institutions and the beginning of organizations such as savings societies and building and loan associations.

In October 1888 the Bank of Monongahela Valley was established by reorganization of the old Merchants' National Bank of West Virginia at Morgantown, located at the corner of High and Pleasant streets.[4]

The Merchants' National Bank, in turn, had been established October 1, 1865, through reorganization of a branch of the Merchants' and Mechanics' Bank of Wheeling. The branch had been reorganized November 6, 1834, and was Morgantown's first incorporated bank.

The War Between the States had placed serious strains on the nation's financial system. A new federal banking law was passed in February 1863 and revised on June 3, 1864. This law provided for the establishment of national banks, chartered by the federal government and under the supervision of the Controller of the Currency, an officer in the Treasury Department. The minimum capital for a national bank in a city of over six thousand people was one hundred thousand dollars, while the minimum for a smaller community, such as Morgantown, was fixed at sixty thousand dollars. National bank notes, unlike the earlier state bank notes, were all printed alike and were uniform in value throughout the nation, issued on the security of U.S. government bonds.

In October 1888, then, the Merchants' National Bank, through reorganization, became the Bank of the Monongahela Valley, with the same capital stock, i.e., $110,000. The first president was Dr. L. S. Brock and the first cashier Dr. E. H. Coombs.

4. Callahan, pp. 213, 254.

The bank drew its patronage not only from the town of Morgantown and most of Monongalia County, but also from the people of Preston County, which had no bank at that time, and even from as far away as Oakland, Maryland. People came from considerable distances to deposit their money here or to exchange it for goods brought to Morgantown stores by packet boats from Brownsville and Pittsburgh. Within a relatively short time the bank built up a surplus larger than its capital and over the next several years paid dividends on its stock every year, even during the hard times of 1893 and 1894.

In 1888, when the Bank of Monongahela Valley was established, Morgantown had one other bank serving the community. This had been chartered as The Morgantown Bank, March 23, 1874. It had been organized by J. H. Hoffman, William Price, George B. Morris, William M. Jones, John Sutton, William Lyons, and others, with William Price as president and J. H. Hoffman cashier (vol. 3, p. 675).

The board later decided to organize as a national bank, at first proposing the name Morgantown National Bank. The name, however, was changed to the Second National Bank, and the new bank was chartered February 24, 1880, with a capital of sixty thousand dollars (see p. 37).

Slowly, Morgantown was awakening from its century of history as a quiet country village. "Gradually," says Callahan, "general indifference retreated from the advance of general interest and general welfare; and old-style gentlemen were replaced by hustling, cosmopolitan business men who arrived from neighboring cities or towns and who earlier would have been called 'foreigners.' "[5]

Colonel James Evans. One of the best known citizens of Monongalia County, Col. James Evans, died November 24, 1888. The son of John Evans, Jr. ("Capt. Jack") and grandson of distinguished pioneer John Evans (see vol. 2, pp. 253-55), he was born in 1798. He married Delia Ray, daughter of Thomas P. Ray, and they had six children, two sons and four daughters, namely: Lucy Strother (married John Dawson), Harvey Anna (married William, son of F. A. Dering), Thomas Ray (married Delia, daughter of Guy R. C. Allen), Gilly Coleman (married O. H. Dille),

5. *Making of Morgantown*, p. 248.

John G., and Delia Belle. He inherited the old Evans homestead by will.

Colonel Evans was well known for his public service and his success as a farmer. In 1839-40 he represented the county in the Virginia General Assembly. He also served as a justice of the peace and as a member of the county court. He was a member of the Wheeling Convention which organized the Restored Government of Virginia in June 1861. Later that year, at the request of Gov. F. H. Pierpont, he organized the Seventh Virginia Volunteer Regiment, which was a part of Gen. Benjamin F. Kelley's corps in the advance south of Grafton, and, after a winter at Romney, was a part of the force which captured Winchester in the spring of 1862. In September 1863, he was appointed as provost marshal, stationed at Grafton, a position he held until the close of the Civil War. He was trained in land surveying and "often rendered useful neighborhood services in settling peacefully and without litigation land-title disputes and was frequently chosen as the court's commissioner in suits involving the assignment of dower and the partition of real estate."[6]

In 1853 he built on the farm a large frame mansion, where he lived until after his retirement from active business (1873), when he built a handsome brick residence on High Street, living there the remainder of his life.[7]

Union Improvement Company. Within three years after the completion of railroad connections with Fairmont many new activities appeared in the county seat town. It was almost as if the coming of the railroad had broken a dam, bringing about a series of changes in the life of the community that soon ended its quiet rural nature.

These activities quickly resulted in the establishment of a series of public utilities. The first of these was gas, and in this activity the town was favored by its location near the developing oil and gas fields about Mount Morris, Pennsylvania.

Outside capital, late in 1888, brought about the formation of

6. *Weekly Post*, December 1, 1888; Callahan, pp. 80, 81; see also Wiley, pp. 527-29. Wiley said of him that he was "an humble and sincere disciple of the Lord Jesus Christ."

7. Callahan, p. 253.

the Union Improvement Company, by Thomas B. Grant, Edward M. Grant, Austin M. Comstock, James W. Rowland, T. B. Gregory, and Lyman N. Hale, of Pennsylvania. The immediate objective was to obtain natural gas for fuel and lighting purposes. After a visit to Col. E. M. Hukill, one of the principal developers of the Dunkard Ridge field, the promoters made arrangements for laying a six-inch pipeline into Morgantown. The town council offered certain favorable and liberal inducements to help bring about this public service.[8]

Two New Post Offices. A post office by the name of Duke was established June 26, 1888, with Walter S. Horner the first postmaster.

Another post office, called Holman, was established March 8, 1888. It was located in Cass District, at the South covered bridge (vol. 3, p. 641) over Dunkard Creek. Dissaway South was the first postmaster.

Dunkard Valley Baptist Church. A church group organized about 1881 in the village of Wise (pp. 49, 50), meeting in the schoolhouse near the covered bridge over Dunkard Creek, by 1888 had become so large that plans were made for a church building. "Materials were taken from the forest nearby and hauled to the sawmill by ox-cart. The building was ready for use the same year. It was decided that this was to be a community church, but since it had to come under some general organization, it joined the Baptist Association. It was the only one in the vicinity at the time. The church was called the Dunkard Valley Baptist Church. Rev. Isaac Wise was the first pastor."[9]

The Floods of '88. Two of the greatest floods in the county's history occurred in midsummer, 1888. At Morgantown it was said: "The great flood of 1852[10] has been eclipsed! The oldest inhabitant remembers no such river as that which spread out before us Tuesday evening, July 10, 1888, when the mighty Monongahela rose to thirty-five feet four and a half inches! the highest water

---

8. Callahan, p. 260.
9. Dodds and Dodds, p. 137. On Sunday, December 15, 1900, just after Sunday school services, the building was destroyed by fire and was never rebuilt.
10. Vol. 3, p. 382.

ever known! All day people were flocking to the suspension bridge watching the rising tide. Thousands of hewed logs and wheat shocks, houses, stables, bridges, furniture, etc., came down all the day long in the seething tide, watched by a multitude of men, women, and children from bridges and riverbanks. The scene was appalling! The destruction awful!—representing thousands of dollars swept away.... The train from Fairmont could not reach us Tuesday evening, the track being under water several feet in many places.[11] The water ran through the streets of Granville like a millrace.... S. G. Chadwick gave everybody toll free to see the sights from the bridge."[12]

Another destructive flood on August 20 and 21 swept away ten thousand dollars worth of bridges on Dunkard Creek. "The Strosnider bridge, about 125 feet span, an iron structure at Strosnider's mill, was swept from its abutments; also the New Brownsville bridge (wooden) over a hundred feet span; also the bridge at A. W. Brown's (wooden, and nearly new), also, the fine iron bridge at Johnny S. Brown's, 150 feet long; and the South iron bridge, 125 feet long.

"A. W. Brown's saw-mill was destroyed, together with about a half mile of his mill dam, and about 300 bushels of wheat were water soaked in his grist mill."[13]

Cass District. A long newspaper account of the mineral resources of Cass District included the following:

"Cassville, the largest town . . . , is a very picturesque village situated at the forks of Scotts Run, seven and a half miles west of Morgantown, at a junction of the Morgantown and Burton pike with the Laurel Point and Mt. Morris road. It has a population of almost one hundred inhabitants. For a small town it has quite an extensive business directory, consisting of three stores, two blacksmith shops, two saddler shops, tannery, carriage factory, hotel, shoe shop, post office and church. The County Infirmary is situated about one-half mile below Cassville, and it is a fine two

---

11. Actually no trains reached Morgantown until Saturday.

12. *Weekly Post*, July 14, 1888. Lizzie Pickenpaugh, widow of Joseph Pickenpaugh, lost her brick house near the old Rogers sawmill on Deckers Creek (*Weekly Post*, July 21, 1888).

13. *Weekly Post*, September 1, 1888. See Mary Jane Lemley, "Brown's Covered Bridge: Flood 1888," a poetic account; *West Virginia Hillbilly*, February 1, 1969.

story brick 30x60. The total cost of building and land was $6,200. The other villages of Cass are Jimtown, Osageville . . . , and Stumptown. Cass District has 11 schools, five of which are situated upon Scotts Run and its tributaries. The District is one of the richest in Monongalia County, especially in minerals, all of which are more easily mined than in many parts of the county."[14]

Clay District. Another account dealt at length with Clay District: "Clay lies directly in the line of the great oil and gas belt. The centre of the District is not more than six or seven miles from the Mt. Morris oil wells, and its territory is sure to be tested in the near future, with the strongest probabilities that paying wells will be found."[15]

Decoration Day. The thirtieth of May, 1888, marked the resumption of "the sacred and revered custom of decorating the graves of Union soldiers," which had not been observed in Morgantown in an official way for several years. At an early hour people began to gather, flags and banners were suspended, the town assumed a holiday garb. The morning train from Fairmont, arriving at 10:30, brought a large number of Odd Fellows of that city, with their brass band. At 1:00 p.m. a procession headed by the University Cadet Corps band formed at High and Walnut streets, proceeded to the Presbyterian Cemetery on Spruce Street, then to the Oak Grove Cemetery, for decoration of graves. A memorial service was held in University Hall at 8:00 p.m.[16]

The Oldest Buggy in the County. "Mr. J. W. Haney, of Stewartstown . . . , has a buggy . . . made, in part, by James M. Kern . . . , which is the oldest vehicle in the county that is still in daily use. It was made about sixty years ago by Mr. Kern when he was an apprentice at the wagon maker's trade, and is still strong and durable. Mr. Haney has been conveying raspberries to town—a distance of six miles—for several days past, in the ancient vehicle, and the buggy bids fair to last several years yet!"[17]

Arnettsville Changes. The village of Arnettsville, long a stagecoach stop, was undergoing numerous changes, now that

14. *Weekly Post*, March 17, 1888.
15. *Weekly Post*, April 21, 1888.
16. *Weekly Post*, June 9, 1888.
17. *Weekly Post*, July 14, 1888.

most travelers between Morgantown and Fairmont went by
train. A local correspondent reported:

"Well, in a few days the hotel sign was transferred to the front
of Jas. W. Teter's residence, where it still remains; and the said

Fig. 21. Interior of a country store. (West Virginia
Department of Agriculture.)

Teter is now a full fledged landlord, and the weary traveller will
find the reputation of the Arnettsville house fully maintained in
its new location; and about the same time the above events were
coming to pass, our stores also changed hands, and Samuel Phillips became proprietor, with Miss Belle McCartney as clerk."[18]

Carraco's Livery Destroyed. One of the most destructive fires in
recent years in Morgantown destroyed "the large and commodious livery stable of Marcellus Carraco." Five horses were destroyed, along with twenty-six carriages, buggies, wagons, and
an omnibus; also twenty sets of harness, collars, saddles, and

18. *Weekly Post,* November 3, 1888.

bridles, along with oats, hay, straw, corn, and various other materials. The total loss was estimated as about eight thousand dollars, with only one thousand dollars covered by insurance.[19]

Municipal Government. "In Morgantown the municipal government was beginning to have a broader conception of its duties and responsibilities, although encountering considerable opposition and indifference. Col. Richard E. Fast, who became mayor in 1888, deserves much credit in initiating this particular phase of development. Under his direction many public improvements were undertaken. A survey of the town was made by W. L. Webb and T. M. Jackson, members of the University faculty. Citizens were encouraged to learn street names and use them. Property owners were ordered to lay brick sidewalks; so successful was this project that the supply of bricks was exhausted."[20]

Miscellany. In 1888: Charles Frederick Lorentz died June 23; he was born in 1860, the son of Allen Wilson and Mary Rebecca (Dering) Lorentz (Callahan, p. 86). . . . W. T. Willey sold his brick office building on Chancery Row to the law firm of Cox and Baker (Callahan, p. 189). . . . In July it was rumored that the Baltimore and Ohio Railroad might secure control of the defunct "Black Bottle" railroad and complete it (Callahan, p. 246). . . . In April the Morgantown Knights of Pythias Lodge was organized in the Odd Fellows Hall (Callahan, p. 258). . . . The lot at the southwest corner of Spruce and Walnut streets was sold by Dr. Elisha H. Coombs to Prof. A. R. Whitehill (Callahan, p. 315). . . . The second church building to serve the Sugar Grove Presbyterian congregation was dedicated by Dr. A. M. Buchanan (Dodds and Dodds, p. 110). . . . Miss Emaline Coleman taught a subscription school in the Dolls Run Christian Church during the summer; these subscription schools, the only type before the Civil War, were now becoming quite rare and would soon disappear (Core, *Chronicles of Core*, p. 127). . . . Thomas Burns in March caught a sixty-pound wildcat on Aarons Creek (*Weekly Post*, April 7, 1888). . . . St. Clair's Grocery advertised that fresh oranges and bananas were received weekly (*Weekly Post*, April 7, 1888). . . . Mrs. M. McVicker opened a millinery goods shop in Morgantown on

19. *Weekly Post*, December 15, 1888.
20. Callahan, p. 263.

May 3 (*Weekly Post,* May 5, 1888). . . . A yellow poplar tree cut on the farm of O. P. McRa yielded over six thousand feet of lumber (*Weekly Post,* September 15, 1888). . . . Joshua M. Davis, of Cass District, died November 19, aged seventy-two years (*Weekly Post,* December 1, 1888). . . . Rev. J. W. Crowl, a Baptist minister and an excellent carpenter (he helped build the John Rogers house; vol. 3, p. 203), died November 25, aged seventy-four (*Weekly Post,* December 15, 1888). . . . Elmer Fetty, a farmer of Indian Creek, Clay District, died May 31, 1888; he was born May 30, 1811 (*Chronicles of Core,* p. 127).

CHAPTER ONE HUNDRED THIRTEEN

1889

January 1, 1889, dawned without any special intimation that it was to usher in one of the most dramatic episodes in Monongalia County's history. True enough, everyone was talking oil, but this had been for thirty years, like the weather, something to fall back on when they could think of nothing else to say. As early as 1865 a well, a few hundred feet deep had been drilled on Dolls Run at the mouth of Pedlar Run but without striking oil. On Dunkard Creek, near its mouth, in Pennsylvania, some oil was found and shipped to Pittsburgh on barges.

The new dramatic chapter in the Monongalia Story opened late in 1888 when E. M. Hukill took a lease on the D. E. and L. Lemley farm on Dolls Run and undertook to drill a well, with a steam engine and equipment vastly improved over that of 1865. Henry Birtcher took the contract of C. C. Wade to furnish coal to the drillers at $6.50 per hundred.

The Oil Excitement. Bad luck delayed the opening of the well. In March the drillers lost a set of tools and in April had difficulty shutting off salt water. But with the advent of mild spring days the very fact that a well was being drilled in the county had a remarkable effect upon the citizens. "The oil boom is on in its full fury now. Oil men are running in all directions to get leases. It is said that the Lemley well is a good one. The whole talk among farmers when they meet is oil and gas. Mr. Hukill has employed his faithful servant, Luther Sanders, to guard the Lemley well and fitted him up with two revolvers and a brier scythe. Luther went over in the dark hours of the night and climbed to the top of the derrick with his field glasses in his hand and viewed heavenward. Soon after reaching the apex he became much alarmed and began firing east and west, north and south, until his ammunition became exhausted. He was given special orders to keep away a certain obnoxious fellow who was on a strike with the noon-to-midnight drillers. Luther performed his part well and has received the eulogies of both the company and the people."[1]

Not waiting for the outcome of the Lemley well, the building of rigs on other farms in the area went forward rapidly. "Mr. Hukill has ordered J. J. Wharton to cut three hundred thousand feet of rig timber for the Dolls Run country. Rumor has it that Jeff Tennant has leased his farm and the parties are to drill soon and if they get oil, they are to pay him $100 per acre and take the farm. A. L. Cole has leased his farm to E. M. Hukill and work has begun on it near the Alphaeus Morris line. C. C. Core and J. V. Pride are hauling the lumber for the rig. The Eliza Morris property was leased yesterday to McCool and $750 was paid as a bonus and one-eighth royalty was also given. Messrs. Alex Lemley, D. S. Morris, A. Garrison, Wm. Core, and J. M. Morford are promised wells in a few days. Hauling pipe for the pipe line from the big

Fig. 22. An oil well derrick.

1. *Weekly Post,* April 27, 1889.

Fig. 23. The Dunkard Ridge Hotel. (Courtesy Walter Davis.)

tank at Mt. Morris to the Lemley well is in progress and will be completed in a few days. Then the Lemley well will be opened and we will all know what it is."[2]

The well was finally brought in on June 6 and started pumping at fifty barrels a day. It had been drilled to the Big Injun Sandstone, at 1,877 feet deep. Services at the nearby Dolls Run Christian Church the following Sunday had to be canceled when it was found the congregation was assembled around the well. "The constant influx of strangers brought here daily by the great oil boom is marked. The news of our county's stride forward in this line has been flashed to all parts of the Union. We are on the upgrade, but there is one wheel locked. It is our miserable public roads."[3]

A Pittsburgh newspaper reported later in the summer: "Only a few miles from the railroad is the oil field of Monongalia County. Already nearly 50 wells have been put down, pipe lines are in the course of construction and not less than one million dollars has been expended up to this time in developing the territory";[4] while on the same day another Pittsburgh paper said: "The Dolls Run oil field is experiencing a greater boom than ever, the prospects for an exceedingly productive territory were never so bright. One 50 and one 70-barrel well came in yesterday. A party of Pennsylvania capitalists have returned from a tour of the field and they are enthusiastic."[5]

On Pedlar Run several Morgantown citizens visited the new David Myers well on a Sunday and reported that "it is certainly a big one. . . . The spray from the oil spread around like a heavy fog on a fall morning and fears of it igniting were looked for. People were there in great numbers. Gray-headed men and women and men and women of all ages were spellbound at this new and curious sight."[6]

Many of the wells were located in the hilly section between Dolls Run and the state line, known as Dunkard Ridge. "On this ridge excitement knows no bounds. The woods, fields, and houses are full of anxious oil men-operators, contractors, speculators, and sightseers, until the farm-houses cannot contain them. So

2. *Weekly Post,* May 9, 1889.
3. *Weekly Post,* July 20, 1889.
4. *Pittsburg Chronicle Telegraph,* August 16, 1889.
5. *Pittsburg Commercial Gazette,* August 16, 1889.
6. *Weekly Post,* August 20, 1889.

Mr. Hukill is erecting as fast as possible a large hotel on the ridge from the road, in the woods where none of us thought six months ago a man would have ventured to build a shanty, much less a fine hotel, on that huckleberry ridge. When you speak of this ridge again call it the city of oil wells, for that is what it really is. For miles each way, north and south, are wells after wells. On the ridge you see them against the hillside, along the rivulets, and along the bottoms, almost nothing but wells for miles each way."[7]

Farm owners, as might be expected, were more excited than anyone else, hoping to lease their oil rights at fancy prices. "Unless you have your pockets pretty well stocked with the root of all evil it is useless to approach any of the honest farmers in the neighborhood of Dolls Run and Dunkard Ridge."[8]

As winter came on, it was reported that "mud is more abundant than oil . . . and is easier to get at. . . . It will hardly be possible to accomplish much while the rainy season continues, as the roads will not permit the moving of boilers and heavy materials."[9]

Gas Lights and Heat. Late in 1888 arrangements had been made by the Union Improvement Company (see p. 118) to bring gas from the Mount Morris oil field into Morgantown for use as fuel. A line was laid from the Evans-Dorsey well near Mount Morris into Morgantown.[10] Mains were laid along the principal streets of the town, and natural gas flowed into these mains on Tuesday evening, February 12, 1889. Gas lamps had been erected along High Street and the enthusiastic citizens, impressed by the brilliant lighting, promenaded up and down the "Great White Way," congratulating themselves on the coming of a new era. Within the next few years the gas industry would indeed transform the town by attracting a large number of industries seeking cheap fuel.[11]

7. *Weekly Post,* November 29, 1889.

8. *Oil City Derrick,* November 26, 1889.

9. *Weekly Post,* March 15, 1890.

10. Two years later, in 1891, the Union Improvement Company brought in a new well on the Wade farm west of the Bowlby's Mill. This well had been drilled by John Kennedy, Joseph McDermott, and others in exploring for oil. When gas was struck, it ignited and remained on fire for a year, a great natural wonder, before the fire was extinguished and the gas was piped into Morgantown.

11. Callahan, p. 260; *Weekly Post,* February 16, 1889.

Arrangements were also made for heating houses with gas, although some citizens had to be assured by Mr. Grant that it would not kill their canaries or house plants.[12]

A Public Water System. Meanwhile the citizens were seeking to provide a system of water works as the next public utility. As early as 1885 this had been proposed by the *Morgantown Post,* with a view to protection against fire and a consequent reduction of insurance rates. At an election held on May 11 of that year the voters responded by a favorable vote of 119 to 36, but no action was taken at the time.

In March 1889, a meeting of citizens was held at the courthouse, and E. M. Grant, manager of the Union Improvement Company, outlined the probable cost of the installation of a water system. Many citizens who had depended for years on John Edwards's water wagon for a supply of wash water (ten cents a barrel) were slow to accept the notion of such a great change, but the town finally accepted the proposal of the company. By September a water line had been laid from a reservoir on Tibbs Run, near Dellslow, to storage tanks at Morgantown. From these tanks it was distributed by lines along the main streets for use of the town and its citizens. Tests showing the high pressure of the water in the lines, and its carrying power, removed the objections of opposing citizens.

The low expense, the convenience, and the reduction of fire insurance rates on property more than balanced the cost to the citizens of installation of the system. All soon agreed that the new system, providing the convenience of kitchen spigots, and encouraging the installation of indoor bathtubs and toilets, was far better than the water wagon system. The Edwards family found compensation for its loss of business by the development of a new type of service—hauling away garbage from homes and businesses.[13]

Coeducation at WVU. West Virginia University went for its first two decades and a little more without regular admission of women to the student body. The Methodist and Presbyterian leaders who had launched the drive for location of the university

12. *Weekly Post,* April 20, 1889.
13. Callahan, pp. 218, 261.

in Morgantown were not opposed to admission of women, and, if they could have had their way, it would have become coeducational from the start. Actually, there was very little discussion of the matter. University enrollment throughout the country was largely confined to men, and there was a good girls' school in town, the Morgantown Female Seminary run by Mrs. Elizabeth Moore.

As usual, the public was indifferent and the president and the faculty were in favor of coeducation, so, in conformity with these attitudes, young women residents of Morgantown, of the proper age, in 1871 were allowed to attend university classes, provided they had the permission of the instructors and provided they were unable to pursue the same courses in any other Morgantown school. A number of young women were enrolled under this arrangement.

One of the strongest arguments of the opposition was the alleged impossibility of enrolling young women, in the absence of suitable housing quarters. Mrs. Elizabeth Moore, principal and owner of the Morgantown Female Seminary, offered to donate it to the state, provided she was permitted to collect customary charges for room and board, to continue her music and art classes, and provided further that she were made university matron. Thomas E. Hodges, principal of the Morgantown Public School, supported this offer, at the head of a group of students, including seminary girls (one of whom he later married[14]). Prof. William P. Willey had already admitted three or four Morgantown girls to his classes in history.

Personalities became involved in a sometimes bitter discussion that continued for several years. Dr. S. S. Adams, a prominent alumnus, advised the regents to "discontinue the premature discussion of coeducation" and to appoint Mrs. Moore to a regular place on the faculty instead of the position as matron, which would subject her to men "her inferiors in intellectual ability, as well as in the ranks of educators." The university administration censured Professor Willey for his independent course; he continued, however, to admit "young ladies" to his classes, and a few other faculty members became equally bold and defiant.

14. Miss Mary Amelia Hayes.

Meanwhile the student enrollment had declined from 159 in 1882-83 to 96 for 1883-84 and coeducation was urged, as it had been in the past, as a means of sustaining the enrollment.

The coeducation bill, on February 20, 1885, was defeated in the house of delegates by a vote of 33 to 30 and a member of the house wrote to the university faculty, expressing the hope that friends of coeducation, having been twice defeated in the legislature, "would give the state a rest."[15]

Under such circumstances, coeducation became a favorite topic for oratory and debate in literary societies of all state institutions of higher learning. Robert A. Armstrong, a senior at the university, in 1885 won the university Parthenon Society's gold medal "with a peroration that was applauded throughout the state." Armstrong wore his medal award until women were finally admitted.

The Female Academy Destroyed by Fire. On April 23, 1889, the building housing the Morgantown Female Seminary, at the corner of High and Foundry streets, was destroyed by "the biggest fire in town since the Woodburn fire of January 25, 1873."

The fire was discovered between 10:00 and 11:00 a.m. by "Aunt Malinda," the colored chambermaid, in the attic of the building; she and several others tried to fight the blaze by throwing water on it, before giving the general alarm. The origin was unknown; some supposed that the roof near the cupola caught fire from a falling spark.

"When a general alarm was sounded the flames had leaped to the cupola, and on account of lack of long ladders and an efficient fire department, all thought of saving the building was abandoned and the surging crowd of men, women, and children set about to remove the household goods."

Fears were felt for the Presbyterian Church, but fortunately the wind was favorable and the building was saved. The residences of Dr. H. B. Lazier, Major William C. McGrew, and Joseph A. McLane were set on fire by flying sparks, but a few buckets of water soon extinguished the flames.

Several pieces of furniture, including pianos, beds, cupboards, etc., as well as books, were saved, but in the excitement of the

15. Ambler, op. cit., pp. 372, 373.

hour many articles were destroyed by being thrown from windows.[16]

Supporters of coeducation claimed that "the fire of uncertain and mysterious origin" was really a blessing in disguise. In view of the generally favorable trend towards coeducation, and prospects that the next legislature would discuss it approvingly, President E. Marsh Turner, in June 1889, little more than a month after the destruction of the girl's school, recommended that the regents approve some conservative policy. The regents without further delay ordered the collegiate departments of the university opened to "female students."

Only ten women enrolled in the fall term, but coeducation was on its way.

The Age of Packet Boats. The dedication of Lock No. 9, on September 29, 1879 (see p. 21), despite expectations at the time, did

Fig. 24. The Packet Boat, *I. C. Woodward.* (Courtesy Roy Moyers.)

16. *Weekly Post,* April 27, 1889.

not immediately insure regular packet boat trips to Morgantown. There was a gap in the river improvements due to the fact that Locks Nos. 7 and 8 had not yet been built. A long series of civic, financial, political, and engineering developments must transpire before they were completed (see pp. 46, 110). But at last the hopes of half a century and more were realized and slack water was completed from Pittsburgh to Morgantown, a distance of 106 miles. Another landmark in Monongalia County history was reached.

On Saturday, November 8, 1889, the large steamboat *James G. Blaine*, and on Monday, November 10, the packet boat *Adam Jacobs* arrived on their first trips to Morgantown. Each boat carried a brass band and a great crowd of people. Saturday was a gloomy, drizzly day, but the ardor of the people was not dampened in the least. (Somewhat remindful of that day, April 29, 1826, more than a half century earlier, when the people had abandoned their church services, and run through the rain to welcome the first steamboat to Morgantown.[17]) When the first boat arrived at the wharf it was greeted by an enthusiastic company under a canopy of umbrellas.

A newspaper reporter for the *Pittsburg Dispatch* told of the events, telegraphing the story from Morgantown: "There were some ludicrous scenes. The genial Captain of the Adam Jacobs took in the antics of the moss-backs with genuine enthusiasm."[18]

The electric searchlight on the *Adam Jacobs* was a never-ending wonder to many Monongalia County residents, who had never before seen an electric light. The captain also gave a display of fireworks which were viewed with great wonder and amusement by the spectators.

Callahan[19] quotes jealous Fairmont visitors as remarking: "These damned Morgantowners get everything: steamboats, electric lights, natural gas, water-works, and booze."[20]

The editor of the *Morgantown Post* said: "Today opens an era of long-looked-for prosperity to our people, thus affording them easy and pleasant traveling, fair facilities and reduced freight rates. There will be from this time on a daily arrival of boats, and

17. Vol. 2, pp. 510-15.
18. *Pittsburg Dispatch*, November 11, 1889.
19. *Making of Morgantown*, p. 249.
20. The town, in May 1889, had voted for liquor licenses in taverns; Callahan, p. 263.

the natural trade between the upper and lower Monongahela that has been for half a century wished for."[21] The next two decades for Morgantown might be referred to as the age of packet boats. Equipped with dining rooms and cabins for passengers, the boats gave comfort and a degree of elegance to the trip to Pittsburgh.

The Buckeye Methodist Church. A growing desire for a church in the Dunkard Creek section of Cass District culminated on March 26, 1889, in a meeting at the Buckeye[22] schoolhouse, with Rev. W. W. Hart presiding, at which a Methodist Protestant society was organized. Among those present were David and Leah Lemley, D. N. and Sophronia Lemley, Isaac and Susanna Bowers, Mattie E. Bowers, Elizabeth LaPoe, James and Hannah Poland, John Wise, Jr., Ida Wise, and William L. Garrison. A second meeting was held in April and plans were drawn to erect a church building across the road from the schoolhouse, on a lot conveyed by Eli L. Bowers.[23]

F. A. Dering. Frederick Augustus Dering, son of distinguished early pioneers Henry and Rebecca Dering (see vol. 2, pp. 350, 351), died in Morgantown in 1889. He was born in 1802. He had held numerous positions of public trust, including service as borough trustee in 1859, 1861, 1862, and 1863, town recorder in 1870-71, and Morgantown postmaster from 1864 to 1882.

He married Julia Lowell Ray (born in 1815, died in 1849), daughter of Patrick Ray and sister of Thomas Patrick Ray (see vol. 3, pp. 215, 326). They had six children, namely, Mary Rebecca (born 1838), Harriet Sophia (1840-41), William Waitman (born 1843), Elizabeth Ellen (1844-45), Martha Augusta (born 1847), and Henry Ray (born 1848).

Beechwood and Bula. A new post office, named Beechwood, was established December 2, 1889, with Clyde E. Hutchinson as postmaster. It was located in Clinton District, in the big bend of the Monongahela River, across from Flickersville, and was served by

21. *Weekly Post*, November 16, 1889.
22. Named for the abundance of yellow buckeye (*Aesculus octandra*) trees along the creek nearby.
23. Core, *Chronicles of Core*, p. 129.

Baltimore and Ohio trains. Beech (*Fagus grandifolia*) trees were common in the area.

Another post office, called Bula, at the forks of Miracle Run, in Battelle District, was established September 16, 1889, with Peter B. Core as postmaster.

Chamber of Commerce. Morgantown was fortunate in having numerous civic leaders at this critical moment in its history, who gave intelligent direction to the general awakening that came with the arrival of the railroad, in 1886.

Among the most prominent of these were George C. Sturgiss, Richard E. Fast, and Dr. I. C. White. Col. E. M. Grant, one of the first to see the importance of gas in the development of the town, was another.

In 1889 Fast, Sturgiss, Grant, and five others, T. Pickenpaugh, William P. Willey, F. A. Hennen, E. Shisler, and John A. Myers, organized the Morgantown Chamber of Commerce, which became active in promoting the growth of the town.[24]

Miscellany. In 1889: More direct railroad connection between Morgantown and Clarksburg was obtained through the opening of the Monongahela River Railroad[25] up the West Fork River, by James Edwin Watson, Johnson N. Camden, and associates (Lough, p. 661; Callahan, p. 245). . . . An addition to the University Agricultural Experiment Station, on Front Street, was completed (Callahan, p. 258). . . . After the destruction of the Female Seminary building by fire, the property was divided into three lots, the upper one purchased by Thomas E. Hodges for enlargement of the Presbyterian Church grounds, the middle one by Robert A. Armstrong, and the lower one by Miss Sadie Coyle (Callahan, p. 315). . . . A new frame building for the Laurel Point M.E. Church, succeeding the old log building (vol. 3, p. 302), was started May 15 and dedicated on November 17 (Dodds and Dodds, p. 104). . . . Lewis Miller died January 24; he was born March 30, 1814, and married Caroline, daughter of Owen and Elizabeth John (*Weekly Post,* February 23, 1889). . . . A revival meeting was held by Elder D. L. Ammons at the Liming Church of Christ, in Battelle District, January 16-27, with thirty-two

24. Callahan, p. 248.
25. This line was acquired by the Baltimore and Ohio system in 1897.

added to the Church (*Weekly Post,* February 9, 1889). . . . A "Court House Ball" was held on February 12 in honor of Judge J. M. Hagans, who opened his first term of circuit court on that day (*The Post,* February 2, 16, 1889). . . . John Robinson's Circus exhibited in Morgantown on June 19; there was a street parade at 10:00 a.m. (*Weekly Post,* June 15, 1889). . . . Mrs. Mary Cordray, widow of Isaac Cordray, died on June 12 (*Weekly Post,* June 29, 1889). . . . By a new agreement, most stores in Morgantown were to close at 7:00 p.m., "giving the clerks a chance to take in the ice cream saloons, moonlight promenades, etc." (*Weekly Post,* June 29, 1889).

CHAPTER ONE HUNDRED FOURTEEN

1890

The eleventh census, recorded in 1890, gave the first faint indication of the great awakening that was about to come to Monongalia County. For more than a century the county's population, largely Anglo-Saxon in origin, had grown very slowly. In 1885, the county seat, one hundred years after its foundation by Zackquill Morgan, had a population of only about 750, and the number was declining.

Actually the population for 1890 had not increased greatly; the total, 15,705, represented less than five percent increase over the 14,985 of 1880. But it did represent the beginning of a trend that was to continue markedly for the next three or four decades.

Three factors during the 1880s contributed to the awakening that was to result in the industrialization of the county: (1) the beginning of more frequent packet boat service following the completion of Lock and Dam No. 9, in 1879; (2) the beginning of railroad service, in 1886; (3) and the discovery of oil, in the Dolls Run and Dunkard Ridge section, in 1889.

The Census of 1890. The population of the seven magisterial districts, with 1880 figures for comparison, follows:

	1890	1880
Battelle	2,452	2,293
Cass	1,495	1,459
Clay	2,827	2,522
Clinton	2,352	2,126
Grant	2,118	2,156
Morgan (including towns below)	2,973	2,722
Morgantown	1,011	745
South Morgantown	285	— —
Union	1,488	1,707
Totals	15,705	14,985

Of the total population, the report showed that 15,631 people were born in the United States; only 74 were foreign born. There were 228 colored people in the county, down from 317 in 1880. Of the 74 foreign born, the countries of origin were as follows: Canada, 3; Ireland, 17; England, 32; Scotland, 4; Germany, 11; France, 41; Italy, 2; and 1 from an unidentified country. Remarkable changes in these data would appear in the next twenty years. Manufacturing was not very important as yet. The seventy establishments reporting showed a total capital of $152,245. The total number of employees was reported as 177, their wages $47,597. Operatives were classified as 109 males (wages $28,417), 4 females (wages $550), and 2 children (wages $100). There were 2 pieceworkers, who made $924. The total value of manufactured products was $210,416.

New citizens were arriving almost daily, bringing new ideas, and there was beginning to be a change in manners and customs of life—a change that was about to be greatly accelerated.

The Oil Field. The new year started off well for developments in the Dolls Run oil field. The Standard Oil Company was building a pump station at the mouth of Pedlar Run, near the brick church, to transport oil produced in the field. Tom Loan was drilling a well nearby. It was believed that "Dolls Run will be the rallying point next summer and it is predicted that inside of a year there will be quite a little village on the stream. It is reported that there will be two or three stores started there in the spring; also a machine shop. C. L. Skinner is thinking of starting a hostelry near the Dolls Run pump station."[1]

"The largest strike is on the G. W. Berry Farm. The J. C. Morris which came in on the 9th is rated at 150 barrels. The well which came in recently near the brick church is a very light producer. There seems to be a determination to develop by the leaseholders but it will hardly be possible to accomplish much while the rainy season continues, as the roads will not permit the moving of boilers and heavy materials."[2]

The weather continued bad and it was a hard spring. "To say that the weather during April and May has been discouraging so poorly conveys any adequate idea of the trials and tribulations of

1. *Weekly Post*, February 15, 1890.
2. *Weekly Post*, March 15, 1890.

Fig. 25. Eureka Pump Station on Dolls Run.

the oil operators, contractors, and teamsters that it seems altogether too tame. The Standard people are laying a line from Mannington via Fairview to Dolls and Pedlar Run."[3] But when the Fetty No. 2 well came in and kept up its regular output at 250 barrels daily, it was "no longer in doubt but fully demonstrated that the oil field in Monongalia is equal to any along the valley of the Monongahela."[4]

Meanwhile prospectors had moved on into Marion County, where the Hamilton well came in on October 20, 1889, near Mannington. On July 30, 1890, the Burt No. 2 well came in, producing 1,600 barrels the first eighteen hours; drilled down to the second pay sand, it continued to produce at the rate of 552 barrels per day. The town of Mannington rapidly grew into a small city.[5] Near Hundred, in Wetzel County, other wells were drilled.

I. C. White and the Anticlinal Theory. What was a boon to industry in Monongalia and Marion counties was also a boon for geologists, the anticlinal structure theory, and the reputation of the first petroleum geologist, Morgantown's I. C. White.

Following the successes in the Mount Morris and Dolls Run fields, prospectors had accepted the advice of Dr. White, who pointed out that these developments were like an arrow pointed in the direction of western Marion and eastern Wetzel counties. When success attended their efforts, the anticlinal theory was generally accepted and the position of I. C. White, and petroleum geologists generally, was rendered secure.

It might be pointed out here that not all later oil men have agreed with the theory. Following the great strikes in Texas in 1901, in Oklahoma in 1907, etc., theories changed as new facts were learned. One authority claimed that "the anticlinal theory of White has done more harm than good in furthering the finding of oil."[6] Another said, "White rode his hobby too hard. It was a sound hypothesis, not an immutable law."[7]

Dr. Price summarizes the status of I. C. White's work, as it appeared nearly a century later:

3. *Weekly Post,* June 14, 1890.
4. *Weekly Post,* January 3, 1891.
5. Thoenen, pp. 201, 202.
6. Sylvain Joseph Pirson, *Elements of Oil Reservoir Engineering,* p. 78.
7. Samuel W. Tait, *The Wildcatter,* pp. 81, 82.

Fig. 26. Portions of the Morgantown Tank Field.

"Dr. White's theory of oil and gas accumulation is in agreement with and included the essentials of oil and gas accumulations as they are known today. It is perhaps unfortunate that the term 'anticlinal theory' was applied to his observations, because they were far more comprehensive. He recognized the part played not only by structure but by sedimentation, fracture, convergence, porosity, and permeability."[8]

The Tank Field. One of the early and very difficult problems in the development of any oil field, including that of Monongalia County, was to develop a system of transportation to get the crude oil from the individual wells to marketing and refining centers. The wells were largely off the main routes of trade and commerce, adding to the difficulty.

Gradually pipelines became the principal medium for trans-

8. Paul H. Price, 1947, "Evolution of Geological Thought in Prospecting for Oil and Natural Gas," *Bull. Amer. Asso. Petro. Geol.* 31:681.

porting the oil on short hauls, to a point of collection. From there railroads or river barges were used to carry it for major distances. Early small producing and refining interests quickly tended to merge into larger concerns, and among these, the one to emerge over all the others as a giant monopoly was the Rockefeller, Andrews and Flagler firm, incorporated in 1870 as the Standard Oil Company of Ohio.

As soon as Standard Oil had at its command the major refinery elements of the industry, it set about to absorb the main trunk lines of the small pipeline companies. By 1879 this absorption was all but completed.

By 1890, when the West Virginia oil fields had reached a point of national importance, the pipeline system had developed so as to relieve railroads and barge lines of their position as major carriers of oil. To move the quantities of oil arising from Monongalia County and other West Virginia pools it was only necessary to connect the individual areas, "as they arose on the oil-producing horizon, with the main pipe trunk lines. Thus the Eureka Pipe Line Company was chartered in West Virginia on December 22, 1890, with a capital of one million dollars. With the remarkable growth of West Virginia production, this company, a Standard Oil Company subsidiary, by April 1892 had expanded its capital stock to five million dollars."[9]

Morgantown at once (in 1890) became a station of the Eureka Pipe Line Company, in its proposal to meet the need for better market facilities by a connecting series of tanks, with a series of pumping stations on a main line to the Atlantic Seaboard.

One of the first lines connected to Morgantown was from the Dolls Run-Dunkard Ridge territory. By 1890 that field had reached a daily production of 1,800 barrels, from twenty-four wells, with many new wells being drilled. On Dolls Run, at the mouth of Pedlar Run, the Eureka Pipe Line Company built a pumping station which was tied into a system of lines leading to Morgantown, to the developing field about Fairview, and by Mount Morris on to Ewing Station, at Washington, Pennsylvania. The Dolls Run Station was handling, from all sources, 15,000 barrels a month. Another main pipeline, in 1890, con-

9. Thoenen, p. 76.

nected Morgantown to Eureka, Pleasants County, about seventy-seven miles.[10]

Just south of Morgantown, along Cobun Creek, the Eureka Company acquired a large acreage, on which the company constructed a pumping station and started building a number of storage tanks to contain the oil in transit.

By the autumn of 1890 there were eight tanks completed, each with a capacity of 25,000 to 30,000 barrels of oil, and work was under way for construction of seven more tanks, on the Ike Hite land.[11]

Eastward from Morgantown to Philadelphia and the Atlantic Seaboard a large trunk line carried the oil over the mountains to the next eastern station, at Watson (thirty-four miles). The main lines were six to eight inches in diameter.

Pittsburg, Brownsville and Geneva Packet Company. Packet boats were now operating between Pittsburgh and Morgantown, a distance of 105 miles "through a rich and beautiful valley, dotted here and there with flourishing towns, and scenery unsurpassed by any other river in the world." Steamers comprising the line were the *Adam Jacobs,* M. A. Cox, master; the *James G. Blaine,* Adam Jacobs, master; and the *Germania.* The boats left Pittsburgh for Morgantown daily at 3:00 p.m., and returning left Morgantown daily at 8:00 a.m.[12]

The boats were 165 feet in length, 47 feet in breadth, with a burden of 297 tons. There were 40 staterooms, with 86 berths.

End of the Thompson Pottery. David Greenland Thompson died, June 15, 1890, at the age of seventy-one, and a long and fascinating chapter in the history of Monongalia County came to an end. James W. Thompson, his great-grandfather, had begun his association with the pottery business in Morgantown about 1785 (vol. 2, p. 129). D. G. Thompson, the son of John W. Thompson, was born in 1819. He studied law under Edgar C. Wilson and was admitted to the bar in 1845, but he took charge of the pottery and mill soon afterwards and continued until his death. He was a

10. In 1892 a line was completed from the Sistersville field. A line from Elm Run, Ritchie County, about seventy-six miles long, was completed in 1897.

11. *Weekly Post,* October 25, 1890.

12. *Weekly Post,* June 14, 1890. A long description of a trip appears in *Weekly Post,* November 30, 1889.

brother of Col. F. W. Thompson, Capt. J. J. Thompson, Mrs.
Charlotte Sears, Miss Mary Thompson, and Mrs. Augustus Haymond. He was never married.[13]

A historian[14] describes the Thompson pottery:

"A more delightful place to rummage would be hard to find.
One hundred and twenty years of pottery making was the inheri-
tance of the long building of rough stone fronting the wharf on
the Monongahela River. . . . Four generations of potters had to
do with the belongings of this shop, which, as was customary in
the days of the trades, formed part of the dwelling house.

"Among the rafters of the old shop were cast-off or disused
tools, thick with dust, molds, stamps, and other articles of the
craft stored in large vessels, while in the garret of the house, in
the dark cellars, and in the living rooms, treasured with loving
hands by a descendant of the potters, were odd pieces of ware of
great historical value. . . .

"When we first were taken into this fascinating workroom,
there were two muddy kick-wheels going, from the center of
which gray jugs were springing up like mushrooms under the
fingers of the potters, to be again abashed and again raised up to
regular forms. Later they showed us how steam has been harnessed to the wheel, to the detriment of those leg muscles on
which the potter prided himself. Aside from this there was but little change from the methods of past generations. . . ."

Nimrod Nelson Hoffman. One of the best known citizens of
Morgantown, N. N. Hoffman, died at his home on November 4,
1890, at the age of sixty-four, after two years in which he had
been bedridden with paralysis. He was a veteran of the Mexican
War and of the Civil War. Besides many other business connections, he had been a partner in the publication of the *Weekly Post*
for nearly a quarter of a century. He had represented Monongalia
County in the legislature.[15]

A. W. Brown. Alphaeus Wilson Brown, son of Andrew (vol. 3, p.
677) and Martha (Worley) Brown, of Brown's Mills, died February 21, 1890. Born August 9, 1822, he attended Greene Academy

13. *Weekly Post,* June 21, 1890.
14. Julia W. Wolfe, *The History of Pottery in America.* Copied by J. H. Lindsay from *The School Arts Magazine,* December, 1928.
15. *Weekly Post,* November 8, 1890.

at Carmichaels, Pennsylvania, and thereafter continued his studies at Monongalia Academy. He then studied medicine in the office of his uncle, Dr. Asbury Worley, at Washington Court House, Ohio, after which he attended lectures in Philadelphia. He practiced medicine for ten years at Washington Court House and then, at the request of his father, returned to Brown's Mills.

Here he built up a large and representative general practice and gained prestige as one of the leading physicians and surgeons of the county, besides being an honored and influential figure in public affairs. He was a delegate to the Wheeling Convention at which the new state of West Virginia was formed and later served two terms as a member of the legislature, besides being a member of the board of supervisors of Monongalia County, later supplanted by the board of county commissioners, of which he was also a member (for ten years), his death having occurred while he was an incumbent of this office. While living at Washington Court House he married Elizabeth Dorsey, of Morgantown, who died only eleven months later. On November 25, 1862, he married Anna Nicholson, of New Geneva, Pennsylvania.[16]

Emrod Tennant. A farmer, merchant, and highly respected citizen of Clay District, Emrod Tennant, died March 12, 1890. He was a justice of the peace at the time of his death. He married Annie Moore and they had fifteen children, ten of whom survived, namely, Marion, Zimri, Simon P., Rebecca, Jacob, George, Alpheus L., Lucinda C., Abraham L., and Savannah A.

Nicholas B. Johnson. The son of Nicholas Johnson, of Pentress, N. B. Johnson, died March 13, 1890, aged eighty years. He married Margaret Minor and they had six children, three daughters, Mrs. William Hibbs, Mrs. Lindsey Blaker, and Mrs. Benjamin Core; and three sons, George W., Perry M., and John L.[17]

The Tygard Foundry and Planing Mill. A feature of the general awakening was the establishment of new industries, several of them every year during the nineties. In May 1890 the Tygard

16. Core, *Chronicles of Core*, p. 147; *Weekly Post*, March 1, 1890; tribute by the county court, *Weekly Post*, March 8, 1890.

17. "Three of the most eminent men of Clay District" had died within a few days of each other—"an event which has caused wide-spread sorrow throughout the county"; *Weekly Post*, March 22, 1890.

Foundry and Planing Mill began operations. Its work included the manufacture of wagons and carriages, moulding and metal work. Located in South Morgantown, its organization was the result of leadership of E. M. Grant, T. W. Anderson, George C. Sturgiss, I. C. White, S. M. and Milton Hirschman, and E. H. Coombs.

The Lough Brothers Carriage Factory was established about the same time.[18]

New Post Offices. Several new post offices were established in Monongalia County in 1890 to handle the increasing volume of mail.

The Bowlby Post Office, on Robinson Run, in Cass District, was established on October 24, 1890, with Edward J. Bowlby as the postmaster.

A post office called Charlotte was established July 21, 1890, in the village generally known as Osageville (p. 121), on Scotts Run. George A. Lemley was the first postmaster.

The Flickersville post office, in the community by that name (vol. 3, p. 100), on Flaggy Meadow Run, was established June 28, 1890, with Margaret McElroy as postmistress.

Uneva Post Office, in the Cheat Neck section, was established July 30, 1890. Alpheus F. Blosser was named postmaster.

The name Andy, for a post office at Brown's Mills, in Clay District, was changed to Worley on February 5, 1890; Alpheus W. Brown, who had been the postmaster at Andy, remained in the position until his death on February 22, after which he was succeeded (on May 2) by Cassius C. Brown.

E. M. Wilson. A former Monongalian, Eugene M. Wilson, died April 10, 1890, in the Bahama Islands. The son of Edgar C. Wilson, he was born December 25, 1833, and moved to Minnesota in 1855. He was instrumental in the attempt to form a Monongalia County in that state (vol. 3, pp. 458-61). He was U.S. District Attorney for Minnesota from 1857 to 1861, and was Democratic candidate for governor in 1888.[19]

The University. The second Morrill Act, passed in 1890, provided $15,000 annually to the university's income, and was scheduled

18. Callahan, p. 251; *Weekly Post,* February 8, 1890.
19. *Weekly Post,* April 26, 1890.

to increase annually at the rate of $1,000 until the total reached $25,000 annually. This, coupled with the $15,000 annual income provided by the Hatch Act (1887), resulted in the university's "first and only embarrassment of riches."

"It mattered not that the Morrill Fund was available only for instruction and aids thereto and on condition that the state provide higher education for Negroes. After they had been cared for, there was a considerable sum left for the university, provided the state erected the necessary buildings and purchased the necessary equipment."[20]

The legislature was disposed to provide the needed funds, so the board of regents devoted their attention to the development of an adequate physical plant. In 1887 they had purchased three tracts across the road to the east of the original campus, comprising in all about ten acres. In the space between two roads[21] the armory had been built, in 1873. Now it was enlarged (in 1889) to provide quarters for the developing Agricultural Experiment Station.

"Of all the additions made at this time, the Agricultural Experiment Station was the most important. From funds derived from the Hatch Act, it was authorized in 1888 and became active in 1889 under the semi-autonomous direction of Dr. J. A. Myers, a native West Virginian who had been trained in Germany and been state chemist of Mississippi. Under Director Myers, the Experiment Station became a center of productive research. Among the contributors, together with their respective fields, were Dr. C. F. Millspaugh, botany; A. D. Hopkins, entomology; F. Wm. Rane, horticulture; Alex. R. Whitehill, chemistry; William Doan, ornithology; B. H. Hite, chemistry; and A. C. Magruder, dairying. The results of their researches were published in a series of university bulletins, some of which were notable contributions to knowledge."[22]

During the 1889-90 term, the first in which women had been admitted as regular students, ten females (seven of them residents of Morgantown) had been enrolled. Commenting on this, President Turner said, in a report dated June 4, 1890: "The admission

20. Ambler, p. 305.
21. Later University and College avenues.
22. Ambler, p. 308. See description of the new building, *Weekly Post,* July 5, 1890.

of ladies seems to have been a successful experiment, so far as it has gone. They have demonstrated their ability to do as thorough work as the young men. Their influence has been wholesome on the young men. I see no reason for making changes in the present regulations.[23]

The Athletic Association. Members of the boat and tennis clubs and of the football and baseball teams, in response to a growing urge, on April 12, 1890, organized the West Virginia University Athletic Association, with E. H. Vickers as president, C. C. Coffman secretary, and William C. Meyer treasurer. One of the main purposes of the organization was to solicit funds to support the athletic teams.

Athletic sports had not developed very rapidly at the university. From the beginning the regents had insisted that farmers' sons had no need of artificial exercise. "Fortunately perhaps, not all the students were farmers' sons and the 'corn fed' among them were not averse to physical contests of the sports variety. Like others, an increasing number of them needed an outlet for what was later called 'college spirit.' In response to this need early in 1890 several upper classmen adopted a 'college yell' and the present college colors, old gold and blue."

Miscellany. In 1890: Henry Lazier built a brick residence on High Street, while W. P. Willey and Mrs. H. H. Pierce built homes on Spruce (Callahan, p. 253). . . . The Protestant Episcopal Church on High Street was dedicated on June 12 (Callahan, p. 257). . . . Lot No. 40 in Morgantown was conveyed from the estate of Dr. Charles McLane to S. S. Wade, James M. Reed, and Luther S. Brock (Callahan, p. 316). . . . The Laurel Flatts Methodist Church (vol. 3, p. 346), on Indian Creek, was closed and the congregation merged with the nearby Mount Hood M.E. Church (Dodds and Dodds, p. 105). . . . The Buckeye M.P. Church (p. 135) was dedicated on August 17 by Rev. D. H. Davis; Rev. L. A. McNemar was the first minister (Dodds and Dodds, p. 115; Core, *Chronicles of Core,* pp. 129, 130). . . . Lewis A. Core, formerly of Cassville, was in India; a newspaper published long letters from him (e.g., *Weekly Post,* February 8, 1890). . . . The natural gas line across the river was broken by a flood on March 22 and Morgantown

23. Ambler, pp. 373, 374.

shivered in darkness (*Weekly Post,* March 29, 1890). . . . John Snider, of near Halleck, died March 8; he was born January 16, 1809 (*Weekly Post,* March 29, 1890). . . . A "floating theatre" exhibited at the Walnut Street wharf April 30-May 2 (*Weekly Post,* May 3, 1890). . . . Benjamin M. Dorsey, son of Benjamin Dorsey, died May 3 (*Weekly Post,* May 10, 1890). . . . There was much agitation for laying a special county levy to improve county roads (*Weekly Post,* May 31, 1890, etc.). . . . James Odbert, of Morgantown, died on November 3, aged seventy-four years; he had been a county sheriff and conducted a saddlery and harness shop (*Weekly Post,* November 8, 1890). . . . Mrs. Mary Donaldson, wife of James Donaldson, of Laurel Iron Works, died November 4, aged sixty-five years (*Weekly Post,* November 15, 1890). . . . Mrs. Cassandra Toothman, of McCurdysville, died October 30, aged ninety-one years (*Weekly Post,* November 15, 1890). . . . William W. Poynter, of Cassville, died November 5; he was born near there May 15, 1810 (*Weekly Post,* November 29, 1890). . . . A certificate of incorporation was recorded to enlarge and conduct the Victor Elevator and Mills Company, with a capital of fifty thousand dollars (*Weekly Post,* November 29, 1890). . . . A new M.E. church building at Cassville was dedicated September 28 by Rev. J. F. Chenoweth (*Weekly Post,* September 20, 1890).

CHAPTER ONE HUNDRED FIFTEEN

1891

A new county courthouse was constructed during 1891. The cornerstone was laid on June 20. It was the fifth regular seat of government for Monongalia County.[1]

The existing building was completed late in 1848 and cost considerably more than the bid of $5,695. After some controversy between the contractor and the court, a compromise was reached and he was allowed $6,500. A statue of Patrick Henry was placed on top of the courthouse in 1851; he had been governor of Virginia when Monongalia County was established (vol. 3, p. 306).[2]

A New Courthouse. By 1884 this courthouse had been pronounced a dangerous place in which to hold public meetings. In 1887 a Pittsburgh architect was employed to prepare an estimate of the cost of erection of a new building and to prepare plans and specifications. Further work on the project was delayed by strong opposition to the project: some objectors proposed temporary repairs until more money was available for a new structure, while others suggested that what the county really needed was improved roads, rather than a new courthouse.

But county officials influenced by some of the prominent civic leaders, on September 13, 1890, made the decision to go ahead with construction of the new courthouse at once. The contract for construction was awarded by the county court to George W. L. Mayers, of Fairmont, for $43,478. The court arranged to rent the Methodist Protestant Church on Walnut Street, for a court room. Here Judge John Marshall Hagans could dispense justice from the pulpit on weekdays, while the Reverend D. H. Davis preached the Word of God on Sundays.

1. For earlier buildings, see vol. 2, pp. xi, 7, 107, 307; vol. 3, p. 277.

2. A long and detailed description of this courthouse, by Walter Hough, appeared in the *Weekly Post*, June 4, 1892.

However, the people of the county were still opposed to the project and voted down a proposal of a bond issue to finance the construction work.

Hereupon the county court resorted to strategy: it authorized the removal of the old building at once and arranged for hasty demolition to begin at midnight, in order to forestall injunction proceedings.

On the evening preceding these activities, Richard E. Fast, the county clerk, directed his deputy, John M. Gregg, to supervise the removal of the county records at an early hour the next morning.

In undertaking the demolition of the building one of the first tasks was the removal of the statue of Patrick Henry. The admirably proportioned wooden statue, nine feet in height, was taken down carefully and stored safely.[3]

With the demolition of the old building completed, the cornerstone of the new structure was laid with fitting ceremonies and the familiar building of today, with the clock in the tower, quickly arose during 1891.[4]

"Its dimensions are as follows: 100 x 78 feet. The basement is to be 7 feet 6 inches high, in the clear, built of native sandstone—broken ashler—a most expensive work. It will contain two large document vaults, absolutely fire proof, 20 x 11 feet, and will be amply large to hold all the old county records. The remainder of the basement will be used for a system of heating by hot air and ventilation (Bennett & Peck's system). . . .

"The first story is 15 feet high, in the clear, and will contain eight rooms, not counting vestibules and corridors.

"Entering from Main Street, to the right is the round tower containing the main stairway to the court room.

"A large corridor, 18 feet wide, divides the building from North to South; on the West side of the corridor are the Circuit Clerk's office—(32 x 21 feet); the vault in this office is 14 x 20 feet . . . ; the Sheriff's office will be 21 x 16 feet; District Attorney's office 17 x 15—with private rooms for both the Circuit Clerk and District Attorney.

3. After many long wanderings, it came back in 1976 to the new courthouse annex, where the governor yet today may be seen displaying the scroll spelling out the establishment of the county just two centuries earlier.

4. Callahan, p. 266.

Fig. 27. The new Monongalia County Courthouse.

"On the East side of the corridor is the County Commissioner's office 30 x 31 feet.

"The County Clerk's apartment will be 20 x 29 feet, with vault 13 x 28 feet, with private room attached. . . .

"A stairway on the South side of the corridor leads to the Jury Rooms on 2nd floor, which are apartments 15 x 21 feet.

"The Petit Jury Room is to be 20 x 21 feet; Consultation and Extra Jury Room 13 x 20; Ladies Waiting Room 21 x 14; Ladies Private Consultation Room 8 x 15 feet.

"The Judge's Private room is to be 16 x 11 feet. There is a complete set of Toilet Rooms and closets for all the apartments. . . .

"In the North end is situated the main corridor from which you enter the Court room.

"The main Court Room is to be 61 x 49, and is 22 feet high. Nearly one-half of the floor surface is to be occupied by the Bar. On the North-East side is situated the Jury Box (elevated seats); the jury boxes are immediately to the right of the Judge's bench."[5]

5. *Weekly Post*, January 31, 1891.

Electric Lights. Even while gas lights were being installed as a great improvement over the old method of lighting by candles or kerosene lamps, efforts were being made to introduce electric lighting into Morgantown. Electricity, an incredible facility that seemed almost as though it had originated in fairy tales, was about to revolutionize the way of life of the entire country.

Thomas Edison, in 1878-79, conducted many experiments trying to find a substance that would give off light when a current passed through it, but would not be reduced to ash. At last he found that carbon was the most satisfactory material. The electric age had begun.

Within a decade after Edison's significant experiments, efforts were under way to install a system of electric lights in Morgantown. These efforts encountered objections and opposition, the chief difficulty being a lack of money. Finally George C. Sturgiss, operating under provisions of a town ordinance dated November 24, 1891, set up on the riverbank near Victor Mills the equipment for a small electric plant.[6]

The Oil Field. Early in 1891 the Standard Oil Company purchased the entire holdings of E. M. Hukill in the Mount Morris and Dolls Run oil fields, for $512,000, and began to push the work of new developments with fresh vigor. Notable new wells brought in during the year were the Andrew Fox No. 2, by Largy & Myers, initial production 80 barrels; C. E. Johnson No. 5, 150 barrels; A. Sutton No. 5, 100 barrels; Moore & Eddy No. 2, by Gann & Garfield, 100 barrels.[7]

The pipeline from Morgantown to Philadelphia was completed on February 20. It was eight inches in size, with a capacity of 15,000 barrels of oil a day. The tank field at Morgantown had a capacity of 500,000 barrels.[8]

The University. Courses in engineering had been offered at the university since 1869 and the extra funds provided by the Hatch Act in 1887 had made possible an expansion of work in that field. The department of civil and mining engineering was created at

6. This plant, by June 1892, was furnishing electricity for lighting the university buildings, the courthouse, and several individual homes. Callahan, pp. 261, 262.
7. Core, *Chronicles of Core*, pp. 143, 144.
8. *Weekly Post*, February 28, 1891.

once and in 1888 Col. T. Moore Jackson was elected to chair the
department. He resigned in 1891 and was succeeded by H. B.
Davenport. The Second Morrill Act made available still more
money and in 1891 a department of mechanical engineering and
mechanic arts was established. Prof. F. L. Emory, a graduate of
Worcester Polytechnic Institute, was appointed to head it.[9]
     In 1891 T. C. Atkeson, president of the new State Board of
Agriculture, appeared before the board of regents to urge the use
of Morrill funds to expand work in agriculture at the university.
"He proved so convincing that the regents detached agriculture
from chemistry and physics, established a 'chair of agriculture,'
and chose Atkeson himself to occupy it. Thus he became the first
professor of agriculture in the University."[10]

The First Football Game. Melville Davisson Post[11] in 1890 succeeded E. H. Vickers as president of the athletic association, and
under the spell of his pen and enthusiasm interest in athletics,
especially football, grew rapidly. The greatest difficulty was the
inability to secure competent coaches, R. F. Bivins, who had been
on the Georgetown College football team, joined the university
team in the autumn of 1891. Prof. F. L. Emory, who had played
for Worcester Polytechnic Institute and Cornell University, volunteered to coach.
     "On November 28, 1891, the team of 'giant misfits' developed
by them met a team from Washington and Jefferson College in
the first intercollegiate game of football played by a University
team and the first of a memorable series fraught with both friendship and bitterness on the part of the contestants.
     "This game was played in a snow storm on the 'showgrounds'
of what was then South Morgantown. . . . It was witnessed by
about two hundred and fifty persons, not all of whom had paid admission and most of whom took an active part in directing the
game. Although the score was 72 to 0 in favor of the visitors, in-

     9. Ambler, p. 306.
     10. Ambler, pp. 306, 307. See biography of Atkeson, *New Dominion*, Septem-
ber 18, 1897.
     11. Post (1871-1919), who received the law degree in 1892, became a famous
Harrison County writer of detective stories, many of them featuring a fictitious
character by the name of Randolph Mason. See Charles A. Norton, *Melville
Davisson Post: Man of Many Mysteries*.

Fig. 28. The first West Virginia University football team. (West Virginia University Library.)

dicating perhaps that the home team kept a safe distance from danger, the Wheeling *Daily Intelligencer* deplored the introduction of football 'in our State University' and suggested that 'the next thing in order will be for the Legislature to establish a hospital in Morgantown.' The first University football team was partly financed through the proceeds of 'Richard III,' an amateur theatrical directed by M. D. Post."[12]

Railroad to Uniontown. After a long and frustrating delay, the work of extending the Fairmont, Morgantown, and Pittsburg Railroad to Uniontown got under way late in 1890. "The building of the abutments at the foot of Walnut Street, Morgantown, and blasting of rock, grading, & c., goes steadily along."[13]

Residents of Monongalia County looked forward to the comple-

12. Ambler, p. 363. See also Tony Constantine (assisted by Dan Miller) *Mountaineer Football,* 1891-1969. 94 pp. 1969. D. A. Christopher, "History of West Virginia University Football," *West Virginia University Alumni Quarterly Bull.,* December 1935; Wayne Schwartzwalder, "A History of Intercollegiate Football at West Virginia University," master's thesis, West Virginia University. 1940.

13. *Weekly Post,* November 8, 1890; December 20, 1890.

tion of this link and being able to go all the way from Morgantown to Pittsburgh by rail.[14]
But work continued at a distressingly slow rate through 1891.

West Virginia and Pennsylvania Railroad. The old expectations of a railroad being built through Monongalia County on the west side of the Monongahela River were being revived in 1891. Stephen B. Elkins visited Morgantown on various occasions in 1890-91 to secure options on large tracts of coal lands on the west side of the river and contemplated for a while the purchase of the rights of the old West Virginia and Pennsylvania Railroad (p. 46, 76) by Davis-Elkins interests. Negotiations failed, largely because of the high price demanded by the promoters.[15]

Brown's Chapel Methodist Protestant Church. A new Brown's Chapel[16] was organized in 1891 as a Methodist Protestant congregation along the Evansville Pike in Clinton District, twelve miles south of Morgantown. It was founded by Rev. J. P. Varner; prominent local leaders were Edson Trickett and Jacob Frederick. Ground for the church was given by the Wilson family and the chapel was named for the Harrison Brown family.[17]

A Long Fox Chase. Fox hunting was a favorite sport of many people, and the rearing and training of foxhounds was an associated pleasant task. "The longest fox chase on record, and one that terminated disastrously for Reynard, took place one day last week. Marshall Crow, with some friends, started to Miller's Rocks, two miles north of Morgantown. They had seven dogs, two of them belonging to Mat. Callahan. The fox was started immediately after the dogs were turned loose."

The fox led the dogs beyond Beaver Hole, on Cheat River, and the next morning the dogs overtook him and killed him. The chase started at two o'clock on Tuesday and ended at eight o'clock Wednesday morning.[18]

14. *Weekly Post*, May 23, 1891.
15. Callahan, pp. 246, 252.
16. The earlier Brown's Chapel was a Presbyterian Church, built in later Union District in 1830 (vol. 3, pp. 108, 109).
17. Dodds and Dodds, p. 141.
18. *Weekly Post*, March 21, 1891.

Blacksville's Building Boom. "Blacksville and vicinity will have a building boom this year. In the village we may notice the following:—Wm. F. Scott, an extensive addition to his stable and wool house; Mrs. Luke Phillips, a new house; Moses Martin, a new house on the South Side (Martinsville). The planing mill is being rebuilt; Bowen Stephens will complete the large frame house on East Washington Street, which Moses Martin erected the past fall and winter. . . . A. I. Strosnider will put an additional story on his business block. . . .

"Oil operations are not moving along as rapidly as we would wish. At Abe John's well the tools are said to be stuck at the top of the oil sand. . . .

"A. Thomas, on Miracle Run, has been having trouble from putting in the last casing too soon."[19]

E. W. S. Dering. Edmund Washington Seahorn Dering, son of John Franklin and Priscilla (Dorsey) Dering, died July 16, 1891. He was born March 7, 1830, on a farm along the river just south of Morgantown. He married Cordelia, daughter of Josiah and Fanny Walker, of Newark, Ohio, and they had four children, namely, Charles, Fanny, Mary, and Fred.

Edmund ran a harness shop and sold farming implements in a store on High Street.[20]

General Pindall. Evan Shelby Pindall, who had been commissioned as brigadier general in the Virginia State Militia in 1830, died in Audrain County, Missouri, in April. He was born in Monongalia County December 5, 1801, the grandson of General Evan Shelby. In Monongalia County he lived on the pioneer Pindall farm in later Grant District. He moved to Missouri in 1852.

He married Drusilla Barker and they had six children, Col. L. A. and Major X. J. Pindall, of the Confederate army, Mrs. John Ball, Mrs. Frank Willey, and Misses Hannah E. and Ethelbert Pindall.[21]

John Bayles. The son of William and Mary Bayles, John Bayles, died December 2, 1891, aged ninety years. His large farm at

19. *Weekly Post,* March 14, 1891.
20. *The 175th Anniversary of . . . Monongalia County,* p. 407.
21. *Saint Louis Republic,* copied in the *Weekly Post,* May 9, 1891.

Easton had an extensive barn and stables and he had a large and commodious dwelling house. His wife preceded him in death. Surviving were three children, William, Magruder, and Agnes.[22]

James M. Kerns. "Our esteemed fellow-citizen James M. Kern was the last of the old stock of Kernses that has been called hence. He died Dec. 30, 1891, at his home here, in the 77th year of his age. For many years he carried on the wagon-making business, and his name and fame as a mechanic are widespread." He was survived by two sons, Thornton and John E.[23]

Evans Race Track. Located one mile north of Morgantown, the Evans Race Track was formally opened on June 6 with a series of grand trotting, pacing and running races. It was a half mile track, in excellent condition. Premiums for the first race, 3.30 trot, were seven dollars for the first horse and three dollars for the second. For the three-minute trot, the purse was fifteen dollars—ten dollars to the first horse and five dollars to the second. A four-minute trot and various other races were held. Thomas R. Evans was the promoter and about three hundred persons attended the first meet.[24] Monthly meetings were planned.

Schools. Martin Luther Brown was reelected county superintendent of free schools, without opposition. He had been appointed earlier in the year to succeed W. E. Glasscock, who had resigned. Presidents of the district boards were: Battelle, J. Robinson; Cass, James Sanders; Clay, George W. Johnson; Clinton, J. S. Watson; Grant, J. D. Cox; Morgan, E. J. Evans; and Union, William Jaco.[25]

Miscellany. In 1891: Prof. S. B. Brown built a residence on North High Street at the edge of the open area (Callahan, p. 253). . . . Dr. W. C. Kelley erected a home at the northwest corner of Spruce and Pleasant streets (Callahan, p. 253). . . . In January the county court added to the size of the courthouse square by purchasing the Henry Lazier property, resulting in a larger frontage on High Street (Callahan, pp. 266, 330). . . . The southwest corner of Lot 37, in Morgantown, was sold in May by Adam W. Lorentz to

22. *Weekly Post,* December 19, 1891.
23. *Weekly Post,* January 9, 1892.
24. *Weekly Post,* May 30, June 13, 1891.
25. *Weekly Post,* May 30, 1891.

David Chadwick (Callahan, p. 315)... Lots 115 and 116 were conveyed in December by George W. McVicker to James M. Reed (Callahan, p. 328)... A. E. Myers, of Bethany, held a series of meetings of Church of Christ adherents in the courthouse (Dodds and Dodds, p. 73)... The second Christian Endeavor Society in West Virginia was organized in the Calvary Methodist Church in Union District by Rev. R. Clark Dean (Dodds and Dodds, p. 150). ... Thomas Howell, of Clinton District, died on January 15; he was born in May 1828 (*Weekly Post*, January 31, 1891)... The *Post* moved into a new brick building on Walnut Street, four doors below T. Pickenpaugh's store (*Weekly Post*, April 11, 1891)... A long history of the Cheat Neck community was published (*Weekly Post*, April 11, 25, May 2, 9, 1891)... The *Germania*, after being overhauled and put in first class condition, took the place of the *Adam Jacobs* on the Morgantown-Pittsburgh run (*Weekly Post*, May 2, 1891)... Graduation exercises for Morgantown High School were held in the Presbyterian Church on May 12; seven girls and two boys received diplomas (*Weekly Post*, May 16, 1891)... A Morgantown Gun Club was formed June 9, with Dr. C. W. Millspaugh, president; B. L. Morgan, secretary; and L. W. Joseph, treasurer (*Weekly Post*, June 13, 1891)... Morgantown's first laundry was started on Front Street by L. J. Holland (*Weekly Post*, June 27, 1891).... By the summer packet schedule to Pittsburgh, effective July 6, boats left Morgantown at 8:00 a.m. and 1:00 p.m. on Mondays, Wednesdays, and Fridays and at 8:00 a.m. on Tuesdays, Thursdays, and Saturdays; the round trip fare, including meals, was five dollars (*Weekly Post*, July 4, 1891)... Rev. Henry W. Biggs, of Chillicothe, Ohio, occupied the pulpit of the Presbyterian Church on August 9; he had been pastor there twenty-seven years earlier (*Weekly Post*, August 15, 1891)... King and Franklin's Circus exhibited in Morgantown on August 25 and John Robinson's on September 23 (*Weekly Post*, August 22, September 12, 1891)... A West Virginia blackberry without briers was named *Rubus millspaughii* for its discoverer, C. W. Millspaugh, of the university (*Weekly Post*, November 28, 1891).

CHAPTER ONE HUNDRED SIXTEEN

1892

In 1785, when Morgantown was founded, sanitation was scarcely thought to be a problem. Most filth could be gathered up and burned, and each house had its own privy or "outhouse" for the evacuation of body wastes. Even the ancients realized that filth had something to do with disease but no one realized what the connection was until in the late nineteenth century, when disease germs were discovered. Sanitary measures were not well organized in the United States until after 1861, when the U.S. Sanitary Commission was founded and even long after that most communities were slow in providing for sewage disposal.

Privies were eventually prohibited in town, for various obvious reasons, and the use of interior plumbing systems for waste disposal became general in the latter part of the nineteenth century. These led into a simple form of individual sewage-disposal, known as a cesspool. This consisted of a sort of a well, lined with loosely laid masonry. Waste was discharged from the house drainage system into the cesspool, from which the liquid wastes gradually soaked or leached into the surrounding ground. The solid wastes underwent bacterial action which gradually liquefied a large portion of them. As the population became denser this system proved less and less desirable.

Program for Sanitation. The growth of the town brought increased emphasis upon plans for improved sewers to drain the surface water and cesspools which were breeders of disease. The voters were slow to respond, however, and after three defeats of a proposed bond issue for sewers, the council studied other ways to begin such sewer developments as were felt needed to protect the people from disease.

In September 1889 the citizens had rejected a proposed bond issue of nine thousand dollars for sewers. Again, in October 1892, "when some immediate action seemed necessary to relieve the collection of waste and refuse on the streets and elsewhere, a proposal to authorize five thousand dollars to lay sewers under the chief streets was defeated by a vote of 80 to 79 (a three-fifths vote being necessary for approval). The question was kept alive, however, with the hope that the increasing needs of the town would educate public opinion and compel the adoption of a thorough and uniform system of sewerage at public cost and under supervision of the municipal government. The wisdom of immediate action was urged as an economic measure, as the difficulty and expense of completion would increase with each succeeding year."[1]

The University. President E. Marsh Turner was having increased difficulties with morale of the faculty. Ambler explains the basis for his problems: "The alleged looseness and naiveness of the Virginia System was exasperating to him and sometimes disturbed his temper. This was particularly true of the wholesale excuses of absences and other delinquencies, as practiced by Professor Reynolds and other 'Confederate Colonels.' The resentments thus provoked on the part of one admittedly friendly to the 'Prep School,' to coeducation, and to the single curriculum, were described as tactless and even imperious."[2]

Differences gradually became irreconcilable. Prof. T. C. Atkeson, for example, when requested to teach either English grammar or bookkeeping in addition to his agriculture courses, in order to provide him with a full load, refused to do either. Temporarily the president himself had to teach English grammar. The president requested that the regents specifically define his powers and duties but the inertia of the board prevented this.

A distinguished member of the staff of the Agricultural Experiment Station from 1889 to 1892 was Dr. Charles Frederick Millspaugh, a botanist, who, during his short stay in West Virginia, thoroughly explored the state and published a book on the *Flora*

1. Callahan, p. 264.
2. Ambler, p. 310. Professor R. C. Berkeley, writing to Governor A. B. Fleming, March 2, 1891, said, "Amid the many stirring times I have been through here I have never seen the whole Board of Instruction so wrought up as now," and added that the only objections he saw against certain professors, resisting the president, was that "they have opinions of their own."

Fig. 29. Eli Marsh Turner. (West Virginia University Library.)

Fig. 30. James L. Goodknight. (West Virginia University Library.)

of West Virginia.[3] He is well known for his widely circulated book, American Medicinal Plants.[4] His dismissal in 1892, on the grounds that West Virginia did not need a botanist, created a minor stir that was fought out in the newspapers.[5]

In 1892 the university, "located partly within the corporate limits" of Morgantown, occupied "grounds comprising about twenty acres. From these grounds and halls a beautiful picture spreads out before the gaze—the broad sweeping river, the town and its suburbs, the long suspension bridge, the green encircling

3. "A Preliminary Catalogue of the Flora of West Virginia." W. Va. Agr. Exp. Sta. Bull. 24. 224 p. 1892.

4. See vol. 3, p. 212.

5. Core, "Contributions of Charles Frederick Millspaugh to the Botany of West Virginia." Proc. W. Va. Acad. Sci. 8(1935):82-93; Weldon Boone, History of Botany in West Virginia (1965), pp. 24-41. See comments in the Clarksburg Telegram, quoted in the Weekly Post, October 1, 1892.

hills, and, in the distance away to the sunrise, the mountains reared in grandeur—a picture where

" 'Not ivy-clad walls that are hoary with time
But God's touch of beauty makes the place sublime.' "[6]

No football games were played during 1892, although the team was kept together. The decisive defeat the previous year, plus indifferent, even hostile attitudes of faculty members and state newspapers were discouraging.[7]

Progress on the FM&P. For several years Morgantown had remained a terminal station on the railway line connecting with Fairmont, while anxiously awaiting construction of the link that would allow service to Pittsburgh. The Baltimore and Ohio Railroad was already in operation from Connellsville to Uniontown and on April 11, 1884, the State Line Railroad was incorporated under the laws of Pennsylvania having the objective of connecting with the Fairmont, Morgantown and Pittsburgh at the state line. Construction began soon after but proceeded slowly and was not completed to Smithfield until 1892.

Meanwhile construction of the West Virginia section of the line had also been delayed, while awaiting the outcome of legal competitive efforts in the strategic struggle between the Pennsylvania and the B&O railways for rights-of-way. Finally, in 1892, the B&O won the battle and construction began more actively at Morgantown, where free right-of-way was granted by the borough council.[8]

Morgantown Building and Investment Company. Some of the same citizens who had a few years earlier organized the Morgantown Chamber of Commerce, seeing that the town's opportunity for development was greatly restricted through the long delay in extending the railroad northward, inaugurated plans to remove some of the obstacles. Among these citizens were Richard E. Fast, Col. E. M. Grant, Dr. I. C. White, and George C. Sturgiss. Their efforts resulted in the organization of the Morgantown Building and Investment Company, which had as its immediate objectives the extension of the railroad and the location of factories in the community. "This company was a large factor in the development and extension of the town. It purchased the briar

6. *Weekly Post,* April 23, 1892.
7. Ambler, pp. 363, 364.
8. Callahan, pp. 242, 245.

fields below the mouth of Falling Run—the entire site upon which Seneca now stands—and, in 1892, opened Beechurst Avenue and provided a free right-of-way for the extension of the railway to Uniontown, offered free sites for glass factories between the river and the railway and on the remainder of the territory surveyed lots" for sale later.[9]

John W. Madera. The son of Francis and Julia Ann (Watts) Madera, John W. Madera, died suddenly February 7, 1892. He was fifty-five years of age. He was well known in Morgantown, being the founder of the Walnut Street News Depot and Confectionery Store. He was twice married, his first wife being Wilhelmina Colebank. They had four children who survived him, Marshall, Walter, Nicholas, and Bernard. His second wife was Mary Murphy.[10]

George D. Evans. The son of Rawley and Marie (Dering) Evans and grandson of distinguished pioneer Col. John Evans, George D. Evans, died May 20, 1892. He was eighty-nine years of age, and had been a very prominent merchant of Morgantown. He married Julia, daughter of Benjamin Dorsey.[11]

John Myers. John, a son of Peter and Sarah Myers, of the Dunkard Creek section, died April 1, 1892, aged sixty-two years. He married Sarah Ann Piles, and they were the parents of several children, including Sylvanus, Vadena, Stacy, Morgan, Sanford, Stella, Malinda, and Lafayette.[12]

Dr. James Way. A longtime popular physician of Monongalia County, Dr. James Way, died in Waynesburg, Pennsylvania, February 6, 1892. He was born at New Geneva, Pennsylvania, October 25, 1815. When he was quite young, his father moved to a farm about a mile from Morgantown, and he later began the study of medicine under Dr. Bernard R. C. O'Kelly. He then graduated from the Jefferson Medical College, in Philadelphia,

9. Callahan, pp. 248, 251. The company also, in 1891 "built the 'Brick Row,' a group of three story buildings on the north side of Pleasant Street above Front Street—an investment which at that time was regarded by many as an unsafe financial venture."

10. *Weekly Post*, February 13, 1892.

11. *Weekly Post*, May 28, 1892.

12. Core, *Chronicles of Core*, pp. 28, 148.

and began the practice of medicine at Smithfield, Pennsylvania. In 1848 he located at Mount Morris but a year later removed to Cassville, where he gained a large practice and was a physician for eighteen years. He then moved to Morgantown, where he had a leading practice until his retirement in 1872. He married Catherine Crawford and they had one son who died at the age of eighteen. He and his wife traveled widely, in Europe and Latin America.[13]

McVicker's Drug Store. John Clarence McVicker, in 1892, opened, on High Street, a drugstore destined to be one of the county's longest enduring commercial establishments. He was a son of George Washington McVicker and a descendant of James Mc-Vicker, who settled here about 1793 (vol. 2, pp. 347, 371, 372).[14]

Madera News-Stand. Walter and Bernard H. Madera were operating the Madera Brothers News-Stand, the first real news-stand in Morgantown's history, on High Street near Walnut; it had been founded by their father, on Walnut Street. Pittsburgh daily newspapers arrived by mail on the stagecoach from the end of the railroad at Fairchance. On Sundays the mail hack did not run and in 1892 the Madera Brothers worked out an arrangement with the *Pittsburg Dispatch* whereby they paid half the expenses of a special rider to Smithfield and return to carry the Sunday papers and thus the Sunday editions, for the first time in history, were received in Morgantown on the day of publication. The rider usually reached town about two o'clock in the afternoon, at which time large numbers of citizens gathered to get their papers.[15]

New Business Buildings. In 1892 Col. E. M. Grant, representing the Union Gas and Water Company, erected a two-story brick office building at the southwest corner of High Street and Bumbo Lane. The Brock-Reed-Wade building at the northeast corner of High and Pleasants streets was built by Dr. Luther S. Brock, James Madison Reed, and Dr. S. S. Wade the same year. About

---

13. *Weekly Post*, February 13, 1892.
14. Frank Mortimer Dent and his brother, Gaylord Hess Dent, sons of Frank M. Dent and descendants of pioneer settler John Dent (see vol. 2), associated themselves with the store in 1908 and purchased it in 1917, after McVicker's death.
15. Callahan, p. 256.

the same time C. A. Hayes erected a new brick building at the corner of High Street and Maiden Alley.[16]

Industrial Enterprises. In successful operation in and near Morgantown in 1892 were: Tygard Manufacturing Company ("Carriages, Sash, Blinds, Doors and Hard Wood Finishings"); one foundry; two furniture factories; the Victor Elevator and Mills Company ("High Grade Corn Goods, Maccaroni, Starch, etc."); Morgantown Brick Company ("Capacity 30,000 per day"); a large roller process flouring mill; five hotels; the Standard Oil Company's Station ("Tanks, Engines, Machinery and Buildings occupy about 70 acres of ground and constitute a town by themselves, lighted by electricity"); a creamery "which numbers among its patrons the President of the United States, the Secretary of War and the Duquesne Club of Pittsburg"; one tobacco factory, etc.[17]

New Post Offices. Rapid changes in the nature and location of the county's population continued to result in establishment of new post offices. Half a dozen new offices were set up during 1892.

Mahanna post office was opened June 20, 1892, with Alpheus B. Mahanna as the first (and only) postmaster. It was located in the Days Run section.

Located on Indian Creek, the Osgood Post Office was established February 10, 1892, with William C. Arnett as postmaster.

On the Evansville Pike six miles south of Morgantown, the Ridgedale Post Office was established December 16, 1892, with Luther J. Howell as postmaster.

The Ruby Post Office, in Battelle District, was opened June 20, 1892. Jacob Shanes was the first (and only) postmaster.

Along the Monongahela River just south of Morgantown, the Scrafford Post Office was opened September 1, 1892, with Alfred H. Gallagher as the first postmaster.

The Triune Post Office, between Halleck and Smithtown, was opened December 22, 1892. Albert T. Bennett was the first postmaster. The name Triune was suggested by Mr. Bennett from the fact that three roads joined at the place (Ellery Brown, *History of Triune*).

16. Callahan, pp. 253, 286.
17. *Weekly Post*, April 23, 1892.

Churches. Rev. A. E. Myers, of Bethany College, conducted a series of meetings in Morgantown for the Disciples of Christ, although there was no church building here.

The Reverend Mr. Summerville succeeded Rev. John Ambler as rector of the Morgantown Protestant Episcopal Church.

The Valley Chapel M.E. Church, in Battelle District, formerly on the Jollytown (Pennsylvania) Circuit, was transferred to the Wadestown Circuit.[18]

Singing School. A social and cultural affair, frequent in the county in the late nineteenth century, was the singing school. A typical event, related in Maple (Battelle District) locals, was one taught by Prof. A. M. Glover, of Glovers Gap, at Mount Tabor Church, which closed with an entertaining concert on the evening of February 27. "After a number of excellent compositions rendered by the class, the audience was highly entertained by Prof. O. M. Smith, of Taylortown, Pa., who sang a vocal solo entitled, 'Poor and old, and only in the way'. . . .

"Prof. Smith being prevailed upon to sing again, responded by rendering the vocal solo, 'Far, far away!' which was loudly applauded by the large audience.

"Prof. Glover then gave his farewell address, and the class sang 'God be with you till we meet again.' "[19]

"Wool Day." State farmers in this section were being urged to raise more sheep, especially larger and hardier breeds that yield larger fleeces of medium grade wool that find a ready market at good prices.

"The wool growing industry in this section of the State must steadily advance. The surroundings are favorable, and the good prices now being received for wool and mutton will have the effect to increase the business."[20]

Buyers appeared in Morgantown chiefly on one day a year, designated as Wool Day. A typical Wool Day was Thursday, June 2, 1892, when "Job Swindler and J. M. Jacobs bought and weighed up more wool than was ever handled in this town in one day. The wool was taken up at John Alexander's new building, Walnut

18. Dodds and Dodds, pp. 73, 75, 136.
19. *Weekly Post*, March 12, 1892.
20. *Weekly Post*, December 27, 1890.

Fig. 31. "Wool Day" on Walnut Street. Note town scales, next to location of the later Morgantown (Junior) High School. (Morgantown Public Library, Moreland Collection.)

street." The price paid was twenty-five cents for unwashed open wool and thirty cents for washed. A list of the names of over one hundred farmers, with the weight of the wool they sold, was recorded, amounting to tens of thousands of pounds.[21]

Miscellany. In 1892: The Eureka Pipe Line Company completed a line from the Sistersville oil field to the Morgantown tank field, a distance of about seventy miles (Callahan, p. 250). . . . Dr. I. C. White erected a large and imposing residence north of North Boundary Street, and Edward Price built far up the hill on Spruce Street an isolated residence (Callahan, p. 253). . . . The Morgantown Baptist congregation sold its property on Bumbo Lane at Long Alley and arranged to hold services in the old Academy building (Callahan, p. 257). . . . George C. Sturgiss, in June, began furnishing electricity for lights in university buildings (Callahan, p. 262). . . . Morgantown voters in April approved a bond issue of

21. *Weekly Post,* June 11, 1892; see also "Josh Smarty," "Wool Day in Morgantown," *Weekly Post,* July 2, 1892.

five thousand dollars to pave the main streets with bricks; the money was found, however, to be insufficient to even start the program (Callahan, p. 264). . . . Rev. A. A. Jimeson, former M.E. pastor at Morgantown, died January 6 at Beverly, Ohio; he was born in Indiana County, Pennsylvania, March 15, 1814 (*Weekly Post*, January 23, 1892). . . . Mrs. Amelia Martin, relict of Turner D. Martin, died in Cass District on January 6 at the home of her son, J. Wesley Martin (*Weekly Post*, January 30, 1892). . . . William Brewer, of Jakes Run, died January 30, aged eighty years (*Weekly Post*, February 13, 1892). . . . At night Morgantown was lighted by "nearly 100 enormous Natural Gas jets" (*Weekly Post*, April 23, 1892). . . . Jesse F. Miller, son of Asa Miller, died April 15 of injuries sustained when a log rolled upon him (*Weekly Post*, April 23, 1892). . . . An oil driller by the name of McClusky was killed May 23 at the D. J. Eddy Well No. 4, on Dolls Run, when hit by a walking beam (*Weekly Post*, May 28, 1892). . . . Nimrod, son of John Protzman, died in Morgantown on May 16, aged fifty-six years (*Weekly Post*, May 21, 1892). . . . Thomas Berry's flour mill at Cassville was destroyed by fire in July (*Weekly Post*, July 30, 1892). . . . The Tygard Manufacturing Company at South Morgantown was burned August 7; arson was suspected (*Weekly Post*, August 26, 1892). . . . Samuel Hickman, of near Wadestown, was accidentally shot and killed as he started squirrel hunting on September 5 (*Weekly Post*, September 17, 1892). . . . Jacob, a son of Fielding Kiger, of the Round Bottom Farm, died October 12 of a heart attack; he was survived by his wife, Elizabeth (Wells), and by three sons and two daughters (*Weekly Post*, October 22, 1892). . . . Dr. I. C. White was elected treasurer of the Geological Society of America on December 28, at the Society's meeting in Ottawa, Canada (*Wheeling News*, December 29, 1892). . . . There were eighteen coke ovens in operation at Beechwood and twenty at Opekiska (*Weekly Post*, January 14, 1893).

CHAPTER ONE HUNDRED SEVENTEEN

1893

As the New Year dawned, the situation for President Eli Marsh Turner of West Virginia University was becoming less and less favorable. The faculty and student body were steadily becoming more unified in their opposition to the president's policies. Even the board of regents began to have doubts, and this was not remedied when the president sponsored a bill in the legislature to decrease the number of the regents, thus necessitating new appointments.

"Armed with exaggerated reports of student demonstrations and with faculty inspired student petitions, protesting parties . . . gained the confidence of the newly elected governor[1] and the legislature. As a consequence, the newly appointed regents were generally opposed to President Turner, and others began to doubt his fitness. Thus, while requesting the faculty and the students to recognize and respect 'the President' as 'the presiding officer of the Faculty,' the regents appointed a committee 'to consider the state of the University.' "[2]

President Turner Is Fired. President Turner precipitated a showdown in June 1893 when he brought to the board of regents charges of incompetence against several faculty members. Two meetings of the board were held to hear the charges but the president failed to prove his case to the satisfaction of the regents, who, in July, approved a motion requesting "the immediate resignation of each Professor, tutor, and the President."

The motion directed the janitor, William ("Doc") Danser, to serve a copy of the order on each and every person concerned. Danser, whose salary was $180 a year, was a direct appointee of

1. William Alexander MacCorkle.
2. Ambler, p. 311.

the board and free from control by the president or the superintendent of buildings and grounds. Often he was said to have been openly defiant and at times impudent to the president and members of the faculty. Thus he was now "in a position, coveted by him, where he could fire the President and the faculty. Tradition has it that he executed the order with a great deal of satisfaction to himself."[3]

This unprecedented action of the regents in discharging the president and the faculty apparently met with approval throughout the state. The editor of the *Charleston Daily Mail* commented[4]: "Matters at the University have been cast into a pretty mess. The *Mail* has the kindest feeling for the trained and able head of the institution, but it appears that the faculty is all split up and the sooner the Board of Regents settles the trouble by firing the whole lot, the better it will be for the welfare of the school."[5]

Most of the faculty members were ultimately restored to their positions but the regents were unable to agree at once upon a successor to President Turner and on July 24, 1893, entrusted the duties of the president to the vice-president, Dr. P. B. Reynolds, who had joined the university staff in 1885.

Powell Benton Reynolds. Dr. Reynolds was born in Patrick County, Virginia, January 9, 1841. He moved to Kentucky and was well along in a law course when he enlisted in the Confederate army. Later he joined the Fifteenth Virginia and saw service with "Stonewall" Jackson. He was captured in September 1864, and spent the remainder of the war period as a prisoner at Camp Lookout, Maryland. During the war he had joined the Baptist church and after the close of the war entered Richmond College to study for the ministry.

In 1872 he became principal of Coalsmouth High School (Saint Albans, West Virginia), which on July 11, 1878, became Shelton College, with Reynolds as the president. He resigned in 1884 to become president of Buckner College, in Arkansas, where he was employed when he was elected to the chair of English in West

3. Ambler, op. cit.
4. June 17, 1893.
5. See also long accounts in the *Weekly Post,* various issues, but especially July 29, August 5, 1893.

Fig. 32. P. B. Reynolds. (West Virginia   Fig. 33. R. A. Armstrong. (West Vir-
University Library.)   ginia University Library.)

Virginia University, where he succeeded Prof. F. S. Lyon. "A vigorous mind and a sense of humor and justice tempered by sentiments of piety and fraternity saved him from the pitfalls of his liberty loving associates."[6]

Acting President Reynolds was also elected to the chair of metaphysics, in addition to English, and his son, W. F. Reynolds, was made his assistant. Prof. J. S. Stewart, having failed of restoration to the chair of mathematics, Prof. R. A. Armstrong was appointed to the position, and Prof. R. C. Berkeley having failed of reelection to the chair of ancient language, B. C. Alderson was given the position. Prof. S. B. Brown replaced Prof. W. P. Willey as secretary to the regents.

Student discipline from the beginning of the university's history had been very strict. All students upon entrance were required to sign an agreement to obey the rules, to conduct themselves with propriety, to be respectful to the faculty, and to de-

6. Ambler, p. 312.

port themselves as gentlemen. This rule was enforced with varying degrees of severity until finally an action of the board of regents, on June 13, 1893, relieved students of the necessity of signing such a contract.[7] The university football team, coached by F. W. Rane, of the faculty, won against Mount Pleasant Institute and the Uniontown Independents, but went down to defeat before the W&J team at Washington on November 30, with one thousand shouting spectators looking on.[8]

Farrow Arms Company. An industrial concern advertised with much fanfare built a two-story brick plant at Morgantown and was ready for work by September 1893. This was the Farrow Arms Company, of Mason, Tennessee, which produced rifles of the target and sporting kind, shotguns, loading tools and ammunition. A repair department was also maintained.[9] Milton W. Farrow, manager of the plant, was widely known as an expert marksman.[10]

Progress on the Railroad. The enthusiasm with which county residents looked forward to completion of the FM&P Railroad to Uniontown was dampened somewhat during 1893 by the slowness with which progress was being made. Strategic right-of-way struggles with other companies was one cause of delay, as all corporations involved were aware of the vast coal resources[11] of the Monongahela Valley and the potential for rail traffic in transporting the coal to market.

But construction on the line between Morgantown and Smithfield, Pennsylvania, was mostly completed during 1893. A bridge across Cheat River at Point Marion, Pennsylvania, remained under construction at the end of the year.

Drake, Stratton Company had the contract to put on the ballast and lay the ties and rails from Smithfield to Morgantown. The grading was completed about July 1. An immense pile of slag and cinders at Fairchance was used for ballast.[12]

7. Callahan, p. 227.
8. Ambler, p. 364; *Weekly Post,* December 2, 1893.
9. Callahan, p. 251. Unfortunately the plant ceased work early the next year.
10. *Weekly Post,* September 23, 1893.
11. See a long description by Dr. I. C. White, *Industrial and Business Survey, Morgantown Chamber of Commerce.* 1921.
12. *Weekly Post,* July 1, 1893.

"We will be running trains through to Morgantown over the State Line railroad in September," a B&O official said to a newspaper reporter in midsummer.[13]

Meanwhile, surveyors were locating the line of a railroad from Brownsville to Morgantown and a Pittsburgh newspaper commented that it is now certain that "the badly neglected West Virginia college town will have two lines leading from Pittsburg instead of one before the snow flies again next November."[14]

The indications were that the Pittsburg, Virginia, and Charleston road was to be immediately extended from Brownsville to the head of slack water.

But all these predictions proved too optimistic and by the end of the year no trains were running on either line (the PV&C was not even started).

Repair the Street? "The teamsters who haul from the F. M. & P. station either fail to look to their interests or are afraid of a dime, for the great hole in the street just below the crossing when they turn into Front street, wrenches their wagons and unnecessarily pulls their horses, when a bushel of broken stone and a little dirt would remedy this. Maybe the town should do this—probably they should, but if the town won't improve it, let those who use it most make this much needed improvement."[15]

Odd Fellows Hall. "The Odd-Fellows of Morgantown have purchased the J. W. Carraco lot and buildings, corner High and Walnut streets, for $8,500. The property fronts 44 feet 5 inches on Main, and 116 feet 0 inches on Walnut, and is considered the best business corner in Morgantown. It extends from High street to the M. P. Church on Walnut, and the rear end of lot is 87½ feet wide. . . . The Lodge will tear down the present buildings and erect an imposing 3 story building—store rooms on 1st floor, offices on 2d floor, and Hall above. . . ."[16]

Tragedy on Pedlar Run. At the head of Pedlar Run a wagon road led, by sharp curves and steep grades, across the hill to the head

13. *Weekly Post,* August 5, 1893; a full-column account of construction work is given.
14. *Pittsburg Dispatch,* February 18, 1893, quoted in the *Weekly Post,* February 25, 1893.
15. *Weekly Post,* April 1, 1893.
16. *Weekly Post,* December 9, 1893.

of Indian Creek. Numerous oil derricks stood on the hillsides and from any elevation in the area as many as fifty or more could be counted.

On July 4, 1893, a tragedy occurred on the hazardous hill road that for many years thereafter caused it to be regarded with dread. "A sad and fatal accident happened in the Dolls Run oil field on the 4th. The oil men had arranged for a picnic at Cassville on the 4th. Mr. John Turner, a pumper who lives at the head of Indian Creek, started with his wife and daughter to spend the day at the picnic. Mrs. Turner hoisted her umbrella, at which the horse took fright and dashed away, becoming unmanageable. In wild flight Mrs. Turner was killed by her head coming in contact with a stake or being thrown from the buggy. She was killed instantly. The little daughter was so severely injured that she died in a short time. Mr. Turner was also severely hurt. The horse broke a leg and had to be shot. Because of the accident few of the oil men attended the picnic. The remains of Mrs. Turner and her child were taken to Clarion county for interment. The accident cast a gloom over the community."[17]

William Wagner. "Wm. Wagner is dead. His familiar figure had been seen upon our streets for over half a century. . . . No man had more warm earnest friends. For many years he was cashier of the old Merchants and Mechanics Bank of Wheeling, and for half a hundred years had been known to Morgantown's people as a banker and business man."[18] He died May 25, 1893. Mr. Wagner was born near Harrisburg, Pennsylvania, August 21, 1813, and came to Morgantown in 1838.

Robert W. Tapp. The son of Festus H. and Mary N. (Cushman) Tapp, Robert W. Tapp, died September 13, 1891. He was born near Maidsville May 18, 1859. He graduated from the public schools and from West Virginia University, receiving an A.B. and an A.M. degree from that institution.

After graduation he became a department head in the Vicksburg city schools and after two years was elected superintendent of schools of that city. He returned to Morgantown after serving one year in that position, becoming principal of the Morgantown schools. In 1890 he was elected principal of the State Normal

17. *Waynesburg Independent,* July 6, 1893.
18. *Weekly Post,* June 3, 1893.

School at Glenville, but served only one year there before dying of typhoid fever.[19]

John T. Fleming. The youngest son of Levin and Mary (Willey) Fleming, John T. Fleming, died at his home near Cassville January 23, 1893. He was born June 8, 1827. He served two terms as Monongalia County sheriff, and was one of the county's most honored citizens. He was a farmer and also a schoolteacher. He married Willimpe T. Smyth and six children survived.[20]

Benjamin McCurdy. The man for whom McCurdysville was named, Benjamin McCurdy, died at his home there on January 6, 1893, aged seventy-nine years. He was the son of John and Mary McCurdy and was born December 15, 1813. He was married twice, the first time to Christena Eddy, the second time to Sarah

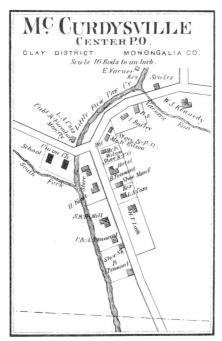

Fig. 34. Map of McCurdysville. (From *Atlas of . . . Monongalia County*, 1886.)

19. *Weekly Post,* January 21, 1893.
20. *Weeky Post,* January 28, 1893; Wiley, p. 713.

Raber. Eight children survived. He was McCurdysville post-master for several years and deputy assessor for two years. "He was a very prominent and much respected man" in his neighborhood.[21]

Church of the Nazarene. The Morgantown Church of the Nazarene was organized in 1893 by Warren C. Jones, a district superintendent. The first pastor was Rev. M. Estes Haney. Meetings were held in a store building on Richwood Avenue.[22]

Miscellany. In 1893: Horatio Dickson McGeorge, of Morgantown, died January 14, aged eighty-two; he married Mary S., sister of Zackwell Morgan III, and they had five children, of whom only Nimrod H. survived (*Weekly Post,* January 21, 1893). . . . William Price of Morgantown, died of apoplexy February 3; he was born in England and was in his seventy-first year (*Weekly Post,* February 11, 1893). . . . George W. Jolliffe, of Brownsville, Pennsylvania, died March 10, aged sixty-eight; he was born at Uffington, the son of Joseph and Harriet Jolliffe, and spent many years on the Monongahela River, shipping timber by steamboat (*Weekly Post,* March 18, 25, 1893). . . . Neighbors protested when William A. Watts proposed to erect a livery stable on his lot at the corner of Spruce Street and Bumbo Lane and other arrangements were made (*Weekly Post,* April 1, 1893). . . . The large barn of T. Pickenpaugh, three miles south of Morgantown, was burned on April 7; the loss, estimated at four thousand dollars, included twenty-five head of cows, five horses, farming implements, etc. (*Weekly Post,* April 18, 1893). . . . Rev. Samuel Hitchens, an M.E. minister of Morgantown, died May 23; he was born in Cornwall County, England, and had been in the ministry thirty-four years (*Weekly Post,* May 27, June 3, 1893). . . . Levi Jenkins, a veteran of the Mexican and Civil wars, died in Marion County on May 27, aged sixty-eight (*Weekly Post,* June 10, 1893). . . . The Knights of Pythias Lodge had a select excursion on the new steamboat *Isaac M. Mason* on July 13 from Morgantown to Brownsville (*Weekly Post,* July 1, 1893). . . . Sarah, widow of William Lantz, of Blacksville, died June 18, aged eighty-four years (*Weekly Post,* July 15, 1893). . . . A new hack line operated by

21. *Weekly Post,* January 21, 1893.
22. Dodds and Dodds, p. 92.

John R. Neill carried passengers daily from Morgantown to Mount Morris, Pennsylvania (*Weekly Post,* July 23, 1893). . . . Many home building lots in Sunnyside were sold at reasonable prices at a special auction on June 28, 29 (Callahan, p. 248). . . . Additional pipelines were constructed to connect the Morgantown tank field with Downs and with the Pennsylvania State Line oil field, a total length of about twenty-eight miles (Callahan, p. 250). . . . The Morgantown Protestant Episcopal congregation enlarged their church building on High Street (Callahan, p. 257). . . . A new church building was erected by the Miracle Run Methodist Episcopal congregation (Dodds and Dodds, p. 133). . . . Barton M. Jones, former county sheriff, died October 10; he was only forty-two years of age (*Weekly Post,* October 14, 1893). . . . Barnum and Bailey's Show exhibited at Morgantown October 19; the show carried 340 women and 960 men, and contracted with T. R. Evans for 275 bushels of oats, 11,000 pounds of hay, and a load of straw (*Weekly Post,* October 14, 28, 1893). . . . One of the earliest photographs to be published in a local newspaper showed the new courthouse (*Weekly Post,* August 5, 1893).

CHAPTER ONE HUNDRED EIGHTEEN

1894

On April 2, 1894, through railroad service was established from Pittsburgh to Fairmont, by way of Morgantown. This new service represented another important step in Morgantown's rapid transition from a quiet country village to a bustling industrial city. The first passenger train out of Morgantown had left on the morning of February 15, 1886.[1] For eight years Morgantown remained a terminal station on the short line connecting with Fairmont, where connections were made with east and west trains between Chicago and Baltimore. More direct connections with Clarksburg via Fairmont was provided in 1889, when a line was completed up the West Fork River.[2]

Active competitive efforts in the strategic struggle between the Pennsylvania Railroad and the Baltimore and Ohio for right-of-way south of Uniontown both delayed and hastened progress. In 1892, after the Baltimore and Ohio had finally won and secured all rights-of-way, the labor force of Lane Brothers appeared for the first work of construction for connecting Morgantown with Connellsville, Pennsylvania.

Construction within the town limits and through Seneca was facilitated by grants of free rights-of-way. The construction of the entire extension to the end of the tracks of the State Line Railroad, near Fairchance, was completed early in 1894.

Railroad to Pittsburgh. The editor of the *Morgantown Post*, like most citizens of Morgantown, was enthusiastic about prospects for the new line. Just before the service started, he commented, quoting in part from the *Pittsburg Dispatch*:

"To show what an important feeder the Morgantown branch

1. Pp. 94, 95.
2. P. 136.

will be, the Baltimore & Ohio people expect to receive from it daily as soon as the road is operated 200 cars of coal, coke and other traffic. The local business is sure to be excellent. In a few years the officials predict that the shipments will reach 500 cars per diem and more.

"The new line is practically finished. The bridge across the Cheat River at Point Marion, which delayed the opening, was completed sometime ago. Drake & Stratton, the local contractors, laid the track. I saw John O'Connor, the field man of the firm, at Point Marion on Saturday. He told me they expected to turn the road over to the B. & O. Co. about April 1. Passenger trains will be run about May 19, when the summer schedule of the B. & O. will go into effect."[3]

A group of West Virginia businessmen, from Clarksburg, Fairmont, and Morgantown, went to Pittsburgh by special train on March 27, returning the next day. The purpose of the visit was to impress "the Iron City's Chamber of Commerce with the importance of establishing closer trade relations with the great rich territory beyond the southern border of Pennsylvania." They went home well satisfied that their mission had been accomplished.

Among those who addressed the Chamber of Commerce meeting was George C. Sturgiss, of Morgantown. Referring to the completion of the new railway link, he told how, more than twenty years before, when he came to Morgantown as a young man, Prof. J. R. Moore had said to him: "Remain here with us. There is a great future before us." Professor Moore had shown him a map and pointed out that one day a railroad would connect the upper Monongahela Valley and its rich resources with markets in Pittsburgh. Mr. Sturgiss was now seeing this dream realized.

The run from Morgantown to Pittsburgh, 101 miles, took over 4½ hours. Lunch and refreshments were served on the train.[4]

Daily passenger service between Fairmont and Pittsburgh began on April 2, on the schedule on page 182.

3. *Weekly Post*, March 17, 1894.
4. *The Post*, April 7, 1894.

SOUTHBOUND (Read down)				NORTHBOUND (Read up)		
2	50	82				
P.M.	A.M.	A.M.		P.M.	P.M.	P.M.
5.50	8.15		Pittsburgh	2.00	8.55	
7.40	10.55		Connellsville	11.35	6.25	
8.10	11.31		Uniontown	11.00	5.50	
8.32	11.52		Fairchance	10.38	5.28	
8.40	12.00		Smithfield	10.30	5.20	
9.18	12.36		Point Marion	9.54	4.44	
9.38	12.55		Van Voorhis	9.35	4.25	
10.00	1.15	5.40	MORGANTOWN	9.15	4.05	12.30
10.08	1.24	5.48	Uffington	9.07	3.57	12.21
10.20	1.35	6.01	Little Falls	8.56	3.46	12.10
10.32	1.47	6.16	Opekiska	8.44	3.34	11.55
10.37	1.52	6.20	Luther	8.39	3.29	11.50
10.41	1.57	6.25	Catawba	8.35	3.25	11.46
10.46	2.01	6.30	Montana	8.31	3.21	11.41
10.51	2.06	6.36	Hoult	8.25	3.15	11.35
10.55	2.10	6.40	F., M., & P. Junction	8.20	3.10	11.30
11.00	2.15	6.45	Fairmont	8.15	3.05	11.25
P.M.	P.M.	A.M.		A.M.	P.M.	A.M.

At Fairmont connections were made with B&O trains east and west and with trains on the Monongahela River Railroad (The Short Line) to Clarksburg.

Meanwhile, steamboat connection with Pittsburgh continued to be available, with packet boats leaving Morgantown daily at 3:00 p.m., the round trip fare, including meals, only five dollars.

Baker's Hardware Store. On April 11, 1894, in the month the first passenger train ran from Morgantown to Pittsburgh, Henry Clay Baker opened a hardware store on High Street. The store was destined to last longer than the train. Baker was a son of Samuel Baker, of Bakers Ridge, and grandson of John Baker, early Monongalia County pioneer.[5]

End of the old Dering Building. To make way for the new Odd Fellows building at the corner of High and Walnut streets, a historic old structure was removed in 1894. Shortly after the

5. John E. Jacobs, a relative of the Baker family by marriage, associated himself with the business in 1899, and in 1902, after Baker's death, the firm was incorporated, with A. G. Baker, son of H. C. Baker, John H. Krepps, and John E. Jacobs as owners.

Revolution Henry Dering had built on the site a log tavern, which burned in 1796. Thereupon he erected the Dering Building, in which he kept a tavern until his death in 1807 and in which his wife Rebecca continued to keep until her death in 1846. And John Dering, their son, kept it for a time thereafter. After 1856 the building was occupied by stores.[6]

Another Sewer Proposal Rejected. The proposal for construction of a complete sewerage system for the growing town was renewed[7] early in 1894 and in June, after a vigorous campaign by civic leaders, the question of a bond issue for $11,000 was submitted to the voters. It was, however, rejected by a vote of 138 to 70.[8]

A few sewers, with inadequate carrying capacity, and also a few street improvements were made by the council, under emergency irregular orders, by small appropriations from the annual tax levies year by year.[9]

The Interim on the Campus. Some important administrative changes were made during the regime of P. B. Reynolds as acting president of West Virginia University. In 1894 control of finances was vested in a business manager ("University Auditor"); Joseph Moreland was the first person appointed to the position. The acting president still was permitted general supervision, but this arrangement relieved him of much drudgery and allowed him more time for teaching, his first love. Alex R. Whitehill was appointed treasurer of the board of regents.

Student extracurricular activities still centered in the Columbian and Parthenon literary societies, although these societies were nearing the end of their period of supremacy. All other student organizations, except the YMCA and the YWCA, were discouraged or even forbidden. To the old educators there was no substitute for the "old time literary society." Their annual contests for regents' prizes, aggregating one hundred dollars, featured commencement week exercises.

6. Vol. 2, p. 351; vol. 3, p. 281. A long description of the old house appears in *The Post,* May 12, 1894.
7. See p. 161.
8. *The Post,* June 1894.
9. Callahan, p. 265.

184 THE MONONGALIA STORY

Athletics, however, were definitely threatening the power and influence of the literary societies. F. W. Rane continued to coach the football team, which won half its games in 1894, defeating Mount Pleasant Institute and Bethany College, losing to the Connellsville Independents and to Marietta College.[10]

New Post Offices. A post office named Hoard was established September 8, 1894, with Virgil E. Hoard as the first postmaster. It was located on the east side of the Monongahela River, at Lock No. 9, in Union District, and was served by B.&O. passenger trains.

Minor Post Office, on Dunkard Creek at the mouth of Days Run, in Clay District, was established June 23, 1894, with Albert G. Chaplin as the first postmaster.

On the east side of the Monongahela River, in Union District about five miles north of Morgantown, the Van Voorhis Post Office was established September 1, 1894. James P. St. Clair was the first postmaster.

In 1894 there were forty-seven post offices in Monongalia County.[11]

Granville. "Ben Hur," in special correspondence to a local newspaper, said that: "This town has a population of 181, and is situated on the west bank of the Monongahela river, two miles northwest of Morgantown. . . .

"Wm. Finnell and sons do a lively business raising vegetables for the Morgantown and other markets. . . ; also, Mr. Mad John raises and sells in the market fine vegetables and fruit. . . .

"We have several carpenters located here; store, hotel, churches and school house."[12]

Baseball. The steamer *Mason* landed at Morgantown on August 28 with a brass band and three hundred enthusiasts, along with a baseball club "picked from the best material from Pittsburg to Morgantown." The local team played them and defeated them soundly: Morgantown, 24, Brownsville, 8.[13]

10. Ambler, pp. 313, 359, 364.
11. *The Post*, March 24, 1894.
12. *The Post*, December 22, 1894.
13. *The Post*, September 1, 1894.

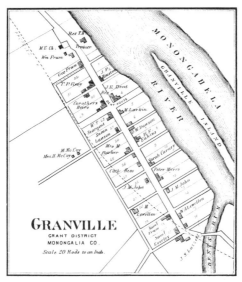

Fig. 35. Map of Granville. (From *Atlas of . . .*
Monongalia County, 1886.)

Lock No. 10. Now that slack water had reached Morgantown, after more than half a century of talk and work, its extension to Fairmont was actively under discussion. The U.S. engineers tentatively located Dam No. 10 just below Morgantown, so close that the town's wharf would be flooded, with little chance of elevating it because of the railroad bridge across Walnut Street near the wharf. Citizens, therefore, filed a petition requesting that the dam be located just above town.[14]

A Pittsburgh newspaper said the stretch from that city to Morgantown, 105 miles, was the longest reach of slack water in the United States.[15]

Newspaper Changes Format. The *Morgantown Post,* on Saturday, February 17, appeared for the first time as an eight-page quarto paper of forty-eight columns, instead of a four-page folio sheet of thirty-six columns, as had been the format in the past. The change had been contemplated for more than a year.

14. *The Post,* May 5, 1894.
15. *Pittsburg Times,* October 4, 1894.

"It is the popular style; it is handy for those who read only the locals and editorials; it is convenient for those who read the news of the day; . . . it is convenient to handle; . . . it is more attractive in every way." The subscription price remained at two dollars a year. The title was changed from *Weekly Post* to *The Post*.

Daybrook Church Is Burned. As the members were assembling for Sunday School on the morning of March 18, the Daybrook Church of Christ was discovered by the janitor, E. W. Piles, to be on fire. Despite frantic efforts to control the flames, the structure was quickly destroyed.[16]

A new building was constructed during the next few months, under the leadership of Noah E. Moore, Marion Tennant, and James McCord.[17]

Hotel Peabody. On May 31 a new Morgantown hostelry, the Hotel Peabody, was opened to the public by the proprietress, L. J. Peabody. On High Street opposite the courthouse, it was located at the very center of town. "A complete modern system of electric lights, gas for fuel, pure mountain water, and all needed and convenient appliances have been put in." Large and commodious sample rooms for commercial travelers were provided and in the dining room none but first-class cooks were employed.[18]

Mont Chateau Hotel. A new tourist hotel, called Mont Chateau, was opened by Ellen Dean, George Hardy, and John A. Dales early in July "at the mouth of the Cheat River canyon, on the Western slope of the Laurel Ridge; in the midst of a country rich in historical events and unsurpassed in the wild beauty of its scenery. . . . The Hotel is built on a rock plateau 150 feet above the clear and beautiful Cheat, surrounded by towering mountains whose sides are clothed with forests as dense and tangled as in the days when it was the favorite hunting grounds of a race who disputed its possession with the hardy pioneer." Cooper's Rock, Cheat View, Rock City, and Quarry Run were scenic features

16. *The Post*, March 31, 1894.
17. Dodds and Dodds, p. 124. The building is still in use in 1980.
18. *The Post*, May 26, June 2, 9, 1894.

Fig. 36. Mont Chateau. (J. L. Keener, Mont Chateau Club.)

within hiking distance. C. J. Pride ran a line of carriages from Morgantown out to the hotel.[19]

Fire at the Tank Field. A spectacular fire occurred near the tank field south of Morgantown at 11:00 p.m. on July 12. Employees of the Standard Pump Station had gone to repair a leak in an oil line nearly a mile from the station, on Aarons Creek. Gas from the oil was ignited from a lantern and in a moment two hundred barrels of oil were ablaze; running down the hill into the creek, it set fire to everything in its way. The home of Madison Hess was saved with difficulty. Two employees, Charles Poland and Tim Hurley, were severely burned. Vivid flashes of light and a towering column of black smoke attracted much attention.[20]

Morgantown Businesses. Among business houses operating in Morgantown in 1894 were Alf. K. Smith, tailor; Phil A. Shaffer, real estate and insurance; A. M. Lazier Medicine Co.; Henry S.

19. *The Post*, June 16, 1894.
20. *The Post*, July 21, 1894.

Hayes, groceries and notions; Hirschman's, clothing; Reed's Drug Store; Morgantown Marble and Granite Works; G. and W. E. Price, furniture; St. Clair Restaurant; Jason Clark, flour and feed; and John H. Hunt's lunch counter.[21]

Joseph P. Keener. A stock dealer of West Morgantown, Joseph P. Keener, died August 4, 1894. He was born in Greene County, Pennsylvania, December 24, 1837, came to Morgantown and married Nancy C., daughter of Moses Kinkaid. They had six children, Waitman W., Joseph L., George I., John F., Grove P., and Myrna. He began his career as a butcher, but gradually became an extensive stock dealer.[22]

Lee Roy Kramer. General Lee Roy Kramer, son of George Kramer, died in Philadelphia on March 20, aged seventy-five years. He was buried in Oak Grove Cemetery. General Kramer was a prominent citizen during the Civil War and assisted in the formation of the new state of West Virginia. He was a member of the first and second legislatures as a representative from Monongalia County, and was speaker of the house of delegates of the first session. He married Elizabeth Hutchinson, of Marietta, Ohio, but they had no children.[23]

"Uncle Jack" Baker. John N. Baker, of Cheat Neck, died July 16, 1894, lacking but one day of his ninety-third birthday, having been born July 17, 1801. One of the oldest and most respected citizens of the county, he was affectionately known by everyone as "Uncle Jack." He joined the Methodist Protestant church in 1833 and remained until his death a faithful member (vol. 3, p. 189; vol. 4, p. 113). He was a son of George and Elizabeth (Norris) Baker.

Francis Marion Durbin. A longtime resident of Morgantown, F. M. Durbin (see vol. 3, p. 341, etc.), died at his home in Parkersburg on November 4, aged fifty-seven years. He was born in Morgantown, the son of William Durbin. He married Abigail Pickenpaugh and they were survived by one son, Charles. He worked in the Merchants' and Mechanics' Bank, in Morgantown,

21. From various issues of *The Post.*
22. *The Post,* August 11, 1894.
23. *The Post,* March 31, 1894.

and later was cashier of the Grafton National Bank, then of the Wood County Bank, which position he held at the time of his death.[24]

Miscellany. In 1894: To provide more convenient communication between the new "Sunnyside" section and Morgantown, P. B. Reynolds and others erected a footbridge across Falling Run near the university (Callahan, pp. 252, 262). . . . A new brick building for the Second National Bank was constructed on High Street at Maiden Alley (Callahan, pp. 253, 254). . . . The Catholic church established a mission in Morgantown (Callahan, p. 257). . . . Sarah (Gilbert) Maple sold the east end of Lot 99, in Morgantown, to George and W. E. Price (Callahan, p. 324). . . . The Morgantown Baptist congregation, having sold its old property at Bumbo Lane and Long Alley, began the construction of a new building on High Street, meanwhile holding services in the old Monongalia Academy building (Callahan, p. 257). . . . James P. Donley, Morgantown stock dealer, died in Philadelphia April 8 (*The Post,* April 14, 1894). . . . The Pittsburgh, Virginia and Charleston Railroad, was surveyed from Brownsville to Morgantown, fifty-five miles, but no construction was done (*The Post,* April 21, 1894). . . . Uniontown department stores advised Morgantown residents to "take the train," "31 miles in 105 minutes," to shop in that city (*The Post,* April 21, 1894, etc.). . . . Rev. Lewis A. Core, son of Barton Core, of Cassville, who had been a Methodist missionary in India for about six years, was married at Moradabad to Mary R. Kennedy on March 21 (*The Post,* May 5, 1894). . . . In grading for Beechurst Avenue a gravestone was removed bearing the name of Henry Petty, who died March 11, 1795 (*The Post,* May 19, 1894). . . . Joshua Shuman, of near Arnettsville, died May 12, aged sixty-seven years (*The Post,* May 26, 1894). . . . William C. Haney, of Easton, died June 19, aged eighty-one years; he married Mary Henry and two daughters survived, Mrs. E. E. Moore and Mrs. Marion Protzman (*The Post,* June 30, 1894). . . . Simon Hirschman, of Baltimore, father of Milton H. Hirschman, of Morgantown, died on July 22 (*The Post,* July 28, 1894). . . . After July 28 local trains leaving Morgantown for Fairmont at 5:30 a.m. daily and arriving in Morgantown from Fairmont at 11:50 p.m. were discontinued (*The Post,*

24. *The Post,* November 10, 1894.

July 28, 1894). . . . A colored camp meeting was held at Round Bottom in August (*The Post,* August 11, 1894). . . . William H. Houston, of Morgantown, died August 11, aged sixty-nine years (*The Post,* August 18, 1894). . . . Emma and Ella Fordyce opened a private school in Morgantown on September 10 (September 1, 1894). . . . Mrs. Eliza B. (Oliphant) Wilson, second wife of Edgar C. Wilson, died September 26 (*The Post,* November 11, 1894). . . . March 20 was one of the hottest March days ever recorded in the county, the temperature reaching eighty-six degrees (*Chronicles of Core,* p. 149). . . . A phonographic concert was given at the Morgantown M.P. Church on November 19, admission, twenty-five cents (*The Post,* November 17, 1894). . . . Captain Henry Holman, who was born and reared in Union District, died at Massillon, Ohio, aged fifty years (*The Post,* November 24, 1894). . . . Emaline, wife of David Musgrave, was found dead in Indian Creek on December 13; foul play was suspected (*The Post,* January 5, 1895). . . . The Morgantown Planing Mill was established (Callahan, p. 251). . . . Daniel Fordyce, a partner in Fairchild, Lawhead and Company's carriage manufactory, died April 30, aged seventy-five years (*The Post,* May 12, 1894).

CHAPTER ONE HUNDRED NINETEEN

1895

The faint beginning of one of the greatest social changes in all human history showed up in Monongalia County in 1895 with the organization of the county's first telephone company.

On March 10, 1876, Alexander Graham Bell had spoken into a sort of mouthpiece connected by a wire with a receiver a considerable distance away: "Mr. Watson, come here, I want you." Thomas A. Watson, his assistant, heard the message clearly; they were the first words transmitted by telephone.

The first telephone line was constructed between Boston and Somerville, Massachusetts, in April 1877. By August of that year about eight hundred telephones were in use and development of the new form of communication had begun.[1]

The Bell Telephone System. During 1895, the Bell Telephone Company, which had been first formed as a voluntary, unincorporated association on July 9, 1877, and had slowly and painfully become a nationwide organization, opened an exchange in the Odd Fellows building in Morgantown for handling long distance calls. Their lines entered Morgantown from Uniontown and calls could be made as far as Pittsburgh.

"Mr. Frank B. Hall, Sup't. of construction of the telephone lines now being put up here, says they will complete the work by April 15th. As soon as the work is completed another force of workmen will give us connection with Pittsburg and all intermediate points, and then we will be within 'talking distance' with all the principal cities east of Chicago. The long distance telephone will be what Morgantown wants, and Pittsburg will be one of our nearest neighbors."[2]

1. See John Brooks, *Telephone: The First Hundred Years* (New York, 1975).
2. *The Post,* March 30, 1895.

The business rate for one telephone on the line was given as thirty-six dollars per annum, and the residence rate thirty dollars.

By the end of the year a line connected Morgantown with Wheeling and the *Wheeling News* reported that it "had the honor of receiving the first long distance message from Morgantown."[3] Actually, long distance service for Morgantown was apparently hardly established for general use until near the end of the year. An open house was held in the offices on December 18, at which Morgantown residents were given the opportunity to talk over the line and receive messages.[4]

The People's Telephone Company. Possibly as early as 1890 a few isolated private telephones were in use in Monongalia County on an experimental basis. H. Fenton Rice is said to have been the first telephone owner in the county, installing the instrument at his store, Rice's grocery, on High Street in Morgantown.

Other persons, in various sections, with crude batteries and instruments hooked together by wires, were having a lot of fun with the new gadget, somewhat like a child's toy.

A group of farmers around Mooresville and Pedlar Run, in 1895, jokingly at first, it is said, later in earnest, signed a contract to support the construction of a line. A few families around Mooresville were connected, then a line was built across the hill to Pedlar Run. Extensions were soon built to Blacksville on the west, to Cassville on the east.

The little company which they formed was called The People's Telephone Company, the first such organization in the county. It was incorporated December 26, 1895, with C. S. Tennant,[5] of Pentress, the president, R. B. ("Dick") Price, secretary, and J. C. Barrickman vice-president.

It did not take the promoters of the new telephone company long to realize that a connection with the county seat would be most desirable, and on November 15, 1895, the first regular telephone line reached Morgantown. The *Morgantown Post* thus hailed this great event:

"The new Franklin Hotel will be the exchange for the People's

3. Quoted in *The Post*, December 21, 1895.
4. *The Post*, December 21, 1895.
5. Later succeeded by Alphaeus Garrison.

Telephone Line. A box was put in the hotel yesterday and the line connected; this gives Morgantown telephone connection with all points in the county on the west side of the river. There are two or three lines which have been consolidated; they cover the following places: Warren to Burton, Blacksville, Fairview, Mannington, Henkins, Stewart's, New Brownsville, Worley, Mooresville, Wright's, Garrison's store, Cassville, Dr. Rinehart's, Charlotte P. O., Osage, Randall, Granville, Morgantown. Capt. Garrison was in Morgantown yesterday superintending the work of putting in the box at the Franklin. The people on the west side are rapidly falling into the procession and the county will soon be cobwebbed with telephone lines. With the completion of the line between here and Uniontown in two or three weeks there will be no place within a circle of a hundred miles that Morgantown cannot reach by telephone, as well as the large cities from New York to Chicago."[6]

Charles Finnell was at that time the manager of the Franklin Hotel and for a while the phone was the only one in town connected to the outside line. Finnell's son, Harry, would carry messages that came in, or race over town to call to the phone someone for whom a call had come. Sam Thralls operated the switch at Blacksville.

About the first of December a line was put in operation between Pedlar Run and Hagans, on Indian Creek, and a little later the Hagans correspondent for the *New Dominion* remarked: "The telephone line from Hagans to Arnettsville is completed and that catnip infested city is now out of the wilderness." The same communication also called attention to a new hazard that came with the telephone: "Luther Eddy recently fell from the top of a telephone pole and was seriously though not dangerously injured."[7]

Still later the Hagans correspondent noted that "our telephone line is doing a good business. Since the young people have got to courting over the line it is bringing in quite a sum of money. Things are quite different now from what they were when Uncle Dave and Aunt Jane were young."[8]

Uncle Dave and Aunt Jane (Morris) could have had no idea about a revolution in living habits the telephone would soon bring

6. *The Post,* November 16, 1895.
7. *New Dominion,* March 7, 1896.
8. *New Dominion,* December 31, 1896.

about. The citizens did not know that the toy they were experimenting with was destined soon to alter social patterns and to become more indispensable to people's daily lives than any other invention; that out of the little system Clay District farmers had built, and a thousand more like it, would emerge the American Telephone and Telegraph Company, the richest corporation on earth, the paradox of a monopoly in a competitive society.

President Goodknight.[9] Acting university President P. B. Reynolds disliked administrative work, particularly that pertaining to discipline, being more interested in teaching and in the Christian ministry. The regents, therefore, began to look for someone to take over his administrative duties. Senator D. S. Walton, of Waynesburg, Pennsylvania, appeared uninvited before the regents in their June 1895 meeting to present and recommend the Rev. Dr. James L. Goodknight as a candidate for the university presidency.

"Thrice married, a matter of concern, in a small college town, 'the Doctor' was a graduate of Cumberland University and of Union Theological Seminary. Following his third marriage he had spent two years abroad in study and travel.[10] With his long mustache and slightly gray hair and with a long clerical coat and sometimes with a silk hat, he made a distinguished appearance. Moreover, he was a Republican and West Virginia was then shifting from the Democratic to the Republican column in both state and national politics."[11]

The board, with a view to liberality and reform, thereupon elected Dr. Goodknight to the presidency and ruled that "the orderly and successful administration of the affairs of the University require that it shall have in fact, as well as in name, an executive head in whom shall be centered power with responsibility."

Results of the Hatch Act (1887) and the Second Morrill Act (1890) having made possible enlarged viewpoints, President Goodknight proceeded to transform what had been known as "the College" into a true university. He thus reorganized "the eight Academic Schools, five Technical and Professional Schools, and four Special Courses" into four colleges, each with its own

9. See his biography in *The Post,* November 2, 1895.
10. See Mrs. J. L. Goodknight, "A Day at the Great Pyramids," *Woman's Edition of the New Dominion,"* December 30, 1896.
11. Ambler, p. 314.

dean, subdivided into schools and departments. The "eight Academic Schools" became the College of Arts and Sciences, with Vice-President P. B. Reynolds as dean. This new college was composed of nine "schools," namely, English, mathematics, ancient languages, modern languages, chemistry and physics, geology, metaphysics, political science, and biology (including medicine). The College of Engineering and Mechanic Arts, with W. S. Aldrich as dean, functioned through two schools. The College of Agriculture had as its dean J. A. Myers, director of the Agricultural Experiment Station. The old School of Law and Equity became the College of Law, with Judge Okey Johnson as dean.

New appointments in 1895 included Prof. R. A. Armstrong to the position of secretary to the faculty; Dr. R. W. Douthat, president of Barboursville College, to the chair of ancient languages; Waitman Barbe as field agent to boost attendance.

"Boarding Forts." Student boarding was increasingly a real problem. A few Greek letter fraternities were organized but the chief resort was to "boarding forts." These places had greater freedom than did authorized boarding houses, which had operated since 1867 under strict regulations that required the owners to keep "genteel and healthful places."

"Each fort fed from twenty to fifty students organized and sponsored by a 'captain' who purchased the food, employed the cook or cooks, and collected and paid the bills. In return for his labor the captain received free board and the privilege of passing his position on to a friend." Among the best known forts were the Davis, the Nuzum, the Tibbs, the Gregg, the Pastorius, the Protzman, the Tuckwiller, and the St. Clair. The usual price of meals was $2.50 a week. Lodging was provided by nearby residents, some of whom made a business of "rooming students." There was generally no rivalry between the forts, except for friendly games of baseball.[12]

Episcopal Hall.[13] Another residence for men students was Episcopal Hall, on North Boundary Street, first occupied in September. This building was made available through the interest of the

12. Ambler, p. 318.
13. See a long history of the hall by James Sheerin, *New Dominion*, April 24, 1897.

Fig. 37. The Pool Boarding Fort. (West Virginia University Library.)

Fig. 38. Episcopal Hall. (H. L. Grant, *Greater Morgantown.*)

Rt. Rev. George W. Peterkin, bishop of the Episcopal Diocese of West Virginia, who wished to provide facilities for students for the ministry, among others. The building had a library, "and such material comforts as bath rooms, well ventilated bed rooms, parlors, steam heat, electric light, etc." Charges for room and board were sixteen to eighteen dollars per month and Rev. James Sheerin, warden, was in charge of the hall.[14]

"The Great Team." The football team of 1895 was known as "the Great Team." With Harry McCrory as coach and William J. Bruner as captain, the team won five games while losing only one. As described at the time, it was the result of "native skill and brawn and two weeks of instruction by a coach of limited experience but of a willing heart," i.e., it was largely self-trained. The later famous Fielding H. ("Hurry Up") Yost played at left tackle. The sole loss (4 to 0) was at the hands of W. & J., the score coming in the final seconds of play and being protested because of interference.[15]

Mont Chateau Hotel. "On the right bank of the Cheat River amid the rocks and forests which characterize the scenery of the western slopes of the Laurel Mountains, stands the Mont Chateau Hotel, the leading summer resort of this part of the state. The hotel is a commodious and well planned structure, capable of accommodating over a hundred guests. . . . The close proximity of the Cheat river furnishes unexcelled facilities for boating, bathing and fishing, and a large fleet of excellent skiffs is always at the disposal of the guests."[16]

Opera House. An opera house was opened in Morgantown and was attracting good crowds. "The manager . . . is to be congratulated. The receptions given to the stage attractions, so far, have been liberal, and our citizens will continue to patronize first class companies."[17]

A Business Review. A business review of Morgantown listed West Virginia University, the Farmers' and Merchants' Bank,

14. *Woman's Edition of the New Dominion,* December 30, 1896. See also *The Post,* May 18, 1895; Callahan, p. 258. The term "warden" was in accordance with the pattern of Oxford and Cambridge, in England.

15. Ambler, p. 364.

16. *The Post,* July 20, 1895.

17. *The Post,* October 5, 1895.

the Union Improvement Company, George C. Steele (dry goods), A. W. Jones (wallpaper, paint, etc.), S. V. Thompson (ice cream parlor), T. Pickenpaugh (clothing), H. F. Rice and Son (grocers), H. L. Smith (meat market), Madera Brothers (stationers), G. W. John and Company (dry goods), W. H. Bailey (hardware), H. C. Baker (hardware), Meminger's (clothier), Wallace House, Stine's Restaurant, Morgantown Building and Investment Company, George C. Hayes and Company (jewelers), St. Clair Restaurant, Morgantown Brick Company, J. F. Weaver and Son (racket store), Posten's Cash Store, The Leader (notions), W. W. Hayes (livery stable),[18] J. Robe and Son, Minnie L. Daugherty ("Bee Hive Store"), W. E. Jolliff (bakery), P. A. Hennen (furniture, undertaker), Davis and Huston (roofing), T. W. Barker (agricultural implements), A. A. Rogers (photographers), Phillips and Lemon Lumber Company, M. Hayes (livery stable), J. J. Wharton (contractor), Jason Clark (flour, feed), Lough Bros. (carriage factory), E. D. Clear Depot Restaurant, Amos Harris (barber), John W. Kincaid (blacksmith), W. M. Platt (groceries, lunches),[19] A. J. Hicks (stoves, roofing), L. V. Keck (lawyer), P. F. Harner (dairy), J. E. Watts and Company (granite works), Lindsay and Grant (stone work), D. C. Hoffman (thoroughbred Jerseys), and T. Pickenpaugh (fine horses and cattle).[20]

The Farmers' and Merchants' Bank. A new financial institution, the Farmers' and Merchants' Bank, opened for business on October 10, 1895, in the old home of the Bank of the Monongahela Valley, at High and Walnut streets, with a paid-up capital stock of $25,000. One of the largest individual stockholders was Senator Stephen B. Elkins. The first president of the bank was A. W. Lorentz, who resigned a similar position at the Bank of the Monongahela Valley to take this one. He had been principal of the old Monongalia Academy (vol. 3, p. 26) and later director of the preparatory department of the university. The cashier was W. E. Davis.[21]

Behler and Shuman Heights. On a high ridge (elevation sixteen hundred feet above sea level) between Pedlar Run and Indian

18. *The Post,* June 15, 1895.
19. *The Post,* June 22, 1895.
20. *The Post,* June 29, 1895.
21. *New Dominion Industrial Edition* (1906), p. 10; *The Post,* October 19, 1895.

Creek, in the still booming Clay District oil field was the main office of the Shuman[22] District of the South Penn Oil Company. Around the office, in this remote spot, were clustered jerry-built residences of numerous oil workers. The hamlet, known as Shuman Heights, was reached by a rude wagon road via Newberry Hollow, off Pedlar Run, or via Clark Wade's farm, from Indian Creek.

Nearby, on the public road leading from Pedlar Run to Hagans, was established, on September 25, 1895, the Behler post office, with Benjamin M. Simpson as postmaster. The post office, located in Simpson's general store, was named, as was his son, Behler Simpson, for a friend in Wheeling.[23]

Wise M.E. Church. A group of Methodists in the village of Wise, under the leadership of J. W. Sanders, W. A. Wiley, J. W. Wiley, and J. W. Woodruff, in 1895 organized a Methodist Episcopal congregation. They bought a lot with a building on it from Mrs. Lincoln Thomas and remodeled the building for use as a church.[24]

Rev. J. T. Eichelberger. The Reverend J. T. Eichelberger, formerly a minister of the M.E. Church, but now retired, died in January, 1895, aged fifty-five. He was residing at the time of his death at Saint Cloud, Battelle District, where he practiced medicine. At the outbreak of the Civil War he was teaching in Ohio but volunteered for service in the Union army, was captured, and spent nine months in Libby Prison. He weighed one hundred eighty pounds when he went in and only ninety pounds when he was released.[25]

Dr. A. B. Mason. A physician of Wadestown, Dr. A. B. Mason, died March 5, 1895. The son of John Mason, he was born June 4, 1844, and raised at Smithtown. He had practiced medicine at Wadestown for several years "and was very successful as a physician and popular as a citizen." He was U.S. Internal Revenue Collector under President Harrison's administration, but was stricken with paralysis about two years before his death.[26]

22. Named for Ezra Shuman, on whose land the office was built.
23. Core, *Chronicles of Core*, pp. 166, 167, 184.
24. Dodds and Dodds, p. 137.
25. *Wheeling Intelligencer*, January 25, 1895.
26. *The Post*, March 9, 16, 1895.

David Herstein. A well-known merchant and restaurant owner of Morgantown, David Herstein (D. H. Stine), died April 12, 1895. He was born in Hesse-Darmstadt November 3, 1829, and came to Morgantown in 1854. He was in the clothing business until the outbreak of the Civil War, when he enlisted in the Quartermaster's Department. He was captured at the battle of Frankfort, Tennessee, but was released because he and his captors were all Odd Fellows.

He married Sisson, daughter of George W. Dorsey, and they had ten children, six of whom survived, namely, George W., Jacob, Dorsey, Richard, Nellie, and Lucy. "He was a great reader, and was well informed on ancient and modern history, as well as on the current news of the day."[27]

Miscellany. In 1895: Alexander Thomas, son of James Grant and Harriet B. (Quarrier) Laidley, died in Charleston; he was born in Morgantown April 14, 1807, and married Dorcas S. Blaine, a cousin of James G. Blaine (Callahan, p. 84; Hardesty's "Kanawha County," Comstock ed., p. 188). . . . The Dering building on Walnut Street was built (Callahan, p. 253). . . . In October the Bank of the Monongahela Valley was moved from its old home at the corner of High and Pleasant streets to the new IOOF building at High and Walnut streets (Callahan, p. 254). . . . Benjamin Liming, son of John and Susannah (Lemley) Liming, of the head of Dunkard Creek, Battelle District, died July 15; born October 2, 1825, he married Zilpha Core (Headlee, *George Lemley*, p. 104). . . . John Barrickman, son of John and Barbara (Pickenpaugh) Barrickman, of Clay District, died in April, aged eighty-two years (Core, *Chronicles of Core*, p. 150). . . . The Liming Church of Christ building, in Battelle District, burned and a new structure was erected (Dodds and Dodds, p. 132). . . . The cornerstone was laid for the Bethel Baptist Church, in Clinton District near Triune (Dodds and Dodds, p. 138). . . . A long history of Easton, by George W. Laishley, was published (*The Post,* February 23, March 2, 1895). . . . Eli White, of Saint Cloud, died March 2; the son of John White, he born December 14, 1835 (*The Post,* March 6, 1895). . . . Thomas Stevens, of Miracle Run, died February 25, aged eighty-seven years (*The Post,* March 16, 1895). . . . Frank Pride bought a new express wagon and now had two to

27. *The Post,* April 20, 1895.

handle his increasing baggage business (*The Post,* March 16, 1895). . . . D. W. Hoffman, of Cassville, died March 15, survived by his wife and five children (*The Post,* March 23, 1895). . . . Lyttle Clayton, the father of Dr. J. P. Clayton, died near Arnettsville, aged eighty-six years (*The Post,* March 23, 1895). . . . Minerva Shuman, wife of W. R. Shuman, of Dolls Run, died of cancer March 17 (*The Post,* March 30, 1895). . . . A Morgantown branch of the Mutual German Savings and Loan Association of Wheeling was organized March 28, with M. T. Sisler president (*The Post,* April 6, 1895). . . . Hirschman's Clothing House, opposite the courthouse, was enlarged and thereafter was referred to as the "Big Store" (*The Post,* April 20, 1895). . . . The new Odd Fellows Hall was dedicated on November 20, with a meeting of the Grand Lodge (November 23, 30, 1895). . . . Silas Wisman, son of Philip and Christina Wisman, died near Lowsville December 25; he was born September 14, 1814 (*The Post,* January 11, 1896). . . . An item in the Washington, Pennsylvania, *Observer* said that a trip to Morgantown on one of the Pittsburg, Brownsville and Morgantown packet boats is hard to beat (*The Post,* August 10, 1895). . . . Lancelot John, of near Stewartstown, died August 9, aged eighty-two years (*The Post,* August 17, 1895). . . . Hundreds of people attended Emancipation Day exercises in Morgantown in October (*Martinsburg Pioneer Press,* quoted in *The Post,* October 12, 1895). . . . The first oil well in Battelle District came in November 6 on the A. J. Corrothers farm near Cross Roads; South Penn Oil Company officials estimate the production at over five hundred barrels a day (*The Post,* November 16, 1895). . . . On February 4 a teamster near Osage rolled a log on the gas line supplying Morgantown; the temperature dropped to four degrees above zero that night, but the gas supply was not restored until next day at 2:00 p.m. (*The Post,* February 9, 1895). . . . Michael Sheets died June 17, aged sixty-two years (*The Post,* July 20, 1895). . . . John Sutton, son of Joseph and Mary Sutton, of Cass District, died Oct. 21, 1895, aged eighty-five years (*Chronicles of Core,* p. 150). . . . Major William W. John, of Stewartstown, died March 12 (*The Post,* March 16, 1895; Wiley, p. 675). . . . John H. Hoffman, Morgantown businessman, died July 8 (*The Post,* July 13, 1895). . . . Morgantown became a station for the M.P. church in 1894 and in 1895 Rev. I. A. Barnes became station minister (Barnes, p. 118).

CHAPTER ONE HUNDRED TWENTY

1896

A new industry came to Monongalia County in 1896, one that would not only be among the leading industries of the county from that time until the present, but also one which would give a distinctive trend to the economy that would make Morgantown's products known internationally.

The Seneca Glass Company. The Seneca Glass Company was first organized in Fostoria, Ohio, in 1891 and operated there for about five years until 1896, when it was moved to Morgantown, the first of several large industrial concerns to take advantage of the excellent inducements offered here. The company, after thoroughly investigating conditions here, readily recognized that few places in the nation provided such favorable conditions for their purpose.

Shipping facilities, with the opening of rail service to Pittsburgh, were excellent. Steamboat transportation on the river was also available. What appealed most to the owners were apparently inexhaustible supplies of natural gas, from the nearby Dolls Run field, still under development. Glass sand was available from Berkeley Springs, West Virginia, and Hancock, Maryland. Choice glass sand also outcropped in the Deckers Creek Valley, a very choice sand which could be used in the manufacture of glass table ware, plate glass, mirrors, and prism glass. A careful chemical test showed that it contained 99½ percent pure silica, with a slight trace of iron oxide. It was almost snowy white in color, sharp and clean cut in grain. Its nearness meant that it would cost the company less than one-third what it had been paying at its previous location.

Another advantage was the site offered, a tract of four acres on a flat along the Monongahela River, and beside the newly opened railroad to Connellsville and Pittsburgh.

Fig. 39. The Seneca Glass Factory.

When first organized the capital stock was $40,000 but this was increased to $100,000 the year of the removal to Morgantown. Among original stockholders were August Boehler, Leopold Sigwart, Otto Sigwart, C. H. Koch, George Truog, and A. Kammerer. These men had backgrounds of years of experience in the manufacture of glass; some of them had been connected with glass factories since their youth. August Boehler, for example, was already among the leading fancy glass operators in the country, and some of the most skilled designers and etchers of the country were on the staff.

The firm turned out many kinds of high grade thin lead, blown, bar and table glassware, including fine cut stem ware, finger bowls, goblets and jugs, water bottles, nappies and tumblers. The ware was cut in thousands of different patterns and was also needle or acid etched in every manner known to glass manufacturing.[1]

1. The plant soon became a fourteen-pot factory, furnishing employment for 250 people—150 men, 50 boys, and 50 girls—100 of whom were skilled laborers. The monthly payroll averaged ten thousand dollars and the weekly product reached three carloads, chiefly lead-blown table ware, all hand-blown. Callahan, pp. 268, 269.

Livery Stables. In 1896, despite the fact that most people were traveling by train on intercity trips, short-distance travel was still on horseback or in light carriages, such as buggies or surries. Morgantown's hotels had livery stables nearby, for accommodations of this sort.

The word livery is related to Old French and Middle English words designating the allowance to servants and peasants of the materials necessary for living, as food, clothing, etc. Later it came to refer to a distinctive dress, as a servant's uniform, and, in another sense, to the equipment essential for travel, including horses, saddles, carriages, and the like.

Travelers stopped for meals or lodging at ordinaries, or taverns, while the "livery" was accommodated in an associated building, or in a nearby establishment under separate management.

In early Morgantown most of the taverns doubtless had stables for the horses on the same grounds. Later, as the population became more congested, it seemed more desirable to have the equipages accommodated some distance away.

Captain William N. Jarrett, a well-known tavern keeper in 1809, ran a livery stable and blacksmith shop associated with his hostelry on High Street at the corner of Maiden Alley (now Wall Street).

But by 1880 the livery stable was mostly separate from the hotel. James Bell advertised that he kept for hire good carriage and saddle horses, single or double teams, buggies, carriages, and sleighs, and also carried passengers to and from all points at reasonable rates.

For several years the Peabody and the Wallace House maintained private livery stables. The Wallace used the W. H. Hayes livery, at the corner of Spruce Street and Maiden Alley.

In 1896 four "first class" livery stables were being operated in Morgantown. The largest and best known was located at the corner of Kirk Alley (later Kirk Street) and Middle Alley, behind the Presbyterian church. It was conducted by Squire Manliff Hayes, who was in the livery business in Morgantown for almost half a century, and whose father, Alexander Hayes, had been one of Morgantown's best known stagecoach operators.

The livery stable of Cel Carrico, at the corner of Court Alley (later Chancery Row) and Middle Alley, was patronized largely by the Franklin House management and enjoyed a good business.

Hotels and Taverns. Up until the 1890s Morgantown was mostly served by five hotels, most of which had been in operation at the same spot for a long time. The Franklin House (vol. 3, p. 82) at the corner of Walnut Street and Middle or Long Alley (now Chestnut Street) was on a site where some sort of tavern had stood since around 1781, serving in pioneer days not only as a hotel, but also as a fort and, later, as a general store. Proprietors included Alex Hayes, C. S. Finnell, and James Hopkins. It was known for its cellar retreat, where there was a fine spring of water, and good liquor was stored.

The Wallace House (vol. 3, p. 644), on High Street north of Walnut, stood on the site where Captain Jarrett had opened a tavern as early as 1805, continuing it until his death in 1828 (and his widow ran the same business until her death in 1849). John Wallace bought the property in 1866, built a brick building, and his son, James C. Wallace, opened the hotel in 1871.

The old National Hotel, on High Street opposite the courthouse, was built in 1798 by Isaac Hite Williams and several persons kept tavern in it, including Hugh McNeely, Elihu Horton, John Addison (who called it the "Old Dominion"), and Addison S. Vance (who named it the "National," in 1847). J. Keener Durr bought the building, tore it down, and erected a new building for the hotel which he named the "Commercial," opening it March 9, 1878. It was later named the Peabody Hotel.

The St. Clair House (vol. 3, p. 203), on the northwest corner of Walnut Street and Front Street, was built by Nicholas B. Madera, and numerous people kept tavern in it, including J. W. Saer, John J. Pierpont, John Devore, Samuel Darnell, and N. N. Hoffman. Samuel Snyder, who was running it in 1869, called it the "Virginia House." In 1873 F. H. St. Clair became the proprietor and named it the St. Clair House.

Another place was the famous "Temperance Hotel," operated by "Granny" Marsh on Front Street.

In 1896 the local hotels appeared to be prosperous, although they had been charging only twenty-five cents for a room and twenty-five cents for meals. Prices were beginning to rise, however.

The University. Under the administration of President Goodknight the enrollment continued to grow, increasing from 283 in 1894-95 to 398 in 1895-96. The public began to predict "a new era for the University," which became a slogan for alumni groups.

The president, who previously had written his own correspondence and recorded student grades, was provided with a secretary in the person of D. M. Willis. The secretary, who was a member of the legislature, was paid fifty dollars a month and in addition to his service for the president, taught bookkeeping, writing, penmanship, and arithmetic in the preparatory school. During 1896 the school of chemistry and physics was divided and Thomas E. Hodges, principal of Marshall College, was made head of physics. Professor A. R. Whitehill remained head of chemistry.

Although progressive in many ways, President Goodknight had problems with student discipline. The faculty, on March 5, 1896, passed an order suspending any student who was absent from chapel three times without an acceptable excuse. Classes began at 8:15 a.m. each school day and students were required to assemble in Chapel Hall at 10:45 each day for roll call and announcements. A short, simple, devotional service followed, which students were not required to attend.

But the students objected to compulsory chapel attendance and found all sorts of excuses for being absent. More and more faculty time was required for disciplinary problems. A note in the minutes of a September 21, 1896, faculty meeting said: "The matter up for discussion was the ubiquitous, perennial chapel question with its attendant disturbances."

The problem gradually resulted in a split, not only between the president and the students, but between the president and the faculty as well.

The Military Ball. In the early years of the school, university-sponsored dances were forbidden. But upon the completion of the gymnasium in 1893 students insisted on using it for dances and, beginning in that year, a military ball was held there. In April 1894 the Military Ball was described as "The Grandest Affair of the Season."[2] In 1896 the faculty voted to use the gymnasium for revival services sponsored by the YMCA and the students held the Military Ball in Professor Hartigan's lecture room in Woodburn Hall.

The regents, in October 1896, voted to leave the matter of student dances in the hands of the commandant of cadets, the super-

2. *Athenaeum,* April 1894.

intendent of buildings and grounds, and the director of the gymnasium. Under their direction student dances were held in the gymnasium during the 1896-97 term.[3]

Football. T. G. ("Doggie") Trenchard, Princeton All-American in 1893, was employed as a regular coach for the football team in 1896. Although the coach placed himself in the lineup at times, and "Hurry Up" Yost continued to play at tackle, the team was not as successful as it had been the previous year. Three games were played with Lafayette College, all of which were lost; two with the Duquesne Country and Athletic Club; and two with the Latrobe Independents.[4]

Destructive Floods. The highest waters since 1888 resulted from several days' rain in July. Streams already high were forced out of their banks by a very heavy rain starting early in the morning of the twenty-fourth. This rain stopped about ten o'clock in the morning, but an additional downpour of near-cloudburst proportions fell on Miracle Run in the afternoon.

"Dunkard Creek came up rapidly and the covered bridge at John Brown's was washed off its abutments, drifting downstream towards the South bridge where G. W. ('Wash') Piles was catching sheaves of oats and wheat that were floating on the water. He escaped just before the big wooden structure struck the iron bridge. Buoyed up by its plank floor, the latter floated around the curve in the creek before it sank to the bottom, a crumpled mass of steel. The wooden bridge floated several miles, finally going aground near Mt. Morris. Later the covered bridge from Brown's Mills came drifting down, mowing off huge trees in its course. Leonard Shanks rescued Mrs. Mary Ann Brown from an upper story window as she facetiously lamented the fact that all 'the fences are washed away and your cows will get in my garden.' "[5]

The loss sustained by county farmers was heavy. Meadows and fields of corn along creek bottoms were flooded. Wheat and oats in stacks were washed away and grass standing and in stack was ruined. Roads were made impassable because of missing bridges

3. Ambler, pp. 317-20.
4. Ambler, p. 365.
5. Core, *Chronicles of Core*, p. 152.

and washed-out stretches of highway. It was feared that it would be necessary to raise the tax rate to repair the damage. One fatality was reported, from Little Indian Creek. John L. Fetty, a prominent and well-known farmer of that section, lost his life: "The creek began to rise at a menacing speed when Mr. Fetty and his son attempted to move a pile of rails that was in danger of being carried away. The bank upon which he was standing gave way and carried Mr. Fetty into the raging torrent, sweeping him away in an instant. A heavy overcoat which he wore became entangled about his head, rendering him helpless and caused him to drown in a very short time. His body was recovered some distance below where the accident happened but life had been extinct for some time."[6]

No fewer than twelve bridges were gone from Dunkard Creek and its branches. On the main stream only one bridge remained from the mouth of Miracle Run to Mount Morris, five large bridges being swept away in a distance of twelve miles. The only one left in this stretch was at Pentress and it was badly damaged.

John A. Dille (Portrait, fig. 139, vol. 3). Judge John Adams Dille died December 18, 1896, in Morgantown. Born July 19, 1821, he was the son of Ezra Dille, of Washington County, Pennsylvania. He moved to Kingwood in 1843 and studied law under William G. Brown, opening a law office in Kingwood in 1844. He married Rachel, daughter of Elisha M. Hagans, who died about three years later, leaving one son, Oliver Hagans. He later married Linnie S., daughter of Thomas Brown, and they had two children, Clarence Brown and Mary McFarland Dille.

He was a member of the Wheeling Constitutional Convention in 1861 and was active in framing the constitution of the new state.[7]

John A. Dille was elected judge of the Second Judicial Circuit and served three terms, from 1863 until 1873.

Dr. H. N. Mackey. One of Morgantown's oldest and best known physicians, Dr. Horatio N. Mackey, died on January 22, 1896. His practice in Morgantown for forty-three years was interrupted only by the time he served in the Union army in a cavalry com-

---

6. *The Post*, August 1, 1896.
7. *One Hundred Seventy-Fifth Anniversary . . .*, pp. 412, 413.

pany. He was born December 19, 1828, in Fayette County, Pennsylvania.[8]

New Presbyterian Church. A new building for the Morgantown Presbyterian Church was dedicated on December 13, 1896. After the burning of the Morgantown Female Seminary the congregation had secured a portion of the property that had been used by that institution, so that more space was available for construction.

The last service in the old building (vol. 3, fig. 109) was held in July 1895, the cornerstone of the new structure was laid October 19, 1895, and on June 28, 1896, they "worshipped for the first time in their new temple."

"The dimensions of the church are 82 x 101 feet; auditorium has bowled floor, and its seating capacity is four hundred. The lecture room adjoins the Auditorium, separated by a rolling partition. This will seat three hundred and in connection with the lecture room are three class rooms and a library. A ladies' parlor, with outside entrance at the rear, is also part of the plan. In the basement are arranged a commodious dining room and kitchen."

The building was constructed of dark red selected brick, embellished with dark iron mottled buff brick and Cleveland stone trimmings. The ceilings were arched and made of clear, narrow yellow pine. The pews were of quartered oak. The interior was made beautiful by art glass windows.[9]

Miscellany. In 1896: Episcopal Hall, on North Boundary Street, was formally opened on January 18 for Episcopal students attending the university (Callahan, pp. 257, 258; *The Post*, January 25, 1896). . . . Isaac Shelby Cox, of Indian Creek, died February 7, aged sixty-eight years; he married Catherine Snider and four sons survived, viz., John D., Elisha M., Dr. N. B., and G. G. Cox (*The Post*, February 15, 1896). . . . The Wadestown Telephone Company elected Elias Eddy president; "the telephone and the POST keep us civilized" (*The Post*, February 22, 1896). . . . Walker Whiteside, tragedian, filled an engagement at the Opera House on February 24 (*The Post*, February 22, 1896).

8. *The Post*, January 25, 1896.
9. Mrs. Lee C. Corbett, *Woman's Edition, New Dominion*, December 31, 1896; James R. Moreland, *First Presbyterian* Church, pp. 38-44.

. . . Members of the Congressional Rivers and Harbors Committee visited Fairmont and Morgantown to study, among other items, extension of slack water to Fairmont (*The Post*, March 28, 1896). . . . Dr. I. C. White made a trip to the West Indies in February and related the events in a long newspaper article (*The Post*, April 4, 1896). . . . William M. Jones, of Laurel Point, died April 12; he was born January 4, 1808 (*The Post*, April 18, 1896). . . . Ring and Company opened a general store at Ringgold, on the Evansville Pike, with E. Ring manager (*The Post*, June 6, 1896). . . . University students established an annual publication known as the *Monticola*; the first volume was dedicated to I. C. White (Ambler, p. 358).

1897

The decade of the nineties was Morgantown's period of transition from a village to a small town, on its way to becoming a small city. On September 7, 1897, the first issue of the first daily newspaper, the *Daily New Dominion*, appeared.

The *New Dominion* had been established as a weekly by Julian E. Fleming and William L. Jacobs in April 1876. The name was an obvious reference to the formation of the new state of West Virginia, less than thirteen years earlier. In full faith of a great future for West Virginia, the founders selected the title, reasoning as Virginia was the "Old Dominion" why should not West Virginia become the "New Dominion"?

Fleming was born in Morgantown, attended West Virginia University, and in 1874, with Jacobs, began the publication of the monthly sixteen-page *University Bulletin*. This periodical ran until 1876, when they started the weekly *New Dominion*.

During commencement week at West Virginia University, in 1876, the *New Dominion* (four pages, thirteen by twenty inches) was issued daily and this continued during that week until 1880, when this function was transferred to a paper, the *University Daily*, issued under the editorial charge of the students. This, in a sense, was the forerunner of the later *Daily Athenaeum*.

The Daily New Dominion. Justin M. Kunkle was the first editor of the *Daily New Dominion*. Announcing the new project, he said:

"The NEW DOMINION has led in newspaper enterprise in this town for the last two decades.

"It has published the largest and newsiest weekly for the least money ever offered in Morgantown. It has maintained the most thoroughly equipped newspaper establishment of any town in the State of the same population. It has the largest and the greatest variety of type, the most complete outfit job material, the most expensive and most modern press machinery, all moved by steam. In short, it has always been the policy of the NEW DOMINION to be up to date if not a little in advance of the procession.

"We have looked forward with some impatience to the time when the local conditions would justify launching a daily edition and giving our readers the news crisp and fresh every day instead of once a week. We now venture upon this new departure relying upon the broad and generous spirit of this growing town to justify the step, and feeling assured that if we are in advance of the town from a numerical point of view we are not in the enterprising spirit which pervades this population. . . .

"The NEW DOMINION is not an experiment, but an established fact from this first number, and if you wish to be up to date, send in your name and we will leave it at your door."

Old Monongalia Academy Burns. One of Monongalia County's most familiar landmarks, the old Monongalia Academy building, was wrecked by fire on January 11, 1897, ending an honorable career extending over three quarters of a century.

"Monday noon the alarm of fire brought the citizens out to witness the partial destruction of old Monongalia Academy. The fire caught up in the cupola and it is supposed to have been due to the carelessness of several small boys who were up there playing. They came rushing down and excitedly told Prof. Jaco that the building was on fire. The alarm was promptly given and before the fire laddies could respond the entire attic was a mass of flames. The attic was piled full of plunder of every description, old desks, boxes and inflammable stuff of all sorts making it one of the best places for the spread of fire that could be imagined. It was sometime after getting on the scene before the water was turned on and when the first stream struck the building it seemed doomed to certain destruction. Owing to its extent, it proved to be a great difficulty to subdue it. The windows affording ingress to the attic were small and but a limited portion could be reached from any one of them. This necessitated a constant change of base and during the intervals the flames would almost regain their former headway. A couple of sections of hose were taken inside the building and the fire fought from the inside. Many of the firemen deserve great credit for their efforts but owing to the smoke and confusion but a few of them were noticed. Chief Christie accompanied by several men fought their way right into

Fig. 40. Burning of the old Monongalia Academy.

the center of the flames and to their work much of the credit must be given. The dangers encountered by many of the men were certainly appalling and were much greater than ordinary on account of the nature of the fire. The high wind which was blowing not only fanned the flames to greater fury but added greatly to the discomfort of the men who in many cases were drenched with the icy water. Their clothing was frozen on them in many instances and the physical discomfort undergone was very great. The fire was finally gotten under control but the entire roof and attic were ruined. The old cupola has almost disappeared and the plastering ruined with the rest of the building by the water. A great many of the school books belonging to the children were also spoiled and many tears shed by the sorrowful urchins over the loss of some dearly beloved, dog-eared volume. . . .''

"The destruction of this building removes one of the old landmarks of Morgantown and in fact of this section of the state. The most complete and satisfactory sketch of the Academy is that contained in the 'Monticola' of last year. . . . It is as follows:

" 'There are many men, and these of the number of our most distinguished citizens throughout our state and other states of the union, in whose patriotic hearts the name of old Monongalia Academy lies enshrined as sacred today as it was in the years of long ago.

" 'The last roar of English guns had not ceased to reverberate on our coasts when our people "west of the mountains" in their desire for a higher education, had secured the passage of an act by the Virginia Legislature of 1814 incorporating the Monongalia Academy.' "[1]

A New School Building? Even before the fire, a movement of citizens had proposed either an addition to the old building or construction of a new one. The loss caused by the fire was estimated at $6,500 and when the insurance company proposed to repair the old building, considerable controversy arose. This controversy was resolved "by the providential destruction of remaining parts of the building by a dynamite explosion of unknown (?) origin."[2]

Following the explosion a new controversy arose when the insurance company refused to pay. The company lost, however, in the resulting law suit which was finally decided by the State Supreme Court, before which Frank Cox presented the case for the board of education.

Meanwhile scattered rooms about town and portions of church buildings were rented for grade school and high school classes.[3]

The Agricultural Experiment Station. The state grange and the state board of agriculture were becoming more and more critical of J. A. Myers, dean of agriculture and director of the Agricultural Experiment Station. He was regarded as too impractical to serve the needs of "dirt farmers" of the state.

T. C. Atkeson, of Putnam County, in January 1897, became master of the state grange and visited his relative, Governor George W. Atkinson, to urge the appointment of a farmer to the

---

1. *Daily New Dominion,* January 16, 1897.
2. Callahan, p. 259. In a footnote Callahan adds: "The origin was known only to a few who kept the secret, but a quarter century later admitted that two young men, filled with the fermented spirits of beer and probably not numbered with those who were accused of being intoxicated with the spirit of progress, performed the dynamic amputation to stop the community argument."
3. Callahan, p. 259.

board of regents. The governor responded by appointing Atkeson himself to the board. Other board members agreed to his proposals to make the university more responsive to the needs of the farmers and appointed Atkeson dean of the College of Agriculture, in succession to Dr. Myers. The next step was to remove Dr. Myers from the directorship of the Experiment Station and to replace him by J. H. Stewart, of Putnam County.[4]

President Goodknight Is Fired. Problems of student discipline at the university continued to become aggravated. The board of regents, in appointing James L. Goodknight as president of the institution, had given him power to enforce rules and regulations. Being reluctant to exercise his authority, the faculty was required to devote much time to disciplinary problems. This led to a three-way friction between the president, the faculty, and the students.

A new board of regents took over in June 1897 and the new president of the board was George C. Sturgiss, "a politician-industrialist and promoter with a penchant for doing things in a big way." S. B. Brown was named secretary. To clear the stage for a "new era at the University," the board, influenced by Sturgiss, called for the resignation of President Goodknight, effective August 9, 1897. Failing to produce the desired result, the regents, in a special meeting on August 6, declared the presidency vacant and revoked the powers and duties of President Goodknight.[5]

Jerome Hall Raymond. The regents had named Robert A. Armstrong as vice-president and acting president, but negotiations were already under way with Dr. J. H. Raymond, who was interested in the presidency. At the meeting on August 6, he was elected to the position and took over his duties, thus essentially nullifying the tenure of Professor Armstrong as acting president.[6]

Dr. Raymond was born in Clinton, Iowa, on March 10, 1869, and received a Ph.D. at the University of Chicago. At the time of his election he was professor of sociology at the University of Wisconsin. He was inexperienced in administration, but "was in

4. Ambler, pp. 321, 322.
5. Ambler, pp. 320, 321.
6. See account of his inauguration, *Weekly Post,* October 20, 1897.

Fig. 41. Jerome H. Raymond.   Fig. 42. James W. Hartigan.
(West Virginia University.)

touch with many educational leaders, which unfortunately
tended to foster his penchant for the faddish, the impractical, and
the extravagant."

The football team in the fall of 1897, made a creditable showing
under the management of T. E. Hodges, a faculty member.
George Krebs, who had been captain of the team the year before,
was the coach.[7]

The Cadet Corps. In 1897 the legislature increased the number of
authorized cadets to 144 and made its first appropriation for purchase of uniforms. At the same time the corps was made part of
the West Virginia National Guard and designated as "the public
guard of the University." After having been raised to school
status in 1895, the courses in military training and tactics were
restored to departmental status in 1897.

The greatest concern was for suitable storage for equipment
and room to drill in bad weather. An armory, built in 1873, was

7. Ambler, p. 365.

Fig. 43-A. The university cadet corps.

Fig. 43-B. University armory.

enlarged and taken over by the Agricultural Experiment Station in 1889. In rainy weather the corridors of Woodburn Hall were used for drill until 1893, when, upon the completion of Commencement Hall, the basement (gymnasium) was made available.[8]

State Geological Survey. On February 26, 1897, the legislature authorized the establishment of the West Virginia Geological and Economic Survey. The need for a state geologist had been noted as early as 1864 and the prospective benefits of a survey had been pointed out by numerous scientists and others (including nonresident capitalists).

A commission to govern the survey was appointed, composed of the governor, the state treasurer, the university president, the president of the state board of agriculture, and the director of the Agricultural Experiment Station.

At the first meeting of the commission Morgantown was designated as the headquarters of the survey and Dr. I. C. White its director. S. B. Brown, of the university faculty, was designated part-time assistant geologist.[9]

New Bridges. The old covered bridge across Deckers Creek near its mouth, a landmark for generations, was replaced in 1897. The bridge, connecting Morgantown with old Durbannah, also served turnpike travelers headed towards Kingwood, Evansville or Clarksburg.

The new bridge was built on the same site, but was much longer and at a higher level so as to avoid the old winding descent from Foundry Street.[10]

Also replaced during 1897 were bridges along Dunkard Creek, some of which, the year before, had been washed away for the third time (1877, 1888, 1896). As previously, the abutments were raised in an effort to prevent a fourth such occurrence.

Town of Blacksville. The town of Blacksville, which had been established by the state of Virginia on February 3, 1830 (vol. 3, p. 42), was incorporated as a municipality under the laws of West Virginia on October 22, 1897. It became the third incorporated

8. Ambler, pp. 377-79.
9. Ambler, p. 381.
10. Callahan, p. 262.

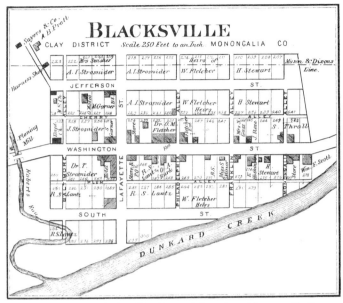

Fig. 44-A. Map of Blacksville. (From *Atlas of . . . Monongalia County*, 1886.)

Fig. 44-B. The Dunkard Valley Bank. (Courtesy Sara I. Scott.)

town in the county. Ira E. Hall was the first mayor, L. L. Thomas the first recorder, Jacob Wells, A. C. Johnson, A. I. Strosnider, Abraham Emery, and William E. Scott the first councilmen.

The Monongahela River Railroad. Since 1889 the Monongahela River Railroad, running up the West Fork from Fairmont, had provided Morgantown residents with a more direct connection to Clarksburg. In 1897 this link became a part of the Baltimore and Ohio system.[11]

Morgantown Savings and Loan Society. Largely stimulated by the influx of factory people, the Morgantown Savings and Loan Society was organized April 3, 1897, the first permanent local institution opening under an approved State Charter (dated February 2, 1897).[12]

The Seneca Glass Works. "This imposing substantial structure with its 18 tributary shops lend an air of busy life to the former quietude of Beechurst Avenue. . . .

"By the present contract 250 people are employed. This business will necessitate them as soon as arrangements can be made to enlarge their factory to 28 shops, when their pay roll will show up in the neighborhood of 500 employees. . . . The output with the present working force in tumblers alone is 3,000 dozen per day. If the natural gas was to go off for one short hour while the glass was being tempered the firm would sustain a loss of $2,000.

"They manufacture only in the white glassware, and their specialties are water pitchers, water bottles, finger bowls, goblets, punch tumblers, sherbet glasses and all kinds of diminutive glasses for cordials."[13]

New Post Offices. Two new post offices for Monongalia County were established in 1897.

A post office named Jaco, in Union District north of the Pierpont community, was set up October 13, 1897, with William L. Jaco as postmaster.

Another Union District post office, called Tyrone, was established December 22, 1897. Located on the road from Dellslow to Ice's Ferry, it had Samuel L. Shafer as the first postmaster.

11. Callahan, p. 245.
12. Callahan, p. 254.
13. *New Dominion*, January 16, 1897.

Contracts Let for New Navigation Aids. With authorization of the U.S. Congress, contracts were let in May for construction of six locks and dams on the Monongahela River between Morgantown and Fairmont, extending slack-water navigation to the very head of the Monongahela, where the West Fork and the Tygart Valley rivers join. The contract went to James McGarron, of Philadelphia, and called for completion of the work in six years. Prices on each lock were: No. 10, $95,059.35; No. 11, $119,618.64; No. 12, $111.953.19; No. 13, $99,785.65; No. 14, $97,905.10; No. 15, $97,862.21.[14]

At the same time Congress awarded the Monongahela Navigation Company the sum of $3,761,715 for the locks and dams which the company had constructed and operated between Pittsburgh and Morgantown. After July 14 tolls were no longer charged and the river was free for its entire length.[15]

In August 1897 the contract to McCarron was canceled by the secretary of war because of the failure of the company to furnish the necessary performance bond.[16] Bids were advertised again and in the fall the contract was awarded to C. I. McDonald, of Pittsburgh. His bids were as follows: Locks 10 and 11, $211,990.23; Locks 12 and 13, $191,951.21; and Locks 14 and 15, $197,272.56.[17]

Joseph Alan McLane. A well-known physician of Morgantown, Dr. Joseph A. McLane, died January 3, 1894, in Steubenville, Ohio, at the home of his son, Dr. Charles H. McLane, where he had lived for two years. He was born at Connellsville, Pennsylvania, March 28, 1820, the son of Charles and Elizabeth McLane (see many references in vol. 3; vol. 4, p. 14).

He studied medicine under his father and completed his course at the age of eighteen in Jefferson Medical College, Philadelphia. "He was engaged in the active practice of medicine in Morgantown for 40 years. His skill attracted attention even at an' early age and gained for him all the practice he could possibly attend to."

Dr. McLane married Mary, daughter of William Lazier, who

14. *New Dominion,* May 29, 1897.
15. *New Dominion,* May 22, 1897.
16. *New Dominion,* August 14, 1897.
17. *New Dominion,* November 24, 1897.

Fig. 45. Dr. Joseph Alan McLane and his children. (From Chandler, *Three Mc-Lane Doctors*, 1951.)

preceded him in death. He was survived by the following children: Dr. Charles H. and Alan E. McLane, of Steubenville; Mrs. Lizzie D. Zollar, of Baltimore; and Dr. William L. McLane, of West Union.

"At the time of the raid of the rebel General Jones [during the Civil War] it was the argument of Dr. McLane, with a committee of Morgantown citizens, that saved the bridge across the Monongahela at that point from destruction. Dr. McLane said to Jones when the latter said he intended to burn the bridge, and his men were already kindling the fire upon it, 'You had better leave the bridge to escape back on if you are attacked and forced to retreat.' The rebel leader thought this good logic and countermanded the order."[18]

Dr. Alex. Martin. The first president of West Virginia University, Dr. Alexander Martin, died December 16, 1893, at Greencastle,

18. *The Post*, January 13, 1894. For another tradition of the saving of the suspension bridge, see vol. 3, p. 543.

Indiana; he had gone to Greenfield to officiate at the wedding of two of his former pupils, and caught a severe cold, which resulted in his death. "Probably no man in Greencastle was so universally respected and loved as Dr. Alexander Martin."[19]

He was born in Scotland in 1822 and in 1867 became president of the institution which became West Virginia University in 1868. He resigned in 1875 and became president of Asbury (later DePauw) University the same year.

He married Caroline C. Hursey and they had five children, James V., John E., Charles A., Edwin L., and Anna.

New Baptist Church. The new Morgantown Baptist Church, on High Street, was dedicated on December 19, 1897, with Dr. W. A. Stanton, of Pittsburgh, giving the dedicatory sermon. He was assisted by Rev. W. E. Powell, of Parkersburg.

Fig. 46. First Baptist Church, Morgantown.
(Photo by Gideon S. Dodds.)

19. *Greencastle Banner Times*, December 16, 1893, copied in *The Post*, December 30, 1893.

A new building had been talked of by the congregation for a quarter of a century, but no active steps were taken until Rev. Ross Ward was called as pastor in October 1891. The old property on Long Alley was sold and a lot on High Street was secured, on which a church was begun in 1894, the contract being taken by Wood and Zearley. At first, work progressed rapidly, then money ran out and the work was stopped. Rev. J. L. McCutcheon was called to the pastorate June 1, 1897, and under his direction the work was resumed and quickly brought to completion.

On the first floor was an audience and Sunday school room, besides three classrooms. On the second floor was the pastor's study and a large general purpose room. The seating capacity was six hundred and the total cost was fifteen thousand dollars.[20]

Sturgisson Methodist Church. Judge G. C. Sturgiss, in 1897, donated land for a church to be located along Deckers Creek about nine miles east of Morgantown. The location had been used for a number of years as a campground for black people. Rev. O. W. Waters was responsible for the organization of a Methodist congregation and the erection of a small frame church, in a beautiful setting of forest trees and shrubs.[21]

Miscellany. In 1897: A main oil pipeline from Elm Run, Ritchie County, was completed to Morgantown, making at least five lines feeding into the tank field (Callahan, p. 250). . . . There was still only one main sewer in Morgantown, emptying directly into the river just above the wharf where packet boats loaded and unloaded their freight and passengers (Callahan, p. 265). . . . Morgantown postal receipts were twelve thousand dollars (Callahan, p. 284). . . . A new church building was erected by the Blacksville M.E. congregation (Dodds and Dodds, p. 125). . . . A new attempt (unsuccessful) was made to set up a new county, with Mannington as the county seat, to include parts of Monongalia, Marion, and Wetzel counties (*New Dominion*, January 23, 1897). . . . Jefferson Tennant opened a flour and feed mill in South Morgantown (*New Dominion*, February 6, 1897). . . . Mrs. Sarah B., wife of Judge J. M. Hagans, died March 6 (*New Dominion*, March 13, 1897). . . . H. L. Swisher opened the Acme Book Store in Morgan-

20. *New Dominion*, December 22, 1897.
21. Dodds and Dodds, p. 89.

town on March 12 (*New Dominion,* March 13, 1897).... Employees of the Seneca Glass Company organized a Turn Verein Chapter, to encourage athletics and good fellowship, and erected a two-story clubhouse with a gymnasium and dancing hall (*New Dominion,* July 24, 1897).... The Peoples' Telephone Company opened a line to Fairmont (*New Dominion,* July 31, 1897) and another to Mont Chateau (*New Dominion,* August 7, 1897). ... Mont Chateau was having its most successful season with eighty guests, a capacity crowd, during the season (*New Dominion,* August 21, 1897).... The Union Improvement Company installed filters to purify Morgantown's supply of drinking water (*New Dominion,* August 21, 1897).... Charles Johnson's flouring mill, near Dellslow, was destroyed by fire on April 7 (*New Dominion,* April 10, 1897).... John S. Costolo, of Laurel Iron Works, died May 6, aged seventy-four years (*New Dominion,* May 15, 1897).... Arrangements were being made to remove remains of 260 persons buried in the old M.E. cemetery, on Front

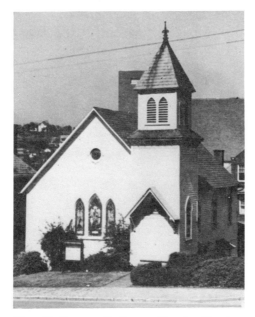

Fig. 47. German Lutheran Church. (Courtesy Saint Paul's Lutheran Church.)

Street, the site of which was to be acquired by the university (*New Dominion*, July 24, 1897). . . . David Shriver, aged fifty years, a brother of Adam, died September 19 (*New Dominion, September 11, 1897*). . . . About one thousand persons assembled at Cassville for the Maccabees picnic on September 4 (*New Dominion*, September 11, 1897). . . . A vast forest fire raged in October from the Cheat River Canyon to near Dellslow in the south and the state line in the north (*New Dominion*, October 20, 1897). . . . A German Lutheran Church was organized by Rev. Ira Wallace, the first pastor (*Evening Post*, May 3, 1901). . . . Morgantown's first Catholic church was built in Seneca, with a seating capacity of three hundred (*New Dominion*, September 25, 1897). . . . The Stanton family became the first Salvation Army family to locate in Morgantown (Dodds and Dodds, p. 97). . . . George, son of Fielding Kiger, died August 13, aged eighty-six years (*New Dominion*, August 21, 1897).

CHAPTER ONE HUNDRED TWENTY-TWO

1898

By order of the Circuit Court, in accordance with the general laws of the state, the town of Seneca was created and incorporated on February 8, 1898, becoming, along with the eleven-year-old town of South Morgantown, an incorporated suburb of the county seat town.

In a sense, this town was the result of long-range activity of the Morgantown Chamber of Commerce, which had been organized in 1889 by Richard E. Fast, George C. Sturgiss, E. M. Grant, T. Pickenpaugh, William P. Willey, F. A. Hennen, E. Shisler, and John A. Myers. This organization became quite active in promoting the growth of the Morgantown community, including the location of the first glass factory.

The Town of Seneca. Following the location of the Seneca Glass Company here in 1896, houses for employees were rapidly built in the new addition. The factory soon employed a large number of people and the town grew rapidly. This in turn stimulated development eastward through Sunnyside, a development which had been aided by the erection of a foot-bridge across the Falling Run ravine in 1894, to provide easier access to the university campus and to the downtown business district.

An election was held on February 5, 1898, by the voters along Beechurst Avenue and in Sunnyside, who voted 70 to 10 for the new incorporation. Sunnyside had previously agreed to become part of Morgantown, but this plan was defeated and it became part of Seneca.

"The new town takes in a large scope of territory and will soon be a very important one. It has within its bounds the University and Morgantown proper can no longer be said to be the seat of that institution."[1]

1. *New Dominion*, February 9, 1898.

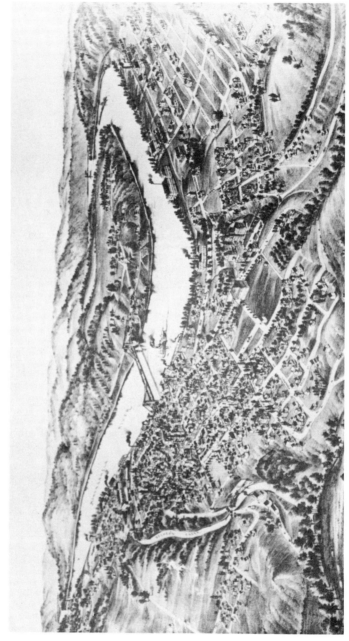

Fig. 48. Morgantown, from a lithograph made in 1897 by Thaddeus Mortimer Fowler (1842-1922), the "bird's eye" artist.

The commissioners, Nicholas Vandervort, John M. Lough, and Leopold Sigwart, set March 21 as the time for the first election of officers for the new town.

The new mayor elected was J. M. Lough, who received 60 votes, compared to his opponent, George Rosenmerkle, who received 50 votes. Elected recorder was G. E. Van Gilder, who received 61 votes; his opponent, J. L. Stoneking, received 47. The candidates for town council were eight in number; the five who received the largest number of votes were declared elected: August Boehler, 84; John Samuel, 86; Rufus West, 89; Ed Lough, 87; Leopold Sigwart, 87; Justus South, 31; Rev. I. A. Barnes, 32; and William Boyd, 39.

The new officers took office on the first of April and at once began to put the machinery of the town into full motion. The tax rate was set and those who voted to stay out of Morgantown to avoid a high tax rate discovered that it cost money even to live in a smaller town.[2]

The Raymond Regime. President Raymond[3] began his administration with buoyant zeal and enthusiasm, determined to avoid some of the mistakes that had proved the undoing of his predecessors. The most difficult disciplinary problems were associated with chapel attendance. Special efforts were made to make the exercises more attractive (for example, it was proposed to install a pipe organ) and, in June 1898, compulsory attendance was abolished.

"The library, 'the heart of the institution,' received attention. It was then housed in a single room in Martin Hall; the shelving was inadequate; the books were unclassified and presented a state of general confusion; and certain departments were again maintaining their own collections. . . . The president recommended the immediate construction of 'a fire-proof building adequate in size and safe in construction, to contain the library and the museums of the University.' For this purpose the regents had already acquired the Methodist Episcopal burial ground."[4]

The purchase of the Fife tract,[5] in March 1898, of about seven

2. *New Dominion,* April 6, 1898.
3. For biography of President Raymond see *New Dominion,* September 4, 1897.
4. Ambler, pp. 327, 328.
5. *New Dominion,* March 22, 1898.

acres, made available two houses ("the Fife cottages") used for classroom purposes. About the same time the university acquired the lots to the rear of the site of the proposed library, for further expansion. The T. J. Gilmore farm of ninety-one acres, on the Mileground, was acquired for use of the Agricultural Experiment Station.[6]

Beginning July 1, 1898, the university year was divided into four "quarters," each of twelve weeks, thus establishing what was then described as the "continuous session." The several curriculums were revised and expanded, so that four bachelor's and four master's degrees were offered in the College of Arts and Sciences, two bachelor's and one master's in the College of Law, and two bachelor's degrees each in Engineering and Agriculture.[7]

Student Activities. The student publication, *The Athenaeum,* which had first appeared in 1887, had gone through various vicissitudes. Under the editorship and management of J. E. Brown and J. G. Stoetzer it was successful in 1888-89, and likewise in 1889-90 under E. H. Vickers and F. W. Clark. A degree of literary excellence was achieved in 1890-91 under M. D. Post and C. C. Hoffman.

But no issues at all appeared in 1894-95. Then the paper was revived in September 1895 and appeared bi-weekly under L. L. Friend and H. L. Swisher. In 1897-98 the Student Publishing Association was organized to take over the ownership and operation of the publication.[8]

Under the direction of Harry M. Anderson, the West Virginia "Snakes" (as the football team was then called) defeated the University of Virginia, on November 14, 1898, by a score of 6 to 0 to win the championship of the South. When word of the victory reached the campus, students, joined by townspeople, celebrated in a "thuse" lasting far into the night. The game was played in Charleston, where residents "went wild with joy."[9]

Work on the Locks. C. I. McDonald, contractor for the new locks and dams, started work without delay. During the winter he built a large warehouse at Morgantown, where he made his head-

6. Ambler, p. 330.
7. Ambler, p. 325.
8. Ambler, p. 357.
9. Ambler, p. 365; *The Monticola*, 1899, pp. 123, 124.

quarters. Cement was to be purchased from the Atlas Cement Company in New York, and shipped here in carload lots, one hundred barrels to a car.[10]

Work on the locks got under way on April 19. Quarries were opened on the west side of the river. Most of the laborers were Italians and wages paid were quite low.[11]

It was expected that the work would be completed in four years and boats would be running all the way to Fairmont.[12]

Hope Natural Gas Company. With the growth of the oil industry in Monongalia County and elsewhere in northern West Virginia, the natural gas industry unfolded concurrently. On September 17, 1898, the Hope Natural Gas Company was incorporated in West Virginia, the immediate purpose being to transport natural gas from the producing areas into neighboring Ohio and Pennsylvania. The company operated as a subsidiary of the Standard Oil Company, and the South Penn Oil Company, another subsidiary, gradually transferred a large number of leases and wells to the new organization. The policy was that companies with mainly oil-producing functions should transfer gas wells to the Hope. A gas transmission system was developed, with compressor stations at strategic points. Several lines crisscrossed western Monongalia County.[13]

Bond Issue for New Streets. Morgantown's citizens were reluctant to provide money for paving streets but the growth of the town was making it necessary. A bond issue for $5,000 was approved[14] in 1892 to pave the main streets with vitrified bricks laid on a concrete foundation, but it was quickly discovered that the available funds were far too meager. On March 21, 1898, the voters approved a bond issue of twenty-six thousand for a similar purpose, the payments to extend over a period of thirty-four years.[15]

10. *New Dominion*, February 2, 1898.
11. *New Dominion*, April 20, 1898.
12. *New Dominion*, June 29, 1898.
13. Thoenen, pp. 112, 113. In 1904 Hope's charter was amended to permit distribution of gas in West Virginia. During the first decade of the twentieth century, Hope was the largest gas producer in the United States.
14. *New Dominion*, April 6, 1898.
15. Callahan, p. 264.

Contract for Street Paving. The first street paving contract in Morgantown's history was awarded by city council on June 20 to J. W. Berry, of Moundsville. He was to pave High, Front, Spruce, and Pleasants streets with vitrified bricks, at a cost of about eight thousand dollars.[16]

Work got under way on "Main" (High) Street on July 21. Hauling of bricks from the railroad was done by Wharton and Hartman (later by Marcellus Carraco). "A great many people have been examining the brick as they are quite a curiosity and have been expected for so long."[17]

By winter the paving had been partly completed, but many people thought the work was poorly done. Much of it was rebuilt the following year, when the contract was completed.

The New Wallace House. John G. Lantz in 1898 purchased the old Wallace House, on High Street north of Walnut, refitted it and changed the name to the New Wallace House. Announced with pride was the fact that hot and cold running water was now available in the washroom.[18] The building had been constructed in 1850 as a residence, and stood on the site previously occupied by an old inn, the Girard House, for more than half a century. The New Wallace House was known chiefly as a commercial hotel.[19]

Admiral Chadwick and the Spanish-American War. The Spanish-American War, with its brilliant flash of imperialism, was over before the country hardly realized it was at war, and the chief influence felt in Monongalia County was the echo of jingoistic speeches. Typical was the remark of a Hagans correspondent: "Our town is the same bustling village it was before the Yanko-Spanko War."[20]

But there was one outstanding figure from Monongalia County involved in the war and that was Chief-of-Staff French Ensor Chadwick (see vol. 3, p. 367), who served under Admiral W. T. Sampson, commander-in-chief of the North Atlantic Squadron.[21] His ship was at Key West when news came of the destruction of the *Maine* on February 15, 1898, and he spent a month on a board

16. *New Dominion,* June 22, 1898.
17. *New Dominion,* July 27, 1898.
18. *New Dominion,* January 26, 1898.
19. Callahan, p. 255.
20. *New Dominion,* September 21, 1898.
21. *New Dominion,* March 2, 1898.

of inquiry as to the cause. The outcome was war with Spain and the squadron took an active part.[22]

Biggest Fire in History. The most disastrous fire in Morgantown's history occurred on the night of April 7, causing thousands of dollars damage to buildings on High Street between Walnut Street and Maiden Alley. Damaged or destroyed were the John and Moorhead building, Capt. J. R. Miller's residence, E. Shisler's hardware store, Jesse Turner's store, and Cox and Baker building, and the C. L. St. Clair restaurant. The origin of the fire was unknown at the time, although it later developed that Miller's shooting gallery had been broken into and it was assumed the fire started there.[23]

New Post Offices. Four new post offices were established during 1898 to serve increasing populations in various areas of the county.

The Core Post Office, at the center of the Dolls Run-Dunkard Ridge oil field, was established May 18, 1898, with Charles H. Core as postmaster.

A post office by the name of John was established on Days Run on August 11, 1898, with Willie F. Moore as postmaster. It was named for John Moore.

On the Evansville Pike south of Morgantown the Ringgold Post Office was established March 7, 1898, with Elias Ring as postmaster.

Leander J. Piles was the first postmaster of the Sandy Post Office, established August 11, 1898, on Days Run.

Catholic Church Is Dedicated. The pioneer population of Monongalia County was made up largely of British, Scotch-Irish, or German people, with Protestant backgrounds. A few persons with Catholic backgrounds assembled in May 1876, at the home of D. H. Chadwick to assist at mass celebrated by Father Lambert, of Fairmont. In 1883 there was only one small organization of

22. Benjamin F. Tracy, secretary of the navy, said of him: "It is proper to refer especially to the untiring and successful efforts of Commander F. E. Chadwick, the first attaché sent out, whose extraordinary ability and judgement during six years of difficult service in England and on the Continent have had a lasting influence upon naval development in this country." *Annual Report of the Secretary of the Navy*, 1889, p. 7.
23. *New Dominion*, April 13, 1898.

Fig. 49. Father Kluser. (Saint Theresa Church.)

Fig. 50. Father Boutlou. (Saint Theresa Church.)

Catholic families in the county, located in the Stewartstown section.[24]

But the coming of the glass factories into the area brought in people of very different backgrounds, chiefly French and German, members of the Catholic church.

After the Seneca glass factory was moved here, Father Boutlou came by train from Fairmont twice a month to celebrate mass in the home of Joseph Stenger, on the corner of Grant Avenue and Sixth Street, or in other homes. Community leaders made the rounds of the families to collect a dollar a month to pay the priest.

"The usual cry of young people in those days was that 'there is nothing to do'—except to dress up on a Sunday and walk 'up town' and home again. The talk of the community was the building of a clubhouse of some kind where they might have entertainment and some social life, to break the monotony and fill some of the empty hours."[25]

"But one woman became upset about such talk, about building a clubhouse, but not about building a church. So she wrote a let-

24. Wiley, p. 448.
25. Marie Ruziska, in *St. Theresa Church, 75th Anniversary*, pp. 6, 7.

ter in her native German to Bishop Donahue (in Wheeling), who was Irish, telling him of the need for a church building.

"Finally, in 1897, the erection of a church was begun on Mc-Lane Avenue, in Seneca, and the next year came the great day—July 17, 1898—when Bishop Donahue himself came to Morgantown to dedicate the building, under the patronage of St. Francis de Sales. Now there was a regular place to worship—but still no resident pastor and no charter as a parish. That was soon to change."[26]

George B. Morris. Morgantown's best known dentist, Dr. George B. Morris, died March 11, 1898. The son of Thomas Morris, he was born at Woodgrove Furnace, Monongalia County, June 30, 1832.

He took up dentistry at an early age. "At that time dentistry was little understood and the returns from practice were meagre. He, however, mastered his profession, as he always did whatever he undertook, and he raised it to a higher plane than was ever before thought up in this locality. In his early practice . . . he traveled on horseback to meet his engagements." He opened an office in Morgantown in 1862, then went to Philadelphia and graduated from dental college in 1867, "thus being the first regular graduate practising the profession" in West Virginia.

He married Ellen Baker, of Laurel Iron Works, and they had one son, Perry, who unfortunately died in 1882, just when he was about ready to graduate from college.[27]

Jarrett Wildman Suicide. Jarrett Wildman, a farmer of Pedlar Run, on whose farm were located about twenty-five oil wells, committed suicide by shooting himself on July 14, 1898. A son of John Wildman, he was born in Pennsylvania April 3, 1837. His wife, Elizabeth, had died May 27, 1879, but he was survived by seven of their children, namely, Sarilda (married George Lynch), Simon (married Mary Henderson), Madison Clark (married Belle Morris), Lewis, Emma, Belle (married J. M. Gay), and Melissa (married Frank Burris).[28]

26. *St. Theresa Church*, p. 7.
27. *New Dominion*, March 16, 1898; Wiley, p. 602.
28. *New Dominion*, July 20, 1898; Core, *Chronicles of Core*, p. 156.

Henry M. Morgan Dead. Great excitement was caused in Morgantown on July 18 when it was learned that Henry M. Morgan, editor of the *Post,* had taken his own life, using the same type of revolver used by Jarrett Wildman a few days earlier. The son of Enos D. and Martha B. Morgan, he was born in Morgantown on April 10, 1843. He received his education at the Monongalia Academy and founded the *Morgantown Post* in 1864, associating Capt. N. N. Hoffman with him in 1865. He married Josephine A., daughter of E. C. Lazier, and they had two children, B. L. and W. H., both of whom were associated with their father in the publishing business.[29]

Miscellany. In 1898: Frank Cox built a palatial brick home at Spruce and Pleasant streets (Callahan, p. 253). . . . W. E. Price built a large brick home on Walnut Street east of Spruce (Callahan, p. 253). . . . A Disciples of Christ Church congregation was organized in Morgantown under the leadership of M. S. Garrison and Rev. A. Linkletter, state evangelist (Dodds and Dodds, p. 73; Core, *Morgantown Disciples,* p. 31). . . . A heavy windstorm on January 22 and 23 damaged houses and trees throughout the county; thirty-five oil derricks in the Jakes Run field were reported blown over, the Falling Run footbridge was wrecked, telephone lines were twisted and tangled (*New Dominion,* January 26, 1898). . . . A charity concert in the Opera House, arranged by Mrs. Milton Hirschman and others, raised about two hundred dollars for relief (*New Dominion,* February 2, 1898). . . . Prof. William A. Pratt, of the University of Delaware, gave a lecture on the Klondike gold region, showing photographs (*New Dominion,* March 2, 9, 1898). . . . Morgantown Lodge No. 411, B.P.O. Elks, was installed March 25 (*New Dominion,* March 30, 1898). . . . The Morgantown Post Office went from third class to second class, with annual receipts of over eight thousand dollars (*New Dominion,* April 13, 1898). . . . Clearing of unsightly livery stables from Spruce Street got under way (*New Dominion,* April 27, 1898). . . . Mrs. Delia, widow of Col. James Evans, died in Uniontown September 9; she was a daughter of Thomas P. Ray (*New Dominion,* September 14, 1898). . . . Col. Philip Golay, U.S. engineer supervising construction of new locks and dams, died suddenly, aged seventy-two years (*New Dominion,* November 2,

29. *New Dominion,* July 20, 1898.

1898).... A memorial service was held November 27 for Dale Grant and Holland D. Thompson, university students who died in the armed services during the late war (*New Dominion*, November 30, 1898).... A fight at Brown's Tabernacle near Mooresville on December 24 between Roscoe Tennant and Will Moore resulted in the death of the latter (*New Dominion*, January 4, 1899).... The Turn Verein Club House was formally opened with a grand ball on May 17 (*New Dominion*, May 18, 1898).... A. J. ("Jack") Houston was the first Monongalia County man to go to the Klondike gold region (*New Dominion*, May 25, 1898).... A new brick factory was built at the lower end of Seneca (*New Dominion*, June 29, 1898).... Asa Lemley, son of Samuel and Rebecca (Snider) Lemley, died January 31, at his home on Dunkard Creek, in Cass District; he was eighty-three years old (Core, *Chronicles of Core*, p. 154).... A new Methodist Episcopal church was dedicated at Wise, in Battelle District (Dodds and Dodds, p. 137).... Christopher, son of Michael and Christena Core, died at Morgantown April 2, 1898; he was born May 22, 1843 (Core, *Chronicles of Core*, p. 154).... Sanford Pickenpaugh, Morgantown tailor, died June 27; he was born on Scotts Run October 30, 1811 (*New Dominion*, June 29, 1898). ... James Madison McVicker, son of James McVicker, died December 23 (*New Dominion*, January 4, 1897; Wiley, p. 658).

1899

Under a headline, "Greenmont decides that it wants to be a town," a local newspaper, early in 1899, said:

"Greenmont voted on the proposition to incorporate on Saturday and the affirmative carried the day by a vote of forty-two to seven. The papers in the case were presented to the court on Monday and he passed on them ruling that they had been prepared in proper form and that the incorporation had been achieved in accordance with the law.

"The town of Greenmont in consequence is now an entity and the first election for town officers will be held within a few weeks

Fig. 51. Greenmont is to the left of Deckers Creek in this excerpt from Fowler's sketch (see Fig. 48).

and the fourth town in the independent school district of Morgantown will begin its fight for continued existence."[1]

The Town of Greenmont. An issue of the same paper, in the spring, carried the news that the officers had been elected and that the town was in business:

"The mayor and council of Greenmont have taken the oath of office and the town government is now in running order. The officers elected all took their places with the exception of Albert Fortney. Mr. Fortney did not appear to qualify and had no desire to do so. The council after investigating the matter decided to elect W. E. Kern who was the opposing candidate to Fortney and he took charge of the office of recorder.

"The town officers of the new government are J. A. Powell, Mayor; W. E. Kern, Recorder; and Lee Gidley, John Smith, Frank Selby, Pierce Hess and Judd Zinn, councilmen."[2]

Greenmont, across Deckers Creek from Morgantown, was connected to the county seat by a bridge near the Morgantown Mills, on a road leading down from Spruce Street. The bridge at that very time was in process of reconstruction. "The Greenmont Bridge is being torn down partially. The sides and top will be removed and everything gotten in readiness to tear it down completely as soon as the iron work of the new structure arrives. This is expected about the fifteenth of the month."

The roads leading into Greenmont in 1899 were essentially dead-end. Kingwood Street, the main thoroughfare, did not lead towards Kingwood but came to an end against the steep hillside. There was no direct connection by road to South Morgantown, without going through Morgantown.

University Advancement. As the nineteenth century drew towards its end, the university continued to make steady advances, in enrollment, in appropriations, in new facilities, in new methods. Approaching his first legislature, early in 1899, President Raymond pointed out that the enrollment had increased from 283 in 1894-95 to 815 for 1898-99, but that the State paid only $19,500 of a total salary expenditure of $62,756 for the previous year, the remainder being paid from federal funds. With the active assistance of Regent G. C. Sturgiss and of Senator R. E.

1. *New Dominion,* February 22, 1899.
2. *New Dominion,* April 21, 1899.

Fig. 52-A. The first Mechanical Hall, built in 1892.

Fig. 52-B. The second Mechanical Hall, built in 1902.

Fast, of the faculty, the appropriation for 1899-90 was increased to $106,000, three times what it had been for 1897-98. Of this, $50,000 was earmarked for a library building, $10,000 for an armory, $3,000 for a school of music, etc.

A loss was sustained March 3, 1899, when Mechanical Hall, on Beechurst Avenue, was destroyed by fire. Plans immediately got under way to construct a replacement on Prospect Street, at the rear of the site for the proposed library building. In April Preparatory ("Prep") Hall was named Martin Hall, in honor of the first president. A pipe organ was installed in Commencement Hall.

The "intellectual awakening" of the Raymond administration was reflected in the admission of the university, in 1899, to membership in the Association of Colleges and Preparatory Schools of the Southern States, the expansion of the work of the College of Agriculture through teachers' and farmers' institutes, the reorganization of university affairs to be handled by twenty-three standing committees, and in numerous other ways.[3]

The first sororities were established in 1899. A group headed by Willa Hart Butcher petitioned the faculty for permission to establish a chapter of the national group, Pi Beta Phi. This was denied, whereupon the group, on November 20, 1899, established Kappa Delta, a local. Another local, Phi Pi Alpha, followed, on Thanksgiving Day, 1899.[4]

Football on the campus was in a precarious situation. The team was coached by Louis Yeager, one of the players, and managed by F. M. ("Tip") Lardin and Howard Cross. Money was scarce and the season's record was not impressive; the four games resulted in two victories and two defeats.[5]

Chadwick Day. A great event in Morgantown's calendar for 1899 was the return of the distinguished native son, Rear Admiral French Ensor Chadwick, on October 10 for ceremonies in his honor. Admiral Sampson attended the ceremony, as did Gov. George W. Atkinson. A sword was presented to him by citizens of Morgantown. Between ten and twenty thousand people attended.[6]

3. Ambler, pp. 329-33.
4. Ambler, p. 360.
5. Ambler, p. 365.
6. *Daily New Dominion,* October 10, 1899.

Fig. 53. Admiral French Ensor
Chadwick.

Fig. 54. D. B. Purinton. (West
Virginia University.)

"The Admiral greatly appreciated the courtesies extended to him and was much impressed by the many changes which indicated that the town had awakened from the simple and isolated life which he had known four decades earlier. It was a fitting occasion to review achievements which had prepared the way for larger achievements of the next period, and to look backward to the victorious struggles and lessons of experience which might prove useful in directing new forward movements and achievements."[7]

A professor of history at the U.S. Naval Academy summarizes Chadwick's life as that of a "superb seaman, intelligence specialist, naturally gifted scientist and technologist, naval administrator, educator, skilled draftsman, and renowned historian —a scholarly warrior."[8]

7. Callahan, p. 267.
8. Paolo E. Coletta, *French Ensor Chadwick: The Scholarly Warrior.* (1980). See also his "French Ensor Chadwick: The First American Naval Attache, 1882-1889." *American Neptune* 39(1979):126-41.

The Madera Hotel. Walter and B. H. Madera, in November 1899, bought the old Franklin Hotel, on Walnut Street, and planned to rebuild it into one of the most up-to-date hotels in the state. Advertised as "One square from boat landing" and "Two squares from R. R. depot," it was strategically located to serve incoming visitors to the university town.[9]

The original Franklin House was built by Fauquier McRa (vol. 2, p. 204), perhaps while Benjamin Franklin was still living.

The Brown Building. S. A. Posten, in 1898, purchased for $4,750 the lot and frame building at the northeast corner of the public square and removed the frame structure.[10] Here he built, at a cost of about $10,250 a four-story brick building (later known as the Brown Building), the first four-story building in Morgantown.[11]

The "Black Bottle" Is Revived. For about a dozen years the proposed "Black Bottle" railroad (p. 108) had lain dormant, except for a multitude of rumors. Finally, in 1899, George C. Sturgiss was able to secure enough capital to get things moving once again. A charter was obtained in January by Sturgiss, J. Ami Martin, and others for a line to be known as the Morgantown and Kingwood Railroad and construction of the line was begun during the summer near Sabraton.[12]

The New Post Office. The new Morgantown Post Office was opened for business early in January. In a new four-story building at the corner of High and Pleasant streets, the location was very convenient.

"Entrance is through a very large roomy door and the lobby in which one finds himself will prevent the squeezing that is incident to trying to get mail in the old office.

"On first going in the registery and money order windows are seen. The drop for mail, the stamp window and general delivery windows are next. . . . The call boxes are next. They number nearly

---

9. Callahan, pp. 88, 255; Wiley, p. 587. A description, with photographs, of the rebuilt hotel may be consulted in the *New Dominion Industrial Edition*, 1906, p. 61.

10. *New Dominion*, March 22, 1898.

11. Callahan, p. 253.

12. Callahan, pp. 246, 251, 252; *Daily New Dominion*, April 21, 1899, July 5, 1899, September 14, 1899, etc.

four hundred and are greatly in excess of the number available in the old office."[13]

The Bridge Is Free! Owners of the suspension bridge across the river having shown no inclination to sell, the county clerk was directed by the county court to contact Senator Stephen B. Elkins and Congressman Alston G. Dayton, asking them to apply for permission to construct and maintain a free public bridge across the river.

Monongalia County citizens, increasingly irritated by the necessity of paying tolls to cross the Monongahela, commended this action, and the owners of the bridge were forced to consider offers by the county to purchase it.[14] On March 10, 1899, the sale was completed, at a price of $24,500, and the collection of tolls on the bridge ceased immediately.[15]

A New Central School. To replace the old Morgantown Graded (and High) School, destroyed by fire in 1897 (p. 212), a new structure was built in 1898-99, by Schallenberger and Fonner, of Pittsburg, Pennsylvania, for $30,988.[16] Funds for its construction were provided by a bond issue of $40,000, sold in New York.

In September 1899 the school opened under new conditions and policies. The new superintendent, W. H. Gallup, at a monthly salary of one hundred dollars, succeeded Harvey Brand, who had served as superintendent and principal at a salary of seventy-five dollars. The length of the school term was increased to nine months. Attendance steadily increased, soon indicating how unfounded were criticisms that the new building was too large.[17]

The Christian Church. On May 21, 1899, a new building was dedicated on Spruce Street by members of the Church of Christ (or Disciples of Christ), a part of the Restoration Movement (vol. 3, p. 125). Leaders of the congregation were Marion Simon Garrison, a former member of the Dolls Run Christian Church, who had moved to Morgantown just before being elected county sheriff; Lewis Cass Woolery, professor of Greek at the university,

13. *New Dominion,* January 4, 1899.
14. See "They Ought to Buy It (And There will be Trouble if They Don't),"
New Dominion, January 11, 1899.
15. Callahan, pp. 266, 267; *New Dominion,* April 5, 1899.
16. *New Dominion,* April 13, 1898.
17. Callahan, p. 259.

Fig. 55. Central Grade School. (From an old postcard.)

Orilas Grant White and Herbert Henry Moninger, students in the university, and several residents of Morgantown. William Henry Kendrick, of Danville, Kentucky, a nephew of Professor Woolery, moved to Morgantown during the summer and became a member of the congregation.[18]

Tennant Memorial Chapel. On Jakes Run, in the Tennant Settlement, Nimrod Tennant, in 1899, gave money for the building of a church, and with the help of several other people, a chapel was erected on his farm and dedicated as a Methodist Church under the name of Tennant Memorial Chapel.[19]

Saint Leo Methodist Church. On the headwaters of Dunkard Creek at Saint Leo, about three miles southwest of Wadestown, a Methodist congregation was organized in a schoolhouse in 1899 by Rev. S. S. White. A building committee was formed, composed of G. D. Leggett, M. Harker, and W. S. Haines. A church archi-

18. Core, *Morgantown Disciples,* pp. 28-42.
19. Dodds and Dodds, p. 127.

tect was employed for fifty dollars to draw up plans for the building, with the result that the church constructed was one with excellent acoustics, very unusual for buildings of that time.[20]

The Daily Post. The *Morgantown Post,* which had been publishing a weekly newspaper in Morgantown since 1864, began a daily edition on December 8, 1899, known as the *Evening Post.* The *Weekly Post* continued to be published as well, going mostly to rural subscribers.

The *Evening Post* was a four-page paper, distributed to about five hundred subscribers in the Morgantown area. Local news and advertising were emphasized, but national and international news items were also carried.

Morgantown now had a morning paper, the *Daily New Dominion,* as well as an evening paper.

The Hartigan Hospital. Hospitals in 1976 were so much a part of life that it is a little hard to believe that Monongalia County went for considerably more than its first century without one. Dr. James W. Hartigan opened Morgantown's first hospital in 1899, at the junction of Kirk and Spruce streets. Dr. Hartigan, a graduate of West Virginia University and Baltimore Medical College, was a professor of biology at West Virginia University.[21]

The Coldest Winter. The winter of 1898-99 was the coldest yet recorded in the county's history. "Last night was the coldest of the year. It was also the coldest night ever experienced in this county so far as the record goes. The mercury has been known to reach some very low points but nothing like as cold as it was last night. The mercury did not get above the zero mark anywhere yesterday except where the sun got a fair strike at it and then it went only a few degrees above that point. As soon as the sun got off of it, it began to go down and during the night it reached points never before touched. In town at 8 o'clock this morning it was 27 below.

20. Dodds and Dodds, p. 135.
21. The first two operations were performed the following year (*Evening Post,* August 9, 1900) and by 1906 there had been three hundred operations, with only two fatalities. There was room in the hospital for twenty patients; *New Dominion Industrial Edition,* 1906, p. 43. In 1890 Dr. Hartigan had published a *Textbook of Anatomy, Physiology, and Hygiene.*

Fig. 56. The Hartigan Hospital.

Arnettsville, Rivesville, and Paradise hold the belt, having reported 38 below."[22]

Daybrook. In Clay District near the head of Days Run a post office by the name of Daybrook was established February 9, 1899, with Jacob J. Moore as postmaster. Actually this was only a change of name of a preexisting post office, Jakes Run, to which Moore had been appointed September 28, 1898. The Jakes Run Post Office had been set up on the stream by that name (sometimes also called Statlers Run, i.e., Jake Statlers Run, vol. 1, p. 184) May 23, 1844. Richard D. Tennant was the first postmaster but his successor, Solomon Wagner (appointed July 2, 1861), lived on Days Run and moved the post office there.

Meanwhile, a post office named Statlers Run had been established September 29, 1876, back on Jake Statlers Run, with Nimrod Tennant as postmaster.

To make the situation still more confusing, Daybrook was

22. *Morgantown Post,* February 19, 1899.

simply a more "respectable" name for the community popularly known as Ponetown (vol. 3, p. 702).

Morgantown in 1899. A newspaper editor summarized some of the features of Morgantown, as the nineteenth century drew toward its close: "Nature has smiled upon the location of Morgantown in a manner to make her famous for her beauty and health. . . . The railroad facilities of Morgantown have added inestimably to her commercial and industrial success. . . . The Pittsburg, Brownsville, Geneva and Morgantown Packet Co. have a line of first-class and elegantly equipped steamboats that arrive and depart daily, affording good passenger and freight transportation. . . . Morgantown is one of the best lighted cities in the state. It is brilliantly lighted from center to circumference by natural gas. . . . Electricity is also a potent factor as a lighting agent, a great many public and private buildings being lighted by it."[23]

Tank Struck by Lightning. Tank No. 16, in the Morgantown Tank Field, was struck by lightning May 3, 1899, and burned in a most spectacular fashion, "the dense clouds of smoke making a sight that was very beautiful and terrible." About fifteen hundred people came out to watch the fire and the efforts of Eureka Pipe Line employes (who came to town by special train) to bring it under control. Shots from a cannon were fired to destroy the tank and spread the oil upon the ground. The oil burned for about twenty-four hours and about fifteen thousand barrels burned up.[24]

Henry Baird Lazier. Dr. H. B. Lazier, a widely known Morgantown physician and druggist, died May 11, 1899. The son of William and Mary Lazier, he was born in Monongalia County January 26, 1831. He was educated in Monongalia Academy and graduated from Jefferson Medical College, Philadelphia, in 1858. At the outbreak of the Civil War he raised Company E, Seventh West Virginia Infantry, of which he was captain. He was severely injured in the battle of Antietam.

He married Mary Agnes Moreland and was survived by two children, Dr. A. M., who succeeded him in the drug business, and Henry B. Lazier, Jr.[25]

23. Justin M. Kunkle, in *Daily New Dominion,* April 29, 1899.
24. *Daily New Dominion,* May 4, 1899.
25. *Daily New Dominion,* May 11, 1899; Wiley, p. 601.

William Hagans. The son of Harrison and Jane Hagans, William Hagans, died January 26, 1899; he was seventy-five years old. He was born in Brandonville, moving in 1881 to Chattanooga, about twelve years later to Chicago, and then to Morgantown about 1893. At Brandonville he had managed two iron furnaces. He married Isabella Lazzell and his wife and one daughter, Mrs. Darius Waterhouse, survived him.[26]

James Lazzelle. James Lazzelle, son of Thomas, Jr., and Rebecca (Bowlby) Lazzelle, died February 1, 1899. He was born December 25, 1810. He was a farmer of Cass District and in 1841 married Eleanor Courtney, a sister of his father's second wife; she had died July 16, 1898, aged eighty-one. Their children were Samuel C., Luther J., Thomas A., Mary E., Rebecca Jane, Isaac Grant, and Vitellius H.[27]

Miscellany. In 1899: The Battelle Oil Company brought in a 250-barrel oil well on the Sarah E. Eddy farm near Cross Roads (*New Dominion*, January 11, 1899). . . . Frank Lazier, the only Morgantown boy at the battle of Manila, died in Pekin, China (*New Dominion*, January 18, 1899). . . . Courtney, McDermott, and Huston bought the Alpha Oil Company, of Jakes Run, with about twenty-five producing wells, for forty thousand dollars, probably the largest cash transaction ever made in the county (*New Dominion*, February 1, 1899). . . . Michael R. Chalfant, of Morgantown, died March 18, aged eighty-two years (*New Dominion*, March 22, 1899). . . . Fred Jennewine, of Laurel Iron Works was killed in battle in the Philippines (*New Dominion*, April 5, 1899). . . . The first volume of West Virginia Geological Survey reports was published (*Daily New Dominion*, April 17, 1899). . . . Morgantown Marble and Granite Works, on Foundry Street, was being operated by J. E. Watts and M. W. Protzman (*Daily New Dominion*, May 2, 1899). . . . The fifth oil well on the Sarah E. Eddy farm in Battelle District came in on May 13, making forty barrels a day (*Daily New Dominion*, May 15, 1899). . . . An early train for Pittsburg, leaving Morgantown at 5:45 a.m., and returning at 8:30 p.m., was added by the B.&O. on June 18 (*Daily New Dominion*, June 7, 1899). . . . David I. B. Anderson, of The

26. *New Dominion*, February 1, 1899.
27. *The 175th Anniversary of . . . Monongalia County*, p. 428.

Flatts, died July 9; he married Martha Coil and they had six children, viz., Mrs. George Parfitt, Mrs. Elza Jacobs, Mrs. George Little, William C., James E., and Robert Anderson (*Daily New Dominion*, July 10, 1899). . . . Street paving continued through the summer in Morgantown (*Daily New Dominion*, July 18, 1899, etc.). . . . The old municipal hall, on a portion of the school ground on Walnut Street, was sold, and a lot on High Street, next to the Baptist Church, was purchased (*Daily New Dominion*, August 1, 1899). . . . The George M. John store moved into the building next to the Second National Bank (Callahan, p. 272). . . . John Wildman, of Pedlar Run, died July 21; he was ninety years of age (Core, *Chronicles of Core*, p. 157). . . . Prof. A. L. Purinton, brother of Dr. D. B. Purinton, died at Smithfield, Pennsylvania, on August 5 (*Daily New Dominion*, August 7, 1899). . . . The John Robinson Circus showed in Morgantown on August 9, with a street parade at 11:00 a.m.; the famous clown, John Lowlow, was along (*Daily New Dominion*, August 9, 1899). . . . The Morgantown Methodist Protestant Church, completed in 1885, was finally dedicated August 20; Rev. I. A. Barnes was pastor (*Daily New Dominion*, August 19, 22, 1899). . . . Prof. S. B. Brown, of the university, brought back from Wyoming the skeleton of an extinct reptile, *Brontosaurus excelsus*, placed on display here (*Daily New Dominion*, August 26, 1899). . . . The Standard Oil Company brought in a well on the Elihu Eddy farm, at Cross Roads, producing at first at the rate of twenty-four hundred barrels daily (*Daily New Dominion*, September 2, 1899). . . . The State Council of the Junior OUAM held its convention in Morgantown (*Daily New Dominion*, September 12, 1899). . . . University enrollment in October reached one thousand for the first time (*Daily New Dominion*, October 4, 1899). . . . Edward Gregg Donley and John Lazier Hatfield formed a law firm (*New Dominion Indus. Ed., 1906*, p. 15). . . . A post office by the name of Mack, near Dellslow, was established October 11, 1899, with Owen D. McMillen as postmaster (U.S. Postal Records). . . . Lock and Dam No. 10 were nearly completed at the close of the construction season; this was the first concrete dam built in the United States (*Daily New Dominion*, October 6, November 13, 1899). . . . The New England Bakery was destroyed by fire November 26 (*Daily New Dominion*, November 27, 1899). . . . To introduce the new pipe organ Prof. Simeon Bissell, director of the Pittsburg Conservatory of Music, gave a concert to a crowded house at the Morgantown Methodist Episcopal Church on November 28 (*Daily New Dominion*, November 29, 1899).

Fig. 56-A. Burning oil tank in the Morgantown Tank Field.

CHAPTER ONE HUNDRED TWENTY-FOUR

1900

At the last stroke of midnight on December 31, 1899, the staid eighteen hundreds came to a close and New Year's celebrants in Morgantown, as elsewhere, enjoyed the novelty of writing the date as 1900 for the first time. Although, contrary to a popular misconception, the twentieth century would not begin for another twelve-month period,[1] people felt that more than usual significance might be associated with the coming of the nineteen hundreds. But the wildest imaginations could scarcely have foreseen the stirring events that lay ahead, nor how marvelous features hitherto restricted to fairy tales were soon to become every-day conveniences of life.

The Census of 1900. The tremendous developments in Monongalia County during the final decade of the nineteenth century, leading to industrialization and diversification, were reflected in the census of 1900, in which the population showed more than a twenty-five percent increase over that recorded in the census of 1890.

In 1890 the total population of Monongalia County was given as 15,705; in 1900 it was 19,049. By far the most significant increases were in Morgantown and its suburbs.

The population of the seven districts, with the incorporated towns, is shown below, with 1890 figures for comparison:

	1900	1890
Battelle	2,760	2,452
Cass	1,444	1,495
Clay	3,149	2,827
Blacksville	180	——

1. "Those who have their doubts as to when the twentieth century does really begin can still have a year to argue over the matter." *Daily New Dominion*, January 2, 1900.

	1900	*1890*
Clinton	2,551	2,352
Grant	2,152	2,118
Morgan	5,356	2,973
Greenmont	349	— —
Morgantown	1,895	1,011
Seneca	723	— —
South Morgantown	405	285
Union	1,637	1,488

Of this total, males outnumbered females, 9,748 to 9,301. The population included 18,746 native-born persons, compared to 303 foreign-born. But in 1890 there were only 74 foreign-born persons and the significant increase reflected the beginning of new industries, particularly the manufacture of glass. There were 18,747 white persons and 299 blacks; the black persons increased from 227 in 1890 but had decreased from 317 in 1880. No persons of Indian descent were recorded, but there were 3 of Chinese ancestry, for the first time in history. One person of Japanese origin had been recorded in 1890, but none in 1900.

Of the foreign-born population in Monongalia County in 1900, the countries of origin were recorded as follows: Austria, 1; Canada, 11; England, 45; France, 21; Germany, 97; Ireland, 14; Italy, 44; Russia, 1; Scotland, 14; Switzerland, 33; Wales, 2; other countries, 20.

Despite the beginnings of industry shown since 1890, agriculture was still easily the leading occupation of the people of Monongalia County. There were 2,259 farms in the county, with an average size of 96.6 acres. The total acreage was 218,114, with 164,306 acres improved. The value of the lands and improvements was given as $7,835,310, plus $1,275,490 for buildings, $219,000 for implements and machinery, and $996,016 for livestock.

The manufacturing industries showed a marked increase over 1890. There were 67 establishments reported, with a total capital of $529,682. The average number of workers was 455, their wages totaling $182,311. The value of products was given as $644,737.

Differences on the Campus. Under the spell of President Raymond's forceful personality and administration, the disciplinary problems that had wrecked the preceding administration were temporarily forgotten. But gradually the glamour began to fade and the president's programs met increasing opposition. Among the bitterest of the dissensions was that involving the College of Medicine. Without regard to the experiences of his predecessors, the president actively promoted the establishment of a medical college. His first step was the appointment of Dr. A. E. Thayer as assistant professor of materia medica, pathology, and bacteriology and his authorization to develop a curriculum for the proposed college. The curriculum was published early in 1900 and on June 22, 1900, the regents established a college of medicine authorized to offer the first two years of a medical course. Professor Hartigan, head of the department of biology, who had not been consulted, opposed the move, in the light of university experiences over the past twenty years. Unable to compromise their differences, Professor Hartigan was dismissed from the faculty on December 18 and on December 20 Professor Thayer was made dean of the College of Medicine. For some reason, however, he did not function in that capacity, his place being taken by Dr. William S. Magill.

The state superintendent of free schools, James Russell Trotter, a Harvard-trained lawyer, joined in the criticism through the medium of *The West Virginia School Journal*, claiming, among other things, that the standards of the university were being lowered.

Differences between the president and his faculty became increasingly bitter. At a meeting of the regents on April 6, 1900, the president recommended dismissal or reprimand for several faculty members. The regents postponing action, President Raymond submitted his resignation. This resignation was laid on the table and on June 21 the president asked leave to withdraw it, which was granted. But he then, the following day, submitted a second resignation, to take effect October 1, 1900. The regents declined to accept this resignation.[2]

In 1900 the first football game was played with the Western University of Pennsylvania, the beginning of a great and glorious series; WUP was held to a score of 6 to 5. The team was coached by Dr. J. C. Hill, of the university faculty. The team was defeated

2. Ambler, pp. 331-35.

Fig. 57. West Virginia University Observatory. (Courtesy Henry W. Gould.)

by Marietta College, 19-6, by Ohio State University, 27-0, and by W. and J., 22-0.[3]

Observatory Hill. In the fall of 1900 a small domed observatory, thirteen feet in diameter, was built on the old Fife property, now owned by the university, on top of the hill at the head of North High Street. Samuel G. Stevens, professor of physics and astronomy at the university, in 1872 had made arrangements for the institution to secure a refracting telescope with a seven-foot focal length and an aperture of five and a quarter inches, but there was hardly a place to mount it.

In 1899 James David Thompson, a graduate of Cambridge University, joined the university staff as professor of mathematics. Soon he established a department of astronomy, discovered the old telescope, and suggested that it be given more suitable hous-

3. Ambler, p. 365.

Fig. 58. William P. Willey.   Fig. 59. George C. Baker.

ing. So the little round-topped structure was built on the hill, observing "the town as well as the skies above."[4]

Waitman Thomas Willey. The best known resident of Morgantown, Waitman Thomas Willey, died on May 2, 1900. A local newspaper summarized the regard in which he was held by the people of the town and the State:

"Great in intellect, great in learning, great in the simplicity of his home life and in the abundant goodness of his heart, he had taken a part in the great drama of life with such men as Lincoln, Seward, Stanton and Chase and on all occasions and under all circumstances he measured up to the very highest expectations of his friends. The great President Lincoln knew him and trusted him as a friend. To the people of Monongalia County Senator

4. H. W. Gould, "History of the old Telescope and Observatory at West Virginia University," *Proc. W. Va. Acad. Sci.* 39(1968): 1-8. Thompson left the following year, however, to join the staff of the Congressional Library, and the observatory apparently was not used much thereafter.

Willey was a father. He was sincerely loved and revered by all. He had lived among us for two-thirds of a century and in all that time had lived a model life."[5]

The Willey family had located in Monongalia County in 1781. William Willey and his family at first settled near Collins Ferry, on the east side of the Monongahela, then moved across the river to Scotts Run, where he died. His son, William, Jr., moved to Buffalo Creek, near the site of the later town of Farmington. William Willey, Jr., by his second wife, Sarah Barnes, became the father of Waitman Thomas Willey, who was born October 18, 1811, in his parents' little log cabin along Buffalo Creek.[6]

He was a member of the First Wheeling Convention and was later elected senator of the Restored Government of Virginia, eventually presenting West Virginia's application for statehood to the United States Congress. He was elected senator from West Virginia in 1863.

In his older years he and his residence were objects of curiosity, intermingled with admiration and respect.[7]

In 1872 Senator Willey was a member of the second State Constitutional Convention (one of the twelve Republican members; see vol. 3, p. 649). In 1876 he was a delegate at large to the National Republican Convention at Cincinnati. His last public office was clerk of the county court, a position to which he was appointed in November 1882, to fill an unexpired term of two years and later, in 1884, was elected for an additional term of six years.

Waitman T. and Elizabeth Willey had seven children: Mary Ellen (married Dr. M. L. Casselberry), Sarah (married John Marshall Hagans), William P. (married Lide Allen), Julia E. (married William Clark McGrew), Thomas Ray, Louisa, and John B.[8]

John Marshall Hagans. Judge John M. Hagans, on June 17, was "summoned to the highest tribunal," and the state of West Vir-

---

5. *Morgantown Post*, May 2, 1900.

6. See many references to him in vol. 3.

7. His principal biography, *Waitman Thomas Willey, Orator, Churchman, Humanitarian*, by Charles H. Ambler, was published in 1954. North Boundary Street, in Morgantown, was renamed Willey Street before his death, providing a well-known memorial to one of Morgantown's greatest citizens.

8. *Evening Post*, May 2, 1900. A biography filling the entire front page and continued onto the second, was published by the *Evening Post*, May 4, 1900.

ginia mourned "the loss of one of its most gifted sons, one of its most cultured citizens, one of its purest and brainiest men. . . . The rich and the poor, the high and the low, the white and the black, were alike his friends."[9]

J. M. Hagans was born at Brandonville August 13, 1838, the son of Harrison and Jane Hagans. He attended Monongalia Academy, then began the study of law in the office of Waitman T. Willey, after which he studied in Harvard University and was admitted to the bar in 1859. He was elected prosecuting attorney for Monongalia County in 1862 and reelected in 1863 and in 1870. He was appointed reporter of the State Supreme Court of Appeals in 1864 and held that position until 1873, during which period five volumes of the leading cases decided by the court were published, now known as *Hagan's West Virginia Reports.*[10]

He was mayor of Morgantown from 1866 to 1869, in 1868 was a Republican presidential elector, and in 1872 was a member of the state constitutional convention. He was elected to Congress in 1873 and to the House of Delegates in 1879 and 1887. In 1880 he was a delegate to the Republican national convention.

In 1888 he was elected judge of the Second Judicial Circuit and was reelected in 1896. His term would have expired in 1904.

Rural Free Delivery. Monongalia County's first rural mail routes went into operation December 1, 1900. There were three routes, serving a population of over two thousand people.

Route No. 1 ran from the Morgantown Post Office by the Fairmont Pike to Stewart's corner, thence via Little Indian Creek to Hood Yost's, thence to the Flaggy Meadow road, to the Laurel Point church and back via the Fairmont Pike to the Red Bridge and the starting point. Length of route, twenty-three miles; population served, 720; carrier, George M. Breakiron.

Route No. 2 carrier served the residents of West Morgantown following the arrival of the morning train, then after the arrival of

9. *Evening Post,* June 18, 1900.

10. A ninety-six page article appearing as a preface to the first volume of these *Reports* gave a history of the movement culminating in the establishment of West Virginia. It was reprinted separately by the author in 1891, with the note that: "If it is tinged with the white heat of the conflict, the afterglow may not be unworthy." It was again reprinted in 1978 by reproduction from an original copy by Jonathan Sheppard Enterprises, Albany, N.Y.

the Pittsburg train, the carrier went west over the old state road to Wisman's corner, then to Flickersville, then to the state road via No. 12 School, thence by the road leading to the Monongahela River and back to Morgantown. Length of Route, twenty-three miles; population served, 625; carrier, Harley Thompson.

Route No. 3 ran from the Morgantown Post Office via the Uniontown Pike to Easton and the Mont Chateau hotel and Uneva, thence to the mouth of Morgans Run and up Cheat River to Ice's Ferry, thence by the Warm Hollow road to Morgantown. The population served was 875, the carrier Oscar C. Gregg.[11]

The M.&K. Railroad. Work on the Morgantown and Kingwood Railroad proceeded rapidly during the year. Track-laying started late in 1899. J. A. Martin, general superintendent, announced the purchase of a forty-two ton, ten-wheeler locomotive.[12] On February 14 a special train was run as far as Dellslow, carrying numerous guests. The big trestle over Deep Hollow, at Dellslow, was crossed safely. The trestle was four hundred feet long, sixty-five feet high, and contained two hundred feet of lumber.[13] Alfred C. Oliver, Pixler and Wittman, and T. Pickenpaugh and Gowing had sawmills in operation along the scenic Deckers Creek Valley.[14]

One of the first wrecks on the line occurred May 8 when two wild cars loaded with crossties ran from the big trestle down to the sawmill, struck the locomotive and damaged it badly.[15]

Bennett and Grinnell, of New York, purchased sixty acres from Gowing Brothers and planned to open a large stone quarry.[16]

On Saturdays during the early fall passenger trains accommodated tourists who could ride as far as Lick Run, then walk to Cheat View, four miles away, to hunt, gather chestnuts, and enjoy the magnificent scenery.[17]

Ground was broken on November 13 for an engine house beneath the South Park bridge. It was to be 18 by 150 feet in size.[18]

By November the end of the track had reached the Preston County line.

11. *Evening Post*, October 9, 1900.
12. *Evening Post*, January 15, 1900.
13. *Evening Post*, February 15, 1900.
14. *Evening Post*, March 3, 1900.
15. *Evening Post*, May 8, 1900.
16. *Evening Post*, July 13, 1900.
17. *Evening Post*, October 30, 1900.
18. *Evening Post*, November 14, 1900.

Through Trains to Clarksburg. A greatly improved timetable for B&O passenger trains went into effect on November 25, with trains running through to Clarksburg, instead of having passengers change at Fairmont to the Monongahela River Railroad, as had previously been necessary.

Train No. 1 left Morgantown at 6:00 a.m., arriving in Pittsburgh at 9:50 a.m. Train No. 2 left Pittsburgh at noon and arrived in Morgantown at 5:00 p.m.

Other north-bound trains left Morgantown at 9:07 a.m. and 3:20 p.m., while south-bound trains left at 10:40 a.m. and 8:35 p.m.[19]

Bridge Across Cheat. The county court, on June 6, let a contract for construction of a bridge across Cheat River at Ice's Ferry. The contract was awarded to Walker Brothers, of Charles Town, for twenty-six thousand dollars. The bridge was to be of steel and wrought iron, 585 feet long, in two spans of 240 feet and one of 105 feet in length. The roadway was to be eighteen feet wide. The piers were of stone to eight feet above low water mark, and on top of them steel cylinder piers extending thirty-five feet above the masonry. The floor line was forty-five feet above the low water mark.[20]

The Greenmont Bridge. Started late in 1899, work on the high-level Greenmont bridge continued through the winter. This was recognized in the community as being a tremendously significant project, since it would, for the first time, make it easy to cross from Greenmont into Morgantown. It seemed impossible: "It is the most stupendous piece of engineering ever attempted here. . . . Holes for the abutments are being dug and in all 25 men and a half dozen teams are at work."[21]

William L. Wilson. Dr. William Lyne Wilson, president of Washington and Lee University and former president of West Virginia University, died October 17, 1900. He was born in Jefferson County in 1843, the son of Benjamin and Mary Whiting (Lyne) Wilson. He was named president of West Virginia University in 1882 but was elected to Congress the same year and resigned the

19. *Evening Post*, November 23, December, 1900.
20. *Evening Post*, June 7, 1900.
21. *Evening Post*, June 18, 1900. This bridge was at Pleasant Street.

presidency to take effect at the end of the term. He was named postmaster general under President Grover Cleveland in 1892 and became president of Washington and Lee University in 1896.[22]

Walter Hayes. One of the best known men in Morgantown, William Walter Hayes, died September 12, 1900. The son of Manliff and Alice Hayes, he was born May 12, 1849. He had been in the livery business since his youth, when he started driving for his father, later engaging in the business on his own, in Clarksburg, Fairmont, and, finally, in Morgantown. He served on the town council and also as justice of the peace.

He married Ona, daughter of Samuel Howell, and they had two children, Miss Flora Hayes, a well-known musician, and Guy Hayes, who was with his father in the livery business.[23]

P. H. Keck. Philip Henry Keck, a prominent Monongalia County lawyer, died April 11, 1900. The son of John Keck, he was born at Reading, Pennsylvania, March 6, 1820. His father brought the family to Monongalia County in 1822, settling on Days Run. Philip read law and was admitted to the bar, practicing law in Morgantown from 1844 until shortly before his death. He was elected prosecuting attorney in 1856.

He married Annie Brown and one son, L. V. Keck, survived.[24]

B. L. Morgan. The son of Henry M. and Josephine Lazier Morgan, Bernard Lazier Morgan, died January 13, 1900, after a long illness. Born August 23, 1866, he had in 1898 succeeded his father as an editor of the *Morgantown Post,* along with his brother, William H. But his career was quite short. He was highly regarded by the people of Morgantown.[25]

"South Park." "The name of the new and beautiful addition to Morgantown, across Deckers creek, is 'South Park.' The commitee of shareholders in the company building the new bridge to their addition decided upon the name Friday morning, after deliberating for several days. South Park was one of thirty names

22. *Evening Post,* October 18, 1900; *W.Va. Heritage Encyclopedia,* pp. 5127-29.
23. *Evening Post,* September 12, 1900.
24. *Evening Post,* April 12, 1900; Wiley, pp. 342, 343.
25. *Evening Post,* January 13, 14, 1900.

Fig. 60. South Park Bridge across Deckers Creek, under construction. (From J. W. Wiles, *Morgantown's Suburbs.*)

suggested by Edward McGrew Heermans, of THE POST's staff, and he wins the $10 prize offered by J. W. Wiles, one of the promoters of the enterprise."[26]

Big Oil Strike. "The biggest oil well ever encountered in the county has been struck by the drill in Battelle District. . . . The drill reached the pay last night and the well at once began to throw the greasy fluid out at a rapid rate. It is now making twelve hundred barrels every twenty-four hours." The well was on the Milo Strosnider farm, three miles from Cross Roads, and was drilled by the Battelle Oil Company.[27]

New Post Offices. Two new rural post offices were established in 1900. One called McMellin, in Union District, began operation December 22, 1900, with Alice B. Barnes as postmistress. The other, named Willey, in Battelle District, was established October 19, 1900, with John W. Haught as postmaster.

26. *Evening Post,* August 17, 1900.
27. *Daily New Dominion,* January 27, 1900; *Evening Post,* January 27, 1900.

New Episcopal Church. The Trinity Episcopal congregation built a new church on Willey Street at the corner of North High, moving there from their old location farther down on High Street.[28]

Sturgiss Methodist Church. A Methodist congregation was organized in the Fairchance Schoolhouse about 1900 about four miles northwest of Masontown, on the old Independence Turnpike (vol. 3, p. 243). Judge G. C. Sturgiss donated land for a church building, which was constructed and named for him. Leaders in the establishment of the congregation were G. M. C. Mayfield, George Kephard, and W. D. McCauley. "This is the highest Church in the county, being well over 2,100 feet."[29]

Miscellany. In 1900: The old gristmill on Deckers Creek at Deep Hollow started by Michael Kerns about 1780, ceased operations; the last owner was Dr. H. M. N. Mackey and the miller was Jeremiah Joseph (Callahan, p. 186). . . . John C. Kincaid started the first wholesale grain business in Morgantown (Callahan, p. 251). . . . A new church building was constructed by the Mount Pleasant M.P. congregation on the Kingwood Pike (Dodds and Dodds, p. 84). . . . The Dunkard Valley Baptist Church, at Wise, was destroyed by fire on December 15, just after Sunday School (Dodds and Dodds, p. 137). . . . The Monongahela River was frozen solidly for a week in January from Pittsburgh to Morgantown; not a boat was moving (*Daily New Dominion,* January 5, 1900). . . . Two brick factories were operating at Morgantown, (*Daily New Dominion,* January 20, 1900). . . . One of the best oil wells ever struck in the state came in on the lands of Seth Tennant and Furman Cook, on Days Run; it made 2,920 barrels the first forty-eight hours (*Evening Post,* January 13, 1900). . . . Morgantown's first labor union, an organization of carpenters and joiners, was effected (*Evening Post,* January 20, 1900). . . . The thermometer registered seventy-eight degrees in the shade at the Acme Book Store today (*Evening Post,* February 8, 1900). . . . The South Penn Oil Company brought in a 1000-barrel-a-day well on the Eli Collins Farm, on Campbells Run (*Evening Post,* March 17, 1900). . . . Local newspapers were carrying daily results of National baseball games (*Evening Post,* April 20, 1900). . . . Citizens

28. Dodds and Dodds, p. 75.
29. Dodds and Dodds, pp. 88, 89.

of Morgantown welcomed persons attending the State Christian Endeavor Convention (*Evening Post*, May 15, 1900). . . . Dr. Allsup[30] was camping at the Charles Morgan gristmill at Uffington (*Evening Post*, June 14, 1900). . . . Five additional oil tanks were built in the tank field, at a cost of ten thousand dollars (*Evening Post*, June 15, 1900). . . . A party of Morgantown society folks narrowly escaped death June 22 when the carriage in which they were returning from Mont Chateau plunged from the Cheat River ferry (*Evening Post*, June 23, 1900). . . . Coleman Straight, of Arnettsville, died as a result of falling from his horse on the way to a gristmill (*Evening Post*, July 23, 1900). . . . Several people died in a typhoid fever epidemic (*Evening Post*, August 27, 1900). . . . Hundreds of persons attended the Grand Lodge sessions of Knights of Pythias in Morgantown (*Evening Post*, October 9, 1900). . . . M. M. Neely, a student in the university, was brought before a justice of the peace, charged with creating a disturbance at Commencement Hall (*Evening Post*, November 1, 1900). . . . Jack Sadler, of Cheat Neck, was killed when thrown from his wagon on a rough road near the Costello Mill (*Evening Post*, November 9, 1900). . . . The Trans-Allegheny Historical Society was organized in Morgantown, under the leadership of Col. R. E. Fast (Society Journal). . . . The Citizens National Bank was organized in Morgantown (Callahan, p. 254).

30. See vol. 3, p. 548.

CHAPTER ONE HUNDRED TWENTY-FIVE

1901

It was in 1901, with the beginning of the twentieth century, that Morgantown finally became a city, incorporating its three suburbs under a single government.

The original Morgan's-Town, or Morgantown, was created by an act of the General Assembly of Virginia in October 1785.[1] It included fifty acres of land, the property of Zackquill Morgan. Government was vested in five trustees, Samuel Hanway, John Evans, David Scott, Michael Kerns, and James Daugherty. An act of the General Assembly on January 4, 1822, amended the act of establishment and redefined the powers of the trustees.[2]

A new borough charter was adopted in 1838 and the number of trustees was increased to seven, elected at large annually in April by a *viva voce* vote. Borough records are complete from the first meeting of this board of trustees.[3]

To remedy defects in the 1838 charter, a new charter was obtained from the General Assembly in 1860 and was adopted by the citizens. This changed the government from a board of trustees to a manager and council.[4]

Morgantown's population grew very slowly. In 1792 it was estimated at 500. In 1850, the first time the census reported the population of the borough, it was 871; in 1860 it had fallen to 749, reached only 787 in 1870, fell to 745 in 1880. In 1890 it had risen to 1,011 and was reported as 1,895 in 1900.

The City of Morgantown. A local newspaper, early in 1901, carried the headline: "A CITY. GREATER MORGANTOWN IS NOW A FACT." The story read:

1. Vol. 2, pp. 123-27.
2. Vol. 2, pp. 489, 490.
3. Vol. 3, p. 159.
4. Vol. 3, p. 500.

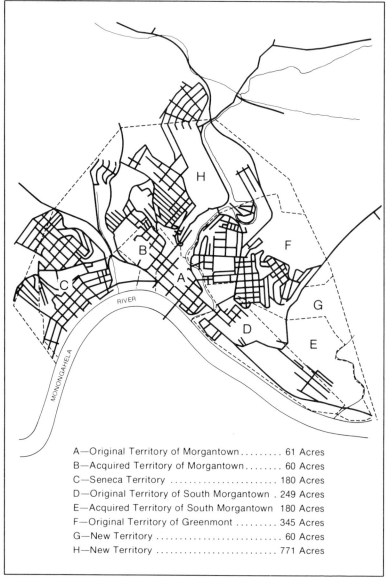

A—Original Territory of Morgantown .... 61 Acres
B—Acquired Territory of Morgantown .... 60 Acres
C—Seneca Territory .... 180 Acres
D—Original Territory of South Morgantown . 249 Acres
E—Acquired Territory of South Morgantown 180 Acres
F—Original Territory of Greenmont .... 345 Acres
G—New Territory .... 60 Acres
H—New Territory .... 771 Acres

Fig. 61. Map of Greater Morgantown, 1901. (Drawn from original sources by Diane Lenhart.)

"The Morgantown charter bill is now a law, except for the Governor's signature, which will soon be affixed. 'Greater Morgantown' is a reality, and that prosperous growing city will show for its true population of 6,000 hereafter, instead of a few hundred, as the census reports show for the old town. . . .

"The signature of the Governor, which has in all probability been appended by this time, will by the wording of the bill make the consolidation of the boroughs date from the day of the passage of the bill, which was Thursday the 24th inst.

"The city of Morgantown will have a population of about 6,000 souls, and an election for officers who will form the government of the new city will occur next spring."[5]

The new city was to be composed of four wards, as follows:

"The first ward shall include the territory within the corporate limits of the town of South Morgantown, together with all the additional territory included in the city limits under this act lying south of the Kingwood Pike.

"The second ward shall include all the territory within the corporate limits of the town of Greenmont, together with the additional territory included in the city limits under this act lying north of Kingwood Pike and south of Deckers Creek.

"The third ward shall include all the territory within the corporate limits of the town of Morgantown, together with all additional territory included in the city limits under this act lying between Falling Run and Deckers Creek.

"The fourth ward shall include all the territory within the corporate limits of the town of Seneca, together with all additional territory included in the city limits under this act lying north of Falling Run on the east side of the Monongahela river."

The election was held on April 4 and the vote was rather light. South Morgantown (the proposed first ward) did not participate at all, feeling the act was unconstitutional. In the second ward 57 votes were cast; in the third ward, 321; and in the fourth ward, 192. George C. Steele was elected the first mayor of the enlarged town and W. E. Arnett the first recorder. The first city council of Greater Morgantown was second ward, Joseph Spurgeon; third ward, Alf K. Smith, H. A. Christy, D. H. Courtney, and M. Hayes; fourth ward, Rufus West.

5. *Evening Post*, January 25, 1901.

These officials, according to the act setting up the new city, were to govern the community until the end of the year, whereupon a new group was to be elected. South Morgantown soon agreed to go along as the first ward.

President Raymond Resigns. Events on the university campus during the winter had added fuel to the already flaming discord between President Raymond and his faculty. The legislature, meeting early in the year, sent an investigating committee to Morgantown, which, after several days on the campus and hearing students in a mass meeting, returned to Charleston with several recommendations, including the removal of the president, who was said to be "too young and inexperienced to deal with men" and whose views and policies were "unsuited to West Virginia conditions." On the other hand, the committee "expressed surprise and gratification at the prosperous condition of the University and commended the zeal and ability of the President."

One of the recommendations was that the governor appoint a new bipartisan (six-three) board of regents, only one of whom could be from the same senatorial district. The new board met on March 17, 1901, and on March 20 accepted the resignation of President Raymond, effective at the end of the spring term, while commending him for his "zeal, tireless energy and great ability." The president and his wife, on a leave of absence with pay, left at once for travel in Europe. A local newspaper noted in a brief headline: "They have gone."

Effective March 21, the powers of administration were vested in Dr. P. B. Reynolds as acting president, who served in that capacity until August 1.

Ambler comments: "Thus ended the Raymond Regime, perhaps the most widely discussed single incident in West Virginia University history. Although it was sarcastically described by a Morgantown newspaper as a 'fruitless effort to Civilize, Christianize and Elevate West Virginia Haw-Eaters,' it had far-reaching and beneficial results,"[6] particularly in directing attention to educators beyond the boundaries of West Virginia and helping to dispel provincialism.[7]

6. P. 338.
7. Ambler, pp. 335-39.

President Purinton.[8] On August 1, 1901, Daniel Boardman Purinton began his duties as the new president of West Virginia University. A native of the state, he was born February 15, 1850, and graduated from the university in 1873. He was a teacher of logic, mathematics, metaphysics, and vocal music on the campus from 1873 until 1890. From March 12, 1880, to June 15, 1882, he had been acting president, was vice-president in 1882-83 and again from 1885 to 1889. On January 1, 1890, he became president of Denison University, at Granville, Ohio.

Harmony, economy, and consideration were watchwords of the new administration. Faculty changes were few; new appointments were largely to replace resignations or retirements. The building program went forward steadily. The "North Wing" extension to "University Building" or "University Hall" was completed in 1901 and the building was renamed Woodburn Hall, for the old Woodburn Seminary.[9]

A cadet band was organized in January 1901, under the direction of Walter A. Mestrezat, a Spanish-American War veteran, who had taught music in the university in 1897 and had seen service as a band director in the Philippines. Members of the band were volunteer cadets, who received the same allowances on the campus as the state cadets. The band brought zest and spirit to university affairs, particularly to athletics, and also figured in state occasions.[10]

A City Hospital. A new hospital, called the City Hospital, was opened for business October 26, 1901, with Mrs. J. Jenifer, formerly of the City Hospital of Baltimore, in charge. She rented for the purpose the Hoffman Building on High Street, formerly occupied by the University School of Music, and fully equipped it as a modern hospital. On the ground floor were two large rooms used as wards for patients unable to pay for private rooms. On the second floor were the private rooms and the operating room. The hospital was open to all doctors and their patients.[11]

Telephone Company Reorganized. In September 1901, Morgantown capitalists bought the controlling interests in the People's

8. *Evening Post,* June 14, 1901.
9. Ambler, pp. 340, 341.
10. Ambler, p. 380. Mestrezat ("Zat") would direct the band for the ensuing forty years.
11. *Evening Post,* October 26, 1901.

Fig. 62-A. Woodburn Hall, with the North Wing added.

Fig. 62-B. Science Hall, built in 1893.

Telephone Company and reorganized it. Work of reconstructing the entire system was commenced at once. New wires and poles were placed and the cable system of carrying wires were installed. A new Imperial switch and distributing board were placed in the central office in Morgantown, which was moved into the Farmers' and Merchants' Bank Building at the corner of High and Pleasant streets. It was expected that the local company would soon rival its competitor, the Bell.[12] In a directory published in 1901, a total of eighty-three phones were listed. Examples were F. and M. Bank, No. 1; Brock and Wade, Physicians, No. 28; William Keener, No. 5-3.

Meanwhile, the American Bell Telephone Company, formed in 1877 by associates of Alexander Graham Bell, and a businessman, Theodore N. Vail, had created a new subsidiary, in 1885, whose function was to build and operate long distance lines. This Bell System had entered Morgantown from Uniontown in 1895 and from Waynesburg in 1900. A line connected Morgantown with Fairmont in 1902. In 1901 the Morgantown city directory listed about 315 subscribers to the Bell system, much larger than the local company.

The First Automobile. "At exactly thirteen minutes and twenty seconds of twelve o'clock today—the time was carefully noted by Mayor Steele—the first automobile ever seen on the paved streets of Morgantown entered the city under a full head of steam. In a moment High Street was crowded with astonished natives. Business was suspended, and the most intense excitement prevailed. Leve Dolton was standing on the corner when he saw the hissing monster bearing down upon him. 'Fire and tow!' shouted Leve, 'Thunder and swort' and hit the bricks for the open country.

"The operator of the vehicle was a geologist engaged in making a Geodetic Survey of the United States. He had left Blairsville, Pa., just before 8 a.m. and arrived here at noon, having travelled 78 miles in four hours."[13]

South Park. A large force of workmen were engaged through the summer in building streets and placing sewers and gas and water

12. *Evening Post,* October 4, 1901.
13. *Evening Post,* September 20, 1901.

Fig. 63. Newly paved Grand Street, in South Park. (From an old postcard.)

lines in the new South Park section. "The remarkable rapidity with which this transformation of green pasture fields to a town with all modern conveniences has been wrought is a high tribute to the energy and progressiveness of Morgantown's enterprising business men."[14]

Progress on the M&K. Business on the M&K was increasing daily, as officials planned to extend the line farther into Preston County. On July 10, for example, fifteen carloads of stone, lumber, and building sand were taken out. Bennett and Grannell had already shipped out over four hundred carloads of stone. The railroad acquired a strip of land a quarter of a mile long beside the right-of-way, two miles from Masontown, in Preston County, with a view of converting it into an amusement park, tentatively named Big Falls Park.[15] By midsummer the line extended only

14. *Evening Post,* August 9, 1901.
15. *Evening Post,* July 11, October 22, 1901. Later designated Oak Park.

six hundred yards into Preston County, where it was being held up by litigation.[16]

About two hundred people rode the train to Coon Hollow on November 17 to witness the explosion of a two-thousand-ton boulder that occupied the right-of-way.[17]

Rev. C. J. Kluser (Portrait, Fig. 40). Members of the Catholic church in Morgantown addressed a petition, dated August 4, 1901, to Bishop Donahue by Jacob Schenck, reading in part as follows:

"We have quite a number of members, enough and more to keep and support a priest. At a recent meeting we held with regard to this matter, we tried to find out what could be done. A committee was appointed to start a subscription list, and we succeeded in getting 62 names who are willing to pay the sum of one dollar per month, . . . and not every Catholic could be seen as yet. We think, therefore, that we are able to maintain a priest, who knows both the German and the English language, as the majority of all Catholics in Morgantown are Germans. . . ." The petition was granted and Rev. C. J. Kluser was sent to take charge of the new parish, which was named Saint Francis de Sales and included all of Monongalia County.[18]

Lutheran Church Dedicated. The dedication of the new Saint Paul's Evangelical Lutheran Church was held May 5, 1901, under the direction of Rev. J. L. Smith, of Pittsburg, with the assistance of Rev. Ira Wallace, the pastor.

The lot on which the church was built, at the corner of Front and Hough streets, was purchased in 1898 from Prof. John A. Myers for eighteen hundred dollars. In July 1900 the foundation of the new building was laid. The building, of frame, was Gothic in style, with natural wood finish inside. It was 32 by 50 feet in size.[19]

New Contract for Locks and Dams. The much-troubled construction of six locks and dams in the Monongahela River between Morgantown and Fairmont, repeatedly stopped when contractors were unable to finish their work, was resumed in 1901, when new

16. *Evening Post*, August 6, 1901.
17. *Evening Post*, November 19, 1901.
18. *Saint Theresa Church*, p. 7.
19. *Evening Post*, May 3, 6, 1901.

contracts were awarded in April. The estimated cost of the whole work was eight hundred thousand dollars. Contracts for dams Nos. 10 and 11 went to Baker and Judson, of Gloversville, New York; for Nos. 12 and 13 to T. A. Gillespie Company, of Pittsburg; and for Nos. 14 and 15 to William A. Howley, of Pittsburg.[20]

Work on the Locks. Baker and Judson, who had succeeded McDonald as a contractor on the locks, quickly went to work on Lock and Dam No. 11 in the Monongahela River, at the old Morgan mill near Uffington. Materials were brought up in barges, tied in on the east side of the river. Sand came from Cheat River and the stone was quarried near Uffington. Carriers (little cars) were operated on cables that crossed the river. The locks and dams were being built of concrete, a relatively new process. Lock No. 10 was complete and the dam nearing completion. The old mill was being used as a stable and storage house.[21]

New Business Buildings. The industrial expansion of the Morgantown area increased the opportunities for various kinds of workmen, such as carpenters, painters, brick and stone masons, electricians, plumbers, etc., as many new commercial buildings were constructed in the downtown section, while residences were built in the outlying districts. Erected in 1901 were the Garlow Building, occupied by the Morgantown Hardware Company, and the Brock-White-Courtney Building, occupied by the Post Office.[22]

Jones Window Glass Plant. On November 5 Miss Bellevernon Jones applied the match to light the fires in a new great industry for Morgantown, the W. R. Jones Window Glass Company. To be the city's largest factory, it had a 48-blower tank, containing five hundred tons of glass. About 36 blowers were to be employed at first and this number was to be increased to 250. The plant was located in Seneca.[23]

Morgantown Ice Company. Deckers Creek and the Monongahela River were, for more than a century, the principal source of ice for the community of Morgantown. The blocks of ice were cut from the streams during the winter and stored in "ice houses" between

20. *Evening Post*, April 18, 1901.
21. *Daily New Dominion*, November 1, 1901.
22. Callahan, p. 271.
23. *Daily New Dominion*, November 6, 1901.

thick layers of sawdust. With the increase in population the streams became polluted and the need for a purer product led to the organization, in 1901, of the Morgantown Ice Company, with a capital stock of thirteen thousand dollars. A plant was established on Beechurst Avenue at Fourth Street and water was secured from two wells about three hundred feet deep.[24]

M. M. Dent. Marshall Mortimer Dent died May 3, 1901, at Granville. The son of Marmaduke and Sarah (Price) Dent, he was born May 2, 1828. He was prominent in politics for nearly half a century. He was editor and proprietor of the *Virginia Weekly Star* from 1856 until 1862. The motto of the paper at first was "Eternal Vigilance is the Price of Liberty," changed in 1860 to "The Federal Union—it must and shall be preserved." He was elected clerk of the county court in 1852 and clerk of the circuit court in 1857. Upon the death of Augustus Haymond, clerk of the circuit court, in 1883, he was appointed to fill out his term.

He was thrice married, to Caroline Roberts (4 children), Louise Holden (1 child), and to Mrs. Ada Baggerly (2 children). Names of the children were Judge M. H., Dr. Arthur, Attorney W. R. D., Mrs. George Woodmansee, Alfred B., Mrs. Charles Montgomery, and Mrs. Lucius Smith.[25]

Miscellany. In 1901: Dora Haught, a member of the West Warren Baptist Church, was ordained as a minister (Dodds and Dodds, p. 132). . . . An oil well producing six hundred barrels the first twenty-four hours was brought in on the Isaac Strosnider farm near Cross Roads by the South Penn Oil Company (*Evening Post,* March 16, 1901). . . . E. C. Bright,[26] former stagecoach driver of Morgantown, died in Keyser April 26; his body was brought to Morgantown by train for burial; he was seventy-two years old. His wife, Ann Isabell, had died January 13, 1882 (*Evening Post,* April 27, May 2, 1901). . . . Adam L. Nye, former postmaster of Morgantown, died June 15, aged seventy-two years (*Evening Post,* June 17, 1901). . . . The stock of the Pittsburg, Brownsville and Geneva Packet Company, with the Mason line of steamers

24. *Post-Chronicle Industrial Edition,* 1913. By 1913 the company was supplying not only the needs of the city of Morgantown but also making shipments on trains to Point Marion, Fairmont, and Kingwood.

25. *Evening Post,* May 3, 1901; Wiley, p. 484.

26. See vol. 3, p. 480.

plying between Morgantown and Pittsburg, passed into the
hands of a new packet company, the Pittsburg, Brownsville and
Morgantown Packet Company, headed by Capt. T. J. Wood,
president; Frank Pride was the local agent (*Evening Post,* July 6,
10, 11, 1901). . . . Three business buildings were in process of construction, the Garlow building on High Street, the Price building
at Walnut and Front, and the Acme Publishing Company building at Maiden Alley and Front Street (*Evening Post,* August 3,
1901). . . . The steamer *Isaac M. Mason* landed 350 excursionists
at Morgantown for an hour's visit (*Evening Post,* August 8,
1901). . . . Commencement Hall was crowded with nearly two
thousand persons on Sunday evening, September 15, for memorial services for President McKinley (*Evening Post,* September 16, 1901). . . . John Alva Myers, former director of the University Agricultural Experiment Station, died April 8 (*Evening
Post,* April 11, 1901). . . . The Morgantown Foundry and Machine
Company later renamed the Romisch Manufacturing Company,
was organized by Anton Romisch (*New Dominion Industrial Edition,* p. 75). . . . The Morgantown City Directory listed the names
of seventeen attorneys, four dentists, one optician, and eleven
physicians. . . . Champ Clark spoke at Commencement Hall on
November 9, but a local editor said his speech was "not much
good" (*Daily New Dominion,* November 11, 1901). . . . The
Methodist Episcopal congregation sold the church building on
Pleasant Street to Dr. I. C. White for ten thousand dollars (*Daily
New Dominion,* November 16, 1901). . . . Four mail deliveries
were being made daily in downtown Morgantown (*Daily New
Dominion,* November 18, 1901). . . . Samuel Thralls died at
Blacksville November 16, aged fifty-four years (*Daily New Do-
minion,* November 20, 1901). . . . George Layton, of Cassville,
died December 5 as a result of being struck by a train in Seneca
(*Daily New Dominion,* December 25, 1901). . . . The county court
let a contract for construction of a bridge across Falling Run to
Sunnyside; the contract went for $11,900 to Walker Bros.,
represented by S. M. Prince (*Daily New Dominion,* December 6,
1901).

CHAPTER ONE HUNDRED TWENTY-SIX

1902

West Virginia University President Eli Marsh Turner, in 1889, had officially described the university library as "a disgrace." Since 1878 Professor J. I. Harvey had been part-time librarian; the single room in University Building (later Woodburn Hall) in which the books, periodicals, and "relics" were housed was "chaotic" and available to readers only a few hours each work day. In desperation some department heads started libraries of their own.

The librarian blamed some of the unfortunate conditions upon the staff of "ex-Confederate colonels," asserting that the institution had steadily declined ever since J. R. Thompson had been forced from the presidency.

To remedy the situation President Turner moved the library into the old chapel room in "Prep Hall" and issued an order requiring all the departmental libraries to be assembled there. Oftentimes in the past, funds budgeted for the library were diverted to what seemed more important current expenses; the president ordered that this was no longer to be done. Greater emphasis was placed on the acquisition and preservation of government documents. A temporary librarian, Margaret E. Morrow, was employed, succeeded in 1890 by Clara Hough.

Jerome K. Raymond, who in 1897 succeeded Dr. James L. Goodnight as president of the university, found the library only slightly improved. It was still housed in a single room in Martin Hall; the shelving was inadequate; the books were scarcely classified and in a state of general confusion; and certain departments were again maintaining their own collections. To deal with the situation, the first professional librarian, Eliza J. Skinner, was employed in 1898 at a salary of seventy dollars a month. About sixteen thousand books and pamphlets were classified according to the Dewey decimal system, while the several departmental libraries were again assembled in the "library room."

The First Library Building. At last steps were taken to provide a suitable home for the university's collection of books and to erect Monongalia County's first library building. President Raymond recommended to the legislature the immediate construction of "a

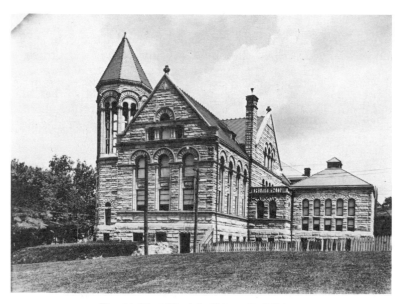

Fig. 64. West Virginia University Library.

fireproof building adequate in size and safe in construction, to contain the library and the museums of the University." The regents had already acquired the old Methodist Episcopal burial ground for this purpose.

The budget approved by the legislature in 1899 included fifty thousand dollars for the new library and museum building. At the same time attention was given to the acquisition of additional land for future expansion. The Fife tract of about seven acres had been purchased in March 1898; it included two small frame houses ("the Fife cottages") which were used for some years for classrooms. About the same time the university acquired lots to the rear of the proposed new library building as the site for a new mechanical hall, to replace the old structure which had been destroyed by fire March 3, 1899.

Daniel Boardman Purinton began his term as president on August 1, 1901, and the building program continued rapidly under his direction. The new library building, a gray Amherst sandstone structure, was completed in 1902 at a cost of about $112,000.[1] William ("Doc") Danser, the eccentric university janitor, who had served for twenty-eight years, died June 10, 1902, and his funeral services were held in Commencement Hall, "an Honor," Ambler says, "never before or since accorded a University employee."[2] The janitor who had been directly responsible to the board of regents and had been a more or less efficient worker, according to his personal likes and dislikes, was soon replaced by a head janitor directly responsible to the superintendent of buildings and grounds.

The M.&K. Railroad. By 1902 the tracks of the Morgantown and Kingwood Railroad had reached Masontown, under the financial management of George C. Sturgiss. In 1902 the line was purchased by Senator Stephen B. Elkins and members of his family, who planned to complete it to connect with the main line of the B.&O. at Rowlesburg.

Other plans of the Elkins family, as announced at a meeting of the directors March 28, 1902, would have made Morgantown a railroad center of considerable importance. One plan included a tunnel from Deckers Creek under the university campus to a proposed bridge across the river and a terminus on the west bank of the river to connect with the long-discussed railroad from Pittsburg up the west side. The Cheat River and Pittsburg Railroad was also purchased by the Elkins interests, who proposed to construct it up Cheat River to connect with the M.&K. at Albright and the B.&O. at Rowlesburg.

1. *New Dominion,* June 24, 1903.
2. P. 341.

The passenger schedule on the M.&K. in 1902 was announced as follows:[3]

M.&K.

East			West	
8.30	4.30	Morgantown	10.41	6.41
8.32	4.32	Marilla	10.39	6.39
8.33	4.33	Pool Rocks	10.38	6.38
8.34	4.34	Johnson	10.37	6.37
8.42	4.42	Rock Forge	10.29	6.29
8.48	4.48	Dellslow	10.23	6.23
8.54	4.54	Oliver	10.17	6.17
8.56	4.56	Sturgisson	10.15	6.15
9.01	5.01	Iron Bridge	10.10	6.10
9.03	5.03	Lick Run	10.08	6.08
9.11	5.11	Cascade Falls	10.00	6.00

Fig. 65. A B&O passenger train at the Union Depot. (Courtesy John Bartko.)

3. *Daily New Dominion*, July 29, 1902.

Developments along the M.&K. By the middle of the year great activity was under way along Deckers Creek on the M.&K. Railroad. The first coal was shipped out July 8 from the A. C. Fullmer coal mine near Woodland, over a branch line. The limestone quarry near Sturgisson was in operation. Work on the sand crushing plant at Sturgisson was under way. The rolling mill and the Marilla Glass factory were under construction. A new highway was being built from the east end of Prospect Street through lands of I. C. White, S. Hirschman, and others to connect the new works to Morgantown.[4]

Sabraton. A new industrial suburb of Morgantown, to be known as Sabraton, or Sturgiss City, was being developed along Deckers Creek, on the route of the M.&K. Railroad. Covering 570 acres, it included the Addison, McClure, Johnson, H. J. Harner, W. T. Harner, and Beall farms.

Manufacturing plants, under construction or proposed, included the Rolling Mill Company, West Virginia Plate Glass Company, Sabraton Automobile Company, Iron and Steel Aluminum Coating Company, and Pressed Prism Plate Glass Company. In the area the Fulmer Coal Company and the Deckers Creek Coal and Coke Company were beginning production.[5]

Over 450 lots were sold in a giant auction on September 10, the highest price being $450, the lowest $50.[6]

B.&O. Passenger Service. By an arrangement between the B.&O. and the M.&K. railroad officials, the Morgantown depot of the B.&O., after April 1, 1902, was used by passengers on both lines, and was thereafter referred to as Union Depot.

Northbound trains on the B.&O. left Morgantown at 5:55 a.m., 8:52 a.m., and 3:09 a.m. Southbound trains were at 11:52 a.m., 5:15 p.m., and 8:46 p.m.

On May 18 a new train was added, arriving at Morgantown at 10:15 p.m., laying over during the night, and departing for Clarksburg at 6:45 a.m.[7]

Pressed Prism Glass. A fourteen-acre site on the M.&K. Railroad a short distance from Morgantown was the location of a new fac-

4. *Daily New Dominion*, July 9, 1902.
5. *Evening Post*, August 12, 1902.
6. *Evening Post*, September 11, 1902.
7. *Daily New Dominion*, January 4, February 28, April 17, 1902.

tory under construction. "It will make prisms. It will be larger than all the other prism factories in the country and will manufacture them under an entirely new process which has just been invented by Prof. F. L. O. Wadsworth of the Allegheny Observatory who is recognized all over the world as a leader in his profession."[8]

New Financial Organizations. Two related organizations were formed during 1902 contributing to the development of the financial life of the community.

The Federal Savings and Trust Company was temporarily organized on May 28 and incorporated on June 5. Officers were elected on June 25, as follows: E. M. Grant, president; Isaac Van Voorhis, vice-president; Alex. H. Tait, vice-president; H. L. Swisher, secretary; E. D. Tumlin, treasurer; and William G. Tait, assistant treasurer. The capital stock was set at two hundred thousand dollars.

The Citizen's National Bank, under the same management and directorship as the Trust Company, but with a separate force of employees, opened for business on October 14 in a building at the corner of High and Walnut streets.[9]

The Acme Publishing Company. A new building was constructed on Front Street in 1902 by the Acme Publishing Company, under the direction of Howard L. Swisher. This company had started in 1897 as a small book store (the Acme Book Store) in the Dering building on Walnut Street. Later it was moved to the Garlow building on High Street and still later was merged with the Acme Department Store, one of the leading mercantile establishments of the growing city.

In 1898 Swisher organized the Acme Publishing Company. This developed into quite an extensive printing concern, and the new building became desirable.[10]

Trolley Franchise Granted. On February 3, 1902, the Morgantown city council granted to the Morgantown Electric Light and Power Company a fifty-year franchise to operate trolley cars on the streets of the town. Members of the company, all "home

8. *Daily New Dominion,* June 21, 1902.
9. *New Dominion Industrial Edition,* 1906, p. 10.
10. *Post-Chronicle Industrial Edition,* 1913, p. 21.

people," were E. M. Grant, W. E. Glasscock, Frank Cox, R. E. Fast, I. C. White, S. D. Hirschman, and J. H. McDermott. They were to pay a percentage of gross earnings to the town. The franchise provided that "no dirty linen is to be transported on the car line," a section that "caused some merriment" when read before council. A big new light and power plant was to be erected.[11]

Plans were made to connect Morgantown by trolley with Fairmont, Kingwood, and Pittsburg.[12]

Guy Brown's Automobile. The automobile, an innovation that at first appeared to be only a fascinating toy, but which in the next half century would completely make over the lives of the American people, had first appeared on the streets of Morgantown in 1901 (p. 271).

In 1902 a young man from Morgantown, J. M. G. ("Guy")

Fig. 66. Guy Brown and his Searchmont automobile, advertising Deering products. (Courtesy Mary Virginia Brown.)

11. *Daily New Dominion*, February 4, 1902.
12. *Daily New Dominion*, July 2, 1902.

Brown was walking down Fifth Avenue in New York City when he saw three horseless buggies in the window of Wanamaker's store. The cars, foreign-made, were of a model known as Searchmont, with a French engine, the Didion. One was painted red, one yellow, one blue.

Mr. Brown bought the red one and it was shipped to him by rail. A man from Wanamaker's came to Morgantown to provide driving instructions. Brown and a close friend, Frank Bannister, both learned to drive and Morgantown was treated to the thrill of witnessing one of the first automobiles in this part of the country, as they drove back and forth on the mostly unpaved streets, scaring the horses, exciting the people, generally having a good time. The car was called for on numerous occasions, in parades and to help draw a crowd.

In late June the two young men decided to make a long trip, to Mount Clemens, Michigan. The roads out of Morgantown were little more than trails, so Brown and Bannister put the Searchmont on the *Adam Jacobs,* a packet steamer that made regular trips to Pittsburgh, and rode with it to that city.

Early in the morning they started out and the first night they made it to Zelienople. On the Fourth of July, after various trials and tribulations, they were in New Castle, out of gasoline. They first tried a drugstore, but unable to find fuel, they were directed to the nearby Atlantic Oil Company refinery, where they secured all the gasoline they needed. They bought some oil, but the employees told them there would be no charge for the gasoline, since they had to dump it in the river anyhow, as a by-product of the refining process.

Nearing Youngstown, they found the tires were beginning to leak badly. So they stopped and wired Wanamaker's to express them immediately four tires. Back came a wire that the tires had been ordered for them from Dunlap's, of Birmingham, England, and they could expect delivery in three to four months. This was the straw that broke the camel's back, and they gave up the trip, had the car hauled to Youngstown by horse, and shipped it back to Martin's Livery Stable, in Pittsburg, for storage.[13]

Rights of Automobiles. Much discussion was being held concerning the rights of the automobile on public roads. A prominent

13. See article in the *Morgantown Post,* July 19, 1958.

local attorney expressed the opinion that, properly operated, they did indeed have a place, but added:

"The question turns upon the inquiry whether it is practicable for the horse and the automobile to use the public highways at the same time without unwarranted interference with each other. It is conceded that the average horse is intolerant of the automobile. His intense fear of it in many instances endangers the life, limbs and property of his owner. It is like taking one's life in his hands to meet an automobile while riding behind some horses. It is the history of the introduction of the automobile everywhere that many serious accidents are occurring every day by its use on the public roads. They are bound to occur here."[14]

The First Automobile Accident. In one of the first automobile accidents reported in Monongalia County history, John Lantz's car was "broken" and a passenger, Henry Demain, slightly injured when the vehicle ran off the road near Uffington. "The machine was backed near the edge of the wall, steam shut off, and before the reverse could be made, the auto rolled . . . over the bank. The occupants telephoned to town for a team, which was sent."[15]

Bad Roads. "Morgantown has fine paved streets in the old part of town, and they are the pride of the city and state. Visitors comment on them every day.

"But she also has about 15 miles of the worst suburban streets any town was ever called upon to tolerate. They lead out in every direction. . . . Some of them are passable and some are impassable for teams. . . .

"The road leading towards Evansville through the First Ward once a fair bicycle track is now so full of 'chuck holes' it is dangerous to drive in a trot over it with a buggy. . . .

"The highway leading to Cheat via Easton, once the pride of the town and the county and on which was the famous mile ground race track, has been well nigh impassable within the city limits. . . ."[16]

Walnut Street Bridge. A contract was awarded by the county court September 3, 1902, for a high level bridge across Deckers

14. *Daily New Dominion,* June 11, 1902.
15. *Evening Post,* August 18, 1902.
16. *Daily New Dominion,* July 10, 1902.

Creek from the end of Walnut Street. The contract price was
$18,632. It was to be 467 feet long, with an 18-foot roadway, and
a 2-foot walk on each side. It was designed to support a twenty-
four-ton street car. Completion was scheduled for June 10, 1903.[17]

The Tank Field. The Morgantown oil tank field was assuming the
status of a station on a main transportation line. To the east a
pipeline from Morgantown already reached Philadelphia and the
Atlantic Seaboard. To the west lines came in from oil fields at
Mannington, Sistersville, Eureka (Pleasants County), and Elm
Run (Ritchie County). In 1902 a main line[18] was extended from
Elm Run to the Kentucky state line (110 miles) to connect with
the Cumberland Pipe Line Company, and a short line was also
laid to Parkersburg (32 miles).

Lynch Chapel. A new Methodist Church was built in 1902 to replace the old Cold Spring Church (vol. 3, p. 319). The Lynch family donated the land and finally paid off the indebtedness on the
building; in gratitude, the congregation named it Lynch Chapel.
It is a small, one-room, frame structure, presenting a pleasant,
peaceful, country scene of a white church amidst green pines.[19]

Snider Temple. A new church building, named Snider Temple,
was erected in 1902 along the old Fairmont Pike at Georgetown.
Included among members of the Methodist congregation which
constructed the building were C. J. Michael, Alvin Michael,
Marion Michael, Davis Arnett, and Mrs. Helen Straight.[20]

Dunkard Valley Bank. The first financial institution in the western end of the county, the Dunkard Valley Bank, opened for business on May 27, 1902. The L. L. Thomas brass band played
music, and the directors invited all depositors to dine with them.[21]
T. J. Collins was the first cashier.

The Centennial Book. In 1902 R. E. Fast published, on the *New
Dominion* press, a 120-page book giving an account of Morgan-

17. *Evening Post*, September 3, 1902.
18. From this a line was laid to developing fields about Hamlin, Lincoln County, in 1909, and later western extensions were laid to connect with Oklahoma,
Texas, and Louisiana fields. Callahan, p. 250.
19. Dodds and Dodds, p. 104; Sylvia Lynch Fetty, ms.
20. Dodds and Dodds, p. 107.
21. *Daily New Dominion*, May 20, 1902.

town's Centennial.[22] Fast explained the long delay in publication of the book:

"It was the intention of the General Committee of Arrangements that a History of the Centennial Celebration of Morgantown, held in 1885, should be published in book form, together with sketches and essays on certain phases of local history to be prepared by individuals to whom the subjects were assigned by the Committee. The task of preparing an account of the celebration and superintending the publication of the essays and papers was assigned to me. Sixteen topics were assigned to as many different individuals, only three of whom ever handed over . . . their manuscripts for publication."

Evidently feeling that sixteen years was long enough to wait, the editor proceeded with the publication, including an account of the celebration and the text of the "Address of Welcome," by William P. Willey and "Historical Address" by Waitman T. Willey. Also included was the Centennial Poem, by Waitman T. Barbe, an article on "Medical History," by Joseph A. McLane, one on "Pioneer History, Tales, Legends, Jokes," by Joseph Moreland, and a short section on "Municipal History," by L. S. Hough and others.

Judge Berkshire. Judge Ralph Lazier Berkshire, a son of William Berkshire, died November 8, 1902. He was born in Bedford County, Pennsylvania, April 8, 1816, and came with his parents to Monongalia County the following year. He worked as a farmer and a carpenter, then studied law under Guy R. C. Allen, and was admitted to the bar in 1841. He was appointed prosecuting attorney in 1847 and was elected to that position in 1852. He was a delegate to the Wheeling Convention in 1861.

In 1861 he was elected judge of the Twentieth Judicial Circuit, serving until 1863, when he was elected as a judge in the West Virginia Supreme Court of Appeals, serving until 1867, most of the time as president of the court. He was elected to the state senate in 1874. He practiced law in Morgantown until shortly before his death.[23]

---

22. "A Fragment. The Centennial Celebration of the Founding of Morgantown. 1785-100-1885. With Addresses and Papers."

23. *Evening Post*, November 8, 1902; Wiley, pp. 323, 324.

Miscellany. In 1902: Telephone lines of the Bell system connected Morgantown with Fairmont (Callahan, p. 285). . . . Frank James, brother of outlaw Jesse James, appeared at the Opera House (*Daily New Dominion*, January 15, 1902). . . . The "Finest Concert ever Heard in Morgantown" was presented by the School of Music under the direction of Miss Russell McMurphy (*Daily New Dominion*, January 24, 1902). . . . Engineers were surveying for a proposed trolley line to connect Fairmont with Masontown, Pennsylvania, via Morgantown and Point Marion (*Daily New Dominion*, January 25, 1902). . . . The First Ward Planing Mill was destroyed by fire (*Daily New Dominion*, January 28, 1902). . . . Edward Utt, aged twenty, was killed in a slate fall in the Meeks coal mine near the Experiment Farm (*Daily New Dominion*, February 5, 1902). . . . The Mackey mill on Deckers Creek, operated by S. N. Pollock, was destroyed by fire (*Daily New Dominion*, February 19, 1902). . . . William Jennings Bryan was a visitor in Morgantown for a reception headed by President D. B. Purinton (*Daily New Dominion*, March 1, 1902). . . . A franchise for supplying gas and water to Morgantown residents was granted by city council to the Union Gas and Water Company (*Daily New Dominion*, March 18, 1902). . . . "The second oldest house in Morgantown," next to the Baptist church, was torn down; former owners included James Shay and Thornton Pickenpaugh (*Daily New Dominion*, April 5, 1902). . . . Rev. Thomas A. Haldeman died May 11 (*Daily New Dominion*, May 12, 1902). . . . The biggest coal sale ever made in the county, involving ten thousand acres of the Pittsburg vein around Ponetown, Mooresville, Hagans, and McCurdysville, was made to Uniontown promoters (*Daily New Dominion*, May 15, 1902). . . . The Monongahela Packet Company joined the Pittsburg, Brownsville, Geneva and Morgantown Packet line in providing service for Morgantown (*Daily New Dominion*, June 4, 1902). . . . About forty new dwellings were constructed in the Peninsula section along Deckers Creek (*Daily New Dominion*, July 17, 1902). . . . In a race from Morgantown to Lock No. 9, the steamers *Elizabeth* and *I. C. Woodward*, laden with 150 passengers, reached and entered the lock together and became stuck (*Daily New Dominion*, July 20, 1902). . . . About two hundred coke ovens were under construction on the Stimmel bottom below Dellslow (*Daily New Dominion*, August 13, 1902). . . . The Morgantown Post Office showed a marked gain in receipts for 1901-02 ($13,299) as compared with 1900-01 ($11,763) (*Evening Post,* September 29, 1902). . . . Dean and Hoffman Company received the contract for construction of four miles of street railway in Morgantown, for about thirty thousand dollars (*Evening Post,* December 17, 1902). . . . The Monongahela Textile Company closed operations on July 1 (*Evening Post,* January 6, 1903). . . . Nellie Barr, daughter of Lewis W. and Zana Thorne Barr,[24] was the first operator for the Wadestown Telephone Company (*Dominion-Post,* January 6, 1973). . . . The United States Window Glass Company, Factory No. 2, was established at Marilla (Callahan, p. 269). . . . Thornton Pickenpaugh, who had operated a store in Morgantown since 1874, died (*Evening Post,* August 18, 1902; Wiley, pp. 573, 583, 604).[25]

24. Born October 13, 1883, she married Milton B. Liming and died January 6, 1973.

25. He was a son of Nicholas Pickenpaugh, whose father, George, had settled on Scotts Run before 1830. See *Sesquicentennial of Monongalia County,* p. 257.

CHAPTER ONE HUNDRED TWENTY-SEVEN

1903

The rapid expansion of the city of Morgantown after 1900 and its extension far beyond the original boundaries made desirable the development of transit lines to carry residents of the outlying sections into the downtown business area.

Fortunately, a new mode of transportation gave promise of providing the system that Morgantown needed.

The first street cars were operated in European cities and were pulled by horses. With the development of electricity inventors began trying to use electric power to propel the cars. Frank J. Sprague opened the first successful electric street railway in the United States in Richmond, Virginia, in 1888 and the electric cars quickly replaced horse cars in American cities.

The street cars got their power from an overhead line suspended from poles, connected to the car by means of a long rod called a trolley. From this the cars came to be known as trolley cars. The usual type of car had a small trolley wheel, or "shoe," riding along the wire, conducting the current down the rod and to the motors under the car. Frequent sparks were caused when the wheel momentarily lost contact with the wire and at night these flashes, like small flashes of lightning, told of the presence of a car in a given section of a city.

The First Street Car Line. Morgantown's first street railway system was constructed in 1903 by the Morgantown Traction and Electric Company. Known as the "Loop Line," it ran the length of High Street, down Foundry to Front, north on Front to Beechurst Avenue, and out Beechurst to Eighth Street, thence back via Beverly Avenue, Prospect Street, and Willey Street to High.

"Promptly at 5.05 o'clock p.m., Tuesday, June 16, 1903, the first electric trolley car was started on Front Street, opposite the

Fig. 67. Loop cars passing in front of the University Library building.

Fig. 68. The "Hickory Tree" Street Car, stopped in front of the residence of George Wells, in Riverside.

B.&O. depot." Among invited guests were I. C. White, George C. Sturgiss, William E. Glasscock, Mayor McGrew, Mr. and Mrs. Walter L. Webb, and others. Charles R. Miles was the motorman on the first car, and Earl Smart was another motorman; both had experience in Parkersburg.

"All along the line people were out . . . gaping in wonder at the moving monsters. . . . On Front Street a team was scared off on the sidewalk. . . . If the ice man did not reach you today you will know the reason why. It took two men to guide the horses past the cars, and left but one to deliver ice."[1]

Operation of the system was actually carried on by the Union Utility Company (p. 299), which, on April 1, 1903, purchased the assets of the Morgantown Traction and Electric Company, together with those of the Union Improvement Company, which had been organized in December 1889, by E. M. Grant, A. M. Comstock, T. B. Gregory, and others, for the purpose of utilizing the gas in the Dunkard Ridge and Dolls Run oil field by transporting it to Morgantown. This company was successful in bringing the first glass factory to Morgantown.

An author a few months later described the trolley system as follows: "The company operates in the city of Morgantown a modern and model street railway system, the construction of which is considered the best that money and experienced talent could obtain. The schedule of the cars, and the first-class appearance and condition of the equipment, together with the care and efficiency of the motormen and conductors has built a considerable traffic, more than is enjoyed by any system in a similarly populated community. . . . The convenience and arrangement of the car barns for the caring of the cars, as well as for repairing the car parts is excellent, and excites favorable comment whenever visited."[2]

The Wabash Railroad. In 1903 there seemed to be excellent prospects that Monongalia County was about to have a third railroad. The Wabash system projected a line south to Fairmont to tap the vast coal fields, just starting to be developed. Finding the right-of-way up the Monongahela River under dispute, it was proposed that the line pass through Washington and Waynesburg.

1. *New Dominion*, June 24, 1903.
2. *The New Dominion Industrial Edition*, 1906, p. 81.

Leaving Waynesburg, the proposed route proceeded through Gump, down the valley of Rudolphs Run to Dunkard Creek near Pentress, thence by a tunnel to the valley of Jakes Run near Mooresville and up that valley to its head, then by another tunnel to McCurdysville and down Paw Paw Creek to the Monongahela River at Rivesville.

In June it was reported: "The people of Mooresville are jubilant over the prospect of having a railroad and are refusing to sell their coal at any price. The Wabash is certainly surveying all possible routes through this county and surely ought to get the best one when it does get down to practical business."[3]

After a summer marked by feverish activity on the part of surveyors, right-of-way buyers, and speculators, construction work finally began on September 3:

"Dirt is flying on the Wabash on Jake's Run today. The work was begun with some ceremony this morning when contractor Ferguson stuck a silver pick into the ground and broke a bottle of champagne. About 30 workmen began the work and in a few days this number will be increased to several hundred. Three big Wabash camps are now located in this county. These are at McCurdysville, Mooresville, and Jake's Run. At the latter place 17 big shanties have been built and a big store room. Similar camps are located at McCurdysville and Mooresville. The people all along the route are excited over the prospects and have a right to be.

"For several weeks big teams of mules have been busy rushing lumber for the camps from Fairmont to McCurdysville. The teams are driven in a trot from the railroad station and back, and, were the animals not the fine specimens they are, dead mules would have strewn the road side between the places. Along with the army of workmen have come the usual number and variety of camp followers, storekeepers, booze peddlers, land scalpers, and men of other callings who hope to make their share out of the enterprise, and the county is swarming with them.

"One year from December 1 trains will be running over the Wabash through this county."[4]

The Morgantown and Kingwood Railroad, then under construction, considered building a line across the river and down the

3. *Morgantown Post,* June 10, 1903.
4. *Daily New Dominion,* September 3, 1903.

Fig. 69. Map showing layout of Pentress Junction. (Courtesy Mabel Henkins.)

west side, thence by way of Scotts Run and Dolls Run to join the Wabash at Pentress (then often called New Brownsville). "The C. E. Johnson heirs who own 140 acres of ground at the village of New Brownsville have been offered $200 per acre for the surface by the Wabash. A depot will be located at New Brownsville which is a fine site for a town and as this land surrounds the village the supposition is, of course, that the Wabash expects a big town to spring up here. If the Wabash secures the land the company will see to the location of factories sufficient to make a good sized town."[5]

"The Conservative Reaction."[6] President Purinton was not slow in making changes in the internal government of the university, deemed advisable for its proper advancement. Policy determining functions were vested in the University Council, a body made up of eleven members, including seven departmental representatives, the commandant of the cadet corps, the registrar, the principal of the preparatory school, and the president himself. The council was responsible for student discipline, courses of study, entrance requirements, and requirements for degrees.

A College of Medicine had been established (on paper) by the regents in 1900, but the order was rescinded in 1901. Courses in anatomy and physiology were offered in Arts and Sciences by William A. Caldwell, succeeded by J. N. Simpson in 1902. An order of the regents, on March 3, 1903, authorized the university to affiliate with the College of Physicians and Surgeons, in Baltimore, "with a view to offering the first two years of a course for the degree of Doctor of Medicine." Without any further authorization, the catalogue announced the restoration of the College of Medicine.[7]

Supervision of the College of Engineering and Mechanic Arts in 1903 was assumed by Will H. Boughton as acting dean. Okey Johnson, dean of the College of Law, died June 17, 1903 and was succeeded by St. George Tucker Brooke as acting dean, beginning September 1, 1903.[8]

The year was a turning point in the history of university

---

5. *Daily New Dominion,* August 27, 1903.
6. Ambler (*History of Education in West Virginia,* p. 340) thus labels the Purinton administration.
7. Ambler, p. 348.
8. Ambler, p. 349; *New Dominion,* June 24, 1903.

athletics. The 1903 football team won, by default, its first victory over W. & J. In the last few seconds the game was tied, 6 to 6, and West Virginia had the ball with one foot to go for a touchdown. W. & J. linemen repeatedly kicked the ball out of the center's hands, even though repeatedly warned by the umpire to desist. The umpire then declared the game forfeited to West Virginia by a score of 6-0. "Already the contest had degenerated into a free-for-all fist fight which was continued from the playing field to the hotel and resulted in interrupted athletic relations during the ensuing two years. . . .

"The holiday in celebration of the event was featured by a bonfire, around which night-shirt clad youths danced and shrieked after the manner of primitive savages celebrating their victories."[9] Speeches were made by the president, the coach, members of the faculty, townsmen. The record that year was 7-1, the only defeat coming from Ohio State.

The First Theater. Morgantown's first playhouse, the Grand Theatre, on Walnut Street between Spruce and High, was opened to the public in 1903.

It is true that various types of entertainment had been associated with campus life ever since the establishment of the university. Even before that, plays were sometimes presented in the auditorium of the Monongalia Academy. Occasionally, theatrical productions were presented there, as also in the Opera House, opened in 1895 (p. 197). Concerts and lectures were presented, open to the public, and were well attended. In the last quarter of the nineteenth century, popular concerts were given by various local bands, including the "Comet," the "Home," and Walter A. Mestrezat's well-known band. The quiet town in those days did not have many forms of entertainment and welcomed productions on the campus, many of which were open to the public.

The building in which the Grand Theatre was housed was constructed by the Odd Fellows lodge in the 1890s. Prior to that time there were few places suitable for a playhouse or even for public meetings except in the courthouse or in assembly rooms in schools or churches. It was to meet this need that a part of the building was constructed.

In 1903 H. A. Christy began the operation of the theater. His

9. Ambler, p. 366.

bookings were the best he could get and the theater quickly grew in popularity.

H. L. Swisher was also operating a theater by 1903. His theater column in a local newspaper listed such attractions as "the popular comedian," Geo. F. Hall, "in his latest Laughing Success, a new western Drama," "An American Hustler,"[10] the "Pretty, Dainty, Petite . . . Charming Little Comedienne," Miss Adelaide Thurston and "her excellent company" presenting "At Cozy Corners,"[11] the "Great Sensational Drama," "The Tide of Life,"[12] etc.

First M.E. Church. A new building for the Morgantown Methodist Episcopal Church, on the corner of High and Willey streets, was dedicated November 27, 1904, by Bishop Charles H. Fowler. The building replaced the one on Pleasant Street (see vol. 3, p. 335), in which the congregation had worshipped since 1850.

The project had been under construction for a number of years, as the need for additional space became more imperative with the rapid growth of the city. Great difficulty was experienced in finding an eligible site, but finally an option was signed and the lot purchased for fifteen thousand dollars.

Ground was broken for the church on Tuesday evening, April 14, 1903, and the cornerstone was laid Monday afternoon, October 19, 1903, with about fifteen hundred people present. About ten thousand dollars was subscribed at the latter service.

"The architectural style of the exterior and the interior follows very early English Gothic. . . . The dimensions of the building are 88 feet wide by 134 feet deep; on the corner of the building at the intersection of the two streets is a tower 114 feet high. This tower contains a chime of twelve bells which are operated from the choir gallery. The auditorium is 67 feet by 78 feet and has an inclined floor and the church is seated with pews, with accommodations for seven hundred sittings. The choir gallery is immediately back of the platform and has sufficient capacity for a large choir, and also contains the gallery. The Sunday School room occupies a space 44 feet by 80 feet and is directly back of the auditorium, and by an arrangement of sliding panels the auditorium and the Sunday school room can be thrown together, forming one large

10. *Daily New Dominion*, April 1, 1903.
11. Ibid., April 3, 1903.
12. Ibid., April 6, 1903.

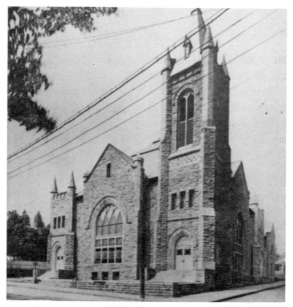

Fig. 70. The First M.E. Church of Morgantown.

room giving a total seating capacity of over one thousand people. Every part of this building is decorated in oil paint and the color scheme is harmonious in every respect, the auditorium being decorated in shades of old rose, and the ceilings being of ivory tint, and this same scheme is carried into the Sunday School room."[13]

The structure was built of cut stone, of a handsome light color, and was secured from a local quarry. The total cost of the completed property was $110,000.

Progress on the M.&K. At a stockholders' meeting of the Morgantown and Kingwood Railroad Company, April 6, 1903, President Davis Elkins reported the purchase of the Cheat River and Pittsburg Railroad and at another meeting on May 11 it was determined to extend the M.&K. to connect with the Cheat River line at Albright. At the same meeting it was agreed that the road should be extended to Rowlesburg to connect with the main line.

13. *New Dominion Industrial Edition*, May 10, 1906.

After a long delay, construction was resumed and the M.&K. was completed to Bretz in September 1903.[14]

Fourteenth Judicial Circuit. By Chapter 20 of the 1903 State Legislature, Monongalia and Marion counties became the Fourteenth Judicial Circuit. Lewis and Harrison became the Thirteenth and Taylor, Randolph, Barbour, and Preston composed the Fifteenth. John William Mason was judge of the local circuit, having been appointed in June 1900 to succeed John Marshall Hagans, deceased, and elected later that year.

Mona and Sturgisson. A post office by the name of Mona was established April 20, 1903, in the village of Granville, with John W. Parker as the first postmaster. The village was established as Grandville by the Virginia general assembly January 22, 1814 (vol. 2, pp. 412, 413), and a post office was set up about 1830, with Melford P. Massie as the first postmaster. It is said that there was already a post office by the name of Grandville in Virginia, hence the name was changed to Granville.[15] The post office was discontinued December 20, 1880, and residents received their mail at Morgantown. When, after more than twenty years, an office was reestablished, there was another Granville in the state, so that name Mona[16] was selected, although the village continued to be called Granville.

To serve workers in the mines, quarries, and sawmills along Decker's Creek, on the new M.&K. Railroad, a post office was established about six miles east of Morgantown on April 17, 1903. Named Sturgisson, in honor of George C. Sturgiss, who had helped bring about many of the developments, the postmistress was Ada L. Van Norman.

The Union Utility Company. On April 1, 1903, the Union Utility Company was formed in Morgantown, acquiring the assets of Union Gas and Water Company (itself the successor of the Union Improvement Company) and the Morgantown Traction and Electric Company. The old Union Improvement Company not only brought the first gas to Morgantown (from the Dunkard Ridge oil field) but also the first water system (from the Tibbs Run reser-

14. Callahan, p. 281.
15. Wiley, p. 721. This statement appears doubtful. The name change was through a gradual loss of the "d."
16. An abbreviation of Monongahela.

voir). These companies were also largely responsible for initiating Morgantown's industrial growth, helping to bring in the Seneca Glass Company (1896), the W. R. Jones Glass Company (1901), the Mississippi Wire Glass Company (1902), and the Economy Tumbler Company (1905).

The company proceeded to construct a large electric plant, replacing the earlier Sturgiss plant (p. 154). The new plant was located along Deckers Creek at the site of the old Kerns (vol. 2, p. 148) and Rogers Mills (vol. 2, p. 509). This plant was designed to supply the normal electric needs of the community, but also to provide power for the new street railway system.[17]

Athens Lumber Company. With a capital of twenty-five thousand dollars, the Athens Lumber Company, of Morgantown, was incorporated in September 1903, by W. W. Graham, W. E. Price, A. F. Gibson, George Jolliffe, J. W. Hinkle, and others. Graham, who became president, had operated a sawmill since 1887. Gibson (born 1850), for many years a general merchant in Tunnelton, became secretary-treasurer, while Price became vice-president.

The plant was located near the mouth of Deckers Creek, with railroad and river shipping advantages. It was formerly operated by the First Ward Planing Mill Company. Some of the incorporators of the new company were also incorporators of the new Graham-Yeager Lumber Company, owner of some of the finest timber land in the vicinity.[18]

A New Water Plant. To supplement the supply of water from the Tibbs Run impoundment (p. 130), now inadequate for the growing city, a new plant and pumping station was established in 1903 along the river just above the mouth of Cobun Creek. The filtration plant used the sand method and other modern purifiers. From a deep well at the plant the water was pumped to a reservoir near the top of the South Park hill, from which it was distributed by lines that reached the entire city.[19]

Colonel Fairchild. Col. Ashbel Fairchild, well-known Morgantown carriage maker, died December 13, 1903. He was born at Smithfield, Pennsylvania, October 19, 1830, the son of Rev. A. G.

17. *New Dominion Industrial Edition*, 1906, p. 5; Callahan, pp. 286, 287.
18. *New Dominion Industrial Edition*, 1906, p. 42.
19. Callahan, p. 286.

and Eliza Fairchild. He moved to Morgantown in 1847 and was a student in Monongalia Academy.

"The well known carriage-making firm of Fairchild, Laughead and Company was founded by Col. Fairchild in 1852 and he remained in the business as senior partner until 1890. At that time he became president and manager of the Tygart Manufacturing Company and continued as such for eight years."[20]

George M. Reay (Portrait, vol. 3, p. 366). George Madison Reay died at his home in South Morgantown on August 15, 1903. The son of John Otho and Elizabeth Reay, he was born October 22, 1813, in what later became Hardy County. He came to Morgantown in 1833 and served as an apprentice to Rev. Joseph A. Shackleford. In 1843 he built a tannery in Durbannah, which he later sold to Fairchild, Laughead and Company, and in 1859 he bought the South Morgantown foundry, which he was still operating at the time of his death. He built the first house in South Morgantown.[21]

Work on the Locks. Construction work on the navigational locks and dams were proceeding at a very slow rate, but some progress was being made.

"The machinery used in the construction of Lock No. 11 is being moved as rapidly as possible to Lock 10 and set up for work. The coffer dam at ten has been finished, and pumps were set to work today to empty the water out of it.

"Lock 11 is finished and the old road along the bank to Uffington is finally closed. A gap in the lock wall was left upon for a long time to allow teams to pass, but this was closed up the other day, and several people who tried to go that way had to turn back. It is impossible to get through now except on foot.

"Between Lock 11 and Lock 12 the river is practically dry. It can be crossed on foot at any point almost without encountering enough water to spoil a pair of white satin slippers. Lock 12 is finished, and the gates are closed. The pool above the lock is filling up, and what little water leaks through is lost in the shuffle before it reaches Lock 11. . . .

"Lock 10 will be finished now in a short time. The conditions

20. *New Dominion*, December 16, 1903.
21. *New Dominion*, August 19, 1903; Wiley, p. 598.

are most favorable for working on the locks now, and every indication is that they will be completed before Christmas."[22]

"Gates have been hung at most of the locks and the rest of the work will be completed before very long and the river opened for navigation. . . .

"T. A. Gillespie Company of Pittsburg have the contract for four of the locks and dams and Baker and Judson of Gloversville, N. Y., have the other two. Each firm has completed its work months before the date which is set forth in the contract. . . ."[23]

First lockmasters to be appointed were: No. 10, Robert A. Foster; No. 11, Walter B. Milliken; No. 12, Frank Miller; No. 13, George W. Anas; No. 14, Harry C. Williams; and No. 15, Stephen E. Enell.[24]

Morgantown Hardware. The Morgantown Hardware Company was incorporated March 16, 1903, by George H. Brown, George C. Sturgiss, M. L. Brown, Frank P. Corbin, and Emil T. Schultz, with a capital of one hundred thousand dollars. John H. Morgan, son of Charles Morgan, was the general manager of the store, located on High Street.

The Town of "Randall." Across the river from the mouth of Scotts Run a new town was being laid out by the Keystone Industrial Company, organized in 1903 with a capital stock of five hundred thousand dollars. The company bought the 123-acre Alfred Yeager farm, as well as the 300-acre David I. B. Anderson farm, and laid out lots and streets.

The Randall Glass Company was organized and incorporated during the summer and a contract was awarded for the construction of a factory.[25]

Dr. McLane Reminisces. Dr. W. L. McLane, of West Union, made a short visit to the town of his birth in the autumn and commented:

"I . . . was reminded of a remark made to me when a boy by my father. We were standing on the brink of the bank, overlooking Deckers Creek and what is now Greenmont, near the spot where

22. *New Dominion*, September 16, 1903.
23. *New Dominion*, November 11, 1903.
24. *New Dominion*, December 16, 1903.
25. *New Dominion Industrial Edition*, 1906, p. 68. The town of "Randall" later became Star City. The Randall Post Office was at Jimtown, across the river.

Fig. 71. Morgantown in the 1890s, from Chancery Hill. (West Virginia University Library.)

Col. Jos. McDermott's residence now stands, when he said to me, 'My boy, the time will come, perhaps in your day, but not in mine, when you will see houses dotted all over the flat across the creek, and clear back to the top of the hill. You will also see tall bridges spanning the deep ravine through which Deckers Creek runs.' ''[26]

Bridge to Chancery Hill. Delayed by injunction proceedings, the bridge over Deckers Creek from the south end of High Street was essentially completed in 1903. By the end of September the concrete work on the piers and abutments had been completed and the contractor was waiting for the steel.[27]

Miscellany. In 1903: The West Virginia University Department of History began a seminar course on local history (Callahan, p. 15). . . . J. M. G. Brown, George Wood, E. M. Grant, Dr. J. P. Fitch, C. R. Huston, and Forney Wade were early owners of auto-

26. *New Dominion,* November 18, 1903.
27. *New Dominion,* September 23, 1903.

mobiles (Callahan, p. 302). . . . The Methodist Protestant congregation on Walnut Street voted to build a new church on Spruce Street (Dodds and Dodds, p. 87). . . . City Council ordered the widening of Chestnut Street by five feet between Pleasants Street and Kirk Alley (*New Dominion*, June 24, 1903). . . . William Montgomery Morgan, professor of Horticulture and Botany at the University, died at City Hospital on July 6, aged twenty-nine years (*New Dominion*, July 8, 1903). . . . A contract was let by Union Utility Company to Dean and Hoffman for construction of a trolley line through West Morgantown to Granville (*New Dominion*, August 5, 1903). . . . A fire on Pleasant Street destroyed Conaway's Millinery, Clyde E. Jacobs' clothing store, V. A. Gloss' candy kitchen, and the People's Telephone central (*New Dominion*, August 5, 1903). . . . Charles Chollet, professor of Romance Languages at the University, died in a gun accident near South Park; he was born in Switzerland in 1863 (*New Dominion*, August 19, 1903). . . . Harry Overfield, nineteen-year-old son of Mr. and Mrs. John Overfield, drowned when he fell from the steamer *Isaac Mason* near Maidsville (*New Dominion*, September 9, 1903). . . . The Marilla Window Glass factory started to make glass at midnight on October 23; about 250 people were employed (*New Dominion*, October 23, 1903). . . . The W. R. Jones Window Glass started at midnight November 11; the town was "full of window glass workers from all over the country" (*New Dominion*, November 11, 1903). . . . The first trolley car from the end of the suspension bridge in West Morgantown to near Granville ran on November 18 (*New Dominion*, November 18, 1903). . . . A. L. Wade's book, *How to Make the Honeymoon Last Through Life*, was published by Lippincott's (*New Dominion*, December 23, 1903). . . . The first woman to study medicine at West Virginia University, Phoebia G. Moore, received her M.D. degree (*Goldenseal*, October-December 1979, pp. 36-41). . . . Levi ("Leve") Dalton, well-known snake-catcher and typical mountaineer, died September 30 at age of eighty-six years (*New Dominion*, October 1, 1903). . . . Simon P. Tennant, of Mooresville, died January 14; he was born December 25, 1831 (*New Dominion*, January 21, 1903). . . . W. H. Bailey was operating a hardware store on Clay Street (*Post-Chronicle Industrial Edition*, 1913).

CHAPTER ONE HUNDRED TWENTY-EIGHT

1904

Another in the long list of newspapers in Monongalia County, beginning with the *Monongalia Gazette* in 1803, was launched in 1904, one hundred one years later.

The Morgantown Chronicle. The daily and weekly *Morgantown Chronicle* was founded June 7, 1904. Directors of the publishing company were I. G. Lazzelle, M. L. Core, Hu Maxwell, W. R. Ludwig, and S. W. Hare. The paper aimed "at giving the news of the city and county fully, and of the state, nation, and of the world only in brief outline."

The *Daily Chronicle* was published six mornings in the week and went "into a majority of the homes of Morgantown before breakfast." The *Weekly Chronicle,* mailed each Tuesday morning, contained, in a condensed form, the news of the daily editions, "edited with special reference to the needs of the reader who does not subscribe for a daily. . . . The *Weekly Chronicle* contains more reading matter than any other weekly newspaper published in West Virginia," never less than 12 pages.[1]

Hu Maxwell was the editor. He was born at Saint George, 1860, the son of Rufus and Sarah Jane (Bonnifield) Maxwell and graduated from the Weston Academy in 1880. He taught school and was in the lumbering business, then became editor of the *Tucker County Pioneer,* a newspaper published at Saint George, then the county seat of Tucker County. For most of the remainder of his life he was an author and an editor. He traveled extensively, visiting every county in West Virginia, and every state in the Union. He published histories of the counties of Tucker (Kingwood, 1884), Randolph (Morgantown, 1898), Barbour (Morgan-

1. *New Dominion Industrial Edition,* 1906, p. 47.

Fig. 72. The Presbyterian Church.

town, 1899), Hampshire (with Howard L. Swisher, Morgantown, 1897), and Monongalia (written and partially printed but never published; see vol. 2, p. 545), and was co-author of two histories of West Virginia, one with Richard E. Fast in 1901 and another with Thomas E. Miller in 1913.

University Affairs. Under the direction of Dean S. L. Wrightson, the School of Music was one of the most effective divisions of the university. Some of the leading national and international artists were featured in a series of "Faculty Concerts"; among them were Max Heinrich, Mrs. Jennie Osborne Hannah, Anton Kasper, William Sherwood, and John Porter Lawrence. In March 1904, Victor Herbert and Richard Strauss[2] appeared in a "Big Musical Event" as directors of the Pittsburgh Symphony Or-

2. *New Dominion*, March 16, 1904; *Daily Post*, May 15, 1924; also Christopher Wilkinson. *Richard Strauss' Visit to the "Kleines Stadtchen" of Morgantown, W.Va.* MS 27, pp. 1980. *WVU Alumni Magazine*, Summer, 1981.

chestra. Following the resignation of Dean Wrightson in 1904, Ross Spence became the new dean.[3] Regular Saturday night student dances were again permitted under President Purinton and in May 1904 the first "Junior Prom" was held. The Military Ball was the big social event of the year.[4] The *Athenaeum* continued to be published as a weekly news sheet, its quality varying from year to year. "Generally, it was a rather high toned and forward looking publication. Among other things, it urged the alumni to increased activity; in the face of an indifferent and in some cases hostile faculty, it actively espoused 'the cause' of athletics; and it even dared to question some of the policies and practices of the faculty and the regents."[5]

A. W. Chez, a graduate of the Harvard School of Physical Training and former director of physical culture and athletics at the University of Cincinnati, was appointed director of physical training, succeeding B. G. Printz, and his wife, Louise Ferris Chez, former director of physical culture for women at the University of Cincinnati, was appointed as assistant director. Thus a departmentalized physical education program was first provided for women.[6]

Because Director Chez was an all-round athlete, responsibility for the football team fell to him (against his wishes) and no coach was employed for 1904. Despite an unusually pretentious schedule, the season showed a 6-3 record. It included, however, a "horrendous" 130-0 loss to the University of Michigan, the largest score ever recorded against a university football team. The Michigan coach, "Hurry-Up" Yost, who had played on the 1895 WVU team, "knew he had his alma mater where he wanted it and showed no mercy."[7] Penn State administered a 53-0 defeat, but there were six victories, including one over Washington University, of Saint Louis, at the World Exposition grounds n that city, closing the season.[8]

3. Ambler, p. 351.
4. Ambler, p. 353.
5. Ambler, p. 358.
6. Ambler, p. 367.
7. Constantine, p. 9.
8. Ambler, p. 368.

A new campus organization, named Mountain in honor of the West Virginia mountains, was founded June 1, 1904, on a ritual provided by Professor C. H. Patterson, which had been used for many years by "Tower Cross," a Tufts College organization. "Beginning with a select group of juniors and seniors eager to attain high standings, as typified by the surrounding mountains, the organization perpetuated itself in the same manner and, with the aid of a few honorary and associate members from the faculty and the state at large, became one of the most constructive factors in University life."[9]

Basketball, invented in 1891 by James Naismith at Springfield, Massachusetts, was first played at the university in 1898, but only as an interclass sport until 1904, when an intercollegiate schedule of seven games was played. A local newspaper described one of the first games:

"A big crowd saw the basket ball game on Friday evening in the Armory. The score as announced at the close of the game was 32 to 12 in favor of West Virginia. East Liberty played what seemed to be a good game and their kicking was at times as fine as usually done by a foot ball team.

"Probably half of the people present knew nothing of the game except the fact that when the ball was thrown into the basket it counted one point. Then they yelled."[10]

Work on the Wabash Is Stopped. A Pentress correspondent reported some disheartening news early in January:

"Work on the Wabash tunnel at this place stopped suddenly last week and without any known cause but it is said there has been a change of contractors and that they have stopped to invoice the work done and will resume in the spring. The prospect of the new town of Pentress Junction is not so bright as formerly; only one new building has been erected on the $13,000 worth of lots sold there by the Pentress land company in October. Although there has been quite a lot of trade in lots since the sale, several of the purchasers having doubled their money on the lots. Rome was not built in a day, neither was Pentress Junction; yet we believe it has a great future before it, as several new buildings, public and private, are to be erected next spring."[11]

9. Ambler, p. 361.
10. *New Dominion*, March 2, 1904.
11. *Morgantown Post*, January 14, 1904.

By the time the work came to a halt, construction was well under way on the two tunnels, and cuts and fills were partially completed for several miles along Jakes Run and Little Paw Paw Creek. When spring came around the resumption of construction was delayed week after week, until finally the dismayed residents of the communities affected were forced to the appalling conclusion that the railroad would never be built. The flurry of construction represented simply the strategy of big business politics to prevent the building of the proposed Buckhannon and Northern Railway along the Monongahela River. But for generations to come the record of this "magnificent gesture" would remain on the scarred hillsides along Jakes Run.

Old Mill Removed. The old Thompson mill at the foot of Walnut Street was removed to make way for the new Chaplin, Warman and Rightmire mill. The old mill, built eighty-five years earlier by John W. Thompson, was the first steam flouring mill in Morgantown, "but for many years before the milling machinery was placed in the building it was used for making stone ware such as fruit jars, cake pans, jugs, milk pans, flower pots, etc." No person in Morgantown had engaged in the pottery business since the death of the proprietor, D. G. Thompson.[12]

Point Breeze Park. Point Breeze Park, overlooking Seneca, was being developed by the Union Utility Company, which ran traction cars to Morgantown's first park. A dancing pavilion, a natural amphitheater, picnic areas, and three miles of winding trails were features offered to the public.[13]

The Locks are Completed. Major W. L. Sibert, U.S. Engineer for the Pittsburg District, in his report for June 30, gave a summary of work on the locks and dams in the Monongahela River in West Virginia. Locks and dams Nos. 7 and 8, completed in November 1899, cost $36,000.00, and Nos. 10 to 15, between Morgantown and Fairmont, started in March 1897 and completed in January 1904, cost $1,167,431.26.[14]

12. *Morgantown Post*, September 1, 1904.
13. *Morgantown Post*, June 2, 1904.
14. *Morgantown Post*, July 21, 1904.

Railroad Schedules. Passenger train No. 1 on the B.&O. R.R. left Morgantown daily at 5:55 a.m. and arrived in Pittsburg at 10:00 a.m. Train No. 2 left Pittsburg daily at 1:30 p.m. and arrived in Morgantown at 6:05 p.m. Other northbound trains arrived at Morgantown at 8:50 a.m., 8:10 p.m., and 10:10 p.m. Southbound trains left at 6:00 a.m., 11:52 a.m., and 8:45 p.m. On the M.&K. R.R. trains left Morgantown daily at 8:30 a.m. and 3:30 p.m. for Bretz. Returning, trains left Bretz at 10:00 a.m. and 4:45 p.m. Stops included Valley Crossing, Marilla, Pool Rocks, Johnson's Crossing, Rolling Mill, Rock Forge, Carter, Dellslow, Bennett's Quarry, Oliver, Sturgisson, Iron Bridge, Lick Run, Cascade Falls, and Masontown.

Richard Post Office. A new post office, named Richard, to serve the rapidly growing population of the Deckers Creek Valley, was established near Dellslow on February 13, 1904, with William P. Haines as the first postmaster. The post office was named for Richard Elkins, a son of Stephen B. Elkins.

The community was developed by the Elkins Coal and Coke Company, which opened mines, operated numerous coke ovens, and constructed a company store and an office building. The town of Richard was unlike many coal camps and was a clean town, with well-painted houses. Women of the community developed a playground for children near the mine office.

Haught's Chapel. On the headwaters of Paw Paw Creek, in Battelle District, a Methodist congregation built a church building on land donated by Alpheus F. Tennant. The group had been founded about 1900 and for a while met in the Paw Paw schoolhouse. Jacob Haught gave a considerable amount of money for the new building and it was named for his family.[15]

Alexander L. Wade. Alexander Luark Wade, distinguished Morgantown educator, died in Richmond, Virginia, May 2, 1904. He was born near Rushville, Indiana, February 1, 1832, the son of George and Anna Wade. The family moved to Monongalia County in 1839.

He was elected clerk of the county court in 1861 and later served eight years as recorder. He became principal of the Morgantown Public Schools in 1871 and in 1875 was elected

15. Dodds and Dodds, p. 132.

county superintendent of schools. He was the author of a widely circulated book, *A Graduating System for Country Schools*, published in 1881. He was principal of the Morgantown Colored School in 1880. In 1884 he discussed by invitation "Supervision in Country Schools" before the meeting of the National Association of School Superintendents, Washington, D.C.[16]

Miscellany. In 1904: Mrs. N. E. Shaffer, a resident of West Morgantown, started a Methodist Sunday school in an old grade school building (Dodds and Dodds, p. 108). . . . William Shanks, a son of Matthew and Martha Shanks, died, aged ninety-one, survived by two sons, Leonard and Andrew (*Chronicles of Core*, p. 168). . . . Col. F. de Nemegyei died in Charles Town, aged seventy-nine (*New Dominion*, February 3, 1904). . . . The plant of the Penn Mirror and Manufacturing Company on Deckers Creek was destroyed by fire on February 17 (*New Dominion*, February 24, 1904). . . . Trolley car No. 10 ran away on a steep grade in Seneca and jumped the track; no one was seriously injured (*New Dominion*, February 24, 1904). . . . The *Gazette*, towing the Quaker City Medicine Company, was the first steamboat to go from Morgantown to Fairmont after completion of the locks (*New Dominion*, March 23, 1904). . . . L. C. Fink's Chinese laundry, operated by Yee Jim, was robbed by a daring burglar (*Daily Post*, April 7, 1904). . . . Morgantown's mayor received $900 annually, compared with Fairmont's $600 and Clarksburg's $720 (*Daily Post*, May 18, 1904). . . . Morgantown's first commercial greenhouse was opened by W. R. P. Stewart in South Park (*New Dominion Industrial Edition*, 1906, pp., 40, 41). . . . Madison W. Bond, aged thirty, was killed June 1 by a falling derrick in Weaver and Zevely's stone quarry in West Morgantown (*Daily Post*, June 2, 1904). . . . A delegation of sixty-eight Pittsburg merchants and manufacturers visited Morgantown by special train (*Daily Post*, July 16, 1904). . . . Mrs. Jane V. McDonald, eldest daughter of Mathew and Margaret Gay, died in Orlando, Florida, on April 30 (*Morgantown Post*, May 5, 1904). . . . The Union Utility Company did a record breaking business on Decoration day, hauling seventy-six hundred passengers on the street cars; half of the passengers stopped at Point Breeze Park, despite the rain (*Mor-*

16. *Daily Post*, May 3, 1904. See further biographical data in vol. 3, p. 684.

gantown Post, June 2, 1904).... Miss Drusilla A. Morgan, daughter of Capt. Zacquill Morgan, died July 5, in the house in which she was born, on March 11, 1815 (*Morgantown Post,* July 11, 1904).... The W. R. Jones window glass plant was destroyed by fire (*Morgantown Post,* October 6, 1904).... The Athens Building and Loan Association was started in January, followed closely (in May) by the Monongalia Building and Loan Association; the latter soon became the largest of its kind in the State (Callahan, p. 280).... Clyde Brand opened a plumbing shop in Morgantown (*Post-Chronicle Industrial Edition,* 1913, p. 53). ... A new builders' supply house, Chaplin, Warman and Rightmire, was formed by B. M. Chaplin, Harlie Warman, A. Rightmire and others (*New Dominion Industrial Edition,* 1906, p. 53).

CHAPTER ONE HUNDRED TWENTY-NINE

1905

Morgantown was changing its complexion daily by 1905, with new houses being built, new streets being opened, new factories starting up. People of many ethnic origins were locating in the growing city, many languages were heard along High Street.

New Businesses. A new law firm, Glasscock and Glasscock, was formed April 1, 1905, having a general practice, but devoting its principal attention to representing important business concerns identified with the prosperity and advancement of the city and county. William Ellsworth Glasscock had served twice as county superintendent of schools and twice as clerk of the county court. In April 1905, he was appointed collector of internal revenue for West Virginia. His brother, Samuel Fuller Glasscock, had graduated in law from West Virginia University in 1893.[1]

Jolliffe Brothers' dry goods store opened for business in Morgantown on December 7, 1905. Their specialty was ladies' ready-to-wear garments. W. S. Jolliffe, the senior member of the firm, had come here from Wheeling, where he was with the Palace Furniture Company, and F. C. Jolliffe had worked for several years with Joseph Horne and Company, of Pittsburgh. Two other brothers, C. E. and J. A. Jolliffe, were financially interested in the firm. The Jolliffe brothers were born near Ridgedale.[2]

C. D. Matthaei, on November 6, 1905, opened the renovated New Wallace House on High Street. The site had been used for hotel purposes since pioneer days. The original Wallace House was opened in 1871 (vol. 3, p. 644). The new hotel had forty-five sleeping rooms and could seat 150 persons in the dining room. There were several toilet and bath rooms, and parlors for ladies.

1. *New Dominion Industrial Edition,* 1906, p. 14.
2. *New Dominion Industrial Edition,* 1906, p. 41.

Mr. Matthaei, born in Baltimore, came to Morgantown from Davis where he had conducted the Howard Hotel.[3]

Mrs. J. M. Hall, on September 20, 1905, opened a millinery parlor at 171 Pleasant Street, handling ladies' hats, along with other ladies' furnishings, including ribbons and trimmings. She had operated a similar establishment in Mannington. Her daughter, Edna R. Hall, assisted her here.[4]

Morgantown was already the leading glass making city in the state, and the Union Stopper Company was the newest addition to the local industry, opening for business March 1, 1905. The company located in the old woolen mill. They manufactured the Briscoe Stopper, patented by C. N. Briscoe, president of the company, born in 1842 in Canada; this stopper was designed to fit any bottle. Thomas L. Waters was the secretary-treasurer, John Z. Middleton, vice-president, and S. D. Kenney, factory manager. Other officers were Harry Farnsworth, bookkeeper, William Hawk, sales manager, H. A. Bridges, foreman of the mold department, and John L. Sellers, foreman of the special stopper department.[5]

The Thomas Wightman Glass Company, one of the largest and oldest glass companies in the country, opened a factory in Sabraton December 20, 1905. They had purchased the buildings and grounds of the West Virginia Bottle and Glass Company, which had gone out of business in 1904. With one tank in operation, 150 men were employed, in two shifts. Thomas Wightman, Jr., was superintendent of the plant, assisted by S. R. Wightman. J. S. Wightman was vice-president and G. H. Patterson treasurer.[6]

Sturgiss Buys the Tin Plate Mill. Announcement was made on July 7 that the United States Circuit Court in Wheeling had confirmed the sale of the Sabraton Tin Plate Mill to George C. Sturgiss. This was most unexpected, as Morgantown citizens were unaware of the progress of events and came as a pleasant surprise, after long frustrating delays. It was anticipated that employment would be provided for perhaps one thousand persons.

When the noon train arrived on the eighth, about two hundred persons, with the city band, were there to greet Mr. Sturgiss

3. Ibid., p. 42.
4. Ibid., p. 72.
5. Ibid., p. 76.
6. Ibid., p. 78.

Fig. 73-A. Sabraton Street Car crossing the Hartman Run Bridge.

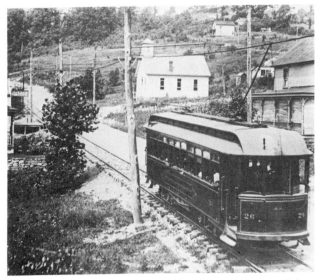

Fig. 73-B. Sabraton Street Car, along Richwood Avenue. Sabra
M. E. Church in background.

when he got off the train, with Frank P. Corbin, his attorney.
"Mr. Smith was there with his automobile into which the two
gentlemen were placed and taken to the home of Mr. Sturgiss,
followed by the band and the citizens. When he alighted from the
automobile the crowd gathered about him and heartily shook his
hand. It was one way of paying respect to a gentleman who has
done so much for this city and proof of the esteem in which he is
held by the public."[7]

The Sabraton Railway Company was incorporated by George
C. Sturgiss on July 10, 1905, for the purpose of building a trolley
line from Morgantown to Sabraton; other incorporators were
Russell L. Morris, president, James H. Stewart, J. Ami Martin,
general manager, Frank P. Corbin, attorney, and L. B. H. Peddi-
cord, secretary.[8]

The Union Utility Company had been the pioneer in Morgantown's street car development and hence controlled the franchise
to the downtown streets. When the Sabraton Railway was projected, a battle ensued with Union Utility for trackage rights
downtown.

Nevertheless, a franchise was granted by the City of Morgantown in August 1905 along the line of Richwood Avenue and construction rapidly went forward. Service was started in November. The first car made its trial runs on November 20, with Albert
Clark at the controls.[9] Regular service started on November 25,
cars running every hour, 6:30 a.m. to 6:30 p.m., from Sabraton
Junction (east end of Prospect Street) to the trestle over Hartman Run.[10] Despite the battle with Union Utility, the Sabraton
Railway was able to borrow two of Union Utilities' single trucker
cars to use until their two railroad-roof double truckers arrived.
The double truckers, numbered 25 and 26 (and named Woodburn
and Appalachia, respectively, a short time later), permitted the
single truckers to return to the city run and were more adequate
to handle the heavy traffic on the line. Soon service was extended
to the Tin Plate Mill.

The line followed Richwood Avenue around its many curves

7. *Daily Post,* July 8, 1905.
8. Ibid., p. 80.
9. *Morgantown Post,* November 23, 1905.
10. *Morgantown Post,* November 30, 1905.

and sharp corners, through Woodburn and Jerome Park, where Hartman Run was crossed by a high bridge, and then proceeded along Sabraton Avenue to the tin plate mill. The car barn was located in Sabraton. At first the cars stopped at the downtown end of Richwood Avenue (Sabraton Junction) and the passengers had to walk the few blocks to downtown. But an agreement was presently made with Union Utility so that the Sabraton cars were able to come on down to High Street.[11]

The President's House. A home for the president of the university was completed in 1905, the first occupant being D. B. Purinton.

The President's House, strange to say, was for years a kind of a nightmare to President Purinton. It had not been authorized by the legislature and was thought by many people at the time to be the product of a shrewd real estate deal. There was no question, however, about the need for such a building, since adequate living accommodations for the president were lacking, and the regents determined to provide it. A number of possible sites were investigated, on property owned by the university, but without success. Finally the regents purchased from Dr. I. C. White a part of the one-half acre "Danser lot," which Dr. White had bought at a court sale in May 1886, for $1,540. His price to the board of regents for the portion fronting on the present University Avenue was $12,500.

At this moment J. M. Guffy, of Pittsburgh, donated ten thousand dollars toward the proposed building and Dr. White agreed to reduce the sales price to seventy-five hundred dollars, with the understanding that the difference was to represent a donation on his part.

Construction did indeed go forward, and the building was finally completed, at a total cost of $42,611.94, only $13,000.00 of which had been donated. About $20,000.00 was paid for out of student fees. Meanwhile the legislature had indeed appropriated about $8,000.00 to pay for retaining walls, walks, etc., and eventually the president moved in.[12]

The University College of Medicine, which had been placing its chief reliance upon its Baltimore affiliation since 1903, was grad-

11. *West Penn Traction*, pp. 150-56.
12. Ambler, pp. 342, 343.

Fig. 74. Footbridge across Falling Run. (West Virginia University.)

ually expanding its local curriculum, mostly by drawing upon other departments. On October 10, 1905, Dr. J. N. Simpson was made professor of anatomy and physiology and "head of the medical faculty at Morgantown."[13]

St. George Tucker Brooke, in June 1905, declined reappointment as dean of the College of Law, and Associate Professor Edwin Maxey was named acting dean.[14]

In January 1905 the constitution of the Athletic Association was amended so as to authorize "W. V." awards to outstanding athletes and the appointment of assistant managers for sports. Under the direction of A. W. and Louise Chez, beginning in 1905, the Annual Gymnastic Exhibition, featuring calisthenics, a band concert, and Swedish folk dances, became a big athletic event. This was a start towards an intramural athletic program.[15] Carl Forkum was appointed football coach and his 1905 team had only

13. Ambler, p. 348; Van Liere and Dodds, p. 18.
14. Ambler, p. 349.
15. Ambler, p. 367.

16 points scored against it, losing only to Penn State, by a score of 6 to 0.[16]

The Fifth Ward. A fifth ward (see p. 267) was created by the Morgantown City Council in 1905, within the limits as prescribed by the charter, comprising the area south and east of Beverly Avenue and the Collins Ferry road to the boundaries of the third ward and Deckers Creek, known in part at least as East Morgantown.

Shriver Post Office. Along the east side of the Monongahela River, about three miles north of Morgantown, a post office was established November 16, 1905, with Frank C. Shriver as the first postmaster.[17]

John J. Brown. John James Brown, of Morgantown, only son of Robert and Annie (Hawthorne) Brown, died August 11, 1905. He was born in Kingwood on November 19, 1825, and moved to Morgantown in 1864. He was one of Monongalia County's best known citizens.[18]

He attended Monongalia Academy and graduated from Washington College, Washington, Pennsylvania, in October 1845. Returning to Kingwood, he became deputy clerk of the circuit and county courts, and studied law under his uncle, William G. Brown. He began the practice of law in partnership with his uncle in April 1849, and the firm soon won a high reputation.

He stood steadfastly with the Union in 1860-61 and made a famous speech in Kingwood on January 26, 1861, when the women of Preston County presented an American flag to an anti-secession convention.[19] He was elected a delegate to the Wheeling Convention of June 1861, which restored the government of Virginia, and was a member of the Constitutional Convention which met at Wheeling in November 1861.

At the first general election under the constitution of West Virginia Mr. Brown was elected to the state senate from the

16. Ambler, p. 368.
17. This post office was discontinued July 1, 1907, and the mail was sent to the Star City office.
18. See biography in Wiley, pp. 283-87.
19. Wiley, *History of Preston County*, pp. 126, 127.

Monongalia-Preston-Taylor senatorial district and was reelected at the expiration of his term.

He moved to Morgantown in 1864 and opened a law office there. He was a director and president of the Merchants National Bank of West Virginia. He delivered one of the principal addresses in 1876, in connection with the centennial of the nation and of the county (vol. 3, pp. 692, 693).

At his funeral William Moorhead made an address, including the following remarks:

"He was one of Nature's gentlemen, in the ancient meaning of that word, gentle man. His life was gentle and the elements so mixed in him that Nature might stand up and say to all the world, 'He was a man.' "[20]

Barton Core. A farmer of Cassville, Barton Core, died October 5, aged eighty-five. A son of Christopher and Hannah (Snider) Core, he was born December 2, 1821. He married Nancy Fleming (1821-1912) and they had eleven children: Martha, married Oliver P. Wade; Mary, married James Sampson Lough; Hannah, married Corbin H. Alexander; Moses Levin, married Martha Smith; Christopher Columbus, married Ella Schultz; William Perry, married Sarah Smith; Salina Jane, died in childhood; Rebecca Arvella, married William A. Loar; Lydia Elmira, married Calvin Cordray; Lewis Addison, a missionary in India, married Mary Kennedy; and Charles Elliott, married Laura Price.[21]

Bank of Wadestown. The Bank of Wadestown opened for business the first of September, with a capital stock of twenty-five thousand dollars. Horace Lee Plum, formerly of the Farmers' and Merchants' Bank of Morgantown, was elected cashier. Directors were Urias Shriver, D. L. Tennant, R. S. Clovis, Benjamin Shriver, E. W. Rose, E. B. Hall, and J. L. Garrison.[22]

Bethel Wesleyan Methodist Church. On Days Run near Daybrook in 1905 a congregation was organized, belonging to an unusual denomination, the Wesleyan Methodist. A meeting had been held under the direction of Rev. John Hillberry and the con-

---

20. *Morgantown Post*, August 17, 1905. The full text of Mr. Moorhead's address is given.
21. *Morgantown Post*, October 5, 1905; *Chronicles of Core*, p. 168.
22. *Morgantown Post*, August 24, 1905.

Fig. 75. Bank of Wadestown. (Courtesy Adelaide Garrison Staggers.)

gregation was organized by Rev. S. Portman. Among interested members were Enos Moore, Rosa Yost, and John Bane. A lot was secured from Morton Conner and a small frame church was built.[23]

Union Methodist Church. A new church building along Flaggy Meadow Run at Flickersville, was constructed in 1905 by members of the Union Methodist congregation. The old building, which had been built in 1856 by a group of Methodists, Presbyterians, and Baptists, was then torn down. Labor and money for the new buildings were donated by members of the community, including Northern and Southern Methodists, Baptists, and Presbyterians.[24]

Beulah Methodist Church. The Beulah Free Methodist congregation, organized about 1905 two miles south of Dellslow, built a frame church building on a high knoll among forest trees, a very pleasing setting. The first pastor was Rev. Herman Baldwin. D.

23. Dodds and Dodds, pp. 129, 130.
24. Dodds and Dodds, p. 108.

H. McDonald, F. M. McDonald, and John McDonald helped in the organization and building of the church.[25]

Miscellany. In 1905: William B. Frum, of Little Falls, died January 3, aged seventy-five years (*Morgantown Post,* January 5, 1905). . . . City Council ordered the installation of twenty new street lights by the Monongalia Oil and Gas Company (*Morgantown Post,* January 19, 1905). . . . Marion C. Ramsey, a farmer of Cassville, son of Ira and Perina Ramsey, died January 26 after being thrown from a sled while his horses were running away (*Morgantown Post,* January 26, 1905). . . . William Barbe, aged eighty-two years, died February 21 at his home near Laurel Point, survived by one son, Elza (*Morgantown Post,* February 23, 1905). . . . Passenger trains on the M.&K. R.R. were running from Morgantown to Reedsville twice a day (*Morgantown Post,* May 4, 1905). . . . Wallace's big railroad show "gave the finest parade that was ever seen in Morgantown" (*Morgantown Post,* May 18, 1905). . . . The city was experiencing an ice famine, consuming four tons a day more than the Morgantown Ice Company and the Madera Hotel, the only two plants, could produce (*Morgantown Post,* June 22, 1905). . . . Announcements were made that the Economy Tumbler Company and the Pressed Prism Plate Glass Company would enlarge their local plants (*Morgantown Post,* July 27, 1905). . . . A contract was let for construction of ten miles of the M.&K. R.R., from Kingwood to Trowbridge's Ferry (*Morgantown Post,* August 10, 1905). . . . The first spike in the Sabraton Street Railway was driven at 2:30 p.m., August 17, by Frank Corbin, assisted by J. Ami Martin (*Morgantown Post,* August 24, 1905). . . . Thomas Warman, aged seventy-nine, of Easton, died August 29, survived by six children, Altha, Sarah, Harlie, Beall, Russell, and Winnie (*Morgantown Post,* August 31, 1905). . . . The Elkins company was operating seventy-five coke ovens at Richard (*Morgantown Post,* September 21, 1905). . . . Charles Henry Cooper, Morgantown chief of police, died November 11, aged fifty-three years (*Morgantown Post,* November 16, 1905). . . . Morgantown High School fielded its first football team (*History of Morgantown High School,* 1935, pp. 79, 80). . . . The name of the Wise Post Office was changed to Wana on April 5, honoring, it was said, an eighteenth century Indian.

25. Dodds and Dodds, p. 76.

CHAPTER ONE HUNDRED THIRTY

1906

The tin plate mill, at Sabraton, opened April 6, 1906, was by far the largest industrial plant to be located at Morgantown. It was perhaps the greatest achievement in the long line of successes won by George C. Sturgiss for the community of Morgantown.[1] Mr. Sturgiss first interested George J. Humbert in the building of a tin mill along the new Morgantown and Kingwood Railroad. He subscribed generously to the stock himself, was instrumental in interesting other capital, and finally the plant, of ten separate mills was a completed fact.

But then financial difficulties arose, and the mill was offered for sale in order to satisfy claims against it. Finally it was put up for sale at public auction under an order from the United States Court. Most of the promoters lost faith in the enterprise, but Mr. Sturgiss continued to work for final victory.

The Tin Plate Mill. The sale of the mill and the battle for its possession is one of the most dramatic incidents in Morgantown's industrial history. For three days the bidding for the property went forward in front of the courthouse. After the sale was made an upset bid was filed. The confirmation of the sale before the Federal Court at Parkersburg was practically complete when a second upset bid was filed. The matter was then taken to the U.S. Court at Richmond, and in a legal battle in which he was pitted against some of the best legal talent of New York City, Mr. Sturgiss won a notable victory.

The people of Morgantown had watched the progress of the battle with the most intense interest, knowing that if Mr. Sturgiss was successful in gaining possession of the plant, it would add materially to the growth of the community. When he re-

1. *Weekly Post,* April 19, 1906.

Fig. 76. American Sheet and Tin Plate Mill.

turned to his hometown he was greeted by a large gathering of enthusiastic citizens, who escorted him to his home and asked him to speak, giving the story of the legal fight (p. 314).

By early spring work was well under way at the plant: "For three years or more the plant in which this industry is carried on has stood partly furnished along the banks of Deckers Creek, about two miles above town. The air of desertion and idleness which a year ago surrounded the tin plate mill has been brushed aside and the hum of industry now enters every nook and corner of the big plant."[2]

The mill was under the ownership and general management of the American Sheet and Tin Plate Company. C. W. Bray was president of the company and Robert Skemp district manager. William C. Loyd was superintendent of the local plant. At the beginning about three hundred men were employed and it was anticipated that when it was in full operation about eight hundred men and women would be given employment.

2. *New Dominion Industrial Edition,* May 10, 1906.

Tin plate, in 1906, was made from pure steel billets, instead of charcoal iron, as had been the practice earlier. The bars were delivered to the mill from steel works at Pittsburgh, and were of various weights, the pieces being about thirty feet long.

Field's Park. On the Tyrone Road near Dellslow a rustic park was being developed around 1906 by Arlington P. Field. It included a large building with a dance floor, large open fireplace, and concessions. There were also summer cottages, large swings, tables for picnics, a ball diamond.[3]

Swisher's Theater. Morgantown's new playhouse, Swisher's Theater, on High Street at Fayette Street was opened on March 26 with a musical extravaganza, *Girls will be Girls*, with Al Leech as the star and Madge Lawrence, Aeline Flavin, and Mary Carr as the Rosebuds. There was also a chorus of forty.

The work of building the theater had begun about a year earlier. The theater occupied a space sixty feet by one hundred

Fig. 77. Swisher's Theater Building on High Street.

3. *Deckers Creek Valley Days*, 1971.

feet in the large building, with an entrance through a wide and commodious lobby. It was leased to H. L. Swisher, one of the promoters who built the building, and was managed by Scott H. Swisher. Manager Scott Swisher said that, besides four parquet boxes and gallery, the theater contained a balcony, all of which together afforded seats for 1,350 people. The total capacity of the theater was 1,700. Mestrezat's orchestra was to furnish music for the new theater, which already had booked eight plays.[4]

"The theatre is a credit to Morgantown and compares favorably with the very best play houses in cities ten times the size of Morgantown. Only the best shows on the road will be booked; a fact which will be appreciated by the lovers of good plays here. The theatre is finely furnished and the seats are so arranged that one can have a good view of the stage it matters not what part of the house he is in. It has a seating capacity of 1,400, this including the eight imposing boxes. The theatre has already been completed and is in active operation."[5]

Street Railways: The "Loop Line." Morgantown was developing pride in its growing system of street railways, particularly the "Loop Line," running down Beechurst Avenue and returning to the downtown section by way of Beverly Avenue, and operated by the Union Utility Company:

"The company operates in the city of Morgantown a modern and model street railway system, the construction of which is considered the best that money and experienced talent could obtain. The schedule of the cars, and the first-class appearance and condition of the equipment, together with the care and efficiency of the motormen and conductors, has built up a considerable traffic, more than is enjoyed by any system in a similarly populated community."[6]

The motormen and conductors, in 1906, were listed as Charles McLain, George Hervey, George Wells, Dent Wilson, Forrest Selby, J. D. Moore, W. H. Calvert, Theodore Farrar, S. R. Newman, and F. C. Martin. J. H. Thorn was car barn foreman, Harry Runner the assistant car barn foreman, and Frank Stewart track foreman.

4. *Morgantown Post,* March 15, 1906.
5. *New Dominion Industrial Edition,* 1906, p. 54.
6. *New Dominion Industrial Edition,* 1906, p. 5.

Fig. 78. Summer Street Car, with Charles McLain at the controls.

The Union Utility Company held the franchises for the principal streets in downtown Morgantown and for a decade, during the period of rapid trolley expansion, engaged in battle with the city and with various other interests trying to promote trolley lines into other sections.

South Morgantown Traction Company. A franchise was granted April 11, 1906, to incorporators of the South Morgantown Traction Company to construct a line from High Street across the South High Street bridge to streets of the Wagner Addition to the Demain lands and through the McGara Addition to Dorsey Avenue at the Oak Grove Cemetery, thence through lands owned by Lorentz, Reay, Madigan, Smith and others to Bridge Street. Incorporators were J. Leonard Smith, John Madigan, Samuel McGara, C. D. Willey, C. N. Reay, and John E. Price.[7]

Morgantown and Dunkard Valley. Among companies planning trolley lines in the county was the Morgantown and Dunkard

7. *Weekly Post,* April 12, 1906.

Valley Railway Company, which was engaged during the summer in making a survey of possible routes. Officers of the company, which was incorporated September 5, 1905, were L. L. Thomas, president; Lee R. Shriver, treasurer; and W. W. Smith, treasurer. C. S. Tennant was right-of-way agent, working with the American Engineering Company, of Indianapolis, on the survey. "The road will run from Morgantown to Mannington by way of Cassville, Blacksville and Wadestown, with a branch line four miles long to Mt. Morris, Pa."[8]

The People's Telephone Company. By 1906 local use of telephones had grown tremendously: "It is owing to the energy and enterprise of the incorporators of the People's Telephone Co., that this community now has the excellent service and low prices they enjoy. When this company was first organized it was not the purpose of the organizers to sell telephone service, but to get service among themselves, as prices prior to the building of the first lines of the People's Telephone Co. were such that only the wealthier class of our citizens could afford to lease telephones from the only company then doing business, on account of the exorbitant charges they made. But the public demand for their service was so great that ere long it was decided to sell their service and the growth of the commodity since they began to put the service on the market has been steady and rapid. . . .

"A larger and more efficient equipment is being installed as the service seems to demand. They have cabled the main parts of the city, and when the Decker's creek industries opened up they were there with the latest equipment, good metallic circuits on a new pole line ready to furnish them with service and in consequence received a very flattering patronage. Until July, 1905, they did not aspire to long distance service, but at that time it was decided to install a long distance line to Pittsburg and work was at once commenced on a line to that place, and it now enjoys the best service possible for any company to give to the greatest manufacturing city in the United States."

In 1906 the officers of the People's Telephone Company were Milton Hirschman, president, Dr. I. C. White, vice-president, and George C. Baker, secretary. On June 5, 1906, William Line was

8. *Weekly Post,* August 9, 1906.

elected general manager of the company. He had been born in Indiana in 1872 and began his telephone career working for the Cumberland Telephone Company in 1889.[9]

President Purinton. On Thanksgiving Day, 1906, President Purinton celebrated the completion and occupation of the new President's House by a turkey dinner attended by faculty members and their wives. Although generally recognized as badly needed, its construction had been involved in much controversy (p. 317).[10]

Another controversy during the year involved the deanship of the College of Law, which had been vacant since the death of Okey Johnson in 1903. St. George Tucker Brooke had been acting dean from 1903 until June 1905, when he was succeeded as acting dean by Associate Professor Edwin Maxey. The regents now determined to appoint a new dean. "Unfortunately, the situation was so tempting to . . . Maxey . . . as to cause him to use 'undesirable and unworthy' methods to attain the deanship. As a consequence he failed of appointment . . . , and C. E. Hogg, a native West Virginian, was made dean at a salary of three thousand dollars, effective September 1, 1906."[11]

It was a period of uncertainty for the faculty, with respect to salaries and general policies, but some outstanding persons were being added. Among them, in 1906, was Dr. Madison Stathers, in romance languages, following the resignation of Dr. Andre Beziat de Bordes.

Star Glass Company. A new addition to the steadily enlarging group of glass plants being located in the Morgantown area was the Star Glass Company, which built its factory along the Monongahela River opposite Randall. The general manager was Louis Kauffield, formerly of the Kauffield Chimney House, Matthews, Indiana, and of the Nilan Glass factory, Point Marion, Pennsylvania. There were four buildings, forming a quadrangle, including a main building for the blow room, lehr room, decorating and machine department and packing room. An office

9. *New Dominion Industrial Edition* (1906).

10. Ambler, p. 343. See also a long report in *Weekly Post,* July 5, 1906.

11. Ambler, p. 349. Charles Edgar Hogg was born on a farm in Mason County in 1853 and studied law at Point Pleasant under Judge C. P. I. Moore, of the Supreme Court of Appeals.

building, a warehouse, and a large building housing the mixing
room completed the group.[12]

Great Scott Coal Company. A nine-foot vein of Pittsburgh coal
outcropped along the west bank of the Monongahela River at
Randall and to exploit this the Great Scott Coal Company was
formed. The company owned 580 acres on the west side of the
river, where a large tipple was built, equipped for loading river
barges. A tramway was built into the coal seam. The company
also owned forty acres on the east side, along the railroad, and
planned to run cables across the river to load railroad cars. A. H.
Tait was president and general manager, William G. Tait, secretary, and D. C. Hoffman, treasurer.[13]

Bank of Morgantown. The rapid industrial development of the
last decade of the nineteenth century and the first decade of the
twentieth resulted in a steady expansion of the banking business.
The Bank of Morgantown opened in 1906 with a good business
which steadily increased and has persisted to the present day.

"Our newest addition to the financial institutions of Morgantown is the Bank of Morgantown, which has been recently incorporated with a capital stock of $40,000. It will do a general bank-
ing business and will be located in the Peabody hotel building on
High Street. Work on the bank has been in progress for several
months past, and it is expected the place will open for business
shortly. . . . Prof. Thomas E. Hodges, of the university, is president of the institution. Professor Hodges is one of Morgantown's
foremost citizens, and is interested in several local concerns. He
is a man of remarkable executive ability, and a better selection
for the head of the bank could not have been made. H. L. Carspecken, manager of the Mississippi Wire Glass Company, is
first vice-president, and C. C. Core, president of the county court,
is second vice-president. M. L. Brown, who for a number of years
has been the assistant cashier at the Citizens' National Bank, is
cashier."[14]

Other Local Banks. Morgantown's oldest and largest financial institution, in 1906, was the Bank of the Monongahela Valley.

12. *New Dominion Industrial Edition,* 1906, p. 70.
13. *New Dominion Industrial Edition,* 1906, p. 70.
14. *New Dominion Industrial Edition,* May 10, 1906; *Morgantown Post,* February 1, 1906.

"In addition to having built up a surplus larger than its capital, it has paid dividends ever since its organization, even during the hard times of 1893 and 1894. Its large capital and surplus afford ample protection to those who have money deposited with it. The officers are E. H. Coombs, president; L. S. Brock, vice-president; and J. H. McGrew, cashier."

The county's second oldest bank was the Second National Bank. "The officers and directors are among the most substantial business and financial men in this community. (The officers are) Aaron J. Garlow, president; W. C. McGrew, vice president; W. E. Arnett, cashier; and W. H. Ashcraft, asst. cashier. . . . This bank owns and occupies the finest structure in Morgantown and is centrally located at the corner of Maiden Alley and Main Street. . . ."

The Farmers' and Merchants' Bank, the third oldest, had opened for business on October 10, 1895, with a paid-up capital stock of twenty-five thousand dollars, and during 1902 and 1903 the capital stock was increased to seventy-two thousand dollars, the new stock being issued on the basis of three hundred dollars per share. "The earnings on the capital stock during 1905, including dividends and all necessary expenses, were about 24 percent. The largest individual stockholder is Senator Stephen B. Elkins." Officers of the Farmers' and Merchants' Bank were A. W. Lorentz, president; Davis Elkins, vice-president, and J. L. Keener, cashier.[15]

Other financial establishments included the Citizens National Bank, organized in 1900, and the Federal Savings and Trust Company, which first opened its doors for business on October 14, 1902. The Citizens National Bank was purchased by the Trust Company, so that thereafter both institutions were under the same management and directorship and both businesses were conducted in the same building, but with a separate force of employees. E. M. Grant was president; Isaac VanVoorhis, vice-president; Alex H. Tait, vice-president; H. L. Swisher, secretary; William G. Tait, assistant treasurer; and E. D. Tumlin, treasurer. The Trust Company was located at the corner of High and Walnut streets.

Train to Kingwood. Effective March 12, 1906, M.&K. trains began running all the way to Kingwood twice a day, leaving

15. Ibid.

Fig. 79. Morgantown and Kingwood Passenger Train.
(Courtesy Lucille Smith.)

Morgantown at 7:30 a.m. and 2:10 p.m., arriving in Kingwood at
9:25 a.m. and 3:47 p.m. Returning, the trains left Kingwood at
9:45 a.m. and 4:00 p.m., arriving in Morgantown at 11:31 a.m.
and 5:37 p.m.

A commuter train to Sabraton left Morgantown daily at 6:40
a.m., arriving in Sabraton at 6:49, returning at once to Morgantown.

Hagans Christian Church. On June 17, 1906, the Hagans Chris-
tian Church was dedicated with an address by Dr. Thomas E.
Cramblet, president of Bethany College. The church was located
at the head of Indian Creek, in Clay District. Among charter
members were Michael Elza and Emily Fetty, Jacob A. Fetty,
John Calvin and Wilhelmina Morris, David F. and Mary Mazella
Morris, Eliza Jane Eddy, Catherine Fetty, Ida Belle and Tida
Ann Fetty, and Etta Morris Jones. Rev. G. H. Ellis was em-
ployed as the first minister, to serve half-time with the Dolls Run
Church.[16]

16. Core, *Morgantown Disciples*, pp. 57, 58; Dodds and Dodds, p. 123.

New Granville Church. A new church building to serve the Granville Methodist congregation was erected in 1906, under the direction of Rev. F. M. Marple. The building replaced an old structure, built about 1850, which was then transformed into a dwelling. Trustees in charge of the new construction were West Snyder, George W. Frum, R. A. Tinnel, Theodore Barker, and Dan Breakiron.[17]

Edwin C. Protzman. Morgantown's well-known photographer and bandmaster, Edwin C. Protzman, died March 15, 1906, aged fifty years. He was a son of William O. and Elizabeth A. Protzman, and lived in Morgantown all his life. Early in life he showed an interest in music and became one of the best cornet players in the state. He organized numerous bands, including the first regiment band of the West Virginia National Guard and the Morgantown Concert Band. At the time of his death he was leader of the Morgantown City Band.[18]

Lewis A. Yeager. A former prominent university athlete, Lewis Armstrong ("Lou") Yeager, died suddenly in Morgantown of a heart attack on December 11, 1906. He was a son of Mr. and Mrs. B. M. Yeager, of Marlinton, and was born September 10, 1878. He graduated from the College of Law, served one term as city solicitor and was practicing law. He was married to Elizabeth Lyman Harvey, daughter of John I. Harvey, who had taught French for many years at the university.[19]

Miscellany. In 1906: A Methodist Sunday School was organized by Rev. Z. B. Musgrove in a church on Statler Run known as Eddy Memorial Chapel (Dodds and Dodds, p. 127). . . . The Philadelphia Baptist Church, in Battelle District, was moved to Bula and renamed the Bula Baptist Church (Dodds and Dodds, p. 130). . . . New Morgantown businesses established were the Guardian Investment Building and Loan and the State Savings and Investment Association (Callahan, p. 280). . . . A bond proposal to build a new bridge across the river at Morgantown was defeated on June 23 by a vote of 858 to 1329 (*Weekly Post,* July 5, 1906).

17. Dodds and Dodds, p. 102. For dedication, see *Weekly Post,* November 22, 1906.
18. *Weekly Post,* March 22, 1906.
19. *Weekly Post,* December 13, 1906.

... Prof. F. S. Lyon, a member of the university faculty from 1867 until 1886 and vice-president from 1878 until 1881, died at Fredonia, New York, March 15, aged eighty-eight years (*Morgantown Post*, March 22, 1906). . . . Dr. Edwin Maxey, of the University College of Law, published an 800-page book on international law[20] (*Weekly Post*, May 24, 1906). . . . Aaron Carothers, of Granville, died June 4, aged seventy-three years; he had been a Baptist minister (*Weekly Post*, June 7, 1906). . . . The Keystone Industrial and Development Company held a public auction of lots at Randall on September 29 (*Weekly Post*, September 27, 1906). . . . Two Union Utility trolley cars collided on Front Street on October 22 but no one was injured (*Weekly Post*, October 25, 1906). . . . City council on October 29 decided to abandon 144 gas flambeaux in use on street corners and bridges and replace them with at least 75 electric lights of 30 or 50 candle power (*Weekly Post*, November 1, 1906). . . . J. W. Wiles was advertising lots in South Park, soon to be served by a new trolley line (*Weekly Post*, November 1, 1906). . . . Richard Scott and Company, of Clarksburg, was awarded the contract for building the South Morgantown Traction Company's trolley line from the High Street Bridge to the southern limits of the city near the Pump Station (*Weekly Post*, November 1, 1906). . . . The grand opening of the Acme Department store on Front Street was held (*Weekly Post*, November 22, 1906). . . . Mrs. Mahala A. Widdows, daughter of John Jacob and Margaret Clause, and widow of Joseph Widdows, a veteran of the Mexican War, died November 26; she was born April 9, 1816 (*Weekly Post*, November 29, 1906). . . . Nine-year-old John Henry Dickinson, son of Charles Dickinson, of Ice's Ferry, died of hydrophobia (*Weekly Post*, November 29, 1906). . . . The main building of the Star Glass Company was destroyed by fire (*Weekly Post*, November 29, 1906). . . . William H. Watts, son of Charles Watts, died December 8, aged sixty-five years (*Weekly Post*, December 13, 1906). . . . Passenger trains were jammed with holiday travelers and extra baggage cars were required to handle express packages (*Weekly Post*, December 27, 1906). . . . Admiral French E. Chadwick published an interesting book, *The Causes of the Civil War* (long review in *Weekly Post*, January 3, 1907). . . . The Smith-Race Grocery Company was

20. *International Law with Illustrative Cases.* St. Louis. 797 pp. 1906.

founded (Callahan, p. 271). . . . Arthur Lee Post, university bacteriologist, "died, aged thirty-three years (*Weekly Post,* May 17, 1906).

Fig. 79-A. High Street about 1910. (From an old postcard.)

CHAPTER ONE HUNDRED THIRTY-ONE

1907

In 1907 there were three theaters in Morgantown and a remarkable new form of entertainment was getting under way, one of the strangest and most controversial products of civilization—the motion picture. C. Francis Jenkins invented the motion picture projector and exhibited the first film, in Richmond, Indiana, in June 1894. On April 23, 1896, a motion picture made by Thomas Edison was shown in New York City, one of the acts in a vaudeville show, the first theatrical showing of a film in the United States.

By 1905 motion pictures were becoming extremely popular. Vacant storerooms in various cities were provided with seats and the films were shown against a wall. The admission price was a nickel, and for this reason these crude theaters were called nickelodeons. Soon there were ten thousand nickelodeons in operation. The sudden growth increased the demand for pictures and companies were formed to produce them; hundreds of pictures were soon being produced each year. Many men engaged in various businesses had their attention directed to the motion picture industry. Among them, in those days, were Adolph Zukor, a furrier, Carl Laemmle, manager of a clothing store, and Lewis J. Selznik, a jeweler.

The First Moving Pictures. Morgantown did not wait long to begin its enjoyment of the motion picture show, at first usually in connection with a play or vaudeville acts.

In 1907 H. A. Christy leased the Swisher Theatre and booked all the plays for that house. He fitted the Grand for the exhibition of motion pictures exclusively. Early in March the Grand was advertising that there were new pictures every Monday and Thursday, "Pictures that are full of enjoyable qualities," "Pictures that are true figures from life," "Pictures that will make you feel good," "Pictures that will make your sides split," "Pictures, Pictures; All kinds of Pictures." Titles of some of the earliest were *Equestrian School, Mischievous Boys, Two Little Scamps,* and *What a Drunkard Saw.*[1]

Another theater, the Arcade, opened at 333 High Street, for the showing of motion pictures. Admission was five cents to all.

The University Reaches Another Crisis. The history of West Virginia University is the account of one crisis after another. A legislative investigation committee, authorized February 22, 1907, reported a number of serious problems. "Among other things, the average number of students taught by each professor was near the minimum for the principal state universities of the country; the enrollment, except in one or two subjects, had declined over a period of years . . . ; and a part of the endowment, aggregating almost $117,000 in 1907, was invested in 'speculative and hazardous securities' in violation of both state and federal laws. . . . The report carried a veiled criticism of recent salary increases of from five to ten per cent and recommended that no buildings be either constructed or repaired until a general plan for expanding the physical plant had been developed and approved."[2]

The investigating committee found the Law College, under Dean Hogg, "one of the very best . . . in the country." The enrollment, however, was declining; the figure of 100, in 1907, was 21 less than in 1902. Dean Hogg made his private library available to students and extended their course so as to include a third year. The moot court, functioning since 1890, took on new life.[3]

Motivated by the legislative investigation, the College of Agriculture was reorganized in 1907 with a view of emphasizing extension work. The Agricultural Experiment Station was making valuable contributions in the field of productive research. Horace Atwood won national distinction in poultry husbandry and, with Director Stewart, published bulletins on such diverse subjects as the cultivation of field crops, the feeding of hogs, sheep, and dairy cows, the production of sanitary milk, and parasites in sheep.

1. *Daily Post,* March 4, 1907.
2. Ambler, p. 354.
3. Ambler, p. 349.

Other researchers were W. E. Rumsey, F. E. Brooks, Bert H. Hite, John L. Sheldon, and N. J. Giddings.[4]

For the accommodation of women students, Episcopal Hall, at Spruce and Willey streets, was leased in 1907 and reconditioned to provide living quarters for forty-two women, under the name of Woman's Hall. "In a sophomore prank, committed in the late hours of the first night of occupancy, it was rechristened 'The Henery' "[5]

The greatest problems continued to be financial. Salaries were low, ranging from twelve hundred dollars for assistant professors to two thousand dollars for professors. The total appropriation for 1906-07 was about eighteen thousand dollars below that of the previous year. The physical plant was congested and in need of repairs.[6]

Among new staff members who joined the faculty in 1907 were O. P. Chitwood, in history; J. A. Eiesland, mathematics; A. M. Reese, zoology; and F. B. Trotter, Latin.

To promote the development of athletics, the regents in 1907 authorized the collection of a five-dollar athletic fee from each regular student. The football team, under the direction of Clarence Russell, was moderately successful, winning six of its ten contests. It lost to Navy by only 6 to 0, to Pitt 10 to 0, to W.&J. 13 to 5, and piled up a total of 236 points to 38 for its opponents.[7]

Building and Loan Societies. Despite a period of depression in 1907, Morgantown's financial institutions continued to do a good business. At the time, spurred by the development of many new factories, the community was quite fortunate in the character of its building and loan associations, perhaps surpassing any other city in the state in the per capita resources available to home builders.

The Athens Building and Loan Association was started in January 1904, seven years after the beginning of the Morgantown Savings and Loan Society, and was followed, in May 1904, by the Monongalia Building and Loan Association, which soon became

4. Ambler, pp. 350, 351.
5. Ambler, p.·352; *The Athenaeum*, September 26, 1907; October, 1907.
6. Ambler, p. 353.
7. Ambler, pp. 368, 369.

the largest in the state. Other organizations were the Guardian Investment Building and Loan, and the State Savings and Investment Association, both founded in 1906, and the Sabraton Building and Loan in 1907.[8]

The M.&K. Is Completed. The line of the Morgantown and Kingwood Railroad, which had been constructed up Deckers Creek to the Preston County line in 1902, and then experienced long delays because of litigation, was finally completed to the main line of the Baltimore and Ohio Railroad, near Rowlesburg, in July 1907. This made possible greatly improved connections for Monongalia County residents traveling to Washington and the Northeast.[9]

Railroad Passenger Service. During the winter of 1906-07, railroad passenger trains on the F.M.&P. R.R. left Morgantown for Connellsville and Pittsburg at 5:53 a.m., 8:32 a.m., and 3:20 p.m. Trains for Fairmont, Clarksburg, and Weston left at 6:00 a.m., 12:02 p.m., and 8:40 p.m. On the M.&K. R.R., trains left for Kingwood at 8:00 a.m. and 2:15 p.m.

Right of Way for the Trolley. Street cars were becoming important to the people of Morgantown, but new construction was encountering problems of rights of way that were often frustrating. The South Morgantown line was an example and a local editor stated his opinion:

"The modern trolley is a vehicle, and it is becoming more and more the vehicle of the people. It should be recognized as such and should be given its fair share of the right of way along all city streets where it may be expected to serve more people than it inconveniences. . . .

"The South Morgantown line should be allowed to secure a right of way for its loop on terms that are financially possible for it to meet. If its franchise needs amendment for the safe-guarding of the city's interests, council is wise in taking time to consider such amendments; but it should not be made possible for rival real-estate interests . . . to block the line under pretext of protecting the public."[10]

8. Callahan, pp. 279, 280.
9. Callahan, p. 281.
10. *Weekly Post*, August 23, 1906.

Carl Hagenbeck and Great Wallace Shows. This show, one of the largest ever to exhibit in Morgantown, arrived in town on Sunday for showing on Monday at the South Morgantown show grounds. The show came in seventy long yellow cars, coming down from Fairmont in three separate trains. About 710 people traveled with the show.

People came in from all the country round about. "The hotels are full, restaurants crowded, the hitching ground packed, and horses tied to every available telephone pole and picket fence in the side streets. At 11.39 the M.&K. excursion train arrived, bringing in 400 happy excursionists from up the Deckers Valley."[11]

New City Parks. Morgantown was becoming a "city of parks." There was Point Breeze, in Seneca, on the line of the Union Utility trolley, Jerome Park, opened May 20, on the Sabraton line, and the proposed new Morgantown and Southern Traction Company was planning a park on the top of South Park hill. The South Morgantown Traction Company opened a park in Round Hollow, near the pump station, which was named Traction Park.[12]

Towards a New River Bridge. On May 10, 1899, the old suspension bridge across the Monongahela River at Morgantown had been freed of tolls. But now new problems developed. The old bridge was soon found to be unsafe for the heavy and increasing traffic which was using it. In this connection, it should be pointed out, the bridge had evidently been constructed under excellent engineering plans for handling the traffic of its day, because no problems were encountered, no accidents were recorded, and only relatively minor repairs were required from time to time.

But now a new day had opened. A railroad ran beneath the bridge, factories lined the riverbanks, the population was increasing steadily. Engineering tests made by W. H. Boughton in 1907 indicated that the bridge was inadequate and unsafe.[13] Furthermore, promoters of various trolley lines, including the Union Utility Company, the Morgantown and Dunkard Valley Railroad, and the Morgantown and Fairmont Traction Company, sought permission to construct their tracks on a proposed new bridge.

11. *Daily Post*, May 20, 1907.
12. *Daily Post*, May 17, 1907.
13. *Daily Post*, April 1, 1907.

At a special election ordered in June 1907, approval was granted for the county court to appropriate funds for the construction of the new bridge. A ferry was established from the bottom of Walnut Street to the west side of the river, and the old suspension bridge, after a long and useful life of fifty-four years, was dismantled.[14] A contract was then signed with the Canton Construction Company for building the new bridge.

The Town of Star City. A new Monongalia County town, Star City, was incorporated on May 17, 1907,[15] with an area of 291 acres. The name had been suggested by Louis Kauffield, general manager of the Star Glass Company, which had located at that place in December 1904. Kauffield was an experienced and widely known man in the lamp chimney business. He was formerly the president of the Kauffield Chimney House, of Matthews, Indiana, and later constructed and managed the Nilan Glass factory of Point Marion. Before owning and managing his own factory, he was for a number of years in the employ of MacBeth and other well-known chimney manufacturers.

The first election for the new town was held on June 14, 1907, and since there was but one slate of candidates, the result was not in doubt.

"By a unanimous majority of 30, all the candidates on the first municipal ticket were elected Friday at Star City. Altogether there were 30 votes cast, all for the citizens ticket. The vote will be canvassed this afternoon by Commissioners Napoleon Boothe, Henry Rettiger and Samuel J. Boyles. Immediately after the declaration of the result, the newly elected officials will take the oath of office and will start in at once upon their duties.

"E. E. Shriver will be the first recorder, and the following councilmen will be convened some time next week for the first council meeting: G. B. Stansberry, R. C. McKinley, F. C. Shriver, U. G. Wright and J. W. Kennedy."[16]

The first school in the community was established in 1905, with James G. Gorman as the first teacher. The building was a two-room brick structure, but at first only one room was used.

14. Callahan, pp. 283, 284.
15. See *Daily Post,* May 11, 1907.
16. *Morgantown Daily Post,* June 15, 1907.

A post office, which had been established in 1905 and named Shriver, for Frank C. Shriver, the postmaster, was now renamed Star City, on July 1, 1907. Shriver remained as postmaster.

Mail From Amos (Fairview). The old community of Amos, on Paw Paw Creek, Marion County, grew rapidly as a result of the oil boom and soon reached a population of one thousand people. Its stores and financial organizations were much used by residents of some parts of Clay and Battelle districts, who were much closer to them than they were to those of their own county seat.

On August 15, 1907, Monongalia County post offices at Daybrook, Miracle Run, Cross Roads, Sandy, and John were closed, and thereafter mail came by rural route from Amos.[17]

Bridge Bonds Approved. In the election for the bond issue to build a new Monongahela River bridge at Morgantown, held on June 1, the bonds carried by 2,154 to 754. The majority in the city, as was to be expected, was higher than in the country, but even in the country there was a narrow majority of 29 votes for the bonds, indicating a decided change in sentiment since the 1906 election.[18]

Burns' Chapel. High on a mountain top five miles southeast of Dellslow, Burns' Chapel, a Methodist church, was dedicated in 1907, having been constructed the previous year. Joseph Burns gave the land for the building and the Reverend Mr. Hodges led the movement to erect the building, taking the place of an old log structure dating from about 1850.

The building committee was composed of Tillman Summers, Bela Davis, Henry Wolfe, Joseph Keenan, Solomon Robinson, Sam Murray, and George M. McMillen, who also did the work of erecting the building. Rev. James Fink and the Reverend Mr. Lowe were in charge of the dedication program.[19]

The Bethel Baptist Church. The cornerstone of the Bethel Baptist Church, on the Halleck Road near Triune, was laid in 1895,

---

17. The name of the post office was later changed to Fairview, to correspond to the name given to the developing town. On May 8, 1908, the Statlers Run Post Office was closed and the residents were served by another rural route from Amos.

18. *Daily Post*, June 3, 1907.

19. Dodds and Dodds, p. 81.

but the small frame building was under construction for several years. Upon its completion, services were held there, but it was considered an outpost of the Goshen Church.

On March 23, 1907, at their own request, about forty persons were dismissed from the Goshen Church for the purpose of organizing a new congregation in the community near their homes. Among these were Ollie Rumble, Gilla Gwynn, Tannie Price, Gracie Moran, T. Fleming Price, Ivy Guthrie, Mary C. Williams, Willie Rumble, and Claude O. Moran. The new congregation was organized in June 1907.[20]

James C. Wallace. A well-known hotel keeper of Morgantown, James C. Wallace, died in the office of the Peabody Hotel on February 25. The son of John Wallace, he came with his father as a small boy from Hopwood, Pennsylvania, to settle in Morgantown. His father bought and operated the National Hotel, on the site of the Peabody, and later built what was known in 1907 as the "Old Wallace House." James assisted and succeeded his father in the operation of these hotels. He was an enthusiastic horseman and kept a stable noted for miles around. He married Lucinda Shay and was survived by one daughter, Mrs. Eleanor Casteel.[21]

Louis Hagedorn. While walking along the M.&K. tracks at Sabraton on June 17, Louis Hagedorn, of Dellslow, was struck and killed by the passenger train bound for Kingwood. He was eighty-two years old and somewhat deaf. He was born in Germany and came here fifty years ago. He married Elizabeth Ann Johnson and was survived by three sons, Marshall, Charles, and Henry, and by four daughters, Mrs. Emma Utt, Mrs. Glenn White, Mrs. John Smith, and Mrs. Lee Gidley. It was the first fatal accident in the history of the M.&K. Railroad.[22]

Miscellany. In 1907: Portions of the B.&O. track between Morgantown and Uniontown were improved by installation of eighty-five-pound rails to accommodate the heavy traffic (Callahan, p. 246). . . . The Donley apartment building, on Pleasant Street, was constructed (Callahan, p. 272). . . . Receipts at the Morgantown

20. Dodds and Dodds, p. 136.
21. *Daily Post,* February 25, 1907.
22. *Daily Post,* June 17, 1907.

post office had increased from twelve thousand dollars in 1897 to twenty-one thousand dollars in 1907 (Callahan, p. 284). . . . The old Deep Hollow bridge in Morgantown was replaced by an earth fill and the ravine was beginning to disappear by being used for the reception of excavations for new buildings (Callahan, p. 298). . . . George Carraco was fined one dollar and costs for driving his delivery wagon at an "improper and dangerous" speed on city streets; he explained that he was hurrying to get the mail on the 2:15 M.&K. train (*Weekly Post*, January 10, 1907). . . . Alexander T. Hess, of Laurel Point, died January 21, aged eighty-six years, survived by his wife Elizabeth, one son, William B. Hess, and one daughter, Mrs. Ora Brand (*Weekly Post*, January 24, 1907). . . . William B. Long, of the West Side, died January 30, aged eighty years, survived by two children, Columbus Long, and Mrs. Emma Thomas (*Weekly Post*, January 31, 1907). . . . Conductor Lloyd Morris, of Union Utility street car No. 11, was seriously injured when the car jumped the track on Eighth Street; the five passengers were not injured (*Daily Post*, January 25, 1907). . . . Judge Frank Cox, president of the state supreme court of appeals, resigned January 28 to return to his home in Morgantown (*Daily Post*, January 28, 1907). . . . Noted pianist Moriz Rosenthal gave a concert in the Swisher Theater on February 8; Clarksburg and Fairmont music lovers came by special train (*Daily Post*, February 9, 1907). . . . Ben Greet starred in *The Merchant of Venice* at the Swisher Theater on February 21 (*Daily Post*, February 22, 1907). . . . William Hinemarch, a coke drawer at the Richard plant of the Elkins Coal and Coke Company, was drowned when he fell from the footbridge over Deckers Creek (*Daily Post*, March 14, 1907). . . . Frank McElroy, the ferryman at the Jimtown ferry, was killed when he fell from a second-story window of Marcus Lemley's store (*Daily Post*, April 19, 1907). . . . Alphaeus, son of Ezekiel Morris, of Clay District, died February 8, 1907; born January 4, 1829, he married Martha Lemley and their children were Etta, Emma, Lemley, Frank, Orpha, George, and Mary (*Chronicles of Core*, p. 169). . . . Noah Pyles, of Pedlar Run, a son of David and Drusilla Pyles, died May 6, 1907; he was born June 12, 1840 (*Chronicles of Core*, p. 169). . . . A Methodist Sunday school was organized in Jerome Park by Rev. C. K. Jenness; sessions were held in a small building on Lincoln Avenue (Dodds and Dodds, p. 85). . . . The congregation of Saint Luke's Church of Christ, at Mooresville, built a small frame church (Dodds and Dodds, p. 125). . . . The Cooley and Hagans show boat gave a concert at the corner of High and Walnut streets, and when the rain began to fall the band boarded a trolley car and "looped the loop" playing the while (*Daily Post*, May 18, 1907). . . . A franchise was approved by city council March 4 for the Morgantown and Southern Traction Company to build a trolley line across South Park Hill (*Daily Post*, March 5, 1907). . . . Charles Jenkins and Virgil Brown formed a partnership to operate a funeral home (*Post-Chronicle Industrial Edition*, 1913).

CHAPTER ONE HUNDRED THIRTY-TWO

1908

By 1908 it might be said that the street car days in Monongalia County were approaching their zenith. A good system of cars served the downtown area and one loop went down Beechurst Avenue to Eighth Street and back through the university campus, while another ran through South Park and South Morgantown, returning to the downtown section by way of Bridge Street and Front Street. A spur ran out to Sabraton, serving the factories and residential areas in that direction. A line went through West Morgantown to a hickory tree in a field owned by Grover P. Keener in what was later the town of Riverside.

This "Hickory Tree" line was envisioned to be extended to Rivesville, there to connect with an extensive system that tied together Fairmont, Fairview, Mannington, Ida May, Wyatt, Clarksburg, Wolf Summit, Bridgeport, and Weston. The interurban electric cars were relatively speedy and operated on frequent convenient schedules, so that many people believed that the day was not far away when the principal cities of the state (and the nation) would be linked together.

Stephen B. Elkins, represented in Morgantown by Harry R. Warfield, obtained franchises for construction of the line to Fairmont and of another to Fairchance, there to connect with a system already in operation to Uniontown, Connellsville, Greensburg, and Pittsburgh.

There was a special lure to the interurban car age somewhat similar to the nostalgic feeling that comes when we contemplate the days of passenger trains pulled by steam locomotives. Maybe it was the thrill of an occasional spark from a glistening wire, maybe it was the fascination of motion and power supplied with such easy control from an unseen source, maybe we just can't put our fingers on it, but many people who remember them wish the

interurban days were still with us. At the time no one could fore-
see that the crude, uncertain automobile then operated as a novelty would not only displace the trolley but would soon seriously
compete with railroads in the transportation of freight and passengers.

Dunkard Valley Traction. Still another line was projected to run
into the Dunkard Creek Valley in the western part of the county,
to connect at Blacksville with a line to be built to Waynesburg
and Washington, where connections were already available to
Pittsburgh, and with Mannington, where connections could be
made with Fairmont. It might even be extended from Blacksville
on to Wheeling.

Organized in 1905, the Morgantown and Dunkard Valley Railway Company was designed as the first link in the projected system. Residents of the Dunkard Valley section heard of the plans
with undisguised joy. A correspondent wrote to a Morgantown
newspaper: "The street cars will be welcome whenever they
choose to come. We who reside in the jungles of Clay District are
tired of the hoot of the owl and are longing for the hum of the industrial wheel."[1]

By the end of the year work was well under way on grading of
the road from Morgantown to Stumptown, on Scotts Run. J. Ami
Martin, president, announced the purchase of 550 tons of
70-pound steel rails, at twenty-eight dollars per ton, to be used in
the construction of the first five miles of the line. The company
had bought over ten thousand cross-ties. Work was under way on
a bridge across Dents Run at Granville. Residents of Mount Morris, Pennsylvania, were attempting to raise twenty-five thousand
dollars to have the line extended from Cassville to that town.[2]

Difficulties with rights-of-way along the route of the proposed
Buckhannon and Northern Railroad and property of the Tait
Coal Company, near Randall, and shortage of funds for purchase
of equipment, delayed construction.

End of the Suspension Bridge. A familiar landmark since before
the Civil War, the Morgantown suspension bridge disappeared
during 1908. With money available for a new bridge, the old

1. *Weekly Post*, March 5, 1903.
2. *Post-Chronicle*, December 17, 1909.

bridge was dismantled and a free ferry was established, crossing the river from the foot of Walnut Street to the West Side. The cables were cut and dropped into the river, and the old bridge dismantled. The contract for the new bridge was awarded to the Canton Bridge Company, and S. M. Prince was appointed as resident representative of the company.

The University. In January 1908, the West Virginia University Council ordered that entrance requisites be expressed in terms of "units" rather than "courses," as had been done previously. The "units" were defined as the work covered in an accredited high school in a class meeting not less than thirty-six weeks for a minimum of forty-five minutes, four or five times weekly. Compliance with such standardizing procedures made it possible for the university to gain membership in the National Association of State Universities.[3]

Changes in the status of various units were made in 1908. The School of Military Science and Tactics, and the School of Fine Arts, became departments in the College of Arts and Sciences.[4]

The School of Music, which, under the deanship of S. L. Wrightson (1902-04), had been one of the most popular and effective units of the university, was also downgraded in 1908 to the status of a department. Ross Spence, who had directed the school after the resignation of Dean Wrightson, featured an ever decreased number of artists, and it was in the interest of economy that the school became a department, with Mabel Constance the only other staff member. In 1907 Music had occupied the third floor of Woodburn Hall, directly above rooms used by the College of Law. Lectures in law were sometimes rendered inaudible, and the lawyers were accused of efforts to abolish "the nuisance" and held responsible for the failure of the legislature to appropriate adequate funds for the 1908-09 session.[5]

The University Commercial School was also abolished in 1908. Established by D. M. Willis in 1895, its enrollment had steadily declined, from 188 in 1902 to 48 in 1908. This was doubtless because of the competition with the numerous commercial col-

3. Ambler, p. 345.
4. Ambler, p. 347.
5. Ambler, p. 351. School status was restored in 1909.

leges which had been established throughout the state, to meet the need for trained clerical help.[6]

Literary societies, which, throughout most of the life of the university had been extremely important, were now definitely losing power and influence. The cause was attributed to various factors, including growing interest in athletics, Greek letter fraternities, the dramatic club, etc. For old-time educators, however, there was no substitute for the literary society, and a determined effort was made to preserve it. Accordingly, in February 1908, two new societies were formed, the Demosthean and the Athenian. They were, however, limited to the preparatory department, of which all students were required to become members.[7] The old Columbian and Parthenon literary societies continued to be active elsewhere in the university.[8]

Student organizations formed in 1908 included a chapter of the scientific fraternity Kappa Psi and of the engineering fraternity, Theta Psi. Aurora Grange No. 372, "the oldest student lodge in the United States,"[9] was reorganized April 28, 1908, by students and faculty of the College of Agriculture as University Grange No. 372. Seo Beowulf Gedryht, organized February 29, 1908, with the assistance of Prof. J. H. Cox, was based on the Anglo-Saxon epic, "Beowulf."[10]

The football team of 1908 was remarkably successful. C. A. Leuder was coach (also an instructor in dairy). With the aid of A. W. Chez and T. B. Foulk, he developed a team that won all but three of its games. The University of Pennsylvania was held to be a score of 6 to 0, Penn State to 12 to 0, and Pitt to 11 to 0. Bethany was defeated by a count of 47 to 0. Basketball had J. H. Jenkins as coach and manager but was abandoned in 1908 as an intercollegiate sport because of inadequate playing quarters. College baseball, however, continued to be popular, both with the students and the townspeople.[11]

6. Ambler, pp. 351, 352. It was revived in 1909 as an Arts and Sciences department.

7. With the discontinuance of the "Prep School" in 1909, they ceased to function.

8. Ambler, p. 359.

9. It was organized at Morgantown June 14, 1876.

10. Ambler, pp. 360, 361.

11. Ambler, p. 369.

Public Schools. The rapid growth of the city of Morgantown was resulting in serious overcrowding in the elementary schools. In the Independent School District a new building had already been constructed in the Third Ward (1899) and in the Fourth Ward (1904). Now, in April 1908, the School Board purchased from John Madigan, for thirty-five hundred dollars, twelve lots along Madigan Avenue, in the First Ward, for school purposes. A bond issue of $150,000 was proposed for construction, but, after much criticism, the amount was reduced to $60,000. Even this was defeated by a popular vote of 459 to 406.

In August, Superintendent William H. Gallup resigned after nine years of successful service.[12]

River Traffic. Traffic on the river continued steady, despite competition with the railroad. "The *Woodward* had an unusually good trip to Fairmont Wednesday. Besides the regular cargo of freight the boat carried two carloads of nails and one carload of paper. . . . The *Jewel* made her first trip Tuesday after being laid up at Pittsburg for repairs. . . .

"The *Marion*, the new towboat owned by McClain Brothers, came to Morgantown yesterday. The new boat towed I. N. Weaver's sand dredger to Granville."[13]

William E. Glasscock, Governor. A Monongalia County native, William Ellsworth Glasscock, was honored in 1908 in being elected governor of West Virginia. He was born December 13, 1862, on a farm near Arnettsville, the son of Daniel and Prudence (Michael) Glasscock.

He attended the Arnettsville School and at the age of eighteen became a teacher, working in Iowa and Nebraska briefly, then returning to West Virginia. He was county superintendent of schools for two terms and was elected clerk of the county court in 1890 and again in 1896. He studied medicine for a short time in Baltimore, then entered West Virginia University for the study of law and was admitted to the bar in 1902, practicing with his brother, Samuel Fuller Glasscock.

In 1900 he became a member of the Republican State Executive Committee and for about eight years was its chairman or sec-

12. Callahan, p. 288.
13. *Post-Chronicle*, November 12, 1908.

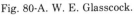

Fig. 80-A. W. E. Glasscock.   Fig. 80-B. James Morton Callahan.

retary, at various times. In 1905 he was appointed by President Theodore Roosevelt as collector of internal revenue for West Virginia and served until his resignation to run for governor in 1908.

Glasscock was nominated as a compromise candidate to break a deadlock between Charles W. Swisher and Arnold P. Scherr. His Democratic opponent was Judge Louis Bennett, whom he defeated by more than 12,000 votes. His administration was destined to be a stormy one.[14]

Automobile Garages. A new word, garage, was entering the vocabulary of American people. Originally from the French, it was a verb referring to the act of putting a boat on the river or canal into a dry dock for repair. It then came to be used on railroads to designate the shunting of cars onto sidings, and then, especially in England, to moving an automobile off a highway into a building prepared for it, which, by transfer, came to be called a garage.

In Morgantown, as elsewhere, automobile garages were beginning to supplant the old livery stables. The first public garage in Morgantown was erected at the Greenmont end of the Walnut Street bridge. This Greenmont garage constructed by the Morgantown Garage Co., provided "electric cab service, . . . storage

14. *West Virginia Heritage Encyclopedia*, pp. 1859, 1860.

and care for automobiles, . . . and a repair shop and depot of supplies." The promoters were Paul McKeil, Charles White, and W. F. Gornall.[15]

Oil Developments in Battelle. During 1908 several sensational producers were drilled to the "deep" or "fourth" sand in the Dunkard Creek headwaters. The biggest strike of the year was in May, when the Wheeling Gas Company brought in a gusher on the Marion Efaw farm on Miracle Run. This well had an average daily production of 650 barrels.[16]

Des Moines Utt. Lieutenant Des Moines Utt, county and city engineer, died suddenly at his home in Woodburn on January 13. At the outbreak of the Spanish War he entered the army as a private in the Forty-fourth Volunteer Infantry and saw service in the Philippines. He was a lieutenant in the state militia.[17]

Mail Service Increases. On December 1, 1908, Morgantown's carrier mail delivery service entered its ninth year. Four carriers, Emerson Carney, Harvey Brand, "Buck" Crawford, and "Dolph" Anderson, who had begun the daily service, were still on the staff, and three others, H. B. Fogle, W. H. Kendrick, and L. A. Smith, had been added. In 1900 the four carriers served a population of 4,000, while in 1908 the population was 8,500.[18]

The Post-Chronicle. Beginning with the issue for June 11, 1908, the *Morgantown Weekly Post* passed away and was succeeded by the *Morgantown Post-Chronicle.* A new management purchased the interests of the majority stockholder, W. E. Glasscock, and combined the two papers, to make possible the publication of a greater paper, "worthy in every respect of Greater Morgantown and of Monongalia County." John E. Day, editor of the *Post,* and W. L. Russell, business manager, were succeeded by Robert R. Green, editor and manager.

The Morgantown Republican. A merger agreement was signed December 31 whereby the morning *Morgantown Republican* which had been in existence only a few months, was to come to an

---

15. *Post-Chronicle,* October 22, 1908.
16. *Post-Chronicle,* January 7, 1909.
17. *Weekly-Post,* January 16, 1908.
18. *Post-Chronicle,* December 3, 1908.

end with its issue of the next day, being absorbed by the New Dominion News Company. Thereafter the newspaper, the *New Dominion*, was to appear as a morning paper, with Gilbert B. Miller as editor, while Julian E. Fleming, founder of the paper, succeeded W. E. Nern as business manager.

By this deal Morgantown was to have only two daily newspapers, the Democratic *New Dominion* in the morning and the Republican *Post-Chronicle* in the afternoon. W. L. Russell, who had been associated with both Republican newspapers, left to take a position in Charleston.[19]

New M.P. Church. The new Methodist Protestant Church, at the corner of Spruce and Fayette streets, was formally opened De-

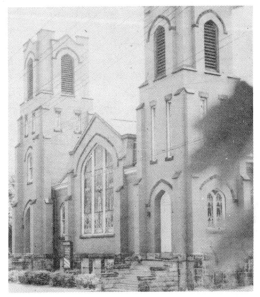

Fig. 81. Methodist Protestant Church on Spruce Street. (Courtesy Spruce Street United Methodist Church.)

cember 6, 1908. The pastor, Rev. James H. Clarke, spoke at the morning service; various ministers of other churches in the city made short talks in the afternoon service; and in the evening Rev. D. H. Davis, of Saint Marys, a former pastor, was the speaker.

19. *Post-Chronicle*, December 31, 1908.

The cost of the construction was about forty thousand dollars.
The large red brick structure succeeded the building on Walnut
Street, which had become too small for the rapidly growing con-
gregation.[20]

Maidsville M.P. Church. A new Methodist Protestant church on
Robinson Run was dedicated in 1908, succeeding the old Westfall
Chapel built in 1858 at Cushman's "Stonepile" (vol. 3, p. 483).
Rev. Willis Hart was the pastor.[21]

Miscellany. In 1908: A new post office, by the name of Sabraton,
was established November 20; Edwin R. Jones was the first post-
master (National Archives). . . . Lonnie E., son of James W. and
Minerva (Morris) Davis, died of typhoid fever on January 23, not
quite twenty years of age; he was an early automobile operator
(*Chronicles of Core*, p. 170). . . . David J., son of James Eddy, died
April 22; he was born May 19, 1835, married Elizabeth Barrickman, and they were the parents of Isaac Luther and James Clark
Eddy (*Chronicles of Core*, p. 170). . . . In August, the South Penn
Oil Company's Alex King Well No. 5, in Battelle District, con-
tinued to hold up at three hundred barrels a day (*Post-Chronicle*,
August 27, 1908). . . . The Morgantown city council passed an ordinance prohibiting the operation of vehicles at speeds greater
than eight miles an hour (*Post-Chronicle*, November 26, 1908).
. . . Dr. Emory M. Henry, Laurel Point physician, died December 1 (*Post-Chronicle*, December 3, 1908). . . . A new insurance
and real estate firm, Sanders and Miller, was formed by Harry
Sanders and Charles E. Miller (*Post-Chronicle Industrial Edition*,
1913). . . . Battelle District oil towns, usually with boarding-
houses or taverns, were Kimberley, Ragtown, and Flyblow, on
Miracle Run (*Battelle District News*, August 12, 1975).

20. *New Dominion*, December 7, 1908.
21. Dodds and Dodds, p. 117.

CHAPTER ONE HUNDRED THIRTY-THREE

1909

On Memorial Day, 1909, a new steel bridge across the Monongahela River at Morgantown was opened to traffic with impressive ceremonies. This replaced the old suspension bridge which had featured prominently in Monongalia County history since before the Civil War.

In pioneer times the Monongahela River had rather effectively divided the county into a western and an eastern section. Numerous ferries, at strategic points, carried people, goods, and livestock across the river, but these at best caused considerable delays and often could not operate at all because of floods or ice. It is not surprising, therefore, that the opening of the first suspension bridge across the river, on December 16, 1854, should have been rated as one of the greatest events in the county's history.

The New River Bridge. The dedication ceremonies were held on Memorial Day (May 29), 1909, beginning at 3:00 p.m. "Congressman George C. Sturgiss presided over the ceremonies. The representative from the Second District delivered a history of the old suspension bridge from the time the money was first raised for its construction until the day it was torn down. The speech was interesting and was delivered in such a way, as to hold the attention of the big crowd of people assembled at the end of the bridge. Congressman Sturgiss was followed by Congressman W. P. Hubbard of Wheeling who delivered a short address."[1]

After considerable discussion, it was decided to place only one set of trolley tracks on the bridge, to be used jointly by cars of the Union Utilities and Dunkard Valley lines. After the opening of the bridge the Union Utilities cars began running from the West Side up onto High Street via Walnut Street. Previously, trolley

---

1. *Post-Chronicle*, June 3, 1909.

Fig. 82-A. The suspension bridge at Morgantown. (Courtesy Louis F. Hiser.)

Fig. 82-B. Dedication of the new steel bridge. (From an old postcard.)

Fig. 83-A. Crossing the river at Morgantown during construction of the new bridge.

Fig. 83-B. Crossing the river at Jimtown. (Courtesy Mrs. Clyde Forbes.)

riders had to walk across the suspension bridge (or, later, to ride the ferry).

Progress on the M.&D.V. Cars on the Morgantown and Dunkard Valley line, however, were still not running despite grandiose visions. At a special meeting of the stockholders of the M.&D.V., on February 10, plans were made to issue bonds for $300,000 to cover the construction of thirty miles of track, from Morgantown to Wadestown. Branches would go to Mount Morris, Waynesburg, and Mannington.

But shortage of funds held up the delivery of steel rails for the track and not even the first short section had been completed by the end of 1909, after being under construction for most of two years.

On the Campus. In 1909 West Virginia University was showing definite signs of progress, notably in the increase in enrollment of students. There were 1,338 enrolled, as compared with only 755 in 1901, when President Purinton's term began.

Nevertheless, his administration had been a kind of a conservative reaction in a general Progressive Era. "In the failure to develop the social sciences, . . . its vision had been circumscribed. By adhering to an economy policy in a determined effort to make an inadequate physical plant adequate, the physical growth had been stunted. Remedial action awaited the formulation of an approved building program which no one was actively trying to develop and powerful interests were trying to keep from developing." Only nineteen new faculty members had been added and the maximum salary for a full professor was only twenty-two hundred dollars.[2]

A committee was authorized in 1909 to prepare plans and specifications for the long discussed "South Wing" on Woodburn Hall; the "North Wing" had been completed in 1901 (p. 270). During 1909 a third floor was added to Science Hall.

A two-year teacher certificate program for domestic science was announced in 1909 by the College of Agriculture, to meet the insistent demand for trained teachers in this field. The entire curriculum of twenty-one courses was developed and taught by Neva

2. Ambler, p. 356.

Augusta Scott, a graduate of the National School of Domestic Arts and Sciences.[3]

The committee on classification and grades, on June 29, 1904, expressed their opinion that the university could not give proper work for the Ph.D. degree and that therefore it should not be offered. The committee at the time was composed of F. B. Trotter, C. Ross Jones, J. N. Deahl, A. J. Hare, and J. M. Callahan. Their chief concern was in maintaining academic standards and since they generally worked concertedly and were dominant in their respective disciplines, they came to be known throughout the state as "the Old Guard."[4]

A secret honorary fraternity named Sphinx was organized on March 9, 1909. Its membership was restricted to fifteen representative men of the senior class. The first group of retiring seniors, on "Link Day" of "Junior Week" in May 1909, each designated a person from the junior class to carry on during the succeeding year, and it was planned to make similar choices annually thereafter.

The 1909 football team, although under the same manager and coach as during the previous year (p. 349), was not so successful, being defeated 12-0 by the University of Pennsylvania, 40-0 by Penn State, and 18-5 by W.&J. Pitt and Bucknell were tied and West Virginia Wesleyan was defeated 49-0.[5]

School Bonds Approved. To meet the rapidly increasing need for more space for school children, a school bond issue of $100,000 was submitted to voters in the Morgantown Independent School District on May 8, 1909. The issue was approved by a vote of 539 to 215.

The board immediately began planning for the construction of several new school buildings, at a cost of eighty-five hundred dollars each. These were to be located in Woodburn, on Wiles Hill, in Second Ward, and on the West Side. For the site of the Woodburn building a lot was purchased from W. G. Smith for twenty-five hundred dollars.[6]

3. Ambler, p. 352.
4. Ambler, p. 355.
5. Ambler, p. 369.
6. Callahan, p. 288.

Community Baseball Teams. One of the most popular forms of recreation in Monongalia County in the first decade of the twentieth century was baseball. Every community had a team, many churches and other organizations had teams, and there was strong rivalry between the teams and great pride in the teams expressed by members of their communities.

By the close of the Civil War the game of baseball was already becoming popular in Monongalia County (see vol. 3, p. 681). During the summer months, for many years to come, many issues of local weekly newspapers had notices of matches between various teams. As is well known, the game is played on a level field marked out as a "diamond." Finding an appropriate place to play was not always easy in a hilly region such as Monongalia County. Often special "ground rules" had to be made up to accommodate for certain features of the field, as a creek or embankment nearby. For Morgantown, in the latter part of the nineteenth century, the best diamond was on the fairgrounds in Greenmont, across Deckers Creek from the town.

Each local community had its own team, often churches and

Fig. 84. Core Baseball Team. (Courtesy Mrs. A. C. Shively.)

Sunday school classes had their own teams, and strong support was given to the teams. Uniforms bearing the name of the team were worn by the players. Wadestown, Daybrook, Blacksville, Pentress, Mooresville, Core, and Cassville were among the communities which supported strong baseball teams, which were eager to take on the town boys from the county seat, who often had a feeling of superiority over their country cousins. One of the best known teams in the county was the Baraca Club, organized and supported by a Sunday school class with that name, in the Spruce Street Methodist Protestant Church.

Union Utilities Building. The Union Utilities Company, whose predecessor in 1892 had built a brick building at the corner of

Fig. 85. Union Utilities Building, at High and Fayette streets.

High Street and Bumbo Lane (p. 166), in 1909 moved the building to the rear of the lot and erected a larger building on the site. This structure, eight stories plus basement, was Morgantown's first steel-frame building.[7]

7. Callahan, p. 286. The name of the company was changed to Union Utilities (from Union Utility) in 1909.

"The frame for the new building comes from Pittsburg, a deal having been closed for the purchase of the steel frame in the eight story structure at the corner of Smithfield street and Sixth avenue."[8]

New Fairgrounds. The first annual fair of the Morgantown Fair Association was held September 28 to October 1 on the new fair-

Fig. 86. Miss Ida crosses finish line first in race at Evans track, September 28, 1909.

grounds on the Evans farm just north of Morgantown. An advertisement announced: "This initial event here will be one of the best of its kind ever held in West Virginia. The arrangements of the grounds have been made with a thought to the pleasure and comfort of all who attend. The farmers will find convenient hitching places outside the grounds." There were balloon ascensions and parachute drops each afternoon by Clara Belmont, as well as special horse races.

The fair was opened at 1 p.m. on September 28, with eighteen hundred people in attendance. Harry R. Warfield, president of

8. *Post-Chronicle,* April 22, 1909.

the fair association, introduced Congressman George C. Sturgiss, who in turn introduced Governor William E. Glasscock, who gave an address full of memories of the old town and country. Hacks and automobiles charged twenty-five cents each way from downtown to the fairgrounds. There were amusement shows and the Morgantown Concert Band (sixteen pieces) rendered musical presentations.

About thirty thousand dollars had been spent in developing the fairgrounds.[9]

Traffic on the M.&K. A new record for traffic on the M.&K. was set March 23, when seventy-six loaded freight cars were pulled out, sixty-one by way of M.&K. Junction and fifteen through Morgantown. Some of the tinplate was being shipped to Honolulu, where it would be used in making cans for canning pineapples. The material went by way of Baltimore, thence by ship around Cape Horn.[10]

The first passenger car in West Virginia to be equipped with gas lights was put into service on the line. Gas lights were regarded as a great improvement over oil lamps.[11]

Oak Park. M.&K. Railroad officials, on June 19, opened an amusement center, Oak Park, along the railroad near Masontown, Preston County. A summer theater was let out to H. A. Christy.[12]

On Sunday, July 11, the railroad operated one train of eight coaches and another of nine coaches to handle the crowds. Another of twelve coaches was run from the park to Morgantown on the next evening. On Sunday over twelve hundred passengers were carried, and over sixteen hundred on Monday, records up until that time.[13] These records were broken on August 25 when over four thousand people were carried in fourteen passenger trains.[14]

The Woodward Is Docked. The packet steamer *I. A. Woodward*, of the Pittsburg and Morgantown Packet Company, made its last

9. *Post-Chronicle*, September 30, 1909.
10. *Post-Chronicle*, April 1, 1909.
11. *Post-Chronicle*, April 8, 1909.
12. *Post-Chronicle*, June 17, 1909.
13. *Post-Chronicle*, July 15, 1909.
14. *Post-Chronicle*, September 2, 1909.

trip from Morgantown to Pittsburg on December 13, 1909, and was docked there for the winter. "The packet company claims that the boat does not pay owing to the expense of keeping it in operation."

The *Jewel* continued to make trips from Pittsburg to Morgantown on alternate days. The *Jewel* had recently replaced the *Columbia* and made the trip to Fairmont once a week. "It is probable that the Fairmont trip will be discontinued entirely."[15]

New Oil Company. A certificate of incorporation was issued June 21, 1909, for the Round Bottom Oil and Gas Company, the incorporators being S. G. Yoke, S. N. Swisher, F. A. Hennen, A. L. Foster, and T. J. McClernan. The capital stock was set at five thousand dollars.

The South Penn Oil Company was continuing to develop its Battelle District territory and brought in its No. 9 well on the Joseph Estell farm, producing 200 barrels a day. The Carnegie Natural Gas Company's well nearby, on the L. E. Hartley farm, was holding up at 225 barrels a day.[16]

Harner's Chapel. At the Dorsey schoolhouse on the Kingwood Pike, Rev. M. H. Steele, a Methodist Episcopal minister, conducted a very successful revival meeting in March and April, 1909. At the close of the meeting, on April 19, a class of fifty members were organized, and investigation was made as to the possibility of establishing a church in the community. Fairchild Harner agreed to donate land for a building site, across the road from the school. A building committee was appointed, consisting of J. D. Anderson, Sr., J. W. Poole, Sr., N. H. McElroy, L. K. McBee, J. F. Smith, and T. Orth Bunner. Men of the community met with teams and necessary equipment to work under the direction of U. S. Fleming and Byron Mitchell, and the frame building was completed later in the year.[17]

Church of the Brethren. Ministers of the Church of the Brethren had come from Preston County in 1883 to start a congregation in Monongalia County (p. 74), but the congregation did not flourish at Mount Union, on the Point Marion road, where it was founded.

15. *Post-Chronicle*, December 23, 1909.
16. *Post-Chronicle*, June 24, 1909.
17. Dodds and Dodds, p. 82.

Since most of the members of the small group lived in Morgantown, it was decided, after much discussion, to locate a new church there.

In 1909, therefore, a lot was secured at the corner of Highland Avenue and Melrose Street, where a brick church was built the same year. Families aiding in the work included the Hamilton, Reed, Rose, Pugh, and others.[18]

"Grandma" Finnell. Lucinda ("Grandma") Finnell, a Monongalia County centenarian, died April 24. The daughter of Isaac and Sarah Hoffman, she was born March 31, 1808, at Strasburg, Virginia. She married S. W. Finnell, Sr., and they moved to Monongalia County in 1849. They had eight children, four of whom survived, namely, Mrs. Margaret Fitch, Mrs. Catherine Johnson, Mrs. Annie Hayes, and C. W. Finnell.[19]

Miscellany. In 1909: The Eureka Pipe Line Company laid a line from Parkersburg to Hamlin, in Lincoln County (eighty-three miles), bringing more oil for temporary storage in the Morgantown Tank Field and necessitating the construction of more tanks (Callahan, p. 250). . . . A new brick church was built at Cross Roads, Battelle District, by members of the Union Baptist congregation, under the pastorate of Rev. Walter Barnes (Dodds and Dodds, p. 131). . . . The Chancery Hill Spring Company was organized by C. D. Willey and others for bottling and daily delivery of water from the famous spring on Chancery Hill (vol. 3, p. 201) (*Post-Chronicle*, March 18, 1909). . . . R. W. West, B.&O. foreman, was struck and killed by a passenger train near Opekiska on March 24 (*Post-Chronicle*, April 1, 1909). . . . At a meeting of the Morgantown City Council Mayor Albert Layton recommended that the city dispose of the heavy fire wagon and horses and purchase a motor car to be used by the fire department (*Post-Chronicle*, April 22, 1909). . . . Discussions were under way by the Waynesburg and Monongahela Street Railway Company to connect Morgantown with Waynesburg and Washington, Pennsylvania, by a trolley line (*Post-Chronicle*, April 22, 1909). . . . James Hood, aged eighty-one years, a business man of Lowesville, died (*Post-Chronicle*, May 6, 1909). . . . The five cars

18. Dodds and Dodds, p. 72.
19. *Post-Chronicle*, April 29, 1909.

on the Union Utility company's loop line carried over four thousand passengers on Saturday, May 29; on an average day there were about one thousand (*Post-Chronicle,* June 3, 1909). . . . Beginning May 31, the M.&K. added one passenger train daily to its schedule between Morgantown and Rowlesburg; trains left Union Station at 6:50 a.m., 12:50 p.m., and 4:50 p.m. (*Post-Chronicle,* June 3, 1909). . . . Work of construction of the line of the long-delayed Morgantown and Southern traction line was postponed again (*Post-Chronicle,* August 5, 1909). . . . Contracts were awarded to the Canton Bridge Company for construction of a bridge over Dolls Run, for $470 and one over Pedlar Run for $440 (*Post-Chronicle,* August 5, 1909). . . . A contract was awarded to W. B. Smith for $1,081 for a new one-room school house at Maidsville (*Post-Chronicle,* September 2, 1909). . . . Among petit jurors for the October term of circuit court was Major Lewis Davis,[20] of Van Voorhis, the smallest man in the state (*Post-Chronicle,* September 9, 1909). . . . H. H. Griffin, of Pisgah, escaped serious injury when his huckster wagon was struck by a street car at High and Willey streets; the horses ran away, scattering eggs and produce along the street and the wagon was demolished against a telephone pole (*Post-Chronicle,* September 30, 1909). . . . The first session of the West Virginia annual conference of the A.M.E. church began in Morgantown October 14; the presiding bishop was the Rt. Rev. W. B. Derrick, of Flushing, New York (*Post-Chronicle,* October 14, 1909). . . . Three men, Clarence S. Johns, Herbert C. Johns, and Clarence Knotts, were drowned November 6 when their skiff capsized by waves from a towboat as they were crossing the river below Lock No. 11 (*Post-Chronicle,* November 11, 1909). . . . Chauncey D. Willey, twenty-eight-year-old Morgantown attorney, son of William P. and Elizabeth (Ray) Willey, died November 3 of typhoid fever (*Post-Chronicle,* November 11, 1909). . . . Judge John W. Mason, of Fairmont, on November 12 attended a reunion at Triune of his old pupils who attended his subscription school there, beginning November 7, 1859; names of thirty-five students appear (*Post-Chronicle,* November 11, 1909). . . . On December 5 the West Virginia University chapter of Phi Beta Kappa was organized, with Oliver Perry Chitwood as president and William Henry Dickinson as vice-president (*Alpha of W.Va.,* 1945). . . . R. R. Chrisman and George H. Goodwin formed a partnership (Chrisman and

20. See pp. 377-78.

Goodwin Foundry) to engage in a general line of foundry jobbing work in iron and brass (*Post-Chronicle Industrial Edition,* 1913, p. 19). . . . Marmaduke Herbert Dent, first West Virginia University graduate (vol. 3, pp. 633, 661), died in Grafton (see John Philip Reid, *An American Judge: Marmaduke Dent of West Virginia.* 1968).

CHAPTER ONE HUNDRED THIRTY-FOUR

1910

The awakening in the last decade of the nineteenth century in Monongalia County had prepared the way for a real transformation of community life during the first decade of the twentieth century. This was stimulated by the opening of new resources and new economic connections and was marked by expansion and improvements in industries, business, transportation, public utilities, educational and religious facilities, social organizations, and activities relating especially to health and safety.

The Census of 1910. Morgantown, the county seat, a town of less than two thousand in 1900, grew to more than nine thousand by 1910. Its percentage of increase of population, which was 87.4 in the decade from 1890 to 1900, rose to 382.8% in the decade from 1900 to 1910. Its real and personal property rose from a valuation of $569,852 in 1887 to $8,938,659 in 1910.

The population of the seven districts in 1910, with the incorporated towns, is shown below, with 1900 figures for comparison:

	1900	*1910*
Battelle	2,760	2,270
Cass	1,444	1,173
Clay	3,149	2,797
Blacksville	180	204
Clinton	2,551	2,415
Grant	2,152	2,495
Morgan	5,356	11,631
Greenmont	349	— —
Morgantown	1,895	9,150
Seneca	723	— —
South Morgantown	405	— —
Union	1,637	1,553
Total	19,049	24,334

It will be noted that in all the districts except Grant and Morgan there was a decrease in population, despite the marked increase in the total population of the county. This indicates a movement of the population from rural into urban areas. The increase in Grant reflects the growth of the suburban area across the river from Morgantown, an area with street car connections to the business district.

Slowly the county's growth was beginning to raise its rank, population-wise, among the fifty-five counties of the state. In 1890 Monongalia County was in nineteenth place, in 1900 it was in eighteenth place; by 1910 it ranked fifteenth.

The growth of the county seat town had been much more spectacular. In 1900 at least sixteen cities and towns in West Virginia had populations greater than that of Morgantown; by 1910 only eight cities were larger than Morgantown.

Despite the tremendous development of industry since 1890, agriculture was still of considerable importance to the people of Monongalia County. There were 2,087 farms in the county, with an average size of 90 acres. The total acreage was 187,822, with 144,121 acres improved. The value of the lands and improvements was given as $8,705,365, plus $1,743,531 for buildings, $212,993 for implements and machinery, and $1,043,436 for livestock. The total acreage reported by the 1900 census was 218,114.

There were 14,531 head of cattle on Monongalia County farms, including 5,227 dairy cows two years old and over. Other farm animals included 4,549 horses, 65 mules, 27,012 sheep, 5,066 swine, and 95 goats. The value of all dairy products was given as $157,359, excluding that which was consumed on the farms where they were produced. A total of 1,848,972 gallons of milk was produced, along with 970 gallons of cream, and 526,353 pounds of butter.

Poultry, including chickens, turkeys, geese, and ducks, numbered 126,191. There were 1,970 colonies of bees, producing 28,959 pounds of honey and 155 pounds of wax. The number of fleeces of wool produced was 19,062.

The production of sorghum molasses, once of considerable importance, was essentially a thing of the past. In 1870, the first census after the Civil War, the production was listed as 36,504 gallons; in 1910 only 38 gallons.

The acreage and production of several field crops is shown below, with figures for 1900 for comparison:

| | 1900 | | 1910 | |
	Acres	Bushels	Acres	Bushels
Buckwheat	483	4,330	525	8,682
Corn	11,341	298,170	9,545	312,989
Oats	3,366	65,410	3,791	74,381
Rye	19	390	39	483
Wheat	9,493	125,990	2,796	36,507

It was in the manufacturing industries that the greatest increases were recorded. In 1900 the total number of establishments was reported as 67, with a total capital of $529,682. The average number of workers, in 1900, was 455, their wages totaling $182,311. By 1910 there were more employees than that in the glass factories alone, in addition to the tinplate mill, with salaries in the millions of dollars.

The University. Control of the financial affairs of West Virginia University, as well as the other state-supported educational institutions, by a legislative act of 1909, was vested in a three-member bipartisan board of control, which was to make its first report to the governor on October 10, 1910, and from time to time thereafter.

The same act abolished the separate boards of regents of the state-supported schools and entrusted their educational policies to a single bipartisan five-member board of regents, including the state superintendent of free schools, ex officio, who served as president.

Biennial appropriations of the legislature for 1909 and 1910 were $160,700.00 for each year. Other sources of income were the Morrill fund, interest on investments, fines, fees, etc. The land grant endowment of $33,828.14 was invested in bonds of the Morgantown and Kingwood Railroad, as it had been for several years.

The regents soon made a change in administration at the university. "Engrossed in metaphysics and philosophy, which he had taught long and well, and in music and fine arts, which had favored places in his program, President Purinton was not well suited to the university presidency in a changing order featured by differences between the new and the old educators, most of whom were chafing under his economy program."[1] With regent George S. Laidley taking the initiative, the board persuaded him that the office should be in more vigorous hands. He thereupon resigned, effective July 31, 1911. On September 22, 1910, Thomas E. Hodges was elected president, effective October 1, 1911.

The university organization at the time included five colleges (Arts and Sciences, Agriculture, Engineering and Mechanic Arts, Law, and Medicine) and several schools, including the Preparatory School, which was in the process of dissolution. E. Dwight Sanderson became dean of the College of Agriculture on September 1, 1910, succeeding T. C. Atkeson.[2]

Dr. Waitman Barbe was made professor of English and director of the summer school.

To clear problems relative to intercollegiate athletics, the university in 1909-10 became a member of the Intercollegiate Athletic Association of Western Pennsylvania and West Virginia. C. A. Leuder, an instructor in dairying, was the football coach. The 1910 season was marked by tragedy. After losing to the University of Pennsylvania and to the University of Pittsburgh, each by a score of 38 to 0, the team was on the point of defeating Bethany College, in a game played at Wheeling on November 12, through the fine playing of Captain Rudolph Munk, when he received an injury resulting in his death. The game was suspended and the team disbanded for the remainder of the season.

The First Airplane. An airplane handmade in Monongalia County is listed among the first fifty to be flown in the United States.

As is well known, the first airplane flight was made by Orville Wright on December 17, 1903, in a plane he and his brother Wilbur had built after several years of experimenting.

Less than ten years later, in the summer of 1910, a local young man, Ben Garrison,[3] aided by a friend, Ralph Kinderman, made and flew an airplane in Monongalia County.

---

1. Ambler, p. 505.

2. For biography of Atkeson, see *New Dominion*, September 18, 1897.

3. Ben Garrison was born in 1888 on Pedlar Run, the son of Marion Simon Garrison, and was actually named Norman Morris, but Dr. Milton Rinehart, the attending physician at the time of his birth, said, "We'll have to call him Ben"; it was the year of Benjamin Harrison's election to the presidency and Dr. Rinehart was a staunch Republican.

Fig. 87. Monongalia County's first airplane. (From an old postcard.)

Charles E. Hodges, an editor of the *New Dominion*, tells of Ben's background:

"Ben was a mechanical genius. He could build anything and make it run. He could solve any of the mechanical problems or ambitions that beset boys. He was recognized as the best in town by all of us boys. Whatever was complicated Ben Garrison understood. . . .

"The automobile soon became too commonplace to Ben. He became interested in flying. One of his pals in this was Ralph Kinderman, formerly of Fairmont, who later moved to Morgantown. Ben and Kin went down to Lock No. 9 at Hoard, just above Point Marion, and there, more or less in secret, the two of them built their own plane. Imagine youngsters nearly 40 years ago building their own plane! Most youngsters of that age today are satisfied to fly one. The knowledge and understanding then was infinitesimal compared to what it is now."[4]

4. Copied by Shelby Young in *Panorama*, June 23, 1974.

A contemporary newspaper[5] describes the airplane which the young men had built, and which they had demonstrated in flight the day before:

"The biplane is quite similar to the type used by Glen Curtiss in his flight from Albany to New York. The two planes (wings) measure 27 feet in length, while those of the Curtiss machine are 28. The two planes are six feet across, with the same space between them. The framework rests on a base upheld by three bicycle-like wheels with pneumatic tires. One of these wheels is in front, while two others are in the rear, on the same scheme as a tricycle. About on a level with and in the middle of the lower plane is the driver's seat. With his feet the aviator regulates the two small stabilizing planes that are located between the larger planes at the two ends of the craft. His hand controls the elevating planes and the rudder, all of which are in front of the driver on a framework of about five feet. . . .

"Except for the engine, the entire plane was constructed by Messrs. Garrison and Kinderman. Work on the craft was started last fall, but the car was not brought to its present degree of excellence until about 10 days ago. All spring and summer the two inventors kept at work, motor and propeller both giving trouble. . . . Being capable of generating only 15 horse power, the engine seemed for some time incapable of moving the machine from the ground. . . ."

But at last it did. The hillside was thickly dotted with scores of people who had come, by B.&O. trains or by auto, to witness the exhibition on the evening of August 9.[6]

The flight, like that of the Wright brothers, actually lasted only a few seconds but it demonstrated that flight indeed was possible. Afterwards the audience crowded around the two inventors, "expressing their satisfaction in the success of the aerial venture."

Progress on the M.&D.V. After having been under construction since 1908, there seemed hope as the New Year dawned that street cars would soon be running on the Morgantown and Dunkard Valley line. A headline in a local paper said "Three weeks will see cars running," and the account stated that: "Rails are now

5. *Post-Chronicle*, August 18, 1910.
6. *Post-Chronicle*, August 10, 1910.

placed a distance of nearly three miles, and within three weeks of working weather the company will have cars running as far as Randall."[7]

Various matters, nevertheless, delayed the opening of the line. Construction was still under way far into the summer. Litigation delayed the construction of the single line planned across the river bridge, to be used jointly by the Morgantown and Dunkard Valley and the Morgantown and Pittsburg cars (the "Hickory Tree line"). In July, M.&D.V. general manager, J. Ami Martin, was still searching for suitable cars.

At last, however, the first cars on the Morgantown and Dunkard Valley line began running, on September 10. The opening run left Morgantown, at the east end of the river bridge, at 10:00 a.m. and arrived at Randall in about twenty minutes. Lawrence Winkler was the motorman. A number of prominent Morgantown citizens were guests of the company on the first run. The schedule called for a round trip between the two points every hour from 6:30 a.m. until 10:30 p.m. The cars did a land office business on the first day of operation.[8]

Two sets of tracks eventually crossed the river bridge. The M.&D.V. cars used the northern set, the M.&P. the southern.

Traction Park. The South Morgantown Traction Company was developing a park at the end of its lines in South Morgantown and prepared to build a new pavilion and a number of seats. New cars were being purchased and arrangements were made to return to downtown Morgantown via Bridge Street, having gone out Madigan Avenue, thus forming a loop.[9]

Looking ahead, in 1910, Morgantown's citizens must have envisioned steadily increasing business for trolley cars. At rush hours "double-headers" were needed to handle passengers on the Sabraton line. They would have had no way of knowing that only one more decade would elapse before a decline would set in.

The Buckhannon and Northern. The county court, on January 18, granted a franchise to the Buckhannon and Northern Railroad for construction of a line across the county along the west side of the

7. *Post-Chronicle*, January 1, 1910.
8. *Post-Chronicle*, September 10, 1910.
9. *Post-Chronicle*, January 27, 1910.

Monongahela River. This had been under discussion for many years, under various situations, and extreme rivalry had existed between competing railroads, anxious to tap the vast unexploited coalfields of the area. "Commissioner Fife stated last night that he felt the court had done the greatest thing for Monongalia County in its history."[10]

The survey was made during the winter and early spring and was completed in May. Some delay resulted from the fact that right-of-way through the federal property at the various river locks had to be cleared in Washington.[11]

Charles Morris was named as right-of-way agent and worked through the summer clearing titles to lands that would be needed.[12] Announcement was made late in the year that a contract would be awarded for construction of the line as soon as a clear right-of-way had been secured.[13]

A site for a Morgantown station was purchased from J. W. Holland for five thousand dollars.[14]

New B.&O. Trains. Two new trains were added to the B.&O. passenger schedule May 29. The southbound train left Connellsville daily at 7:30 a.m., arrived in Morgantown at 9:30, and in Fairmont at 10:30. Returning, the train left Fairmont at 4:30 p.m., Morgantown at 5:30, and arrived in Connellsville at 7:30.

The complete schedule of Morgantown departures follows:

Northbound for Connellsville and Pittsburg: 5:53 a.m., 7:59 a.m., 2:39 p.m., and 5:30 p.m.

Southbound for Fairmont: 5:45 a.m., 9:30 a.m., 12:04 p.m., 6:33 p.m., and 8:04 p.m.

On the M.&K., trains were leaving Morgantown daily at 6:50 a.m., 12:40 p.m., and 2:55 p.m.

Railroad Traffic Heavy. The B.&O. ticket agent was very busy during the month of December. Many Morgantown people spent the vacation out of town, adding to the usual number of ticket sales. The greatest number of one-way fares was to Fairmont, totaling 1,318; round-trip fares were 159. There were 1,017 round-

10. *Post-Chronicle*, January 19, 1910.
11. *Post-Chronicle*, May 5, 1910.
12. *Post-Chronicle*, May 28, 1910.
13. *Post-Chronicle*, November 24, 1910.
14. *Post-Chronicle*, August 18, 1910.

trip tickets to Point Marion, many people going there to purchase liquor; Morgantown was dry. In addition, 987 one-way tickets were purchased to Point Marion, although most of the people were going on to Pittsburg, buying two tickets to take advantage of special rates. Other sales were to Little Falls, 207; Wheeling, 123; Grafton, 76; Moundsville, 16; Charleston, 15; Elkins, 18; Connellsville, 68; Saint Petersburg, Florida, 2.[15]

Road Maintenance Problems. County commissioners were debating the relative merits of various types of equipment used to smooth the surface of the county's dirt roads. The county owned seven road machines, each of which required two men and six horses to operate and cost $13.50 for a nine-hour day. Drags, on the contrary, did just as good work, perhaps even better, and required only one man and two horses. Both methods continued to be used.[16]

General Woodworking Company. Early in the spring of 1910 a new lumber company was organized in Morgantown, by the name of the General Woodworking Company. Officers were G. E. Laishley, president; E. R. Baker, vice-president; Charles C. Robinson, secretary-treasurer; and Charles P. Thorn, general manager. The plant was located on Beechurst Avenue below Fourth Street and was equipped with modern machinery operated by electricity. They carried a general line of builders' supplies and turned out mill and detail work, making a specialty of cabinet work.[17]

Board of Trade. A new Morgantown Board of Trade was formed February 1 at an enthusiastic meeting in the circuit court room, with an initial membership of 508. Dr. I. C. White was elected president and James H. McGrew treasurer. Vice-presidents, by wards, were, first, A. W. Lorentz; second, S. A. Posten; third, J. H. Stewart; fourth, Aug. Boehler; fifth, E. M. Grant; West Side, T. P. Reay; East Side, at large, David Mansberger.[18]

Public Schools. The Morgantown Independent School Board contracted to pay $34,497 for the erection of a public school building

---

15. *Post-Chronicle*, January 5, 1910.
16. *Post-Chronicle*, March 23, 1910.
17. *Post-Chronicle Industrial Edition*, 1913, p. 35.
18. *Post-Chronicle*, February 2, 1910.

Fig. 88. General Woodworking Company.

on Wilson Avenue at Kingwood Street, in the Second Ward, to accommodate the increased population in South Park.

Susannah Cobun. Monongalia's oldest woman, Mrs. Susannah Guseman Cobun, aged 101 years, died at the home of her granddaughter, Mrs. Ammon H. Jarrett, on Kingwood Street, on March 20. She was a daughter of Abraham Guseman, a Revolutionary War veteran, and was the only "real" daughter of the American Revolution in the county. She was survived by one daughter, Mrs. Elizabeth Lazzelle.[19]

William Davis. A farmer from near Van Voorhis, William Davis, died July 4, 1910. The son of John W. Davis, he was born in this county. He married Louisa Sutton and they were the parents of Oliver J. (married Mary Myers), Teresa (married Arthur Hough), Nevado (married Nelson Hugus), Eva (married E. B. Eblon), and Katherine.

Lewis Davis, a brother of William, was a dwarf four feet tall,

19. *Post-Chronicle*, March 21, 1910.

weighing 96 pounds, and, under the name of "Major Green," traveled with Barnum and Bailey and other circuses as "the world's smallest man," often in company with a fat man weighing 640 pounds. He visited every state of the time except Maine.[20]

Captain Parker. Captain Eli Lynch Parker died at his home in Granville on April 10, aged seventy years. He served in the Civil War, entering as a private, then as captain in the Twelfth Virginia Cavalry. He served in various public offices in Marion County and after moving to Monongalia County, about 1890, served as justice of the peace for about fifteen years.[21]

Jerome Park M.E. Church. A frame church building[22] was constructed in 1910 along Richwood Avenue, in Jerome Park by a Methodist Episcopal group which had been organized in 1907 by Rev. C. K. Jenness. Meetings were held in a small building on Lincoln Avenue which David Thistle helped to secure; he was the first superintendent of the Sunday school and his daughter was organist and teacher of the beginners' class. Zora Wilcox taught the girls' class and J. W. Hackney the boys'.

A committee was organized to secure money for a church building and the drive quickly succeeded. Helpers in the drive were Dr. R. Douthat, J. C. Wilcox, Vena Jane Snyder, and W. R. Robinson.

The lot was donated to the congregation by Judge G. C. Sturgiss, who later transferred his membership to this group.[23]

Fort Martin Church. The congregation of the Fort Martin Methodist Episcopal Church, in Cass District, constructed a substantial brick building in 1910, replacing one that had been in use since 1834. The new building had a bell tower and basement.[24]

The congregation was organized by Charles Martin in 1778 and is the second oldest in the county. It was visited by Bishop Asbury in 1785 (see vol. 2, p. 162).

20. *Chronicles of Core*, p. 170; *Awhile Ago Times*, vol. 2, no. 8.

21. *Post-Chronicle*, April 11, 1910.

22. A few years later this building was replaced by a substantial brick structure just across the street.

23. Dodds and Dodds, pp. 85, 86. The name of the church was later changed to Sabra M.E. Church, at the suggestion of Judge Sturgiss, as a memorial to his wife (see p. 315).

24. Dodds and Dodds, p. 116.

Valley Chapel. Two miles west of Wadestown a group of Methodists had formed a congregation in 1875 and built a church. By 1910 the well-to-do farmers who constituted the membership decided the building was not good enough, compared to their own homes, and built a new structure on an adjoining lot conveyed to the trustees by Urias Shriver. The total cost of the building was thirty-one thousand dollars. The bell was given by C. E. Hennen and J. W. Smith.[25]

Miscellany. In 1910: A small group of persons interested in Christian Science began meeting every Sunday in the millinery shop of Mrs. Lucy M. Dering, on Price Street, reading the authorized "Lesson Sermons" of The Mother Church (Dodds and Dodds, p. 75). . . . A new brick church was built by the Arnettsville M.E. congregation (Dodds and Dodds, p. 101). . . . Ex-sheriff Theodore W. Barker and his daughter Beulah were badly shaken up when thrown from their sleigh in Riverside (*Post-Chronicle*, January 8, 1910). . . . An auto belonging to A. N. Briscoe and driven by Jesse Jenkins was badly damaged in a collision with Union Utilities car No. 8, Luther Reed, motorman (*Post-Chronicle*, January 10, 1910). . . . A stone house belonging to Mabel G. Haymond, used by the Rightmire-Shriver planing mill, was destroyed by fire (*Post-Chronicle*, January 11, 1910). . . . Jacob Arnold, a well-known Union District farmer, was frozen to death when his wagon overturned and pinned him beneath (*Post-Chronicle*, February 2, 1910). . . . The steamer *Woodward* resumed twice-a-week trips from Pittsburg to Morgantown, once-a-week to Fairmont (*Post-Chronicle*, February 11, 1910). . . . Coming home with a new Ford auto he had purchased in Pittsburg, Aaron J. Garlow wanted to test the speed of the vehicle; the indicator was registering fifteen miles an hour when the car struck a bump and Garlow suffered a scalp injury when his head hit the top (*Post-Chronicle*, February 14, 1910). . . . The steamer *Columbia* was destroyed by fire at Pittsburg (*Post-Chronicle*, February 18, 1910). . . . Harry R. Warfield purchased the Sabraton trolley line and proposed extending it to Cheat Haven to connect with a projected line from Pittsburg (*Post-Chronicle*, February 28, 1910). . . . Later in the year Warfield transferred ownership of the Sabraton line to the Union Utilities (*Post-Chronicle*, July 21, 1910). . . . Running at a speed of eight miles an hour, an auto driven by Dr. David H. Hott

25. Dodds and Dodds, p. 136.

collided with a garbage wagon driven by William Holland; both vehicles were badly damaged (*Post-Chronicle*, April 7, 1910). . . . By a new arrangement, mail from the Sabraton post office was dispatched twice a day by street cars and placed on B.&O. trains at the Morgantown depot (*Post-Chronicle*, April 22, 1910). . . . A program of races was held at the fairgrounds on Memorial Day (*Post-Chronicle*, May 31, 1910). . . . The Bell Telephone Company was installing a new exchange in the Odd Fellows Building (*Post-Chronicle*, June 4, 1910). . . . The first fatal accident at the M.&K. shops resulted in the death of thirty-year-old Harry Murphy (*Post-Chronicle*, June 23, 1910). . . . Horse racing and a balloon ascension featured the second annual fair of the Morgantown Fair Association, August 16-18 (*Post-Chronicle*, August 18, 25, 1910). . . . A heavy storm on July 4 did a great deal of damage to buildings and growing crops, besides killing several head of stock (*Chronicles of Core*, p. 171).

CHAPTER ONE HUNDRED THIRTY-FIVE

1911

On Columbus Day, October 12, 1911, by an act of the Circuit Court for the County of Monongalia, the city of Westover was established, with Wilbur F. Waters, David C. Reay, and Parker S. Johnson named as commissioners to hold an election for mayor, recorder, and councilmen within sixty days.

The City of Westover. The petition for the establishment of the city had been signed by N. Hamilton Steele, Albert Shuman, Thomas P. Reay, Joseph L. Keener, John Shriver, Columbus J. Long, Wilbur F. Waters, A. J. Cook, William E. Martin, Jasper Steele, Harvey J. Weaver, Thomas C. Lough, Cal Hawkins, and M. E. Boyles. The petitioners represented that "no newspaper is printed within the limits or boundaries" of the proposed city, but that a legal notice of the proposal had been posted for at least four successive weeks "on the front door of Hall Brothers Feed Store; at the store room of Earl Smyth's store; and on the front door of the Blacksmith Shop of Luther Fox, the same being three of the most public places in said territory." Following that, a public meeting was held on September 30 in "the office of Hall Brothers Feed Store, situate on Tower Lane," at which a majority of the voters in the territory approved the proposed incorporation.

As approved by the circuit court, the corporation contained 287.44 acres, or .4478 square miles. A census taken on August 18, 1911, indicated that the population within the corporation limits was "more than one hundred (100) persons."

At the first city election, held on November 25, John Shriver was elected mayor, Louis C. Snyder recorder, and Ira E. Hall, C. J. Long, L. L. Keener, L. L. Jamison, and M. H. Steele councilmen. The first council meeting was held on Friday evening, December 1, 1911.

Two streetcar lines passed through the new city of Westover, when it was established in 1911. The first, operated by the Union Utilities Company, went up Holland Avenue and out West Park Street, thence through the University Woods to Dunkard Avenue and out through a field to a hickory tree on the farm of Grover P. Keener. Its promoters expected that some day it would lead on to Fairmont, but it never got beyond that point and was popularly referred to as the "Hickory Tree Line."

The other trolley line, operated by the Morgantown and Dunkard Valley Railway Company, did a bigger business. It left Holland Avenue at Tower Lane and ran through several fields, then reached Dunkard Avenue, passed through Granville and Jimtown, then up Scotts Run to end at Cassville.

West Morgantown, after 1868, was included in the Morgantown Independent School District, and children from the community walked across the bridge to attend classes at the old Monongalia Academy building, at the corner of Spruce and Walnut streets.

Finally, in September 1911, at the same time the promoters were setting up the new city of Westover, the board of education let a contract to the Smith Construction Company for a school building in Westover, at a price of $18,500.[1]

President Hodges. Thomas Edward Hodges was inaugurated as president of West Virginia University on November 3, 1911, currently described as the greatest event in the history of the institution. It was featured by an address by William Howard Taft, president of the United States, speaking from the steps of Martin Hall to a crowd that overflowed the Circle.[2] The exercises lasted for three days; practically all state elected officers were present, with Governor W. E. Glasscock and State Superintendent of Schools Morris P. Shawkey presiding over parts of the program. Presidents of several other universities and colleges were present and some of them made addresses. "Morgantown and the University were elaborately decorated for the occasion which was featured also by playing bands, by reminiscent oratory, and by scores of good wishes."[3]

1. *Post-Chronicle*, September 7, 1911.
2. *Post-Chronicle*, November 3, 1911. Taft was the first United States president to visit Morgantown during his term of office.
3. Ambler, p. 507.

Hodges was born December 13, 1858, in Upshur County. He obtained his primary education in district schools and at French Creek Academy, then graduated from West Virginia University in 1881. He had an impressive educational career. From 1881 to 1886 he was superintendent of the Morgantown public schools; from 1886 to 1896 he was principal of Marshall College; and from 1896 to 1909 he was professor of physics at the university. He was appointed as a member of the state board of control in 1909. He had valuable business training as secretary-treasurer of the Morgantown Savings and Loan Society and as president of the Bank of Morgantown. He was an able speaker, an athletic enthusiast, and an inspiring teacher, popular with students and alumni. He had visited several institutions of higher education in the Middle West and it was said that West Virginia was getting "a bigger view of things educational."

President Purinton moved out of the President's House on July 31, 1911. Dr. Hodges's term officially began on October 1 and Alexander R. Whitehill served as acting president during the interim. Purinton continued on the university staff as professor of philosophy. The new president's salary was fixed at five thousand dollars, minus eight hundred dollars annually for the use of the house.

As expected, President Hodges made a number of changes in administrative policies and there were marked gains. Policy-determining powers were restored to the faculty. The South Wing of Woodburn Hall, started in 1909, was completed in 1911 and the old curfew bell and university clock were moved from Martin Hall to the belfry tower on Woodburn Hall. The freshman class of 1911-12 was 20 percent larger than in any previous year. E. H. Vickers, who had been a teacher in a Japanese university from 1898 to 1911, was appointed professor of economics. In the College of Agriculture, N. J. Giddings was appointed plant pathologist and L. M. Peairs entomologist.

C. A. Leuder continued as coach of the football team, which won six games against two defeats. One of the special victories was over Washington and Jefferson, the second ever, by a score of 6 to 5. The game was played on the home grounds, at the time of the inauguration of President Hodges, a football enthusiast, and was the occasion of much rejoicing. Lt. H. M. Nelly, who had been assistant coach at West Point, was assistant to Coach Leuder.[4]

The Buckhannon and Northern Railroad. As early as 1881 a railroad had been projected to run from Pittsburgh south along the Monongahela River to tap the vast coal deposits of the upper Monongahela Valley. Finally, in 1886, the Baltimore and Ohio opened a spur line from Fairmont to Morgantown, extended by 1894 to Connellsville, where connections were made to Pittsburgh.

This line, however, reached Pittsburgh by an indirect route, and furthermore ran on the east side of the river, whereas the coal was mostly on the west side. Efforts continued, through various agencies, to build a line on the west side. The move by the Wabash Company has already been described (p. 308).

At last a subsidiary of the Pennsylvania Railroad, the Buckhannon and Northern Railroad, was formed, with the announced intention of constructing a line connecting the Pittsburgh and Lake Erie Railroad (another Pennsylvania subsidiary) at Brownsville with the Baltimore and Ohio Railroad at Fairmont and to terminate at Buckhannon.

Work of construction got under way early in the year, and by the end of April it was reported that some sections of the grade were about complete. Patterson, Moran, and Luck, the general contractor,[5] had its own boats, barges, and flats, with shantyboats for its laborers. The steamer *Gazelle* moved the various craft from place to place. Between Morgantown and Lowesville, at various sites from time to time, a dinky engine with eight or ten cars, moved excavated materials.[6]

Plans were being drawn for a passenger station and a freight depot just north of the river bridge. The railroad company secured land enough for the buildings and freight yards.[7]

In August six steam shovels were at work grading the line; Patterson, Moran and Luck had two working near Jimtown. Of the subcontractors, Williams Brothers and Sales, had one shovel opposite Little Falls, Weaver, Gilmore and Company had one at

4. Ambler, p. 577; Constantine, p. 11.
5. *Post-Chronicle*, February 21, 1911.
6. *Post-Chronicle*, March 2, April 27, 1911.
7. *Post-Chronicle*, May 11, 1911.

Lock No. 10 and one just below Westover, while Hunter and Hinds were working farther down the river.[8] Dynamite blasts on the Jimtown hill, set off by an electrical mechanism connected with the trolley wire of the Dunkard Valley streetcar line, caused some damage to the car line and also to the highway, between the car line and the railroad.[9]

In September the first shipment of ties for the new line was received in Morgantown. Three carloads, containing twenty thousand ties, were unloaded, hauled across the river and distributed along the grade.[10]

Grading was essentially completed by the end of the year by the Patterson, Moran and Luck Company. Two bridges, across Parkers Run and Robinson Run, were completed. Riveting was under way on the bridge across Dents Run at Granville, and work was under way on the bridge across Scotts Run and that across Indian Creek, the largest on the line.[11]

New Trolley Projects. "Spring is bringing forth the usual number of trolley projects this year, and should promoters build all the roads which are now being discussed, Morgantown will be one of the greatest trolley centers in this section of the country."[12]

Lines being considered, in addition to the expected extension of the Dunkard Valley system to Blacksville, were one from Blacksville to Waynesburg, from Morgantown to Point Marion, from Morgantown to near Smithtown, and a line by the Morgantown and Southern company around South Park Hill.

A race was under way to see which line would get to Blacksville first, the one from Waynesburg, or that from Morgantown.[13]

Construction work on the Waynesburg-Blacksville line was contracted to the Bardella Construction Company[14] and most of the grading was completed when money ran out and the project was abandoned.

The Masontown (Pennsylvania) and Morgantown Street Rail-

8. *Post-Chronicle,* August 17, 1911.
9. *Post-Chronicle,* August 8, 1911.
10. *Post-Chronicle,* September 14, 1911.
11. *Post-Chronicle,* December 7, 1911.
12. *Post-Chronicle,* June 8, 1911.
13. *Post-Chronicle,* April 20, 1911.
14. *Post-Chronicle,* July 11, 1911.

way Company and the Mount Morris and Morgantown Railroad Company were formed, but nothing came of either endeavor.[15]

Trolley to Cassville. The Morgantown and Dunkard Valley streetcar line was completed to Cassville in November. Cars had been operating first to Charlotte (Osage) and then to Stumptown (Barker) and now began running to the lower end of Cassville. The company now had eight miles of track, the longest trolley line in

Fig. 89. The first M.&D.V. trolley car is stopped in front of Ed Goodrich's Store in Osage. (Photo courtesy Willis E. Lough.)

the county. The fare from Cassville to Morgantown was twenty cents, cash, with a half fare school rate; tickets, bought 250 or more at a time, were sixteen cents each. Many people from farther west drove in buggies or wagons to Cassville, there leaving their teams at Dr. Milton Rinehart's livery stable, which did a thriving business. During December 18,068 cash fares and 11,228 tickets were taken up by the conductors.

During the line's first year of operation, from September 1910

15. *Post-Chronicle*, July 6, 1911.

Fig. 90. M.&D.V. trolley at terminal on Pleasant Street.

until September 1911, over 205,000 fares were collected.[16] Plans were being made to continue it to Core.[17]

South Morgantown Trolley Extension. Plans for a two-mile loop as an extension of the lines of the South Morgantown Traction Company were announced in October. "The company plans to abandon its present trolley line on Prairie Avenue and Wagner Street as far as Allen street.[18] Instead the line will proceed directly from the South High street bridge, over the new street opened to Dorsey avenue, to Allen street, thence through the new street to Euclid avenue in South Park, thence over Euclid avenue to the Second ward school building and down through Homeside. Circling back the road is to strike Brockway street and thence to the Walnut street bridge, completing the loop."[19] A car barn was built at the South Morgantown terminus.[20]

16. *Post-Chronicle*, September 9, 1911.
17. *Post-Chronicle*, April 6, 1911.
18. Now called Simpson Street.
19. *Post-Chronicle*, October 12, 1911.
20. *Post-Chronicle*, April 13, 1911.

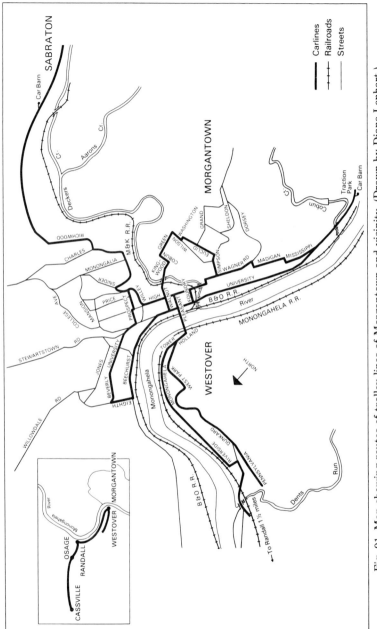

Fig. 91. Map showing routes of trolley lines of Morgantown and vicinity. (Drawn by Diane Lenhart.)

Loving Furniture Company. The J. F. Loving Furniture Company was located in Morgantown in 1911, one of a chain of large furniture stores, mostly in the Southeast. Officers of the company were S. P. Jones, of Richmond, Virginia, president; C. S. Ream, Salisbury, North Carolina, vice-president, and J. F. Loving, Morgantown, secretary-treasurer. Loving, who came to Morgantown from Charlottesville, Virginia, was manager of the local store, located at the corner of Chestnut Street and Chancery Row.[21]

Lough-Simpson Grocery. Morgantown's leading wholesale grocery in the first quarter of the century was the Lough-Simpson Grocery Company, organized in the spring of 1911. Incorporators were R. A. Lough and W. T. Simpson. Officers were James F. Campbell, president; W. H. Bailey, vice-president; R. A. Lough, manager and treasurer; W. T. Simpson, assistant treasurer; Charles W. Evans, and I. N. Lough, directors. The company located on Clay Street.[22]

Twenty-third Judicial Circuit. By Chapter 11 of the 1911 State Legislature Monongalia and Marion counties became circuits by themselves, Monongalia being the Twenty-third, while Marion remained the Fourteenth. Judge John W. Mason, who lived in Fairmont, was to continue serving both circuits until the end of his term of office.

The Grand Theater. One of the most popular playhouses in Morgantown was the Grand Theater, in the Odd Fellows Building on Walnut Street.

In 1911 H. A. Christy canceled his lease on the Swisher Theatre and gave his entire attention to the operation of the Grand. "The pictures used are always the most expensive and of the highest class. The Grand has easily led in that line from the beginning of motion pictures exhibited in the city. Its success is due to the constant care and industry of its owner. He studies all conditions and is thoroughly conversant with all phases of the business. He chooses only the most trustworthy assistants, those who discharge their duties with the greatest care and in the most satis-

21. *Post-Chronicle Industrial Edition,* 1913.
22. *Post-Chronicle Industrial Edition,* 1913.

Fig. 92. Grand Theater on Walnut Street.

factory manner. Mr. Christy is a native of Morgantown and has a host of personal friends who are always interested in his success."[23]

Cheat Haven and Bruceton Railroad. Organized for the purpose of building a railroad from Cheat Haven to Albright, the Cheat Haven and Bruceton Railroad Company, of Ice's Ferry, was incorporated August 6, with a capital of seventy-five thousand dollars. Incorporators were Gilmore S. Hamil, Sr., Gilmore S. Hamil, Jr., Stuart F. Hamil, and Scott T. Jones, of Oakland, Maryland, and Frank Cunningham, of Somerset, Pennsylvania.[24]

Paved Streets for Wadestown. The county commissioners traveled to Wadestown by automobile on September 8, along with county engineer Robert D. Hennen for a meeting in the Bank of Wadestown building with about forty Wadestown people. The local representatives had asked for the paving of about twelve hundred

23. *Post-Chronicle Industrial Edition* (1913).
24. *Post-Chronicle,* August 10, 1911.

feet of the main streets of the village and the commissioners assured them that this would be done.[25]

Casing-head Gas and Drip Gasoline. Oil and gas producers early learned that when a gas line passed through a cooled area, vapors in the gas condensed and accumulated in lower levels of the line. Drips, or outlets, were maintained on the lines at various points to drain off this "drip" gasoline. This was particularly true in the Appalachian fields, where the gas issued from the well, mostly between the tubing, which carried the oil, and the outside casing, for protection of the tubing, and was known as casing-head gas.

In both oil and gas lines, operators had to deal with this accumulation of gasoline (and also water) in the lines. At first both the gas and the drip gasoline were considered as nuisances. The gas was burned in colorful flamboyants or used in lease houses and farm dwellings for lighting, heating, and cooking. The gasoline, water, and solid impurities were drained off at the drips as wastes.

But with the advent of the gasoline engine, field producers and refiners began to think of harnessing this "drip" gasoline as fuel for the developing automobile. Between 1903 and 1911 there was much experimentation in the region in the production of "drip" or "natural" gasoline. The existence and basic properties of this substance had been known from the beginning of the petroleum industry; the only thing new was that for this highly inflammable fuel a practical use had now been found. A substance long rejected as waste now had a rapidly expanding market. As the demand grew, refineries enlarged facilities and made technical advancements.[26]

In 1911 West Virginia produced 3,660,165 gallons of gasoline, more than Pennsylvania, Ohio, and Oklahoma combined. Early producers quickly learned that production could be enhanced through a simple compression process, and numerous small compressor plants were put into operation.

"Recent developments in the manner of operating oil properties when there is a surplus of gas, lead to the installation of compressors for the transforming of this surplus gas into a commodity which is in almost as great demand as the gas itself—

25. *Post-Chronicle*, September 9, 1911.
26. Thoenen, *History of the Oil and Gas Industry in West Virginia*, pp. 241, 242.

namely, gasoline. This is manufactured at slight additional cost
and with little labor in addition to that required in operating the
wells, and operators claim it increases the flow of oil, thus not
only increasing the output of the well, but adding a valuable by-
product which is very profitable."[27]

It would not be long, however, until automobile operators
would be demanding a more refined product and these early compressor plants would fade from the picture.

Rock Forge. A post office by the name of Rock Forge was opened
April 26, 1911, with Edward J. Cosgrove as the first postmaster.

Construction of the M.&K. Railroad brought new life to the old
community (vol. 2, p. 268). Coal mines were opened by the
Connellsville Basin Coal and Coke Company and coke ovens were
put into operation.

John A. Thompson. A well-known Morgantown resident, J. A.
Thompson, died suddenly on December 13 while attending a
meeting of the directors of the Second National Bank. He was
born at Laurel Point March 19, 1845. He served in the Civil War
under Capt. Alphaeus Garrison and a good part of the time was
company mail carrier. He married Jane Fleming and they had
two children, Mrs. Morgan Lemasters and J. Harley Thompson.[28]

Margaret Gregg. The wife of T. M. Gregg, Mrs. Margaret M.
Gregg, died May 31, from a stroke. She was born July 29, 1839,
in Washington County, Pennsylvania, and was married in 1857.
The couple came to Morgantown in 1883. They were survived by
five sons and two daughters, namely, Oscar C., John M., Ira L.,
Roma P., Jesse P., and Mrs. Bessie L. Wilbourn and Mrs. Mary
E. Dawson. Two other sons died earlier.[29]

Miscellany. In 1911: One of the oldest stone houses in Morgantown, on Lot 1 at Walnut and Front streets, was removed to provide space for the Rightmire Building (Callahan, p. 188). . . . Production capacity of the Morgantown Ice Company was doubled,
to fifty tons daily (Callahan, p. 271). . . . The White Apartment
Building, on upper High Street, was constructed (Callahan, p.
272). . . . A postal savings service was begun at the Morgantown

27. *Wheeling Register,* April 8, 1911.
28. *Post-Chronicle,* December 13, 1911.
29. *Post-Chronicle,* June 1, 1911.

post office on September 19 (Callahan, p. 285). . . . The Morgantown and Southern Railway Company, after a long delay, announced plans to resume construction of a streetcar line from the South Morgantown tracks at the southeast corner of the Oak Grove Cemetery to Hess Lane and Sheldon Avenue, thence to the South Park barn (*Post-Chronicle*, October 26, 1911). . . . The Pittsburg, Fairmont and Morgantown Packet Company discontinued operations on the Monongahela River with the last trip of the *Woodward* to Fairmont on October 15; the steamer *Wabash* continued operation between Morgantown and points in Pennsylvania (*Post-Chronicle*, October 19, 1911). . . . The Rev. H. Aley was employed as minister of the Dolls Run Christian Church and delighted and horrified his congregation with his superb handling of his new motorcycle (*Chronicles of Core*, p. 171). . . . Arthur M. Lucas and Company paved twelve hundred yards on Bridge and Kingwood streets and on Prairie Avenue (*Post-Chronicle*, September 9, 1911). . . . Two automobile accidents, neither resulting in fatalities, occurred in Morgantown in less than a week, one when a Maryland car, driver unknown, scared a horse pulling a buggy occupied by Mrs. H. C. Protzman and Miss Ethel Robinson, the other when an automobile driven by C. A. Singer collided with a motorcycle driven by J. E. Hunter (*Post-Chronicle*, August 14, 1911). . . . The four-day Monongalia-Preston Fair opened at the fairgrounds north of Morgantown August 29; it featured horse racing and motorcycle events (*Post-Chronicle*, August 17, 24, 31, 1911). . . . Harry C. Allender, an engineer at the tinplate mill, was scalded to death in an accident on August 2 (*Post-Chronicle*, August 3, 1911). . . . Antonio Mancini was killed near Dellslow when hit by an Oak Park excursion train on the M.&K. (*Post-Chronicle*, July 23, 1911). . . . The plant of the Acme Publishing Company was sold at public sale to Harry S. Green and the *Post-Chronicle* moved into the building (*Post-Chronicle*, July 6, 1911). . . . Mrs. Laura McFadden Hartigan, wife of Dr. J. W. Hartigan, died suddenly on June 29 (*Post-Chronicle*, June 30, 1911). . . . A new street, an extension of High Street, was opened through the Chancery Hill Company's property to Dorsey Avenue (*Post-Chronicle*, June 22, 1911). . . . By a new state automobile law the speed limits for automobiles on country roads was set at twenty miles per hour (*Post-Chronicle* June 8, 1911). . . . Dr. Samuel Marmaduke Dent, aged thirty-four, son of Mr. and Mrs.

James Dent, of Granville, died May 31; a graduate of West Virginia University, he was "one of the best pitchers the Old Gold and Blue ever had" (*Post-Chronicle*, June 1, 1911). . . . A public meeting was held at Core to push the sale of bonds for the Dunkard Valley Railway; J. Ami Martin, general manager, was the speaker (*Post-Chronicle*, May 18, 1911). . . . "Aunt Prissie" Clark, a former slave in the family of George Washington Dorsey, died at the age of 101 years (*Post-Chronicle*, May 18, 1911). . . . Z. M. Barker, of Georgetown, died on May 4; he operated the Georgetown mill for many years (*Post-Chronicle*, May 4, 1911). . . . William Jennings Bryan spoke on April 10 to a standing-room-only crowd in Commencement Hall on "The Prince of Peace" (*Post-Chronicle*, April 13, 1911). . . . John W. Armstrong started a restaurant in Blacksville (*Post-Chronicle*, March 9, 1911). . . . Madame Schumann-Heink gave a concert in the Swisher Theatre (*Post-Chronicle*, February 24, 1911). . . . Mrs. Julia (Davis) Barbe, wife of George Barbe and mother of Clyde Barbe, died February 16 (*Post-Chronicle*, February 16, 1911). . . . United Woolen Mills opened a branch store in Morgantown (*Post-Chronicle*, February 16, 1911). . . . The M.&K. shops were destroyed by fire on February 7 (*Post-Chronicle*, February 8, 1911). . . . The steamer *Bessie Smith* arrived at Morgantown on January 19, for the first time since the river was closed by ice early in December (*Post-Chronicle*, January 19, 1911). . . . The Valley Chapel Methodist Church, near Wadestown, was dedicated (Dodds and Dodds, p. 136). . . . The Athens Glass Company, in Seneca, was opened (Callahan, p. 269). . . . The Labor Building and Loan Association was founded (Callahan, p. 280). . . . A second Seneca Glass factory, Factory B, began production in August, making lime blown tumblers (*Post-Chronicle Industrial Edition*, 1913). . . . Samuel Lemley, of Charlotte, died January 20; he was an enthusiastic fife player (*Post-Chronicle*, January 20, 1911).

CHAPTER ONE HUNDRED THIRTY-SIX

1912

Morgantown and all Monongalia County looked forward eagerly to the coming of the New Year. Under the heading, "Nineteen Twelve," a local editor wrote:

"The new year opens with bright augury for the continued growth of Morgantown. . . . With the spring will come the rapid completion of construction work on the new railroad up the west side of the river and the opening of the new road for traffic, and then the means will be at hand for the development of the rich coal fields of the western half of the county. The coming year should see also the completion of the west side trolley line to Blacksville, bringing the county seat at last into touch with Battelle and all the west end of the county."[1]

The B.&N. Railroad. A transportation enterprise of great importance to the future development of Monongalia County was completed in 1912. This was the Buckhannon and Northern Railroad, running from Brownsville, Pennsylvania, to Fairmont, a distance of about seventy miles. It was built to provide an outlet for the immense coalfields on the west side of the river, a development which would be stimulated only a few years later by the great demand for coal during the World War. Morgantown would soon feel the effect of the increased business brought by this new railroad.[2]

By the end of January structural work on the bridges had been completed and work was continuing on the excavations for the grade.[3]

Laying of rails got under way soon after April 1, beginning at Rivesville and coming down the river. At that time it was planned

1. *Post-Chronicle*, January 1, 1912.
2. Callahan, p. 282.
3. *Post-Chronicle*, January 3, 1912.

to run into Fairmont over the B.&O. tracks to the B.&O. depot.[4] The Hurlay Track Laying Machine Company had the contract for laying the track.[5] Work of laying the rails began at the Rivesville end in April and proceeded rapidly.[6] By the end of May the track-laying machine was at Lock No. 13; about a mile a day was being laid.[7] At the end of June the machine was at Jimtown and it was estimated the work would be completed in a month. A New York Central engine and caboose, with a string of thirty boxcars, stood on the track opposite Morgantown on June 29 and attracted much attention.[8] The last rails to the state line were laid by the middle of July, leaving only six miles in Pennsylvania to be completed.[9] The final link was laid on July 30.

The University Under Hodges. As at all times in its history, 1912 saw a continuing struggle between new and old educators on the university campus. The former were inclined to accept practical courses in high school curricula for accrediting purposes, as a substitute for the standard courses. Also, state normal schools were expanding their courses, often beyond their facilities, and there were differences of opinion as to how much should be accepted for university credit. Discussions were held and an agreement reached in 1912.

During 1912 the semester system was substituted for the old quarter system which had been followed for many years. E. Dwight Anderson was made director of the Agricultural Experiment Station, succeeding J. H. Stewart. The department of medicine in the College of Arts and Sciences was converted into the School of Medicine, with J. N. Simpson as dean.[10]

There was a substantial improvement in student morale. In 1909, it was said, there had been "a good bit of drinking and licentiousness"; in 1912 "there was little of either"; moral and social life were on a high plane. The Military Ball in February was "a big social event," and the Alda-Bispham concert was well received.[11]

4. *Post-Chronicle,* March 20, 23, 1912.
5. *Post-Chronicle,* March 28, 1912.
6. *Post-Chronicle,* April 24, 1912.
7. *Post-Chronicle,* May 31, 1912.
8. *Post-Chronicle,* June 29, 1912.
9. *Post-Chronicle,* July 22, 1912.
10. Ambler, pp. 507, 509.
11. Ambler, p. 508.

Fig. 93. Commencement Hall and University Library, 1912.

Dr. William P. Edmunds, a product of "Hurry Up" Yost, was football coach in 1912. The team won six games and lost three, but one of the losses was a 9 to 12 defeat by West Virginia Wesleyan, the first defeat by Wesleyan. Since the game determined the state championship, the result was quite a shock to university fans.[12]

The City of Riverside. Only a few weeks after the incorporation of the city of Westover, the adjoining area along the Monongahela River was approved for incorporation by the circuit court as the city of Riverside, on February 27, 1912.

Residents of the proposed new town went to the polls on March 31 to express their opinion and voted 40 to 2 in favor of incorporation. The limits of the proposed town, as shown by the survey made by William H. Brand, of Laurel Point, comprised 202.4 acres. A census indicated sixty-nine voters resided within the area.

Lee Shriver and Vint Guthrie were the candidates for mayor, Charles Woodhull, Florence Chisler, and Hukill Calvert for re-

12. Ambler, pp. 577, 578; Constantine, p. 11.

corder, A. J. Shriver, Charles Fox, Luther Donley, Henry Malott, Samuel Lovell, I. McGallagher, Levi Mason, William Keener, John Chisler, Frank Blowers, and Rufus Raber for councilmen.

"Several reasons are advanced for the incorporation of Riverside, which borders upon the recently incorporated 'city' of Westover. The principal reason assigned, however, is for the betterment of the sanitary conditions of the settlement along the placid Monongahela. The citizens are anxious to be empowered with the privilege of laying sewers and to provide for a municipal waterworks system. It it the idea of Riverside residents to erect a fairly large sized water tank somewhere near the town and to pump the water into the tank from the river, by means of a small pump. This would give sufficient water for sanitary purposes."[13]

The first election was held May 11, resulting in the election of Lee Shriver as mayor, Charles Woodhull as recorder, and Rufus Raber, Frank Blowers, John Chisler, Henry Malott, and William Keener as councilmen.

The new town had excellent connections with the county seat, where many of the residents commuted to work in glass factories or business establishments, to shop, or to attend classes at the university. Two trolley lines ran through the town, providing frequent service to downtown Morgantown.

A Methodist Protestant Church organization was formed in 1908, meeting in the school building at first. The Sunday school led to the organization of a congregation. Among those responsible for the organization were Eli Parker, Marion E. Adkins, Josephine Barrickman, Levi Mason, Mr. and Mrs. Bennett Mason, and Alice Lovell. A lot was secured and a church built.

New Automobile Agencies. Automobile garages were gradually replacing the old livery stables. The Walnut Street garage (p. 351) was the first in town. Three others were opened in 1912. The Ford Garage was erected by the Central Auto Corporation on Chestnut Street at Kirk Alley.[14] About the same time Leonard Smith opened another on Chestnut Street at Poplar Alley. Still another was erected by the Chaplin-Dille Motor Company on Spruce Street opposite the Central School building and was ready for occupancy in September.[15]

13. *Post-Chronicle*, March 29, 1912.
14. *Post-Chronicle*, November 5, 1912.
15. Callahan, p. 273.

Livery Stables. With the rapid increase in the use of automobiles, Morgantown's livery stables were passing out of the local scene and even the name was becoming somewhat derogatory. Years later a citizen[16] reminisced concerning their one-time place in the community:

"What an ignoble reference to an institution of the past! The Councilman was referring to Davidson's Livery Stable, albeit no doubt innocently. What a wealth of adjectives we can apply to this institution: indigenous, innate, inborn; second in Morgantown in tradition, memory, importance and love to only the University itself. . . .

"Davidson's Livery Stable was on Chestnut Street where the Davidson Garage now stands. It was by all odds the most important place of business on the street; the Hotel Madiera ran a poor second as a gathering place. The fragrant aroma of a livery stable is a thing of the past and hardly a memory to those whose experience goes back that far. There were spirited horses, and many a young swain rented a rig to drive his co-ed date over Cheat to the dances at Mt. Chateau, to go for a swim, or to have a picnic.

"Davidson's Livery Stable was owned and operated by Henry (Ek) and George Davidson, both amiable gentlemen with more friends than a politican. In the evenings you would find gathered in the small office the most important and the best known citizens of Morgantown. In those days life was simple—the automobile was only coming into popularity and there were no distractions like TV. . . . To drop by Davidson's and talk with the boys was a satisfactory evening activity. All political, social, athletic, and economic problems were discussed and usually solved."

Standard Adds New Tanks. The Standard Oil Company in October was in the process of constructing ten additional storage tanks at Morgantown, each holding about 36,000 barrels. The plant at the time consisted of the pumping station and forty-six tanks, holding from 16,000 to 37,000 barrels each. The tanks were widely spaced in the Tank Field, so that in case of fire only one tank will burn. More than a million barrels of oil were stored and

---

16. See editorial in the *Morgantown Post,* March 21, 1962. The anonymous citizen was B. B. Laidley and the reference was to a report given in city council that a certain building was once "used as a livery stable."

more than 60,000 barrels were pumped daily to the Atlantic seaboard. In addition, nearly 100,000 barrels monthly were delivered to the Pure Oil Company pumping station, located between Morgantown and Star City.[17]

South Morgantown Street Car Line. By midsummer work was well under way on the new loop being built in the Second Ward by the South Morgantown Traction Company. This line crossed the Walnut Street bridge on the Union Utilities tracks, went up South Walnut Street to Cobun Avenue, out Cobun to Green Street, up Green to Wilson Avenue, up Washington Street to Euclid Avenue, and then by what was then called Allen Street[18] down to South High Street. The new line eliminated the sharp curve up Prairie Avenue.

Track was being laid in November on Cobun Avenue, Green Street and Wilson Avenue.[19] On November 28 service was started from Washington Street to downtown Morgantown; Charles McClain was motorman on the first car and John Madagan conductor.[20]

The company announced that it was applying for a franchise to build a line from Greenmont to Sabraton, by way of Marilla.[21]

The Morgantown and Southern was also constructing a line forty-four hundred feet long from a junction with the South Morgantown line on Dorsey Avenue to a point just over the brow of the South Park hill.[22]

The M.&D.V. Dunkard Valley streetcars carried mail for Mona, Randall, Charlotte, and Cassville, beginning April 1.

Clay District voters, on June 22, approved a bond issue of $200,000 for extension of the line to Blacksville. The issue carried by a vote of 396 to 190.[23]

Bids for extension of the line were opened on June 6, but they exceeded funds available and had to be reconsidered.

The M.&D.V. schedule, effective August 25, showed cars leav-

17. *Post-Chronicle*, October 14, 1912.
18. Now Simpson Street.
19. *Post-Chronicle*, November 5, 1912.
20. *Post-Chronicle*, November 29, 1912.
21. *Post-Chronicle*, December 30, 1912. This line was never built.
22. *Post-Chronicle*, July 6, 1912. This, too, was never completed.
23. *Post-Chronicle*, June 24, 1912.

ing Morgantown for Cassville at 6:30, 8:15, and 10:30 a.m., and at 1:30, 2:45, 4:30, 6:30, and 11:00 p.m., while numerous other cars ran only to Randall. **Night Train Is Started.** Morgantown's first sleeping car service went into operation on December 15. The train consisted of a baggage car, combination smoker and ladies coach, and sleeper, each vestibuled, the sleeper electrically lighted. Northbound, the train left Clarksburg daily at 10:00 p.m., Fairmont at 11:30 p.m., Morgantown at 12:30 a.m., Connellsville at 2:30 a.m., and arrived at Pittsburg at 6:55 a.m. Southbound the train left Pittsburg at 11:55 p.m., Connellsville at 3:45 a.m., Morgantown at 5:45 a.m., Fairmont at 6:50 a.m. and arrived in Clarksburg at 8:20 a.m. A. E. Lewis, of Morgantown, bought the first sleeping car ticket ever sold in Morgantown. The city now had fourteen trains daily carrying mail.[24]

Cheat River Railroad. Work was started in June for the Cheat Haven and Bruceton Railroad up Cheat River, from a junction with the B.&O. at Cheat Haven. The contractor was Younkin and Wilson, of Fairchance. About seventy-five men were working.[25] By September the first mile had been graded and bids had been received for the extension to Ice's Ferry.[26]

Wadestown Paving Completed. The paving of twelve hundred feet of Wadestown streets, by the Pietro Paving and Construction Company, was completed June 3. The last brick was laid by M. J. Garrison, who also laid the first brick. It was anticipated that this improvement would lead to additional road building projects in the area.[27]

The Flood of 1912. Exactly sixteen years to the day from the date of the flood of '96 (p. 207), on July 24, 1912, another destructive flood hit the county. Fences, crops, bridges, buildings, roads, telephone lines, etc., felt the power of the surging waters.

"With none of the more appalling displays of natural forces to

24. *Post-Chronicle*, December 9, 17, 1912. A Pullman car was later named "Morgantown" (*Post-Chronicle*, January 4, 1913).
25. *Post-Chronicle*, June 22, 1912.
26. *Post-Chronicle*, September 4, 1912.
27. *Post-Chronicle*, June 4, 1912.

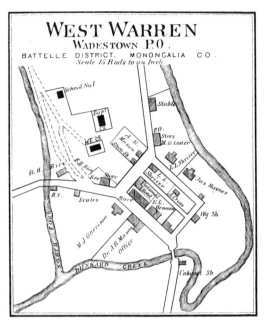

Fig. 94. Map of West Warren. (From *Atlas of . . .
Monongalia County*, 1886.)

give warning of its devastating power, a storm broke over this
section of the Monongahela Valley Wednesday afternoon and in
less than two hours had caused damage which can only be guessed
at, but which it is certain must reach into hundreds of thousands
of dollars. The storm was without destructive force and the lightning was not so threatening as to cause serious alarm, but the
rain fell in such torrents that within two hours the face of the
country had been changed along water courses and the work of
man wrought by months of toil had been swept away. Railroads
are washed out and covered with mud and debris, telephone and
telegraph lines were destroyed, bridges and houses are swept
from their foundations, factories are inundated and closed, fields
of growing crops are devastated by the floods, gardens are washed
bare of soil and vegetation, roads are made impassable and
general havoc is wrought wherever the floods were confined by
natural or artificial barriers.

"People who observed the approach of the storm tell of two
clouds, low, but apparently not very dense, that approached from
opposite directions, rolling and curling like steam escaping from

a huge pipe. The clouds hung low and when they met there were almost constant flashes of lightning, followed by the heaviest downpour ever observed here.

"Scotts Run and Core's Run, draining a large water-shed and uniting at Cassville, did a large damage. The waters rose with incredible swiftness and the entire territory along their banks was flooded before the people realized there was any danger. Ross Core's house at Cassville was washed from its foundations and demolished. His store building was picked up, turned around, and carried into the middle of the street, where it now reposes. The line of the Morgantown and Dunkard Valley Railroad between Jimtown and Cassville is out of commission for two or three days. There isn't a bridge left on Scotts Run and there isn't anything else, was the way one man put it last night."[28]

Mount Hermon Baptist Church. A congregation of black people was organized in Jerome Park in 1908, under the leadership of Rev. Alonzo Payne. The group at first met in a building on Hartford Avenue, then secured a lot on Richwood Avenue and built a substantial red brick church in the residential section in 1912.[29]

Manliff Hayes. A well-known businessman of Morgantown, Manliff Hayes, died December 8, after a long illness. The son of Alexander and Phoebe Davis Hayes, he was born December 24, 1826, at Randall. As a boy he learned the trade of a tailor and followed it until 1855, when he engaged in the livery business, following it for over fifty years. He was elected president of the county court in 1872 and served two terms. He was mayor of Morgantown three times, served eleven years as recorder, and was a member of the board of education. He married Alice, daughter of Nelson Berkshire, who survived him, along with four children, Mrs. Thomas E. Hodges, Mrs. Annie L. Johnston, Mrs. Winona B. Wilson, and Curtis R. Hayes.[30] His wife died on December 17.[31]

J. M. Brand. John McCray Brand, sheriff of Monongalia County from 1863 to 1867, died March 2, 1912, at his home in Cass District. The son of James and Elizabeth (Wade) Brand, he was born

28. *Morgantown Post,* July 25, 1912.
29. Dodds and Dodds, p. 71.
30. *Post-Chronicle,* December 9, 1912.
31. *Post-Chronicle,* December 17, 1912.

April 10, 1826. He married Sarah, daughter of Rev. G. F. C. Conn, and was survived by his widow and three children, Harvey, George C., and W. C. He was a cattle dealer and frequently took large droves to Baltimore. On one trip early in the Civil War he was captured by the Confederates at Harpers Ferry and his cattle confiscated. He was, however, released the next day and given an order on the Confederate government for the value of his cattle, which he was able to sell to a Confederate at a 10 percent reduction.[32]

A. F. Laughead. Ashbel Fairchild Laughead (Lawhead) died January 12, 1912, at the age of eighty-six. He was born in Fayette County, Pennsylvania, and moved to Morgantown in 1870, helping to found the well-known Fairchild, Laughead and Company, manufacturers of carriages, with factories in Uniontown, Morgantown, and Clarksburg. His first wife was Jeannette R. Hite, who died in 1858. Three years later he married Mary A. Lee. He was survived by his widow and seven children, W. B., Dr. J. H., Mrs. H. G. Jackson, Gay, Sara, Guy, and B. M.[33]

A. W. Lorentz. Adam Wilson Lorentz, a member of the staff of Monongalia Academy and of West Virginia University, died September 27, 1912; he was born May 28, 1836. He was educated in the Monongalia Academy and graduated from Washington and Jefferson College. After serving two years in the quartermaster's department in the Civil War, he went into the mercantile business in Morgantown. He became principal of the preparatory department of the university in 1877, a position he filled until 1893. He became president of the Farmers' and Merchants' Bank in 1895.[34]

Sarah R. Coyle. Miss Sarah R. Coyle, a member of one of Morgantown's most prominent families, and for thirty-five years a teacher in Morgantown schools died July 1, 1912; she was born at Greensboro, Pennsylvania, May 3, 1840.[35]

Miscellany. In 1912: The Brown Building was constructed on the northwest corner of High and Fayette streets (Callahan, p. 272).

---

32. *Post-Chronicle*, March 2, 1912; Wiley, p. 737; Brand, *Brand Family*, p. 219.
33. *Post-Chronicle*, January 13, 1912.
34. *Post-Chronicle*, September 27, 1912; Wiley, p. 419.
35. *Post-Chronicle*, July 1, 1912.

... A new cemetery, East Oak Grove, was opened (Callahan, p. 293). ... Charles B. Morris was appointed to take charge of the county home, effective April 1 (*Post-Chronicle*, January 6, 1912). ... The coldest weather since 1898 was recorded; it was thirty-eight degrees below zero at Pedlar Run and at Maidsville (*Post-Chronicle*, January 13, 1912). ... Harry M. Warfield opened a sales agency in Morgantown for the Maxim Tricar, a three-wheeled truck selling for $395 (*Post-Chronicle*, January 15, 1912). ... A cab belonging to Liveryman H. A. Davidson, pulled by two black horses, was badly damaged when it upset over an embankment along Forest Avenue, but the riders escaped (*Post-Chronicle*, January 29, 1912). ... Efforts were still being made to extend the M. and D. V. from Cassville to Mount Morris (*Post-Chronicle*, April 6, 1912). ... Lucian P. Smith, of Morgantown, went down with the *Titanic*, although his bride, the former Miss Eloise Hughes, was saved (*Post-Chronicle*, April 17, 1912). ... Repairs were made to the South Park bridge, which had been closed for over fifteen months; when it was opened again, it was conveyed by the Morgantown Bridge and Improvement Company to the county (*Post-Chronicle*, April 27, 1912). ... The steamer *Woodward*, after being laid up for extensive repairs, resumed service; three trips weekly from Pittsburg to Morgantown and one to Fairmont were scheduled (*Post-Chronicle*, May 9, 1912). ... The tinplate mill was making the biggest shipments ever, with about seventy-five carloads leaving weekly (*Post-Chronicle*, May 28, 1912). ... Political campaigners George C. Sturgiss, Ellis A. Yost, and John Shriver, returning from meetings at Daybrook, Wadestown, Wise, Blacksville, etc., had problems with their auto on muddy roads, and left it at Cassville, chartering a trolley to come on to Morgantown (*Post-Chronicle*, May 30, 1912). ... The city purchased two acres from Mr. and Mrs. Frederick Christon on the west side for a garbage disposal plant (*Post-Chronicle*, June 11, 1912). ... Dr. George Washington Dent, of Granville, born October 23, 1840, son of Dr. Marmaduke and Sarah Dent, died of a stroke (*Post-Chronicle*, June 13, 1912). ... The new road up the river from the western end of the bridge was opened, following its relocation by the B. and N. (*Post-Chronicle*, June 21, 1912). ... In one of Morgantown's first hit-and-run accidents, the buggy in which Mr. and Mrs. Raymond Hachat were riding was hit and upset on Bridge Street by an auto which kept on going

(*Post-Chronicle*, July 3, 1912). . . . Main line Chicago-to-New York passenger trains were detouring through Morgantown because of an accident in the Sand Patch tunnel (*Post-Chronicle*, July 10, 1912). . . . The county court authorized paving of the street from the city line through Jerome Park to the Hartman Run bridge (*Post-Chronicle*, July 16, 1912). . . . Oscar Brindley ascended two thousand feet in an airplane at the fairgrounds (*Post-Chronicle*, July 30, 1912). . . . The fourth annual fair was held October 1-4 (*Post-Chronicle*, September 30, 1912). . . . Billy Sunday, revivalist and orator, spoke in Morgantown November 1, traveling in a special railroad car (*Post-Chronicle*, November 1, 1912). . . . Harry O. Cole, civil engineer in charge of construction on the Pacific division of the Panama Canal, was in Morgantown with his wife and daughter, visiting his mother; he predicted the canal would be completed by 1914 (*Post-Chronicle*, October 19, 1912). . . . Postal carrier delivery was extended to Woodburn (*Post-Chronicle*, October 19, 1912). . . . Solomon H. Shriver, aged eighty-four, prominent business man of Wadestown, died October 29 (*Post-Chronicle*, October 31, 1912). . . . An epidemic of diphtheria was raging on Jakes Run, with two or more deaths (*Post-Chronicle*, November 7, 1912). . . . Samuel C. Baker, of Cheat Neck, died November 2, aged sixty-six years; he had read the Bible through thirty-seven times (*Post-Chronicle*, November 13, 1912). . . . Mrs. Martha Ammons Garrison, wife of M. S. Garrison, died November 19, aged fifty-nine years (*Post-Chronicle*, November 19, 1912). . . . Joseph Hilton, a black man, veteran of the Civil War, died in Morgantown, aged eighty-one years (*Post-Chronicle*, November 21, 1912). . . . The first mail delivery by auto in Monongalia County was made November 23, on Rural Route 2, J. Harlie Thompson, carrier, with Ben Garrison at the wheel (*Post-Chronicle*, November 25, 1912). . . . Rev. Charles Kelley Jenness, pastor of the Morgantown M.E. Church, published a book, *The Pilot Flame*, a study of religious experience (*Post-Chronicle*, November 25, 1912). . . . A new public water reservoir on Tibbs Run was completed, after being under construction nearly two years; to supply Morgantown with mountain water, it had a capacity of 90 million gallons (*Post-Chronicle*, December 27, 1912). . . . The steamer *I. C. Woodward* was tied up at Fairmont and service suspended for the winter; the *Wabash* continued to make daily trips from Morgantown to Martin, Pennsylvania (*Post-Chronicle*, December 7, 1912). . . . Samuel P. Huston, aged seventy-six, died December 21, about three weeks after his wife; they were survived by three children, Chauncey W., C. R., and Mrs. Louis T. Krebs (*Post-Chronicle*, December 21, 1912). . . . Jacob Sine, Jr., a Dolls Run farmer, died (*Chronicles of Core*, pp. 148, 171).

CHAPTER ONE HUNDRED THIRTY-SEVEN

1913

In 1913 Morgantown had two developing hospitals, both started by private enterprise. Both were founded at about the time Morgantown was developing from a village into a city, among the many aspects of change appearing in those years. Dr. J. W. Hartigan had opened the community's first hospital on Spruce Street at Kirk in 1899 and Drs. Luther S. Brock and S. S. Wade the second in 1900, at first on the Keck property on the west side, then in the Hoffman Building on High Street.

Morgantown Hospitals. The two institutions grew steadily and were well established by 1913. The Hartigan Hospital was described as follows:

"Dr. J. W. Hartigan was the first to recognize the need for a hospital in the town of Morgantown—it is now a city—and eleven years ago opened and equipped an institution of that kind. It was a success from the beginning. As many as eight hundred cases have been treated in a single year. . . .

"The establishment of this hospital filled a need which had long existed here and its continuance is assured. The people of the community owe much to it and they are not slow in recognizing the fact. Dr. Hartigan is a genial man but a modest one when his abilities or accomplishments are referred to. He has the respect of every one as a surgeon and as a man and stands high in the community. . . .

"The hospital has not the air of a house of sickness. It is bright and cheerful, more like a fine house than a hospital. The surroundings are attractive. Everything is for the best results to the one who needs them. The presence of the genial Doctor is a tonic in itself and few fail to appreciate and profit by it."[1]

1. *Post-Chronicle Industrial Edition,* 1913.

Fig. 95. The City Hospital.

By 1913 Brock and Wade's institution had been incorporated under the name of the City Hospital and Training School for Nurses and was located in a large house on the Purinton property at the corner of Willey and Prospect streets, under the direction of Dr. Irvin Hardy and Dr. T. Jud McBee. Both men were graduates of the College of Physicians and Surgeons, Baltimore, Maryland.

"The property, while located near the central part of the city, is well isolated from the congested residence and business districts. Here no time is lost in conveying patients to the institution in emergencies, and yet the location is so admirable, that privacy and quiet is assured. The training school for nurses has been given careful thought and attention, in all provisions therefor, the course consisting of three years which are required of students before graduation. Miss M. S. Smylie, the head nurse in charge, is a graduate of one of the largest hospitals in London, England, and has had several years of experience in hospitals abroad, and in Philadelphia."

"The building, formerly the residence of the Purinton family, has been entirely remodeled and is at present equipped to take care of thirty-five patients, besides the student nurses and nursing staff. Nice private, well lighted rooms, with perfect ventilation, have been provided and everything has been secured for the convenience and comfort of the patients. The new operating room is one of the best appointed in the state, being equipped with all the modern appliances."

"The grounds surrounding the beautiful and commodious building are ideal for convalescents during warm weather, being abundantly supplied with shade trees and beautiful lawns."[2]

The University. The effectiveness of President Hodges's administration was beginning to be questioned. He adhered to an economy program that resulted in very little money being spent for campus improvement; the $60,000 appropriation for buildings was not used. Complaints were voiced that "only a few of the buildings were provided with drinking fountains; despite the increased emphasis on physical training, the gymnasium was that in name only; . . . lights in University offices were saved at the expense of research, and requests for dictionaries, maps, and laboratory supplies were scrutinized in such a manner as to reduce such requests to a minimum."[3] State Superintendent of Schools M. P. Shawkey expressed disappointment with the administration of university affairs and did it so forcibly as to disturb the president.

In 1913 the Short Course in coal mining became a regular feature of the Summer School. The courses in elocution in the English department were elevated into a separate department of public speaking. A school of mines was established in 1913 and another of good roads, both sponsored by the College of Engineering. Dean C. E. Hogg of the College of Law resigned; Prof. G. F. Wells became acting dean. Rudolph Wertime was named head of the piano department.

Football was beginning to be a dominant interest on the campus and among the alumni. E. R. Sweetland succeeded Dr. W. P. Edmunds as coach, and the 1913 team had a very disappointing season, losing to the University of Pittsburgh 40-0, to Washing-

2. *Post-Chronicle Industrial Edition,* 1913. Dr. Hardy bought Dr. McBee's interest in 1914 and became the sole owner; *Post-Chronicle,* December 30, 1914.
3. Ambler, p. 509.

ton and Jefferson 34-0, to Washington and Lee 28-0, and to West Virginia Wesleyan 21-0. Among the few victories was that over Davis and Elkins, 43-0, in the first contest with that school. As the state championship was lost again, the alumni were "aroused as never before," and authorized an investigation.[4]

Mail Service Grows. With the growth of the town the amount of mail handled continued to increase and plans were under way to build a new building to handle the operations. Morgantown, in 1913, became the sixth first class post office in the state. Its receipts had tripled in the decade since 1903. On January 2, 1913, Stamp Station No. 1 was opened in Seneca. Twelve daily mails were received by train and a night force was added to facilitate the dispatch of mail.[5]

Postmaster Frank L. Bowman turned over the first spadeful of earth on March 24, as work got under way on the new post office. John G. Unkefer and Company were contractors for the construction.[6]

A new service, parcel post, was started on January 1 and a steady stream of packages was received; 256 were mailed between 10:00 a.m. and 11:00 a.m. Packages were delivered to homes and businesses in the city by horse and wagon.[7]

Morgantown and Wheeling Railroad. A reorganization of the Morgantown and Dunkard Valley Railway, suffering from financial woes, resulted in the organization of a new company, the Morgantown and Wheeling Railroad, to which the property of the M.&D.V. was sold. Officers of the new company were Dr. L. S. Brock, president; H. L. Carspecken, vice-president; James H. McGrew, treasurer; J. Ami Martin, general manager, and Frank P. Weaver, secretary.

By a remarkable change in plans, the construction of a trolley line from Cassville to Blacksville was abandoned and the company proposed to build a railroad to Wheeling.[8]

The B.&N. The Buckhannon and Northern company purchased forty acres of land between Jimtown and Maidsville and pro-

4. Ambler, p. 578.
5. Callahan, p. 285.
6. *Post-Chronicle*, March 21, 1913.
7. *Post-Chronicle*, January 2, 1913.
8. *Post-Chronicle*, January 11, 1913.

posed to construct the Morgantown assembling yards on that location.[9]

Construction of the railroad led to great enthusiasm on the part of local developers. Coupled with recent coal developments, there was indicated "an unprecedented season of industrial prosperity for this section according to business men conversant with such matters."[10]

Plans were being made to enter Fairmont by a line of their own through Palatine, rather than over the B.&O. tracks through Rivesville. This necessitated construction of a bridge across the Monongahela River at the mouth of Pricketts Creek.[11] Monongalia County residents were anxiously awaiting the beginning of service on the line but July came without any further word.[12]

In a surprising development later in the year, it was announced that the Monongahela Railway, owned jointly by the New York Central and the Pennsylvania lines, would purchase the B.&N. property for $10 million and would plan to begin service as soon as possible.[13]

Oil Field Developments. Increased activity in the oil fields of western Monongalia was resulting in more freight business for the M.&W. line between Morgantown and Cassville. Ten wells were being drilled near Cassville and all the casing for the wells was being hauled on the trolley freight cars. Three joints of thirteen-inch casing makes a load for a two-horse team, so the trolley saved heavy traffic on the roads. Wells being drilled in Battelle District brought in materials by other routes. On Miracle Run, the South Penn Well No. 3 on the L. V. Tennant farm, was holding up at ninety-five barrels a day.[14]

Geology of Monongalia County. The West Virginia Geological Society, under date of 1913, published another in its series of contributions to the geology of the state, this one dealing, in part,

9. *Post-Chronicle*, January 14, 1913.
10. *Post-Chronicle*, January 20, 1913.
11. *Post-Chronicle*, April 3, 1913; May 22, 1913.
12. *Post-Chronicle*, July 16, 1913.
13. *Post-Chronicle*, July 29, 1913.
14. *Post-Chronicle*, November 14, 1913.

with Monongalia County.[15] The volume included detailed accounts of the historical and industrial development, the physiography, the stratigraphy, the mineral resources, clay, road material, sand, building stone, iron ore, water power resources, and forests. There were more than thirty full pages of plates and three folded maps under separate cover.

"History of West Virginia." West Virginia was celebrating its fiftieth anniversary in 1913 and as a fitting accompaniment James Morton Callahan, professor of history and political science, West Virginia University, published a book[16] on the state's history that has been a much-consulted reference ever since. The volume is divided into two parts, the first (pages 1-302) being a history of the area from its first settlement through the formation of the new state down to the time of writing. The second part (pages 303-593) included special articles on the development and resources of West Virginia contributed by about twenty-five different authorities.

A Centennial. On February 10, 1913, Morgantown Union Lodge No. 4, A. F. and A. Masons, celebrated the one hundredth anniversary of the lodge's first meeting (see vol. 2, pp. 399-401).[17] An elaborate program was presented and the Master Mason's Degree conferred on John B. Mitchell. At the banquet, served at 10:00 p.m. at the M.E. Church, about 450 were in attendance, and music was furnished by Cox and Corey's Orchestra.

New Buildings. Numerous new brick business buildings continued to be constructed as Morgantown's economy expanded. A second Brown building was completed in 1913, nearly across High Street from the first, as well as the new Chadwick, under the McCrory lease, the Weiler on Front near Walnut, the Erd on High.[18]

Ice Manufacture. The Morgantown Ice Company was experiencing a steady increase in production. By 1913, in addition to sup-

15. Ray V. Hennen and David B. Reger. *Marion, Monongalia and Taylor Counties.* 844 pp. 1913.
16. *Semi-Centennial History of West Virginia.* Published by the Semi-Centennial Commission of West Virginia. 1913.
17. See *Post-Chronicle*, January 24, 1913.
18. Callahan, p. 272.

plying the needs of the city, the company was making shipments on the M.&K. as far as Manheim and on the B.&O. to Point Marion and to Fairmont. Large quantities were also supplied to B.&O. passenger trains passing through Morgantown.[19]

Oak Park. Although not in Monongalia County, Oak Park, near Masontown, in Preston County, provided important recreational facilities for local people and, indeed, for people over a wide area. Excursion trains were operated from as far away as Pittsburg and in 1913 thousands of people would visit the park on a favorable day.

Developed by the M.&K. Railroad, the entrance at the train stop was marked by a large iron gate and archway. The park had a carnival atmosphere. There were slides for all ages, a dance and concert pavilion, shooting galleries, cotton candy. Across Deckers Creek there were picnic tables, roller coasters, merry-go-rounds, and a baseball diamond. There was also boating on Deckers Creek.[20]

Kramer's Chapel. An interesting story is told of the origin of this church, in Clinton District:

"This church originated through a dream of Mrs. Harriet Jolliffe Kramer. For years she had worried because there was no church in the little village of Smithtown, and none closer than two miles. With this on her mind, one night she dreamed that a beautiful little church stood on the site where the church now stands. On awaking she told her husband, Dr. S. E. B. Kramer, of her dream. He promised to give her the ground if she would collect money to build the church. This she did by asking anyone and everyone for a subscription to build the chapel. It was erected and was dedicated in 1913 as a Methodist Protestant Church."[21]

Joseph Moreland. Judge Joseph Moreland died at his home on High Street on December 2, after a long illness. The son of John and Priscilla Rogers Moreland, he was born near Connellsville, Pennsylvania, May 26, 1842. He was a student at Monongalia Academy and graduated at Washington and Jefferson College in

19. Callahan, p. 271.
20. *Deckers Creek Valley Days,* 1971.
21. Dodds and Dodds, pp. 139, 140.

1866. He came to Morgantown the following year and entered the practice of law. "He was kind and gentle and a friend to everyone" and so completely had he won the confidence of the people that he was familiarly called "Honest Joe." He was frequently appointed as a special judge in legal cases.

He married Mary E. Brown and they had two children, Eleanor and James R.[22]

He had made substantial contributions towards recording the history of Monongalia County, especially through his fifty-two page book, *Morgantown. Its Practical Jokes and Jokers; Its Thrice Told Tales; Legends, Ghost Stories, Exaggerations, Doings and Sayings, Marvelous and Incredible; Its Fun, Wit, Humor, Etc.* (vol. 3, pp. 258-60), published in 1885 in connection with Morgantown's centennial.

G. W. McVicker. Captain George Washington McVicker died at his home in South Park on January 4, 1913. The son of James Madison and Catharine McVicker, he was born October 20, 1831. He married Alcinda Rude, then Mattie Clear, and was survived by five children, J. C., Clark, Mrs. Charles A. (Ella) Reed, Mrs. J. L. Wharton, and Mrs. J. B. Whidden.

During the Civil War he organized Company D, Third West Virginia Cavalry, in 1862, and served as captain for the remainder of the war. He was present at Appomattox when Lee surrendered.

He was prominent in civic affairs and was elected sheriff three times.[23]

W. R. Jones. Walter Roselle Jones, a national figure as a window glass manufacturer, died at his home in South Park on January 15. The only son of Samuel C. and Mary A. Jones, he was born in Clyde, New York, on February 28, 1846.

Practically all his business life was spent in the manufacture of window glass. He owned and operated large factories in Ohio and Indiana, and when the natural gas failed in those states he moved to West Virginia, where new supplies had been found, becoming a pioneer in his line here.

The W. R. Jones Window Glass Company located in Morgantown in 1901. The large factory was destroyed by fire in 1904, but

22. *Post-Chronicle*, December 3, 1913.
23. *Post-Chronicle*, January 4, 1913.

immediately rebuilt. He also operated a distributing company in Columbus, Ohio.

He married Lydia Davidson and they had five children, two of whom survived, namely, A. W. Jones and Mrs. Burt E. Taylor.[24]

Miscellany. In 1913: The Union Utilities Company was merged into the West Virginia Traction and Electric Company, with headquarters in Wheeling (Callahan, pp. 286, 287). . . . Samuel Barrickman, of Cass District, died April 23; the son of Michael and Mary Barrickman, he was born November 3, 1855 (*Chronicles of Core*, p. 173). . . . Morgantown's oldest store, Chadwick's, opposite the courthouse, was closed by D. Chadwick, the owner; it began business in the 1840s (*Post-Chronicle*, January 4, 1913). . . . Rural route No. 7, serving 110 families in Grant District, was started April 1 from the Morgantown post office (*Post Chronicle*, February 4, 1913). . . . Motorman James Madigan lost control of a South Morgantown trolley on Allen Avenue near Wagner Road, the car jumped the track, and four persons were slightly injured (*Post-Chronicle*, February 21, 1913). . . . A daily newspaper comic strip, "The Nut Club," by F. R. Morgan, was being carried (*Post-Chronicle*, March 7, etc., 1913). . . . Joseph Jacobs, aged forty-seven, died March 17 as the result of an accident when the mules pulling the Baker Hardware delivery wagon ran away on the South Park bridge (*Post-Chronicle*, March 15, 17, 1913). . . . The West Virginia Traction and Electric Company brought in a three-million-foot gas well on the A. N. Eddy farm in Grant District (*Post-Chronicle*, March 20, 1913). . . . Barley Foods Company of Adrian, Michigan, opened a factory at Sabraton (*Post-Chronicle*, May 2, 1913). . . . For the first time ever, wireless messages transmitted from the government aerial station at Arlington were intercepted at the university wireless station, constructed under the direction of Dr. C. W. Waggoner (*Post-Chronicle*, June 24, 1913). . . . The state convention of Christian Endeavor societies was held at the Morgantown Presbyterian Church; an auto trip to Cheat River was featured (*Post-Chronicle*, June 26, 1913). . . . Fifty persons fell into Deckers Creek June 26, when the Marilla swinging bridge collapsed; no one was seriously injured (*Post-Chronicle*, June 27, 1913). . . . A bridge on the M.&D.V. line at Boyer's mill, on Scotts Run, was washed out by a flood

24. *Post-Chronicle*, January 15, 1913.

(*Post-Chronicle,* July 17, 1913). . . . About five thousand people attended the races at the fairgrounds on August 6; hundreds came in autos from nearby towns, others by train (*Post-Chronicle,* August 6, 1913). . . . Dr. Charles H. Ambler published a book entitled *Thomas Ritchie,* a study of Virginia politics (*Post-Chronicle,* August 21, 1913). . . . Black people of Morgantown and surrounding towns on September 22 celebrated the fiftieth anniversary of Emancipation Day with a parade and other festivities (*Post-Chronicle,* September 22, 1913). . . . Elias J. Eddy died at Bula on September 27; born January 22, 1840, he married Acha Thomas and was a successful farmer and businessman (*Post-Chronicle,* September 27, 1913). . . . Morgan District voted by nearly 80 percent to issue bonds to support the development of local street car lines (*Post-Chronicle,* September 29, 1913). . . . An unusually early snowstorm broke down telephone and telegraph wires, caused difficulty for streetcars and trains (*Post-Chronicle,* November 10, 1913). . . . A charter was granted to the Morgantown and Fairmont Railway Company to build an interurban line between the two cities; it was announced that only thirty-one miles of road was needed to connect Weston and Pitts-

Fig. 96. Saint Luke Church of Christ, destroyed by fire in 1913. (Courtesy Roxie L. Jones.)

(*Post-Chronicle,* December 4, 1913). . . . Dr. I. C. White said the state's supply of natural gas will last thirty years or longer, contradicting more pessimistic statements (*Post-Chronicle,* December 5, 1913). . . . Wadestown was the "only place in the county" to observe the state's semi-centennial; Kate Garrison was the community leader (*Post-Chronicle,* December 15, 1913). . . . The Saint Luke Church of Christ at Mooresville was destroyed by fire as the morning service began on January 19 (*Post-Chronicle,* January 20, 1913). . . . Rev. William Hampton Hart, who was born near Maidsville, became president of the West Virginia Conference of the M.P. Church (Barnes, p. 140). . . . In a fight at a public function at Hagans, Ira Cordray was killed March 3 (*Chronicles of Core,* p. 173).

CHAPTER ONE HUNDRED THIRTY-EIGHT

1914

The completion of the Morgantown and Dunkard Valley trolley line to Cassville, in 1911, led to a flurry of proposals for extension of the system. Residents of Mount Morris, Pennsylvania, asked that the line be built to that town, thence up Dunkard Creek to Blacksville and beyond. Citizens of Mannington and of Waynesburg, Pennsylvania, proposed construction of an interurban line to connect those communities, joining the Dunkard Valley line at Blacksville. At Mannington a system already in operation extended to Fairmont, Clarksburg, and Weston. But lack of ready financing prevented initiation of any of these projects.

What actually happened, in the extension of the line from Cassville, was very different from what had been planned when the Morgantown and Dunkard Valley Railway Company was organized in 1905. Visionary promoters, with grandiose ideas, organized the Morgantown and Wheeling Railway Company, and on January 12, 1913, took over the property of the M.&D.V., and asked permission to extend the line all the way to Wheeling!

The reasoning behind the change in plans was to provide an outlet for the vast coalfields of western Monongalia County and western Greene County and also to give a more direct connection to the Ohio Valley at Wheeling.

George C. Sturgiss, a leading advocate of an interurban line to Wheeling, was in that city in May to publicize plans for the road. He said:

"We have eight miles of road in actual operation from Morgantown to Cassville. We have under contract and construction being pushed as rapidly as possible a section of 14 miles, from Cassville to Blacksville, which will be done by November 1st. . . . We have taken out a Pennsylvania Charter and made surveys and locations very complete from Blacksville . . . to Elm

Grove . . . a location with so few curves and slight grades that it can be, with little additional cost, converted into a standard gauge steam-railroad."

It was apparent that promoters were still not certain if the M.&W. would be a steam railroad or a trolley line. A trolley branch would go from Blacksville to Waynesburg. Concerning this, Mr. Sturgiss continued:

"On this latter road over $200,000 has been expended, and the grading is nearly completed. The masonry for the bridges is also nearly completed, and seven steel bridge structures are on the ground ready to be erected."[1]

The Morgantown and Wheeling Railroad. Construction began early in the season, the contract for the section from Cassville to Blacksville having been awarded to Keeley Brothers and Gilmore.

By midsummer it was estimated that the sixteen-mile section of the line from Cassville to Blacksville was 35 percent com-

Fig. 97. Lemley Hill cut on the M&W Railroad.

1. *Post-Chronicle*, May 25, 1914.

pleted, so far as grading and masonry were concerned. The contractors were concentrating on the big cut at the top of the hill between Cassville and Core.

"A steam shovel, two dinky engines, and about a mile and a half of track are in use in making the cut through the hill, the cutting being about the heaviest of its kind ever attempted around here. . . . From Cassville to Core the grading is practically completed, except where heavy fills are being made with dirt taken from the cut. From Core to the mouth of Dolls Run no work has been started, as all of these rights-of-way are involved in present proceedings before circuit court. From the mouth of Dolls Run to Pentress the grading is practically finished. From Pentress to Blacksville the grading is almost done except for the mile nearest Blacksville."[2]

On September 3 the *Post-Chronicle* reported: "There is one spot in Monongalia County where the sun never sets. That spot is the Lemley Hill, where the big cut on the line of the M. & W. is under way. Last night the contractors had several big searchlights playing over the cut and a double shift was put to work in order to rush the job through. . . . The cut is to be about 200 feet wide at the top and 22 feet at the bottom, the depth averaging about 70 feet and the banks sloped back at about 45 degrees. The task is the heaviest of its kind ever undertaken in the county. . . . Yesterday a track laying machine reached Randall over the B. & N. Some track laying will be started in about 15 days. Today the M. & W. has stored at Randall several tons of rails and 20,000 ties, enough to lay several miles of track. As soon as the cut is completed it is expected that track laying will progress at the rate of half a mile a day. The track laying engine will take out a load of ties and rails each morning and return at night for another load after laying half a mile of track."[3]

B. M. Chaplin was the contractor on the bridges, which were constructed of concrete, or of concrete and steel.

At Jimtown a connection was completed August 22 on a track connecting lines of the B.&N. and the M.&W. Heavier rails were being placed on the M.&W. tracks up Scotts Run, in anticipation

2. *Post-Chronicle*, July 14, 1914.
3. *Post-Chronicle*, September 3, 1914.

of the opening of coal mines. A new steel span, across Scotts Run, 108 feet long, replaced the old wooden trestle.[4]

A New Post Office Building. A new federal building in Morgantown, housing United States post office facilities, was dedicated on November 2, 1914. This building provided space for the greatly increased business which had overcrowded the large room in the Brock-White-Courtney Building on High Street near Pleasant, where the facilities had previously been housed.

Fig. 98. New post office building, Morgantown.

The beautiful new building, on High Street at Kirk, begun in 1913 and finally completed in 1915, cost nearly $150,000 to construct. In addition to the post office it provided offices for other government officials, such as the internal revenue collector, government engineers, civil service examiners, and also the National Red Cross.

In 1913, a newspaper account had said:

"Twelve railroad mails are received daily. There are six rural

4. *Post-Chronicle,* August 22, 1914.

free delivery routes, eight office clerks, and eight city carriers. The postmaster is Frank L. Bowman, and the assistant postmaster is Amos L. DeMoss. The office clerks are Annie L. Johnson, W. G. Johnson, W. H. Kendricks, W. E. Martin, Carl Newbraugh, J. E. Protzman, James E. Reed and John M. Wildman. The sub-clerk is Sardis M. Cordray. The city carriers are D. A. Anderson, Harvey Brand, Lloyd Bunten, Emerson Carney, Homer B. Fogle, C. Leslie Hall, Linn M. Jaco, and Lee A. Smith. The substitute carriers are Frederick S. Dorrell and Robert L. Poland. The rural carriers are Oscar C. Gregg, J. H. Thompson, George C. Birtcher, Daniel M. Hoard, Isaac A. Morris, and John W. Pool, Jr. The manager of Stamp Station Number 1 is Joseph H. Kaszer.

"At an early day the Morgantown post office will be housed in the Federal building for which an appropriation of $137,000 has been made. The site on High Street was purchased of Hon. George C. Sturgiss for $37,000, and the frontage of the building on the said street will be 88 feet. The height will be two stories. The sum of $99,000 is now available as a building fund. The supervising architect of the United States Treasury Department is now preparing the plans. Bids for the construction have been received, and the actual work will begin at an early date. Rock from the Kingwood quarries will very possibly be used."[5]

Of Frank L. Bowman, the first postmaster in the new building, the account said that he "was born at Masontown, Pennsylvania, January 21, 1879. In 1902 he was graduated from the West Virginia University with a degree of A. B. Then for two years he was teller in the Farmers' and Merchants' Bank of this city. Graduating also from the law department of our university, he became in May, 1909, associated with the law firm of Glasscock and Glasscock. His present position he assumed July 1, 1911. As a student, Mr. Bowman enjoyed a brilliant career, winning as orator and debater in inter-society contests. He is a member of the Masonic order and of the Presbyterian Church. His wife was Miss Pearl Silvers, daughter of a Presbyterian minister of Pittsburgh, Pa."

After the construction of the new building a night force was established to facilitate the dispatch of mails.

5. *Post-Chronicle Industrial Edition*, 1913.

President Hodges Resigns. The "bigger view of things educational," eagerly foreseen at the beginning of the administration of Thomas E. Hodges as university president, by 1914 had not developed into a reality. Instead, the president found himself trapped between his support for traditional educational standards and the demands of the new educators. His political friends provided an escape by nominating him for election as West Virginia congressman-at-large. His acceptance of this nomination, on July 18, 1914, was coincidental with his resignation as president. With expressions of "regret and appreciation," the regents hastened to accept his resignation and appointed Dean F. B. Trotter as acting president, his services to begin at once.[6]

The Agricultural Extension Division was undergoing significant revision. C. R. Titlow was director; C. H. Hartley (1914), assistant director; M. J. Abbey (1913), professor of agricultural education, Nat T. Frame (1914), state agent in charge of county agents; W. H. Kendrick (1912), in charge of boys' clubs; W. H. Alderman (1914), professor of horticulture; Nell M. Barnett, instructor in home economics; and Sadie R. Guseman in charge of girls' clubs.[7]

A revitalization of the football team was expected when the athletic board hired as coach Sol S. Metzger, of the University of Pennsylvania, who had developed a team there that defeated "Hurry Up" Yost's eleven. Optimism was encouraged through a preseason training camp and "the influx of raw material." The optimism was not justified, however; the season was not far advanced before the coach broke his leg[8] and was incapacitated the remainder of the year. The team lost to Washington and Jefferson and West Virginia Wesleyan. Its five victories were over relatively insignificant teams.[9]

The B.&N. The long-delayed passenger train service on the Buckhannon and Northern Railroad was still not started during 1914. Work was under way on construction of the extension into Fairmont, on the east side, by way of a bridge across the river near

6. Ambler, p. 510. Dr. Hodges failed in the election; in July 1915, he was appointed Morgantown postmaster, a position he held until his death on July 13, 1919.

7. Ambler, pp. 531, 532.

8. He fell from a moving automobile on October 9.

9. Ambler, p. 580; Constantine, p. 11.

Catawba. This was scheduled for completion by the end of the year. Freight service was under way, however, and was growing rapidly.[10]

The contract for the steel work on the bridge was awarded to McClintic-Marshall Company, of Pittsburg, and erection of steel began August 27.[11] A big cut was made at Pricketts Creek, in Marion County, and the line then ran through a tunnel into East Fairmont. The tunnel was completed in November and the track was nearly completed to the Fairmont depot by the end of the year. Passenger service from Brownsville to the state line was started October 30.[12]

Packet Boat Service. In January Morgantown businessmen were starting a movement to have packet boat service resumed between Morgantown and Fairmont.[13] Noting that nearly two years had passed without regular packet boat service between Morgantown and Pittsburg, Captain G. W. C. Johnston in June announced plans to enter the steamer *Lorena* in service on that route.[14]

The *Lorena* left Pittsburg September 16 on a special excursion to Morgantown and Fairmont, the first steamer in the Monongahela headwaters in more than two years. "Old rivermen recall . . . when two packets daily did a thriving business. With the railroads paralleling the river on either shore, the trade . . . gradually declined, until about two years ago . . . it was practically abandoned."[15]

The Strand Theater. Morgantown's old theater, the Swisher, was sold in October to Harry Davis and John P. Harris, theatrical men of Pittsburg, and was closed for a few weeks while it was overhauled, redecorated, renovated, and refurnished. Col. Theodore Roosevelt spoke in the theater on October 27, to an audience of two thousand people. At first it was proposed to call it the Princess Theater, but the name Strand was given when it reopened on November 16. It was planned to show mainly motion pictures but occasionally drama and vaudeville.[16]

10. *Post-Chronicle*, July 3, 1914.
11. *Post-Chronicle*, August 27, 1914.
12. *Post-Chronicle*, November 6, 1914.
13. *Post-Chronicle*, January 2, 1914.
14. *Post-Chronicle*, January 2, 1914.
15. *Post-Chronicle*, September 16, 1914.
16. *Post-Chronicle*, November 13, 1914.

A New City Hall. For many years before 1914 the Morgantown city government occupied rented quarters on Walnut Street near Spruce. Early in 1914 the Watts property, grounds and frame buildings, at the southwest corner of Spruce and Fayette streets, was purchased by Russell L. Morris, John M. Gregg, and Robert D. Hennen on behalf of the city, which had no funds for the purpose. The object was for the city, by annual payments from the levy, to obtain a free title to the property. Meanwhile the buildings furnished quarters, however inadequate, for the police and fire departments, and for a so-called "city jail."[17]

Jerome Park. A popular summer recreational area was Jerome Park, developed by the West Virginia Traction and Electric Company along its trolley line between Morgantown and Sabraton. It was named for Jerome Rogers, a popular, unmarried resident of the area, born at Pisgah, Preston County. The park was on what is now Jerome Street, and had a merry-go-round, sand slide, refreshment stand, see-saws, tables, benches, swings, a gas range to warm lunches or make coffee. In addition, there was a dancing pavilion with a piano, all provided by the Traction Company.

Highland Park Methodist Church. In 1913 a small group of people on Wiles Hill asked permission of the board of education to hold religious services on Sunday evenings in one of the rooms of the Wiles Hill school. The request was granted and the group increased in size until the school board felt the building was not safe for so large a crowd. Prayer was made that a place of worship might be found.

Highland Park, at that time, was an open grove owned by Clark Hoffman. He laid it out in lots for the development of a residence section, and came to Rev. E. J. Heller, who was in charge of the church group, with an offer to donate a lot. Feeling their prayer had been answered, they accepted the lot, and broke ground early in 1914 for the erection of a church. The cornerstone was laid on July 4 and the church was dedicated January 24, 1915.[18]

O. H. Dille. Oliver Hagans Dille, son of Judge John A. and Rachel Jane (Hagans) Dille, died November 22, 1914. He married Gilly

17. Callahan, p. 294.
18. Dodds and Dodds, p. 83.

Coleman Evans and soon after his marriage bought the old Evans farm north of Morgantown, which thereafter remained the Dille home. They had six children, Elisha M., Thomas Ray, Jennie, James Evans, Maud, and John.

He graduated from West Virginia University in 1871, read law with his father and was admitted to the bar in 1872, practicing law as a member of the firm Dille and Son. He was also engaged in the livestock business.[19]

Dr. P. B. Reynolds. Powell Benton Reynolds died December 29, 1914. He was born in Patrick County, Virginia, January 9, 1841, the son of James Bartholomew and Roxana Reynolds. He graduated from Richmond College, then received the A.M. degree from West Virginia University in 1887 and the D.D. degree from Richmond in 1890. He was ordained a Baptist minister in 1866 and from 1872 to 1884 he was president of Shelton College, then president of Buckner College for one year.

In 1885 he became professor of English at West Virginia University, serving in that position until 1889, when he became vice-president and professor of metaphysics. In 1893 he was appointed acting president, serving two years, then was appointed to the chair of metaphysics and political science. After another two years, he became professor of philosophy in 1897 and professor of economics and sociology in 1901, which position he held until his retirement in 1911.

His writings were primarily in the form of articles appearing in various educational journals. An editor of *West Virginia School Journal* said of him: "A man of sweet spirit and a great mind, also a ripe scholarship."

Miscellany. In 1914: Lough-Simpson Grocery Company doubled their space by expanding into a new addition to their building (Callahan, p. 271). . . . Harner's Chapel Methodist Church, which had been started in 1909, was completed and dedicated in September (Dodds and Dodds, p. 82). . . . Two residents of Core died, Oliver Perry Morford on February 14 and Harry Michael Core on March 23 (*Chronicles of Core,* p. 180). . . . A baby was born on M.&K. passenger train No. 18 to Mrs. Scott Lantz (*Post-Chronicle,* January 10, 1914). . . . J. A. Blaney opened a shoe

19. Callahan, p. 80; Wiley, p. 357.

store in Morgantown (*Post-Chronicle*, January 17, 1914).
... Father C. J. Kluser, pastor of the Morgantown Catholic
Church, was transferred to Mannington and was succeeded by
Father Peter Flynn, of Mannington (*Post-Chronicle*, February 16,
1914).... Madame Teresa Carreno presented a piano recital at
Swisher's Theater (*Post-Chronicle*, February 20, 1914).... Tom
Walker, black chef at the Ridgeway Hotel, was instantly killed
and nine others injured when the bobsled they were riding, which
started on the hill above the university, wrecked on Front Street
in front of the home of E. L. Mathers (*Post-Chronicle*, Febru-
ary 21, 1914).... Albert Gallatin Brown, aged forty-two, died
when he fell five floors through the elevator shaft of the Main
Street Building (*Post-Chronicle*, March 10, 1914).... Albert
Scopic, a Polish miner, was murdered at Round Bottom (*Post-
Chronicle*, April 13, 1914).... Jacob Adams, aged ninety-four, of
Cheat Neck, died, survived by these children: John, George,
Robert, Charles, William, Mrs. Carry Bowers, and Mrs. Cora
Barndell (*Post-Chronicle*, April 17, 1914).... W. E. Slaughten-
houpt, owner, closed the Acme Department store (*Post-Chronicle*,
May 13, 1914).... Samuel McGara, aged eighty-four, a retired oil
promoter, died in Morgantown (*Post-Chronicle*, May 25, 1914).
... A contract was let to W. F. Blair for construction of a con-
solidated four-room school building at Daybrook (*Post-Chronicle*,
June 27, 1914).... A new highway bridge across Dunkard Creek
at Pentress was built to replace the old covered bridge (*Post-
Chronicle*, July 24, 1914).... Railroad passenger traffic through
Morgantown was the heaviest in history; 306 round trip tickets
to Point Marion were sold on a Saturday afternoon and a crowd of
one thousand was handled in an Odd Fellows outing at Oak Park
(*Post-Chronicle*, July 27, 1914).... More than one hundred
horses were entered for races at the fairgrounds (*Post-Chronicle*,
August 3, 4, 5, 6, 1914).... In August, no oil was going east from
Morgantown through Eureka Pipe Line facilities because of suspension of exports resulting from the outbreak of war in Europe
(*Post-Chronicle*, August 18, 1914).... Bids were received by the
Morgantown Interurban Company for construction of a trolley
line to Point Marion but there were insufficient funds available to
pursue the project (*Post-Chronicle*, August 28, 1914).... Numerous Morgantown tourists caught in the European war zone returned home safely, but had some thrilling stories to tell (*Post-

Chronicle, September 4, 1914). . . . Battelle District voters approved, on September 22, by 304 to 171, a bond issue of $175,000 for extension of the M.&W. railway (*Post-Chronicle,* October 2, 1914). . . . About 150 university students "rushed" the Grand Theater following a "thuse" on the campus (*Post-Chronicle,* October 16, 1914). . . . The university football team traveled by Pullman to Raleigh for a game with North Carolina A.&M. (*Post-Chronicle,* October 17, 1914). . . . President Daniel Willard of the B.&O. visited Morgantown by special train (*Post-Chronicle,* October 24, 1914). . . . Col. Theodore Roosevelt came to Morgantown by special train and spoke to about six thousand people at the courthouse square (*Post-Chronicle,* October 27, 1914). . . . Night classes in commercial subjects were started for the first time by the High School (*Post-Chronicle,* November 9, 1914). . . . Movies of Morgantown and vicinity were taken by N. E. Merhie, of Charleston, for showing at the Panama-Pacific Exposition (*Post-Chronicle,* November 17, 1914). . . . Motorman William Forman was injured in a car collision on the M.&W. line at Barker (*Post-Chronicle,* November 19, 1914). . . . Vice-President Thomas R. Marshall spoke at the university, arriving in Morgantown on the M.&K. (*Post-Chronicle,* November 23, 1914). . . . Samuel McVicker, aged eighty-one, died in December near Morgantown (*Post-Chronicle,* December 9, 1914). . . . The first goblets to be successfully made from lime glass were being manufactured by the Athens Glass Company, in Seneca (*Post-Chronicle,* December 26, 1914). . . . Cole Bros., Inc., were awarded the contract for constructing the new Front Street bridge over Deckers Creek, for $53,330.70 (*Post-Chronicle,* December 28, 1914). . . . The University Scientific Society held its first meeting on May 19, 1914, under the initiative of Profs. A. R. Whitehill, A. M. Reese, S. B. Brown, J. L. Sheldon, C. W. Waggoner, and J. A. Eiesland (Nelle Ammons, *History of the W.Va. Academy of Science* (1963), p. 6).

CHAPTER ONE HUNDRED THIRTY-NINE

1915

A new separate building for the growing enrollment in the Morgantown High School was authorized by a bond issue for $150,000 passed by the Morgantown Independent School District May 29, 1914, by a 572-381 vote.[1] After considerable discussion concerning the best location for the proposed new building, the board of education finally chose the fine lawn in front of the old Central Building, at the corner of Spruce and Walnut Streets, although there were strong objections that a beautiful site was being destroyed. The contract for construction was awarded to R. R. Kitchen.

Morgantown High School. By autumn of 1914 the excavation had been completed[2] and construction proceeded rapidly. The building was completed and opened for public inspection on September 25, 1915. It was described as follows:

"It is a square brick building of modern type. Steel lockers were installed in the main corridors. Clocks are run by air and a most acceptable form of heating and ventilating system was installed. Steps leading to the street are at each end of the hall. The ground floor contains the boiler room, machinery, coal space, cold storage room, janitors' workshop, manual training department, and domestic science department. The gymnasium is in the center of the building. On the first floor was the commercial department, principal's office, superintendent's office, board of education, waiting room, and several other rooms. The second floor contains the library, study hall, medical inspection room, and an auditorium which seats seven hundred and fifty persons.

1. *Post-Chronicle,* May 29, 1914.
2. *Post-Chronicle,* October 9, 1914.

Fig. 99. Morgantown High School, completed in 1915. (From an old postcard.)

On the third floor is the science department, as well as class-rooms for other departments."[3]

The Morgantown High School had been established in 1882 and the first principal was Thomas E. Hodges. In 1904 there were still only sixteen four-year high schools in the state, the largest being Parkersburg, with 299 students. Morgantown High School, in 1904, had 72 students enrolled. By 1915, when the new building was completed, the number had increased to 470.

High school students at first shared rooms in the old Monongalia Academy, until its destruction by fire in 1897, and then in the Central building, completed in 1899, but from the beginning were forced to use space rented in other buildings.

"The Trotters." On the university campus acting president F. B. Trotter was getting well under way on his outstanding administration. Ambler says that he "was not a profound scholar even in his chosen field, but he appreciated scholarship in all fields. In University affairs he worked in close cooperation with his brother, James Russell Trotter, who was state superintendent of

3. *Post-Chronicle*, October 9, 1914.

Fig. 100. James R. Trotter.   Fig. 101. Frank Butler Trotter.
                                     (West Virginia University.)

free schools from 1897 to 1901, a University regent from 1901 to
1908, and a professor in the University College of Law from 1908
until his death, July 5, 1925. Their somewhat uncanny memories
for family names and educational data contributed to their effectiveness in dealing with state legislators and with the public in
general, and their habit of attending weddings, funerals, family
reunions, and fairs was due to their innate interest in West Virginians and not to proneness to demagoguery. . . . 'The Trotters'
worked in close cooperation with J. S. Lakin, president of the
state board of control."[4]

The acting president kept well in the background of university
affairs, while helping the regents find a "proper person" for the
presidency. He gave his first attention to needed buildings and
land. At the time numerous persons and organizations were seeking to bring about the removal of the university to "a more desirable location." A resolution proposing its transfer to Charleston was proposed to the legislature in February 1915, and was
seriously considered.

Dr. J. L. Coulter was appointed dean of the College of Agriculture, effective February 1, and the college was making steady
progress. In order to thwart the proposals to remove the university from Monongalia County, the county commissioners offered

4. Ambler, p. 511.

to raise $75,000 for the purchase of land needed by the college for instructional and research purposes. The 1915 legislature appropriated $100,000 for an agricultural building. The 1915 football season, under coach Sol S. Metzger, was quite successful and the coach was hailed as "the Miracle Man." The team lost to the University of Pennsylvania by a score of 7 to 0, held Washington and Jefferson to a 6 to 6 tie, and forfeited a game with Washington and Lee because of a dispute over an umpire's decision. All other games were won. More importantly, the alumni were aroused and had placed West Virginia on the football map.[5]

Passenger Service on the Monongahela. After months of waiting, regular passenger service was initiated November 1, 1915, on the Monongahela Railway, formerly the Buckhannon and Northern. The B.&N., a West Virginia corporation, and the Monongahela, a Pennsylvania company, were consolidated into one company.

The first train "arrived at 7:45 a.m., in charge of engineer James Ryan, fireman F. M. Vankirk, conductor C. E. Booth, baggagemaster T. A. Hicks, and brakeman George Vickers. Clyde E. Jacobs bought the first ticket, from Morgantown to Brownsville. Dr. I. C. White was among the first passengers."[6]

Direct service to Pittsburg was provided, running over the Monongahela to Brownsville and on to Pittsburg over lines of the Pittsburg and Lake Erie Railroad. Trains left Morgantown for Pittsburg at 7:58 a.m. and 5:03 p.m. and arrived from Pittsburg at 11:40 a.m. and 8:30 p.m. A buffet parlor car serving breakfast was attached to the morning northbound train and dinner was served on the evening southbound train.[7]

To meet the competition, the B.&O. changed one of its accommodation trains to an express, supplied with modern dining cars and Pullman coaches.

During the summer the passenger station in Westover was built by Ben Chaplin. It contained a ticket office, operators' room, and men's and women's waiting rooms. A long cement platform was built along the tracks, sixteen feet wide and covered

5. Ambler, pp. 580, 581.
6. *Post-Chronicle*, November 1, 1915.
7. *Post-Chronicle*, December 9, 1915.

with umbrella sheds. Steps were erected up to the river bridge and a paved driveway led from Holland Avenue to the depot.[8]

Freight service was started August 31. H. C. Williams was named chief clerk of the local station and R. E. Foltz ticket agent.[9]

Progress on the M.&W. End-o'-track on the new railroad to the Dunkard Valley reached Core on February 17, 1915, and the first "iron horse" puffed into the village. Track laying proceeded westward and the line was expected to reach Blacksville before many months. Each day a puffing dinky engine (M.&W. No. 3) went out from Randall with a load of ties, rails, and men, returning in the evening after a day of track laying.

Local freight service was soon established, with the western terminal always the constantly advancing end-o'-track, where materials were unloaded from boxcars onto road wagons, mostly operated by merchants of the western end of the county. A passenger and freight depot was constructed at Core and another at a station named Price, at the mouth of Jakes Run, along Dunkard Creek, with sidings by each depot.[10]

Martin Resigns. J. Ami Martin resigned as general manager of the M.&W. R.R., effective December 4. He had been in railroad development in northern West Virginia for twenty-seven years, beginning with the West Virginia Northern from Tunnelton to Kingwood. He came to Morgantown in 1898, helped Judge Sturgiss with the development of the first eighteen miles of the M.&K., managed the Sabraton street railway from its inception, then took charge of the M.&D.V. At that time the company had been discredited by repeated unsuccessful efforts to finance it, but he was able to have the road built and put into operations as far as Cassville.[11]

The Last Fair. The final annual fair on the Evans farm was held in the fall of 1915. The Morgantown Fair Association had been incorporated October 24, 1908, by W. A. Ream, E. D. Tumlin, Alf K. Smith, B. H. Madera, and T. R. Evans. The layout, of about eight acres, was on the Evans farm, near the site of the later

8. *Post-Chronicle,* July 8, 1915.
9. *Post-Chronicle,* August 31, 1915.
10. *Chronicles of Core,* pp. 179, 180.
11. *Post-Chronicle,* December 7, 1915.

Monongalia General Hospital. There were stables with stalls for about 100 horses, a wooden grandstand seating about 2,500 people, and a half-mile oval racetrack. The track was over a smaller one which Thomas Evans had built for training horses.[12]

University Song. Students at the university, in a vote on June 2, 1915, selected "West Virginia," as the official song of the school. The words were written by F. B. Deem, of Parkersburg, and the music by Ed McWhorter and Earl Miller, of Charleston. "The music is very catchy and the students took to the song with a rush this morning."[13]

The Masonic Temple. Morgantown's Masonic lodge, Union Lodge No. 4 A.F. and A.M., through its trustees, John M. Gregg, Frank L. Bowman, W. E. Arnett, W. S. Carrothers, and P. C. White, in February 1915, purchased from George Rogers a lot 41x139 feet, at the corner of High and Willey streets, and prepared to build a Masonic Temple. The lodge at the time was meeting in the Brock, Reed and Wade Building.[14] The cornerstone of the new building was laid on July 22.

New Deckers Creek Bridge. A concrete viaduct across Deckers Creek was completed in 1915 by Cole Brothers Construction Company. This bridge extended directly from Front Street, of the original borough of Morgantown, to Bridge Street, of South Morgantown, and eliminated a curve that had existed since pioneer times, when the first covered bridge had been built from Foundry Street, farther up the creek, as had been succeeding bridges, including the steel bridge which the new concrete one replaced.[15]

Highways Need Attention. With more automobiles using streets and roads, it was becoming more important to keep the surfaces smooth. Dirt roads were mostly impassable in winter but in spring, as the mud began to dry, drags were used to assure smooth roads for the coming season. The tarvia road, part of the "Stewartstown pike," of "the usual tar and gravel construction,"

12. See Al Babcock, *Morgantown Post,* July 8, 1948.
13. *Post-Chronicle,* June 2, 1915.
14. *Post-Chronicle,* February 11, 1915.
15. Tracks of the South Morgantown streetcar line were later built across the bridge.

was in need of special repair to keep it from going to pieces. There were suggestions that a motorcycle cop was needed, especially on the Point Marion road, since people returning from the saloons there "often imbibe pretty freely before starting back."[16] On June 21 an autoist was arrested on the Cheat road for exceeding the twenty-mile speed limit.[17]

Dr. Buchanan Resigns. Rev. Aaron Moore Buchanan, who had been pastor of the First Presbyterian Church in Morgantown since May 1886, resigned in the fall of 1915. He was born July 7, 1856, in Beaver County, Pennsylvania, and graduated from Western Theological Seminary in 1882. His alma mater conferred the degree Doctor of Divinity upon him in 1899. He was an able preacher and was active in enlisting university students in church programs.

"Dr. Buchanan was a remarkable pastor. . . . He probably knew every man, woman, and child in Morgantown at that time. He knew them by name and made them feel that he was a friend. His efforts to assist those in distress was not confined to members of his church."[18]

Saint Markella Orthodox Church. One development resulting from the great influx of people from southern and eastern Europe was the establishment of church groups where the members could feel at home with each other.

In 1915 there were hundreds of Slavonic people residing in and near Sabraton and, under the direction of Emeri Zatkovich, bishop of Uniontown, a church body was organized. A small but substantial building, constructed of tile, was erected on the hill overlooking the tinplate mill. A cross on the steeple identifies it.[19]

Star City Methodist Church. In the spring of 1915 E. J. Heller, a divinity student who was taking courses at West Virginia University, gathered a group of Methodists in the developing town of Star City into a Methodist congregation. Mr. and Mrs. W. C. Anderson deeded a lot for a building to the trustees, W. C. Anderson, G. W. Stiles, Maude L. Keener, Elizabeth A. Cobun, Jacob

16. *Post-Chronicle,* April 15, 1915.
17. *Post-Chronicle,* June 21, 1915.
18. Moreland, *First Presbyterian Church,* pp. 55-58.
19. Dodds and Dodds, p. 78.

Calvert, William Garner, and Richard Riley. On this lot a church was erected.[20]

Jehovah's Witnesses. The religious group known officially as the Watch Tower and Bible Society, and popularly as Jehovah's Witnesses, located in Morgantown in 1915, meeting in the Garlow Building. They do not regard their group as a church, but emphasize the reading of the Bible and are required to "publish" or "witness" their belief to others, handing out literature, Bibles, and tracts of various kinds.[21]

Sheriff Wallace. John Bullen Wallace, sheriff of Monongalia County, died suddenly at City Hospital August 2, 1915, following an operation for appendicitis. He was born April 26, 1875, in Fair Spring, Maryland, and moved to Morgantown in 1893. He married Mary Jolliffe and they had four children, Marion, Marjorie, John, and Jean. He began his duties as sheriff January 1, 1913. Deputy E. E. White was appointed to succeed him.[22]

J. C. McVicker. A well-known Morgantown businessman, John Clarence McVicker, died February 17, 1915. The son of George Washington McVicker, he was born in Monongalia County in 1859.

He graduated from the Philadelphia College of Pharmacy about 1884 and was associated with the J. M. Reed pharmacy, on High Street, before starting a drugstore of his own, in 1892. He had inherited considerable property and by business acumen added to it, until he became moderately wealthy. He served four terms as county sheriff. He married Mrs. Alice Kramer, of Pittsburg.[23]

Thomas Jerome Meeks. A retired farmer and Morgantown storekeeper, Thomas J. Meeks, died February 12, 1915. The son of Joseph and Sarah Meeks, he was born in Mansfield, Ohio, March 9, 1838, and was brought to Morgantown by his parents about 1845. He married Miss Linnie Vance, daughter of Addison and Mary Vance.[24]

20. Dodds and Dodds, p. 88. The church was dedicated in 1916 by Rev. Daniel Westfall.
21. Dodds and Dodds, pp. 79, 80.
22. *Post-Chronicle*, August 2, 1915.
23. *Post-Chronicle*, February 17, 1915.
24. *Post-Chronicle*, February 12, 1915; vol. 3, pp. 561, 680, 701.

Virginia Berkshire. Mrs. Virginia Berkshire, daughter of Zackwell and Elizabeth Morgan, died February 17, 1915. She was born September 29, 1843. She married Nicholas W. Berkshire, who died in 1903, and was survived by four daughters, Mrs. Stella (John M.) Gregg, and Mrs. Elizabeth (W. E.) Rumsey, Mrs. Mayme (Robert) Woodhull, and Mrs. Mattie (F. M.) Dawson.[25]

Miscellany. In 1915: Virginia, wife of Isaiah Warren, died in April; she was a daughter of Dr. Charles McLane and was born in 1836 (Callahan, p. 97). . . . The Dixy Theatre opened in the Brock-White-Courtney Building, in the space formerly occupied by the post office (Callahan, p. 279). . . . A great revival was held at the new Highland Park Church in February (Dodds and Dodds, p. 83). . . . Morgan District voters on September 18 approved a road bond issue by a tally of 1,168 to 565; Union District rejected a similar proposal by a vote of 154 to 108—a three-fifths majority was required (*Post-Chronicle,* September 20, 1915). . . . The Highland Park M.E. Church was dedicated on January 24; the pastor was Rev. E. J. Heller (*Post-Chronicle,* January 25, 1915). . . . George W. Gamble, farmer and horse dealer of Rock Forge, died February 4; he was born May 2, 1827 (*Post-Chronicle,* February 5). . . . John Stein, a Star City glassworker, was killed when struck by a B.&O. train (*Post-Chronicle,* April 6, 1915). . . . Morgantown's "great white way," consisting of sixty-six pedestal lights along High Street, was turned on July 17; the street will probably be "the best lighted . . . in the world" (*Post-Chronicle,* July 17, 1915). . . . The Nelson Glass Plant at Van Voorhis was constructed, to manufacture preserving jars (*Post-Chronicle,* July 22, 1915). . . . The Clay District board of education voted to build a high school building, at a cost of about eight thousand dollars (*Post-Chronicle,* July 23, 1915). . . . Horse racing at the Morgantown track, scheduled for mid-August, was canceled because of rain and poor attendance, leaving owners disappointed (*Post-Chronicle,* August 13, 1915). . . . A lodge known as Figli del Sole was organized by local Italians (*Post-Chronicle,* August 16, 1915). . . . Professional auto races were featured at the fairgrounds on September 25, but only a small crowd attended (*Post-Chronicle,* September 27, 1915). . . . City Council awarded a contract to B. M. Chaplin to construct an eighteen-inch sewer along

25. *Post-Chronicle,* February 17, 1915.

High Street from Pleasant to Walnut and down Walnut to Chestnut (*Post-Chronicle*, October 14, 1915). . . . A new oil well at Mooresville, drilled by the Carnegie Natural Gas Company on the Pierce Tennant farm, came in as a good producer (*Post-Chronicle*, October 30, 1915). . . . Equal Suffrage meetings were being held by women (*Post-Chronicle*, November 27, 1915). . . . Charles Montgomery Babb, Morgantown civic leader, died June 10 (*Post-Chronicle*, June 10, 1915).

CHAPTER ONE HUNDRED FORTY

1916

In a way, 1916 marked the beginning of a very dramatic new chapter in the history of Monongalia County. The long-talked-of program for the construction of paved roads finally got under way.

The lid-opener in this program was the Morgan District bond issue. It was to be expected that the first construction would tie onto the few paved streets of Morgantown and extend outwards from the center of the community.

Towards Good Roads.[1] In February John M. Gregg, county clerk, prepared the bonds for the $300,000 bond issue, and W. S. Downs, engineer in charge of the work, announced that the first roads to be improved would be the Beverly Pike, the Deckers Creek road, Charles Avenue, the Cheat River road, the Star City road, and the Van Voorhis road. The entire length of the planned construction was fifteen miles and the estimated cost was $20,000 per mile. The roads were to be fourteen feet wide, except for the Cheat road, which was to be sixteen feet wide.

Bids were advertised, beginning March 1, for 8.6 miles of improvement. The bids received ranged from $14,000 to $18,000 per mile for concrete and from $20,000 to $24,000 for brick. Contracts were awarded in April to the Hottell Company, of Pulaski, Virginia, for portions of the Cheat River, Beverly, and Deckers Creek roads, and to the McCormick Company, of Morgantown, for the Star City and Van Voorhis roads. The Deckers Creek and Van Voorhis roads were to be of concrete and the others brick on a concrete base.

Trouble arose immediately. The difficulty was the same as that

1. See Core, "Out of the Mud," *Westover Observer*, July 12, 1956, first of a series of weekly columns.

which was to confront road builders for a decade and more to come: the selection of the proper route. Sixty residents appeared before the county court to protest a proposed change in the Deckers Creek road, which was to begin on Brockway Avenue and extend by way of the Deckers Creek bridge and the Sulphur Spring to Sabraton. Without a similar situation from past experience to fall back on, the county court took the easy way out and approved the demands of the protesters. The court was later to regret this decision.

McCormick started grading the Star City road on April 13, planning to finish the grading before starting to pave the road. The grade was to be twenty feet wide, providing a three-foot shoulder on each side of the fourteen-foot roadway. By May 2 it was reported that the grading was 40 percent completed. A teamsters' strike on May 5 delayed work on this project and on the Easton road. The teamsters demanded a wage increase from five dollars to six dollars a day and a working day of nine rather than ten hours. The strike lasted only one day, however, for rural teamsters were hired at the old wage scale. Then McCormick "went modern" and purchased two motor trucks to supplement the work done by the teams and wagons. But operations in Star City were then held up because the town council asked a minimum grade of 15.5 percent on the river hill, while the county court proposed a grade of 13.9 percent.

Work on the Easton road was started on April 22 and fifteen hundred feet had been graded by May 2. About forty laborers, imported from Virginia, were living in temporary shanties near the scene of operations.

On May 19 the work of grading the Deckers Creek road began at The Hogback but by June 26 the county court had again changed its mind about the location of the road and decided to follow the original plan, in order to avoid three railroad crossings, improve the alignment and keep the road above high water. Forty residents of the area went angrily away from a second meeting with the court and appealed to the State Supreme Court for an injunction restraining the county commissioners from making the change. The injunction was granted on August 5; litigation continued to hold up the work throughout the summer and fall and, finally, L. V. Harner and others won a second injunction against the proposed relocation.

Winter now brought a close to the road building activities of 1916. Only a feeble start had been made, despite the enthusiasm with which the work began. Pioneering, inefficient methods, inexperienced laborers, and endless litigation had combined to waste the taxpayers' money, delay construction, and produce unsatisfactory results.

M.&W. Passenger Train. On January 27, 1916, the first passenger train, with invited guests, ran over the line between Cassville and Price, a distance of about six miles. At Core, the only village on the section, the one-coach train was excitedly greeted by welcoming citizens who waved their hands to the train crew or

Fig. 102. M.&W. passenger train at Cassville. (Courtesy Grace Rinehart Worley.)

crowded to the station to be on the first scheduled train. Stacy Stephens, teacher in the Core one-room school, dismissed his pupils from their classes to see the village's first passenger train. The regular schedule went into effect on January 31. The train left Cassville for Price at 8:10 a.m. and 3:40 p.m., weekdays, and at 2:10 p.m. Sundays. Returning, the train left Price at 9:05 a.m. weekdays and at 4:35 p.m. daily. Immediate connection was made at Cassville with interurban cars for Morgantown. Freight service was made three days a week.[2]

Ex-governor William E. Glasscock, on August 26, was appointed receiver for the railroad, which had declared bankruptcy. It was hoped that the receivership would make possible the extension of the line to Blacksville. From Price westwards the grading was nearly completed, ready for track laying.

The construction had been authorized following the passage of bond issues by Morgan and Clay districts, whereby $325,000 worth of bonds were accepted. Several stockholders retired $123,000 of the company's $500,000 bonded indebtedness by giving their personal obligations.[3]

In November a contract was signed with H. D. Eichelberger, of Richmond, Virginia, for completion of the railroad from Price to Blacksville. At Blacksville, it was hoped to utilize the old trolley grade (p. 385) to Waynesburg, thence to build to Elm Grove and Wheeling as a coal-carrying railroad.[4]

West Virginia University. Two significant events in the history of the university took place in 1916. First and foremost, Frank Butler Trotter was made president, effective July 1. For two years he had served as acting president (and as dean of the College of Arts and Sciences), while the board of regents sought the "proper person" for the presidency. Without putting himself forward, during these two years, he had been able to secure funds for the needed expansion of the institution. The 1915 legislature had made appropriations for a new agriculture building, for a woman's hall, for a School of Medicine building, and to enlarge the engineering building.

By the spring of 1916 the search for the "proper person" had practically ceased and in June M. P. Shawkey, of the board of regents, announced that they had interviewed twenty to thirty persons for the position, and that they had selected the acting president as "the best one available." In accepting the appointment, which paid a salary of $4,800, President Trotter said that the search for the "ideal man" would continue and that his resignation would be available when he was located.[5]

2. *New Dominion,* January 28, 1916.
3. *New Dominion,* August 28, 1916.
4. *New Dominion,* November 4, 1916.
5. Ambler, p. 542. See *Post-Chronicle,* June 14, 1916.

The second significant event was that, for the first time in history, the student enrollment passed the one thousand mark at the beginning of the 1916-17 term. It was noteworthy that this school year marked the fiftieth anniversary of the establishment of the institution.[6]

Dr. J. M. Callahan was named dean of the College of Arts and Sciences, to succeed the president. The university purchased 590 acres of land on the "Mile Ground" for use by the college of agriculture, at a cost of $66,978.30, paid by Monongalia County. Prof. C. B. Canaday was made head of the Latin department. Alex H. Forman was made head of the electrical engineering department, following the death of Prof. William E. Dickinson on November 4, 1915, and, also in 1916, J. B. Grumbein became head of steam, gas, and experimental engineering. Leo Carlin was appointed to a law professorship. G. A. Bergy was placed in charge of the department of pharmacy.

The new Medical Building, on Beechurst Avenue, was com-

Fig. 103. Medical Building on Beechurst Avenue. (West Virginia University.)

6. *New Dominion,* September 21, 1916.

pleted and occupied in 1916 and at the time was considered "admirably adapted" to the needs of a two-year medical course.[7]
Coach Sol. S. Metzger resigned in the spring of 1916, a big disappointment for football promoters. Elzie Tobin and Mont M. McIntire were made co-coaches and developed an outfit that did well against formidable Eastern teams. WVU lost to the University of Pennsylvania by a score of 3 to 0, tied 7 to 7 with Dartmouth, tied 0 to 0 with Rutgers. West Virginia Wesleyan was defeated by a score of 54 to 7.[8]

First Chautauqua. Morgantown's first chautauqua ended on July 6, with a song recital by Mme Dora de Philippe, of the Chicago Grand Opera. "In this city where good music is always received with enthusiasm and correct appreciation, the singer made a lasting impression on the great audience which filled the seats under the chautauqua tent."[9]

Modeled on a system of popular education developed at Chautauqua Lake, New York, beginning in 1874, the local chautauquas featured lectures, plays, music, etc., and were quite successful at the time. National lyceum booking agents supplied lecturers and musicians who traveled from one community to another to appear at the approximately four hundred local chautauquas.

Gasoline Supplies. In 1916 drip gasoline (p. 391) was being produced at various places in Monongalia County, including Core and Statler Run. From Core, some of it was shipped in tank cars over the M.&W. railroad; from both plants, considerable quantities were hauled away in drums on wagons and trucks.

In October the Morgantown community was suffering from a gasoline shortage and on Sunday, October 29, not a single gallon was available. One dealer gathered up his drums and brought in a supply from the Core gasoline plant, the only gasoline available on Monday.[10]

The Masonic Temple. The new Masonic Temple, at the corner of High and Willey streets, was opened March 16. Special trains supplemented the scheduled trains in bringing hundreds of

7. Ambler, p. 540.
8. Ambler, p. 581.
9. *New Dominion*, July 7, 1916.
10. *New Dominion*, October 31, 1916.

Fig. 104. Monongahela Railway Depot, Westover. Note streetcar. (From an old postcard.)

visitors from nearby communities in West Virginia and Pennsylvania.[11] Formal dedication ceremonies were held on May 30, with Lewis N. Tavenner, of Parkersburg, delivering the dedicatory address.

The original charter was dated December 15, 1812, when the Most Worshipful Solomon Jacobs, Grand Master of the Most Worshipful Grand Lodge of Virginia, granted it to Morgan Town Union Lodge No. 93 (vol. 2, p. 399).

The lodge was rechartered December 16, 1846, after a period of dormancy, by the Grand Lodge of Virginia, signed by Most Worshipful Sidney S. Baxter, Grand Master, naming Worshipful Peter T. Laishley, Master; John Bowlby, Senior Warden; and John Beck, Junior Warden.

The Virginia charter was endorsed by the Grand Master of West Virginia on May 11, 1865, the date of the formation of the Grand Lodge of West Virginia. A new charter was granted January 24, 1867, signed by Most Worshipful William I. Bates, Grand

11. *Post-Chronicle*, March 17, 1916.

Master, and Right Worshipful Thomas H. Logan, Grand Secretary. Officers of the lodge at the time were Worshipful William A. Hanway, Master; William W. Dering, Senior Warden; and William P. Willey, Junior Warden.

The number of the lodge was changed from 93 to 4, and the designation thereafter was Morgantown Union Lodge No. 4 of Ancient Free and Accepted Masons.[12]

Evansdale. "Morgantown's modern suburb," Evansdale, was opened to the purchasing public in October, as real estate promoters immediately began to capitalize on the as-yet-incomplete Star City road. The Evansdale Corporation had laid out numerous streets, with water mains and sewers, and had built fifteen hundred feet of concrete sidewalks.[13]

Greer Post Office. A new post office, named Greer, was established May 14, 1915, on the M.&K. Railroad on Deckers Creek, about eight miles east of Morgantown. Roy M. Clear was the first postmaster. The office was named for Herbert C. and Agnes Greer who had established the Greer Limestone Company at that point.

Rock Forge Methodist Church. The old Rock Forge Church, built about 1872, was extensively renovated in 1916, while Rev. G. P. Federer was pastor. A sum of twenty-five hundred dollars was collected, the building was raised about four feet, a stone foundation was laid, and a furnace installed. Much of the labor and equipment was donated. The church was dedicated on Thanksgiving Day.[14]

Auto Accident Results in Death. The Ford automobile which Grover Conner was driving slipped on a muddy road on Days Run and went over a steep declivity, resulting in the death of his sister, Mrs. Maggie Conner Morgan, who was pinned beneath the car. Others in the car escaped injury. They had been out for a Sunday afternoon drive and had been caught in a rain, but had placed chains on the wheels to finish the journey.[15]

12. Information from *Special Communication Commemorating the 150th Anniversary of the First Charter from the Grand Lodge of Virginia.*

13. *New Dominion*, October 19, 30, 1916.

14. Dodds and Dodds, p. 85.

15. *New Dominion*, July 25, 1916.

Thomas Reiner. A well-known citizen of Morgantown, Thomas Reiner, died April 11, 1916; he was born near Connellsville, Pennsylvania, October 31, 1838. He was a schoolteacher and cashier of the Bank of Dunbar. He married Elizabeth Porter and they had four children, Ada, Sarah May, Phineas Porter, and Pearl. The family moved to Morgantown in 1902 in order to educate their children.[16]

E. L. Mathers. Eugene L. Mathers, prominent Morgantown printer, died August 16. The son of Dr. Joseph Ray and Drusilla Ann Morgan Mathers, he was born in Monongalia County August 19, 1854. He was a grandson of Rev. E. Mathers, a pastor of the Morgantown M.P. church and a great-grandson of Zackquill Morgan, the founder of Morgantown. He learned the printer's trade, worked for the *Morgantown Post* and later with his son, Max, established a shop of his own.

He married Arthelia Morgan and they had six children, Mrs. George Walsh, Mrs. George Rust, Mrs. Homer Hoffman, Max, Harry H., and Carl.[17]

George Hall. One of the oldest and best known citizens of Morgantown, George Hall, died on December 1. He was born at Uffington, January 25, 1829, and came to Morgantown in 1845. He was apprenticed to James Kerns, in the trade of building wagons and engaged in the work at Uffington for a short time on his own. In 1850 he started for California, got as far as Portsmouth, Ohio, worked at his trade there for a year, and then returned to Morgantown, where he married Alcinda Cunningham. He worked with Fairchild, Laughead and Company until the outbreak of the Civil War, during which he was employed in the quartermaster's department under Capt. E. P. Fitch in repairing wagons. After the war he reentered the service of Fairchild, Laughead and Company.[18]

Miscellany. In 1916: Cox and Baker erected a three-story building on High Street on the site of the Stag Restaurant (*Post-Chronicle*, January 1, 1916). . . . Lynn Hastings was selected as county superintendent of schools, to fill the unexpired term of

16. *Post-Chronicle*, April 12, 1916.
17. *New Dominion*, August 17, 1916.
18. *New Dominion*, December 1, 1916.

Harry E. Brookover, deceased (*Post-Chronicle*, January 8, 1916).
. . . A total of forty-nine manufacturing establishments was located at Morgantown (*Post-Chronicle*, January 10, 1916). . . . An M.&W. interurban car bound for Cassville crashed into a locomotive at Boyers Mill; engineer P. H. Trevillian stopped the engine quickly, averting a more serious accident; no one was hurt (*Post-Chronicle*, February 29, 1916). . . . Because the franchise had expired, the city of Morgantown began tearing up tracks of the Morgantown and Southern on Grand Street extension and Dorsey Avenue; Mayor James A. Cox said that "it was his candid opinion . . . that the building of the line was a scheme to aid in the sale of lots by J. W. Wiles" (*Post-Chronicle*, April 29, 1916). . . . Robert August Andris, aged seventy-six, a former window glass blower, died at the home of his daughter, Mrs. N. B. Weibel, of Morgantown; he was born near Charleroi, Belgium (*Post-Chronicle*, May 23, 1916). . . . E. S. Baumgartner, manager of the Dixy Theater since its opening, resigned and was succeeded by E. B. Shaffer (*Post-Chronicle*, June 19, 1916). . . . Miss Eudora Ramsey, of Greenville, South Carolina, gave a speech on woman suffrage to a large crowd on the courthouse square (*Post-Chronicle*, June 19, 1916). . . . Nora Bradley was drowned in the river near Lock 11 (*New Dominion*, July 24, 1916). . . . Eureka Tank No. 62, in the Tank Field, was struck by lightning and ten thousand barrels of oil destroyed in a spectacular fire (*New Dominion*, July 24, 1916). . . . Rev. M. H. Steele, son of Moses Steele, died in Westover; he had been a teacher and an M.P. minister (*New Dominion*, July 8, 1916). . . . Harrison Groves, a student in the university, was drowned in the Monongahela River at Granville when his skiff collided with a motor boat (*New Dominion*, August 12, 1916). . . . With fifteen students enrolled, a high school for black boys and girls opened on Beechurst Avenue; Roscoe C. Clarkson was teacher (*New Dominion*, September 22, 1916). . . . The tinplate mill was being prepared for burning coal instead of gas (*New Dominion*, September 16, 1916). . . . Mrs. Carrie Chapman Catt gave an address on woman's suffrage in Morgantown (*New Dominion*, October 31, 1916). . . . The Tait mine at Jimtown was sold by the Great Scott Coal and Coke Company to Fred Tropf (*New Dominion*, October 24, 1916). . . . Morgantown city council granted a franchise to the Morgantown Interurban Railway Company, which proposed a trolley line to

Point Marion, Pennsylvania (*New Dominion,* October 3, 1916). . . . The old Wightman glass factory was sold to a new company to operate as the Beaumont Glass Company (*New Dominion,* October 3, 1916). . . . Admiral French E. Chadwick delivered the Phi Beta Kappa address on December 4 (*New Dominion,* December 4, 1916). . . . The Scotts Run Coal Company, of Morgantown, was incorporated (*New Dominion,* December 23, 1916). . . . The Union Building and Loan Company was established July 1 at Morgantown (Callahan, p. 280). . . . Major H. B. Van Voorhis, a Civil War veteran, died in Riverside February 22 (*Post-Chronicle,* February 22, 1916). . . . Frank P. Hummel, fifty-eight, minister at the Spruce Street M.P. Church, died at the pulpit on January 20, just as he finished the morning sermon (*New Dominion,* January 21, 1916). . . . Morris J. Garrison, well-known businessman and civic leader of Wadestown, died February 18; he was born August 24, 1843 (*New Dominion,* February 19, 1916).

CHAPTER ONE HUNDRED FORTY-ONE

1917

In 1914 nearly half a century had gone by since the close of the bitter and agonizing American Civil War. For the world as a whole nearly a century had gone by since the close of the Napoleonic wars, when many nations had been involved in conflict simultaneously. This long period of world peace was rudely brought to a close in midsummer of 1914 when German troops marched into France. An astonished world which had come to believe war was outmoded could scarcely believe the black headlines that brought the fearful news day by day. It quickly became evident that the most terrible and destructive war in human history was under way.

At the first the war was largely confined to Europe. In the United States the initial feeling of surprise gave way to excitement and a throbbing of increased enterprise as the economy reacted to huge war orders that kept factories working at full production. For Monongalia County this boom was expressed, during the next two or three years, most notably in the opening of the vast coal resources on the western side of the river, chiefly in the Scotts Run area of Cass District.

World War. Gradually it became apparent that the United States would not escape a more serious involvement in the war. On April 7, 1917, Congress declared war against Germany and her allies and a more sober feeling settled over the nation. No longer were our citizens just reaping huge benefits from the war—now Americans, too, would contribute, in anxiety and agony, in human lives. Congress enacted the selective draft law in May 1917 and many young men, some of whom had never been away from home before, marched off to serve, to fight, some to die.

Registration Day for men of military age was June 5, and in Monongalia County 2,685 men were enrolled. A two-billion-dollar

451

Liberty Bond issue was being offered; Monongalia County's
share was about $300,000. Monongalia County's share of an
American Red Cross drive was $15,000; by the end of June the
county had raised $23,000.

War gardens were planted, cultivated, harvested, and canning
schools were held for women, under the direction of Miss Ada
Compton.

Reports soon began filtering back of the deaths of men in the
service. Sergeant Barton Core, Company L, of the National Guard,
died of pneumonia on July 14, the first in a long list from the
county.

Names began to be drawn on July 20 for induction into the
armed services, and Charles W. Moore had the distinction of
being the first one drawn in the county. By August 21, 182 men
were ready to be sent to the camp of mobilization. The first six to
leave were Roy Nelson, Wardney C. Snarr, Louis Gidel, Marcelus
M. Rokos, Fred H. Hood, and John L. Barnes. Banquets were
being held in churches for the departing men. Thousands of
people turned out to bid the contingents farewell at the railway
depot. For the fourth time, on October 27, the people turned out
to say farewell to a contingent; this time it was colored people:
Richard D. Warrick, Irvin White, Randolph Hardy, and Charles
Edwards.

The Fiftieth Anniversary. In the midst of the expanding war effort, West Virginia University observed its fiftieth anniversary
with fitting ceremonies. In one of his first appointments after becoming president, Dr. Trotter had named a committee to prepare
the program. The committee's program was held in 1917, but a
controversial feature was postponed, namely, the awarding of
honorary doctorates upon seventeen persons of distinction, mostly natives of the state. The committee had ignored the fact that
former President Raymond had outlawed such practices which
some persons described as a desecration of the purposes of the
university (rather than a recognition of merit, as the committee
maintained).

Prof. E. N. Zern, professor of mining engineering, resigned in
1917. He had been responsible for the introduction of mining extension instruction for the Short Course in mining, first offered in
the 1913 Summer School, and helped pave the way for an Engi-

neering Experiment Station.[1] He was succeeded by A. C. Callen, a graduate of Lehigh University, an aggressive and ambitious leader. Prof. R. L. Morris was named head of railway and highway engineering and surveying.

Prof. F. C. Butterfield, head of the piano department in the school of music, was given leave for service with the YMCA with American troops in France.[2]

The Reserve Officers Training Corps[3] was expanding rapidly, largely under the stimulus of the war. The 1915 legislature authorized the admission of six hundred cadets, entitled to specified privileges, exemptions, and benefits, and also with opportunity of working for incentive awards. Because of the increased enrollment the corps was organized as a regiment of infantry, with "Field, Staff, and Band, and twelve companies." The office of cadet colonel was set up; colonels named were Dorsey Brannon (1916-17) and D. A. Christopher (1917-18). The old gray uniform was suspended and the regulation olive drab U.S. army uniform was adopted. A rifle team, composed of D. A. Christopher, A. M. Miller, A. K. Carroll, C. W. McDowell, and K. L. Marshall, made a perfect score in the last contest of 1916-17, and thereby won a world record.[4]

West Virginia was attracting national attention through its football team, which in the 1917 season won six games, tied one, and lost three. The team defeated Navy, 7-0, the first defeat of famed Coach Gil Dobie in twelve years. The hero of the game was Frank Harris, a back who ran thirty-five yards for the only touchdown.[5]

Telephone Merger. Morgantown's two telephone systems were merged during 1917 into the newly formed Chesapeake and Potomac Telephone Company, operating under a domestic West Virginia charter bill. The properties of the Central District Telephone Company and the Consolidated Telephone Company were joined to make for greater efficiency in operating and developing the constantly growing system. F. R. Dunning was local manager

1. Established by order of the state board of education June 24, 1921.
2. Ambler, pp. 514, 534, 547.
3. The old University cadet corps became the ROTC with the passage of the National Defense Act of 1916.
4. Ambler, p. 561.
5. Constantine, p. 15.

454 THE MONONGALIA STORY

for the new company.[6] A dual franchise was thereby eliminated and all telephones in Morgantown were tied into the same central board.

All over West Virginia a similar sort of telephone development was being worked out. Small, local, independent companies would be formed before the Bell system reached the communities and the Bell system would acquire the local companies by purchase. Local citizens would realize that their home companies were being gobbled up by a constantly growing conglomerate which looked upon the independents with lofty disdain but they could not complain because the nature of the commodity furnished was such that the monopoly was in a position to give better service.

"The perfection of techniques making possible unlimited long-distance conversations instantly and radically changed the place of the telephone in American life—socially, economically, and politically. Suddenly it was a national rather than a local phenomenon—one that almost immediately came to be regarded as a national rather than a local necessity. People assimilated national telephone into their minds as if into their bodies—as if it were the result of a new step in human evolution that increased the range of their voices to the limits of the national map."[7]

The actual change-over took place on Saturday evening, September 1. Operators answering calls from Consolidated (the old People's) company telephones in the Odd Fellows building (where they had been since the beginning, in 1895) requested that Bell instruments be used.[8]

The Scotts Run Coal Field. Despite the fact that outcrops of coal had been noted in the Monongahela Valley in pioneer days,[9] Monongalia County was nearly a century and a half old before mining on a substantial scale was begun. Up to the time of the Civil War, coal in western Virginia, in general, was used only by a cross-roads blacksmith or by a settler whose cabin stood near an outcrop.

By the close of the Civil War coal "banks" were beginning to be

6. *New Dominion*, January 5, 1917.
7. John Brooks, *Telephone: The First Hundred Years*, 1975, pp. 141, 142.
8. *Post-Chronicle*, September 1, 1917.
9. See vol. 3, pp. 133-37.

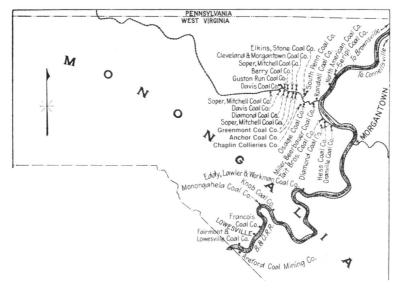

Fig. 105-A. Map showing location of the Scotts Run Mining Field. (Morgantown Chamber of Commerce.)

Fig. 105-B. Pursglove Mining Camp. (Courtesy Mary Behner Christopher.)

opened for local sale in Monongalia County. In southern West Virginia operations on a fairly large scale began in 1873, when the Chesapeake and Ohio Railroad was completed across the state. The production of coal in West Virginia rose from 444,648 tons in 1863 to 1,000,000 in 1873 and 1,225,833 in 1883.

In Monongalia County the first important commercial operations began in 1886 at Beechwood where mines were opened and coke ovens constructed shortly after the completion of the railroad from Fairmont to Morgantown.

But not until 1917, when the United States entered the World War and there came a sudden unprecedented demand for coal did Monongalia County become a large-scale producer. Almost overnight Scotts Run, in Cass District, by a remarkable boom, became one of West Virginia's greatest industrial districts, with a pronounced influx of population.

Dr. I. C. White, state geologist, had pointed out the basic reason for this development:[10] "First, at the base, and lying approximately 100 feet above the Monongahela river, . . . at the mouth of Scotts Run, comes the great Pittsburgh bed, 8 to 10 feet thick with its wealth of pure coal famous all over the world, for steam, gas, coke, and general fuel purposes. It passes below drainage level about one mile up Scotts Run, but underlies the entire course of [the M.&W.] railway at easy shafting depths, being only 500 feet below drainage at Blacksville. Hence, the line of the railway [then projected to run to Wheeling] will pass over the widest and richest belt of virgin Pittsburgh coal between Morgantown and Blacksville and on to Wheeling yet remaining undeveloped anywhere in the United States. . . . Then, only 40 feet above the Pittsburgh seam comes the Redstone coal, 4½ to 5½ feet thick of wonderfully pure fuel, . . . while only 60 feet higher comes another coal bed, the Sewickley, or Mapletown of the oil well drillers, with its 5½ to 6½ feet of matchless steam, domestic and general fuel, so that here on Scotts Run, we often have twenty feet of splendid merchantable coal all in the same hill above water level."

Dr. White was writing to ex-Governor William E. Glasscock,

10. Morgantown Chamber of Commerce, *Industrial and Business Survey* (1921), pp. 10, 12. A long article by Dr. White, on the coalfields of West Virginia and Monongalia County had appeared in the *Weekly Post* as early as March 24, 1888.

who was then receiver for the Morgantown and Wheeling Railroad, already beset by financial woes. Traffic was very light, and the prospective mining operations seemed most promising. "As your railway passes up Scotts Run," Dr. White continued, "one after the other of these three beds dip down and pass under water level, and at two miles up the same all have disappeared below the grade of your railway, but they are present at moderate depths until a fourth seam, the Waynesburg, makes its appearance in the hills near Cassville. . . , at a vertical interval of 260 feet above the Sewickley bed, with a thickness of 7 to 8 feet. True, the coal in this bed is not so pure as in the three others, . . . but it is a valuable fuel and a large area of it is accessible above water level along your railway. It passes below the grade of the same near the high bridge over a branch of Scotts Run, one-half mile above Cassville.

"One would think that these FOUR splendid coal beds are all that any district should claim, but not so with this one. At 175 feet above the Waynesburg bed, and cropping out along this railway from the deep cut at the summit above Cassville, all the way to Pentress, . . . we find another coal bed, the Washington, not so pure or valuable as the others, but nevertheless having a large quantity of good fuel with a thickness of three to four feet. . . .

"Nowhere else in the entire Appalachian basin are four coal beds of merchantable dimensions present in the Monongalia series . . . , so that having seen all the great coal districts of the country, the writer has found nothing to equal in fuel wealth the region tributary to the Morgantown and Wheeling Railway."

During 1917 and 1918 dozens of coal tipples were erected along the first two miles of Scotts Run and near Granville and Maidsville, along the river. The Monongahela Railway ran along the river, serving the mines there, but up Scotts Run there was only the trolley line to handle the traffic.

The enormous increase in freight was too great a burden for the light rails and the uneven, poorly ballasted roadbed. Wrecks were frequent.

Tipples constructed in 1916 included the Berry, near Cassville, and the Haymond, at Barker. During 1917 many others were built, including the Randall (at Randall), Elkins (Osage), Osage (Osage), Cleveland and Morgantown (Barker), Scotts Run (Pursglove), Liberty (Berry), Gilbert (Gustin Run), Higgins (Cassville), and Cassville (Cassville).

At Charlotte (later Osage) and Stumptown (later Pursglove) many residences were hastily built to accommodate the rapidly increasing population. The men could walk to the nearby mines; men, women, and children either rode the passenger trains (two a day) or walked one or two miles to Jimtown to catch the trolley for the trip to Morgantown. The highway up Scotts Run was unpaved and a sea of mud during the winter.

"The opening of the vast coal resources furnished labor for an ever-increasing number of operations and miners. . . . During the period of the World War several coal operators and coal brokers accumulated comfortable fortunes in the abnormally high prices of coal; and workers in the mines, with only short periods of experience and training, received wages far in excess of the modest salaries paid to college professors who had spent years in preparation for their work."[11]

Road Building. By the beginning of 1917 a total of $129,261.07 had been spent of the contract price on the Morgan District road projects, with the program still far from completion, delayed by injunctions and inexperienced workmen. In March the county court opened bids for the construction of the remaining roads designated in the 1916 bond issue. The experience of 1916, and the sharply advancing price rises due to a war-time boom, resulted in much higher costs than in the previous year. The bids were not less than $24,000.00 a mile for concrete and $35,000.00 per mile for brick.

In February Judge George C. Sturgiss handed down a decision favoring the county court in the case of L. V. Harner et al, plaintiffs against the court concerning a proposed relocation of the Deckers Creek road. Further opposition by the group of protestants, nevertheless, led the State Supreme Court, in May, to grant a permanent injunction against the county commissioners, restraining them from changing the road.

The construction season was already well advanced and work continued to be delayed by many debates and issues. People were demanding the completion of the Deckers Creek road, "already half done," to accommodate hundreds of employees of the Ameri-

11. Callahan, p. 275.

can Sheet and Tin Plate mill in Sabraton, and in August, representatives of several manufacturing plants in the area appeared before the court asking for resumption of work on the road, "in the direction it was originally laid out."

But highway construction only faintly interested Monongalia County residents in 1917, with all activities being directed towards stopping the Kaiser.

Of the twelve projects contemplated in the original Morgan District bond issue proposal, only four had been completed by the end of the year, and only one other was under way. Even the completed roads were in poor condition, with slips and slides, poor drainage, broken pavement, and even totally impassable sections.

The Cheat Road had been built to the Union District line at Easton, a distance of 2.57 miles. The Beverly-Evansville pike had been paved to the Clinton District line, 1.25 miles. The Star City road had been built to the railroad crossing at the ferry, 2.56 miles. Finally, the Van Voorhis road had been extended 0.55 of a mile from the junction of the Star City road towards Van Voorhis. This represented only 6.93 miles out of the ambitious fifteen-mile program originally outlined. The Deckers Creek road, subject of months of bitter disputes, was half completed and virtually impassable. The other four projects included had not even been started.

Probably only the overwhelming interest in the progress of the war saved the members of the county court from more severe criticism. They were doubtless little to be blamed, since they were the pioneers in a new field of endeavor. Later supervisors were to profit by the mistakes and failures, as well as the less-emphasized successes of these beginners.[12]

Christian and Missionary Alliance. A new congregation, the Christian and Missionary Alliance Church, was formed during the summer of 1917 as the result of a tent meeting conducted by Rev. D. Hayes Permar and Rev. A. R. Fesmire. The Rev. Mr. Permar became the first pastor of a group of twenty-five members. A lot was purchased on Kingwood Street and a building was constructed before the end of the year.[13]

---

12. Core, "Out of the Mud," *Westover Observer*, July 19, 1956.
13. Dodds and Dodds, p. 73.

Fire Chief Killed in Blaze. James H. Kennedy, chief of the Morgantown fire department, was killed November 14 in fighting a blaze that destroyed the Hirschman Building on High Street. A portion of the front wall fell on him as he was directing the work. He was survived by his wife and two sons, Harold and Robert. The building housed a pool room and barber shop.[14] John R. Hare succeeded Kennedy as fire chief.

M.&W. Schedule Changes. The development of the Scotts Run coal field had a serious effect on the line of the Morgantown and Wheeling Railroad. Many mines were opened, tipples built, sidetracks constructed, and the traffic soon proved too great a burden for the uneven roadbed and the worn-out rolling stock, hitherto serving only a sparsely settled countryside.

At first coal trains were operated under the trolley wire but the danger was apparent, and after the summer of 1917, the trolley operated only between Randall and Morgantown, while the passenger train met it at Randall, instead of Cassville. The passenger service, meanwhile, had been extended from Price to Blacksville. But with many wrecks of coal trains, the passenger service by October had become most untrustworthy.[15]

New Railroad Started. In an apparent attempt to divert coal traffic from the ailing M.&W., the Monongahela Railway early in December was working vigorously at three different places near Randall on the grade for a spur line up Scotts Run. The legality of the line was questioned by the M.&W., however, and the work was stopped before Christmas.

Robert Cushing White. Robert C. White died on February 17, 1917, aged eighty years. He had bought the first railroad passenger ticket into Morgantown (p. 94). He and his wife, Mary Ann (DeWitt), had sold their 320-acre farm in Ohio to move to Morgantown in order for their family to have the educational advantages afforded by West Virginia University. In 1886, shortly after his arrival, he started Morgantown's first horse-drawn dairy delivery (milk five cents a quart) and traded in coal and timber lands. His wife was an amateur botanist and the family

14. *Post-Chronicle,* November 14, 1917.
15. *Chronicles of Core,* p. 182.

spent much time camping along Cheat River, where she died of a stroke on her sixty-seventh birthday, August 13, 1901.

They had six children, DeWitt, Prescott Cushing, Charles Louis, Anna Bancroft, Stella Sexton, and Bennett Sexton, all of whom had graduated from the university by June 1897, the largest family of children graduated by the institution in its first half century.[16]

John W. Mason. Judge John William Mason died in Fairmont April 23, 1917. He was born in Clinton District, Monongalia County, January 13, 1842, and was educated in and taught in the public schools of that district. He served as sergeant in Battery F, West Virginia Artillery ("Maulsby's Battery") during the Civil War. After the war he served one year (1867-68) as principal of the preparatory school of West Virginia University.

Fig. 106. John W. Mason.   Fig. 107. Thomas E. Hodges.

In 1889 he was appointed by President Benjamin Harrison as commissioner of internal revenue and in June 1900 was appointed as judge of the circuit court to succeed John M. Hagans, deceased. He was later elected to the office and moved to Fairmont in 1901. He was reelected in 1904 and served until January 1, 1913.

16. *175th Anniversary...*, p 454.

Rev. J. A. Selby. At the West Virginia Methodist Conference Meeting in Morgantown in 1917 James Alfred Selby was elected president. He was born April 17, 1865, near Easton, the son of William and Sophia Selby. He joined the church at a revival held at Avery by Rev. John M. Conaway, son of Thornton and Elizabeth (Laishley) Conaway. He preached his first sermon at Eden. The first year of his ministry was in the Muskingum Conference, Ohio, and he served as president of that conference, so that his later election at Morgantown put him in the unusual position of having headed two separate conferences.[17]

Miscellany. In 1917: George S. Vance died on January 12 (*New Dominion*, January 12, 1917). . . . The largest public benefaction in the history of West Virginia took place in February when the trustees of the Lawrence A. Reyman estate transferred a 931-acre farm in Hardy County, with a herd of registered Ayrshire, to West Virginia University (*New Dominion*, February 13, 1917). . . . Morgantown and Fairmont businessmen were discussing formation of a company to operate packet boats to Pittsburgh (*New Dominion*, February 24, 1917). . . . Through their efforts the packet *Valley Gem* left Pittsburgh March 9, at 5:00 p.m. for Fairmont (*New Dominion*, March 7, 1917). . . . J. W. Wiles was still trying to build the Morgantown and Southern trolley line to South Park (*New Dominion*, March 20, 1917). . . . Richard E. Fast's 500-volume historical library was presented to the West Virginia University Library by Joseph H. McDermott (*New Dominion*, March 19, 1917). . . . Carl R. Beebe was named chief of police in Morgantown; James Kennedy was fire chief (*New Dominion*, May 2, 1917). . . . The residence of Dean C. R. Jones, on McLane Avenue, was destroyed by fire; two small children of Mr. and Mrs. R. E. Kerr were burned to death (*New Dominion*, May 4, 1917). . . . W. H. Davis was named manager of the Sabraton Tin Plate plant, now working at full capacity; the pay roll for the past two weeks was $52,000 (*New Dominion*, May 30, 1917). . . . James Deusenberry, a Cass District farmer, was killed on July 14 when hit by a Morgantown and Wheeling trolley car (*Post-Chronicle*, July 16, 1917). . . . A South Morgantown street car loaded with passengers was knocked out of commission when hit by an automobile at the corner of Cobun Avenue and Walnut

17. Barnes, pp. 129-33.

Street (*Post-Chronicle,* October 20, 1917). . . . Mrs. Nancy Hoffman, widow of N. N. Hoffman, died November 4; she was born February 27, 1844, the daughter of Josiah W. Saer (*Post-Chronicle,* November 5, 1917). . . . "Bringing Up Father," featuring Jiggs and Maggie, was a daily feature in the *New Dominion.* . . . William Sidney Laidley, of Charleston, died; an attorney, he was a son of John Osborn Laidley, and was an authority on state and local history (Callahan, p. 84). . . . The Cox and Baker Building, on High Street, was completed (Callahan, p. 272). . . . The Morgantown city council, influenced by the popularity of the commission form of government, which had been adopted by several state cities, appointed a charter committee which submitted a draft for a new charter; it was not approved, however (Callahan, p. 295). . . . Robert Garlow, son of John M. Garlow, was killed when hit by the B.&O. flyer near Star City on July 29 (*New Dominion,* July 30, 1917). . . . The Star Glass Company plant was destroyed by fire on December 11 (*Post-Chronicle,* December 11, 1917).

CHAPTER ONE HUNDRED FORTY-TWO

1918

The weather in Monongalia County is not often very spectacular but once in a while there is an exception. There was "the year without a summer" (1816), the big June frost (1859), and the year the river dried up (1930). The winter of 1917-18 was also remarkable.

From Christmas on the weather had been unusually cold and a thick layer of ice formed on the Monongahela River (and the Cheat, as well). By February, it was reported:

"Perhaps this city was never more completely ice-bound than it has been since yesterday morning shortly after it began to rain. . . . The streets were completely covered with clear ice. . . . Those living in the hill sections were practically marooned, as it was almost impossible to walk on the hilly streets. Grand and Park streets in South Park, which have been used for the past several weeks for coasting, were practically impassable and business today is almost at a standstill. Only a few teams and trucks are working."[1]

The Big Ice Gorges. The rain was raising the water level in streams and fear was felt that the heavy ice would form gorges and cause great damage. The *Post-Chronicle* on February 9 said an ice gorge had formed on Deckers Creek "at the short bend at Marilla" and was "backing the water up around the houses on the peninsula near the United States Window Glass company plant." The swinging footbridge across the creek was destroyed.

Shortly after midnight on Sunday morning, February 10, the huge bridge across Cheat River at Ice's Ferry was carried away by the ice.

"The ice gorge had been piled to a height of about 20 feet for

1. *Post-Chronicle,* February 7, 1918.

several days and there had been great uneasiness for the safety of the bridge for the past two weeks and shortly before midnight Saturday the immense gorge which extended from about a mile below the bridge to Albright began to move and the weight was irresistible and the large steel structure was swept away. . . .

"The first part of the bridge to give way was the long span on the Morgantown side of the river, which went out about 11 o'clock, as an automobile passed over the bridge as late as 10 o'clock at night. . . . Only part of the short span on the east side of the river is left hanging. . . .

"Both of the long spans of the bridge have completely disappeared as they seem to have been carried some distance down stream with the immense ice jam. The steel work on the bridge was 499 feet long, being composed of two spans of 240 feet each and a short span on the east side of the river of 119 feet. . . ."[2]

The bridge had been built in 1900 at a cost of about twenty-six thousand dollars. The destruction of the bridge cut off all travel

Fig. 108. Highway Bridge across Cheat River at Ice's Ferry.

2. *Post-Chronicle*, February 11, 1918.

between Cheat Neck and Morgantown except by way of Cheat Haven, Pennsylvania, where residents could get a train to the county seat. A ferry was established in the spring, when the ice disappeared.

At Morgantown: "The Valley Gem is still at the local wharf with its prow high and dry on the bank with one side and the rear of the boat under water. The house boats of the Monongahela Pleasure Craft company are high on the bank but surrounded by cakes of ice."[3]

Fig. 109. The packet boat *Valley Gem*, wrecked by ice gorge.

The *Valley Gem* was one of the last of the packet boats that ran between Morgantown and Pittsburgh. Freight was carried on the lower deck and passengers had staterooms lined with railed walkways on the upper deck. A dining room was provided. The boat, 150 feet long, usually left Morgantown in the early evening, arriving in Pittsburgh in the morning. But the packet boat service, started in 1889, was already well on the way out and scarcely

3. *Post-Chronicle*, February 12, 1918.

Fig. 110. M.&W. streetcar, with the big ice gorge in the Monongahela River.

survived the big ice gorge. Railroad passenger trains made the trip to Pittsburgh in only two or three hours and travelers were mostly in too big a hurry to use the leisurely, luxurious service provided by packet boats.

The gorge at Maidsville held for several days, closing the highway between Granville and Jimtown, and also closing the tracks of the trolley between those two points. When the water finally went down, the road and the trolley tracks were still impassable, covered with huge irregular blocks of ice that required a vast amount of hard work to remove. The road was open by February 17 but the trolley did not get through until the next day.

The War Comes to an End. The principal thought of Monongalia County people during 1918, as throughout America, was the war in Europe.

Daylight Saving Time began for the first time at 2:00 a.m. on Sunday, March 31, adding "one hour of daylight to the nation's efforts to win the war." Although expected to cause some stir, it was predicted that within a few days, "no one will note the difference."[4]

4. *Post*, March 30, 1918.

Monongalia County's share of the Third Liberty Loan was set at $575,000.[5] A group of 26 men entrained for war service on May 15, with fitting ceremonies.[6] Many others left, week after week. A huge parade, perhaps the greatest in numbers in Morgantown's history, was held on May 26 to mark the successful conclusion of the Red Cross drive.[7] On the second national registration day, June 5, a total of 255 Monongalia County men were registered.[8]

Citizens were encouraged to raise Victory Gardens. A thirteen-year-old boy, Robert Dugan, "the pride of Bridge Street," raised dozens of roasting ears, forty bushels of potatoes, etc.[9] Mrs. R. E. Lantz, doing her best to "can the kaiser," had put up 140 cans of tomatoes, one hundred glasses of jelly, etc.; she had picked three and a half bushels of blackberries.[10]

Mr. and Mrs. Solomon Wright, of Clay District, had the honor of having the most sons in the army; Leslie W., William, and Jesse G. were in service and a fourth son, James E., had died at Camp Lee.[11]

C. S. McNeill, son of E. W. McNeill, of Morgantown, was named lieutenant colonel, perhaps the highest rank held by any county serviceman.[12]

Through the summer and fall of 1918 it became apparent that the war was nearing its end. But as the prospect of peace shone brighter and brighter, the dread specter of influenza rode across the land, like one of the Horsemen of the Apocalypse. By the twenty-fourth of October, 298,275 cases had been reported in the army, with 16,174 deaths. In Morgantown 543 cases were reported by October 11;[13] on October 21 it was reported that 504 new cases had developed in the past three days, with 11 deaths.[14]

West Virginia University was closed on October 5. Church services were suspended; theaters and schools were closed. Terror gripped the populace; physicians were powerless.

5. *Post*, April 12, 1918.
6. *Post*, May 15, 1918.
7. *Post*, May 27, 1918.
8. *New Dominion*, June 6, 1918.
9. *New Dominion*, August 22, 1918.
10. *New Dominion*, August 23, 1918.
11. *New Dominion*, September 5, 1918.
12. *New Dominion*, September 17, 1918.
13. *Post*, October 11, 1918.
14. *Post*, October 21, 1918.

Gradually the plague subsided, schools, churches, etc., were reopened and on November 11, 1918, the World War came to its close with the signing of the Armistice. The news, flashed to Morgantown by telegraph, electrified the population and a noisy parade marched up and down the rough brick pavements of High Street.[15] Like all Americans, the citizens hoped the world had been made safe for democracy.

Training for War on the Campus. West Virginia University had been quickly affected by the war. "As never before training men for armed services was directed to the production of engineers, machinists, and technicians for the construction of railroads and buildings and for repair work. The normal supply of trained men being insufficient for these purposes, the War Department asked cooperating colleges to accelerate their training programs. In response thereto, most of the graduating class of 1917 entered the armed service at once; the 1918 class was graduated in December, 1917; and the succeeding classes were accelerated in like manner."[16]

The supply still being short, the War Department organized the Committee on Education and Special Training to hasten the program. In response to this, the university enrolled 921 students in three detachments, in June, August, and October 1918. At first the men used the Armory and the Agricultural Pavilion as barracks; the "Ark" (the basketball building) was used as a mess hall, with John Hunt, a well-known local chef, in charge. Later Barracks No. 1, No. 2, and No. 3 were built on Beechurst Avenue near the mess hall.

The most unique service centered in the College of Arts and Sciences, which was largely responsible for the Students' Army Training Corps (SATC). In this service all physically fit men students over the age of eighteen were allowed to enlist in the regular army but to remain in college for a given period. Their training program was coordinated with that of the ROTC, so they were thus potential officers in the regular army.

With the ROTC and the vocational students already on the campus, the 585 SATC students enrolled by October 1, 1918, converted the campus into a military camp. Established academic

15. *New Dominion*, November 11, 12, 1918.
16. Ambler, p. 564.

customs gave way to regimented life in barracks. The College of Engineering was taken over completely, and Woman's Hall, then nearing completion, in part. In addition, a number of fraternity houses were requisitioned for living quarters.

Growth of the University. Despite the war effort, growth of the university steadily continued. A dormitory for women, large enough to house nearly two hundred students, was completed in 1918 and named Woman's Hall. An agricultural building was also completed the same year and named Oglebay Hall, in honor of E. W. Oglebay, a member of the board of regents. Partly as an aid to the war effort, the annual State Farmers' Week (held this year January 7-11) had the largest attendance to date.[17]

Fig. 111. Woman's Hall, West Virginia University.

Although the war had a disconcerting influence on the School of Medicine, diverting both instructors and students to other activities, the school did not close. Instructors who remained on the

17. Ambler, p. 513.

campus cared for SATC soldiers and an increasing total number of university students in the campus dispensary.[18]

At a mass meeting on May 6 university students voted to form a student council, to be headed by the president of the student body. They thus began to bring a measure of cooperation into their social affairs.[19]

Because the campus had been converted into a military camp, the football schedule for 1918 was canceled. Basketball was played, under the coaching of Harnus P. Mullennex, but the team was not very successful, losing all but one of the games played on other courts and winning only three at home.[20]

The State Road Commission. Spurred by the phenomenal development of the automobile as a means of transportation, the people of Monongalia County and of all West Virginia, by the end of the World War, in 1918, were determined that something had to be done about the public roads. Highways in the Mountain State were not good under the best of circumstances; in winter they became absolutely impassable to motor cars.

Actually, as early as 1913 the legislature had created a State Road Bureau, of four members, setting a trend for road improvement under a centralized authority. A report made by the bureau in 1914 said that West Virginia had "the worst roads in the United States."

The legislature of 1917 revised the state road laws and replaced the State Road Bureau with the State Road Commission, to be composed of two members to be appointed by the governor. The duties of the commission were to collect and report to the governor information concerning "Class A" roads; all inter-county or main county roads were known as "Class A," whereas all other roads were known as "Class B." No county could have more than two "Class A" roads; they were selected by the county court, and, in most cases, ran from border to border, east and west, and north and south."

Talk of Road Building. The county's infant highway construction program made only slight progress during 1918, with war activities continuing to hold the major interest of the people.

18. Ambler, p. 541.
19. Ambler, p. 567.
20. Ambler, pp. 582, 593.

The long-drawn-out course of construction of the Morgan District road program still held the attention of the county court and, more than two years after the ratification of the bond issue, the commissioners, in February, called for bids on the completion of the Sabraton road project, estimated to cost above forty thousand dollars. Much criticism of the court had come from officials of the Tin Plate mill, and others, relative to the failure to construct this important highway. Nevertheless, shortage of funds once more delayed initiation of work on the project.

The court received another blow immediately. The city of Morgantown refused to accept portions of the roads completed within the city limits. On the Deckers Creek road, it was stated, the concrete slab above the Standard Glass Specialty Company had sunk; that a slide was half-way across the road for 230 feet at the same point; and that another slide had occurred at The Hogback. On the Star City road, the complaint stated, there were numerous slips, the gutters were filled, walls were falling, alleys blocked, properties had caved in, and sewers were broken; while on the Cheat road many slips had occurred and the ditching was closed at many points.

At last, almost exactly two years after the original beginning of work on the 1.66-mile-long Deckers Creek road, the court awarded a contract for the completion of the road from the end of the concrete, across the M.&K. railroad tracks and Hartman Run, via the sulphur spring to the town of Sabraton at the Harner Run bridge; the total distance was forty-seven hundred feet. The road was completed during the summer and provided the first paved road connecting Morgantown with the busy industrial suburb of Sabraton.

Roads West of the River. Summer brought the beginning of road construction on the west side of the Monongahela, where the only paved roads were about a mile of old brick paving from the end of the river bridge to the top of Westover Hill, and about another mile of similar paving through the village of Wadestown, in the far western part of the county.

The first attempt at road construction in Grant District had come in the spring of 1916. In March of that year a petition, bearing 211 names, had been presented to the county court, asking for an election to consider a $300,000 bond issue. The petition was approved, and the election was held on April 15, 1918. Sentiment was not yet strong enough, however, and the proposal was defeated by a vote of 198 favorable to 336 against.

But a tremendous drive for a road down the river from Westover through Riverside and Granville was resulting from the development of the great Scotts Run-Maidsville coalfield in 1917. It was estimated that by the first part of 1918 there would be two thousand people living in the area. In August of 1917 a delegation of fifty businessmen had appeared before the county court asking for an improved road to Maidsville.

Early in the spring the court worked out plans for the construction of the highway. In April 1918, it was announced that a sixteen-foot-wide concrete road would be built from Westover to Randall, a distance of 2.6 miles. Class A Road and Federal funds were to be used, and the work was to be done by county forces, since bids submitted by contractors were unfavorable.

Actual construction proceeded slowly, but, in general, satisfactorily, throughout the season, until closed down in December. The grading had been essentially completed and the concrete slab had been laid from the end of the brick pavement in Westover to the Monongahela Railway crossing in Riverside. This section was opened for traffic on December 7, 1918.

Trolley Service Reduced. Reporting a loss of five thousand dollars in 1917, the West Virginia Traction and Electric Company announced a drastic cut in local trolley service, effective August 18. Joseph K. Buchanan, manager, said that one loop car would run daily between 10:00 a.m. and 3:00 p.m. only, to comply with the city franchise which required twelve round trips a day. The Granville line, from the head of High Street across the river bridge to a point ("the hickory tree") across Dents Run from Granville, was discontinued entirely. This line was owned (p. 374) by the Morgantown and Pittsburgh company but operated by West Virginia Traction.[21]

End of the Post-Chronicle. The issue of February 7 was the last for the afternoon newspaper, the *Morgantown Post-Chronicle.* Thereafter the paper was issued under the name *Morgantown Post.*

The significance of the change was announced in an editorial:

21. *New Dominion,* August 28, 1918.

"The Morgantown Post Chronicle is published today under the management and control of the Morgantown Press Company recently incorporated and organized by a number of citizens for the purpose of publishing a newspaper that could play its part in the upbuilding of the community. It was originally their plan to launch a new afternoon Republican paper to be known as the Morgantown Press but the plan was abandoned when it became possible to purchase the Post-Chronicle, and to continue its publication at the new plant recently installed in the Blackstone building on Chestnut Street with Ralph G. Hess in charge of the enterprise."[22]

Rotary Club. A Rotary Club was organized in Morgantown December 9, 1918, with forty-eight original members. S. F. Glasscock was the first president and Ralph G. Hess the first secretary.[23]

M.&W. Extended. The extension of the line of the Morgantown and Wheeling, nominally under a separate company, the Blacksville and Western, from Blacksville to Brave, Pennsylvania, was completed in August. The big plant of the People's Natural Gas Company, at Brave, had brought about the extension, in order that coal might be shipped from Scotts Run to fire the furnaces of the compressing station, and that gasoline, a by-product, might be shipped out to refineries.[24]

The M.&W., by a special court decree, was granted the privilege of issuing $150,000 in receiver's certificates to upgrade the railroad through Scotts Run. "It is believed that when the proposed improvements are made . . . that this railroad will be capable of taking care of all of the enormous business on Scotts Run."[25]

A hearing was held in New York on May 16 on a petition of the Monongahela Railway to spend $225,000 to build a spur line from Randall to serve the Osage Coal Company and the Cleveland and Morgantown Coal Company. The M.&W., whose line paralleled the proposed new route, was protesting,[26] and won its case.

22. *Post-Chronicle*, February 7, 1918.
23. See Frederick Carspecken, *Morgantown Rotary. The First Fifty Years. 1918-1968*, 130 pp., no date.
24. *Chronicles of Core*, pp. 182, 183, 185.
25. *Post*, February 27, 1918.
26. *Post*, May 16, 1918.

Contracts for improving the M.&W. tracks through Scotts Run were let to Keely Brothers, of Clarksburg, and Cole Brothers, of Morgantown, the work to be finished within three months. Heavier steel for the rails, and three new bridges were included.[27]

County Bridge Collapses. The highway bridge across Scotts Run at Boyer's Mills collapsed on March 21; it was used by the M.&W. Railroad and went down when cars loaded with coal were passing over it. "The bridge was built five years ago from the long span at the end of the old suspension bridge across the Monongahela. It was regarded as of sufficient strength for the use of the trolley cars . . . , but at the time it was built, it was not expected that cars loaded with coal would be hauled over it."[28] The railroad was able to maintain traffic by using the siding of the Randall Coal Company, running alongside, but highway traffic had to be detoured.

Saint Francis School. A parochial school, Saint Francis de Sales, in 1918 moved into a new building on Beechurst Avenue. Operated by Saint Theresa's Parish, the school had begun in 1915, during the pastorate of Father Peter Flynn. "Through the deep interest of Father Flynn and Mr. Joseph Falter, Mother Angela of the Ursuline Sisters in Louisville, Kentucky, was convinced that she should send several Sisters to work in Morgantown. . . . Mother Angela chose, for this work, Sister Angelina, Armella, Isadore, and Gregory."[29]

The school, including elementary classes only, continued to hold its sessions in a McLane Avenue residence until 1918, when the move was made to the new building.

Saint Luke's Church. Members of the Saint Luke's Church of Christ, at Mooresville, built a new brick church and dedicated it in 1918. The original church, built of logs, was constructed in 1871.[30] Later, about 1907, a frame church was erected on a site nearby, on the Daniel Moore farm, which was destroyed by fire in 1913. An oil well stood on the church property and revenue from it was used for church purposes.[31]

27. *New Dominion*, July 2, 1918.
28. *Post*, March 22, 1918.
29. From *St. Theresa Church, 75th Anniversary* (1976).
30. Wiley, p. 751. See pp. 34, 417.
31. Dodds and Dodds, p. 125.

Fig. 112. Saint Francis School and newly finished convent, 1922 (St. Theresa Church, 75th Anniversary).

Miscellany. In 1918: The big car of the South Morgantown Traction Company, which was damaged in an accident several weeks ago, started running again on February 16; while it was out of service, small cars of the loop line had been used (*Post*, February 16, 1918). . . . Efrem Zimbalist, celebrated Russian violinist, gave a concert in the Strand Theater on January 15 (*Post*, February 28, 1918). . . . The Walnut Street bridge was closed for repairs and the light South Park structure was dangerously overcrowded (*Post*, March 13, 1918). . . . A ferry at old Ice's Ferry was put into operation on March 27, while a new bridge was being built; Harry Hall was ferryman (*Post*, March 27, 1918). . . . The Economy Tumbler Company, one of Morgantown's oldest glass plants, was planning to double its capacity (*Post*, March 28, 1918). . . . The Star City Glass (Seneca) Company, Plant B, went back into operation (*Post*, April 1, 1918). . . . Leonard and Corrothers (Harry C. Leonard and Brady Corrothers) took over Nathan's Fashion Shop (Nathan J. Cohen) (*Post*, April 27, 1918). . . . Morgantown's Annual Redpath Chautauqua was held July 2-8 (*Post*, May 3, 1918). . . . Several Morgantown people were on the Clarksburg-to-

Pittsburgh express due here at midnight when it wrecked six miles north of Clarksburg; no one was injured (*Post*, May 14, 1918). . . . Streets were suffering more destruction in Morgantown than in any other town in the state, due to overloaded coal trucks (*Post*, May 15, 1918). . . . B.&O. train No. 70, from Pittsburgh to Clarksburg, due at Morgantown at 8:10, after July 3 ran only to Fairmont (*New Dominion*, July 3, 1918). . . . Monongalia County's largest contingent of servicemen to date, 193, entrained for Camp Meade, Maryland, on July 22 (*New Dominion*, July 22, 1918). . . . Ralph H. Saunders was the first Monongalia County soldier to be killed in action; four had died in service (*New Dominion*, August 6, 1918). . . . The street leading through Greenmont to Valley Crossing was named Brockway Avenue by city council (*New Dominion*, August 28, 1918). . . . The first airplane flew over the Morgantown area on November 7 (*New Dominion*, November 8, 1918). . . . The Morgantown Printing and Binding Company moved from the Acme Building on Front Street into a new building at the corner of Chestnut and Kirk streets (Callahan, p. 271). . . . The Nathan Cohen Building on High Street was constructed (Callahan, p. 272). . . . The Morgantown Building Association was incorporated; Glenn Hunter was president, C. W. Huston vice-president, Morris L. Clovis treasurer, and Don K. Marchand secretary (*New Dominion*, November 20, 1918). . . . Rev. Andrew Harsanyi, pastor of the Uniontown Hungarian Evangelical and Reformed Church, started services for miners and their families in Osage and Brady (Dodds and Dodds, p. 79). . . . John E. Price, son of William Price, died November 17 (*New Dominion*, November 18, 1918). . . . Perry C. McBee, a coal operator, died May 5 (*The Post*, May 6, 1918). . . . Under the direction of Charles Morris, superintendent, the county infirmary was moved from Cassville into a new building on the Flatts; the facility had been located at Cassville since 1874 (see vol. 3, pp. 676, 677).

CHAPTER ONE HUNDRED FORTY-THREE

1919

With the war over, business still on a good level, money relatively easy to come by, and a growing sentiment for better roads, it is not surprising that the new year brought some very encouraging advances.

Automobiles were becoming more abundant and Monongalia County citizens were anxious to see the day when they could drive their cars all year long, instead of closing down for the winter months.

Long distance travel was still by train. Local transportation was by streetcar, and the Monongahela Valley Traction Company was still planning an extension of their extensive interurban system from Fairmont to Morgantown.

County and District Road Building. In April the county court undertook to complete the Morgan District road program, now drawn out into its fourth season, and called for bids on 5,160 feet of the Sabraton-Dellslow road, 4,400 feet of the Stewartstown road, 7,990 feet of the Chestnut Ridge road, and 3,200 feet of the Charles Avenue project. Bids were opened in May, but when it was discovered that the contractors had asked for double the amount of money the fund had available, the projects were again dropped.

In April, Cass District, faced with its rapidly growing coal industry, passed by an overwhelming majority a proposal to issue $300,000 in road bonds. The proposal contemplated construction of three roads completely across the district, to be paved with a concrete slab sixteen feet wide. One road would start at Randall and run through the booming Scotts Run mining section to the Clay District line west of Cassville. Another would start at Randall, follow the Monongahela River to Maidsville Landing, then proceed up Robinson Run via Bowlby and across the hill to

Wades Run, ending at the state line. The third would proceed down the river from Maidsville Landing to the state line near Rosedale.

In midsummer Grant District tried again, after its first bond issue proposal had been defeated (p. 472). The new proposal was for $325,000 and was approved by a vote of 344 to 202. Roads to be improved were the Fairmont Pike from Westover to the Marion County line, the river road from Westover to Lowesville, the road up Indian Creek from Lowesville to Arnettsville, and one mile up Dents Run from Laurel Point.

In September Union District approved a proposal to issue bonds for $150,000 to construct certain roads in that section. Union thus became the third civil subdivision to vote bonds during the year and brought to $750,000 the amount authorized during the year for new highways.

Meanwhile, the county court was completing the road to Randall, started the year before. The new road reached the entrance to the Scotts Run mining district, paralleling the M.&W. trolley line. To provide an all-weather outlet for Maidsville area, slag was placed on the road from Randall to Maidsville Landing, a more permanent road being postponed until the completion of the giant Maidsville railroad yards, then under construction to serve the developing mining industry. In September the county court contracted with the Chaplin, Kerr, and Van Voorhis Corporation to construct three miles of road leading down the river towards the state line; work was started at the cattle pen opposite Van Voorhis. Construction had already been started on the Robinson Run road and concrete was being poured in September, although progress was slow due to the difficulty of securing concrete. Funds for these two projects came from the Cass District bond issue.[1]

Progress Under President Trotter. Following the close of the war President F. B. Trotter launched a million dollar building program on the university campus designed to provide adequate quarters for the College of Law, for the department of Chemistry, for a boys' residence hall, a gymnasium, a women's building, a new armory, and a larger commencement hall.[2]

1. Core, "Out of the Mud," *Westover Observer,* August 2, 1956.
2. Ambler, p. 515.

Personnel changes were numerous during the year. W. J. Kay succeeded C. Edmund Neil as head of public speaking; H. H. York followed J. L. Sheldon as head of botany and bacteriology; Nat T. Frame became director of agricultural extension, following C. R. Titlow; G. P. Boomsliter succeeded F. L. Emory as head of mechanics. New additions were E. A. Livesay and C. V. Wilson, animal husbandry; H. E. Knowlton, horticulture; J. L. Hayman, pharmacy; M. L. Bonar, pharmacology.

The 1919 football season was one of the greatest in the university's history. Although defeated by Pitt (26-0), and by the "praying team" of Centre College, Kentucky (14-6), it won all the other games and had only seven points scored against it. Rutgers was defeated 30-7 and W.&J. 7-0, only the fourth victory over that team in eighteen years. The high point of the season was the defeat of Princeton, 25-0. Walter Camp said: "It is safe to say that no team . . . will stage a finer exhibition of versatile, finished football than that displayed by West Virginia under the leadership of the great Captain, Rodgers." Already Ira Errett ("Rat") Rodgers was being proclaimed "West Virginia's Greatest Athlete." He was captain and fullback on Camp's mythical All-American team of 1919 and his team-mate, Russell Bailey, was center on the second team.[3]

The Astronomical Observatory. An unexpected result of the university football team's victory over Princeton was the destruction of the Astronomical Observatory on Observatory Hill, overlooking Morgantown.

"The team was met by a committee yesterday and quietly escorted home in automobiles, the students having decided not to break the decorum of the Sabbath with their celebration. Last night, however, shortly after midnight, some one set a torch to the old Observatory on Observatory Hill and paid homage to the great University eleven as the ancient old structure went up in smoke."[4]

---

3. Ambler, p. 582.
4. *Post,* Monday, November 3, 1919. H. W. Gould, "History of the Old Telescope and Observatory at West Virginia University," *Proc. W. Va. Acad. Sci.* 39: 1-8. 1968. See also *W.Va. Univ. Magazine,* Summer, 1971. Arthur Beaumont and Helen Purinton Pettigrew recalled seeing Halley's Comet through the telescope in the spring of 1910, under the direction of Dr. John Arndt Eiesland, professor of mathematics. Professor Eiesland salvaged fragments of the telescope after the fire and these are still preserved.

Memorial Services. A memorial service was held on March 6 in Commencement Hall to honor the forty-two servicemen from West Virginia University who lost their lives in the war. Addresses were made by President Frank Butler Trotter and by President Samuel Chiles Mitchell, of Delaware College.[5]

A poem, "Stars of Gold," was read by Prof. Waitman Barbe at the services, which some critics regarded as the most exquisitely beautiful tribute paid to those who made the supreme sacrifice. It was reprinted in France and was in great demand there among American soldiers. A portion of the poem follows:

> With cheers for every star, we flung
> Our flag a year ago and sung
> The songs of marching men;
> And all the season through
> We proudly filled the flag with stars
> Until they crowded field and bars,
> And still we cheer'd—for then
> Our stars were all of blue.
>
> But now in silence do we raise
> Another flag too dear for praise,
> And every head we bow
> And for awhile withhold
> Our cheers for banners filled with blue:
> Another color shineth through
> The field and bars—for now
> These stars have turned to gold.

A giant parade and "welcome-home" was held in Morgantown on July 4 in honor of Monongalia County soldiers in the war.[6]

Improved Railroad Service. Beginning April 20, the B.&O. added one round-trip passenger train to Fairmont to the schedule. The train left Morgantown at 8:00 a.m., arrived in Fairmont at 9:10 a.m, then, returning, left Fairmont at 6:30 p.m. and arrived in Morgantown at 7:40 p.m.

The M.&K. train formerly leaving Morgantown at noon was

5. *New Dominion,* March 7, 1919.
6. *New Dominion,* July 5, 1919.

changed so as to leave at 3:30, allowing people along the M.&K. more shopping time in Morgantown.[7]

Efforts to Improve Street Car Service. Mayor Charles T. Hickman gave an ultimatum to Morgantown street car lines to either improve their service or get out of town. A suggestion to consolidate the South Morgantown system with that of the West Virginia Traction came to naught and operators of both lines said they were losing money and could not afford to make any improvements.[8]

City council approved a raise of fares from five to six cents for the West Virginia Traction and the company thereupon resumed full service.[9]

Traffic on the M.&W. With the renovation of the old trolley line on Scotts Run, the M.&W. was beginning to handle the immense coal shipments more effectively, with much fewer accidents.

Passenger service was finally resumed on January 25, 1919, with trains running on Mondays, Wednesdays, and Saturdays. Passengers between Morgantown and Randall continued to be carried by trolley.

On May 14 passenger service was extended to Brave, Pennsylvania, the trains operating on the following schedule, Mondays, Wednesdays, Fridays:

East			West	
P.M.	A.M.		A.M.	P.M.
9.00	12.00	Morgantown	6.30	4.00
8.30	11.30	Randall	7.00	4.30
7.45	10.45	Core	7.45	5.15
6.50	9.50	Blacksville	8.40	6.10
6.30	9.30	Brave	9.00	6.30

The passenger coaches were usually pulled behind a string of perhaps a dozen freight cars, mostly coal or gasoline, and so were frequently stopped by a derailment of a freight car ahead.[10]

During 1919 it was confidently expected that service would

7. *New Dominion,* April 19, 1919.
8. *New Dominion,* January 10, 1919.
9. *New Dominion,* January 28, 1919.
10. Core, *Chronicles of Core,* pp. 186, 187; see also Canfield, *West Penn Traction,* p. 158.

soon be opened from Blacksville to Waynesburg, Pennsylvania, on the grade already partially built (p. 385). On April 13 it was announced that arrangements had been completed and finances had been secured. On June 1 final authority was granted in a decree issued in circuit court by Special Judge James A. Meredith. But finances again proved inadequate and the project was suspended.

The Dann Boarding House. To provide space for the proposed new College of Law Building, a well-known old house was moved to a new location at the rear of the President's House. This was the boarding house built by William Dann in 1874 at the corner of Front and Hough streets. The old boardinghouse, after having been used for the purpose for many years, later became the residence of E. M. Grant and still later was occupied by the music school.[11]

New Industries. New Morgantown businesses established in 1919 included the Cook Copper Process Company, the Morgantown Broom Company, and Jackson and Grow Machine Company.

Fighting Fires. The Morgantown city charter of 1901 had made provisions and established regulations for both police and fire protection but lack of funds prevented the acquisition of much new fire-fighting equipment. For the most part, it was limited to a few hose-carts and a fire truck and ladder wagon drawn by teams of horses. A new power truck was purchased in 1919, against the reluctance of many citizens, who felt the horses were more dependable. The truck proved inadequate, due to lack of pumping equipment, especially when compelled to operate at distances far from fireplugs, and provoked comments of "I told you so." The truck even seemed slower than the horses had been.[12]

Sturgiss City. Citizens of Jerome Park, Sabraton, and West Sabraton, on June 28 voted 95 to 6 in favor of incorporating the three communities into a municipality to be called Sturgiss City, in honor of Judge George C. Sturgiss, who had founded the principal industries responsible for its growth. It became the sixth in-

11. Callahan, p. 226.
12. Callahan, p. 296.

corporated town in the county, the others being Morgantown, Blacksville, Star City, Riverside, and Westover.[13]

M. L. Childs was elected the first mayor and Paul Mansberger the first recorder. Appointed officers were Donald Lazzelle, attorney; P. L. Glover, treasurer; and Dr. R. A. Long, health officer.

Seventeenth Judicial Circuit. By Chapter 132 of the Acts of the 1919 Legislature it was declared that Monongalia County was to be known as composing the Seventeenth Judicial Circuit after January 1, 1921. Lewis and Harrison were to constitute the Fifteenth Circuit and Marion the Sixteenth. George C. Sturgiss was judge.

Smail Post Office. The Hagans post office, near the head of Indian Creek (p. 112) was closed January 31, 1918, and was reopened March 14, 1919, under the name of Smail. Clarence M. Smail was a young, popular minister who had preached at irregular intervals at the Hagans Christian Church and married Miss Catherine Fetty, who had been a charter member of the church. Because of his popularity the new post office was named for him. Michael E. Fetty was the first postmaster (see p. 332).[14]

Marilla Plant Destroyed by Fire. The big Marilla plant of the United States Window Glass Company (Factory No. 2) was destroyed by fire on the afternoon of November 30, at an estimated loss of $200,000. The plant had been idle for about five weeks, except for one small tank used in making light glass; it was this tank which fell in, causing the fire. Firemen saved the warehouse and clay house, but twenty carloads of lumber on a nearby siding were destroyed.

The Marilla plant was built in 1902 and operated for several years as a cooperative business. In 1913 it was taken over by the United States Window Glass Company and greatly enlarged. In 1919 Walter A. Jones, of Columbus, Ohio, was president of the company, B. E. Taylor, of Detroit, vice-president, and J. L. Keener, of Morgantown, secretary-treasurer.[15]

New Ice's Ferry Bridge. A contract was awarded by the county court on October 8 for piers and abutments for the new Ice's

13. *New Dominion*, June 30, 1919.
14. Core, *Morgantown Disciples*, p. 58.
15. *Post*, December 1, 1919.

Fig. 113. Marilla Window Glass Factory. (From J. W. Wiles, *Morgantown's Suburbs*.)

Ferry bridge across Cheat River, to replace the one destroyed by the ice gorge last winter. The contract went to the H. C. Gilmore Company for $30,654.

T. E. Hodges. Thomas Edward Hodges, a former president of West Virginia University, died July 13, 1919. He was born in Upshur County December 13, 1858, the son of John Henry and Melissa Humphreys Hodges. He obtained his primary education in district schools and at French Creek Academy. He graduated from West Virginia University in 1881 and then had a remarkable career as an educator. From 1881 to 1886 he was superintendent of the Morgantown schools; from 1886 to 1896 he was principal of Marshall College; and in 1896 he joined the staff of West Virginia University as professor of physics. He became treasurer of the state board of control in 1909, the date of its organization, and served until 1911; he was largely responsible for getting it started on a sound financial basis. He was an impressive speaker and was frequently invited to appear before church, educational, and other gatherings.

On September 22, 1910, Hodges was named president of West Virginia University, effective October 1, 1911. President W. H. Taft spoke at his inauguration, which was described at the time as "the greatest event . . . in the history of the University." Many good things were indeed accomplished, but the effectiveness of his administration was not sustained, disagreements developed, and finally he tendered his resignation, accepted by the regents effective September 1, 1914.

He was a good businessman with much valuable experience, serving as secretary-treasurer of the Morgantown Savings and Loan Society and as the first president of the Bank of Morgantown. In July 1915 he was appointed postmaster of Morgantown, in which capacity he served until his death.

He married Mary Amelia, daughter of Manliff Hayes, and was survived by two children, Mrs. O. F. Gibbs and Charles Edward Hodges.[16]

French Ensor Chadwick. Rear Admiral French Ensor Chadwick, U.S. Navy, retired, died in New York on January 27 and was buried in Morgantown on January 30.[17] The son of Daniel C. and Margaret Chadwick, he was born in Morgantown on February 29, 1844, and was one of the most distinguished natives in Monongalia County's first two centuries.

Chadwick was admitted to the U.S. Naval Academy, then at Newport, Rhode Island, on September 28, 1861. He learned the mysteries of shipboard life on the *Constitution* and the *Macedonian*. At graduation, November 22, 1864, he ranked fifth in academics out of a class of forty men.

From 1864 to 1882 he served on the *Susquehanna, Sabine, Tuscarora, Juniata,* and *Guerriere.* He rose rapidly in rank, through the grades of ensign, master, lieutenant, and became lieutenant commander in 1869. He became commander in 1884.

His first shore duty was teaching mathematics at the Naval Academy for three years, and he then served as executive officer on the *Powhatan.* While on leave, on November 20, 1878, he married Cornelia J. Miller, of Utica, New York. They had no children.

In 1882 he was ordered to duty in London as the first naval attache and served there until 1889. Upon his return home in 1889 he was given command of the new gunboat *Yorktown,* which as a member of a squadron toured the Mediterranean until 1891, gathering intelligence about harbors and ships.

He served as chief intelligence officer in 1892 and 1893, then as chief of the Bureau of Equipment until 1897. He was promoted to captain in 1897 and given command of the armored cruiser *New York.*

16. *New Dominion,* July 14, 1919.
17. *New Dominion,* January 28, 31, 1919.

The ship was at Key West when news came of the destruction of the *Maine* on February 15, 1898. With W. T. Sampson he spent a month on a board of inquiry as to the cause of the tragedy and the outcome of their report was war with Spain. Sampson became commander-in-chief of the North Atlantic Squadron and chose Chadwick as his chief of staff. The squadron blockaded Cuba from March until July 1898.

Following the war he was honored in Morgantown on October 10, 1899, in a program of parades and speeches—a great homecoming day (p. 241).

From 1900 through 1903 he was president of the Naval War College and on March 22, 1904, he was named commander of the South Atlantic Squadron and sailed with the squadron on a round-the-world cruise. In 1905 he joined the North Atlantic Squadron and became rear admiral. He retired February 28, 1906, and thereafter lived at Twin Oaks, Oakwood Terrace, Newport.

He was a prolific writer and published many short articles, as well as numerous books, including *Ocean Steamships* (1891), *Causes of the Civil War* (1906), a three-volume work on Spanish-American relations (1909, 1911), and a short history, *The American Navy* (1915).

His death brought to an end "the life of a superb seaman, intelligence specialist, naturally gifted scientist and technologist, naval administrator, educator, skilled draftsman, and renowned historian—a scholarly warrior."[18]

W. C. McGrew. Major William C. McGrew, a prominent citizen of Morgantown (and of West Virginia), died October 30. He was born in Kingwood April 21, 1842, the son of James Clark and Persis (Hagans) McGrew. On November 9, 1864, he married Julia E., daughter of Senator Waitman T. Willey, and they moved six years later to Morgantown, where he engaged in the mercantile business. He helped bring about the construction of the Fairmont, Morgantown, and Pittsburgh Railroad, and was its first Morgantown agent. He helped establish the Morgantown Glass Company (later the Economy Tumbler Company) and served as its president. He was vice-president of the Second National Bank.

---

18. Paolo Coletta, *French Ensor Chadwick: Scholarly Warrior.* (University Press of America, 1980), 256 pp.

He was a member of the state senate and of the house of delegates. He served five terms as mayor of Morgantown.[19]

Miscellany. In 1919: Jascha Heifetz gave a concert at the Strand Theatre on January 14 (*New Dominion,* January 14, 1919). . . . Preliminary plans for a new Morgantown hotel were submitted by a Wheeling architect (*New Dominion,* April 5, 1919). . . . Lawrence M. Cox became county road engineer, succeeding W. S. Downs, who resigned to go with the State Road Commission (*New Dominion,* April 10, 1919). . . . Thomas R. Lewis, aged forty, a foreman at the Tin Plate mill, was fatally injured when his automobile hit a stump on the Mileground road (*New Dominion,* April 26, 1919). . . . The 1920 *Monticola* was dedicated to Dr. Alexander Reid Whitehill, chemistry chairman at the university, the oldest active member of the faculty, having come here in 1885 (*New Dominion,* April 26, 1919). . . . In October the M.&K. Railroad was purchased by the B.&O., with the financial cooperation of the Bethlehem Steel Company (Callahan, p. 281). . . . An attempt to revise Morgantown's city charter was defeated by the voters (Callahan, p. 295). . . . Matthew B. Jones, of Hagans, died April 7; a son of Henry Jones, he was born August 31, 1839 (Core, *Chronicles of Core,* p. 186). . . . A Baptist Church congregation was organized in Sabraton by Rev. T. C. McCarty, Rev. P. L. Gloxes, and G. W. Parsons (Dodds and Dodds, p. 71). . . . Isaac Buckner, proprietor of Buckner's jewelry store, committed suicide; he was the son of Saul and Esther Buckner, and had been in ill health (*New Dominion,* May 7, 1919). . . . Mont Chateau Hotel, which opened for the summer in late May, with Frank J. St. Clair as manager, had one of its most successful seasons (*New Dominion,* June 2, 1919). . . . Adam Bowers, Morgantown barber, died June 1; he was born in Germany in 1852 (*New Dominion,* June 2, 1919). . . . Alberto Salvi, "the wizard of the harp," gave a program at the Strand Theater (*New Dominion,* June 4, 6, 1919). . . . Thomas W. Anderson, seventy-four, Morgantown insurance and real estate agent, died June 21 (*New Dominion,* June 23, 1919). . . . The annual Chautauqua opened July 9 with a big attendance; the tent was pitched on the university campus just behind the library (*New Dominion,* July 10, 1919). . . . The Peabody

19. *Post,* October 30, 1919.

Hotel was sold by Mrs. T. J. Peabody to Charles E. McCray, Jr. (*New Dominion,* July 22, 1919). . . . Capt. Charles H. Thompson's yacht, with a remarkable collection of marine life, was anchored at the City Wharf for public viewing (*New Dominion,* July 24, 1919). . . . Some excitement was aroused when the South Penn Oil Company, on Dunkard Creek, brought in A. B. Price Well No. 2 on July 30, with thirty barrels daily production and No. 3 on September 9, with ten barrels daily (*Chronicles of Core,* p. 189). . . . Special trains on the M.&W. took people from Morgantown to Blacksville for a county Sunday school convention September 23, 24 (*Post,* September 19, 1919). . . . Two special trains on the Monongahela took fans to the Pitt game in Pittsburgh on October 10 (*Post,* October 18, 1919). . . . About four thousand miners were idle in Monongalia County, defying a federal injunction (*Post,* October 30, November 1, 1919). . . . Aaron J. Garlow, receiver for the bankrupt South Morgantown Traction Company, was attempting to resume service on the line shut down since the middle of October (*Post,* November 4, 1919). . . . Service was resumed November 29 and the fare raised from five to eight cents (*Post,* November 14, 1919). . . . Newsboys' price of the *Post* sold on the streets was raised to three cents (*Post,* December 9, 1919). . . . A joint concert was presented in the Strand Theater by Alessandro Bonci, distinguished Italian tenor, and Eleanor Brock, a native of Morgantown (*Post,* December 12, 1919). . . . Prof. Frederick Lincoln Emory, of the university engineering staff, died December 31 (*New Dominion,* January 2, 1920; biography in *New Dominion,* September 18, 1897). . . . James Henderson, a farmer of Dunkard Ridge, Cass District, died December 29, 1919 (*Chronicles of Core,* p. 185); a son was Joseph Lindsay Henderson (see his *Educational Memoirs,* 335 p., Austin, Texas, ca. 1940).

CHAPTER ONE HUNDRED FORTY-FOUR

1920

The remarkable growth in population of Monongalia County which had characterized the first decade of the twentieth century was continued unabated throughout the second decade. The factories which had been responsible for the earlier growth were still recording high employment and production rates, stimulated by America's participation in the World War, and the university steadily increased in enrollment and in services rendered. In addition, a new industry, that of coal mining, brought thousands of new people into the county.

The Census of 1920. Monongalia County, which remained unchanged in its area, at 358 square miles, in 1920 had a population of 33,618, an increase of 38.2 percent over the 1910 population of 24,334. The population in 1900 had been only 19,049 and the rate of increase during the first decade was 27.7 percent.

The population in 1920 was classified as 12,127 urban and 21,491 rural. There was 93.9 people per square mile.

The population of the seven magisterial districts in 1920, with the incorporated towns, is shown below, with 1910 figures for comparison:

	1920	*1910*
Battelle	2,059	2,270
Cass	3,160	1,173
Clay	2,581	2,797
Blacksville	218	204
Clinton	2,016	2,415
Grant	4,807	2,495
Riverside	326	——
Westover	721	——

Morgan	16,934	11,631
Morgantown	12,127	9,150
Star City	823	318
Sturgiss City	1,389	— —
Union	2,061	1,553

It will be noted that the strictly rural districts, Battelle, Clay, and Clinton, showed decreases in population. Agriculture, which for more than a century had been almost the only occupation of the people, was now declining rapidly. The county seat town, on the other hand, continued its rapid increase, and the suburban towns, Riverside, Westover, Star City, and Sturgiss City, were likewise growing rapidly. But by far the most spectacular growth was in Cass District, influenced by the tremendous development of coal mining in the Scotts Run area, where the population had tripled.

Steadily the county's growth was continuing to raise its rank, population-wise, among the fifty-five counties of the state. In 1890 Monongalia County was in nineteenth place, in 1900 it was in eighteenth place, and in 1910 it was in fifteenth place. In 1920 it was tied with Marshall (both were recorded as having 33,618 people) for the twelfth place.

Morgantown, among the cities of the state, was eighth in size with respect to population. Wheeling was the largest city in the state, followed by Huntington, Charleston, Parkersburg, and Clarksburg. Other cities larger than Morgantown, in 1920, were Bluefield, Fairmont and Martinsburg.

The number of farms in the county had steadily decreased since 1900; in that year there was 2,259; in 1910, 2,087; in 1920, only 1,805. The average acreage per farm was 90.5. The total acreage in 1920 was 163,332, down from 187,822 acres in 1910. The improved acreage was only 123,932, down from 144,121 acres of improved land ten years earlier. The total value of all farm property, however, was $13,335,315, up from $11,705,325 in 1910.

The industrial census, taken in 1919, showed that Morgantown had 61 manufacturing establishments, up from 49 in 1914. The average number of wage earners in these establishments, in 1919, was 1,303, earning wages of $1,482,000. The value of the products manufactured was reported as $4,643,000. For the entire county there were 104 establishments, with an average of 2,771 wage earners and a total value of products of $16,333,355.

The most spectacular industrial development in the past two decades, mostly in the past two years, had been in the production of coal. Production in Monongalia County, by tons, for each year since 1900 was reported as follows:

1900	82,148	1910	414,992
1901	75,589	1911	464,319
1902	130,371	1912	381,164
1903	148,074	1913	426,137
1904	194,540	1914	400,046
1905	178,752	1915	319,947
1906	196,074	1916	501,101
1907	292,596	1917	751,403
1908	271,843	1918	1,687,153
1909	235,816	1919	2,158,219

In 1919 there were sixty-one mines in production, with 2,521 employees, compared with two mines and 107 miners reported in 1900.

Road Building Slows Down. Despite the promising record of 1919, road building activities throughout 1920 proceeded with discouraging slowness. The important Scotts Run road, the outlet for the rapidly growing mining area, was closed to traffic in February, when two steam shovels began grading on the hill above Randall.

While grading was in progress up Scotts Run, resulting in impassable conditions most of the spring, work on the Robinson Run road slowly continued. As late as September, concrete was still being poured between Maidsville Landing and Maidsville, a short stretch which had already been under construction for more than a year.

A contract had been awarded to Cole Brothers for the grading, draining, and paving of a six-mile section of the Fairmont Pike between Westover and Little Indian Creek, the contract price being $305,402. Grading operations got under way during the summer, and thus three major highways, leading south, west, and north from Morgantown, were all under construction at the same time. There were times when motorists approaching Morgantown on the west side of the river could scarcely find an open road into the city. That fall, heavy traffic on the new grade of the Scotts Run road cut out such deep ruts that when winter came even empty wagons got stuck in the mud and had to be abandoned, and small children were cautioned not to attempt crossing the road.

Good Roads Clubs. Thus another year drew to a close, with the addition of only a very short section to the county's paved road map.

Nevertheless, an event occurred during the fall that was soon to pay undreamed-of dividends in the way of roads. For several months "Good Roads Clubs" throughout the state had urged the development of a system of state highways. In July the West Virginia Good Roads Federation published a Primer stating that there were only nine hundred miles of paved roads in the state, with only two county seats connected (Wheeling and Moundsville), and that one thousand miles more were needed to connect all fifty-five county seats. The Primer advocated ratification of a proposed state bond issue for $50 million to develop a state highway system. Jean Billingslea, a West Virginia University student, starred in a film promoting improved roads, entitled *The Road Ahead for West Virginia.*[1]

This was but typical of a general educational campaign being carried on over the state, and no one was greatly surprised that the vote, on General Election Day in November, resulted in approval of the proposal by a ten-to-one majority. Monongalia County would soon participate in the sharing of the dividends.[2]

President Trotter, Administrator. Much of the success of President F. B. Trotter as an administrator on the university campus lay in his ability to secure salary increases for key personnel. In 1919 the maximum salary for professors was $2,900, for heads of departments $3,100, and for deans $4,200. All were given a 10 percent bonus for 1919-20 and 20 to 30 percent increases effective July 1, 1920.[3]

The president, however, narrowly missed being replaced. The regents seriously considered appointing State Superintendent of Schools M. P. Shawkey for the position, and the appointment was scheduled for a special meeting of the board to be held in Parkersburg in November. Two members of the board, H. M. Gore and L. W. Burns, objected strenuously, however, maintaining that

1. *New Dominion,* February 17, 1920.
2. Core, "Out of the Mud," *Westover Observer,* August 9, 1956.
3. Ambler, p. 516.

President Trotter should be given time to develop his building program and the change was again postponed.[4]

New appointments included A. L. Darby, who was raised from an assistant to Madison Stathers in romance languages to the rank of professor; Dr. H. O. Henderson, who would make notable contributions in dairy husbandry; and Rebecca L. Pollock, who was promoted to assistant professor, with L. B. Hill, promoted to professor, both in education.[5]

The football record for 1920 was not impressive, with "Rat" Rodgers, Russell Bailey, Andrew King, Clay Hite, Frank Ice, and other stars out of the line-up. Mont M. McIntire continued as coach, but had "too much raw material." Victories were won over Washington and Lee, Rutgers, Bethany, George Washington, and West Virginia Wesleyan. Defeats were inflicted by Pitt, Yale, Princeton, and Washington and Jefferson. Lehigh was tied.[6]

Twenty-Four Passenger Trains Daily.[7] An average of one passenger train each hour of the day served Morgantown, including eight on the Monongahela, ten on the B.&O., four on the M.&K., and two on the M.&W. (although the latter gave very irregular service).

Maidsville Yards. The Monongahela Railway Company had under construction a giant layout of railroad yards along the Monongahela between the mouths of Scotts Run and Robinson Run. This facility was to serve the immense coal production of Scotts Run and the increasing output of other mines in the vicinity, as well as the proposed future development of the territory along the river south to Lowesville and up Indian Creek to Arnettsville.[8]

Construction of the yards was greatly delayed because of a controversy with the county court over highway locations, resulting in great congestion of traffic in Scotts Run and elsewhere, since the railroad had no place to put loaded coal cars while moving in empties.[9]

4. Ambler, p. 515.
5. Ambler, pp. 527, 533, 543.
6. Ambler, p. 583; Constantine, p. 21.
7. *New Dominion*, June 22, 1920.
8. Callahan, p. 276.
9. *New Dominion*, October 13, 14, etc., 1920.

Indian Creek and Northern Railroad. A new railroad, the Indian Creek and Northern, was incorporated with the announced intention of constructing a line from the Monongahela Railway up Indian Creek to Arnettsville, to allow the development of vast coal reserves in that section.[10]

Trial Run of River Packet. The Pittsburgh Navigation Company, on August 16, began packet service between Fairmont, Morgantown, and Pittsburgh, on a trial basis. It was planned to make three trips to Pittsburgh weekly from Morgantown and one to Fairmont. The boat used was the *Leroy*, 36 by 136 feet, William Syphers, captain.[11]

Country Club. A country club was being developed in Evansdale, on a high knoll overlooking Morgantown, on an eighty-acre tract of land owned by Joseph H. McDermott. A nine-hole golf course was laid out by Joseph J. Walsh, of the Maryland Country Club, and C. J. Chisholm, of Pittsburgh. The property fronted on the Star City road and the Willowdale road and on the north was bounded by the old fairgrounds. A club house was being planned, to be about eighty feet wide, with large social and dining rooms, and various other facilities.[12]

Morgantown Kiwanis Club. A local Kiwanis club was formally organized at a meeting of Morgantown civic leaders on October 1, 1920, in the Hotel Madeira. Officers chosen at the meeting were E. M. Grant, president; E. H. Gilbert, vice-president; Charles H. Baker, secretary; M. T. Sisler, treasurer; Dr. I. C. White, trustee.[13]

Armorcord Rubber Plant. The Armorcord Rubber Company, a Morgantown corporation, built a plant across the river from Seneca to produce blowout proof tubes for automobile tires. It was expected that the plant would produce one thousand tubes daily on the eighty-acre site. Capital stock was set at $500,000. J. H. McDermott was president of the company, E. D. Tumlin treasurer, and D. C. Reay, J. M. Wood, and W. A. Ream directors.[14]

10. *New Dominion*, November 17, 1920.
11. *New Dominion*, August 16, 1920.
12. *New Dominion*, August 2, 1920.
13. *New Dominion*, October 2, 1920.
14. *Post*, October 9, 28, 1919.

Ground was broken on December 2, 1919, and a siding built to connect with the M.&W. trolley line.[15] Production began on November 6, 1920.[16]

The Salvation Army. In 1920, with Capt. George Riley in charge, the organization known as the Salvation Army purchased the building on Walnut Street where meetings had been held since 1900. Morgantown's first Salvation Army members, the Stanton family (James and Elizabeth, with their daughter, Tessie, who had been born in England April 26, 1880), came here in 1897 from Fostoria, Ohio, where they had been active soldiers. The Seneca Glass Company had moved here from Fostoria the year before, bringing many glassworkers along.

Fig. 114. Salvation Army Headquarters, Walnut Street.

During the first two decades of the century Morgantown was progressing from a village of a little more than one thousand people into a town and then into a small city. Many people were

15. *Post,* December 3, 1919.

16. *New Dominion,* November 8, 1920. Unfortunately, the plant did not prove successful.

coming and going, attracted by the dozens of factories that were being built here. The army found its work to be most fruitful. Among those who had charge of the work during that period were Captain and Mrs. J. M. Edgell (1901), Captain and Mrs. J. Black (1902), Captain and Mrs. John Kissell (1909), Captain and Mrs. David Moreland (1910), Captain Katherine Hartman and Lieutenant Emma F. Collins (1910).

The work was officially closed for three years, from 1911 until 1914, but local people kept it going on an informal basis. Tessie Stanton, who had been only nineteen years old when her family moved to Morgantown in 1897, had already been enrolled for three years. In Morgantown she married James Madigan and they were given the rank of Envoys, keeping the work going while no regular officers were on duty.[17]

The work was reopened March 7, 1914, conducted by Captain and Mrs. Richard Ives and Captain and Mrs. William Ayers. Other officers, during the next few years included Captain Ida Raymond (1915), Captain and Mrs. John Bamford (1916), Lieutenant Hilda Raab (1917), Captain Merritt Eisenhardt (1919), and Captain and Mrs. George Riley (1920). Some of these leaders, through promotions and transfers, rose to higher posts elsewhere.

From one family in 1897, the army had grown by 1920 to dozens of workers who were always to be found in the forefront when need arose or when disaster struck, such as, for example, serving coffee and sandwiches on a ladder to firemen fighting a blaze in the middle of the night.

But the program carried on by the army in the community mostly dealt with matters much less spectacular—a day in and day out service that mostly attracted little attention: carrying good news into jail cells, to lonely people in the midst of crowds on the street, into remote rural areas, into taverns and bars, and, of course, through church services actually held in the citadel. The full religious program included numerous services each week, along with classes for young people.

17. Incidentally, Tessie remained active as a local officer in the Morgantown corps until her death in 1969, having been a faithful and dedicated officer of the army for three quarters of a century.

New Banking Facilities. On March 31, 1920, occurred the consolidation of the Citizens' National Bank with the Federal Savings and Trust Company, a movement prompted by economy in operation and opportunities for increasing the capital stock. The Citizens' National Bank had operated under a federal charter and the Federal Savings and Trust Company had conducted its business under a state charter. This consolidation reduced the number of banks in the city to five. Two others, one in Blacksville, one in Wadestown, made the total number in the county seven.

But a new bank, the Union Bank and Trust Company, opened on November 1, 1920, occupying the space used by the post office until 1915, thereafter occupied by the Dixy Theater until its closing early in 1920.[18]

Financing the Fire Department. Late in 1920 the Chamber of Commerce and the Morgantown city council considered a plan to finance the purchase of modern fire-fighting apparatus, equipped with a chemical engine, ladders, hose, and pumps. But the question was again postponed because of a lack of funds in the city treasury and the unwillingness of private citizens to provide more adequate financial support.[19]

New Editor for the Dominion. L. E. McKenzie, editor of the *Donora* (Pennsylvania) *Evening Herald* and a writer for various magazines, including the *Saturday Evening Post,* on August 8 succeeded R. S. Reid as editor of the *Morgantown New Dominion.* He was a native of Zanesville, Ohio, and formerly a professional baseball player on the Pacific Coast.[20]

Aerial Circus. An aerial circus was presented over the Fourth of July weekend by the Gilbert Air Line Company and the Zenith Aviation Company. The planes landed on a field near Evansdale or on the Carrico tract on the Mileground, and gave scores of local men and women their first ride in the air. Capt. W. L. G. Smith was one of the pilots. Two minor accidents occurred because of the soggy field at Evansdale but no one was injured.[21]

18. Callahan, pp. 278, 279.
19. Callahan, pp. 296, 297.
20. *New Dominion,* July 31, 1920.
21. *New Dominion,* July 3, 6, 1920.

Pursglove P.O. To serve the rapidly increasing population on Scotts Run, a new post office, named Pursglove, was established November 27, 1920. It was named for the Pursglove Coal Company, operated by Samuel Pursglove, and others, nearby. John P. O'Connell was the first postmaster. The post office was at the mouth of Wades Run, at the site earlier known as Stumptown.

A. G. Baker. Albert Griffin Baker, head of the Baker Hardware Company, died on March 4 at his home on Spruce Street. He was the son of Mr. and Mrs. H. C. Baker. His father founded the hardware company April 11, 1894, and upon his death in 1900, Albert assumed direction of it. He married Ida Jacobs, who survived him.[22]

Mary Ella Brown. Mary Brown, a member of one of Morgantown's best known pioneer families, died on January 18. She was the daughter of Mathew and Margaret Smith Gay, and married John J. Brown September 30, 1868. They had three children, Margaret (married Dr. Herman G. Stoetzer), Alexandria Gay, and J. M. G. Brown. She was prominent in civic affairs.[23]

Dr. Coombs Dies. Death brought an end to the useful career of Dr. Elisha Hoffman Coombs on February 18. He was born on a farm near Frostburg, Maryland, in January 1840, and moved to Morgantown about 1855. After studying medicine in Hahnemann College, he returned to Morgantown in 1862 to begin the practice of medicine. He was also prominent in civic affairs, was cashier and president of the Merchants' National Bank (later the Bank of the Monongahela Valley). He married Mary Lazier and they had one daughter, Mrs. Jessie Coombs Davis.[24]

George Rogers. A great-nephew of John Rogers, well-known Morgantown citizen during the earlier 1800s, died December 13, 1920. He was a son of Thomas and Mary (Meason) Rogers and was born in Fayette County, Pennsylvania, May 26, 1857. John Rogers, having no children of his own, had persuaded Thomas to come to Morgantown to help with his business.

George was educated in the Morgantown public schools and in

22. *New Dominion,* March 5, 1920.
23. *New Dominion,* January 19, 1920.
24. *New Dominion,* February 19, 1920.

West Virginia University. He was a real estate dealer, helping to develop the Woodburn and East Morgantown residential sections. He was also interested in Cass District coal development. He married Louise Clemson Brown and they had two daughters, Mary Washington (married Bradford B. Laidley) and Louise Clemson (married Harlan B. Selby).[25]

Miscellany. In 1920: The Second National Bank completely renovated its former quarters, installing new fixtures of the latest kind, and providing better facilities in the remodeled and greatly enlarged banking room (Callahan, p. 277). . . . Albert Edward Hayes was killed in an accident at the A. L. Black Coal Company tipple at Randall on January 24; born March 16, 1864, he was the son of Henry S. Hayes (*New Dominion*, January 26, 1920). . . . For the third time in three years, Morgantown voters on January 27 rejected, 431 to 646, the proposed new city charter (*New Dominion*, January 27, 28, 1920). . . . Mrs. Albert Stillman published a biography of pioneer settler David Scott (*New Dominion*, January 28, 1920). . . . The Strand Theater Building was sold by the Morgan Realty Company to Morton Van Voorhis and Asa Sterling for $165,000 (*New Dominion*, March 11, 1920). . . . Ream's Drug Store, corner of High and Walnut streets, was sold by W. A. Ream, proprietor, to Robert R. Pierce and others, of Thomas (*New Dominion*, March 15, 1920). . . . The greatest display of the aurora borealis in memory was witnessed in the county; telegraph wires were put out of commission (*New Dominion*, March 23, 1920). . . . A deed drawn up February 28, 1798, by Charles and Cynthia Ferry, attesting the sale of two hundred acres of land at the mouth of Jakes Run to Michael Core for "22 pounds 10 shillings," was recorded at the courthouse (*New Dominion*, March 27, 1920). . . . The Morgantown Laundry Company was organized by Dr. I. M. Austin, Aaron J. Garlow, William E. Arnett, Virgil A. Brown, and Charles C. Jenkins (*New Dominion*, April 8, 1920). . . . The Commercial Candy Company opened for business at Morgantown (*New Dominion*, April 22, 1920). . . . The West Virginia Traction and Electric Company, in receivership, was reorganized as the West Virginia Utilities Company (*New Dominion*, April 23, 1920). . . . Ellis Parker Butler,

---

25. *The 175th Anniversary . . . of Monongalia County*, pp. 442, 443. The date of his death is misprinted as 1921 in that work.

author and humorist, spoke at the university (*New Dominion*, April 24, 1920).... The J. J. Brown property in South Park was sold to the city board of education as the site of a future high school building (*New Dominion*, June 24, 1920).... Albert M. Holland, a contractor, was killed when his truck was hit by a Monongahela passenger train (*New Dominion*, June 24, 1920). ... The Ever Bright Mirror Company, which planned to manufacture special mirrors, took over the plant formerly used by the Morgantown Broom Company (*New Dominion*, August 7, 1920). ... Layman W. Ogden, of Clarksburg, was killed when his automobile slid off the muddy Grapevine Hill road (*New Dominion*, August 13, 1920).... A new street, called Maiden Lane, was opened on the university campus in front of Woman's Hall (*New Dominion*, September 1, 1920).... Vice-presidential candidate Franklin D. Roosevelt spoke at the Strand Theater on September 29 (*New Dominion*, September 30, 1920).... Sousa's Band gave two concerts in the Strand Theater on October 6 (*New Dominion*, October 8, 1920).... The United States Window Glass Company announced that it is moving from Morgantown to Shreveport, Louisiana (*New Dominion*, October 12, 1920). ... The Monongahela Railway announced plans to double-track its lines from Brownsville to Fairmont (*New Dominion*, October 20, 1920).... Jere Johnson, local coal operator, was killed when his truck was hit by a shifting engine in Westover (*New Dominion*, November 4, 1920).... John L. Alexander, national young peoples' Sunday school worker, spoke at the First M.E. Church in Morgantown (*New Dominion*, November 11, 1920). ... Curtis C. Jackson and Adam Grow planned the immediate rebuilding of their plant in Westover, destroyed by fire on December 15 (*New Dominion*, December 17, 1920).... A private club of Pittsburgh men purchased the Mont Chateau Inn, which had been owned and operated by Mr. and Mrs. Alexander Voight since January 5, 1898 (*New Dominion*, March 9, 1920).

CHAPTER ONE HUNDRED FORTY-FIVE

1921

At the beginning of the second century of Monongalia County's history, very few of the residents were foreign born and nearly all of these were from northwestern European countries. The 1890 census showed only 74 were foreign born, out of a total population of 15,705. Of these, 3 were born in Canada, 17 in Ireland, 32 in England, 4 in Scotland, 11 in Germany, 41 in France, 2 in Italy, and 1 in an unidentified country.

The Ethnic Mix. But by 1921, the nature of the population was rapidly changing in Monongalia County, as in most other parts of the country. Beginning just before 1900, a vast wave of immigrants from new sources surged into America, attracted by our tremendous industrial development. Eighty percent of the 18 million newcomers who arrived in America in the quarter century before World War I came from southern and eastern Europe. Italians headed the list, followed by Jews, mostly from Russia, then by Poles; Magyars, Greeks, Armenians, Syrians, Turks, all came pouring in.

Most of the immigrants settled in the large cities of the Northeast and the Midwest, concentrating in areas where they found the most jobs. In New York, Chicago, Boston, the native-born Americans suddenly realized they were in the minority. Like it or not, residents of these cities faced a bewildering ethnic variety in the sudden presence of so many new arrivals eager to get ahead in their new land.

Economic opportunity magnetized the new immigrants (as, indeed, it had beckoned our earliest pioneers), drawing them off worn-out lands and out of the ghettos of crowded European cities. Once arrived here, they generally started at the bottom of the occupational ladder, doing America's dirty work—construction, mining, smelting, factory work, domestic service. So far as

502

possible they arranged themselves in tight ethnic communities, finding security in an enforced segregation.

Mystified by the overwhelming variety of immigrant life, progressive Americans developed schemes for "Americanizing" the new immigrants. A hopeful immigrant, Israel Zangwill, looking forward to the day of total assimilation, in his popular play, "The Melting Pot," described the "American symphony," the "seething crucible—God's crucible," where a new amalgam was being forged over divine fires. "Yet Zangwill told progressive audiences what they wanted to hear, not what they saw around them." Some, like Theodore Roosevelt, deplored the "tangle of squabbling nationalities" as "the one certain way of bringing the nation to ruin."[1]

In Monongalia County, as elsewhere, the new arrivals were regarded with suspicion and were referred to by disparaging nicknames, such as Dagos, Hunkies, or Polacks. They were felt to be illiterate and culturally deprived. They held to a form of benighted Catholicism or they were dedicated to the overthrow of capitalist society. Only a minority of the "old timers" welcomed the newcomers as adding richness and variety to the mostly Anglo-Saxon community.

In 1920 there were 3,279 persons of foreign births in Monongalia County, compared with 74 thirty years earlier. Of these 384 were from Austria, 94 from Belgium, 21 from Canada, 106 from Czechoslovakia, 149 from England, 43 from France, 128 from Germany, 155 from Greece, 406 from Hungary, 22 from Ireland, 802 from Italy, 168 from Jugo-Slavia, 41 from Lithuania, 246 from Poland, 10 from Rumania, 211 from Russia, 30 from Scotland, 24 from Spain, 31 from Switzerland, 5 from Syria, 146 from Wales, and 57 from various other countries.

Nearly one-third of the foreign born lived in the city of Morgantown itself, and the remainder were mostly in Sabraton, Star City, Westover, Riverside, and in the Scotts Run mining district. Only four cities in West Virginia, Charleston, Clarksburg, Fairmont, and Wheeling, had more foreign-born people than Morgantown.

The ethnic groups soon formed social clubs, such as Sons of

1. Bernard Bailyn, David Brion Davis, David Herbert Donald, John L. Thomas, Robert H. Wiebbe, and Gordon S. Wood, *The Great Republic,* (1977), p. 952.

Italy, or Turn Verein, but especially church groups, where services were often held in the language of the group, and where matters of common interest could be discussed.

A Hungarian Baptist Church was formed at Evansdale, meeting in homes. Rev. Andrew Harsanyi, of the Hungarian Evangelical and Reformed Church, started holding services in Osage and Brady in 1918. An important lay leader was Nicholas Molnar. An Orthodox Church, Saint Markella, was organized in 1915 at Sabraton by Bishop Emeri Zatkovich. Roman Catholics began holding services as early as 1901 and built a church in Seneca in 1914. Many of the early members were French, German, or Italian.

Americanization Activities. By the end of the nineteenth century American agricultural opportunities had considerably lessened. With half a million newcomers arriving in the United States annually, there was no longer farm land on which they could locate. They could only settle in the urban areas, where they hoped to obtain jobs in factories or other industries. Most of them had been farmers at home, so their difficulties in adjusting to life in America, already great because of language differences, was aggravated because they now must live in crowded towns or cities. Hostilities often developed between longtime residents and the newcomers because of communication problems and other factors.

But in Monongalia County, as in many other places, there were some who worked unselfishly to make life easier for the new people, to help them understand American ways and to adjust to them.

The community of Sabraton displayed a good example of this type of program. At the big tinplate mill around one thousand workers were employed, many of them from abroad. The foreign families were often criticized because they did not maintain their homes according to American standards. One reason for this was that they had never seen American homes; furthermore, they were mostly poor, unable to afford fine houses. The women spent most of their time in their kitchens, which doubled as nurseries, dining rooms, laundries, and sitting rooms.

Morgantown churches undertook programs to alleviate the unfortunate conditions. One of the most active leaders in this work was Mrs. Josie M. Hurxthal, who began working with the children, giving them outings and picnics, getting to know the parents through their children. The value of this work was soon recognized by the management of the tinplate mill and Mrs. Hurxthal was placed on the payroll.

Next, in September 1919, a visiting nurse was employed and, with the assistance of Mrs. Hurxthal, soon gained the confidence of the people living in the community.

"Assistance was given to any one in distress, whether or not they were employees of the American Sheet and Tinplate Company. The genuine, unselfish interest the nurse has taken in this people has awakened a desire in them to please her. She has been so intent in helping them that they have assisted in the cleanup campaigns by ridding up the backyards of rubbish, improving their cellars, and removing their pigpens and cow stables from the doorways."[2]

The company built, on the hill near the clock office, a demonstration home with quarters for the nurse, in order to show the immigrant mothers the proper conditions under which a home should be conducted. The house was furnished simply but neatly, with equipment within the means of the lower paid employees. There was a living room, a kitchen, and a bedroom, open to visitors at all times. The basement was so constructed that it had a room, twelve by twenty-four feet in size, entirely above ground. This was used as a kindergarten during the day and as a club room in the evening. Girls were taught sewing, bedmaking, the planning and preparation of meals.

All this is not to imply that conditions were by any means perfect. The first two decades of the twentieth century brought problems hitherto unknown in Monongalia County. There were problems of communication, only partly because the newcomers spoke a different language. Part of it resulted from the fact that they came from entirely different environments and an entirely different culture. It was difficult for them to understand the rules and requirements of the new society in which they found themselves. There were bitter arguments and fights, often between immigrants of different ethnic origins, sometimes resulting in fatalities.

Only the passage of time would demonstrate that the descendants of some of these immigrants would be among Monongalia's leading citizens as the county's bicentennial approached.

2. *Morgantown Chamber of Commerce Publ.* (1921), p. 52.

City Manager Government. One of the most pressing needs of the city of Morgantown as the 1920s approached was a new charter to overcome difficulties incident to the charter of 1901, which in many respects was a compromise between the towns of Morgantown, South Morgantown, Seneca, and Greenmont, when they combined to form a city. This charter was soon outgrown and difficulties were experienced in plans for improved streets and sewers, and with respect to equalization of taxation.

In 1917, influenced by the popularity of the commission form of government which had been adopted by some other cities of the state, the city council named a charter commission consisting of five members to draft a new charter. After much investigation and discussion this commission submitted a draft which the voters, however, reluctant to make a change, turned down. Again in 1919 and in 1920 other attempts were made to revise the old charter, or to draft a new one, but these attempts also met with strong opposition, particularly in the Fourth Ward, the old town of Seneca.

In December 1920, a more determined drive was started to solve this difficult problem of the city. New features proposed by representative committees from the voters in all parts of the city were given publicity almost daily in the columns of the two daily newspapers, the morning *New Dominion* and the afternoon *Morgantown Post.* Gradually the outlook became more promising. Finally, early in 1921, after three months of arduous work and discussion, the terms of a new charter were adopted by the several committees of citizens and at a general mass meeting, and were promptly approved by the legislature.

The new charter placed the municipal authority in a rotary common council of two members from each ward, each selected for a term of two years. By terms of the charter, the council members selected one of their number to act as chairman and as mayor, whose term lasted for one year. The council appointed the city manager and the city clerk, whose terms were of indefinite length. The city manager was the administrative head of the city government and responsible for the efficient operation of all departments (except, of course, the council). The city clerk kept the records of the council and all departments of the city government, and acted as clerk of the municipal court, prepared the assessment rolls, and collected all funds due the city.

The new charter also authorized special assessments against abutting property owners for street improvement, and thus made possible a new era of street paving. Coincident with this change, more adequate funds were obtained by bond issues and by increased taxation, especially through higher assessments, according to the true value of its property, in accord with the state law and the 1901 report of the state tax commissioner. While these changes did not correct all the problems contained in the old charter, they did result in more efficient government and more adequate funding.

The city manager plan was placed in operation in 1921 and the first manager was Charles E. Sutherland. Following the inauguration of the city manager plan of government, the city council authorized a complete survey of the city and the publication of a map showing a comprehensive plan.[3]

The University Comes of Age. Under the administration of President Frank Butler Trotter, it might be said that West Virginia University finally came of age. In the early days of its history it had been largely ignored by most citizens of the state; more recently, strong and determined efforts had been made to remove it to a more suitable location, in response to claims that Morgantown was very difficult to reach, besides being only a few miles from the Pennsylvania line.

But events of the administration of President Trotter virtually nailed it down to Morgantown. It was partly that the institution had now been more than a half a century at this location; partly that new buildings had been added, new investments made, rendering a move more and more costly.

Meanwhile, President Trotter was earning his cognomen as "The Builder." Although he did not complete his program of physical building, he did much to transform the institution from college to university status. Much of President Trotter's success as an administrator was through increases in faculty salaries. Before 1919 maximum salaries had been $2,500 for professors, $2,600 for department heads, $3,600 for deans. In that year these figures were raised to $2,900, $3,100, and $4,200, respectively. The next year all faculty members were given a 20 to 30 percent increase to meet rising costs of living.

3. Callahan, p. 296.

These increases made it possible to attract new faculty members of a high level in the rapidly expanding staff. In 1919 W. J. Kay became head of the department of speech, L. D. Arnett of library science, P. I. Reed of journalism. F. E. Clark became head of chemistry in 1918. Important scholarly contributions in Arts and Sciences during this period were also made by A. M. Reese, O. P. Chitwood, J. H. Cox, J. A. Eiesland, J. M. Callahan, W. P. Shortridge, R. A. Armstrong, and a host of others. Appointments in other fields were J. W. Madden, dean of law and, E. J. Van Liere, professor of physiology, both in 1921.

The State Road Commission. A new era of road construction was ushered in by the adoption of the Good Roads Amendment. The 1921 legislature passed a law authorizing the designation, construction, and maintenance of a state road system "to connect at least the various county seats and with important roads of adjoining counties." A State Road Commission of three members was provided for, not more than two from the same political party. Sale of $15 million of road bonds was authorized to get the program under way.

The 1921 legislature also abolished the old "Class A" and "Class B" system of public roads. In the new system there would be "state roads" and "county-district" roads, the "state roads" to include as much as was necessary or advisable of the old "Class A" system.

State "routes" were designated, but these remained as "county-district" roads, as far as maintenance was concerned, until they were taken over by the State Road Commission for construction; thereafter they were to be maintained by the state as "state roads."

In Monongalia County there were two state routes, designated, as elsewhere in the state, by numbers. State Route 4 ran north and south, connecting with Uniontown via a Pennsylvania route at Point Marion, and with Fairmont via the old Fairmont Pike through Laurel Point and Arnettsville. Route 7 ran east and west through the county, connecting with Kingwood, in Preston County, and, via the old Dunkard Creek Turnpike, with Hundred, in Wetzel County, and (later) on to New Martinsville, the county seat.

The principal road improvement in 1921 was the paving of the road up Scotts Run from Randall through Osage to Gustin Run.

The sixteen-foot-wide concrete highway, two miles in length, was opened for traffic in August.

Trolley Cars and Omnibuses. By 1921 the trolley car system of Monongalia County had reached and passed its zenith and was beginning to experience a serious competitor in the field of public transportation, the curious omnibus, or bus.

The omnibus was at first a horse-drawn carriage carrying a number of passengers, on streets of European cities, particularly London. Using a modification of these vehicles, specially built carriages propelled by gasoline motors were being used for sight-seeing tours in New York as early as 1902. The word omnibus (a French word, from Latin) was quickly shortened to merely bus.

In 1921, a Monongalia County corporation, the Star Bus Company, applied to the state for a license to operate between Morgantown and Scotts Run.

Fig. 115. Scotts Run bus passing through Riverside. (Courtesy Edith L. Peterson.)

The new road up Scotts Run had immediately begun to be used by a host of independent taxi drivers, transporting thousands of people to work or to the shopping centers. In December, when the

state granted an "exclusive franchise for taxicab privileges" to
the Star Bus Company over the road from Morgantown to Gustin
Run, twenty-seven independent drivers filed a protest. They were
informed, however, that the company was complying with the
state law. Thus there came into existence the county's first bus
line, and soon the first odd-looking buses were rolling from
Morgantown towards the mining district.[4]

A prime organizer of the company was Nelson E. Peterson, who
was born on March 6, 1880, in Trelleborg, Sweden. He came to
America about 1900, searched for gold in Alaska, did truck farming in Florida, then came to Morgantown in 1920 to work in the
developing coal mines. He married Hilda Hokeson, of Pennsylvania.

Tiring of coal mining, Peterson conceived the idea of forming a
company to transport people back and forth from Morgantown to
the mining field. In this enterprise he was assisted by his father-
in-law, Martin Hokeson, and by his brother, Oscar Peterson. Also
involved in the company was Fred Fiorini and a small group of
dependable bus drivers, who kept the buses running on a frequent
schedule from 5:00 a.m. or earlier until past midnight on work
days. Hilda Peterson did the accounting work, ran a candy and
cold drink stand in the bus terminal on Front Street, and operated a roller rink over the bus barn.

Fred Fiorini was born February 9, 1895, in Arnara, Italy, and
married Frances Turino. He, and some of the other drivers, had
operated taxi lines from Morgantown to Gustin Run and intermediate points, and came to see the advantages of a vehicle that
would transport a larger number of passengers than could be accommodated in an ordinary automobile.

In 1921 the days of the trolley were about over and the days of
the bus were just beginning. Buses, or motor coaches, would
presently develop into a billion-dollar industry, connecting most
cities and towns in America.

But these were still pioneer days for bus operators: "There was
no such thing as a bus, wagon makers turned into truck body
builders by the advancing tide of gasoline power had to learn

4. The line carried mostly miners, many of foreign origin, to and from the
mines and carried their families to the stores of Morgantown and Osage. By 1925
it was carrying over one million passengers in a year, the first line in the state to
reach that volume.

Fig. 116. N. E. Peterson.   Fig. 117. Oscar DuBois.

another set of new skills to satisfy early bus entrepreneurs. Parts were hard to get, if not impossible, and were often made in the neighborhood, not infrequently by blacksmiths. Tires, which never lasted long on the roads of the day, were seldom interchangeable between vehicles of different makes and modes. A much bigger business in the early days of motoring than later on was tire recapping and rebuilding, and tires constituted a major element in bus operating expense."[5]

Development of Sturgiss City. "Water and gas and sanitary sewers are being provided for as fast as labor can be had. Sturgiss City will have a population of 3,000 within two years. Manufacturing plants already in successful operation include the Sabraton works of the American Sheet and Tin Plate Co., Mississippi Glass Works, Pressed Prism Plate Glass Works, Barley Food Co., Beaumont Glass Works and Morgantown and Kingwood Railroad shops. The city wants and has sites for automobile factory, glass works and additional tin plate works."[6]

New Post Offices. Two new Monongalia County post offices were established in 1921, serving increased populations resulting from

5. Albert E. Meier and John P. Hoschek, *Over the Road. A History of Intercity Bus Transportation in the United States* (1975), pp. 8, 9.
6. *Industrial and Business Survey.* Morgantown Chamber of Commerce (1921), p. 8.

mining activities. Along the west side of the Monongahela River just north of Lowsville was Brady, named for Samuel Brady, president of the Brady Coal Company. Ulric D. Hawley was the first postmaster, appointed August 27, 1921.

On Indian Creek the Everettville post office was established February 26, 1921, with John Dawson Fultz as postmaster. The office and town were said to have been named for a Mr. Everett, an executive of the New England Fuel and Transportation Company, which established a mine there.

Monongahela Building. The largest office building in Morgantown (and in Monongalia County) was completed in 1921. This was the Monongahela Building, at the corner of High Street and Chancery Row, an eight-story building constructed by the Bank of the Monongahela Valley and others. It provided more than 200 offices in addition to space for the bank on the ground floor. "The construction of this building marked a departure from a long established condition of conservation on the part of businessmen of the city."[7]

Fig. 118. Monongahela Valley Bank Building, under construction.

7. Callahan, p. 279.

Charles W. Finnell. One of the best known residents of Morgantown, Charles Wesley Finnell, died October 30, 1921. The son of Rev. Charles W. Finnell, he was born in Virginia June 24, 1846, and came to Morgantown at the age of two. He served as clerk of the county and circuit courts and was a successful businessman. In 1872, with John H. Hoffman, he formed a stock company which became the Farmers' Bank, immediate predecessor of the Second National Bank. He operated the Franklin House from 1892 until 1899. He married Lucy E., daughter of John Hoffman, and they had two children, Mrs. Page A. Gibbons and Harry W. Finnell.[8]

Indian Creek and Northern Railroad. Authority to purchase the Indian Creek and Northern Railroad was being sought by the B.&O. The road was originally planned to run from Lowsville up Indian Creek via Arnettsville and Hagans, thence through a tunnel to Jakes Run and down that stream to Dunkard Creek and on to Blacksville. The company was organized with five hundred shares of stock at a par value of one hundred dollars.[9]

A portion of the road had been built, primarily by the New England Fuel and Transportation Company, to develop its coal lands on Indian Creek.

End of the M.&W. A new passenger schedule on the M.&W. R.R. was instituted on April 5, 1921, with the train crew spending the day at work in the Scotts Run section, then returning to their homes in Brave in the evening. This schedule, the most satisfactory ever used by the line, was as follows:

East A.M.		West P.M.
8:46	Randall	3:30
7:00	Brave	5:00

At Randall connections were made with main line Monongahela Railway trains to Morgantown. Mail for the towns along the line was carried by trains after May 23.

8. *Post,* October 31, 1921.
9. *Post,* September 23, 1921.

In November the name "Morgantown and Wheeling" passed into oblivion, as the hopes of its ultimate completion had long since died. At that time it was acquired by the Monongahela Railway and became known as the Scotts Run Branch. Passenger service continued good; despite the fact that about 175 cars of coal left Scotts Run daily the improved track and rolling stock did the job.[10]

Miscellany. Morgantown audiences again crowded the chautauqua sessions (*Post,* July 5, 1921). . . . Grading for five new oil storage tanks at the Morgantown Tank Field was under way by the South Penn Oil Company; they were to be of 75,000 barrels capacity each (*Post,* July 20, 1921). . . . Paul Rogers, of Charleroi, Pennsylvania, opened a new drugstore in Morgantown (*Post,* July 28, 1921). . . . Rev. A. Boutlou, first rector of the Saint Francis de Sales Catholic Church, died in Baltimore on September 25; a botanist of note, he was born at Landerneau, France, April 21, 1850 (*Post,* September 26, 1921). . . . Two new Morgantown stores, the Quality Meat Market and Kropff Brothers Jewelry, opened (*Post,* September 30, 1921). . . . Shipments of coal from Scotts Run in October amounted to 230,000 tons, a new record (*Post,* November 1, 1921). . . . M.&W. R.R. bonds worth $325,000 were sold on November 21 by the county court to Samuel Pursglove, acting for the Monongahela Railway (*Post,* November 21, 1921). . . . The contract for the new Ice's Ferry bridge across Cheat River was awarded to the Independent Bridge Company, of Pittsburgh, for $51,240 (*Post,* December 8, 16, 1921). . . . Asa Henderson, a farmer of Wadestown, died June 24; a son of David and Elizabeth (Morris) Henderson, he was born May 15, 1842 (*Chronicles of Core,* p. 191). . . . The old home of John Rogers (vol. 3, p. 203) was rented to the board of education; following Rogers it had been owned and occupied by Judge John A. Dille (1864-96), then by his daughter, Mrs. F. L. Emory (Callahan, p. 96). . . . The Everbright Mirror Company's plant was destroyed by fire (Callahan, p. 269). . . . The name of the Barley Foods Company was changed to Morgantown Macaroni Company (Callahan, p. 271). . . . The holdings of the Elkins Coal and Coke Company in Monongalia County were transferred to the Penn-Mary Company, a sub-

10. *Chronicles of Core,* pp. 191, 192.

sidiary of the Bethlehem Steel Company (Callahan, p. 276). . . . The Morgantown and Kingwood Railroad was transferred from the Elkins interests to the Baltimore and Ohio Railroad (Callahan, p. 281). . . . Membership of Morgantown's largest churches was reported as: Methodist Episcopal, 2100; Catholics, 900; Methodist Protestants, 700; Baptists, 585; Presbyterians, 557; Christians, 310; Lutherans, 200 (Callahan, p. 293). . . . A new humorous magazine, *Moonshine,* appeared on the university campus; because some of the alleged humor was regarded as obscene, it met with a storm of protest (Ambler, p. 569). . . . Alexander Reid Whitehill, head of the department of chemistry at the university, died October 25 (*New Dominion,* October 26, 1921). . . . Bert Holmes Hite, chemist at the Agricultural Experiment Station since 1895, died October 6 (*The Post,* October 6, 1921). The Lemley Coal Company opened a small mine and built a mining town at Lemley Siding (*Chronicles of Core,* p. 191).

CHAPTER ONE HUNDRED FORTY-SIX

1922

West Virginia University was making the most rapid growth in its history, up to this time. Additional acreage was purchased and new buildings were under way or planned. Land acquired about 1922 included sites for a Law Building (begun in 1921), a Field House, and a Music Building. The total appropriation for the 1921-23 biennium was double that for any previous such period and for the first time exceeded $2 million.

A New President? "To some persons these achievements seemed to mark a fitting end for an administration that from the outset had been regarded as temporary. Moreover, . . . former regent Shawkey was still regarded by his friends as the 'ideal man' for the presidency of the University. . . ."[1]

President F. B. Trotter again reminded the regents that he intended "eventually" to resign from the "heavy burden." It was again rumored that Shawkey, then superintendent of the Beaver Pond (Bluefield) school district of Mercer County, was about to be appointed as the new president. "But President Trotter adroitly sidestepped the issue by announcing his intention not to resign until his building program had been completed and until the board felt that his withdrawal would not injure the University."[2]

New appointments during 1922 included Dr. G. R. Lyman as dean of the College of Agriculture; Dr. L. H. Leonian, professor of plant pathology; and Dr. P. I. Reed as head of the newly established department of journalism, in the College of Arts and Sciences. Harry E. Stone, of Erie, Pennsylvania, was made dean of men, effective September 1. F. Roy Yoke, a 1903 alumnus, be-

1. Ambler, p. 515.
2. Ambler, p. 516.

came the first full-time alumni secretary. Pi Lambda Psi, a Jewish fraternity, was opened on May 28.

An amusing incident which attracted national attention occurred on the campus in 1922. Evolution was a red-hot subject during the early twenties, culminating in the famous John T. Scopes trial at Dayton, Tennessee, in 1925, in which William Jennings Bryan participated.

Early in 1922 Rev. John Roach Stratton, pastor of the Calvary Baptist Church in New York City, began a campaign to have textbooks teaching the "Darwinian theory" excluded from the schools of that city. Dr. A. M. Reese, head of the zoology department of West Virginia University, attacked the Reverend Mr. Stratton's views, stating that the minister was "talking rank folly" and "evidently seeking notoriety." Rev. O. W. Baylor, pastor of the Spruce Street Christian Church in Morgantown, came out in opposition to Dr. Reese and arranged a debate on the subject of evolution, which was held in the Presbyterian Church on March 1. Dr. Reese spoke on the subject, "Why I should believe in evolution," and another university professor, C. W. Waggoner, head of the physics department, spoke on "Why I should not believe in evolution."

This was followed, on March 11, by a lecture by the "silver-tongued orator" himself, William Jennings Bryan, who addressed an overflow audience in Commencement Hall on "The Bible and its Enemies."

In his address, "Bryan was so sure of his position that . . . he offered a prize of one hundred dollars to any professor, who could reconcile evolution with the Bible. When Professor R. C. Spangler, of West Virginia University, said he could, he sent him one hundred dollars but then reminded him of certain questions that he must answer; including the first, 'Do you believe that you are the descendant of an ape?' ' "

"Spangler answered all these questions affirmatively except the first, for 'The biologists of today do not teach that man descended from the ape of today, and no one believes it except those ignorant of the facts of biology.' "[3] Furthermore, Spangler asserted that the questions were not part of the original terms laid down by Bryan in his speech. Bryan thereupon accused

---

3. Paolo E. Coletta. *William Jennings Bryan* (3 vols., 1969), vol. 3, pp. 219, 220.

Spangler of "cowardly evasion" and Spangler demanded a public retraction. And thus it stood. Spangler, however, cashed the one hundred dollar check, which had been written out on a scrap of paper.

The 1922 Mountaineer team reached "the pinnacle of football fame in West Virginia." Under Coach C. W. Spears the team won every game except for a 12-12 tie with Washington and Lee. Old rivals Pitt and Washington and Jefferson were defeated and a post-season game with Gonzaga College, at San Diego, California, resulted in a 21 to 13 Mountaineer victory. Stars on the team included Charles C. ("Trusty") Tallman, Joseph Setron, Homer Martin, Gustavus Ekberg, Fred ("Jack") Simons, Nicholas Nardacci, Russell Meredith (captain), Walter Mahan, Philip Hill, and Pierre Hill.

To further emphasize athletics, the Woman's Athletic Association was organized in 1922, with a membership of about two hundred.

Pullman to Charleston. An important new train service was provided, beginning on December 17, 1922, by the B.&O., furnishing the best connection yet between Morgantown and the state capital. Two new trains, Nos. 57 and 58, carried through coaches and parlor cafe cars from Grafton to Charleston and drawing room sleeping cars between Pittsburgh, Morgantown, Grafton, and Charleston. Southbound, the train left Pittsburgh at 5:00 p.m., Morgantown at 8:15 p.m., and arrived in Charleston at 8:30 a.m. Northbound, it left Charleston at 8:20 p.m., Morgantown at 7:58 a.m., and arrived in Pittsburgh at 11:35 a.m. Six berths were assigned to Morgantown.

A local editor commented: "This will greatly facilitate business trips to the state capital and will save at least 24 hours on the trip."[4]

Monongalia County Hospital. Hundreds of county residents gathered on October 22, 1922, for the opening of the new Monongalia County Hospital,[5] on the second floor of the County Infirmary, on the Van Voorhis Road. The new hospital was established through the cooperation of the Morgantown Woman's Association and the county court and was said to be the first in the

4. *New Dominion,* December 18, 1922.
5. By a 1930 act of the legislature the name was changed to Monongalia General Hospital.

Fig. 119. Monongalia County Hospital. (Courtesy Mrs. Wayne Batteiger.)

country to be formed through the sponsorship of a woman's association. Charles Morris, superintendent of the infirmary, was also in charge of the hospital, Miss Della Main, head nurse, and Dr. J. R. Hughart, county health officer. The hospital had a capacity of seventy-five. There were operating rooms, a kitchen, nurses' quarters, etc.[6]

Road Building Controversies. The county's Good Roads program was at last moving along at full speed. The experimental period was drawing to a close and actual "good roads" were beginning to appear. The new year was to bring substantial extension of the paved road system, but disappointment in Morgantown's main objective—an all-weather connection to the nation's highway system.

In February the State Road Commission promised enough money to complete U.S. Route 19 to Fairmont and U.S. 119 to the Pennsylvania line, towards Uniontown, provided the county completed the section from Laurel Point to Little Indian Creek. But funds assigned to that project had been exhausted, threaten-

6. *New Dominion,* October 21, 1922.

ing to leave a two-mile gap unpaved. Morgantown civic leaders quickly suggested transfer of Grant District funds earmarked for the River Road to the Fairmont Pike; residents along the River Road were just as quick to oppose the transfer and Judge I. G. Lazzelle in April granted an injunction against the transfer. Meanwhile the county found other funds and Cole Brothers, the contractors, resumed work on the project, and the work was completed before the end of the season.

Sisler and Morse, however, the contractors on the remaining section to the Marion County line, were making scant progress, chiefly because of lack of paving materials. A mile of pavement between Georgetown and Arnettsville was completed by the end of the season, but without connections at either end.

In April Sisler and Morse were awarded a contract for improvement of 3.8 miles of the road towards Point Marion. The grading was completed during the season and all of the concrete poured except for about one mile between Cartwright's and Easton. All fall Morgantown citizens had watched the work, with hope gradually dying for an outlet before winter.

Meanwhile people in the western end of the county were proposing construction of north-south highways, connecting Pittsburgh and Fairmont. They were closer to shopping centers in Fairmont and Waynesburg than in Morgantown. A meeting held in Wadestown in April proposed a north-south road via Blacksville and Cross Roads, and Stephen Mason, of Daybrook, suggested a route via Blacksville, Daybrook, and Fairview. A Battelle District road bond issue proposal, however, was defeated at an election on August 19. Morgantown people were interested in a road through Blacksville and Wadestown towards the Ohio River.[7]

WHD. West Virginia's first radio station was established on the University campus on March 16, 1922; on that date Dr. C. W. Waggoner, head of the physics department, obtained a license to operate a broadcast transmitter on 360 meters with 250 watts power for unlimited time. The call letters WHD were assigned

7. Core, "Out of the Mud," *Westover Observer*, August 30, 1956.

and Dr. Waggoner soon began conducting experimental work in broadcasting.[8]

The Jewish Community. The first Jewish family came to Morgantown in 1879, when the place was still only a village, with fewer than a thousand inhabitants. It was in 1879 that the Hirschman family came from Philadelphia with the view of locating in business in what promised to be a rapidly growing community.

At first only two young men of the family, Simon and Milton, located here. Their father came along for a while, to help them get started in business. Their first store was a small one in a frame building that stood on High Street on the site of the Odd Fellows building. Later they moved to 279 High Street, where they presently bought the property, built a new building, and developed Morgantown's largest department store, known as "The Big Store."

The Morgantown city directory, in 1901, lists three members of the family, Louis, Milton, and Simon, residing at 467 High Street.

In the mid 1890s a brother-in-law, M. J. Sonneborn, also moved to Morgantown and presently became the general manager of The Big Store. It was said of him that he "has a handsome home in South Park. He is devoted entirely to his family, a wife and daughter and his business."[9]

Shinedling gives numerous references to the story of the Morgantown community. In 1898, he says, there were four Jewish families residing in Morgantown. In 1901 Milton Hirschman was listed as the only subscriber in Morgantown to the Jewish Publication Society of America. In 1905 Morgantown was named as one of eight West Virginia cities having a Jewish community. In 1908, an enumeration reported a total of 1,500 Jews in West Virginia. By 1920, this number had grown to 5,440 (out of a total

8. See Colee Twigg, in the *Daily Athenaeum*, February 22, 1973. The signal probably never extended beyond the campus, broadcasts were sporadic, and confined to the experimentation. In 1923 the university allowed the license to lapse, because of a belief that radio was a commercial concern and its educational value had yet to be established.

9. Abraham L. Shinedling. *West Virginia Jewry: Origin and History* (1850-1958). 3 vols. 1963.

population of 1,463,701) and there were 120 Jewish people in Morgantown, sufficient to have organized a Morgantown Congregation, and a local lodge of the B'nai B'rith (one of eight in West Virginia).

At that time the Morgantown congregation held its religious services in Phillips Hall, on Pleasant Street. Services were conducted in Hebrew. There was no rabbi but the congregation had a school which met for one session weekly; there were three teachers and sixteen pupils. The congregation, Shinedling speculates, was Orthodox, saying that there appears to have been later a Reform congregation and that the two congregations presently merged to form the Tree of Life congregation.

The Morgantown Temple Sisterhood affiliated with the National Federation of Temple Sisterhoods on November 12, 1922, with twenty members. At that time its president was Lillian (Mrs. Samson) Finn and its secretary was Mrs. Daisy Weil.

Among early Jewish citizens of Morgantown, listed by Shinedling, were the following:

Samson Finn came to Morgantown from New Castle, Pennsylvania, in 1915 "and began his mercantile career . . . as a small merchant, operating a ladies' clothing store." In the course of the next forty years "he acquired a reputation as a notable merchant, and became the owner of considerable real estate, playing a role in the development of the city."

In a list entitled "Jews of Prominence in the United States," published in the American Jewish Yearbook for 1922-23, there is mentioned Aaron Arkin, a pathologist at West Virginia University, who was born in Russia in 1888.

French and Belgians. In 1920 there were more than one hundred persons living in Monongalia County who gave France or Belgium as the country of their birth. Of these, eighty said they were born in Belgium, while thirty-five gave France as their natal home. Since the Belgians were virtually all French-speaking, it could be said that in the first two decades of the twentieth century there was a good-sized French community in and around Morgantown.

The majority of these people were from northern France and Belgium and came to Monongalia County because of the glass industry here. An exception was Medard Albertazzie and his family, who came from Grenoble, France, and located in the Scotts

Run coalfield, at Cassville. A notable scion of the family is Ralph Albertazzie, pilot of Air Force No. 1.[10]

Europeans who had learned the techniques of glass making in their home communities were often attracted by news of the developing industry in America and developed a desire to cross the Atlantic, where they thought prospects were better for them.

Oscar DuBois was one of these. His recollections provide the basis for the early history of the Belgian and French glass workers in Monongalia County. Oscar was born in 1879 at Charleroi, Belgium, which at that time boasted that it was the window glass capital of the world. His maternal grandfather, Dominque Andre, was making glass in Charleroi by 1850.

Charles DuBois, Oscar's father, first came to America in 1880, along with several of his neighbors who were solicited by a representative of the Swindel Glass Company, of Baltimore. Charles had learned the trade in northern France in 1870 with his uncle, Charles Avrenne, who operated a plant there.

Charles DuBois made seven round trips across the Atlantic, working at various plants in the United States. Finally, in 1901, he brought his wife and two children, Oscar and Earl, to Morgantown, where they took two thousand dollars stock in the new Marilla cooperative glass works.

Among other early Belgian or French workers in and around Morgantown were Camille Rassart (whose daughter, Laura, became the wife of Oscar DuBois), Alidor Houche Collart, Emile Raspillaire, Alfred and Louis Zellers, Leopold Lefevre, Edmund Brasseur (who became a foreman at W. R. Jones Window Glass Company), Arthur Laurent (who started the Morgantown Glass Company, on Chestnut Street), Rene Bousiflet, and Alexander Rousseau. Carl and Christian DuBois (no relation to Oscar) were among other newcomers.

John F. Heiner points out two kinds of glass largely made at Morgantown.[11] Soda lime glass contains a large proportion of sodium hydroxide and calcium hydroxide; tableware, jars, containers, and window panes are examples. Lead glass (flint glass) contains lead oxide, potash, etc., and is distinguished by its clar-

10. J. F. ter Horst and Col. Ralph Albertazzie, *The Flying White House*. 350 pp. 1979.

11. *Morgantown Crystal Glassware Guide* (1978).

ity, sparkle, and tone; thin walled pieces have a resonant, bell-like ring when gently tapped.

The Seneca Glass Company produced flint glass. In Europe, Liege, Belgium, was a center for flint glass manufacture and most of the French-speaking flint glass workers came here from that city, although a few came from Alsace-Lorraine or Switzerland. The Morgantown Glassware Guild and Beaumont were also flint plants.

Among early flint glass workers here were Aime and Joseph Defrere, Emile Melphis, Gabrielle Henri, Leon Jacquet, Emile Bernier, Arthur Gillot, Joseph Libert, Arthur Licot, Octave Detaille, John and Oscar Grandchamps, John DeCoster, and Dennis Leroy.

Oscar DuBois tells in poetry how Morgantown was a place

> "Where workers mingled as a clan
> And they were highly paid
> And training their apprentices
> They kept the tricks of trade.
> "The trade was old and started back
> Beyond the Middle Ages
> When windows even one foot square
> Commanded princely wages.
> "Then in the land of many hills
> Was lime and sand and gas
> And West Virginia had in plenty
> The things to make the glass."[12]

Courthouse Changes. Behind the courthouse the jail, constructed in 1881, was enlarged to make room for an increasing number of prisoners and was connected with the courthouse by a bridge from the second story for the convenience of the sheriff in escorting prisoners to the court room.

About the same time the trees in front of the courthouse were removed and the entire space was paved, "against the protests of botanical members of the civic clubs and a few remaining lovers of nature."[13]

Canyon Sunday School. To serve the religious needs of residents of the Canyon mining community, a union Sunday school was or-

---

12. *Lichen and Moss and Other Poems* (1976).
13. Callahan, p. 300.

ganized in 1922 by Oscar Clingan, assisted by Robert Eddy, V. E. Mazzocco, and Minerva Shelby. At first they met in homes but later arranged to meet in the Canyon Schoolhouse.[14]

The Apostolic Faith Church. A congregation known as the Apostolic Faith Church was organized in 1922. It was sometimes called the Pentecostal Church and was a unit of the United Pentecostal Church.

The local body came into existence as a result of prayer by Rev. and Mrs. H. I. Goodin, of Akron, Ohio. They felt called to do some kind of special religious work and had a vision that there was a place for them in the West Virginia coalfields. They came to Morgantown in 1922, the minister going to work in the mines, where he made friends with many people. Prayer meetings were held wherever possible, a tent was erected on Sabraton Avenue, in Norwood, and a six-weeks revival was held. About seventy people joined the group and a church building was started before the revival was over, and dedicated in December.[15]

St. Mary's Russian Orthodox Church. A new congregation of Slavonic Christians was organized in 1922, through a split in the membership of Saint Markella's Orthodox Church in Sabraton. The split was political in origin, rather than religious, chiefly in reaction to political conditions in Europe following the World War. The new congregation located in Westover.[16]

The Community Building. The Women's Christian Temperance Union, with the aid of a community fund drive, began the construction on Fayette Street of a large Community Building.[17] The structure was to be equipped with an assembly hall, kitchen, gymnasium, rest rooms, and numerous dormitory rooms. The cost was about $110,000 for the building; the lot and the equipment brought the total cost to $150,000.[18]

The Lions Club. The Morgantown Lions Club was organized May 11, 1923. Its first president was Attorney Minter L. Wilson,

14. Dodds and Dodds, p. 154.
15. Dodds and Dodds, p. 69.
16. Dodds and Dodds, pp. 78, 111.
17. To clear the site, the old decaying building formerly housing the Kiger Tannery was removed. Callahan, p. 121.
18. Callahan, p. 272.

with J. Clyde Smith as secretary-treasurer. Weekly luncheon meetings were held each Tuesday in the Community Building.[19]

Miscellany. In 1922: Rev. Stephen Borsos became the first regular minister of the Hungarian Evangelical and Reformed congregation in Monongalia County (Dodds and Dodds, p. 79). . . . A new frame building was constructed to serve the Highland Methodist congregation on Klondike Hill, in Battelle District (see vol. 3, p. 590) (Dodds and Dodds, p. 133). . . . The name of Sturgiss City was changed to Sabraton, in honor of George C. Sturgiss's wife, Sabra J., daughter of Col. Addison S. Vance; she had died May 22, 1903. Sturgiss's mother was also named Sabra. . . . John L. Hatfield rebuilt for his residence the old Evans home on the historic lot at the corner of Spruce and Willey streets, where the Monongalia Academy began (Callahan, p. 273). . . . The Bank of Morgantown on August 14 purchased the adjoining four-story building from the old Farmers' and Merchants' Bank, which had been consolidated with the Bank of the Monongahela Valley (Callahan, p. 277). . . . The Morgantown post office had ten city carriers and thirty-four office employees (Callahan, p. 284). . . . There were seven rural free delivery routes (Callahan, p. 285). . . . The tank-flow of the Morgantown water system was 2.5 million gallons, the daily consumption about 133 gallons per capita (Callahan, p. 286). . . . The enrollment at Morgantown High School reached 842, necessitating the rental of additional space, including the old John Rogers home on Foundry Street (Callahan, p. 288). . . . A Morgantown hotel stock company was organized by Judge Frank Cox, Dr. I. C. White, Dr. D. H. Courtney, Dr. L. S. Brock, James H. McGrew, Judge I. G. Lazzelle, Rufus Lazzelle, James R. Moreland, Harry O. Cole, and others (Callahan, p. 301). . . . Charles E. Hodges became owner and publisher of the *New Dominion* in May (Callahan, p. 272). . . . Alvin C. Michael, of Hagans, died (*Chronicles of Core,* p. 192). . . . A special Pullman train was operated to Charleston for the Washington and Lee football game on October 28 (*New Dominion,* October 16, 1922). . . . William P. Willey, retired professor of law at the university, died December 19 (*West Virginia Law Review,* January 23). . . . Chauncey William Waggoner, head of the university department of physics, died October 26 in Shreveport, Louisiana, as a

---

19. See manuscript history of the club by Charles E. Moore.

result of being thrown from a horse (*New Dominion*, October 27, 1922). . . . Dr. Charles McLane, son of Dr. Joseph A. McLane, died at Morgantown April 18 (Chandler, *Three McLane Doctors*, p. 272).

CHAPTER ONE HUNDRED FORTY-SEVEN

1923

The year of 1923 was the most memorable one of all in the history of Monongalia County's road-building activities. Hundreds of people had already experienced the thrill that came from watching the paving crew reach their homes, and the sense of security that resulted from living on an all-weather road. Now the city of Morgantown and the entire area of the county served by paved roads were tied into the nation's highway system. It represented a climax to the checkered story of labor, hope, dissension, and discouragement that had characterized road building efforts of the past several years.

The Point Marion Road. Work was slow getting under way in the spring and the State Road Commission had to remind Sisler and Morse, the contractors, that there might be a forfeit if there was further delay. In May concrete pouring was started on the gap near Easton but only about twenty-five feet had been laid when the concrete mixer broke down. All things come to an end, however, and on July 7 the last concrete on the project was poured and Morgantown was at last connected with the outside world by a hard surfaced highway.[1]

In a ceremony on July 20, the road was opened for traffic. At least three hundred autos were parked for the program and thousands of people passed over the new road later that day. Point Marion was clogged with cars from 5:00 p.m. until midnight, with traffic officers on the job.[2]

The Fairmont Pike. Meanwhile, the same contractors were at work on the Fairmont road. In May concrete pouring started at

1. Core, "Out of the Mud," *Westover Observer,* September 6, 1956.
2. *New Dominion,* July 21, 1923.

Little Indian Creek, with traffic detoured up the creek and back to the pike near Georgetown, thence over the one mile of paving completed the previous fall, to Arnettsville, where another detour was necessary between that place and the Marion County line, because of another paving crew at work.

After the completion of the Point Marion road the contractors were able to concentrate their efforts on the Fairmont road and by the beginning of August only about two thousand feet remained to be paved. About three hundred feet was laid on a good day's work.

At last, on September 7, the road was opened for traffic, and with it motorists could travel the entire stretch from Clarksburg to the Pennsylvania line, over fifty miles, one of the longest stretches of paved road in the state. Residents of Clarksburg, Fairmont, and Morgantown joined in a giant ceremony held near Arnettsville. Gov. E. F. Morgan and Major C. P. Fortney, chairman of the State Road Commission, were present. The ribbon was cut by Miss Alice Brett (Miss Marion County) and Miss Elizabeth Malamphy (Miss Monongalia County). Speaking from a truck, part of the time with an umbrella over his head because of intermittent showers, Governor Morgan said:

"I know that you have become impatient on account of the delay and have criticized the State Road Commission and the contractor, but now the magnificient highway has been completed, you are ready to excuse the delays and show by this wonderful gathering that you are deeply appreciative of the completion of this great task. And while the road has cost millions of dollars, you are all satisfied and happy. When we drive on this magnificent highway and reflect that less than a century and a half ago the entire territory extending from Clarksburg to Morgantown was practically a wilderness and penetrated only by the wild beast and the savage, we are amazed at the progress that has been made."

The newly completed roads were immediately choked with heavy traffic. On Sunday afternoon, September 13, between 5:30 and 6:30 p.m., 530 automobiles crossed the river bridge at Morgantown, and 448 between 7:30 and 8:00 p.m. Over that weekend twenty-six cars were wrecked in Morgantown and vicinity, as inexperienced drivers tried to negotiate the crowded roads and streets.

State Routes. State routes through the county had been designated in February as (1) the road from the state line near Point Marion to Morgantown, thence (2) "generally with the Brandonville and Fishing Creek turnpike" to the Marion County line; (3) from the Marion County line via Smithtown and Uffington to Morgantown; (4) from the state line near Mount Morris via Bowlby to Morgantown thence (5) via Deckers Creek through Dellslow to the Preston County line; and (6) from the Wetzel County line to Wadestown, "down the West Virginia fork of Dunkard Creek to Wise, thence crossing the divide by way of Bula to Dunkard Creek, thence generally with Dunkard Creek to Dolls Run, and thence with Dolls Run to Core; thence crossing the divide to Cassville, and thence down Scotts Run to the State route at Randall."

The road from the state line near Point Marion through Morgantown and over the Fairmont Pike to the Marion County line was designated as State Route No. 4; it led across the state to Bluefield. The road from the Wetzel County line to the Preston County line was State Route No. 7; it led east and west across the state from Ohio to Maryland. The road from the state line at Mount Morris to Morgantown was State Route No. 30, and that from the Marion County line through Smithtown to Morgantown was State Route No. 73.

During the summer the course of these routes across the county was indicated by road crews who painted red and white markers with black route numbers on telephone poles across the county.

Roads for Battelle. A petition with the signatures of four hundred Battelle District residents affixed was presented to the State Road Commission early in the year, asking for the improvement of their road to the county seat. As a follow-up, a group of Battelle men drove in buggies in March to Brave, Pennsylvania, and took the passenger train to Morgantown to ask the Chamber of Commerce for help. The chamber promised to help but W. S. Downs, of the SRC, said the Kingwood section of Route 7 had priority.

End of the Loop Line. The days of the trolley cars were numbered, as paved roads continued to be built. In April 1923, the last street car on the famous city loop line made its circuit for the final time, as contractors prepared to engage upon a big street improvement program.

Bus Line to Fairmont. For two decades there had been talk of building an interurban trolley line to connect Morgantown with Fairmont, as that city was connected to Clarksburg and Weston. But in April the West Penn Company, operators of that line, announced that they would first test the territory by operating a bus over the new highway. On September 26 the SRC heard the application of the company and in October it was announced that the company would soon start hourly service over the newly completed Fairmont Pike, between 6:30 a.m. and 11:30 p.m., between Morgantown and Rivesville, changing to a trolley at Rivesville.

Motorman Stops Car as Chasm Yawns. An accident which might have resulted in the greatest catastrophe in the history of Morgantown occurred on Saturday evening, December 1, 1923. The Union Utility Company's streetcar, bound for Greenmont and South Morgantown, jumped the track on the Walnut Street bridge, plunged toward the guard rail, and was only stopped on the brink of a drop of eighty feet to the waters of Deckers Creek below. About twenty to thirty passengers were on the car and no one was injured except Circuit Court clerk Garfield Davies, who jumped from the rear platform and sustained slight cuts. Motorman Charles McClain and Conductor J. L. Beach were in charge of the car and catastrophe was averted only through Motorman McClain's prompt use of the handbrake.[3]

Italian-Americans. In 1890 there were two people in Monongalia County who were born in Italy. In 1920 there were 802 persons who gave Italy as their birthplace and doubtless a few thousand others who were born in America but of parents who were born in Italy. Of the 3,279 persons of foreign birth in the county it is obvious that 25 percent of them were from Italy. In the ethnic mix that Monongalia County had become, the Italian-American community was by far the largest.

It was, of course, the opportunity for employment in the county's dozens of new factories that brought these people to Morgantown. America was a land of golden opportunity. Italians were

3. *New Dominion,* December 3, 1923.

flocking to America by the hundreds of thousands; a few of them chose Monongalia County.

"The United States has a government that is entirely satisfactory to at least several foreigners who reside in or near Morgantown. They are anxious to renounce their allegiance to their foreign rulers and become citizens of the best country in the world, the country ruled by President Taft and the pleasant smile.

"Tuesday Rocco Lepera filed his petition for naturalization with the clerk of the circuit court. Mr. Lepera had already filed his declaration of intention of becoming a citizen of the United States and now files his second and final paper. The applicant is a merchant and for several years has conducted a fruit store in Morgantown. At the present time he is located at the eastern end of the new bridge. Mr. Lepera came here from Naples, Italy, September 9th, 1899.

"Six more subjects of sunny Italy have tired of the rule of Victor Emmanuel or have come to regard the United States as the greater country and have filed their declaration of intention of becoming citizens of it. . . .

"Luigi Lepera, aged 31, a native of Apriglianno, Italy, now of Morgantown, thinks he can have more success as a merchant in America and filed his declaration Tuesday. Monday Rocco Pisegna, age 25, who is a subject of the Italian king and formerly lived in Callordonga, Italy, took the first step to becoming a full-fledged citizen of the United States. Mr. Pisegna is a merchant at Dellslow.

"Carlo Paolone is another Italian, 25 years of age, who loves America. Mr. Paolone lives in Dellslow and emigrated from Scanno, Italy. His application was left with the circuit clerk Monday.

"Carmel Centofanti and Frederick Paolone are two more former residents of Scanno, Italy, who prefer dear old Dellslow to their first residing place. Centofanti is 28 years of age and is a stonemason, while Paolone is a baker and gives his age as 23. Both applications were filed last Saturday.

"The last of the present number of applicants filed his application July 11th, 1908, and his name is Joe Lambardo. Mr. Lambardo is a laborer and hails from Messina, the scene of the terrible earthquake. He gives his age as 24."[4]

4. *Post-Chronicle,* November 27, 1909.

Luigi Lepera ran a hotel and restaurant across the street from the B.&O. depot and many newcomers from Italy came in to see him and ask for directions for finding relatives and friends in the area. John Zan, a boy from Parella, Piedmont, arrived in Morgantown May 12, 1912, to be with his uncle, Mike Tinivello, who had been here about ten years. Mr. Zan worked for him at his Walnut Street store and on various occasions directed new arrivals to their destinations. On one such occasion, in 1917, a young girl, Margaret Sabodo, got off the train and asked how to find her aunt, who was married to Jacint Henri, a Belgian glassworker in Seneca. John showed her the way and five years later married her. She was from Loranze, a town only two or three miles from John's hometown, although they had never met in Italy.

Emilio Ferrara, from Palena, Abruzzi, came to Morgantown in 1912 to work in the tin mill at Sabraton. He had met and married in New York a young girl, Filomena Purificato, from Formia, Latina (where, legend says, Aeneas landed on his way home from the siege of Troy).

Andrea and Maria Anna Constantine, from Chieti, located at an early date in Morgantown, where their son, Tony, was born in 1908.

Domenick Furfari, Sr., came to Morgantown April 2, 1902, from Cerasi, Calabria. His wife, Josephine Catalano, from the same town, followed in 1914. They had several children, including Domenick ("Mickey") Furfari, Jr., in 1976 sports editor for the *Morgantown Dominion-Post.*

Thoney Pietro came to Morgantown in 1901 and established the Pietro Paving and Construction Company, inducing his brothers, James, Henry, and Lawrence, who had settled in Pennsylvania, to join him. The Pietro family migrated from Attelata, in Abruzzi. Among early construction jobs done by the company were the brick pavements from the end of the Pleasant Street bridge up Grand Street to the top of the hill, in 1902, and from the end of the river bridge to the top of the Westover hill, in 1910. James married Maria Donetteli and their son, Lawrence, still lived in Morgantown in 1976.

Members of Italian families often changed the spelling of their names to Anglicize them, or even to translate them into the English equivalent.

Among dozens of other Italian families locating in Morgantown during the first two decades of the twentieth century were

Fig. 120. Domenick Furfari, Sr.   Fig. 121. George Comuntzis.

the Masciola, Chico, Farinetti, Chioso, Beata, Furfari, Quagliotti, Salucci, Bartoluzzi, Pisegna, Biafora, Antonio, Annonio, Carbarino, Benvenuto, Rich, Gianola, and Vecchio families. Many started as laborers, then went into commercial ventures. Second and third generations members of the families contributed significantly to the county's professional and commercial life.

Greek-Americans. George Peter Comuntzis came to Morgantown in 1909, from Sparta, Greece; he had married Angelina Caravasos, also of Sparta. In Morgantown they established a restaurant that soon became known as the best in town. In 1976 the family was still in the restaurant business in Morgantown.

Nick J. Kugoulis was one among numerous Greeks who came to Sabraton, attracted by the big tinplate mill. He started a store across from the factory, which far outlived the tinplate mill itself.

Nicklous Costianes was another early Greek immigrant. He was born in 1895 at Zoupana, Greece ("a nine hour walk from Sparta") and came to the United States in 1907, locating at first in Pennsylvania. He was decorated with the Distinguished Service Cross by General Pershing on July 29, 1918. He had raided an enemy machine gun nest held by twelve Germans.

John and Theodore Batlas, who were born in Greece, came to Morgantown and operated the Boston Confectionery, then founded the Morgantown Florist Company.

Theodore Delardas went into various business enterprises, including real estate, and built the Delardas Apartments (1923), on Spruce Street.

Another Greek immigrant, Nicholas Papapetrou, was a well-known local book-binder, working for various concerns, including the Morgantown Printing and Binding Company. In 1912 he learned from Athens, Greece, that he was an heir to an estate and was about to be declared legally dead. He was able to prove that he was alive.

Language was a real barrier, in addition to the normal suspicion or hostility the people encountered. Persons who encouraged the immigrants to come to America and who made money from their labor were usually not interested in their education or welfare. There were some happy exceptions, however, here, as elsewhere. At Sabraton, nurses were provided by the American Sheet and Tin Plate Company, a demonstration home for immigrant mothers, home gardens on the factory grounds, a kindergarten for children. The immigrants usually were not well educated and their poor command of English often made them seem much more ignorant than they actually were. Old-timers frequently were greatly surprised, a few years later, to see the supposedly ignorant immigrants making more money than they were.

The new immigrants, from Greece, as elsewhere from southern and eastern Europe, were slow to adopt American ways, and the often hostile attitude of their neighbors made them cling even more closely to their own traditions.

City Planning. The Morgantown city government was giving more attention to city planning, with a view towards establishing better connections between different areas or additions laid out by real estate companies. The widening of certain streets and the removal of obstructions in the congested business district were also considered.

Under a state legislative act of 1923, prohibiting the platting of lots on additions whose streets do not connect with neighboring streets already established, city councils were empowered to require real estate promoters to make their streets conform with neighboring streets. "Under this act, which has revolutionized street planning, the city authorities can put rings in the noses of realtors who seek to resort to 'dead end' or 'dead line' strategy for selfish purposes."[5]

Morgantown's First Park. A movement was beginning for the development of parks and playgrounds and, especially in urban areas, for directed recreation and play in summer. "The first municipal ownership of land for a park within the corporate limits was obtained by the donation of a 'dingle side' area in East Morgantown by Dr. I. C. White in 1923."[6]

Schools. The Morgantown Independent School District voted an issue of $600,000 in bonds for the erection of a new high school building in South Park, east of Grand Street.

On Scotts Run, to accommodate the rapidly growing mining population, temporary buildings were provided (at Guston Run, Barker, Chaplin, Bailey, etc.). The two-room Scottdale School was built at Jere. Three schools were provided for black students (Continental or Forest Hill, Pursglove or Stumptown, and Randall).

Galilee Free Methodist Church. On White Day Creek near the Marion County line a group of lay people in 1923 constructed and dedicated a church building for use of the Galilee Free Methodist congregation. The group had its origin about 1918; Mr. and Mrs. B. F. Stevens, Mr. and Mrs. W. J. Newell, Mr. and Mrs. J. D. Stevens, and Mr. and Mrs. Samuel Estel were among early leaders. Meetings were held for a time in schoolhouses. An early pastor was Rev. Boyers Boyce.[7]

Westover Methodist Church. Members of the Westover Methodist Church, under the leadership of Rev. James A. Shultz, built a large brick building at the corner of North and West Highland streets. The building, an attractive structure with stained glass windows, cost seventy-five thousand dollars.

The congregation had its beginning in 1904, when Mrs. N. E. Shaffer started a Sunday school meeting in a school building. Rev. C. B. Meredith later started a preaching mission in connection with the Sunday school. When the new school building was

5. Callahan, p. 298.
6. Callahan, p. 299.
7. Dodds and Dodds, p. 140.

erected, the congregation bought the old building, which stood on the opposite corner from the new church, and used it for holding services.[8]

National. A new post office by the name of National was established June 23, 1923, with James Hanford as postmaster. It was located on Flaggy Meadow Run in the old Flickersville community, where an office was established in 1890 but discontinued in 1900, when a rural route from Morgantown took its place. The new post office took its name from the National Fuel Company, developers of coal lands in the community.

Miscellany. In 1923: New buildings constructed in Morgantown included the Cox Building, the Duncan-Conner Building, the Palace Hotel, the Batlas Building, and the Community Building (Callahan, p. 272). . . . Two new financial institutions, The Fidelity Building and Loan and The Peoples' Building and Loan, were established in Morgantown (Callahan, p. 281). . . . The West Virginia Utilities Company obtained from city council a fifty-year franchise under which it built a twelve-inch water main from a large Tibbs Run reservoir into Morgantown (Callahan, p. 286). . . . A. A. Hall was succeeded as Morgantown city manager by

Fig. 122. The College of Law. (West Virginia University.)

8. Dodds and Dodds, p. 108.

George H. Bayles (Callahan, p. 296). . . . The Hungarian Evangelical and Reformed congregation built a church on Harding Avenue, in Evansdale (Dodds and Dodds, p. 79). . . . The Yellow Cab taxi company was formed (Callahan, p. 302). . . . The new West Virginia University College of Law building was completed (Ambler, p. 538).

CHAPTER ONE HUNDRED FORTY-EIGHT

1924

Although Morgantown had entered the winter of 1923-24 with paved road connections to the north and to the south, the city itself was literally torn inside out during that season, with High Street closed for repaving and resembling a long, gigantic trench, while great piles of earth edged over onto the sidewalks and became oozy mud through which pedestrians sloshed and splashed. The concrete base between Kirk and Foundry streets was completed on January 10, 1924, but the entire street was not finished until May 26.

High Street Repaved. The improvement had included the placing of larger sewers, new water mains, and new gas lines beneath the street. From Willey Street to Foundry Street the street was widened to forty feet, leaving thirteen feet on each side for sidewalks. Clusters of five lamps on ornamental posts were placed seventy-five feet apart on each side of the street. The paving was a concrete base with a willite surface. All shade trees were removed in the widening.[1]

The Kiwanis Club sponsored a big celebration, with a program under the direction of H. R. Cokeley, chairman of its public affairs committee, which was scheduled for May 29 but because of rain was not held until June 2. It was a real thanksgiving day.

A single track was left down High Street to Walnut for the Sabraton streetcars, but, although citizens hesitated to admit it, the days of trolley cars were coming to an end. In April of 1923 the last streetcar on the famous city loop line had made its circuit for the final time, as contractors prepared to start work on the big street improvement program, involving not only High Street but also Spruce, Pleasant, Walnut, and Front streets.

1. Callahan, p. 297.

The Kingwood Road. The main interest in good roads during the year was in getting a paved road to Kingwood. Very early a debate arose as to the route to be followed. The State Road Commission had announced its decision to build the road up Deckers Creek from Sabraton, but many citizens felt the road should follow the old pike across the mountain, basing their claim to a very great extent upon scenic and historical features. But it was generally recognized that ten times as many people would be served by the proposed new route. "From the end of the paved road in Sabraton to Masontown the new state road will run through the wilderness. There are no roads following that route at the present time and the new state highway will be new in every sense of the word" (SRC news release).[2]

A Road to Dunkard Valley? Meanwhile, people from the western end of the county, far from the county seat, were becoming impatient, as they witnessed miles of paved highways creeping out from Morgantown, but not in their direction. From Wadestown it was easier to reach Fairmont than Morgantown, and from Blacksville, Waynesburg was much closer. Some citizens from Clay and Battelle districts wanted to concentrate their efforts in those directions, since much less paved road construction was necessary.

William B. Haught, cashier of the Dunkard Valley Bank, at Blacksville, who came to Morgantown on the passenger train from that town in December 1924, severely criticized Morgantown's attitude in opposing roads to Fairmont or Waynesburg, saying that "We are not seeking to get away from Morgantown but we do want a main state road through our section by way of Fairmont, Fairview, and through Blacksville to Waynesburg and Washington, Pa. At Blacksville we can reach a paved road into Waynesburg by traveling over six or seven miles of earth road, and we are just about the same distance from a paved road to Fairmont. We fear that this road from New Martinsville to Morgantown cannot be built in many years to come. You cannot blame our people for wanting paved roads now."

The road he was talking about, from Morgantown to New Martinsville, was State Route 7, which Morgantown leaders were promoting. In March 1923, a group of Battelle citizens had come to

2. Core, "Out of the Mud," *Westover Observer*, September 20, 1956.

Morgantown to talk about it, riding in buggies over muddy roads to Brave, then taking the passenger train to the county seat to ask the Chamber of Commerce to assist in getting their road paved. They were told that the state would match Battelle's money, if they would approve a district bond issue, which would expedite matters.

Other Road Work. Although much of the road development during the year was only talk, considerable progress was actually made. About a mile of Holland Avenue in Westover was rebuilt by Sisler and Morse, SRC contractors, the old brick pavement (p. 543) having gone to pieces under the immense volume of traffic flowing over it. It was a difficult task to build the road and at the same time handle the long lines of vehicles but the work was completed during the summer.

County road forces were also busy. Work was started on grading two miles of the Scotts Run road from Gustin Run to Cassville. A new concrete road was built from the end of the brick paving on Stewart Street to intersect the Point Marion road at the top of the Cartwright Hill, furnishing motorists from the north with a second approach to Morgantown.[3]

Inter-City Bus Lines. On April 1 the Monongahela West Penn Company started bus services over the new Fairmont Pike from Morgantown to Rivesville, where passengers were transferred to trolley cars for the continuation of their trip to Fairmont or Clarksburg. Hourly trips were made from 6:30 a.m. to 11:30 p.m. daily.

By December the White Star Lines had started running an auto bus six times daily to Washington, Pennsylvania, via Mount Morris and Waynesburg. A considerable portion of this route was still over dirt roads and only ordinary motor cars could be used on the runs, often canceled in winter.

A line to Uniontown was also started in 1924, by John Clark and Ralph Frankhouser, with buses leaving each city every two hours, from 7:00 a.m. until 11:00 p.m.

New Publishing Home. The *New Dominion* and the Morgantown Printing and Binding Company jointly occupied a new building at the corner of Chestnut and Kirk streets in late spring, 1924.

3. Core, "Out of the Mud," *Westover Observer*, September 20, 1956.

The newspaper had started in 1876 in a building on Pleasant Street and expanded into the Fleming Building, "Morgantown's first skyscraper," about 1904. W. R. Ludwig was manager of the Printing and Binding Company, and Charles E. Hodges was editor of the newspaper.[4]

Metropolitan Theatre. One of the most beautiful playhouses in West Virginia, the Metropolitan Theatre, was opened July 24, 1924, on High Street by Comuntzis Brothers, its owners, and by Charles Hoskins, the manager. A super-vaudeville attraction featured the opening night, with a parade of "Midgets" at noon. The "Carnival of Venice" included musicians, dancers, and singers.[5]

Monongalia Historical Society. The Monongalia Historical Society was organized December 3, 1924, at a meeting called by Thomas Ray Dille. Others present at the meeting were L. D. Arnett, F. M. Brand, J. M. G. Brown, Samuel B. Brown, J. M. Callahan, D. C. Clark, I. G. Lazzelle, Gilbert Miller, F. P. Weaver, and W. C. Kelley. Dr. Kelley was elected the first president, Mr. Dille secretary, and Prof. S. B. Brown treasurer.

The objectives of the society were to mark and preserve historic spots, gather data, and encourage research and publication on the history of the area.

The word "County" was purposedly omitted from the name of the society, since the county, in early pioneer times, included all or parts of more than twenty present-day counties, and it was felt that the research could justifiably be applied to the entire region, rather than being restricted to the area of Monongalia County as it exists today.

Academy of Science. The West Virginia Academy of Science was organized on the campus of the university on November 28, 29, with sixty-five charter members. G. R. Bancroft was the first president; B. R. Weimer, vice-president; J. A. Eiesland, secretary; and A. S. White, treasurer.[6]

4. *New Dominion,* July 23, 1924.
5. *New Dominion,* July 24, 1924.
6. See Nelle Ammons, *A History of the West Virginia Academy of Science,* 1963.

Fig. 123. The Metropolitan Theater. (From the *Grand Opening Souvenir Program*.)

Slavonic Americans. The Slavs, or Slavonians, are a large group of people of eastern Europe, including Russians, Poles, Ruthenians, Czechs, Slovaks, Croats, Serbians, Bulgarians, and so on.

The 1920 census showed, in Monongalia County, 106 who gave Czechoslovakia as the country of their birth, 168 from Jugoslavia, 10 from Rumania, 211 from Russia, and 246 from Poland.

Slavonic people, being so far away from America, were in general later than the French, Germans, Italians, in arriving here. And by 1920, with Communism established in Russia, many Russians were regarded with suspicion and Congress was passing harsh discriminatory laws to limit their further immigration.

In the face of all this antagonism, the courage required for Slavs to locate in Monongalia County (as elsewhere in America) must have equaled that of the early Anglo-Saxon pioneers who came here in Indian times. They were far from home, almost wholly on their own, surrounded by unknown dangers.

John Pavlech, a Slovak who first came to America about 1906, was among the miners who located in the Booth section about World War I times. The family recalls that they came by passenger train on the Monongahela Railroad, and rode a coal car up a steep incline on the river hill to the site of their new home at Booth. At first four families lived in one four-room house; then, as new houses were built in the company town, one family after another would move out into more ample quarters. To supplement the uncertain income of miners, they raised a garden, kept chickens and a cow.

Among the dozens of Slavonic families, many of whom have reached considerable distinction in Monongalia County, may be named the Panzi, Galik, Pasko, Rockis, Racin, George, Gansor, Sanetrik, Petrick, and Hlad families. Vassily Luczak, of Mukachevo, Hungary (now a part of the USSR), married a neighbor, Anna Manyak, and they came to Jere in 1921.[7]

Arsenty Osetzky, from Leipaja, Russia, married Marina Osadchuck and they came in 1920 to the Scotts Run mining field, where their names were Anglicized to Mr. and Mrs. Samuel Osecky. Their descendants still live in the county.

Johan Krajnyak was born in Androvia, Austria (now Czechoslovakia), and came to America in 1890, where he married a girl who had recently emigrated from the same general region. As their children grew up they simplified the family name by spelling it Crynock. Among their children in Morgantown today are physician Dr. Peter D. Crynock and Attorney John E. Crynock.

Ukrainians, as well as other Slavic groups, had fellowship together in church activities and in lodges and clubs. Frank Petryszak, later a mayor of Morgantown, recalled how church groups, going caroling on Christmas Eve (January 6), sang songs in Ukrainian. Some Monongalia County people still speak Ukrainian at home.

Hungarian-Americans. The 1920 census listed 406 Monongalia County residents as having been born in Hungary. Not all of

7. Their son, John Luchok, is West Virginia University editor and a trustee of Saint Mary's Church. John's wife, Anna, is the daughter of Charles Babich, who came from a town about fifty miles from Mukachevo; Anna's brother, Lt. Peter O. Babich, was killed in action during the battle of Leyte, in 1944. John Rockis was a well-known Morgantown athlete, playing for Saint Francis High School, then Notre Dame and WVU. His brother, Edward, was one of the owners of the City Pharmacy. Louis Hlad was principal of Morgantown Junior High School.

them, of course, were Hungarians, in the strict sense of the word. Up until World War I Hungary had been a part of the great Austro-Hungarian Empire and many of the people who listed Hungary as the land of their birth called themselves Czechs, Slovaks, Croats, Rumanians, or other Slavs.

Hungarian people came to Monongalia County primarily to work in coal mines or in factories. By the mid-1920s there were many of them at Jimtown, Osage, Pursglove, Jere, Cassville, in the Scotts Run section. South of Morgantown, along the Monongahela, there was a large Hungarian population at Edna and Booth, still others along Indian Creek, at Everettville and Crown. Many others lived at Sabraton.

Two churches were organized by Hungarian families, the Hungarian Reformed, which bought a property on Harding Avenue, in Evansdale, on which a small frame church was erected in 1923, with the aid of a ten-thousand-dollar loan from the Hungarian Reformed Federation. Rev. Stephen Borsos became the first minister.[8]

Another group of Hungarian families formed the Hungarian Baptist Church, meeting in homes for worship and fellowship in this new land, at first quite strange and unfriendly to them. Later they rented the Reformed Church building for services three or four times a month. These services, as in the Reformed Church, were in the Hungarian language.[9]

Among Scotts Run miners, at Jere, Pursglove, Osage, etc., were Joseph Kun, George Vereb, Paul Buda, Pete Nagy, Gabor Szarks, Steve Lakatos, Nick Chernok, Nick Molnar, Andy Balaza and Janos Danicsko, some of them among the miners' union leaders in the early days of bitterly contested struggle for better working conditions. Dallas Hall was a center for union meetings, as well as for social affairs. For the Hungarian families, one of the social highlights of the year was the annual fall Hungarian Grape Harvest Dance.

8. Ministers, succeeding the Reverend Mr. Borsos, who retired in 1938, have been Arpad Bernath, Alexander Jalso, Zoltan Novace, and Helen and Laszlo Borsay; Dr. Borsay has provided abundant material for this account.

9. In 1935-36 they built a church of their own, also on Harding Avenue, about a block from the Reformed Church. It is an excellent commentary on how well assimilation has taken place to note that services in both of these churches are now rarely held.

At Sabraton, working in the Tin Plate Mill, were many Hungarians, including Zigmond Farkas, a foreman, whose daughter, Irene Sakalo, has been one of the prominent leaders of Monongalia County's Hungarian community for many years. Other Hungarian workers at the Tin Plate Mill were Steve Barkaszi, Andy Grosz, Joseph Takacs, Michael Sakulo, Alex Sabo, Joseph Vargo, Joseph Bahus, Charlie Meszaros, and Joseph Bence.

All these are names of men. There were about as many women. They were just as important, they worked just as hard, but mostly they were at home, taking care of the house, raising the children, perhaps keeping boarders to help with household expenses. Only a few were factory workers.

John Kish ran a store and butcher shop at Sabraton, where Hungarian families could buy ethnic foods, such as hurka and kolbasz. Steve Deak, near the M.&K. railroad yards, had a furniture shop where he made special materials on order; some families still treasure items he made, as noodle boards and children's rocking chairs. After work and in evenings workmen assembled for social hours at Jim Deak's pool room. The Old Silk Mill[10] was an important center for Hungarian dances and other community affairs.

Polish-Americans. By 1920 there were 246 persons living in Monongalia County who had been born in Poland (at least in the territory called Poland after the close of the World War), and many other second-generation Poles. The Poles represent the westernmost branch of the Slavic race, in Central Europe, but, although holding to their ancestral tongue, they have often been ruled by other nations.[11]

The majority of Polish immigrants fell in the class of unskilled laborers and were welcomed in America, finding employment in mines, factories, and steel mills.

10. Built about 1925 for a silk mill that never materialized—now the Norwood Fire Department.

11. Theresa McCormick, a Monongalia County schoolteacher, has prepared an excellent account of the Old World background and the New World settlement of the Polish people, and most of the material for this account is taken from her essay, prepared for Dr. Joe Simoni, in a course (Sociology 191A) given at West Virginia University.

Polish immigrants were industrious, thrifty, ambitious to own homes, and in general made good citizens. Second-generation Polish people grew up quite independent of Old World family customs and adapted well to the language and customs of the United States. The Roman Catholic Church was their most important social institution, although most Polish parents preferred to send their children to public schools, rather than to parochial schools.

In 1924 there were many Polish people in Monongalia County who still spoke Polish in their homes, sang Polish songs, and prepared Polish food, such as sauerkraut, kolbasi, and perogies.[12] Joe Wrobleski's father, Adam, came to America in 1910; his mother, Zofia Grabkowski, was born in Wloclowsk, Poland, in 1890. They met in Chicago and were married, coming to West Virginia in 1924, where Adam secured work in the coal mines. Polish, of course, was the language in their home and the children grew up speaking and reading it, although they later lost this ability, for lack of practice.

In the first two decades of the twentieth century there were numerous Poles and Slovaks concentrated in Sabraton and Star City. The two languages are similar and the groups intermingled freely at dances and special events, interchanging information received in letters from the Old Country. Mike Sikora, of Star City, was one of the early Slovaks to locate here.

Anthony ("Tony") Cheslock arrived at Star City in 1922. He was born in 1896 near Krakow, Poland (then in the German Empire), and came to America in 1913, working in Pennsylvania coal mines and in Detroit factories. He met his wife, Nellie, also Polish, in Detroit, married her, then came back to work in the coal mines. Living at Star City, Tony crossed the river by ferry to work in the Osage, Arkwright, and other mines. At first he made five dollars for an eight-hour day, or fifty-seven cents a ton. There were no mining machines and the work was mostly done by hand. He and his wife had eight children.

Frank Gwozdziewicz and his wife Anna arrived in Scotts Run in 1920 from Andrychow, Poland, a village in Wadowice Province.[13] His name was difficult to spell and pronounce and his new

12. McCormick.
13. Later home of Pope John Paul II.

neighbors had shortened it to Nels when he was naturalized in 1932—a good example of many such changes. He and his wife established the Monongahela Valley Bakery at Liberty.[14]

Reiner and Core. The oldest men's store in Morgantown, in point of continuous service, was Reiner and Core. It was founded in 1907 as a business called "The Spot to Buy," located in the Donley Building, a three-story red brick structure on the east side of High Street between Fayette and Wall. The store from the beginning dealt in quality merchandise and was quite successful.

In 1915 Phineas P. Reiner and Lewis S. Core, two of the town's prominent bachelors, purchased the business and with it a lease for the large storeroom, with twelve years yet to run at eighty dollars a month. Under the new management the store was renamed "Reiner & Core" and continued to prosper, coming to be recognized as one of the finest men's specialty shops in the state.

Hale Posten reminisces:[15] "During the teens and into the twenties the store gained a popular reputation as an information center for University athletics. It was sort of a downtown club for many of the coaches and townspeople who were interested in University athletics. This group of 'Monday-morning quarterbacks' included such well-known community names as Joe McDermott, Sam Chadwick, Bernie Madiera, Charles Herd, Charles Hodges, John Tait, Roscoe Posten, and Paul McKeel." Ken Miller[16] recalls that university football teams often owed a considerable financial support to this group.

Wilkins Motors. In 1924 Frank H. ("Cap") Wilkins opened a Chrysler-Maxwell automobile agency in Morgantown. He had served as a riverboat captain on the Ohio and Mississippi rivers, then purchased the Star City ferry and operated it until 1922. He then bought the Westover Service Station and began serving a rapidly growing new field. Then in 1924, when the Chrysler Motor Company was organized, he became a charter agency and began to sell cars at his service station. Chrysler had just taken over Maxwell Motors and his first arriving shipment included

14. A son, Stanley J. Nels, is associate editor at West Virginia University.
15. Pers. comm.
16. Pers. comm.

both makes. In those days automobiles were shipped by railroad boxcar, about four automobiles to a boxcar.[17]

The Morgantown Country Club. Forms and methods of recreation, indicating an increase of wealth and leisure, were changing rapidly. A country club was organized in 1923 and a fine tract of land was purchased, located around a high elevation just north of the Wiles Hill section of Morgantown. Upon this tract a clubhouse was erected, formally opened in September 1924, and golf links were being developed.[18]

A New City Hall. In 1924, the city of Morgantown voted a bond issue of $150,000 for the erection of a modern municipal building, which would provide space for all departments of the city government. In August the old frame structure on the lot at the corner of Spruce and Fayette streets was removed preparatory to beginning the excavation for the new building.[19]

Churches. In February 1924, the congregation of the Saint Francis de Sales Church abandoned its old building in Seneca, constructed in 1898, and moved into a newly completed chapel over classrooms in the Saint Francis School, on Beechurst Avenue. The chapel accommodated 450 and three masses were said each Sunday.[20]

Morgantown Presbyterians were considering plans for the sale of their church property on High Street and the erection of a larger building on their old cemetery lot on Spruce Street.[21]

The Morgantown Christian Science Society, in January 1924, having a sufficient number of members in The Mother Church, was authorized to become a full-fledged branch and adopted the name, The First Church of Christ Scientist, of Morgantown, West Virginia. Arrangements were made to conduct services in the Masonic Temple.[22]

Under the leadership of Allen Jones and James Walker a small group of black people of Osage organized the New Hope Missionary Baptist Church in 1924. A small frame house, on a hill-

---

17. See *Dominion-Post*, December 7, 1975.
18. Callahan, p. 299.
19. Callahan, p. 294.
20. Callahan, p. 292.
21. Callahan, p. 293.
22. Dodds and Dodds, p. 76.

side among miners homes, was donated by the Chaplin Collieries Company and converted into a church.[23]

Schools. The enrollment in Morgantown High School reached 925 and the new building was already too small.[24]

Plans were being drawn for a new school complex consisting of four separate buildings arranged in a capital V around the outside of a twelve-acre tract of land in South Park, purchased from the estate of John J. and Mary Ella Brown. The planners said: "The administration building and the gymnasium are adaptations of the modern colonial style and are strictly American. As Morgantown is one of the oldest settlements west of the mountains, this style of architecture is particularly fitting."

In September the Saint Francis parochial school opened with a teaching staff of eight sisters and an enrollment of 230 children—209 in the grades and 21 in the high school.[25]

New Bridges Proposed. The Morgantown city council and the Monongalia County Court were considering plans for building new bridges across Deckers Creek at Pleasant Street and at High Street. The existing bridges, built in horse-and-buggy days, were not strong enough to support safely the increasing volume of motor traffic. Incidental to these plans, the city council, with a view to securing better street connections with the southern end of the proposed new Pleasant Street Bridge, instituted judicial proceedings for purchase of the South Park home of E. H. Gilbert, "which in accord with the strategic methods of some early real estate promoter had blocked the way for a lateral street which was needed to connect with Greenmont."[26]

New Post Offices. A post office by the name of Frum was opened on Scotts Run September 10, 1924, in the town generally known as Osage. Peter H. Karanfilian was postmaster.[27]

Further up on Scotts Run a post office by the name of Jere was opened May 28, 1924, with Benjamin Wakefield as postmaster. The office was named for Jere Johnson, a local coal operator.

---

23. Dodds and Dodds, p. 113.
24. Callahan, p. 288.
25. Callahan, p. 292.
26. Callahan, p. 283.
27. The name of the post office was soon changed to Osage.

Miscellany. In 1924: Sherwood Eddy, noted religious worker among college students, spoke in Morgantown (*Post,* January 17, 1924). . . . Charles P. Berkshire, son of Judge Ralph L. Berkshire, died at age sixty-five (*Post,* January 18, 1924). . . . Cole Brothers Construction Company built a three-story and basement store building for A. R. Price and Company on Walnut Street (*Post,* February 26, 1924). . . . An Austrian miner, Frank Wollenchenk, aged fifty-four, was found murdered on railroad tracks in Scotts Run (*Post,* March 3, 1924). . . . The Sanitary Milk Company opened a new plant at the corner of Chestnut Street and Reed Alley, with Hu S. Vandervort general manager (*Post,* April 17, 1924). . . . Jack J. Wick opened a plumbing shop on Kirk Street (*Post,* April 25, 1924). . . . The C.&P. Telephone Company purchased the old Hayes property (earlier the Female Seminary property), at the corner of Fayette and Chestnut streets, with plans to erect a building later (Callahan, p. 285). . . . The publication office of the *New Dominion* was removed from Pleasant Street to a new building at the corner of Chestnut and Kirk streets (Callahan, p. 272). . . . The south end of the steel bridge across Falling Run had to be moved slightly eastwards to permit construction of the new University Stadium (Callahan, p. 283). . . . The Moore-Tex Oil Company drilled several successful oil and gas wells in western Monongalia County, using gas engines, a new form of power (*Post,* April 26, 1924). . . . Fairmor, a new subdivision on the Fairmont Pike, was laid out (*Post,* May 7, 1924). . . . The Sabraton Baptist congregation built a basement where meetings were held; a building over the basement was planned (Dodds and Dodds, p. 72). . . . A small group of black people met in the home of Irene Trimberlak, at Edna, and organized the Shilo Baptist Church (Dodds and Dodds, p. 99). . . . The Pisgah Methodist Church, near Smithtown, was destroyed by fire on August 3 (Dodds and Dodds, p. 144). . . . Elisha Clarence Allender died May 28, aged seventy-six (*Post,* May 29, 1924). . . . Aaron Moore Buchanan, for thirty years a Presbyterian minister in Morgantown, died June 20; he was born July 7, 1856, in Beaver County, Pennsylvania (*Post,* June 20, 1924). . . . The General Woodworking Company built a new plant in Westover; Charles P. Thorn was general manager (*Post,* June 24, 1924). . . . The Morgantown *Post* moved into a new building on Spruce Street (*Post,* June 28, 1924). . . . The Morgantown Christian Science Society became the First Church

of Christ, Scientist, of Morgantown (Dodds and Dodds, p. 76).
. . . William A. Ream opened a pharmacy at High and Walnut
streets (*New Dominion*, August 2, 1924). . . . The annual Tennant
Family Reunion was held at Pentress, with over three thousand
people present (*New Dominion*, August 19, 1924). . . . Charles
Orr, one of the proprietors of Orr Brothers Department Store,
died August 24 (*New Dominion*, August 25, 1924). . . . William
E. Brooks, of Allentown, Pennsylvania, became minister of Morgantown's First Presbyterian Church, succeeding Edward
August Krall, who had been pastor since 1916 (Moreland, pp. 58,
59).

CHAPTER ONE HUNDRED FORTY-NINE

1925

On November 14, 1925, the new football stadium of West Virginia University was dedicated with fitting ceremonies and a new chapter in university athletics began. The stadium had been the product of one of the best planned and executed programs in university history.

The Mountaineer team of 1922 had reached "the pinnacle of football fame in West Virginia." C. W Spears, Dartmouth All-American guard of 1915, was the coach, assisted by Ira Errett ("Rat") Rodgers and by Robert H. C. Kay. It was the only unbeaten football team in the long history of university athletics. All games were won except that with Washington and Lee, which ended in a 12-12 tie. Both Pitt and Washington and Jefferson, old rivals, were beaten and a post-season game with Gonzaga College, at San Diego, California, resulted in a 21 to 13 victory for the Mountaineers.

Practically all members of the team were stars. Among those mentioned most frequently were Charles C. ("Trusty") Tallman, Joseph Setron, Homer Martin, Gustavus Ekberg, Fred Simons, Nicholas Nardacci, Russell Meredith, Walter Mahan, Philip Hill, and Pierre Hill. Setron was given a place at guard in Walter Camp's third All-American team for 1922.

Mountaineer Field. Despite the fact that many people in the state and throughout the nation were insisting that too much emphasis was being placed on football, compared to educational programs at institutions of higher learning, Athletic Director Harry A. Stansbury was spurred by these successes to undertake the most ambitious project yet considered in the university's athletic history. He proposed construction of a vast new football stadium to replace "Splinter Stadium" erected around the old athletic field at the rear of the Library and Commencement Hall.

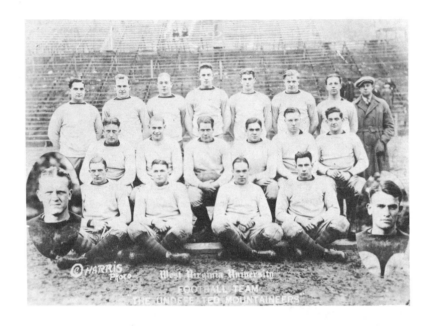

Fig. 124-B. Mountaineer Field under construction.

Director Stansbury had the assistance of Alumni Secretary F. Roy Yoke and of Dr. I. C. White, a prominent alumnus who resided at Morgantown. Although they had no specific building plans or cost estimates, they thought that five hundred thousand dollars would be sufficient for their purposes and in the fall of 1923 they launched a campaign to raise that amount, all of which they expected would be subscribed during the intermission between halves of the regular Thanksgiving Day game with W.&J., which fell that year on November 29.

The 1923 team was regarded as even better than that of the previous year. Most games were won by unusually large scores; football profits were in excess of seventy-five thousand dollars; Trusty Tallman was given a place at end of Camp's second All-American team. Up until Thanksgiving the team had won all its scheduled contests except for a 13-13 tie with Penn State.

Although plans for the campaign were hastily conceived, details were not neglected. Publicity was given to pledges by I. C. White and E. W. Oglebay for ten thousand dollars each; about six thousand letters were sent to people not expected to attend the game, asking them to subscribe not less than twenty dollars each; and three hundred students were provided with blanks to be used to solicit the crowd. Efforts were made to assure a record attendance.

When the big day arrived, the attendance, thirteen thousand, and the gate receipts, thirty-eight thousand dollars, were indeed record-breaking, but the rest of the plans did not work out. The rain fell in torrents; largely through the masterly playing of a black student named Charles West, the Presidents were ahead at half-time 7-0. Only about one hundred thousand dollars of the expected goal was subscribed; many of the rain-soaked subscriptions were illegible.[1]

Regardless of the dampened enthusiasm, the stadium sponsors proceeded with their plans. The West Virginia University Stadium Corporation, a non-profit organization, was incorporated early in 1924, with Brooks Fleming as president. The state board of control authorized the corporation to use the valley of Falling Run, alongside "The Circle." Objections on the part of some that it would mar the scenic beauty of the campus were dismissed as

1. Ambler, p. 586.

nonsense; to those who had worked so hard to bring it about, the stadium, indeed, would be a thing of beauty far surpassing that of its site, the rugged Falling Run Hollow long adored by many for its natural beauty.

Work began at once and set an example for contractors for all time to come. Two steam shovels were just about all the labor-saving equipment used on the job. Wagons pulled by teams of horses moved most of the materials. Nevertheless, in only about eighty-five working days, the two sides of the stadium were completed, ready for the opening of the football season in September 1924. The corporation had by that time collected about three hundred thousand dollars and had subscriptions totaling about two hundred thousand dollars, more than enough to finance the program, according to the original plans. Work was well under way on the curved portion to join the two sides.

The 1924 team was another outstanding one, placing among the high-scoring outfits of the country with a total of 282 points against the opponents' 47. Except for a 14-7 loss to Pitt, the record would have been better than that of 1922. The Thanksgiving Day game with W.&J. resulted in a 40 to 7 rout of that ancient foe, avenging the embarrassment of the previous year. The attendance at this game was twenty-four thousand, by far the largest number to witness a football game here up to that time. This was Spears's last year as coach; he was succeeded by his assistant, "Rat" Rodgers.

On November 14, 1925, the completed stadium was dedicated with fitting ceremonies. Under a benignly clear sky, with seventeen thousand spectators looking on, President Fleming, of the stadium corporation, with a sound amplifier, presented the structure to Governor H. M. Gore, who accepted it in the name of the people of the state. Grateful students would have named it Stansbury Field but the modest director of athletics preferred Mountaineer Field. To round out a perfect day the football team defeated Penn State by a score of 14 to 0.[2]

University Honoraries. Many fields of study on the campus were represented by an honorary organization in which membership

2. See West Virginia University Alumni Quarterly Bulletin, December 1925; Ambler, pp. 582-87; Constantine, *Mountaineer Football*, pp. 27-33; *New Dominion*, November 16, 1925.

was based on demonstrated ability. Among these, with dates of establishment, were: Entre Nous, 1919, French; Alpha Zeta, 1922, agriculture; the English Club, 1900; Seo Beowulf Gedricht, 1908, English; Phi Alpha Delta, 1925, the Order of the Coif, 1925, and Phi Delta Phi, 1922, law; Theta Kappa Psi, 1922, and Phi Beta Pi, 1922, medicine; Tau Beta Pi, 1922, engineering; Phi Lambda Upsilon, 1924, chemistry; Kappa Psi, 1925, pharmacy; Phi Upsilon Omicron, 1923, home economics; Matrix, 1924, journalism; Scabbard and Blade, 1916, military.[3]

Waitman T. Barbe. Dr. Waitman Barbe, one of West Virginia's best known literary figures, died October 30, 1925. In his memory a new public library in Morgantown was named and, a few years later, a junior high school in the community in which he was born.

The son of John and Margaret Esther (Robinson) Barbe, he was born November 19, 1864, near the later community of Booth. His father was of French descent and his mother of English.

After completing the course of study in the rural one-room school, Grant District School No. 12, known as the Barb School

Fig. 125. W. T. Barbe. (Morgantown Public Library.)

Fig. 126. G. C. Sturgiss.

3. Ambler, p. 574.

(in early Monongalia County the name was spelled without an e), he attended the Preparatory Department of West Virginia University, and then the university itself. He received his A.B. degree in 1884, and A.M. degree in 1887, and a M.S. degree in 1897. He was a graduate student at Harvard University in 1900-1901 and in 1908-09 he studied at Oxford University. In 1904 he received the honorary degree of Doctor of Letters from Dennison University.

From 1889 to 1895 he was city editor and managing editor of the Parkersburg *Daily State Journal* and managing editor from 1915 to 1921. During this period he wrote many distinctive editorials, as well as numerous instructive and inspiring activities on literature.

On June 6, 1894, he was united in marriage to Miss Clara Louise Gould, of Parkersburg.

He became a member of the faculty of West Virginia University in 1895, serving as professor of English and assistant to the president. He also served as director of the summer school; under his leadership the school increased in enrollment and in its standards of instruction and scholarship. He was an inspiring teacher and through his scholarly and sympathetic interpretation of literature won the hearts of thousands of men and women who had the privilege of receiving his instruction.

But Dr. Barbe was known not only as an interpreter of literature—he was also an author in his own right. His first book was *Ashes and Incense,* a volume of poems published in 1891. The *Saturday Review,* of London, England, said of it: "We note a true singing capacity, and an unlabored strain like the song of the thrush of which the poet sings in 'An Old Love Song.' "

In 1896 he published *In the Virginias,* a volume of stories and sketches in which he presents with rare insight and sympathy various types of people. This work has been highly praised for its excellent characterization and charming style.

Perhaps his best known work of criticism was *Famous Poems Explained* (1909). This, along with *Great Poems Interpreted* (1913) was written for use in college classrooms. These books included historical sketches and background for the poems, as well as interpretation for the edification of the novice. A large portion of the work included in the two volumes had previously been published in the *West Virginia School Journal.* They were widely used throughout the United States.

In *Going to College* (1899) Dr. Barbe presents the advantages of higher education so convincingly that many people looked back on the reading of the book as the turning point in their lives, on the road to success. Some chapters were translated into two or three foreign languages.

The Hotel Morgan. Morgantown's hotel facilities, after being inadequate for many years, were finally brought into line with the great increase in population and volume of traffic through the completion of the Hotel Morgan in October 1925.

During the first two decades of the twentieth century the two chief hotels were the Madera and the Peabody. The Madera Hotel, at the corner of Walnut Street and Long Alley (now Chestnut Street) stood on a site where there had been some sort of a

Fig. 127. The Hotel Morgan. (From Callahan's *Making of Morgantown.*)

tavern about as long as Morgantown had been in existence. The Franklin House had been built there by Fauquier McRa, perhaps while Benjamin Franklin was still living. The old building was rebuilt several times, most recently by C. W. Finnell in 1895 and by Walter and Bernard Madera in 1899; the two latter rebuilt it into a first class hotel for the period, advertising its strategic location, only one block from the boat landing and two blocks from the railroad depot. Across High Street from the courthouse Isaac Hite Williams had built the National Tavern in 1798; it was later (about 1812) operated by John Addison, who called it the Old Dominion. J. Keener Durr bought the old building, tore it down, and erected the Commercial Hotel, which he opened for business March 9, 1878. The Peabody family later took it over and developed it into a family and boarding hotel, catering to a high class trade.

The first hopeful active step in a long delayed new hotel enterprise was taken late in 1922 by the organization of a stock company including in its membership Judge Frank Cox, Dr. I. C. White, Dr. D. H. Courtney, Dr. L. S. Brock, James H. McGrew, Judge I. G. Lazzelle, Rufus Lazzelle, James R. Moreland, Harry O. Cole, and others.

Plans were finally completed for the construction of a modern eight-story hotel on the old Chadwick lot on High Street, adjoining the post office, and work was begun in 1924. Progressing at a satisfactory rate, it was completed in the autumn of the following year.

The hotel was opened to the public on October 16, 1925, with a dinner and a ball, which more than three hundred persons attended, while two thousand others inspected the facilities. Guests for the dinner were greeted by J. W. Poling, president of the Morgantown Hotel Company, Harry O. Cole, secretary of the company, Houston Bond, manager of the new hostelry, I. W. Poling, associate manager, Mrs. Ivan W. Poling, hostess, W. G. Andrews, chief clerk, and M. G. Poling, clerk.

"Despite the most inclement weather of the fall season the formal opening of the Hotel Morgan last night proved to be one of the most auspicious affairs in the history of Morgantown. Never did Morgantown townspeople and scores of visitors turn out in such an enthusiastic manner to celebrate the introduction of a new institution to the city.

"The hour for the opening of the hostelry was set for 6 o'clock but long ere that time the hotel lobby, the several floors, the ball room—in fact the entire building was crowded with eager visitors bent upon exploring every nook and cranny of the establishment."

"One of the most imposing rooms in the hotel is the magnificent lounge on the first floor, with its woodwork of oak and columns of solid oak. Lavish use of large chairs, divans and tables give an air of luxury to the rooms, and a grand piano in one corner, adds to the home atmosphere. Handsome velours and needlepoint tapestry are used in the coverings of the furniture, and tones of which blend and harmonize with the grayed colors in the heavy drapery and rugs. . . ."[4]

On January 16, 1925, at a meeting of the Monongalia Historical Society, a committee had been appointed to interview the directors of the new hotel, then about completed, and ask to have it named in honor of Zackquill Morgan, the founder of Morgantown. As a result of these efforts it was named Hotel Morgan.

George Cookman Sturgiss. The Honorable George C. Sturgiss, who had figured more than any other single person in the transformation of Morgantown from a nineteenth century village to a twentieth century city, passed away on February 26, 1925. He was eighty-three years of age.

The son of the Reverend and Mrs. Albert Gallatin Sturgiss, he was born August 16, 1842, in Mahoning County, Ohio. His first and middle names were for the distinguished clergyman, Rev. George Cookman, who went down with the ill-fated steamer, *President,* while crossing the Atlantic in 1841.

His father died when he was only three years of age and he was reared on the farm of his mother's father, in Ashtabula County, Ohio.

On November 11, 1858, he came to Morgantown for a temporary visit with the family of Col. A. S. Vance, whose wife was a sister of his father. Upon the urgent invitation of Colonel Vance and his family, and the magnetic inspiration of Rev. J. R. Moore, principal of the Monongalia Academy, he was induced to prolong his visit and to enroll as a student in the academy.

After his work in the academy came to an end, he read law in

4. *New Dominion,* October 16, 1925.

the office of Waitman T. Willey. A son of Mr. Willey, William P., was a fellow student in the office, and during 1863 the two young men edited and published a local newspaper, the *Weekly Monitor*, which was not, however, very successful.

The legislature of the new state of West Virginia had provided for a system of free schools. Rev. Henry W. Biggs, a Presbyterian minister, was elected as Monongalia County's first superintendent, but removed from Morgantown before his term began. Sturgiss was named by the school board to serve in his place and at the expiration of that term was elected by the people for another two-year term. He was thus concerned with the organization of the free school system for the county, being responsible for the establishment of more than one hundred, mostly one-room schools.

In 1869 he was elected to the legislature and was reelected for two successive terms thereafter. During this time he was acting secretary for a time of the board of visitors of the new state university and was helpful in securing what was looked upon then as liberal appropriations.

In 1872 he was elected prosecuting attorney for Monongalia County and was reelected in 1876. In 1880 he was an unsuccessful candidate for governor. In 1889 he was appointed as U.S. attorney for the West Virginia District, and in 1906 was elected to Congress from the Second West Virginia District, being reelected in 1908.

In 1897 he was appointed as a member of the university board of regents and served four years as president of the board. Including time on the earlier board of visitors, he served a total of seventeen years on the board.

But it was as a private citizen that Sturgiss made his greatest contributions to the development of Morgantown. He helped stir interest in building the first telegraph line into Morgantown, in 1866, and the first railroad, in 1886. He went to Washington to urge appropriations for building locks and dams in the Monongahela River south of the Mason-Dixon line, with the result that daily packet boat service to Pittsburgh was started in 1889.

After numerous other men had failed, he was successful in building the long-talked-of railroad from Morgantown up the Deckers Creek Valley to Masontown and on to Kingwood and Rowlesburg, connecting with the main line of the Baltimore and

Ohio Railroad at the latter point. Along this line, the Morgantown and Kingwood Railroad, he helped to develop a large number of important industrial operations.

In the spring of 1902 Sturgiss purchased several hundred acres of land along the railroad about three miles east of Morgantown and laid out a suburb which was at first known as Sturgiss City, then named Sabraton in honor of his wife, Sabra J., daughter of Colonel Vance; she died May 22, 1903, without issue.

Sixteen acres of this land were donated to the Morgantown Tin Plate Mill Company, which went into bankruptcy in 1903, with the proposed factory still incomplete. Sturgiss bought the layout for two hundred thousand dollars and sold it to the American Sheet and Tin Plate Company, which completed the plant and operated it for more than a quarter of a century. As a part of the consideration to induce the company to come, Sturgiss promised to build and operate an electric street railway from the plant into downtown Morgantown, which was built and operated until 1934.

Among other corporations he helped to organize were the Federal Savings and Trust Company, the Farmers' and Merchants' Bank, and the Morgantown Creamery Company. At Sturgisson, on the M.&K. Railroad, he started the Deckers Creek Stone and Sand Company, producing sand for glass manufacture. He foresaw a great future demand of limestone from the Deckers Creek valley for use in the manufacture of Portland cement.

He also operated a planing mill in South Morgantown and was president of the Morgantown Hardware Company. He owned and operated the first electric light plant in Morgantown and helped to bring in public water and gas supplies. He helped found the Penn Mirror Company and later the West Virginia Bottle Factory.

For his second wife Sturgiss married, on November 25, 1908, Charlotte Cecilia Kent, of Alameda, California, and they had four children, Katherine, Kent, Helen, and Marie.

Osage. In 1910, before mining activities began, Cass District, in which Scotts Run is located, had a population of 1,173 people, mostly living on farms. By 1920 the census showed 3,160 and by 1925 there were probably 5,000 people in the district, most of them in Scotts Run, nearly all of them newcomers to the county.

As a matter of fact, many of the farming people who had been living there moved away as the boom began.

Osage was the principal business and social center. The narrow two-lane street was crowded with cars, trucks, buses. The railroad track went down the main street; hundreds of coal cars went by daily; often it was impossible, for long stretches, to cross the street.

At one end of the town, on the right coming from Morgantown, was the Osage School. Then came John and Peter Karanfilian's drugstore (later run by John Preston), followed by Nick Hrinsin's grocery. Levinson's department store came next. Levinson later sold out, to Max Levine, who built a large building across the street and ran Max's department store there for many years. Restaurants were run by Egway Rossie, and others. Joseph and Sara Lee ran a highly-regarded butcher shop. Frank Amato was another grocer. Across the tracks was the Osage Coal Company store, run by John Angotti. And across the bridge, towards Chaplin Hill, was Francis Laszlo's grocery.

For entertainment there was the Osage theatre, run by Dixy Downes. For a time there were two theaters, the other being the Liberty, in a building owned by Sidney Melnikoff. Besides, in the Moose Hall, run by Mike Shiel, vaudeville and medicine shows were presented (and Catholic religious services were held on Sundays.) There were also bowling alleys and "hangouts," where miners gathered to drink and play cards.

Various people operated barber shops and there were dentists' offices and coal company doctors. Almost anything needed could be bought in Osage. For shoppers who wanted more browsing space, buses left for Morgantown every few minutes, from early in the morning until late at night.

Road Building. There was a great deal of road building activity during the year but most of it was on paper. The most important piece of work actually accomplished was from the end of the paving at Gustin Run to the old county home just below Cassville. The section through the village had to wait until railway tracks were moved to permit widening of the street.

On September 5 Battelle District ratified a bond issue providing $360,000 for the construction of Route 7 from Wadestown to Bula and also for a road from Wadestown through Crossroads to the Marion County line.[5]

5. Core, "Out of the Mud," *Westover Observer*, September 27, 1956.

End of the Dunkard Valley Trolley. On May 9 the Morgantown-to-Randall trolley made its last run. The project that had started out so ambitiously less than two decades earlier to build a line from Morgantown into the Dunkard Valley came to a quiet end. The days of the trolley had come to a close. On September 10, 1910, a number of prominent Morgantown citizens had been on the first car to Randall (p. 374); hardly anyone noticed when the last car ran.

Passengers and mail on the passenger train to Blacksville and beyond now made transfers to Monongahela Railway trains at Randall for the remainder of the trip to Morgantown. But some transferred to buses at Gustin Run and the Star Bus Company ran a special each morning to meet the train.

Black Monongalians. Black Monongalians have had their share in the building of the community in which they live. In the years before 1925 they had never constituted a very large percentage of the population but they nevertheless added richness to the Monongalia society and performed many useful tasks.

Blacks, of course, did not begin arriving here with the twentieth century. They have been here since early in the county's history. Black men played a role in the defense of the Virginia frontier against Indian attacks; some of them may have been runaway slaves. Henry Dorton, a free black, settled in what later became Clinton District about 1790; he was a veteran of the Revolutionary War.

It is interesting to note, as Dr. Steel points out,[6] that in the years before the Civil War the black people had no voice in the shaping of politics, and appeared powerless, yet arguments over their status brought on the greatest political crisis of the United States in the nineteenth century. It could not be said that they were without influence.

Although blacks decreased in number in the county in the days before the war, because of reduction in the number of slaves held here, a new chapter in their history began with the close of the war and the number began to increase under the stimulus of the new conditions.

In the new economic set-up the black people, mostly illiterate,

6. Edward M. Steel, Jr., "Black Monongalians: A Judicial View of Slavery and the Negro in Monongalia County 1776-1865," *West Virginia History* 34 (1973):331-59.

struggled to find a place. Many of them, especially females, became servants or housekeepers. Some became farmers, although few could afford to buy farms. Many of the men were artisans or laborers.

Cultural affairs developed slowly. Although the constitution of the new state of West Virginia provided for "separate but equal" education for black children, there were so few of them in the county that it was difficult to provide schools for them. At first teachers were provided in the Jones Methodist Episcopal Church, on Chestnut Street, then a school was built on Beverly Avenue. Numerous other churches were established later.

Fig. 128. George Blue. (McCormick, *Monongalia Blacks Speak.*)

Fig. 129. Gabriel Holland. (McCormick, *Monongalia Blacks Speak.*)

Among black leaders in Monongalia County may be mentioned George Blue, who began shining shoes in 1907, at the age of fourteen; Paul Hall, who recalls that his Model T Ford was Sabraton's first fire truck; Gabriel Holland, who went to work in a glass factory about 1910 and played a French horn in World War I; Cora Williams, a council member and town recorder of Sabraton, the first black woman in the state to be a member of a town council; and Juanita Cranford, who attended a black school on Scotts Run.[7]

Slowly and painfully, in the years before 1925, black people were developing a better life for themselves.

Churches. Morgantown church organizations were extending their activities into neighboring industrial districts, including Scotts Run, where their work was supplemented by the university YMCA and YWCA and by student pastors from various denominations.[8]

A group of black people of the Shriver community, on Scotts Run, met in July 1925 and organized the Saint Stephen Baptist Church, largely under the leadership of the Reverend Mr. Bird. A small frame building was erected across Scotts Run from Route 7.[9]

A new building for the Pisgah Methodist Church was dedicated on August 23, 1925, by Presiding Elder William Shultz. It was a beautiful brick building surrounded by a large yard. An earlier building had been destroyed by fire about a year before, but the new structure, largely financed by Mrs. Eva Garlow, was already under construction about 150 feet away.[10]

Miscellany. In 1925: Morgantown's real and personal property was valued at $33,974,205 (Callahan, p. 268). . . . A new industrial concern, the Tryon Silk Mills Company, was promoted by solicitation of subscriptions (Callahan, p. 271). . . . A large brick residence was constructed by R. M. Davis on Park Street (Callahan, p. 275). . . . The Tibbs Run water reservoir was tied into Morgantown's water system by July, finishing an adequate supply of pure mountain water (Callahan, p. 287). . . . Morgantown voters approved a bond issue of $400,000 for additional street improvements (Callahan, p. 299). . . . Morgantown houses of the type selling for $5,000 in 1907 now brought $15,000 (Callahan, p. 302). . . . Fire destroyed the building used as a Methodist settlement house in Osage (Dodds and Dodds, p. 118). . . . Charlotte,

---

7. Theresa McCormick, Ed. *Monongalia Blacks Speak. Part I. Black Men. Part II. Black Women.* Monongalia County Board of Education. 1977.

8. Callahan, p. 294.

9. Dodds and Dodds, p. 113.

10. Dodds and Dodds, p. 144.

Fig. 130. Hall of Chemistry, West Virginia University.

widow of Capt. Alphaeus Garrison, died at Core on March 29, aged ninety-two years, and a special train was run from Randall for the funeral (*Chronicles of Core,* p. 195). . . . The large new chemistry hall was completed on the university campus (Ambler, p. 516). . . . The Baltimore and Ohio Railroad was planning to build a new passenger station in Morgantown (*New Dominion,* July 3, 1925). . . . The Cheat River bridge at Ice's Ferry was raised and lengthened to allow for higher water resulting from the Cheat Haven dam (*New Dominion,* July 29, 1925). . . . William Edwin Brooks, chief of the Willite Construction Company here, succeeded G. Harry Bayles as Morgantown City Manager on September 1 (*New Dominion,* August 3, 1925). . . . The Tryon silk mill was located on Sabraton Avenue by Associated Industries (*New Dominion,* August 3, 1925). . . . Morgantown voters approved a $400,000 bond issue for paving and also approved city collection of garbage (*New Dominion,* August 7, 1925). . . . Mrs. Garlow, wife of Marshall J. Garlow, died at age sixty-four; she was a director in the Bank of the Monongahela Valley (*New Dominion,* August 17, 1925). . . . The Morgantown Elks Club dedicated their new home on Walnut Street (*New Do-*

minion, September 14, 1925). . . . The O. J. Morrison Company leased a High Street building, former home of H. F. Austin dry goods and the National Woolen Mills, and planned to open a department store here next year (*New Dominion,* September 25, 1925). . . . Jabez B. Hanford, born in England June 4, 1864, died at Morgantown September 22; he was one of the organizers of the National Fuel Company (*New Dominion,* September 23, 1925). . . . The Eastmont Tuberculosis Sanitarium was built through leadership of the Monongalia Tuberculosis Association; A. M. Reese was president; Mrs. John Samsell, vice-president; Daisy Godlove, secretary; and Mrs. S. F. Glasscock, treasurer.

CHAPTER ONE HUNDRED FIFTY

1926

How time flies!

So it must have seemed to Dr. I. C. White, perhaps Monongalia County's most widely known citizen at the time, who had participated in the centennial celebration in 1876 and was still living in Morgantown at the time of the sesquicentennial.

While the nation was quietly observing its sesquicentennial in 1926, Monongalia County was separately celebrating its own sesquicentennial. As side attractions the city of Morgantown observed its 141st anniversary and the Baltimore and Ohio Railroad Company joined in helping to note the fortieth anniversary of the completion of its line to the city.

The Sesquicentennial. The observances were integrated through committees appointed by Dr. W. C. Kelly, president of the Monon-

Fig. 131. Sesquicentennial Parade on High Street in Morgantown.

galia Historical Society. The general committee was composed of George C. Baker, S. A. Barker, A. A. Hall, Miss Susan M. Moore, and Mrs. D. C. Clark, ably assisted by numerous special committees responsible for the different features of the observance.

The principal programs were held on October 20, 21, and 22, with a football game on the university campus representing the closing activity, on the twenty-third.

The opening program was held on Wednesday evening, October 20, in Commencement Hall, with Dr. Daniel Boardman Purinton, former president of the university, as chairman. This program featured music by the Apollo Club, a chorus consisting of forty male voices, and a song, "My Heart's in West Virginia," written by Elizabeth Davis Richards, and presented by Edna Leyman Morris.

A poem, "Monongalia, 1776-1926," was read by Rose M. Sweeney, its author. Sample lines include:

> "Look to the East, o'er the mountains misty,
> See in the sunrise slow-moving trains,
> Oxen and wagons in tireless processsion,
> Pushing their way toward the western plains
> Where is now the peaceful village
> Nestling tranquil 'neath her trees?
> Where the form of Patrick Henry
> Standing guard o'er law's decrees?
> Where the timber wheels so laden,
> Where the wagon and the sled?
> Where the winding roads from town,
> Dust in summer, mud in winter,
> As the creaking stage rolls down?
>
> "All are gone—and in their places
> See the flashing rails of steel,
> Hear the clanging locomotives
> Drawing long trains to and fro . . .
> Smooth roads thronged with motor cars,
> Streets congested, traffic, parking,
> Air oft cleft by giant wings."

But the principal feature of the evening's program was a long address on the history of Morgantown by Dr. J. M. Callahan, head of the Department of History at West Virginia University.

His address filled twenty-three closely printed pages in the book published by the Monongalia Historical Society giving the proceedings of the celebration, and was full of rolling oratory and humorous references to events in the long history of the community.

Dr. Callahan explained why we observe anniversaries: "To the past . . . the present owes a debt, and in paying it by proper recognition of its services and achievements we benefit ourselves at least by gaining a useful perspective which gives intelligent purpose and balance to our attitudes and our efforts."

As were most of his contemporaries, Dr. Callahan was overwhelmed by the changes and transformations that had taken place in the century and a half: "We now live in a closely united world and in a fast age which is far different from previsions of the most advanced dreams of the age of Zackquill Morgan and George Washington. Rapid trains of the Baltimore and Ohio system transport us to Washington or Baltimore or to Cincinnati or Chicago while we take 'a night's rest in sleep.' Automobiles on modern paved roads pass us like shooting stars. Telephone wires transmit to us immediately the verbal messages of friends speaking in Atlantic coast cities or in the Middle West, and wireless transmissions, far distant voices and far distant music furnish us in our own homes the enjoyment of listening to the best sermons and concerts and the proceedings of great conventions in the larger cities of the United States and even in Europe. Each day we receive at our homes the current news from the most distant parts of the civilized world."

The second day of the celebration was featured by the presentation of "Ellen and the Old Songs" in Commencement Hall by the Woman's Music Club, under the direction of Mrs. Clarence B. Dille. Billed as "A Romance in Song and Story," the program featured presentations by Mrs. Charles Baker, Mrs. S. J. Morris, Miss Pauline Mattingly, Mrs. Nathaniel Barnard, Mrs. J. J. H. Cather, William Price, and numerous others.

At 7:00 a.m. on Friday, October 22, 1926, the ringing of court house, church and school bells alerted the population to the Governor's Salute and the Grand Parade and Street Pageant to follow. "Past, present and the hopeful future of old Monongalia county passed in review before city, county and state notables in the stand on the court house square. A squadron of airplanes circled overhead to give a military air to the occasion, motion picture cameras clicked at every corner and bands of all descriptions blared forth martial music. . . .

"What will be in future pageants? What will they gaze upon when, fifty years hence, there is another Big Parade? How many of the present-day customs and conveyances will be looked upon with a mingling of wonder and tolerant scorn?"[1]

The parade featured fife and drum corps, bands, the cadet corps, an old covered wagon, numerous floats, including a one-room school, a log cabin, "Mother Monongalia" and her twenty daughters (counties), a B.&O. old-time engine, etc.

In the afternoon, at 2:00 p.m., the official program was held in the Metropolitan Theatre, with George C. Baker as chairman. Remarks were made by Governor Howard M. Gore, by ex-Governors John J. Cornwell, William A. MacCorkle and Ephraim F. Morgan, and numerous others. Margaret Mathers Barrick unveiled a portrait of Zackquill Morgan, her great-great-great-great-grandfather.

The evening featured a reception at the Elks Club, a carnival on High Street, and a ball at the Hotel Morgan.

On Saturday, at Mountaineer Field, ten thousand people watched as WVU defeated West Virginia Wesleyan by a score of 7 to 6.[2]

"The Making of Morgantown." A most important contribution to the history of Monongalia County, in connection with the celebration of the sesquicentennial, was the publication of a small book, *History of the Making of Morgantown, West Virginia. A Type Study in Trans-Appalachian Local History,* by James Morton Callahan, head of the Department of History and Political Science at West Virginia University. The illustrated book, of 335 pages, was the result of many personal interviews with older citizens and careful investigations by the author and his students over a period of more than twenty years.

The book, arranged in chronological order, in contrast to Wiley's county history, begins with a long discussion of the value of the study of local history: "The study of history, like charity, should begin at home." It is noteworthy, however, that relatively few of the historians who have been on the university staff have been interested in local history.

1. *Morgantown Post*, October 22, 1926.
2. The events of the celebration were presented in a book, *Sesqui-centennial of Monongalia County, West Virginia.* 275 pp. Charleston. No date.

Fig. 132. Ira Errett ("Rat") Rodgers.   Fig. 133. Harry A. Stansbury.
(West Virginia University.)

The account stresses the development of early institutions, such as churches, schools, taverns, banks, newspapers, etc., describes the quiet evolution of society during the middle period, and then lays stress on the rapid progress made after the "awakening" in the last decade of the nineteenth century.

"Although the historian whose foresight must be considerably restricted by his hindsight cannot properly assume the role of a prophet, nor assume the exaggerated views of the real-estate agent, yet by interpretations from the relentless logic of the achievements of the past and the active and potential forces of the present, including new utilization of neighboring water power and plans for better facilities for communication, he can safely conclude that the community growth of the next quarter century may far exceed the expectations of the latest quarter century" (Preface).

History of the M.P. Church.[3] A history of the Methodist Protestant Church was published in 1926 by Rev. I. A. Barnes who had

3. I. A. Barnes. *The Methodist Protestant Church in West Virginia.* 514 pp. Baltimore, 1926.

been pastor of the M.P. Church in Morgantown from 1895 to 1901. The twenty-one chapters contain basic information on most of the churches of the state, with about forty pages on Monongalia County.

In addition to the Morgantown congregation, there are treatments of the Zion, Calvary, Eden, Avery, Westfall Chapel, Buckeye, Guston Run, Riverside, Hopewell, Mount Calvary, Brown Chapel, Harner Chapel, Sturgiss, Burns' Chapel, Mount Union, and Mount Pleasant congregations, with abundant biographical material.

Progress of the University. In June President F. B. Trotter again offered to resign when the board of regents found "a suitable person." The board settled on Dr. J. W. Withers, dean at New York University, who had been born at Ben Lomond, Mason County, West Virginia, September 23, 1868, and offered him the position at a salary of fifteen thousand dollars.

But M. P. Shawkey protested. As previously noted, he had been considered for the position at various times in the past, while serving as a member of the board of regents and as state superintendent of schools. But he had now removed himself from the picture, having been elected president of Marshall College on June 28, 1923. Before this time he had aided significantly in the university's development; now he strongly advocated a separate program for the "normal school bloc," with particular reference to southern West Virginia. The university, he maintained, could not adequately serve the state because of its location and conservatism. To many friends of the university, this was an alarming turn of events.

President Shawkey's opposition to the appointment of Dean Withers as head of the university was based on the size of the salary promised, far out of line with other West Virginia educators and regarded as unfair to them. His letter of protest, to State Superintendent George M. Ford, on October 27, 1926, and to members of the state board of education was regarded as the determining factor in Dean Withers's rejection of the offer.[4]

New appointments to the staff during 1926 included S. L. Galpin as head of geology and mineralogy; A. P. Wagner, who succeeded C. B. Canaday as head of the Greek Department; H. G.

4. Ambler, pp. 517-19.

Knight as dean of the College of Agriculture; J. W. Simonton as professor of law; and J. E. Bohan professor of education.[5]

One more in the president's long list of building achievements, a new chemistry hall (Fig. 130), had been completed in 1925.

Controversies Over Athletics. The growth in importance of athletics at the university, associated with the completion of the new stadium, resulted in bitter conflicts throughout the state and the accusation on the part of some that "the tail was wagging the dog." State Superintendent G. M. Ford envisioned the state's educational system as a unit, with the university as the capsheaf and, when the West Virginia Athletic Conference was organized, in January 1925, he instructed President Trotter to take the proper steps for the university's membership.

To his surprise, a vigorous protest came from Director Harry A. Stansbury on the grounds that membership would restrict university athletics almost entirely to West Virginia and that the university, because of its financial obligations, could not afford to curtail possible sources of income from meeting opponents from outside the state. The controversy continued, with neither side yielding ground.

President Trotter was placed in a dilemma between the state board of education on one hand and the state board of control on the other, and it was under these conditions that he again offered to resign and the board of regents began in earnest to look for a successor.

The 1926 football season started off well but then lost to the University of Missouri (27-0) and went into a slump, losing all the remaining games except that with Centre College. The overall net for the season was about seventy thousand dollars.[6]

Building Roads. The year again saw most substantial progress in the county's program for improvement of its highway system.

The Keeley Construction Company, early in 1926, was given the contract to build the 8.3 mile stretch up Deckers Creek to the Preston County line. The work of grading proceeded rapidly through the spring and summer and then paving was started.

Work on the Preston County section of Route 7 was also under

5. Ambler, pp. 528-49.
6. Ambler, pp. 588-90.

way and was completed by the end of August, so that a paved road led all the way from the county line through Masontown and Reedsville to Kingwood.

Early in November it was announced that only 1,600 feet of road remained to be built. The gap remaining was between Greer and the Preston County line, with a short stretch on each side of the newly completed bridge over Deckers Creek at Dellslow. On November 11, 240 feet of concrete was poured, and 200 more the following day. Work was delayed because the road bed became frozen during the night. The contractor tried mixing calcium chloride with the concrete to induce it to dry more quickly. Finally, on November 13 the last gap was joined, as paving forces labored into the night. On November 22 the road was opened to light traffic, although there were two short sections where one-way traffic was necessary. These caused enormous traffic jams the following Sunday, as thousands of Monongalia and Preston county residents hastened to try out the new road.

Morgantown was now connected by paved roads with three neighboring county seats in three different directions, north, south, and east.

On Route 7 west the road was paved through Cassville, on Scotts Run, providing an important artery for the developing coal field. In Battelle District, using funds from a district bond issue, work was under way on the section from Wadestown to Bula.

In April Grant District voted approval of an additional road bond issue to build the road from Morgantown to Flickersville, from Flickersville to Lowsville, with a spur to Brady, from Lowsville to Arnettsville, from the Fairmont Pike to Lynch Chapel, and from the Fairmont Pike to Zoar Church.

Agitation was started early in the year to secure the improvement of the 3.7-mile gap between Morgantown and the state line near Mount Morris, there to connect with the newly completed road to Waynesburg, "one of the finest and most modernly-built highways in this section of the country." A contract was awarded in August to the Consolidated Construction Company for grading of the important link.

Work was also under way in Clinton District to extend the paved road from near Dorseys Knob to Uffington and, on the

Fig. 134-A. Unimproved Route 7 along Dolls Run.

Fig. 134-B. Paved Route 7 along Deckers Creek.

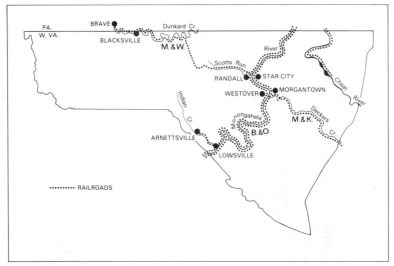

Fig. 135. Map showing principal railways of Monongalia County, 1926. (Drawn by Diane Lenhart.)

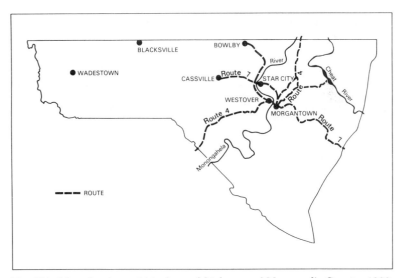

Fig. 136. Map showing principal paved highways of Monongalia County, 1926. (Drawn by Diane Lenhart.)

other end of the east-side Fairmont road, from the Marion County line through Smithtown to Pisgah Church.[7]

The Cheat River Dam. The State Line Dam, constructed in 1924-26, transformed the historic old Cheat River, in Monongalia County, into a lake. "The old lower Cheat from Squirrel Rock and

Fig. 137. Lake Lynn Power Station and Dam. (From *The Stewartstown Story*.)

Grassy Island to the Pennsylvania line—the Cheat which was known to the Indians for centuries before the white man came, to the Deckers and Morgans and the early pioneers, to George Washington, and four generations after the founding of Morgantown—is now only a memory. Its channel, cut by the flow of water for centuries, is now partly hidden in the bottom of the lake. . . . Its contour has changed to something new and strange. Its sandy beaches, along which children for generations have waded and played and splashed in dark waters, and where youth has bathed and sunned and made love, have been obliterated. Some of its great bordering rocks, where men and women have lounged and dreamed and chiseled their names, have been covered by the waters of the new lake. The old river, so long chiefly

7. Core, "Out of the Mud," *Westover Observer*, October 4, 1956.

useful as a playground, has been transformed into a reservoir of power and harnessed for the work of the new industrial era."[8]

The Cheat River enterprise had been discussed for many years, almost as far back as the very beginning of the use of electricity in the county. Morgantown's first tiny electric plant, on the Monongahela River near the university campus, went into operation in June 1892, furnishing lights for the university buildings, the courthouse, and several private homes. Demand for electricity, for light and power, increased rapidly; soon a larger plant was built on Deckers Creek.

Cheat River, with its great and rapid fall, was early looked upon as a source of cheap and abundant power. The river rises in northern Pocahontas County at an elevation of considerably over 4,000 feet above sea level, and falls to 780 feet at its mouth. From Parsons to Rowlesburg the river falls from 1,630 to 1,360 feet in a distance of 33 miles, at the rate of about 8 feet a mile. From Rowlesburg to the state line it falls from 1,360 to 787 feet, in a distance of 40 miles, or at the rate of 14 feet to the mile. The total area of the drainage basin is over 1,400 square miles and the rainfall ranged from forty to sixty inches, so that it was recognized that there existed a great potential for power development.

"A project of hydro-electric development, gigantic in its scope, to augment the immense West Penn Traction and Water Power Company plants of J. S. and W. S. Kuhn, of this city, is progressing in the Cheat River district whereby practically the whole river is to be harnessed to supply three big power plants. The first of these, located near Cheat Haven, just over the West Virginia state line, is now under construction, and two other plants of equal capacity are to follow as soon as this initial plant is put into operation.

"Work is now in progress on a monster dam on the Cheat River to be located about a mile above Cheat Haven. This will be known as the State Line Plant. Situated 58 miles south of Pittsburgh and 60 miles from Wheeling, it is planned from this central location to run high-tension light, power and heat lines that will supply practically every town and public service company within its radius. In addition, a standard-gauge railroad is now being built

8. Callahan, p. 299.

up the bank of the Cheat River from the Baltimore & Ohio Railroad to the mouth of Big Sandy, in the Cheat Mountains."[9]

Other dams were projected at Beaver Hole, nine miles above the state line, and at the mouth of Big Sandy Creek, seven miles farther on. It was estimated that these three power plants would have a capacity of 150,000 horsepower. The company had already a capacity of 50,000 horsepower from steam generators, so this would give it a total of about 200,000 horsepower.

These plans, however, were slow in developing and in the end only one dam was constructed. Although, in 1912, the prediction was that all three would be completed within three years, it was really nearly a decade and a half before the first one was done.

By the dam, which was essentially completed in 1926, the river was backed up so as to create a lake about thirteen miles long and from one quarter to one half of a mile wide. It was named by the power company Lake Lynn (honoring Albert M. Lynn, president of the West Penn Company), but was always referred to by the general public as Cheat Lake.[10]

Cheat Lake has a surface area of 1,730 acres and at the time of impoundment had a total capacity of 73,000 feet. The head-water elevation of the reservoir was 870 feet, the tail-water elevation 782 feet, the normal power head 81.5 feet. The hydroelectric plant was normally operated during week-day afternoon peak load periods and the reservoir refilled during the off-peak periods. When the stream flow was greater than usual, the plant was operated to obtain maximum energy from the available water.

Recreational uses, as boating, bathing, and fishing, were expected to develop coincidentally with the industrial uses, but these were delayed somewhat by the timber and heavy vegetation which covered the riverbanks and flooded bottomlands, and which was not removed before flooding. Dead tree trunks and other debris for some time created hazards for boats and bathers. Fishing was to be a permanent disappointment.

Window Glass Plant Sold. The United States Window Glass Company, with properties located in Seneca, Marilla, and Gran-

9. Pittsburgh *Dispatch*, quoted in *Post-Chronicle Industrial Edition*, 1913.

10. On maps published by the U.S. Geological Survey the name Lake Lynn appeared, but in 1976, yielding to general usage, the name was officially changed to Cheat Lake.

ville, valued at about seven hundred thousand dollars, had been closed by receivership proceedings in May 1925 and in July 1926, by order of the Federal Court, was advertised for sale from the doorsteps of the county courthouse. The sale was held on August 5; the chief bond holders purchased the property with a view to reopening the plants.[11]

Morgantown High School. The new Morgantown High School complex, in South Park, was nearing completion. It was to consist of four buildings, an academic and administrative building, the auditorium, the gymnasium, and the shop, with the athletic field at the center of the complex. Contracts for buildings Nos. 1, 3, and 4 had been awarded to Charles D. Keyser and Company, of Bellaire, Ohio, for $640,000. The total cost of the project was over $1 million.

Coal Production Increases. Coal production in the county reached an all-time high in 1926 and the increase was reported by the West Virginia Bureau of Mines as follows:

Year	Production (tons)	No. of Mines	Total No. Employed
1920	3,223,418	75	3,236
1921	4,926,800	90	4,682
1922	4,104,305	79	5,267
1923	7,180,273	101	6,906
1924	7,445,657	83	6,880
1925	8,338,038	83	6,614
1926	9,350,364	84	7,070

Quota Club. A woman's civic luncheon club, the Quota Club of Morgantown, corresponding to the men's clubs, such as Kiwanis, Lions, and Rotary, was organized in 1926. Ruth C. Wood was the first president. Among its objectives were the development of good fellowship and friendship and service to country and community.

The City Hall. At last, early in 1926, the new city hall, at the corner of Spruce and Fayette streets, was ready for occupancy. It contained quarters for council meetings, offices for the city man-

11. Callahan, p. 269.

ager, city clerk, police department, city jail, etc., with two large
rooms on the ground floor for fire-fighting equipment. It was constructed from the proceeds of a $150,000 city bond issue, adopted
in 1924, and replaced an old-frame structure on the same site,
which was removed in August 1924.[12]

Jakes Run Methodist Church. With a decline in population resulting from reduced oil production, the old Eddy Chapel and
Tennant Chapel congregations on Jakes Run, in June 1926, combined their Sunday Schools and decided to construct a new building, at a more central location. A building lot was secured from
Mr. and Mrs. P. W. Moore, and a building constructed, with the
first service held on December 12, with Rev. Oliver Hatfield as
pastor. Final services were held in Eddy Chapel on December 5,
and in Tennant Chapel on August 29, although it was planned to
retain the old Eddy Chapel as a place to conduct funerals.[13]

Booth. A mining town was growing up in the old Barbe community on the "river road," the coal being lowered in cars down
steep inclines for loading on coal hoppers on the Monongahela
Railway. On December 24, 1926, a post office named Booth was
opened with Earthy G. Bean as postmaster.

Miscellany. In 1926: There were fifty-five oil tanks in the Morgantown Tank Field (Callahan, p. 250). . . . New buildings constructed including the G. J. Papandreas Building on Walnut
Street and the Corey Building on University Avenue (Callahan, p.
272). . . . C. L. Chenoweth built a stone mansion on Wilson
Avenue (Callahan, p. 275). . . . The Union Bank and Trust Company purchased the Brock-White-Courtney Building, formerly occupied by the post office, then by the Dixy Theatre (Callahan, p.
279). . . . Streets repaved under the Morgantown street improvement program included Spruce, Pleasant, and Walnut and a portion of University Avenue (Callahan, p. 298). . . . A new system of
free garbage and ash collection and disposal was put into operation in Morgantown (Callahan, p. 299). . . . A swimming pool on
the Morgantown Country Club grounds was opened in May
(Callahan, p. 299). . . . Roman Catholics of Star City dug a basement and prepared to build a house of worship (Dodds and

12. Callahan, p. 294.
13. Dodds and Dodds, p. 127.

Dodds, p. 96). . . . The distinguished university geologist, Samuel Boardman Brown, died September 18; he was sixty-six years old (*New Dominion,* September 19, 1926). . . . A public library, the Waitman Barbe Memorial Library, was opened by the Morgantown Women's Club at their club rooms, 356 Spruce Street, on June 28 (*New Dominion,* June 29, 1926). . . . The 1925-26 Polk's City Directory listed for Morgantown: 1 chiropractor, 18 dentists, 11 druggists, 53 lawyers, 2 opticians and optometrists, 2 osteopaths, 40 physicians, and 2 veterinary surgeons.

APPENDIXES

Appendix A

UNITED STATES POST OFFICES AND POSTMASTERS MONONGALIA COUNTY, 1876-1926

The dates following the names of the postmasters indicate times of their appointment.

Andy

Alpheus W. Brown, October 21, 1889
  Discontinued, January 20, 1890

Arnettsville

Calvin W. Miller, January 15, 1875
James P. Arnett, July 31, 1888
Lavinia Arnett, September 17, 1889
M. Angie Smith, May 15, 1893
Jonathan C. Glasscock, June 8, 1897
William E. Price, November 15, 1898
James P. Arnett, February 13, 1900
Mary E. Beatty, July 31, 1902
West Virginia Hayward, September 11, 1904
  Discontinued, July 31, 1907

Beechwood

Clyde E. Hutchinson, December 2, 1889
Edward Snider, September 6, 1895
Robert J. Patterson, May 12, 1898
Webb W. Ferguson, January 12, 1901
Wayman Collins, January 11, 1906
Charles L. Abel, May 5, 1910
Albert L. Bowman, April 15, 1914
Wayman Collins, March 18, 1916
Arthur G. Goodwin, September 28, 1918
Allen W. Wolfe, August 1, 1919
John B. Gregory, December 1, 1920

587

Behler

Benjamin M. Simpson, September 25, 1895
John W. Kennedy, October 10, 1899
    Discontinued, November 15, 1918

Blacksville

William Lantz, September 4, 1866
M. Headlee, February 10, 1881
Arthur Strosnider, August 24, 1882
Remembrance S. Lantz, May 19, 1885
Arthur Strosnider, April 3, 1889
Remembrance S. Lantz, April 26, 1893
Caroline V. Fletcher, May 12, 1897
John W. Scott, August 15, 1911
Laura Russell, November 26, 1918
James Powell, acting, January 16, 1923
Grace Powell, March 6, 1923 (name later changed by marriage to Grace
    Wells)
George H. Howard, December 10, 1923

Blaine

Ezekiel Trickett, July 7, 1881
    Discontinued, July 17, 1882

Booth

Earthy G. Bean, December 24, 1926

Bowlby

Edward J. Bowlby, October 24, 1890
Leander D. Boyles, September 17, 1904
    Discontinued, January 31, 1915

Brady

Ulric D. Hawley, August 27, 1921
Lawrence A. Floyd, February 9, 1925
Howard R. Pigott, April 1, 1926

Bula

Peter B. Core, September 16, 1889
Clarence E. Sidwell, November 18, 1901
Sanford C. Hilberry, January 14, 1904
Mary A. Kent, March 24, 1904
    Discontinued, May 15, 1912

Cassville

John W. Tucker, March 21, 1867
Mrs. Elizabeth Lough, July 10, 1885
John W. Tucker, February 8, 1890
Edwin O. Wiedman, April 16, 1894
Joseph S. Pickenpaugh, July 26, 1898
Myrtle Lough, April 22, 1909
Myrtle L. Ramsey, April 10, 1916
John W. Kennedy, December 12, 1918
Clarence L. Cialella, April 15, 1921
Carl H. Schenck, June 25, 1924
Albert E. Adams, January 19, 1925

Cedar Valley

William N. Stewart, March 8, 1876
Harry E. Miller, April 1881
  Changed to Georgetown, 1882

Center

Hezekiah Lough, January 4, 1877
Theodore V. Coleman, August 11, 1879
George Brookover, March 25, 1880
Theodore V. Coleman, April 22, 1880
Christopher Toothman, April 16, 1883
McKendrie Wilson, December 15, 1884
Hiram Kent, July 20, 1889
William Freeland, May 26, 1892
  Discontinued, March 31, 1908

Charlotte

George A. Lemley, July 21, 1890
Clark R. Lemley, October 28, 1897
Thomas Brewer, March 20, 1906
  Discontinued, November 15, 1913

Clinton Furnace

Omer B. Johnson, July 25, 1867
Omer C. Johnson, December 1, 1891
  Discontinued, April 30, 1908

Core

Charles H. Core, May 18, 1898
Spencer C. Pyles, December 28, 1908
Charles H. Core, September 11, 1909

Cross Roads

Griffin S. Cross, June 17, 1878
Amos J. Ammons, January 20, 1887
Thomas J. Collins, April 8, 1887
Nancy C. Haught, January 2, 1890
Sarah C. Haught, March 4, 1890
G. S. Cross, April 3, 1894
Sarah C. Haught, April 30, 1898
George W. Barr, November 17, 1903
   Discontinued, August 15, 1907

Daybrook

Jacob J. Moore, February 9, 1899
Eliza W. Piles, November 4, 1900
   Discontinued, August 15, 1907

Dellslow

James P. Burbridge, July 26, 1886
Thomas M. Pixler, October 20, 1897

Duke (Granville)

Walter S. Horner, June 26, 1888
John Stewart, September 6, 1890
Eli S. Parker, January 23, 1891
Alfred S. Barker, April 21, 1893
Eli S. Parker, April 30, 1899

Easton

Thomas W. Anderson, June 3, 1867
Melvill C. Courtney, May 2, 1884
Lot Stewart, September 17, 1889
Joseph J. Pomroy, May 25, 1894
L. J. Reppert, October 9, 1896
   Discontinued, September 30, 1904

Everettville

John Dawson Fultz, February 26, 1921
David N. Richeson, November 1, 1923
Edwin R. Horner, May 1, 1924

Flickersville

Margaret McElroy, June 28, 1890
   Discontinued, May 15, 1895

Harley Thompson, October 8, 1897
   Discontinued, October 25, 1900

Frum

Peter H. Karanfilian, September 10, 1924
   Name later changed to Osage

Georgetown

Harry E. Miller, March 8, 1882
Lizzie Kennedy, April 12, 1886
Henry Clay Miller, February 3, 1890
Terressa Chipps, October 27, 1891
Horatio Chipps, May 12, 1894
Daniel Y. McElroy, July 8, 1897
Alfred R. Wilcox, July 5, 1901
William L. McElroy, April 23, 1902
Melville L. C. Pratt, March 10, 1906
   Discontinued, July 31, 1907

Granville (see Duke, Mona)

Marmaduke Dent, May 28, 1873
   Discontinued, December 20, 1880

Greer

Roy M. Clear, May 14, 1915
Edward E. Williams, January 2, 1920
Otis M. Mayfield, January 8, 1921
David J. Kelly, November 17, 1922

Hagans

Michael E. Fetty, February 2, 1887
James L. Jones, July 23, 1897
John C. Morris, April 10, 1899
   Discontinued, January 31, 1918

Halleck

Charles H. Duncan, March 18, 1880
James Miller, May 3, 1893
Charles H. Duncan, December 10, 1896
   Discontinued, April 30, 1908

Hoard

Virgil E. Hoard, September 8, 1894
Miss S. E. Hoard, November 4, 1914

Holman

Dissaway South, March 8, 1888
Robert B. South, June 3, 1891
John S. Brown, May 25, 1892
Lewis Lemley, May 18, 1901
Norman S. Fetty, November 4, 1907
    Discontinued, July 31, 1908

Jaco

William L. Jaco, October 13, 1897
    Discontinued, July 1, 1904

Jakes Run

Benjamin Wilson, March 19, 1868
Abraham Mosier, June 15, 1877
Felix Bell, January 3, 1878
David Wilson, June 18, 1880
Thomas Williams, January 2, 1884
John Shriver, December 10, 1891
Jacob J. Moore, September 28, 1898
    Name changed to Daybrook, February 9, 1899

Jay

Milton Hall, April 23, 1887
    No papers, May 18, 1887

Jere

Benjamin Wakefield, May 28, 1924

Jobe

Remembrance Thomas, July 16, 1874
John R. Robinson, November 29, 1878
Peter B. Core, December 12, 1879
Abraham J. Eddy, July 13, 1880
    Discontinued, July 18, 1881

John

Willie F. Moore, August 11, 1898
Odis C. Moore, June 6, 1901
Alpheus L. Tennant, July 15, 1905
    Discontinued, August 15, 1907

Laurel Iron Works

Nathaniel H. Triplett, March 11, 1868
William Kussart, October 26, 1885

Francis P. Lyons, April 5, 1889
Hugh A. Dickinson, May 26, 1891
Charles Dickinson, May 10, 1893
Hugh A. Dickinson, May 12, 1899
    Discontinued, October 19, 1900

Laurel Point

Thomas L. Miller, May 26, 1873
Henry C. Miller, February 8, 1876
R. E. Thomas, January 6, 1879
Henry C. Miller, February 19, 1879
Miss Mary C. Rice, July 16, 1879
Charles Martin, June 30, 1897
    Discontinued, October 25, 1900

Lewisville

John B. Cunningham, August 25, 1885
    Changed to Dellslow, July 26, 1886

Little Falls

J. Marshall Jacobs, November 9, 1885
Hugh Hood, April 13, 1893
Benson Jacobs, April 30, 1897
John L. Stansberry, March 18, 1915
Norval D. Crow, July 14, 1926

Lowesville

John Hood, December 16, 1874
Joseph A. Hood, March 13, 1879
Alice M. Clayton, January 28, 1891
    Discontinued, January 15, 1892
James Hood, October 31, 1893
John B. Lough, June 11, 1900
Joseph A. Hood, December 11, 1901
Robert B. Satterfield, July 12, 1909
Claude A. Snider, November 17, 1917
Raymer W. Barker, August 3, 1918
Bryon W. Wistran, January 24, 1921
Mrs. Lenora V. Good, January 16, 1926

Mack

Owen D. McMillon, October 11, 1899
Peter A. Anderson, March 27, 1901
John L. Shaw, October 5, 1901
    Mail to Dellslow, November 11, 1901

McMellin

Alice B. Barnes, December 22, 1900
Calvin C. Nabora, August 8, 1902
  Mail to Cheat Haven, Pennsylvania, May 30, 1903

Mahanna

Alpheus B. Mahanna, June 20, 1892
  Mail to Statler Run, April 17, 1894

Maidsville

Lorenzo Davis, December 8, 1874
David B. Waters, February 21, 1881
John Ridgway, December 13, 1886
Colman T. Lazzell, January 27, 1898
E. E. Murphy, December 11, 1903
  Discontinued, January 27, 1904
William L. Murphy, September 24, 1921
Mrs. Antoinette Masciola, June 8, 1925
Kester W. McCartney, October 11, 1925

Maple

Simon L. White, January 6, 1887
  Mail to St. Cloud, January 15, 1915

Minor

Albert G. Chaplin, June 23, 1894
  Mail to Pentress, April 21, 1897

Miracle Run

William Tuttle, Jr., January 19, 1863
Leroy Lemley, April 23, 1907
  Discontinued, August 15, 1907

Mona (Granville)

John W. Parker, April 20, 1903
Paul H. Trevillian, April 8, 1919
Arlington W. McGinnis, October 10, 1919
Samuel M. Wood, April 6, 1921
Sidney S. Sapper, March 29, 1922
Mrs. Lessie W. Trevillian, October 19, 1925

Mooresville

Simon G. Tennant, February 2, 1870
Harman L. Sine, July 22, 1885

James B. Furman, February 15, 1889
Sarah A. Furman, July 7, 1906
William S. Tennant, October 17, 1910
Peter R. Moore, March 16, 1926

Morgantown

Frederick A. Dering, February 11, 1864
Adam L. Nye, April 6, 1886
James A. Davis, March 20, 1890
Joseph L. Wharton, June 11, 1894
James P. Fitch, May 24, 1898
A. Posten, March 1, 1907
Frank A. Bowman, May 25, 1911
Thomas E. Hodges, April 14, 1915
Amos L. Demoss (acting), July 23, 1919
Edwin M. Grant (acting), July 1, 1921
Earl Pepper, January 24, 1923

National

James Hanford, June 23, 1923

O'Neal

John N. Conway, May 28, 1883
J. Marshall Jacobs, August 1, 1884
  Discontinued, November 7, 1885

Opekiska

Thomas F. Watson, April 14, 1886
Miss Emma Tibbs, April 27, 1889
Mary C. Heston, January 20, 1890
Henry W. Martin, June 2, 1894
Cornelius Heston, April 14, 1897
Page D. Heston, October 5, 1912
Cornelius Heston, March 26, 1923
Thomas Faulkner, November 3, 1924

Osage (Frum)

Peter H. Karanfilian, September 10, 1924

Osgood

William C. Arnett, February 10, 1892
  Discontinued, September 8, 1894
Dora Arnett, October 8, 1897
K. Arnett, August 6, 1898

Willie C. McElroy, December   8, 1900
    Discontinued, May 15, 1902

Pedlars Run (Pedlar)

Alpheus Garrison, June 22, 1874
Jacob R. Hough, January 25, 1884
David L. Garrison, January 9, 1891
Jacob R. Hough, April 30, 1895
John C. Barrickman, October 23, 1897
Alpheus Garrison, May 2, 1898
    Discontinued, June 15, 1909

Pentress

Titus Lemley, May 28, 1889
John O. Clark, April 21, 1897
Titus Lemley, December 12, 1898
Christopher S. Tennant, December 4, 1902
Perry M. Johnson, March 24, 1904
Christopher S. Tennant, January 31, 1905
Claude H. Johnson, April 3, 1906
Guy Lemley, April 4, 1907
Herbert C. Johnson, February 21, 19—
Gertrude Johnson, September 25, 1915
Grace F. Johnson, March 22, 1917
Milton Adams, August 19, 1917
James L. Downey, January 14, 1919
S. A. Litman, September 20, 1924
Clyde M. Johnson, January 15, 1925

Pleasant Valley

Charles H. Holland, January 24, 1876
    Discontinued, November 19, 1877

Pursglove

John P. O'Connell, November 27, 1920
Harry A. Pittigrew, February 2, 1923
James J. Keegan, June 30, 1924
James A. Cunningham, October 17, 1924
Earl Morris, January 28, 1925
Miss Helen D. Cox, April 5, 1926

Randall

Isaac N. Furman, April 13, 1874
Genie Corothers, August 24, 1880

William L. Robins, November 29, 1880
Isaac N. Furman, June 2, 1881
Thomas Lazzell, November 2, 1882
David Wiedman, February 11, 1887
Melville C. Courtney, December 9, 1889
Alex J. Tait, July 13, 1892
Annie F. Cobun, August 21, 1895
Jessie F. Cobun, September 9, 1895
Alex J. Tait, January 30, 1897
John J. Lemley, June 14, 1899
Marcus C. Lemley, July 29, 1903
Lewis Lemley, November 30, 1907
Frank W. Parker, April 10, 1911
    Discontinued, November 15, 1913

Richard

William P. Haines, February 13, 1904
Walter L. Corey, September 3, 1904
Thomas F. Protzman, May 17, 1906
Harry C. Botsford, September 28, 1907
George P. Corey, May 4, 19—
Charles B. Ross, October 27, 1915
    Discontinued, December 15, 1921

Ridgedale

Luther J. Howell, December 16, 1892
    Discontinued, March 6, 1908

Ringgold

Elias Ring, March 7, 1898
    Discontinued, July 31, 1901

Rock Forge

Edward J. Cosgrove, April 26, 1911
Sarah J. Keller, May 5, 1914
    Discontinued, September 30, 1916

Ruby

Jacob Shanes, June 20, 1892
    Mail to Wadestown, February 21, 1894

Sabraton

Edwin R. Jones, November 20, 1908
Leonard H. Jones, May 16, 1914
Charles J. Parsons, October 8, 1922

Saint Cloud

John H. Six, August 5, 1873
Martin L. White, September 17, 1889
  Discontinued, April 15, 1915

Saint Leo

Joseph M. Hall, May 18, 1887
George N. Stockdale, August 16, 1890
Samuel J. Hall, December 27, 1895
William Furbee, January 2, 1900
Clark Youst, January 7, 1901
Myrtle L. Haught, July 30, 1903
Myrtle A. Liggett, January 6, 1904
Libbie Haught, February 16, 1905
  Discontinued, June 15, 1908

Sandy

Leander J. Piles, August 11, 1898
Fletcher B. Wilson, December 15, 1902

Scrafford

Alfred H. Gallagher, September 1, 1892
William H. Gorman, February 11, 1895
Henry L. DeVault, May 28, 1900
Loyd C. Brand, March 7, 1902
Ira Prickett, December 28, 1903
John E. Price, July 1, 1905
  Discontinued, August 14, 1909

Shriver

Frank C. Shriver, November 16, 1905
  Name changed to Star City, July 1, 1907

Smail (Hagans)

Michael E. Fetty, March 14, 1919
Ross Hawkins, March 9, 1921
Fred Hawkins, November 1, 1921
George R. Michael, June 21, 1922
  Discontinued, February 15, 1923

Star City

Frank C. Shriver, July 1, 1907
Ernest E. Shriver, December 9, 1913
Frank Hamilton, July 1, 1918
Franklin E. Hall, August 1, 1919

Harry A. Higgins, June 16, 1920
Ralph S. Kauffield, March 14, 1922
Andrew O. Goldstrom, November 29, 1924
John H. Shay, February 23, 1925

Statlers Run

Nimrod Tennant, September 29, 1876
Samuel J. Snyder, February 3, 1897
Perry W. Moore, September 9, 1897
Discontinued, May 8, 1908

Stewartstown

John G. Conn, June 22, 1874
Elisha M. Snyder, December 20, 1877
Alpheus Dilliner, August 16, 1886
Daniel W. Darling, September 17, 1889
Edson Hare, September 20, 1893
Discontinued, September 23, 1909

Sturgisson

Ada L. Van Norman, April 17, 1903
Discontinued, February 14, 1925

Triune

Albert T. Bennett, December 22, 1892
Alma Bennett, August 11, 1895
John D. Summers, May 11, 1899
William H. Gwyn, April 23, 1902
Discontinued, May 15, 1907

Tyrone

Samuel A. Shafer, December 22, 1897
Discontinued, June 30, 1903

Uffington

James S. Watson, July 8, 1873
Solomon Frum, July 22, 1885
James S. Watson, January 26, 1889
George C. Watson, February 18, 1889
Allen R. Price, January 21, 1890
Amos L. Demoss, April 9, 1895
Mary B. Watson, March 15, 1901
Mary B. McDaniel, July 30, 1906
Stanley C. Watson, December 28, 1910

Frank R. Sapp, September 20, 1916
Willey G. Phillips, April 18, 1919
C. Lester Hartzell, September 7, 1920
Willey G. Phillips, January 31, 1921
Anna Jolliffe, April 7, 1922
Clarence L. Hartzell, June 28, 1922

Uneva

Alpheus F. Blosser, July 30, 1890
Mary L. Blosser, April 30, 1898
Discontinued, October 19, 1900

Van Voorhis

James P. St. Clair, September 1, 1894
John F. Ross, May 26, 1903
Wilda McClure, November 26, 1904
William E. Rush, July 8, 1909
Lloyd D. St. Clair, May 30, 1921

Wadestown

Mark G. Lester, June 24, 1867
Lot L. Shriver, February 28, 1877
Mark G. Lester, September 11, 1885
Morris J. Garrison, March 30, 1889
Theodore W. Barr, April 28, 1893
Nancy J. Barr, June 17, 1899
Morris J. Garrison, March 20, 1900
Winfield S. Kern, May 5, 1916
Miss Blanche Cowell, August 1, 1919 (Name changed by marriage to
    Mrs. Blanche Shriver, November 26, 1924)

Wana

John R. Robinson, April 9, 1908
Joseph L. Robinson, June 2, 1908
Charles E. Hennen, October 18, 1912
George M. Whitehill, September 30, 1913

White Day

William C. Wilson, January 16, 1867
Charles D. Malone, November 10, 1880
William B. Jolliff, September 4, 1885
Lillie J. Hutchinson, April 16, 1889
Leeroy C. Beals, August 14, 1893
John N. Conway, May 7, 1897

Fletcher N. Conway, December 18, 1905
Joseph E. Gwyn, May 4, 1906
  Discontinued, May 16, 1907

Willey

John W. Haught, October 19, 1900
  Discontinued, August 16, 1907

Wise

John R. Robinson, May 2, 1881
M. J. Lantz, January 21, 1886
William L. Harker, May 5, 1886
John W. Sanders, March 9, 1894
John R. Robinson, April 25, 1898
  Name changed to Wana, April 9, 1905

Worley

Alpheus W. Brown, February 5, 1890
Cassius C. Brown, May 2, 1890
  Discontinued, February 28, 1905

Appendix B

Circuit Court Judges

Charles L. Lewis	Mar. 10, 1872	to	Mar. 15, 1878
Brooks Aretas Fleming	Mar. 15, 1878	to	Feb. 12, 1889
John Marshall Hagans	Feb. 12, 1889	to	June 18, 1900
John W. Mason	June 18, 1900	to	Jan. 1, 1913
Geo. Cookman Sturgiss	Jan. 1, 1913	to	Jan. 1, 1921
Isaac Grant Lazzelle	Jan. 1, 1921		

Clerks of the Circuit Court

Augustus Haymond	Jan. 1, 1873	to	Jan. 1, 1879
William S. Cobun	Jan. 1, 1879	to	Oct. 12, 1883
Marshall M. Dent	Oct. 12, 1883	to	Jan. 1, 1885
Richard E. Fast	Jan. 1, 1885	to	Jan. 1, 1891
W. E. Glasscock	Jan. 1, 1891	to	Aug. 23, 1906
John Shriver	Aug. 23, 1906	to	Jan. 1, 1921
Garfield Davies	Jan. 1, 1921	to	Apr. 3, 1925
John Shriver	Apr. 3, 1925	to	Aug. 31, 1926
Joseph L. Keener	Aug. 31, 1926		

Prosecuting Attorneys

G. C. Sturgiss	Jan. 1, 1875	to	Apr. 16, 1880
Waitman W. Houston	Apr. 16, 1880	to	Oct. 11, 1887
Joseph Moreland	Oct. 11, 1887	to	Jan. 1, 1888
Frank Cox	Jan. 1, 1888	to	Jan. 1, 1892
Geo. C. Baker	Jan. 1, 1892	to	Jan. 1, 1896
I. G. Lazzelle	Jan. 1, 1896	to	Jan. 1, 1900
C. A. Goodwin	Jan. 1, 1900	to	Jan. 1, 1904
C. W. Cramer	Jan. 1, 1904	to	Jan. 1, 1908
T. Sutton Boyd	Jan. 1, 1908	to	Jan. 1, 1912
C. A. Goodwin	Jan. 1, 1912	to	Jan. 1, 1916
Stanley Cox	Jan. 1, 1916	to	Jan. 1, 1920
R. P. Posten	Jan. 1, 1920	to	Jan. 1, 1924
French Hunt	Jan. 1, 1924		

Sheriffs of Monongalia County

1876—Samuel Hackney
1880—George W. McVicker
1884—Ira Bailey
1888—Barton M. Jones
1892—Silas W. Hare
1896—Marion S. Garrison
1900—Greenberry Barrickman
1904—Theodore W. Barker
1908—William H. Brand
1912—John B. Wallace
1916—E. E. White
     John L. Dougan
1920—William M. Yost
1924—J. F. Rodeheaver

Mayors of Morgantown

Borough

1877—S. G. Chadwick
1878—Joseph Moreland
1879—Joseph Moreland
1880—Jesse J. Fitch
1881—Manliff Hayes
1882—Manliff Hayes
1883—Manliff Hayes
1884—John C. Wagner
1885—John C. Wagner
1886—John C. Wagner
1887—John C. Wagner, resigned August 2
     Richard E. Fast, elected August 19
1888—Richard E. Fast
1889—Richard E. Fast
1890—Richard E. Fast
1891—Richard E. Fast

Town

1892—Joseph Moreland, elected in January instead of May
1893—F. K. O'Kelley, resigned May 31
     I. G. Lazzelle, appointed by council
1894—Richard E. Fast
1895—S. A. Posten
1896—Joseph Moreland

1897—L. V. Keck
1898—William E. Glasscock
1899—William E. Glasscock
1900—S. A. Posten
1901—E. B. Stewart, elected in January
    —George C. Steele, elected by people April 4, 1901

City

1902—George C. Steele
1903—W. G. McGrew
1904—Joseph J. Wharton
1905—A. E. Lazier
1906—John L. Hatfield
1907—I. N. Lucas
1908—Albert Layton
1909—Albert Layton
1910—E. G. Donley
1911—E. G. Donley
1912—Fred C. Flenniken
1913—Terrence D. Stewart
1914—James D. Gronniger
1915—James A. Cox
1916—Frank L. Bowman
1917—Charles T. Hickman
1918—Charles T. Hickman
1919—Charles T. Hickman
1920—William H. Gilmore
1921—Charles F. Sutherland, resigned to be city manager
        Theodore Warrick, first elected by council
1922—Theodore Warrick
1923—Theodore Warrick
1924—Edward G. Donley
1925—Jefferson L. Smith
1926—Jefferson L. Smith

On June 21, 1921, the city voted 2,074 to 750 for the city manager form of government. C. F. Sutherland was appointed by council.

Appendix C

Monongalia County Members
of the State Senate
1876-1926

Ralph L. Berkshire, 1875-77
William C. McGrew, 1879-85
Joseph Snyder, 1887-89
Alpheus Garrison, 1891-93
Richard E. Fast, 1897-99
Joseph H. McDermott, 1905-07
John L. Hatfield, 1913-15
Edgar B. Stewart, 1919-21
Dennis M. Willis, 1925-27

Monongalia County Members
of the House of Delegates
1876-1926

John M. Gray, 1877
James T. McClaskey, 1877
James R. Hare, 1879
J. Marshall Hagans, 1879-87
James S. Watson, 1881
Henry L. Cox, 1881-83
John E. Price, 1885
Edward W. St. Clair, 1889-91
James M. Anderson, 1893-95
George W. Laishley, 1897
E. M. Grant, 1899-1901
Lewis C. Snyder, 1903
Altha Warman, 1903-05
Zimri Ammons, 1905-07
William C. McGrew, 1907
Simon L. Wildman, 1909-11
Ellis A. Yost, 1909-13
David H. Courtney, 1911

Sylvester Arnett, 1913
David C. Clark, 1915
James R. Moreland, 1915
Perry C. McBee, 1917
William S. John, 1917-19
Franklin M. Brand, 1919-
R. Earle Davis, 1921
D. M. Willis, 1921-23
G. T. Federer, 1925
I. M. Austin, 1925

Clerks of the County Court

1873-78	W. S. Cobun
1879-82	John W. Madara
1883-90	Waitman T. Willey
1891-96	William E. Glasscock
1897-1902	John E. Price
1903-	John M. Gregg

County Assessors

1877-80	George Barb
1881-92	Barton M. Jones
1893-96	M. S. Garrison
1897-1900	Sylvestor Arnett
1901-04	David F. Morris
1905-08	Peter B. Core
1909-12	E. W. Griffith
1913-16	Norman Garrison
1917-20	James E. Gaskins
1921-24	E. E. White
1925-	James E. Henry

County School Superintendents

1875	Alexander L. Wade
1879	Bruce L. Keenan
1881	Benjamin S. Morgan
1885	Virgil Vandervort
1887	William E. Glasscock
1891	Martin L. Brown
1893	D. Benson Waters
1899	Stephen Mason
1903	Jesse H. Henry
1911	Harry E. Brookover
1916	Lynn Hastings

Selected Bibliography

Ambler, Charles H. *History of Education in West Virginia.* 1951.

Ambler, Charles H. *Waitman Thomas Willey.* 1954.

Anonymous. *St. Theresa Church, 75th Anniversary.* 1976.

Anonymous. *Sesqui-Centennial of Monongalia County, West Virginia.* n.d.

Barnes, I. A. *The Methodist Protestant Church in West Virginia.* 1926.

Boone, Weldon. *History of Botany in West Virginia.* 1965.

Brand, Franklin Marion. *The Brand Family.* 1922.

Brand, Franklin Marion. *The Fleming Family.* 1941.

Brand, Franklin Marion. *The Wade Family.* 1927.

Brown, Lloyd L. *The Life of Dr. Israel Charles White.* Master's thesis, 1936.

Butcher, Bernard L. (and others). *Genealogical and Personal History of the Upper Monongahela Valley.* 1912.

Callahan, James Morton. *Semi-Centennial History of West Virginia.* 1913.

Callahan, James Morton. *History of the Making of Morgantown.* 1926.

Canfield, Joseph M. *West Penn Traction.* 1968.

Carspecken, Frederick. *Morgantown Rotary. The First Fifty Years. 1918-1968.*

Coletta, Paolo. *French Ensor Chadwick: The Scholarly Warrior.* 1980.

Conley, Phil, and William Thomas Doherty. *West Virginia History.* 1974.

Constantine, Tony (assisted by Dan Miller). *Mountaineer Football, 1891-1969.* 1969.

Core, Earl L. *Morgantown Disciples.* 1960.

Core, Earl L. *Chronicles of Core,* 3 ed. 1975.

Core, Earl L. "Out of the Mud," a series of weekly columns in the *Westover Observer,* beginning July 12, 1956.

Dodds, Dr. and Mrs. Gideon S. *The Churches of Monongalia County* (in *175th Anniversary . . . of Monongalia County*). 1954.

Fast, R. E. *The Centennial Celebration of the Founding of Morgantown.* 1902.

Gillespie, William H., Ira S. Latimer, Jr., and John A. Clendening. *Plant Fossils of West Virginia.* 1966.

Gluck, Joseph C. (and others). *Forks of Cheat Baptist Church.* 1975.

Hagedorn, Charles A. *History of Dellslow.* Typescript, n.d.

Hastings, Lynn. *School and Local History* (typescript). 10 vols. 1960.

Headlee, Alvah J. W. *George Lemley and wife Catharine Yoho and Their Descendants for Two Centuries.* 1975.

Headlee, Alvah J. W. *The Headlee Family.* 1980.

Hennen, Dorothy T. *Hennen's Choice.* Vol. 1, 1970. Vol. 2, 1972.

Hennen, Ray V., and David B. Reger. [Geology of] Marion, Monongalia, and Taylor Counties. 1913.

Hoard, Clifford B. *House of Hoard.* 1965.

Lathrop, J. M., H. C. Penny, and W. R. Proctor. *Atlas of Marion and Monongalia Counties, West Virginia.* 1886.

Lee, Howard B. *The Burning Springs and Other Tales of the Little Kanawha.* 1968.

McCormick, Theresa, Ed. *Monongalia Blacks Speak. Part 1. Black Men. Part 2. Black Women.* 1977.

McCormick, Theresa. *Polish-Americans.* Typescript. 1978.

McRae, Elijah. *History of Halleck Community.* Typescript, n.d.

Millspaugh, Charles Frederick. *Flora of West Virginia.* 1892.

Monongalia Historical Society. *The 175th Anniversary of the Formation of Monongalia County, West Virginia, and Other Relative Historical Data.* 1954.

Moreland, James R. *The First Presbyterian Church of Morgantown.* 1938.

Moreland, James R. *Anecdotes, . . .* etc. Typescript, 2 vols. 1914.

Moreland, Joseph. *Morgantown, Its Practical Jokes and Jokers.* 1885.

Morgan, French. *History . . . Of the Family of Col. Morgan Morgan.* 1950.

Owens, Ivan C. *Easton-Avery Community History.* 1964.

Reeder, Benjamin Garnet. *Book of Reeder.* Typescript, n.d.

Reid, John Philip. *An American Judge. Marmaduke Dent of West Virginia.* 1968.

Robinson, Felix G. *Monongalia County Issue, Tableland Trails. Vol. 2. No. 3. Summer, 1958.*

Shively, Norman B. *Index to Samuel T. Wiley's History of Monongalia County, West Virginia* (1883). 1976.

Tennant, J. Ross. *Memories.* 1, 1942; 2, 1945; 3, 1946; 4, 1948.

Thoenen, Eugene D. *History of the Oil and Gas Industry in West Virginia.* 1964.

Van Liere, Edward J., and Gideon S. Dodds. *History of Medical Education in West Virginia.* 1965.

Wade, Alexander A. *A Graduating System for County Schools.* 1881.

Weltner, Fred Hamilton, and Harry Leroy Jeffries, Sr. *The Stewartstown Story.* 1971.

Wilding, George Cleaton. *Promoted Pioneer Preachers of the West Virginia Conference of the Methodist Episcopal Church, and a Sketch of Her Early Ministers Who Were Transferred to Other Fields.* 1927.

Wiley, Samuel T. *History of Monongalia County.* 1883.

Index

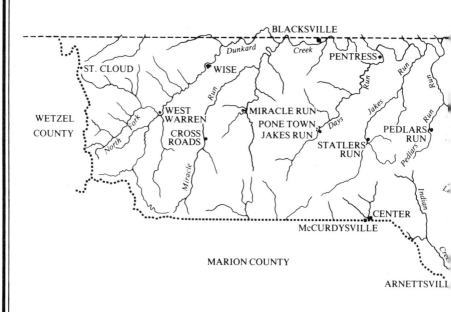

BLACKSVILLE

Dunkard *Creek*

PENTRESS

ST. CLOUD

WISE

Run

Run

Run

Jakes

WETZEL
COUNTY

WEST
WARREN

Run

North Fork

MIRACLE RUN
PONE TOWN
JAKES RUN

Days

PEDLARS
RUN

Run

CROSS
ROADS

STATLERS
RUN

Pedlars

Miracle

CENTER

Indian

McCURDYSVILLE

MARION COUNTY

Creek

ARNETTSVILL

MONONGALIA
COUNTY
1886

N